The Signifying Eye

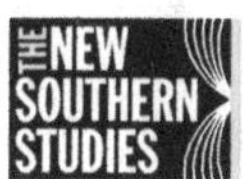
THE NEW
SOUTHERN
STUDIES

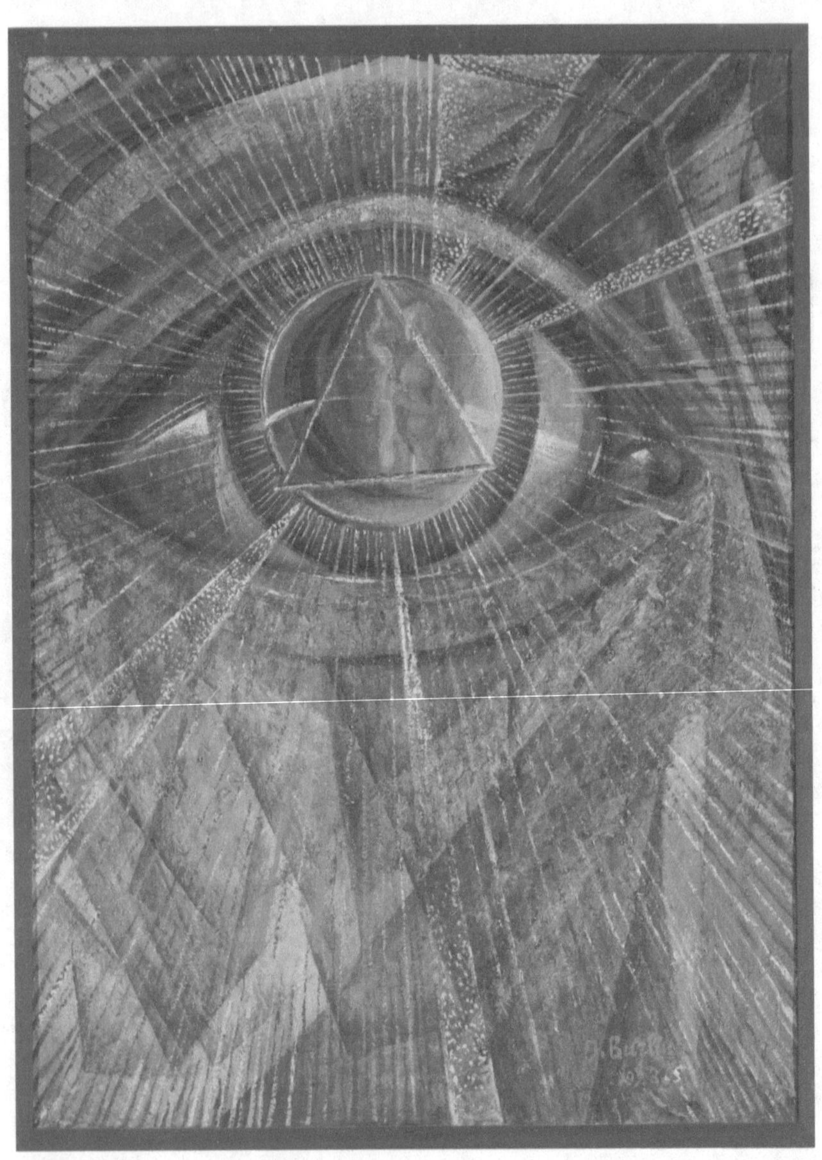

The Signifying Eye

Seeing Faulkner's Art

Candace Waid

The University of Georgia Press
Athens

Frontispiece. David Davidovich Burliuk, *The Eye of God*, 1923–25. Courtesy of the Yale University Art Gallery, Gift of Collection Société Anonyme.

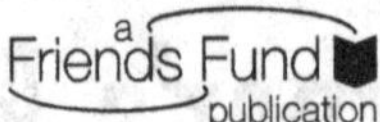

Publication of this work was made possible, in part, by a generous gift from the University of Georgia Press Friends Fund.

Paperback edition, 2017

Athens, Georgia 30602
www.ugapress.org

Set in Sabon MT Pro by Graphic Composition, Inc., Bogart, Georgia

Most University of Georgia Press titles are available from popular e-book vendors.

Printed digitally

The Library of Congress has cataloged the hardcover edition of this book as follows:
Waid, Candace.
The signifying eye : seeing Faulkner's art / Candace Waid.
xvi, 383 pages : illustrations (some color) ; 24 cm. — (The new Southern studies)
ISBN-13: 978-0-8203-4316-7 (hardcover)
ISBN-10: 0-8203-4316-1 (hardcover)
Includes bibliographical references (pages 297–367).
1. Faulkner, William, 1897–1962—Criticism and interpretation.
2. Abstract expressionism—Influence. I. Title.
PS3511.A86Z98525 2013
813'.52—dc23 2012047666

Paperback ISBN 978-0-8203-5055-4

For Dawn, Daniel, Donna, and Patricia

Contents

Illustrations

Figures

Plates (following page 238)

Acknowledgments

The South was not a country . . . but a battle cry.
Karl Marx

The word "South," like the words "Midwest" and "West," is capitalized in this book: the words "southern" and "war" are not. The anxiety around this act of capitalization is explained in the epigraph from Marx that identifies the nationalist and indefensible ambition of a war fought as an effort to preserve slavery. The capitalization of the word "South" here is a regional recognition of the multiple Souths that are visible in cultural and literary forms of a diabolical richness, carved from a shared history of economic and other poverties. Not a nationalist concept, this plural South is not demarcated by state borders or border states. I thank the University of Georgia Press for allowing the book within the book: the substantive note structure that provides a foundation of both oral and written sources, in particular with regard to the mysteries of social mores and labor history.

More than one colleague in the academic community has asked with genuine disbelief: "Are people still reading Faulkner?" The excision of Faulkner (whether through burial in curricular canons or the refusal to read) may lie in the denial of an agrarian, backwoods, rural modernism: the common confusion of modernism with not only an excluding realm of "high modernism" but also with the idea of a modernity located in the urban. (Whatever its ranking in the dictionary's digitally constructed chain of being that excludes saying, "get" is still a noun that descends from the biblical "begats," a word that is used and spoken in the ranch pens of California and the farm country of north Mississippi.) Paulo Moreira and Kimberly Benston have understood that this richness of orality and intense localism makes the transnational backwoods a place of change that gives voice to the formal complexities of modernism. Meanwhile, the answer to the question about the reading of Faulkner at the University of California, Santa Barbara takes the form of my three graduate seminars: The Experimental Faulkner; Deeper into Yoknapatawpha; and Faulkner: The Bad, the Ugly, the Unpleasant, and the Unread. I am grateful for the conversations occasioned by these encounters as well as those precipitated in my decades of teaching Southern Literature: Language and Culture.

My acknowledgements reside in this century and in the last. I thank R.W. B. Lewis, C. Van Woodward, Peter Brooks, David Minter, Kai Erickson, Trudier Harris, Carolyn Porter, Wai-Chee Dimock, Richard Brodhead, Harry Aldridge, David Lowe, Virginia Praytor, Rose Gladney, Emily Bernard, Harriet Swift, Wanda Suitts, Michele Stepto, Elizabeth Meese, Julia Erhardt, Anne Abadie, Carl Smith, Rachel Bowlby, Doreen Fowler, Brian T. Edwards, Marie-Christine Lemardeley, Margaret Ferguson, Anne Goodwyn Jones, Judith Babbitts, Mimi Katzenbach, Pamela Jones, Sara Suleri, Anne Ullmo, James Snead, Martin Kreiswirth, William Ferris, Hortense Spillers, Michael Zeitlin, Charles Montgomery, Robert Stepto, Rudolf Byrd, Howard Lamar, Robert Penn Warren, and Cleanth Brooks for memorable conversations about Faulkner, Porter, and Hughes and for insights into the deeper sources of narrative and cultural struggle in my home region.

I am fortunate to have spent my life in places that recalled the cultural richness of Baton Rouge in the 1930s, notably the mountains of north Alabama and the Black Belt that pulled southward on the book-centered Tuscaloosa through the work of Francis Walter and the Selma Inter-Religious Project. I benefited from southern studies and the continued dedication of scholars, writers, and activists to the civil rights movement in Birmingham, Chapel Hill, Washington, D.C., New Haven, and New Orleans and the third coast, as well as among the scholars and activists of the central coast of California.

I thank my colleagues at the University of California, Santa Barbara, along with others in my California community who have encouraged this project, especially Laura Kalman, Elizabeth Heckendorn Cook, Stephanie LeMenager, Stephanie Batiste, Yunte Huang, Bishnupriya Ghosh, Mark Rose, Porter Abbott, Elliott Butler-Evans, Jeremy Douglass, Giles Gunn, Carl Gutiérrez-Jones, Richard Helgerson, Kay Young, Zachary Horton, Russell Samolsky, Shannon Brennan, Elisa Tamarkin, Kristin McCants, Janis Caldwell, Claire Colquitt, Rita Raley, Katie Berry Frye, Sonja Magnuson, Paulo Da-Luz-Moreira, Sara Gerend, Jamie Andrews, Nathan Henne, Amanda Phillips, Laura Adams, Karina Evans, Laurie Monahan, Kim Coonen, Chip Badley, Nissa Cannon, Natalie O'Brien, Patrick Mooney, Susan Stanfield, Judy Shanks, James Gracer, and Randy Garr. I thank Alan Liu, who declared that it was time for this book to be finished. The book exists because of Daniel Pecchenino's intelligence as a consultant, interlocutor, and advisor: he has read more than his Faulkner and he understands Faulkner's fiction as it pushes the boundaries of narrative theory.

Although the erasure of my hard drive was challenging, I hope (and partially believe) that I have succeeded in reconstructing the layers of debt recorded in those older note structures. In more than practical ways, I thank the University of Georgia Press and its gifted editorial and design divisions. I am grateful for the uncompromising intelligence and support of Nancy Grayson, Beth Snead, Daniel Simon, and John Joerschke. Steven Moore brought a remarkable list of rhetorical terms to the index. The visual components of this project benefited from the help of many individuals at the University of California, notably Jackie Spafford, Christine Fritsch-Hammes, Susan Moon, and Tom Moon. George Riser and his colleagues at the Faulkner Collection in the Small Library at the University of Virginia, and the librarians at the Harry Ransom Center at the University of Texas, the Special Collections in the J. D. Williams Library at the University of Mississippi, and the Birmingham Public Library were crucial to the making of this book.

Those who supported this project over the years include: Cynthia Blakeley, Susan Allein, Phil Teague, Clinton Cunningham, Estelle Gracer, Helene Marshall, Kayvon Mazooji, Manina Dubroca, Karina Jougla, Audrey Kliman, Deborah Welch, Doris Salem, Amy Girling, Aliki St. Denis, John Grear, Brian Sciacca, Judy Karin, Karen Marshall, Shela West, Tommie Bass, Tom Moore, Cindy Marshall, Kathy Pillsbury, Donald Lehr, Inez Lollar Jones, Harold Jones, Dorothy Tullos, Hannah Rose Blakeley, and Rolf Tullos. My thanks to Andrea Kaufman, Howard Babus, Muriel Satzinger, Oliver Wheeler, and Arthur Marshall who contributed directly to the completion of this project. I have been moved by Prima Luke, Marianna Jaye, Donna Waid, Elizabeth Beck, Asher, Cadence, Ashton, Sevy, Winnie, William, Nadia, Donny, and Alani Day Sciacca: these inspiriting beauties join Jane Johnson, whose kindness and faith continue to be a destination.

Lillian Hellman understood that art, like memory's dream of transparency, is layered: a matter of materials, time, and revelatory weather that (in *Pentimento*'s echoing phrase) provokes "seeing and then seeing again." Jean-Christophe Agnew, Jennifer Greeson, Jennifer Wicke, David Marshall, Paul Fry, Karen Bowie, Randall Wilhelm, Harriet Pollack, Harriet Chessman, Bryan Wolf, Susan Donaldson, Harry Reese, Sandra Liddell Reese, Alan Trachtenberg, Shirley Samuels, Dick Hebdige, Brigitte Peucker, Miriam Hansen, Patricia Saik, and Carly Day Andrews—painters, photographers, seers, and theorists of art and politics—opened my eyes to the visual arts. Lee, Jo Dee, and Marcus Musselman and Dawn, Steven, and Tim Thompson (beset by Katrina and challenges to breath itself) in their humor and intelligence have taught me about the resilience of life and the passion to make art in north Alabama. This last—art, Alabama, the world—speaks to the great labor historian, music man, and poet Allen Tullos, who introduced me to our South as a place of multiple imaginaries, to where I lived and what I live for.

David Marshall (in addition to responding to the originary germ for this project) read the manuscript in its nascent form and suggested a crucial rearranging of chapters. I thank him for reading, observing, and participating on an individual level in the work of my colleagues in the arts, in letters, and in creative performance. His work has been essential to the forging of a vital interdisciplinary community of ideas at the University of California, Santa Barbara.

Finally, I thank Rhoda McGraw, Augusta Harper Cunningham, Patricia Saik, James Clyde Waid, Elizabeth June Wofford, Ida Canterbury Waid, Paula Ballard, Kathleen Bagley Tanner, Claudelle Howton, Amelia Heron Lynch, Jere Lynch, William T. Jones, Dawn Michelle Thompson, Donna Waid, Daniel Waid Marshall, Billie Jones Waid, and my raconteurs: Harriet Lynch Jones and Donald Waid. There should be more names. I have remembered not to forget you. These acknowledgments name debts to partners in the arts, silent and narrating.

Bay St. Louis, Mississippi

INTRODUCTION

The Marionettes

Prefacing *The Signifying Eye*

His drawings here are perhaps the most subtle challenge, for they say, in concrete images, what he cannot say in words.
—Judith Sensibar, writing about Faulkner's *The Marionettes*[1]

In a 1933 introduction that was written but never used for *The Sound and the Fury*, William Faulkner begins by announcing: "Art is no part of southern life . . . We have never got and will probably never get, anywhere with music or the plastic forms." Writing about what he calls "visibility," the author of seven novels (up to that point) insists that in his home region art "must become a ceremony, a spectacle; something between a gypsy encampment and a church bazaar given by a handful of alien mummers who must waste themselves . . . until there is nothing else with which to speak . . . for a show to be held on Friday night and then struck and vanished, leaving only a paint-stiffened smock or a worn out typewriter ribbon in the corner" (228, 229).[2] Faulkner, who had scripted courtroom and sanctuary dramas, an on-page castration, and scenes of sex being played out while an impotent watcher drools, sees southern art as a play that is over, leaving behind the evidence of painting and writing.

As a founding member of a theater troupe at the University of Mississippi called "The Marionettes," Faulkner painted sets and wrote poetry and at least one play. The earliest and most remarkable project that the young Faulkner undertook was the writing and illustrating of *The Marionettes: A Play in One Act*, the hand-lettered text interleaved with pen-and-ink drawings. Faulkner's play, potentiated and elaborated by Beardsley-inspired illustrations, tells the story of a virgin in a garden: Marietta is being seduced by the lovesick clown-poet, Pierrot, from the classic tradition of *commedia dell'arte*. The events of Faulkner's symbolist play are depicted as the drunken reveries of Pierrot, who is always present as a sleeping figure on stage while his dreams take shape on the page in an enacted plot of seduction. Of the four extant versions of this work, three are almost identical copies, replicated and distinguished from the original version by their streamlined aesthetic.[3] Notably, the pen-and-ink illustrations of *The Marionettes* contain drawings that allude to race as a comic component of female sexuality, and the closing articulation of this racially nuanced iconography reveals that this humor, like the bodily experience of sexuality itself, has fatal consequences. Meanwhile, the raciest of the illustrations, "The Apotheosis of Marietta" (see fig. 1, page 4), remains virtually unchanged in all of the versions. Flanked by identical white peacocks that have walked on her, Marietta's very sandals seem to have been imprinted by her animal totems' sharp and inky talons. Her costume burlesques active, if not aggressive, female sexuality. This Marietta in her decadent sartorial cage may be part of Pierrot's fantasy or a drawing that illustrates her released sexuality, but in either evocation, this inked-in, bird-inscribed woman is a joyous dominatrix.[4] Having crossed over into the knowledge that pleasure and pain are close kin, what should be frightening, or at least edgy, in Faulkner's body-baring illustration, "The Apotheosis of Marietta," has instead become comic.[5] Marietta's exposed body reveals the smirking features of an animal face. With her ecstatic arms upraised, Marietta bares her breasts that have become pendulous eyes, punctuated by nippled Os that themselves echo the mouthed O of her navel to complete the minstrel-like face of a simian creature. Although Faulkner will become the author of Medusa-like female characters, Beardsleyesque and debased, this displaced animal face does not elicit fear. Still, reflection and repletion lead to death in Faulkner's fiction. As Randall Wilhelm has pointed out, the autumnal "Marietta at the Pool" sees a reflection that does not show her head. This drawing of reflection and repetition, suggesting that Marietta will follow the path of her mother to pregnancy and death (or just death), is pictured in the final drawing of the play in which a simian-jawed Pierrot, seen in partial profile from the back, gazes at himself and the sacrificial Marietta laid out before him on a slab. Together, these figures compose the tableau of a looked-upon death ostensibly visible to Pierrot alone as he gazes into the reflective space of the oval looking glass that vertically balances and visually echoes the slab-like bier demarcated by the supine and seemingly dead female body.

The most dramatic field/space drawing in *The Marionettes*, "The Kiss" (see fig. 2, page 5), is directly cued by a line in the play that refers to "the white statue of Hermes [as] an island in a sea of ink" (52). This drawing, an embodied vase/face construction, would have been particularly compelling to an artist who conceived of art itself as a vase and who repeatedly alluded to Keats's "Ode on a Grecian Urn" in acts of homage that celebrated the female body caught in a circle and driven by cycles of desire that can only be contained in the stasis of art. Frozen, reified, and rigidified forever at the moment of possibility, the shape of the uncircumcised penis whose tip is partially exposed is the hidden thing articulated by and enclosed within the ink of "The Kiss," but this modern "herm" is finally not closed off.[6] Rather, the unusual shape of Marietta's breast in this drawing and the recognizable features of a double silhouette that are inscribed above the couple's leaning lips reveal another hidden figure.

The silhouetted lovers that form the "sea of ink" have made a woman who (in a version of the familiar vase/face conundrum) is herself a container. A formidable older woman (a mother figure), doubling with the phallus, haunts the inkless interior. Humanly sized—a force to be reckoned with—this matron cuts a figure more frightening than the phallus. In her full stature, she is a tiny-headed, hatted figure of a woman wearing long skirts. Her distinctive bodice sports a peplum that is strangely proportioned but undeniably present. As her double-profiled head presents the features of a face (the rounded chin looks backward while the most carefully cut face of her two-sided features looks forward), the story that is being told recognizes the existence of a circuit that nonetheless favors—in hat, bodice, breast, and chin—a direction. As surely as the maiden will become the crone, the girl will become the mother in an archetype mandating that Little Red Riding Hood will be devoured not just by the wolf but by the grandmother herself (the old woman, who [long-nosed and hairy] remains living inside the wolf's belly): age does not wait to devour youth. All the forewarned young Mariettas, with their gravity-defying "breast points" (*Marionettes* 21), are destined to become mother to the mother herself. This central maternal figure signifying her past through her fallen breast embodies age just as surely as her jutting peplum models outmoded fashion. Janus-profiled, this stalwart female (according to the tilt of her hat) has her eye on the future: her gaze is directed toward Marietta. And, inevitably, between the impending action of the arcing lips, this maternal figure with her tiny head and tiny hat will be decapitated when the lovers kiss: "The Kiss" will complete the narrative circuit that leads to the headless woman and headless work of art. This trope of the headless female—from the focus on the broken maidenhead (Caddy in *The Sound and the Fury* and Temple in *Sanctuary*), to actual acts of drilling into the mother's face (Addie Bundren in *As I Lay Dying*), to the decapitation of women (the Baritone's unnamed wife in *Sanctuary* and Joanna Burden in *Light in August*), or the related feminization accomplished through the castration of men (Joe Christmas in *Light in August*)—rises to the level of an obsession in Faulkner's fiction.

The original version of *The Marionettes*, dedicated to Ben Wasson, is more raucous (the precise word is *puerile*) in several other particulars. In the three later copies, Faulkner's drawing "Marietta and the Statue" features multiple crosses in a trellis that is foregrounded in this garden scene (see figs. 3 and 4, pages 8 and 9). In the close to identical drawings referred to among themselves as the copies, the naked female statue stands in the middle of the garden's pool holding her breast with one hand while her other arm fluoresces upward into the monumental form of an Easter lily. This statue, depicted as cupping her breast in all four versions, occupies a different symbolic landscape in the original volume. Here, the Christological elements have not been covered over or transformed: they have simply not been drawn or developed. In the original drawing of "Marietta and the Statue," the trellis is just a trellis. Unlike the illustration carefully

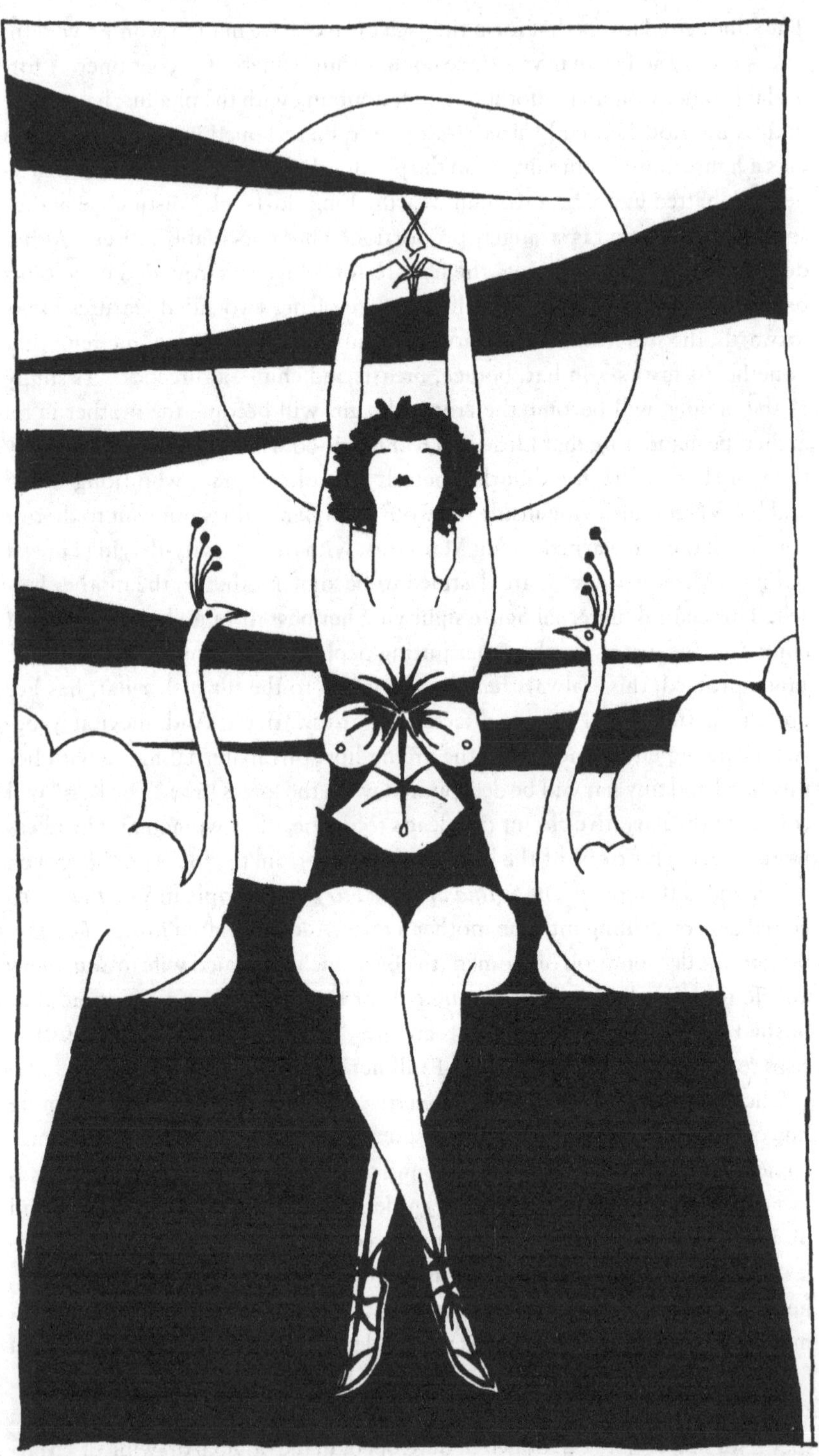

Figure 1. "The Apotheosis of Marietta," from William Faulkner, *The Marionettes: A Play in One Act*. Used by permission of W. W. Norton & Company, Inc. Original in Albert and Shirley Small Special Collections Library, University of Virginia.

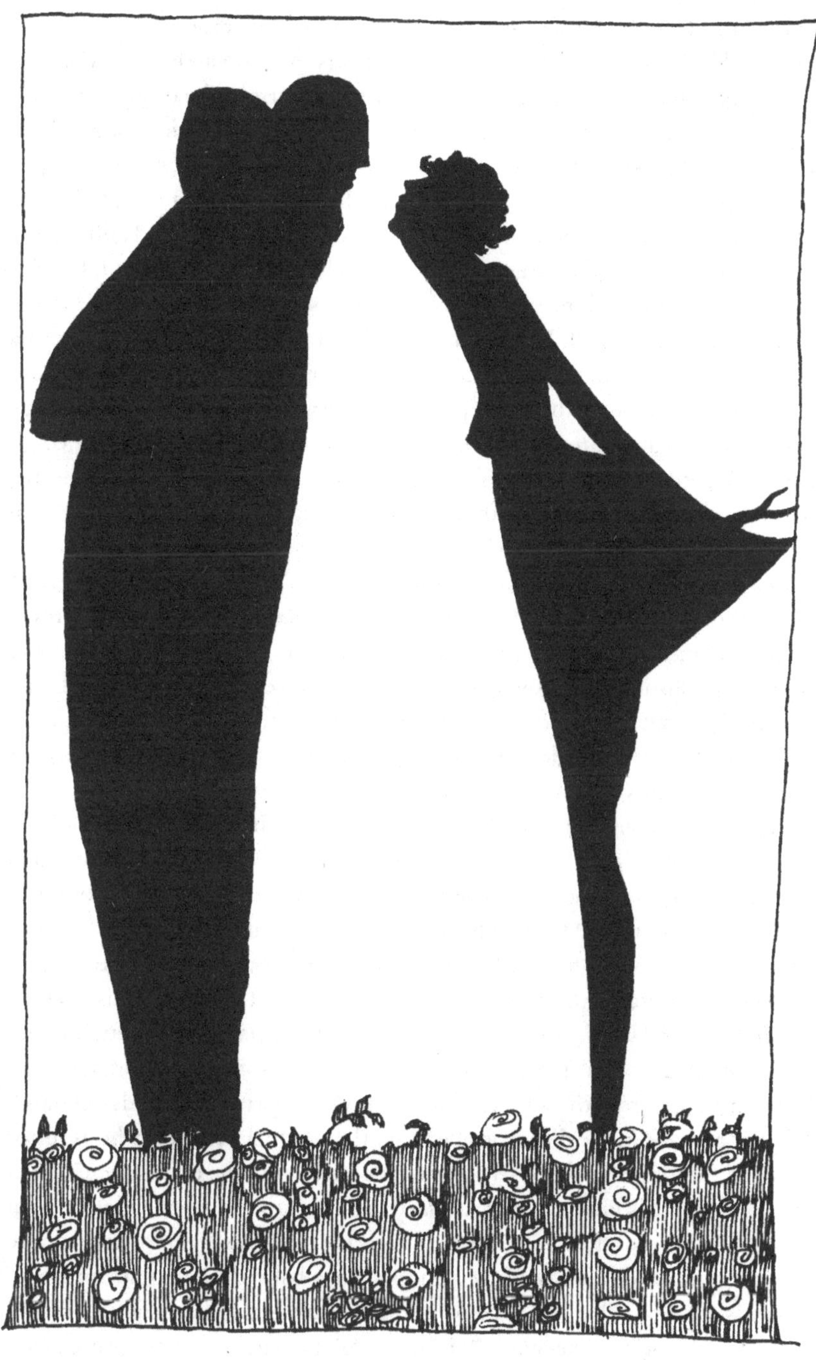

Figure 2. "The Kiss," from William Faulkner, *The Marionettes: A Play in One Act*. Used by permission of W. W. Norton & Company, Inc. Original in Albert and Shirley Small Special Collections Library, University of Virginia.

redrawn and repeated in the other three, this earlier illustration does not locate the inky black swath of the river so that it bisects the vertical thrust of the poplar tree to complete a large and central cross. In contrast, the original illustration is jocular, sporting a social-realist critique that anticipates the Faulkner who would choose some seven years later to open his second novel, *Mosquitoes*, by presenting a feminized man and his discomfiting and unwontedly personal relationship to another man's gender-coded, empty, and used milk bottle. The female statue in the earliest version holds her breast in one hand, but this gesture is defined and mocked by the fact that she holds a milk bottle in the other. This hand, which blooms upward into a floral excrescence connoting purity and Christological sacrifice in the later versions, is attached here not just to a debased but rather to a replaced maternity. While the later lily-shape here may indicate water springing from the stone maiden's hand, the original is sculpted as an ejaculatory fount. Spouting milk from this iconic bottle, the eruptive breast has become that of a consuming middle-woman rather than a primal source. The mother's milk alludes in the earliest version to the displaced fluid of female nurturance—displaced by the geyser-like plenitude of mass production. The iconic bottle replaces the female vase, maternal or erotic, with a defiling narrative that alludes to milkmen. Aside from the narrative shift accomplished by removing the factory-made bottle that has turned milk into water, a major detail distinguishes the content, radically transforming the narrative of yet another drawing as the original version diverges from the later three. This signifying discrepancy consists of a drawing within a drawing, a telling element consciously remarked by Faulkner as he chose to excise it from the stylistically elegant and simplified images he produced and reproduced in the three relatively standardized versions of *The Marionettes* that followed.

While the figure of Marietta herself varies significantly across the four versions of this drawing for the "Frontispiece" (see figs. 5 and 6, pages 10 and 11), the most noteworthy alteration appears in the first version of this opening illustration for *The Marionettes*. All four renditions portray Marietta as a resisting maiden, and in all the versions of this "Frontispiece," Marietta demurs by pulling away from the advances of an amorous Pierrot who holds her hand. What is at stake in the difference between the original Marietta who is introduced in this drawing seems to be a fashion detail, but the issue articulated in black and white is finally more than sartorial. This narrative emendation—an act of conscious exclusion in the variations that followed—amounts to more than the removal of the would-be seducer's black balls: the balls that appear on Pierrot's shoe as well as on his clown suit. Certainly, the most significant ball present in the original version's "Frontispiece" (in a gesture that is once again anticipatory of Faulkner's later fiction) is a female ball (see fig. 5). In his conscious act of editorial excision, Faulkner chose to remove the corresponding ball that links the maiden's modern apparel to Pierrot's stylized and traditional garb. In the three later versions, this inked-in ball that corresponds to Pierrot's traditional clown accoutrements has been removed from its provocative perch atop the side slit of Marietta's skirt. In the original, Marietta's blackened leg is exposed to the top of the slit where the most textured of all the black balls punctuates Marietta's direct connection to the sexual longings of Pierrot. With its distinctive nap, this ball manages to solidify the textured wildness of hair while emphasizing the diminutive elements of a facial profile: Marietta's ball forms the head of a silhouetted and sculpted Africanist female. Naked and high in the hip, this figure (visibly articulated through the blacked-in leg) struts toward rather than away from the pursuing poet, exposing what is depicted as Marietta's racialized and clearly ready sexuality. While traces of race and racially suggestive bodily features are consistent elements—nuances—in all the versions of several illustrations in Faulkner's 1920 play, race in the earliest version of this drawing is used to narrate this ingénue's willing sexuality. Indeed, Marietta embodies the first step toward the racial typing (a stratified coloring not just of histories of female vulnerability and the depredations of slavery and class but also the cultural blackening of desire and experience) that would color the white females who are presented as sexually active in Faulkner's novels. A list limited to four years of the early period includes many of the most prominent of Faulkner's fallen and racially colored women, notably Caddy Compson, Temple Drake, Dewey Dell, Lena Grove, and Joanna Burden. Why Faulkner chose to eschew this racial nuance by erasing Marietta's black ball and leg—parts that join to form a body unto themselves—is unknown, but the initial presence of this figure hidden within the figure is a telling point of origins for the coloring of female sexuality in his fiction.[7]

Meanwhile, the strangest and most experimental component of the visually active narration of *The Marionettes* has been carefully maintained in all four of the versions of Faulkner's handmade and carefully mastered volume. This dynamic relationship is accomplished by and through "Pierrot's Two Visions" (see figs. 7 and 8, pages 14 and 15). Here, an enactment of intimacy reveals the experimental Faulkner's understanding of the physicality, the stasis and motion possible in the form of the book itself. Located in a double-page spread, these visions were designed to face each other. While one side pictures Pierrot's dream and the other pictures him sleeping and dreaming his dream, Pierrot dreaming is surrounded by his equally real reality. Closed, these "Two Visions" tell a different story depending on whether the joined and superimposed images are seen from the front or the back. In each instance, the view offers a glimpse through a productively translucent blank back of a page that reveals what is going on literally inside the book. Whether seen closed from the front or the back, the Pierrot of the vision flings his arm around the isolated Marietta who stands alone in Pierrot's so-called reality (see fig. 8).

From both the front and back, the subtly translucent pages demarcate a more intimate story. Seen from the front, the palimpsest of the overlapped drawings cut off the top of Marietta's body with a clear diagonal that centers

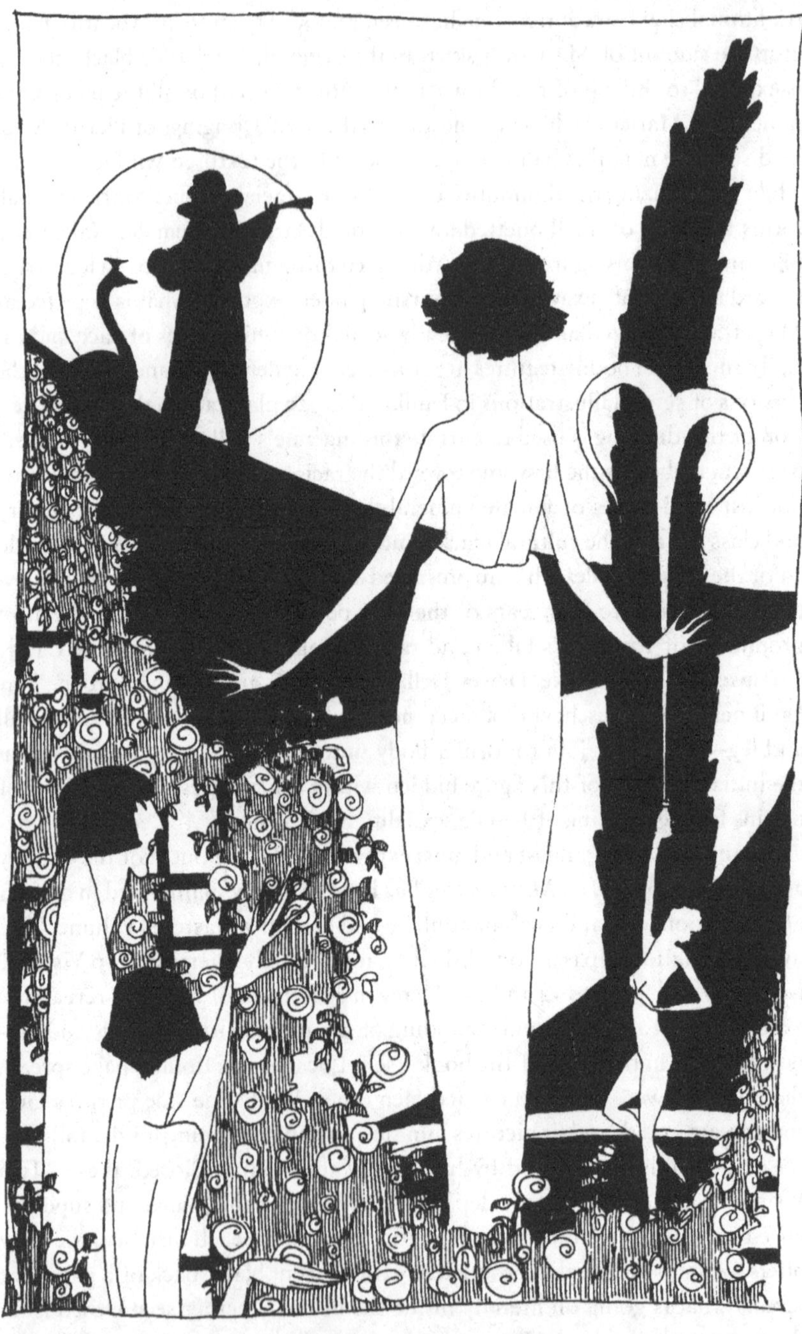

Figure 3. "Marietta and the Statue," from William Faulkner, *The Marionettes: A Play in One Act*. Used by permission of W. W. Norton & Company, Inc. Original in Albert and Shirley Small Special Collections Library, University of Virginia.

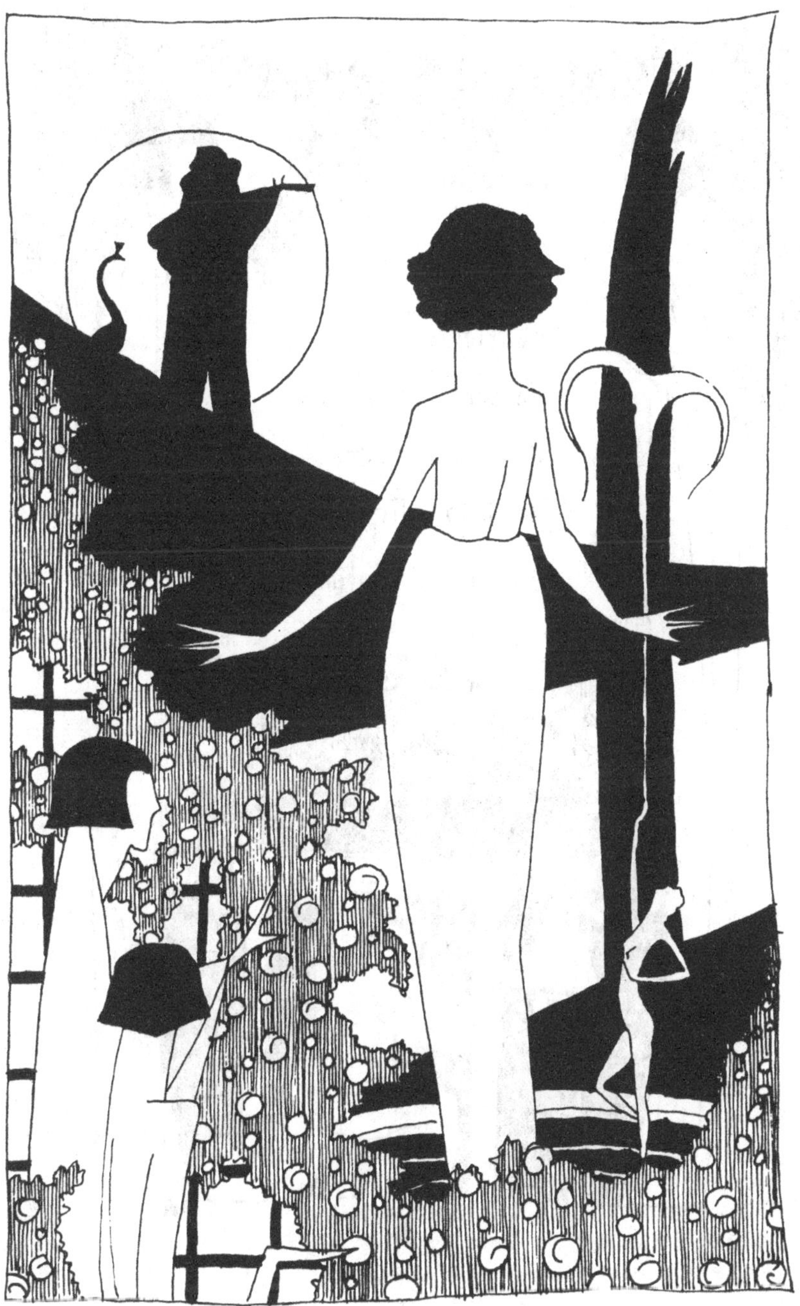

Figure 4. "Marietta and the Statue," from William Faulkner, *The Marionettes: A Play in One Act.* Used by permission of W. W. Norton & Company, Inc. Original is the second copy of two copies held in the Faulkner Collection, Harry Ransom Center, University of Texas at Austin.

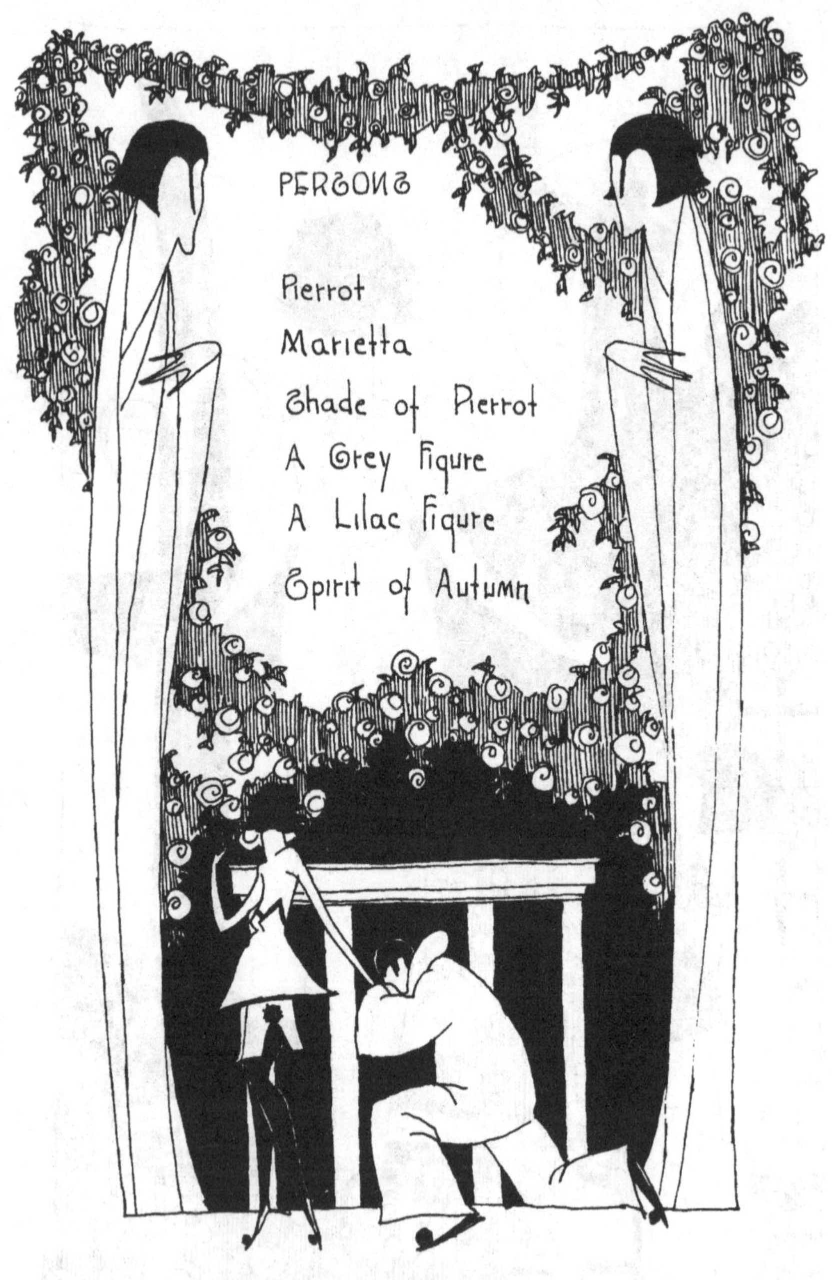

Figure 5. "Frontispiece" or "Dramatis Personae," from William Faulkner, *The Marionettes: A Play in One Act*. Used by permission of W. W. Norton & Company, Inc. Original in Albert and Shirley Small Special Collections Library, University of Virginia.

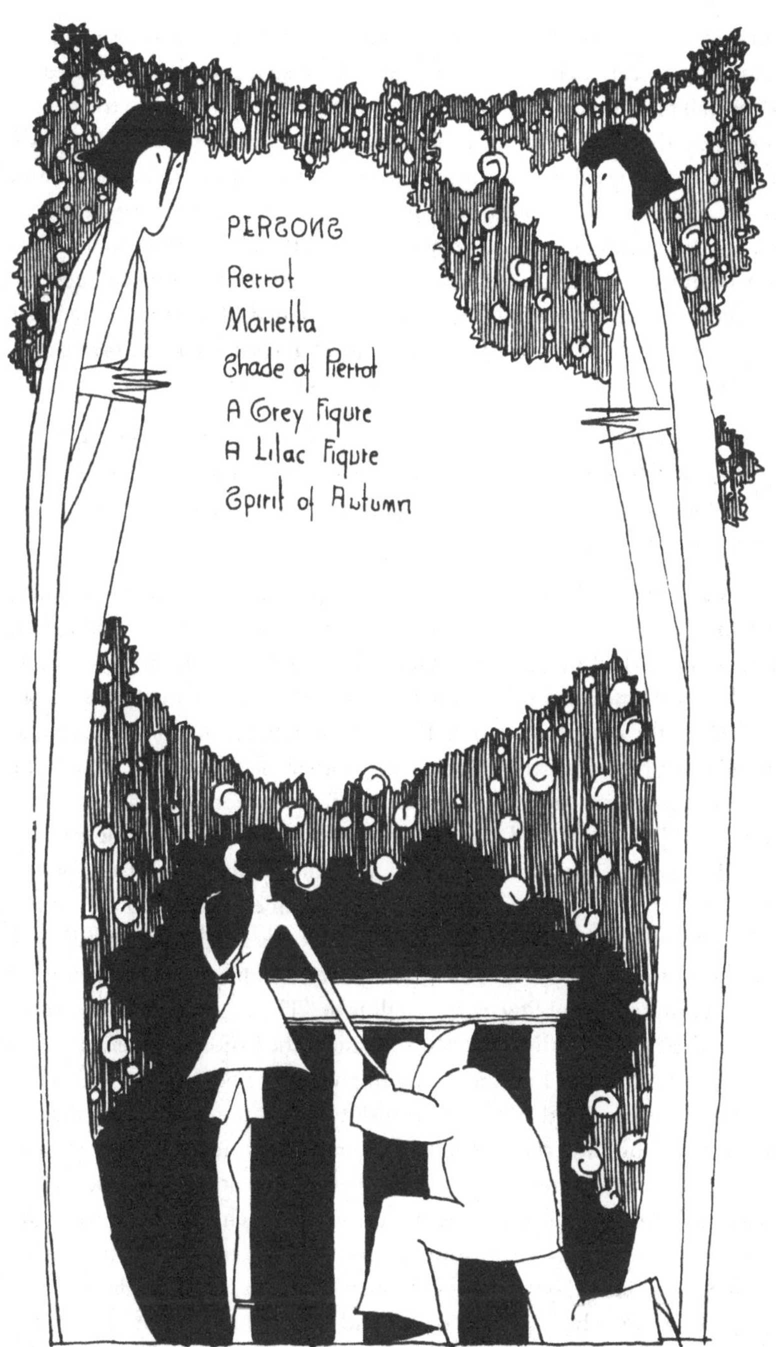

Figure 6. "Frontispiece" or "Dramatis Personae," from William Faulkner, *The Marionettes: A Play in One Act*. Used by permission of W. W. Norton & Company, Inc. Original is from the second copy of two copies held in the Faulkner Collection, Harry Ransom Center, University of Texas at Austin.

and makes sense of the buttockslike front of her labially suggestive, more grotesque than erotic, clown costume. Starkly sliced, this centrally revealed torso, both labial and mammary, has been reversed—framed off—to become the posterior, the part of the body that (despite covering the front of her body in the drawing) it has always most resembled. Viewed from the unprinted and blank backside, there is a more dominant, albeit less cleanly cut or framed, body part that asserts itself. Seen from the back, the overlapping collage features a rounded arc that points forward toward the fatal consequences of seduction: the feared maternal fate that has orphaned Marietta. As the illicit fluorescence of her dead mother's dance, Marietta has become her own warning about dancing, the fatal repetition that leads to reproduction:

> The she returned, my mother sweet, / And slow and sad were her white feet; / yet slower still, till from her grave / There sprung a flower, sweet and brave / — The flower was I, so say my aunts / And I must never learn to dance. (*The Marionettes* 23)

Shadowing forth the dominating feature of maternity, the collaged palimpsest of an emergent shape articulates the subtle yet solidified curve of a giant breast demarcated by an aureole that identifies this maternal feature as pointing to the right toward continued reading and the already inscribed death, which will be the end of her story. This breast signifies the immanence and inevitability of becoming the internalized mother of "The Kiss." Like "The Kiss," both the internalized figure of the mother and that of the fore-skinned phallus are right-facing, and this view points toward the inevitable ending. In *The Marionettes*, the moon is likened to "a dismembered breast upon the floor of a silent sea" (6). This emerging image, while pointing to the future, provides what might be called hindsight. It bears repeating (and a reading of these drawings is revisited) that this collaged breast, like the phallic mother (the mother literally doubling as the phallus in "The Kiss"), points the story toward its determinist ending.[8] At the same time, the fusion of "Pierrot's Two Visions" joins the dream and the reality to picture the possibility inherent in fiction as well as life: the dream is the translating lens, a way of seeing that always colors and overlays even the most rational of realities. When the slender volume of *The Marionettes* is closed in each of the extant versions, the Pierrot of his own dream is always embracing Marietta. When the pages are being turned, Pierrot swings his arm from one page on top of another to accomplish what, in the closed book, is a permanent embrace. Unlike the lovers "on" Keats's Grecian urn, blessed with desire and doomed to pursuit, *The Marionettes*, as long as the book remains unopened, inscribes the hidden fact of an embrace, the consummated dream, with page lying forever on intimate page.

While detailed readings of Faulkner's fiction fill separate rooms of houses (O. B. Emerson's sanctum in late-twentieth-century Tuscaloosa included color-coordinated spines and lit candles) and aisles of university libraries,

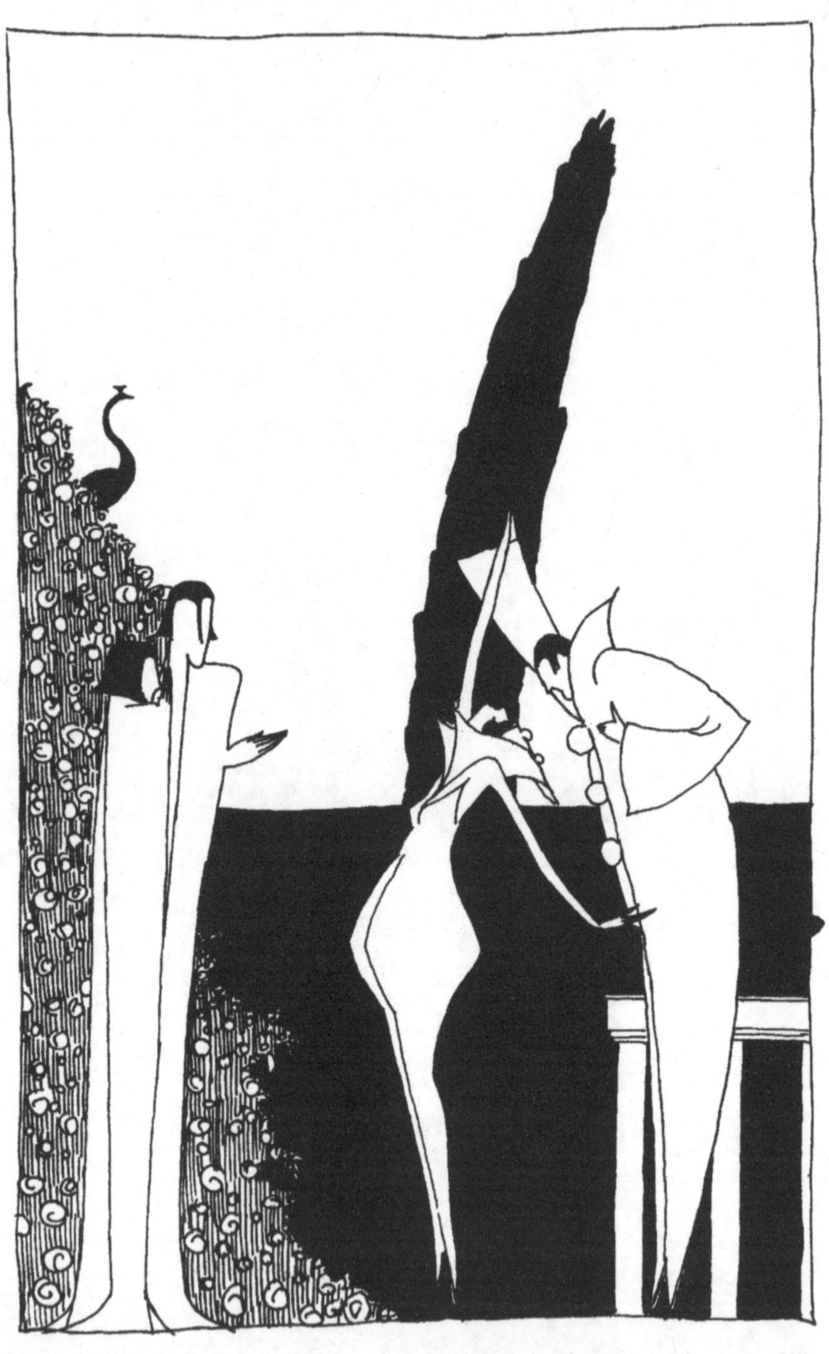

Figure 7. "Pierrot's Two Visions," from William Faulkner, *The Marionettes: A Play in One Act*. Used by permission of W. W. Norton & Company, Inc. Original in Albert and Shirley Small Special Collections Library, University of Virginia.

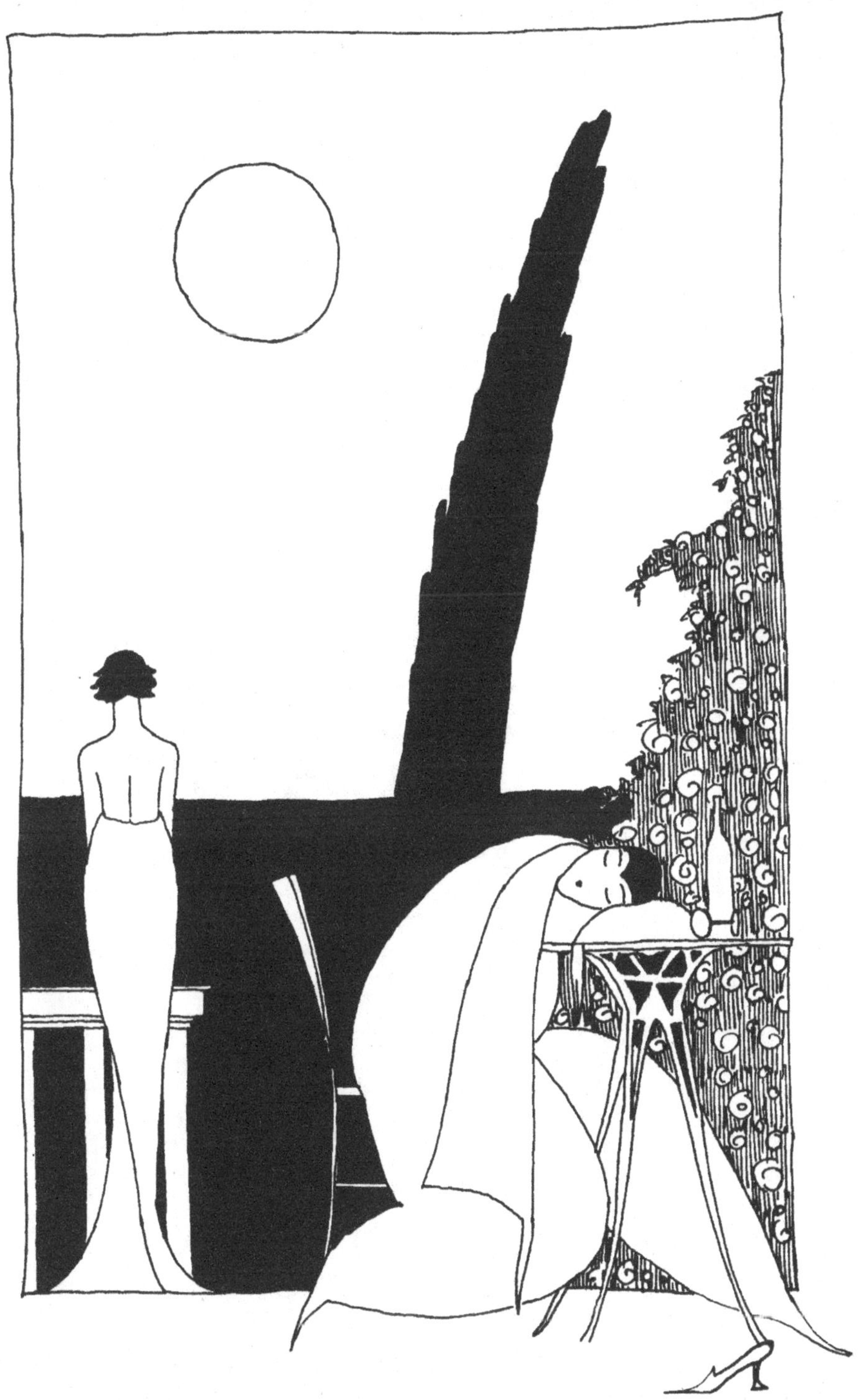

Figure 8. "Pierrot's Two Visions," from William Faulkner, *The Marionettes: A Play in One Act*. Used by permission of W. W. Norton & Company, Inc. Original in Albert and Shirley Small Special Collections Library, University of Virginia.

close readings of his drawings are rarer.[9] In retrospect, these early works, which have been seen as mimetic Beardsleys and have been respected for their technique and balance, teach us how to read Faulkner. Displaying Faulkner's deep obsession with the image, these illustrations reveal a strange but ultimately recognizable psychic iconography, a visual vocabulary that sharpens the experimental edge to much of his fiction. It is predictable that Faulkner's drawings would predicate his fiction. William Faulkner came from a family with strong interests in the visual and verbal arts. Ensconced within the wilds of Mississippi, Faulkner's maternal grandmother was offered a scholarship in the late nineteenth century to study sculpture in Rome. No less a figure than Henry James noted this peculiar herding in the arts that made female sculptresses from America as numerous as "sheep on the Palatine." As a boy, under this grandmother's watchful eye, Faulkner carved villages into the mud of Mississippi in his early efforts to shape a world out of what he would later call his "little postage stamp of native soil."

If devotion to the visual arts spun its insistent thread from the distaff side, then writing (along with violent heroics and drinking) was the male legacy left to Faulkner by his most notorious progenitor, his great-grandfather and namesake, William Clark Falkner. The acknowledged model for his Colonel Sartoris and the other larger-than-life dead avatars whom Quentin imagines arranged on the Valhalla-like hill of a Confederate heaven, Faulkner's great-grandfather, in addition to raising two militia units during the Civil War and building a railroad in the postwar chaos, wrote books and narrative poems, most notably his commercially successful and popular novel, *The White Rose of Memphis*. Before he was gunned down himself on the streets of Ripley, Mississippi, Faulkner's great-grandfather had already killed two men before the war without being brought to law. And in the violence that continued to be accepted practice in postbellum Mississippi, the outraged business partner who killed the Old Colonel was never prosecuted.

Maud Butler Falkner, Faulkner's mother, aside from going to church and managing the household, devoted her time to painting and reading.[10] Of the four Faulkner sons, William and his brother John drew on these aesthetic legacies. Like his brother, John Wesley Faulkner, a painter who was known for his "Vanishing South Series" (incomplete at the time of his death) and to a lesser extent for such novels as *Men Working* (1941) and *Dollar Cotton* (1942), William Faulkner was a writer called to words that in his hands gained the color and motion of painting and the dimensional quality of sculpture. Both brothers made art that gained solidity through the realization of absence and loss, and both Faulkner brothers understood the words' intimate brothering with what had long been familiarized as the sister arts.[11]

Before he was a recognized writer, William Faulkner was drawn to the visual arts. His first publications were poems and elegantly stylized drawings for student publications at the University of Mississippi. While some of these efforts remain lost, others damaged by fire and water have been preserved in fragmentary forms. Faulkner's *Mayday*, featuring reproductions of his own fanciful watercolors, was, like *The Marionettes*, eventually published.[12] In *Mayday*, Faulkner drew an Apollonian set piece of a knight and his lady driving a chariot drawn by dolphins through a sea of sky. The stylized dolphins harnessed together echo the multiple and pendulous breasts of the statue of Diana of Ephesus. Explicit in his early work, the visual arts continued to be integral to Faulkner's creativity, which emerged with clarity as he began to picture and, in formal terms, quite literally to sculpt his experimental fiction. The young Faulkner who traveled through Italy to France with his painter friend Bill Spratling in the fall of 1925 continued to include drawings with the letters, stories, and poems that he sent home to his mother.[13] Well into the 1920s, Faulkner was still traveling with the conscious goal of spending time on his drawing as well as his writing.[14]

Seeing Faulkner's Art

Introducing a major collection of critical responses, Robert Penn Warren described what was for him "the first, powerful impact of Faulkner's work" as "immediate intuition" not mediated "by the exegesis of critics": "The great images which the novels contain, and are—spoken in their own always enigmatic and often ambiguous terms, an awakening of awareness, by a kind of life-shock."[15] In many ways, the image in Faulkner, in its excess and elaboration, appearing and disappearing, is Faulkner's great canvas. What *The Signifying Eye* proposes is a return to the shock of Warren's encounter with the image on the page. Like his mad Quentin Compson, Faulkner saw and wrote in pictures. More than most writers, Faulkner's fiction has refused the Balkanization common to literary studies because his work itself insists on the chiastic relationships between and among race, sexuality, gender, region, religion, community, class, and animals. This list is partial, limiting and expansive, generating meaning through binaries to go beyond the oppositional and into the realm of dialectics. *The Signifying Eye* is concerned with all these subjects, but its vision locates the experimental quality of Faulkner's fiction as a visually rendered,[16] synesthetic prose that speaks both through and in the physicality of the word as image.

Faulkner's words carve, shape, accrete, creating meaning and motion through as simple an act as radical parataxis. Adjectives, designed in English to be static descriptors, are set in tumbling motion in their undivided (comma-less) multiplicity. Faulkner appears not to have understood that Choctaw, Chickasaw, and many of the new world's resident languages are verb-based, but he understood that adjectives could gain the power of verbs. In the madness of Quentin and Darl, as well as in the inner thoughts of other less definitively crazy characters, punctuation and capitalization appear and disappear. The ordering principle of hypotaxis that inscribes and maintains family boundaries in language locates and controls meaning by separating elements of thought. Refining (and to some degree, redefining) "parataxis" as a rhetorical term that finds its apex in modernism's lists undivided by commas, sentences unmarked by periods and capital letters, Faulkner establishes grounds for illicit intimacies: laying the fertility for multiple meanings. In *The Sound and the Fury*, form carries meaning beyond sanity to convey the condition of grammatical incest. This intimacy creates too much meaning rather than presenting meaninglessness or a mere method to convey madness.

Faulkner's people and places are made of words, but they press the limits of language to become telling portraits, abstract as well as representational. Signifying to the eye even as they form in the reader's mind and mouth shapes to fill the ear, subjects in Faulkner are objects that have the capacity to breathe: "to . . . stand on their hind legs and cast a shadow."[17] *The Signifying Eye* invites shared acts of seeing sound and hearing the words on the page to discover the revelatory in the mundane as a method for looking into the hiding places of creation. The focus of *The Signifying Eye* is on the physicality and the motive potential of language: to see these "great images" with the "life shock" of Warren's first vision, a vision that leads to Willem de Kooning's generative concept of the "slipping glimpse" found in seeing and seeing again.

The Signifying Eye

To begin to understand Faulkner's magnificent reach as he incorporates textual, visual, oral, and historical currents in his created world of Yoknapatawpha, this introduction has focused on Faulkner's drawings to enter his pictures, sculptures, and worlds made of words. Clearly, the game has already begun before chapter 1, which opens by proposing a definition of southern literature countering the resilient claim that the Southern Literary Renaissance is a white mystery. Building on a view of American literature that recognizes the importance of the oral and written traditions of the nineteenth-century slave narrative and slave novel as well as the continued and profoundly related popularity of the captivity narrative, chapter 1 redefines southern literature as a reverse slave narrative in which protagonists (to borrow a phrase from Whitman) go "South" to "the living soul." This journey, deeper into the past and into a racial and racially mediated sexual consciousness, takes characters toward an interiority located in the South. Journeys bring liberation or death in works by Twain, Toomer, and Wright, and notably in the case of Brown, Chopin, Hurston, and Faulkner's protagonists, this liberation comes directly through death. Finally, chapter 1, like this introduction, provides the context for Faulkner's emergence as a highly visual avant-garde writer concerned with the origins as well as the violable limits of language.

In what has been called the book inside the book, chapter 2, "Burying the Regional Mother: Faulkner on the Road to Race through the Visual Arts," insists on the significance of the female as well as the African American lineage of U.S. literature. Edith Wharton and Willa Cather are located at the experimental and misogynist headwaters of an aesthetic movement that sought to go beyond the visceral embodiment associated with the mother and the still influential tradition of female local color. "Burying the Regional Mother" explores the paradigm of abstract art that is generated after two men have collaborated to bury a woman. While Edgar Allan Poe's "The Fall of the House of Usher" plays a major role as the book returns to Wharton in chapter 6, this gothic story of a primal burial underwrites *The Signifying Eye*'s project of charting the flow as well as the genealogy or, more precisely, the family dynamics of U.S. literary history. Chapter 2 examines the association of race and corporeally blackened sons in *As I Lay Dying*, sacrificed as they attempt to frame and preserve the body of the dead and rotting mother at the center of art.

Chapter 3, "Dewey Dell, Dead Center," locates *As I Lay Dying* as a paradigm-changing book in relation to Wharton's and Cather's (and even Faulkner's own provisionally presented) parable of art. This story of Dewey Dell, who occupies the literal and metaphysical "dead center" of the novel, rewrites the family romance of art that insists on the burial of a visceral mother by shifting the focus from male sacrifice to *As I Lay Dying*'s other embedded concern: the sacrificial daughter. "Dewey Dell, Dead Center" analyzes *As I Lay Dying*'s feminist revision of the story of the sacrificial daughter. Eric Sundquist's insight that the dead Addie Bundren's largely unspoken diatribe "is an extreme example of the way in which the novel's other acts of speech should be interpreted—as partially or wholly detached from the bodily selves that appear to utter them"[18] casts light backward on the radical incorporation of voices that literalize the concept of narrative preoccupation in Dewey Dell's section 30. A figure of heretofore undisclosed meaning, Dewey Dell by her final section, the fifty-eighth, has been emptied of the rich, lyrical eroticism and interiority of her past sections to dwell in an empty existence that consists almost entirely of the spoken word. Section 30, the novel's dead center, bears the secret of *As I Lay Dying*'s contention over the artist's and the mother's competing claims to the female womb. The closest of close readings in this volume, "Dewey Dell, Dead Center" provides a genetic analysis of Faulkner's intellectual intentionality and his creative genius. Meanwhile, with equal historical specificity, Dewey Dell's narrative development is pregnant with agricultural meaning. Her unwilling progression into the mysteries of female reproduction is both a paradoxical counter to and an elaborator of the seasons of production: the brutal march of the cotton calendar framing the sanctity of the cash crop in an upland patch in north Mississippi during the Depression.

Chapter 4, "The Signifying Eye: Faulkner's Artists and the Engendering of Art," views such early works as "Elmer," "Portrait of Elmer" (begun in the mid-1920s), and *Mosquitoes* (1927) as aesthetic primers that reveal crucial components of Faulkner's parable of art and the artist in which the visceral flesh is opposed and juxtaposed to the sterility and impotence of the word. This chapter considers the significance of Faulkner's major pictorial interventions in his novels: the in *The Sound and the Fury*, the in *As I Lay Dying*, and the ∇ or delta stood on its head in "Delta Autumn," the penultimate story of *Go Down, Moses* (1942). In addition to looking at word-shaped blank spaces (the most notable one is the space where Addie Bundren insists her virginity used to be), this chapter explores Faulkner's integral use of the shapes inhabited and articulated by letters themselves in print as well as in cursive writing, letters that picture the arrival of death in *The Wild Palms* (1939).

Chapter 5, "Echoing Back to *Absalom:* Quentin's Reverie in *The Sound and the Fury*," considers patterns of words on the page as an audibly visible and visual phenomenon. This Faulknerian device of the echo formation, identified here as the narcissistic fold, is seen as the textual and reflective mirror of Quentin Compson's madness. Located near the close of Quentin's section in *The Sound and the Fury*, this madman's longest reverie is revealed as the formal site for the origins of Faulkner's masterpiece, *Absalom, Absalom!* (1936). A prolonged act of "slow reading," "Echoing Back to *Absalom*" likens Quentin's suicide to that of a heroine from classical antiquity while insisting on the importance of the bridge as the literal location for both Quentin's reverie and for his leap into a drowning death that finally stops the words. The Quentin of *The Sound and the Fury* does not want to cross the bridge into what waits in the twentieth century: Quentin refuses to breathe the cloyingly familiar air of a bellicose and annihilating modernity that has already been conceived in the sartorial sign of the brown shirt.[19]

Chapter 6, "Bonfires of the Masculinities: Wharton and Faulkner in the Glare of Whistler's *Falling Rocket*," has its origins in the most racist passage in all of Wharton's work, her critique of a mongrel and miscegenated art. This passage is punctuated by what was, for Faulkner, a provocative reference to "a Whistler Nocturne" in Wharton's *Twilight Sleep*. Returning to the very passages of *As I Lay Dying* singled out in chapter 2 for having framed the mother at the center of art, chapter 6 locates these scenes as textual descendants of Wharton's prose in her Pulitzer Prize–winning *Age of Innocence* (1920) and her lesser-known diatribe that joins failed maternity to "bad" aesthetics in her critically declaimed 1927 novel, *Twilight Sleep*. Indeed, Faulkner's fiction turns again and again in his writing to Whistler's most significant contribution to modern painting and to the history of abstract art: the scene of fires (the infamous fireworks) that light the night sky in Whistler's *The Falling Rocket*. In the context of its use in Faulkner's work, this Whistler painting, along with several of Beardsley's illustrations, reveals the profound connections between Faulkner's hypermasculine and racially blackened illegitimate sons: Jewel of *As I Lay Dying* and Joe Christmas of *Light in August*. As the title intimates, this chapter is concerned with the sacrificial destination of male identity, using this trope as a way of understanding the impact of race and the visual arts in *Light in August*, Faulkner's 1932 novel, which would inspire Willem de Kooning in his epiphany that became a transformative turn in Abstract Expressionism.

Chapter 7, "De Kooning's Faulkner Trilogy: *Light in August*, *Black Friday*, and *Black Untitled*," proves that Faulkner provided the narrative fuse for a painting that has been recognized as a turning point in mid-twentieth-century abstract art. While Willem de Kooning could not have been familiar with Faulkner's Beardsleyesque drawings from *The Marionettes*, Faulkner's writings inspirited the word-loving de Kooning who, seeming to follow Faulkner's lead in *As I Lay Dying*, made a career of laying rotting and rottingly effulgent women on canvas. Arguably, de Kooning, along with William Faulkner and Jackson Pollack, was able (in Allan Stone's apt language) to a "liquefy cubism." Chapter 7, which considers over a dozen of de Kooning's works, focuses on three of de Kooning's "black" paintings from his field-changing black-and-white period. These black paintings, including *Black Friday* and *Black Untitled*, continue the pictorial conversations initiated by de Kooning's *Light in August* (1946–47) to complete the circuit of the painter's brilliantly cartographic mapping of the Picassoid history of art. De Kooning's pictorial vocabulary of race, including Africanist sculpture and the shape of the dark continent itself, implicates Faulkner (abetted by Picasso and Gorky) in de Kooning's transformation of his portrait-focused art that emerged with the power of an abstract idea in the years immediately following World War II. The fact that Faulkner had already embedded pictures of racialized and maternally fatal sexuality in field/space drawings in *The Marionettes* suggests that these elements transfigured into the highly visual and, at times, electric complexity of Faulkner's prose drew de Kooning to Faulkner's words.[20] Epiphanic metamorphoses, seeing and seeing again, inscribe motion in stasis, and de Kooning's major collage portraits that incorporate this potential are found in two of this artist's trilogy of Faulkner-inspired paintings. Like his influential interlocutor, de Kooning was moved to picture the midcentury crisis in masculinity not just in these "black" paintings but also in the genealogy of the male-destroying arm of his obstreperous *Woman I*.

In the epilogue, "Collateral Damage, Collating Strange: Canned Death, Collage Portraits, and Uncanny and Uncannable Beauty in *Intruder in the Dust* and *The Town*," Faulkner is seen as entering these post–World War II novels through his own early work, notably *Sanctuary* and *The Sound and the Fury*. As Faulkner draws on his pictorial vocabulary, whether in the telling juxtaposition of montage or through the collating drift of objects that lead to characters' constructed portraits and the ordered art of graves, his visually obsessed work emerges in greater clarity after it has been framed, given a context, by de Kooning's great black and whites. Ultimately, William Faulkner's art can be seen in his drive to incorporate the pictorial, the sculptural, and the accretions of collage to present print and its figuring of absence as a signifying medium.

CHAPTER ONE

Envisioning Faulkner and Southern Literature

The Reverse Slave Narrative

Down there a poet is now almost as rare as an oboe-player, a dry-point etcher or a metaphysician. It is, indeed, amazing to contemplate so vast a vacuity . . . And yet, for all its size and all its wealth and all the "progress" it babbles of, it is almost as sterile, artistically, intellectually, culturally, as the Sahara Desert . . . If the whole of the late Confederacy were to be engulfed by a tidal wave tomorrow, the effect upon the civilized minority of men in the world would be but little greater than that of a flood of the Yang-tse-kiang. It would be impossible in all history to match so complete a drying-up of a civilization.
—H. L. Mencken, "Sahara of the Bozart," 1917

Everyone in the South has no time for reading because they are all too busy writing.
—William Faulkner

Penning his infamous critique of the state of art, letters, and literacy in the cultural desert he dubbed "The Sahara of the Bozart," H. L. Mencken quotes a "true poet," one J. Gordon Coogler, whom he calls "the last bard of Dixie": "Alas for the South! Her Books have grown fewer. / She was never much given to literature."[1] Surveyed as an "awe-inspiring blank" in every category of literacy and aesthetics, art in Mencken's South has suffered the fate of the aristocracy: "[Y]ou will not find a single southern poet above the level of a neighborhood rhymester." Leaving aside James Branch Cabell—whom Mencken designates as "a lingering survivor of the *ancien regime*: a scarlet dragonfly embedded in opaque amber," the sharp-tongued critic asserts: "you will not find a single southern prose writer who can actually write."[2] According to Mencken, the South, which he locates between "the Potomac mudflats and the Gulf," is so intellectually arid that the region does not even have a "bad" historian, sociologist, or philosopher. Just over a decade later, this region defined as a desert by Mencken would emerge as the literary home to a concentration of the most gifted writers of prose in the history of the United States.

These writers included sociologists and historians who wrote like novelists: Howard Odum, who began by imagining the strongly voiced journey of a "Black Ulysses,"[3] and a young C. Vann Woodward, who understood the rhetorical device of irony as a mode that was essential to his fact-based account of his region, writing a first book dedicated to the strange career of Georgia's white populist in *Tom Watson: Agrarian Rebel* (1938). Robert Penn Warren, a writer of such gifts that he would become the only individual to be awarded the Pulitzer Prize for fiction (for *All the King's Men* in 1946) as well as for poetry (in 1958 and again in 1979), emerged in 1929 as the author of a volume of questionable history, *John Brown: The Making of a Martyr* (1929). In their earliest books, these men emphasized portraiture and biography, respectively, to underline the place of narrative in the social sciences and in letters.[4]

Whatever else may be said, these white men were writing under the influence of signifying writers of color who were addressing the problem of the South as a site of troubling inheritance during the creative genesis known as the Harlem Renaissance. Arriving in New York at the height of the renaissance, the young Arkansas-born and bred Vann Woodward, who would write his dissertation on Watson at Chapel Hill (inspired by the work of the creatively driven sociologist Odum), had gotten a scholarship to Columbia designed to help impoverished students from the state of Mississippi. Woodward, speaking about his early years, confessed modestly that he "had played a role in the Harlem Renaissance." Unable to remember the name of the play (which had not become famous), Woodward recalled the work's author, Langston Hughes, the poet and playwright who had asked the history student from the South to perform the role of an unmemorable, but by definition evil, plantation master.

While the self-identified southerner (born in Alabama and raised in the Florida panhandle) Zora Neale Hurston was among the early-twentieth-century African American writers, her work is considered to be somewhat late in the temporal period assigned to the Harlem Renaissance. Hurston, who continued to write into the 1950s (her last novel was *Seraph on the Sewanee* [1948]), added to the social-science credentials of these gifted southern authors, deepening the voice and complexity of analysis that was shaping the narratives of the region. Hurston, after being trained by Franz Boas in the still young field of anthropology, returned to the South after her stint at Barnard; her role in both settings was and would continue to be that of a participant observer. Speaking her native patois as she collected stories, songs, humor, and rhymes from turpentine camps before entering into her serious study of older religious practice (she went through the ritual to become a practitioner, a voodoo doctor, some eight times) and writing works of front-porch lore such as *Mules and Men* (1935), Hurston became a major novelist who wrote works that are known for their orality as well as their understanding of "intimate gate[s]" and their back-porch content. Unlike the elite narrators of social science and the new field of psychoanalysis, Hurston specialized in the exploration of the interior lives of women. Drawn by both totem and taboo to speculate on the voice of Miriam in the Exodus and the psyches of economically struggling white as well as black women, Hurston ventured into Freud's territory to examine the mystery he had located as the "dark continent" of femininity and femaleness.[5]

In terms of history and race-defined and race-driven psychoses of loss, William Faulkner was considered by novelist Ralph Ellison as the authority for understanding the African American past.[6] It may have been by design that Faulkner's portrait was the only visible image in Vann Woodward's academic study at Yale; the most gifted and honored southern historian used Faulkner here as he used him in his beautifully written, ironic, and transformative works of history: to back him up. If the social scientists of the region were writing like novelists and, in the instance of Hurston, becoming a noted novelist, Faulkner began to read them and to lead them as early as the late 1920s. Historically and culturally awake in ways that still drive observers to pained distraction, Faulkner was the novelist who wrote like a painter while he dynamically sculpted his work through the carved bodies and congealed breath of his created people. Likening himself to Shakespeare and occasionally to God, Faulkner wrote like Cézanne, the painter to whom he is most often compared by scholars of the visual. Writing to his mother from Paris in the fall of 1925, where he reported visiting galleries and private collections, Faulkner announced: "Cezanne paints with light."[7] It is perhaps not an accident that Willem de Kooning, the earliest and most insightful figure to apprehend the visual power of Faulkner's fiction, wrote and delivered the first speech of his life on "Cezanne and the Color of the Veronese." De Kooning would later argue that "innovators come at the end of a period," concluding "Cezanne gave the finishing touches to Impressionism before he came face to face with his 'little sensation.'"[8] In narrative terms, de Kooning is right: endings provide the sites where beginnings ("sensation[s]" large and small) are most starkly visible. Scholars, trying to place Faulkner's work in the traditions of the visual arts, have quarreled over whether *As I Lay Dying* is a "cubist" (focusing on structure) or "expressionist" (focusing on emotional color and tonalities) novel.[9] Seen as a symbolist in his own early drawings in his 1920 hand-illustrated and hand-lettered work, *The Marionettes: A Play in One Act*, the relation between symbol and image has been outlined by Robert Musil in his "Visual Imagination of William Faulkner": "When images are connected to a larger pattern of meanings, they become symbols . . . capable of [being] translat[ed] into the visual arts." Encyclopedic and historically immersed in the remnants of past lives found in plantation diaries and account books, Faulkner is "a pictorial writer" who used language to challenge and to enter the multidimensional and carved realm of the visual and plastic arts.[10]

The Southern Renaissance

The Southern Renaissance has been declared by critics as having begun in 1929, the year that saw the publication of major works by Robert Penn Warren, Thomas Wolfe, and William Faulkner.[11] From the outset, poet and sometime novelist Allen Tate questioned the appropriateness of the word "renaissance," concluding that this literary outpouring "was more precisely a birth, not a rebirth." Building on Tate's insights, C. Vann Woodward, introducing "[t]he second and more common historical usage of [the term] 'renaissance'" to refer to "the evocation of the ghost of a dead civilization, as the ghost of Hellenic culture was evoked in thirteenth- to fifteenth-century Italy," insisted that "surely nothing of that sort took place in the South." Woodward's assessment in 1975 was not unlike that of Faulkner in 1933, who quipped that the South would never accomplish anything in "music and the plastic arts." Faulkner is famous for not acknowledging individual or cultural influences on his writing, so his assessment of the state of "music and the plastic arts" in his region is Menckenesque and unsurprising. However, he did feed on the cultural ferment that gave voice and shape to the Mississippi of his time. As Thadious Davis has documented, Faulkner regularly heard the dance rhythms and art of what had become W. C. Handy's "franchise" of bands, traveling ensembles that played the southern college circuit.[12] While Robert Johnson has become a household name through the rise of recorded music and his acknowledged influence on Eric Clapton and other British rockers, the names of blues queens alone—Ma Rainey (billed as "Mother of the Blues" and "Songbird of the South"), Bessie Smith ("Empress of the Blues"), Billie Holiday ("Lady Day")—frame Faulkner's South as "birthplace" and wellspring rather than the tonal dearth of art that he and Mencken conjured. The Mississippi that once sported the nostalgic slogan "The Magnolia State" is pointedly nationalist now, declaring itself on license plates to be "The Birthplace of America's Music."[13] The Faulkner who in 1927 published his second novel, voiced by vapid aesthetes and desperate artists trapped together on a stalled yacht in Lake Pontchartrain, might not have been aware of the existence of Shearwater Pottery in Ocean Springs, Mississippi, and he could not have been aware of the still-to-be discovered psychotropic watercolors awash in water and light generated by his contemporary, Walter Anderson, a figure who was known for his pottery and who made madness into art. This being said, the William Faulkner who had any interest in art could not have spent time in Pascagoula without having heard about the work of George Ohr, the storied "Mad Potter of Biloxi"; this self-taught artist created pots, playing in bright shapes, ultimately (like Faulkner after him) favoring form over color. Faulkner's artist figures that focused on glassblowing and the ideal shape of the female vase are telling when seen in a Mississippian, let alone a southern, context that would include the remarkable beauty fired from the clay of the late-nineteenth-century Carolina Piedmont.[14] Faulkner's disparagement of music in 1933 (unlike his bad-faith but self-preserving denials of the influence of the words of Joyce and the theories of Freud) speaks to his unfathomed consciousness or absence of consciousness of the art he imbibed as mother's milk. Thadious Davis, addressing the dynamic and changing field of American popular music, has understood the cross-racial synergy of an era in which blue notes, elegy, and the changing emphases of syncopation had striking implications for literature. Writing about the late 1910s and 1920s, Davis identifies an intense "period of reverse acculturation, in which aspects of the minority culture moved into the dominant one with the accumulative effect of transforming the majority." "Cultural diffusion," an aesthetic force that fertilized art as it crossed the color line, brought a "revitalization . . . witnessed perhaps most vividly in the New Negro or Harlem Renaissance."[15] This vitality constituted the living matrix that birthed the Southern Renaissance. The language of Faulkner's region, like the music, was the air that his ears breathed. This being said, it would be wrong not to acknowledge that this southern literary emergence in 1929—so surprising to the literate white world—was indeed based on "the ghost of a dead civilization," the diabolically vital and haunting specter of slavery recorded and recounted in the written word of the slave narrative and the slave novel.[16] These ghosts, along with the writers of the Harlem Renaissance, precursed and begat what we now think of as southern literature.

While Louis Rubin notes that critics could "justly feel uncomfortable . . . talking about an entity known as 'Southern Literature'" as opposed to individual authors, he insists on the necessity of addressing this phenomenon, placing Faulkner as only "the most distinguished" among what he recognizes as "a galaxy of accomplished literary artists."[17] If the quantity of literary production is impressive in the twentieth-century South, the quality is shocking. An apostolic twelve, cut crudely from the end of an alphabetized list, reads like a pantheon: Lee Smith, Elizabeth Spencer, William Styron, Allen Tate, Peter Taylor, Jean Toomer, Alice Walker, Margaret Walker, Robert Penn Warren, Eudora Welty, Thomas Wolfe, and Richard Wright were producing works that defined twentieth-century southern (as well as American) literature.[18] Partial and incomplete, the much longer list in the note favors novelists while acknowledging the centrality of the short story and in particular the story-cycle novel to a literature that has its provocation in orality. This literature, paradoxically emerging from poverty and illiteracy to challenge hierarchies of art, has created the South, and page by page it both answers and begs the question of southern distinctiveness.

William Faulkner (who, quite drunk, once resisted going further north than he had already been on the subway system in Manhattan) had an unerring sense of direction. Faulkner never denied being southern, and he was among the first to acknowledge the existence of southern literature as a phenomenon. African American writers and Harlem Renaissance figures other than the most famous of the untoward—Zora Neale Hurston—chose to identify themselves as southern while some, wary of the taint of whiteness and insult in the term, pointedly did not. Alice Dunbar-Nelson (best known for her New Orleans stories in *The Goodness of St. Rocque* [1899]) enunciated the grounds of her own race-blind ambition, expressed in her desire to surpass George Washington Cable as a great "Southern writer."[19] Jean Toomer, the most influential ancestor of southern modernism, published *Cane* (1923), a prose-poem cycle that has increasingly been understood as an innovative novel. This lyrical masterpiece, seen as a culmination of the experimental promise of the Harlem Renaissance and the extensive African American exploration of the collage form, was written by an author who pleaded unsuccessfully with his publisher, Horace Liveright, to keep *Cane* from being marketed as a work by an African American.[20] Toomer claimed that he was a "new American," and wanted to be true to all of the bloods that ran in his veins.[21] Stating a modernist fact (a geography of creativity that would have included Taos, New Mexico, in its locations), Toomer openly acknowledged that he had journeyed south in the 1920s to be closer to the "sources" of his art.

Alice Walker, taking a course on southern literature that consisted of works by Faulkner, Welty, and McCullers at Sarah Lawrence College in the 1960s, recalls her epiphany in reading the assigned works of Flannery O'Connor. Walker credits O'Connor's fiction with having taught her that she did not want to live and write in the poverty of a segregated literature. Born in a sharecropper's shack (unbeknownst to her, just down the road from the family dairy farm where the terminally ill O'Connor wrote and died), Walker was capable of imagining a literary estate that did not cede territory. Able to distinguish the adjective "southern" from meaning white, Walker noted that there were no black southern writers taught in this racially focused and no doubt (given the precociousness of this female-dominated canon) politically conceived course.[22] While C. Vann Woodward argued that the region would come of age when the adjective "southern" came to refer to the region's black population as well as its rebellious white inhabitants, Woodward and others continued to see the emergence of the Southern Renaissance as a white mystery rather than the progeny of aesthetic miscegenation inherent in William Faulkner's, as well as Alice Walker's, literary genealogy.

Even the most conservative conception of the Southern Literary Renaissance, one that names a figure such as William Styron as Faulkner's heir, necessitates a consideration of the formal influence of Robert Penn Warren, finally placing both Warren and Styron in the tradition of the slave narrative. Styron's first novel, *Lie Down in Darkness* (1951), has been understood as being Faulknerian in theme while being indebted in formal terms to Warren's *All the King's Men* (1946), the most successful of his ten novels. Warren's fifth novel, *Band of Angels* (1955), concerns an elite light-skinned woman who discovers that she is a slave at the time of her father's death. Here, Warren rewrites the story of the "tragic mulatta" told in slave novels such as William Wells Brown's *Clotel; or the President's Daughter* (1853) and Frances E. W. Harper's *Iola Leroy; or Shadows Uplifted* (1892), to give the heroine of color a voice as the narrator rather than as a courageous and painfully exposed character.

A dozen years after Warren published his fictionalized slave narrative, William Styron penned a first-person account that gives voice and interiority to the most feared revolutionary in U.S. history. It speaks to the origins and materials of southern literature that Styron's *Confessions of Nat Turner* (1967), considered his most successful work, is written in the threatening voice of a resisting slave, a character whose motivations include psychosexual torments in the form of fantasies about white women. In his novel, Styron, who would later speculate that he had "unwittingly created one of the world's first politically incorrect texts,"[23] revealed the heightened racial tensions over black masculinity that reached a white heat in the late 1960s. While Styron's *Confessions* precipitated controversy, his work has not approached the productively provocative place of Faulkner's varied and offensive representations of race, whether as static stereotype or troubling paradox. As Anne McKnight has argued, contending with complex Japanese hierarchies as her mediating context, racism is difficult to translate:

> Faulkner's texts, with all of their hauntings of the racial hysteria, [inscribe] the sprawling structure of materiality, sensory mechanism and figure that is his inscription of the "South." The narration of Faulkner's south is always in the process of uneven growth, of slapping up another textual building . . . , in the process of re-reading and re-presenting itself as a (not always successful) strategy of bringing the effects of this racial hysteria into a field of legibility.[24]

As Craig Werner prophesied, this continued response by black writers to Faulkner's irritations and incitements is far from a joyous coming to voice, but Faulkner's fiction seems destined to remain a generative place of productive dialogue about race and racism.[25]

The neo-slave narrative,[26] often in novels set in the United States or the Caribbean, forms a suggestive parallel to the southern novel, as it continues to develop as a site of political fiction that uses the "not dead" past to reflect on problems in the present. In many ways, Faulkner's *Light in August*, as it located this crisis of masculinity and incarceration within a body defined by race rather than color, provided a crucial turning point for writing about the violence inherent in the enforcement of racially delimited identities. The embodied conflict of Joe Christmas ignited political writers, often male, across the wavering and full spectrum of the color line, and the white woman is a pregnant presence in Faulkner's narrative of violence. Describing Lena Grove as "a wistful staging of a myth," André Bleikasten argues that

> when the procession of identical wagons in which Lena is traveling is likened to a procession "moving forever and without progress across an urn" (7), Faulkner's pastoral calls attention to itself as a work of art. And, revealingly, the reference here is to a plastic medium, to the arts of space, whose privileges Faulkner must have sometimes envied and with which he seems to have competed with more vigorously in *Light in August* than in any of his other novels.

Seen here as an ekphrastic act as it sculpts and structures Keats's "Ode on a Grecian Urn," Faulkner's *Light in August*—framed by the flesh of men and women sculpted by pregnancy and other forms of bodily violence—is understood by Bleikasten to be Keats's poem "reread and rewritten in and by the novel."[27]

The Southern Literary Renaissance, positioned at the cusp in 1929, also ushered in a decade that would become known for its nostalgic idealizations of a plantation South, a mythology canonized in Margaret Mitchell's bestseller *Gone with the Wind* (1936), and given heft in over seventy Hollywood films trading on the popular and highly marketable longing for an "Old South."[28] Mitchell's novel, which contains only one mixed-blood character, the significantly named Dilsey, avoids issues of race while promoting regeneration through capitalism. Known for its sentences of over eighty lines in search of a paragraph, Faulkner's *Absalom, Absalom!*, published the same year as *Gone with the Wind*, places race and miscegenation at its center. In fictions that often did not provide solutions or consolations, Faulkner created a world that could not satisfy the programmatic desires of the Depression era, but would inspire later writers of varying colors and classes to create their own complexly articulated Yoknapatawphas.[29] From the 1970s to the present, with a steadily decreasing emphasis on the fast-aging adjective, critics have touted the "New Regionalism." However, this literary movement continues, in the culturally deep tracks of Faulkner and Eudora Welty, to represent regions within this region remains the most distinctive, productive, and accomplished literary area of the United States.

Yoknapatawphas All

Raymond Andrews was forty-four when he published *Appalachee Red* (1978), which chronicles life after World War I in his fictional Muskhogean County, Georgia, a world that he examines in more depth in *Baby Sweet's* (1983), a novel set in a local brothel during the era of the civil rights movement.[30] More political and situated in a plantation past, Ernest Gaines's eight novels take place in the fictional environs based on the actual River Lake Plantation in Louisiana, where his family has lived for seven generations, framed by a narrative history that begins in slavery. The author of *The Autobiography of Miss Jane Pittman* (1971), which charts a woman's transition from bondage into the challenging freedom of the twentieth century, Gaines, like Faulkner, is known for multivocal narrations, in particular *A Gathering of Old Men* (1983),[31] a work that, like Faulkner's *As I Lay Dying*, is presented through the first-person accounts of fifteen named narrators. (In Gaines's novel, his "Candace" bears the more usual nickname "Candy," and she is one of the narrators, unlike the close to voiceless Caddy [Candace] in Faulkner's *Sound and the Fury*. As more than one observer has noted, the "Old Men" of Gaines's title have become more potent than the Compsons or even Jewel of the Bundrens. Class, if not race, is equalized as these men come bearing guns.) Faulkner remains recognizable as a formal presence for Randall Kenan in his creation of Tims Creek, a community whose fictional template, directly recalling *Go Down, Moses*, includes layered stories, letters, and journal entries, to build a late-twentieth-century Yoknapatawpha. Regions within regions, geographically conceived as well as narratively populated with voices, are important for naming Yoknapatawphas, and Kenan's Tims Creek locates a fictional community in the swampy low country of North Carolina.

Faulkner's work has been acknowledged as and is a source for this creative outpouring, the wellsprings of cultural regions distinguished by their creators' capacities to voice their own communities of fiction. In terms of ethnic and race-based fictions, Faulkner was and continues to be a major influence. Even the most cursory glance at the late-twentieth-century fictional masterworks treating Native American experience reveal his acknowledged presence as a formal as well as thematic forebear, recognizable in the works of the brilliant and voice-based experimental authors N. Scott Momaday, Louise Erdrich, and Ray A. Young Bear Jr. *The Sound and the Fury* is alluded to explicitly in Momaday's Pulitzer Prize–winning novel, *House Made of Dawn* (1964), while Erdrich has created complex and interrelated historical communities that include islands of the very real and mythic past, a place pockmarked by the slaughterhouses and bingo palaces of more recent acts of survival committed amid and despite depredations. Erdrich's encyclopedic oeuvre provided provocation for Young Bear's strong language-based entry. Ironically, Young Bear, the separatist author of two novels with alternating sections in syllabic (spoken) Mesquakie, is a poet and a drummer who, despite the fact that he may never have read Faulkner's work, is more Faulknerian than Erdrich in his tribal-based fiction's challenge to decipherability. Young Bear conveys and withholds cultural knowledge through his inclusion of transliterated orality.

Language—the difficulties of dialect as words become the medium of resisting incorporation into a national or narratively flattened body—is crucial to the most productive uses of racially inflected class consciousness and the unanswerable hysterias of insulted humanity. Paulo Da-Luz-Moreira has revealed the pained vitality of a contact zone that I think of as "the inland triangle." This is a modernism with Faulkner at its northern apex as backwoods narrators struggle against the encroaching codifications of bureaucracy, articulating cultural resistance in João Guimarães Rosa's Brazilian backlands of Minas Gerais and Juan Rulfo's deep south Mexico in Jalisco. The challenges inherent in comparatist analysis are foregrounded by the state of translation. As Rodrigo Bauer reveals, the most recent Brazilian translation of *As I Lay Dying* is in high-church Portuguese rather than the rich dialects nourished in internal regions such as the dark corner known to Faulknerians as the "Deep North" of Brazil.[32]

Of the fictional worlds generated in Faulkner's wake, the Japanese Yoknapatawpha created in the novels of Nakagami Kenji (that, like Young Bear's work, is rooted in textual documents which go back centuries) is uncompromisingly dedicated to the juncture where the profoundly oral vessel of culture meets literacy and the written word. Born in 1948 into the despised *burakumin* (considered the lowest and most defiled or polluted caste in the highly stratified and hierarchical structures of traditional Japanese culture),[33] Nakagami, according to his own account, was distinguished in his village for being able to read his own name. Nakagami's work, in what Kato Yuji has called "[t]he lushness of language,"

> repeat[s] the images of the random growths of plants and roots . . . [to] constitute what might be called a culturally transplanted Yoknapatawpha saga . . . polyphonic mixtures of random voices and pieces of vernacular narrations of his almost anonymous characters. His images reverberate with the memories of the texture of Faulkner's writings: rumors, fragmented narrations, voices of isolated, orphaned characters, coming out of no specific origins. Nakagami echoes these Faulknerian textual idiosyncrasies so persistently that they come to constitute the very essence of his writings.[34]

Nakagami emphasizes the crucial importance of oral narrative and the sound of words as a dimension that resists and delights in the incorporation of the vocal into the written word, inscribing difference and distance from the imperial claims of Kyoto as well as those of the metropolis, a Tokyo that is even further to the north. As he translates the underlying forces, thematic and formal, locating a world of a Japanese "South" in the Kumano region of the southern Kii peninsula, Nakagami creates an inassimilable region that defines the opposing concept of nation. The most Faulknerian of Nakagami's work, his trilogy, is not a Snopesian chronicle of the advance of capitalism and modernization; rather these novels are rooted in the concerns of *Absalom, Absalom!*, featuring brother and sister incest and a narrative where brother kills brother. And neither of these heinous acts provokes the desired acknowledgment from the patriarch who, Sutpen-like, builds monuments to try to pass in terms of caste.[35] Arguably, capitalism was both too ubiquitous and too mundane in postwar Japan to generate the "luxuriating" response to the primal miscegenation that joins the spoken to the written word. This is the crossroads, vernacular and oracular, that discovers class as race in modernism's multiplicity of voices.

Faulkner's Faulkner: Making Art

The only one of his novels that Faulkner felt was narratively terminal—the novel that he had no desire to rewrite—was his wonderfully offensive *Mosquitoes*, which features artists, their would-be patrons, and hangers-on, talking about aesthetics and sex (often at the same time) while addressing such pressing questions as the development of advertising schemes for selling a good laxative.[36] Faulkner's most popular novel (arguably his only work that could merit classification as "popular" at all), *Sanctuary*, was initially considered to be a book that, with its lurid brothel and courtroom revelations, most shockingly the rape of a judge's daughter named "Temple" with a corncob, could have landed both its author and publisher in jail. Deified and damned, Faulkner was an author of considerable influence, even though his work (with the exception of *Sanctuary*) was essentially out of print in 1946. Faulkner's own assessment of his career in 1945 is telling: "My books have never sold, are out of print; the labor (the creation of my apocryphal country) of my life, even if I have a few things to add to it, will never make a living for me."[37]

After making what many have classified as an unfortunate marriage to his newly divorced childhood sweetheart, Faulkner, who had acquired the ruin of a modest antebellum mansion, needed money to support his family. Not surprisingly, the author of the notorious *Sanctuary* was offered a job as a writer for Hollywood, where he worked intermittently on screenplays (1932–53). The most notable of these remain Faulkner's adaptations of Chandler's *The Big Sleep* and Hemingway's *To Have and Have Not*, both successful collaborations with Howard Hawks, Humphrey Bogart, and Lauren Bacall that featured fast and loose (if wordy) dialogue.[38] While the Warner brothers would brag that they had the best writer in America on contract for slave wages, critics (largely in agreement with his Hollywood employers) have seen this period as a fallow time during which Faulkner's imaginative resources were sapped for lesser purposes by the lucrative film industry.[39] While Faulkner did produce fewer and less critically celebrated works during the fifteen years between his publication of *Go Down, Moses* (1942), his powerful and experimental story cycle, and his return to the Snopes trilogy in *The Town* (1957), any four of his nineteen novels (*Soldiers' Pay* [1926], *Mosquitoes* [1927], *Sartoris* [1929], *The Sound and the Fury* [1929], *As I Lay Dying* [1930], *Sanctuary* [1931], *Light in August* [1932], *Pylon* [1935], *Absalom, Absalom!* [1936], *The Unvanquished* [1938], *The Wild Palms* [*If I Forget Thee, Jerusalem*] [1939], *The Hamlet* [1940], *Go Down, Moses* [1942], *Intruder in the Dust* [1948], *Requiem for a Nun* [1951], *A Fable* [1954], *The Town* [1957], *The Mansion* [1959], or *The*

Reivers [1962]) sampled in chronological sequence would garner him a place in the history of the novel as a genre, irrespective of national boundaries. Taken together, the Snopes trilogy, which Daniel Pecchenino has termed "the economic Faulkner," represents the great, late Faulkner.[40] Distinguished by his mytho-driven outbursts of poetry in *The Hamlet* (1940), Faulkner, in the period following the Second World War, returned to the Snopes family's descent into spiritual vapidity through materialism in *The Town* (1957) and *The Mansion* (1959).

Ironically, the reputation of Faulkner's post–World War II work has suffered because of his earlier virtuosity. Critics have compared the late Faulkner with the iconic Faulkner, rather than seeing his late novels as works with a different purpose that should be contrasted with other economic taxonomies in novels such as Frank Norris's *The Octopus* (1901), Theodore Dreiser's *The Financier* (1912), or John Steinbeck's *The Grapes of Wrath* (1939). Had Faulkner narrated nothing else concerning the dramatic changes precipitated by the war, his *Intruder in the Dust* (1948) would constitute a literary landmark for its treatment of black masculinity and manhood, presenting the threat of lynching through the constant odor of gasoline to reveal a United States where men of color cannot expect justice. If in 1948 the United States was not ready to acknowledge that there was a race problem in the South, if not in America, the reception in 1960 of Harper Lee's only novel, *To Kill a Mockingbird*, suggests the importance of history to fiction and fiction as a means of serving and helping to write history.

During the nightmare of the war years in occupied France, intellectuals and artists, notably the distinguished philosopher of existentialism, Jean-Paul Sartre, and the Algerian-born novelist Albert Camus, who had published *L'Étranger* in 1942, were reading Faulkner and cutting their teeth on the very difficulty of his novels that U.S. reviewers had earlier panned as "signifying nothing." More than half a century later, South African–born J. M. Coetzee celebrated the experimental novels of Faulkner, placing his forebear as "a writer to whom the avant-garde of Europe and Latin America would go to school."[41] Encouraged by the interest of the French intelligentsia and other dedicated readers, Malcolm Cowley in 1946 single-handedly brought Faulkner's immense accomplishments back before the American public in the form of *The Portable Faulkner*. Cowley's influential edition achieved what Faulkner had not; *The Portable Faulkner* made the United States' most aggressive experimentalist readable and even palatable for a new (by definition select and self-selecting) generation of readers.

Signifying *Sound*

In his hand-drawn map of Yoknapatawpha County, which initially appeared in *Absalom, Absalom!* (1936), Faulkner proclaims himself "sole owner and proprietor" by locating and listing characters and events from what critics have increasingly recognized as one long novel. Faulkner's long novel begins in 1929 with the publication of the two major works, *Sartoris* and *The Sound and the Fury*, that introduced the world to what he would call his "own little postage stamp of native soil."[42] Short of Faulkner's own exclamation of pride to Ben Wasson that he had written a novel that was "a real son of a bitch," David Minter provides the most succinct assessment of Faulkner's departure from novelistic as well as psychological norms, concluding that "*The Sound and the Fury* is thematically regressive, stylistically and formally innovative."[43]

Faulkner was inspired by Wharton's and Cather's experiments in voice in their regional novels *Ethan Frome* (1911) and *The Professor's House* (1925).[44] Indeed, *The Sound and the Fury* and *As I Lay Dying* are direct descendants of Wharton's and Cather's experiments in framing first-person narration. Cather's Tom Outland offers an allegorical name for the emptiness of materialism that is the wages of modernity, in the same way that dismemberment and death is the destination, if not the motive definition, for modernism.[45] *The Sound and the Fury*, Faulkner's most signifying novel (in part because it took even a post-Joyce—a *Ulysses*-apprised world—by surprise), originates from questions about time raised by Edith Wharton in a 1925 diatribe against modernism, condemning this movement for being located in a "pathological world where the action, taking place between people of abnormal psychology, and not keeping with our normal human rhythms becomes an idiot's tale, signifying nothing."[46]

Faulkner's breakthrough, as he described it in retrospect in two 1933 introductions written for, but not used in, the Modern Library edition of *The Sound and the Fury*, grew out of rejection. Arthur Kinney has argued persuasively that Faulkner's manuscript version of *Flags in the Dust* is a carefully balanced work of art that was chopped into an inferior product.[47] Seen as too long, with too many storylines, the manuscript that Ben Wasson would edit into *Sartoris* tried the patience of those who (expecting the readable if not the palatable) had not yet become accustomed to Faulknerian prose. Faulkner would later recall his conversation with Wasson, who was engaged in cutting down this ambitiously balanced novel that had been accused of being six novels at once:

> I said, "A cabbage has grown, matured. You look at that cabbage; it is not symmetrical; you say, I will trim this cabbage off and make it art; I will make it resemble a peacock or a pagoda or 3 doughnuts. Very good, I say; you do that, then the cabbage will be dead."
>
> "Then we'll make some kraut out of it." he said. "The same amount of sour kraut will feed twice as many people."[48]

Whatever else happened in Manhattan in 1928, the fact that *Flags in the Dust* (published uncut almost half a century later in 1973) was rejected for publication some eleven times caused William Faulkner to return to first terms.

There has been controversy over Faulkner's presentation of his creative development, a questioning of his own mythologizing of the place of *The Sound and the Fury* as a point of origin that begins with a primal scene.[49] However, the novel's regressive theme of genital sexuality and procreation is a fundamental site of modernism, a movement that is itself profoundly concerned with origins. To condense (and extend) David Minter's insight, the brilliance of *The Sound and the Fury* is that Faulkner's formal innovation *is in itself* regressive. According to Faulkner, the novel "began with the picture of the little girl's muddy drawers, climbing that tree to look in the parlor window" onto a scene of death.[50] As Caddy views the body of "Damuddy," the dead grandmother whose name is a seamless syllabic joining of daddy and mother, the strange moniker recalls a primal scene of language for Faulkner himself. "Damuddy," coined by Faulkner as the name for his own maternal grandmother (the prerogative of the first grandchild), is the first of many words invented by Faulkner in his fiction.

In an excessive act that points to the centrality of a type of primal language, *The Sound and the Fury* joins the mute and seemingly languageless (literally "infantile") Benjy, a thirty-three-year-old idiot, to the crescendo of the black chorus at Dilsey's church on Easter morning, as they shout together and are made one by spiritual ecstasy. The call offered up to God in the novel's fourth section is the primal sound for food: "Mmmmmmmmmmmmmmmm." Moreover, the only language that Benjy understands is not the word "Caddy" but the primal sound for fear: "shhh" or, in its English form, "hush."[51] Primal sounds that range across the northern continents of Europe and Asia, these human articulations for food and fear speak to the dream of universal utterance. The water-splashing scene, viewed widely as a microcosm of the novel as a whole, reveals a return to these utterances associated with first terms that is telling, providing evidence of Faulkner's lingual imagination as well as his striking intentionality. Primal language is crucial to Benjy's version of the children playing in the branch. Initially, this scene (at least to the uninitiated) seems to suggest that Benjy may understand language:

> "I'll run away and never come back." Caddy said. I began to cry. Caddy turned around and said "Hush" So I hushed . . . Caddy was all wet and muddy behind, and I started to cry and she came and squatted in the water.
>
> "Hush now." she said. "I'm not going to run away." So I hushed. Caddy smelled like trees in the rain. (*SF* 12)

Deceptively simple, this passage, which appears to be mere description, reveals the control that underwrites the novel as a whole. Arguably, the appearance that Benjy understands Caddy's threat gives way to the more plausible claim that the idiot brother, like an intelligent dog, may be responding to Caddy's tone of voice. Here, Caddy's primally hissed "hush" combines with the removal of the visually disturbing display of her soiled drawers to silence her "bellering" brother. Speaking this word of first utterances and concealing the harbinger of her coming "change" cued by absence (the stained drawers that are no longer visible), Caddy reveals the complexity within Benjy's seemingly simple perceptions. The words on the page in Benjy's section go beyond words to articulate the physicality of the aural and the visual. Indeed, the spoken word, capable of congealing and casting a shadow in *As I Lay Dying*, gains the materiality of an object that can be seen and felt and that signifies without being diluted by meaning. This emptying out of meaning precedes Addie Bundren's infamous diatribe against language, as Faulkner has Fairchild, his writer from *Mosquitoes*, speculate about "Words" as "a kind of sterility . . . You begin to substitute words for things and deeds . . . and pretty soon the thing or the deed becomes just a kind of shadow of a certain sound you make by shaping your mouth a certain way" (*M* 210). The description of Benjy's section requires recourse to the connection between the visual and the aural rather than between words and their meanings, signifiers and signifieds. Benjy's narration is like an impossible photographic plate in which sounds and scenes, associated by proximity rather than temporality or meaning, create his experience.

Stating the "worst case," Eric Sundquist argues, "[T]here is reason to believe that without Faulkner's work of the next ten years *The Sound and the Fury* would itself seem a literary curiosity, an eccentric masterpiece of experimental methods and 'modernist' ideas."[52] But it must be argued (as Faulkner himself did argue) that his work of the next ten years would not have been conceivable without his having written *The Sound and the Fury*. Louis Rubin makes an inspired observation that links this novel to the Faulkner that Sundquist recognizes as the great Faulkner—the one who writes about "the problem of miscegenation."[53] Rubin contends that in writing *The Sound and the Fury*, Faulkner "extended and expanded" "his own sympathies," "eliminating . . . any elements of local color quaintness and folksy caricature."[54] As Rubin points out, Faulkner's entry into the first-person consciousnesses of an idiot without language, a suicidal madman with too much language, and a sadistic and impotent capitalist hoarder whose language consists of quoting himself, allowed him to imagine the interiority of others. This process offers an important insight into *The Sound and the Fury*'s transformation of Faulkner's understanding of voice, an understanding that had implications for his representations of race across the color line. Critics have been critical of Dilsey's larger-than-life status as a monumental and fallen "ruin" (165), but her prepossessing figure in "April Eighth, 1928" transforms stereotype into archetype. Sexless and Sybil-like, the Dilsey who fills the door at the start of the closing section of *The Sound and the Fury* is a force of culture rather than nature and, as such, counterbalances the goddesslike fecundity suggested by

Caddy Compson and more fully embodied later by Eula Varner (*The Hamlet* [1940]), another promiscuous daughter of the white elite.

Ethnographic Regions: Slave Narrative / Slave Novel

In the 1930s, cultural geographer Rupert Vance set some key parameters with his own unanswerable question about literary categories: "What is the difference between local color and regionalism? Is regionalism just better?" As Vance understood, history is important in the mapping of culture, and this history is essential for understanding the role of place in fiction. While local color was criticized as a descriptive literature concerned with surfaces that included voices speaking in a vernacular located in the sentimental sites of cottages and mansions, the southern branch of this literary movement from the outset included cabins, most famously Uncle Tom's, and fleeing women, lust, threatened rape, bloodhounds, and violence. The gentle ethnographic impulses of the local color tradition that insisted on recording and preserving a disappearing past can be said to have returned with a vengeance in Toni Morrison's love-hungry and dissatisfied baby ghost (Beloved), who comes back with a woman's appetites, remembering the "sixty million and more" who suffered and died during the Middle Passage. As it rose to the highest level of articulation, southern local color became political local color. Voice itself was the bearer of culture, and narrative, whether spoken or written, provided the only means through which a people who had been legally established as things could assert their humanity. As local color became regionalism, this literature revealed codes and rules encoded in language offering worlds to be decoded by readers who could find in fiction what anthropologist Franz Boas termed "cultural relativism."

Faulkner's contribution to the ethnographic novel of manners is to expose a world that is highly nuanced and less genteel than the gentle analyses of culture said to be characteristic of local color.[55] Faulkner's work considers individuals, families, and communities in his Yoknapatawpha County as sites and subjects of anthropological inquiry. Just as Galsworthy's Forsytes and Wharton's Marvells and Dagonnets as well as her Archers and Wellands represent complex cultures, provincial aristocracies that can degenerate, Faulkner's Compsons, Sartorises, Sutpens, and McCaslins generate and degenerate from their cobbled-together self-fashionings as biblical patriarchs in plantation fictions. The Snopeses, the Gibsons, and the Beauchamps in their endurance could have provided mere grounds for local color, but instead these families introduce and frame the presence of others, individuals who are the disinherited of the earth. Faulkner's Mink Snopes, his Rider, and his Dewey Dell Bundren are feeling subjects who might have remained unexamined because each is (in Patricia Yeager's moving term) a "throwaway body."[56] These detailed cultures—exposed by figures such as Toomer and Faulkner—open the sluice for Henderson, Hurston, Wright, and Welty, ethnographers all. The best southern writers understand the crucial quality of the grotesque in a world where people are categorized as animals, brutes defined by their race and class.[57] The poor, the black, the pregnant, the female, the insane, the suicidal, the homicidal, and even the speechless idiots of Faulkner's Yoknapatawpha occupy and witness a complex, multivalenced and multivocal world that has been painted through writing. This sensitivity to the "wretched of the earth" primed the pump for the least expected of voices who would write in the tradition of McCullers and O'Connor. While emerging from what are ultimately very different works, the voices of the teenage protagonists from Bobbie Ann Mason's *In Country* (1985) and Dorothy Allison's *Bastard Out of Carolina* (1993) carry the burden of Dewey Dell Bundren into the final decades of the twentieth century.

In formal terms, the southern novel is birthed by the major nineteenth-century tradition of African American letters in which the slave narrative gave rise to the slave novel, establishing a direct line of descent that leads to Twain's *Adventures of Huckleberry Finn* (1885), Toomer's *Cane* (1923), and Faulkner's *Light in August* (1932) and *Absalom, Absalom!* (1936). These last are the most southern of Faulkner's novels, because they (like the texts that precede them) both continue and invert the slave narrative by sending protagonists south toward a fatal knowledge of the racial secrets that have imprisoned them. While Kate Chopin's *The Awakening* (1899) and Zora Neale Hurston's *Their Eyes Were Watching God* (1937) present this journey toward racial knowledge as one of sexual epiphany, Faulkner's *Light in August* serves as a renewed point of origin for mid-twentieth-century narratives that turn to the South to explore the violent narrative of black masculinity. Seen from this perspective, Wright's most southern novel is his memoir, *Black Boy* (1945), narrating his psychological journey south to his childhood as he writes his run toward freedom. Ralph Ellison's *Invisible Man* (1952), a novel for which Faulkner expressed his unqualified admiration, is the culminating work in this tradition of the journey into the psychological heart of darkness, to know and experience the prison of race for whites as well as blacks.[58] While *Invisible Man* clearly riffs on Faulkner's *As I Lay Dying* through the life story of a character named Trueblood who dreams he is having relations with a woman in white in a grandfather clock, Ellison's man of color recalls waking to discover that he is violating his own daughter. The lives of Faulkner's poor whites are first the dream, then the nightmare, come true for Ellison's blacks. *Invisible Man* identifies the source of enslaved minds in the southern history of incarceration, but this self-confinement, like the potential for liberation, takes place underground in 1930s Harlem, suggesting that invisibility may cease as the unnamed narrator, "the invisible man," emerges from underground into the Harlem, rather than the southern, Renaissance. As an orally inspired literature, southern journeys into narrative are laden with the curse of slavery, and the burden of southern history is the burden of southern literature: memory. All these works involve the story of a journey south toward a potentially fatal identity located at the crossroads of art and race.

While this is inscribed in *Absalom, Absalom!*, *Light in August* is clearly Faulkner's signifying novel in terms of presenting the crisis of black manhood. Joe Christmas can only be confirmed in his otherwise unknown and unknowable racial identity at the moment that his manhood is sacrificed, literally cut away in an act of castration.[59] Joe Christmas goes in circles; Rider of "Pantaloon in Black," drunk with grief that cannot be assuaged by whiskey, acts to resolve the problem of being unable to "quit thinking" by generating a white lynch mob (*GDM* 154). Ulysses is black in the early-twentieth-century South. Arriving in Ithaca can be tantamount to death in a culture in which white social observers such as Howard Odum and Alan Lomax look to wandering men of color (bluesmen poets) as a desideratum of male fantasy. The journey in the slave narrative, as Robert Stepto has argued, is toward literacy and the free North.[60] Yet as Stepto has taught me, these venturing characters sometimes are driven to go back. What I am defining here as a "reverse slave narrative" is a return to repression undertaken to face the repressed—to go back into the trauma of social slavery to escape the captivity of its psychological bonds—to realize freedom or die trying.

The Female and Poetical Mainstream: Porter and Faulkner

In addition to his influence on writing about masculinity, Faulkner's work is central to the continued force of the female-dominated mainstream in the history of the twentieth-century U.S. novel. These headwaters not only flow from the regionalist fictions of Wharton and Cather;[61] they also pour from authors who focus on female cultures and the paradoxical necessity of a matriarchy that assigns patriarchy its place by defining and insisting on the rigid terms of male protection and its unspoken corollary, race- and class-based predation. To understand this period in southern letters and in the development of the novel, it is necessary to introduce another innovator who was coeval with Faulkner. Katherine Anne Porter, born into the dry world of Indian Creek, Texas, drew on family stories and her grandmother's transport of her grandfather's bones through three removes, to invent a southern girlhood in her story cycle, *The Old Order* (1944).[62] If *The Old Order* can be said to be flawed thematically because it sentimentalizes race in the unacceptable mode of the plantation novel,[63] it is revelatory in its experimental project as it becomes a bildungsroman for the form of the short story itself. This cycle of sketches culminates in the formally complete short story "The Grave." A series of maturing vignettes, *The Old Order* enacts an imitational fallacy as it parallels the development of Porter's most famous protagonist, Miranda Gay. Porter, regarded as one of the finest stylists in the history of U.S. letters, was most successful in her development of what she (eschewing the femininity of words such as "novella" and "novelette") called the "short novel," most notably *Old Mortality* (1937), *Noon Wine* (1937), and *Pale Horse, Pale Rider* (1939).[64]

Written before *Absalom, Absalom!* was published (her own publication dates aside), Porter's work anticipated the startling lyricism of Faulkner's *The Hamlet*, which along with *Absalom, Absalom!* opened the world for Carson McCullers and Eudora Welty, as well as the later mythopoetical, post-Welty Yoknapatawphas of Toni Morrison and Louise Erdrich. Faulkner commits a feminist act by exposing the predation inherent in the pastoral as he writes his most extravagant paean to love pictured in an idiot Snopes's narrative of eloping with a cow. This Faulkner, who writes in "The Long Summer" of *The Hamlet* in the tradition of Porter's beautiful descriptive prose and with the erotic florescence of Wharton's earlier *Summer*, is the Faulkner who could write this sentence that provokes and opens a place for the lyrical miracle of Eudora Welty:

> Roofed by the woven canopy of blind annealing grass-roots and the roots of trees, dark in the blind dark of time's silt and rich refuse—the constant and unslumbering anonymous worm-glut and the inextricable known bones—Troy's Helen and the nymphs and the snoring mitred bishops, the saviors and the victims and the kings—it wakes, up-seeping, attritive in uncountable creeping channels: first, root; then frond by frond, from whose escaping tips like gas it rises and disseminates and stains the sleep-fast earth with drowsy insect-murmur; then, still upward-seeking, creeps the knitted bark of trunk and limb where, suddenly louder leaf by leaf and dispersive in diffusive sudden speed, melodious with the winged and jeweled throats, it upward bursts and fills night's globed negation with jonquil thunder. (200–201)

This Stravinsky-like passage reveals multiple Faulkners: the excessive Joycean Faulkner, the embodied Freudian Faulkner, the poetic Keatsian Faulkner, as well as a great deal of what Ellen Moers would identify as the "female gothic." In its accretive power, this single sentence in form and content is the closest articulation in words of more than one painting by Walter Anderson, the artist who was thundering light at the same time in a different state of Mississippi. Uniting all these Faulkners is the Faulkner who so shocked Robert Penn Warren: the Faulkner who creates highly visualized images that contain and bear the content of his fiction. The voice that announces "jonquil thunder" is not Quentinian or nationalist, but Faulknerian: sensually and sonorously visual.

William Styron and Walker Percy are Faulkner's primary heirs in relation to a nationalist conception of southern literature, proceeding from a notion of "southern" as white and male and predicated on the existential narrative that attends the southern male's self-immolation because of the failure of aristocratic honor. Yet in the most significant turns of words and structural forms, Welty and Morrison are Faulkner's strongest and most direct heirs because they are relentlessly experimental and because they (like Faulkner himself) descend from so many mythologies and literatures, so many heard voices and read volumes. Welty's work is most like Faulkner's in its difficulty and depth, picturing the seemingly unnamable. There is mystery in this act of visual naming that calls on more than one voice in works that become audible by insisting that the listener and reader must be present at the very scene of the multivocal. Morrison, fearless in her own encyclopedic creativity, draws from the spoken and the written, but she often reserves her most visual prose for the diabolical beauty of the pastoral from hell: a past that is not Africa but rather is located in the environs of the violent and still violating remains of a slave South.

Although there are specific riffs that indicate a Faulknerian presence or, at least, provocation in Morrison's fiction (she wrote her master's thesis at Cornell on suicide in the fiction of Virginia Woolf and Faulkner),[65] Morrison most resembles Faulkner in her epic portrayal of multigenerational family narratives, most notably *Sula* (1973), *Song of Solomon* (1977), and *Beloved* (1987), works that radically shift the focus to the development of female identity in families dominated by women. Faulkner's *Absalom, Absalom!*, with its narrative of female isolation that places the novel's childless women as "unsistered Eve[s]," contains his most detailed (albeit vague) account of women and daughters located in the female household of Judith, Clytie, and Rosa. These weird sisters gather together in silent survival to demarcate a significant set of relationships between (and among) women that are rare in Faulkner's extensive treatment of southern life and culture.[66] This is a territory that Morrison and Welty own.[67] If Quentin Compson, like the young Richard Wright, makes his journey south through remembering words and scenes from the perspective of his young manhood, *Absalom, Absalom!* reveals another aspect of this journey southward toward the place of a mystery whose solution may be fatal. While *Light in August* centers on literal journeys that are racial, sexual, and psychological, *Absalom, Absalom!* insists on the centrality of language in a narrative journey: the unraveling of a mystery contained in versions of a pictured past—the novel's "might-have-been . . . more true than truth." In terms of southern literature, *Absalom, Absalom!* is the hinge that swings forward to reveal that *Song of Solomon* is the Ohio-born Morrison's diasporic southern novel.

The southern novel, defined here as a journey into a past that is located in the South, achieves its Faulknerian apotheosis in Eudora Welty's *Losing Battles* (1970). Fusing the family saga with an experimental form devoted entirely to the oral and the visual, *Losing Battles* is Welty's answer to *Absalom, Absalom!* In this last, longest, and most experimental of her novels, Welty accomplishes the most radically innovative work in this tradition by setting *Losing Battles* not just in the past but in the isolated and preserved past of the Mississippi mountains during the Great Depression. With over thirty-five named speakers, *Losing Battles* is arguably the most oral novel in the history of the English language. Created entirely from the spoken word and descriptions of the physical world, from the materiality of sound and sight, *Losing Battles* conveys interiority through the relentless portrayal of what can be heard and seen. Realism with a narrative vengeance, *Losing Battles* provides absolutely no access to any character's interior thoughts, and yet this is a work of remarkable emotional depth. It is no accident that the reader is invited to the family reunion that comprises *Losing Battles* in the antagonized position of a reluctant participant, more precisely, as an in-law. Welty's novel provides a taxonomy of language, denoting the incursions of modernity not only through the diction of advertising ("World Wonder Number Two" rope and "Coca-Cola") but also by distinguishing cultural distance embodied by various listeners and tellers on the basis of whether they are foreign enough to this mountain family's mores to need to be offered a moral for the stories they are being told.

Faulkner's Renaissance

In a definition that still works, Allen Tate defined southern letters as a literature "conscious of the past in the present."[68] And how could it not be? In his effort to explain southern identity, C. Vann Woodward insists on "the burden of Southern history," and he, like Faulkner, is clearly aware of the black man's burden within it. From the origins of this "world the slaves made," men and women were not free.[69] Founded from the history of slavery, the South was defined by race and the very American struggle for freedom through literacy that generated one of the great literary lineages of the nineteenth century: the slave novel. These novels of incarceration and escape, with their powerful links to the gothic as well as the still popular prism provided by the captivity narrative, turn on accounts of the acquisition of literacy, a very specific act of seeing, which engenders the modernist move into transcribing the vernacular. Framed by fictions of race, this intersection of the written, oral, and visual is the primary crossroads for any claim to a peculiarly southern tradition of letters. Variously defined through a delineation of dialectics—rural and urban, agrarian and industrial, past and future (with contentions over the present)—the major claim for southern distinctiveness is found in its complex and complexly interrelated multivocal literary tradition amid a heightened consciousness of the coloring of class.

The mystery of William Faulkner was at the core of the defining debate between the Fugitives (the poets of Vanderbilt University who included Tate and Warren) and the culture-rooted regionalists (the geographers and sociologists of the University of North Carolina at Chapel Hill that included Rupert Vance and Howard Odum). As these noted figures representing schools of thought engaged in a debate centered on the question of "Why William Faulkner?" or, more to the point, "How could William Faulkner exist?" the critically astute poets of Vanderbilt framed the question based on the reputation of Faulkner's home state. Mississippi had and continues to have the highest rate of illiteracy, seemingly stuck in perpetuity on the lowest rung of what is still called the "educational ladder." Here, "The Fugitives," who had already begun to eschew flight and stand their ideological ground under a new creed, becoming known nationally and internationally as "The Agrarians," faced off with the social scientists of Chapel Hill who were known for their influential journal, *Social Forces*, and for their consciousness of the social milieu. What was at stake for both in understanding the meaning of William Faulkner was the meaning of the South's long history of poverty, and what was increasingly being seen by many as a bizarre, if not entirely inexplicable, florescence of art.

While the Vanderbilt poets took a belletristic position that touted the concept of genius, offering Faulkner and his oeuvre together as incontrovertible fact, Odum's team of social scientists, joined by then graduate student in history C. Vann Woodward, argued that a William Faulkner was created, made possible, by the same social conditions that made him impossible. Reflecting after the belated recognition of the enormity of his accomplishment, Faulkner himself speculated on the origins of his art:

> And now I realize for the first time what an amazing gift I had: uneducated in every formal sense, without even very literate, let alone literary, companions, yet to have made the thing I made. I don't know where it came from. I don't know why God or gods or whoever it was, selected me to be the vessel. Believe me, this is not humility, false modesty: it is simply amazement.[70]

Wherever he came from, William Faulkner, to borrow a phrase from *Absalom, Absalom!*, did not come out of nowhere, "out of the soundless Nothing." Rather, he was spawned by a world that was like William Shakespeare's, a world where Elizabethan English was still spoken and where the heightened narrative intelligence of those who were not readers and writers, but hearers and listeners, talkers and tellers, and observers and seers, generated a story-centered culture. This orality arising from the conditions that made speech itself essential to proving the humanity of people who were sold as things is key to Faulkner and Faulkner's contribution to the history of the novel. And in Faulkner's *As I Lay Dying*, language continues to gain substance, rising, congealing, and casting shadows that confound the great fact: the rotting materiality of the mother. This mother, difficult to bury, would exhume local color and the intense localism of the inland modernisms of the Americas. William Faulkner, ironically residing in one of the leading vase-making states in the union, a potter's paradise, saw himself as "selected" by "God or gods" "to be the vessel" "to have made the thing I made." Crossing over like the vase-making (and vase-kissing) artist figure of *Sartoris*, Horace Benbow, who finds himself replaced in *Sanctuary* by the violated virgin of his ink-vomiting mind, Faulkner understood the incestuous origins of art that made his beloved works sisters and daughters: Faulkner's art is the get of God or the more intimate progeny of mating with the maternal muse.

CHAPTER TWO

Burying the Regional Mother

Faulkner on the Road to Race through the Visual Arts

We did not know his legendary head
in which the eyeballs ripened. But
his torso still glows like a candelabrum
in which his gaze, only turned low

holds and gleams. Else could not the curve
of the breast blind you, nor in the slight turn
of the loins could a smile be running
to that middle which carried procreation.
—Rainer Maria Rilke, "Archaic Torso of Apollo"

American literature in the early decades of the twentieth century seems obsessed with defining the nation by burying or revealing the burial of some troubling past.[1] In this recurring family romance, the narrative of the nation has become a story of art that insists on the burial of a woman: a failed, infertile, or dead mother. As men collaborate, broken and feminized bodies—smashed and severed—litter the scene of art. In these works, ruptured bodies are the source of art, often bearing broken heads that evoke and provoke speech. "[C]happing"—Anse Bundren's spoken word for procreation that his wife Addie recalls in *As I Lay Dying*—links the "splitting" of bodies in birth to the production of chapters, a process that calls attention to this spate of highly embodied books, generated by works that insist on the presence of books within books. A paradigm of death and preservation reigns in these narratives in which male narrators eviscerate and bury the furniture of female interiority (emptying houses like wombs as well as wombs from houses) in order to pursue a masculine identity found in the carving out of a man-made art. This is a head game, and it takes two men—the character of the narrator and the character he is creating—to play.

As William Faulkner began to publish novels in the United States during the mid-1920s, the ambitious young writer from Mississippi was faced with the specter of a female-dominated literature headed by women whose writings were obsessed with their own mortuarial and matricidal version of the anxiety of influence. This scene of a burial was important to the William Faulkner of 1930 who, with his genius for excess, devoted an entire novel to the burial of the effulgently rotting body of the mother. In 1929, the year of the publication of Faulkner's *Sartoris* and *The Sound and the Fury*—the year critics would claim for the birth of the Southern Literary Renaissance—Edith Wharton and Willa Cather were unanimously recognized as the most distinguished living American authors.[2] This fact runs upstream from the widely accepted revisionist river that privileges youth and wounded virility by naming Hemingway and Fitzgerald as the men of the age. This is not to suggest that Hemingway and Fitzgerald have been without progeny in the highly reproductive literary marketplace of the twentieth century. Rather, this view highlights that the burial of mothers, like Wharton and Cather and even Irving, James, and Anderson, is an ideological burial perpetrated by both artists and critics. As Faulkner waded into a stream whose headwaters were dominated by older women, he surveyed a literary landscape that was obsessed with the problem that the female body—the aging and demanding maternal body—posed for art and for the increasingly vulnerable head of the male artist.

Faulkner Sounding the Misogynist Mainstream: Wharton and Cather

What was at stake for Wharton and Cather was the laying away of the matrifocal tradition of "local color," the burial of the late-nineteenth-century tradition of the regional mother who ruled the hearth in fictions authored by powerful cultural mothers. Reeling from the violent history of southern nationalism, Faulkner was born into a cultural milieu in which regional sensibility and literary proclivities battened on poverty itself. As Faulkner lifted his head to breathe in the backwaters of fin-de-siècle Mississippi, he was awash in the voices that were too fecund in memory and too burdened with intelligences overripe from illiteracy. As the record suggests, Faulkner kept his mouth shut (except to drink) and watched and wrote. Faulkner, like Wharton and Cather, inherited the legacy of an increasingly entrapping binary that gendered aesthetics. Here, at this unforgiving juncture, in Susan Donaldson's words, "the male artist's own incarceration [took place] within the shrinking definitions of masculinity forever bound to definitions of femininity," and all were circumscribed "within a regional art largely defined by women."[3]

Edith Wharton's autobiography, *A Backward Glance*, named Sarah Orne Jewett and Mary Wilkins Freeman as Wharton's "predecessors." In their fictions that valorized older women, these leading local colorists were known for their New England characterized and given heft by a social world of independent spinsters, childless widows, and undying mothers who held sway over childless elderly children. Their writing was not just fiction; it located the Yankee counterpart to the environs structured by the Miss Rosa Coldfields and Judith Sutpens and Aunt Jenny DuPres—the wide spectrum of white women who were known as the type of the "Civil War Aunt": the anchors of the steeled and resilient matriarchy of the South that William Faulkner inherited. At the turn into the twentieth century, the larger-than-life sibyl, embodied in the childless herbalist mother of Jewett's *The Country of the Pointed Firs* set on the seacoast in Maine, found its visual articulation in Winslow Homer's forceful paintings of larger-than-life women working along the coast of New England. This sibylline power, with its quality of type and stereotype as a force of nature, is found in the dominating figures of Dilsey in *The Sound and the Fury* and Clytie in *Absalom, Absalom!* (These women were actual aunts as well as figures who were referred to as "aunt" or "auntie" in this race-based respect title, which was ubiquitous in the hierarchy-driven South.) Forces of culture, Faulkner's icons of black maternal authority fill passageways and, like the mythical Cerberus, control and watch houses. Both New England and the South were depicted as feminized in the stasis and demise of their power during and after the war. Faulkner's fiction abounds in narcissistic child-mothers and strong (sometimes angry or mad) white women of the South who fit the regionalized and only slightly revised type of the Yankee schoolmarm (Addie Bundren of *As I Lay Dying* and Joanna Burden of *Light in August*) as well as the strong and un-husbanded social arbiters, widows or spinsters (Aunt Jenny DuPre of *Sartoris*, Miss Rosa Coldfield of *Absalom, Absalom!*, and Miss Habersham of *The Unvanquished* and *Intruder in the Dust*). All these white characters who are strong, even the seemingly least likely woman on this list, Addie Bundren, are intimately linked to people of color and the story of black bodies. What distinguishes Faulkner's incorporation of Addie's story is the powerful presence of the black mother known through her racialized blackening of sacrificial sons who try to preserve her at the center of the frame of art.

Noting the power of "the traditional position of women in Southern art and literature," Donaldson, quoting Faulkner, writes that "art in the South 'was really no manly business'" (74). As Father's (Mr. Compson's) narration indicates in *Absalom, Absalom!* the "lost cause" was for some men seen as the loss of a sybaritic style, a masculine elegance that approached the feminine through the birthright familiar to this cultured aristocracy. Through his nuanced creation of the figure of Charles Bon, Quentin's father acknowledges that a man born to silk could also be seductively feminine in his masculinity, suggesting that manly desire is not limited to the homosocial bonds native to the condition and practice of hypermasculinity. Arguably, the frontier-edged and, in many ways, faux aristocratic South had become a functioning matriarchy because of the vested interest of elite white women in the control of male violence. These stalwart "ladies" used the stability of the patriarchy and the tradition of a defined class of sexually exploited women to maintain a rigidly preserved hierarchy that held fathers and brothers in place. Quick to scent insult and quick to kill, men who played starring roles in what Wharton called the "tottering stage-fictions of . . . a chivalrous South" were expected to perform the courtesies that passed as social graces.[4] White men, who were and were not part of the aristocracy, practiced the dominant culture's habits of protection and predation. Following the Civil War, the female and feminized identity of the settled regions, New England and the South, was enunciated by and established through what was widely acknowledged at the time as the "feminine note in fiction."[5]

Kate Chopin, in *The Awakening* (1899), created a protagonist whom Cather herself reviewed as a "Creole Bovary."[6] As Cather's reference to Flaubert suggests, Chopin was participating in a critique of bourgeois experience that went well beyond the borders of the United States. But Chopin's novel also underlined the political potential of local color by demonstrating the dangers of fictions of maternity and sexual passion that had the power to destroy men as well as women and art. While Wharton and Cather were not the first to expose the animality inherent in femaleness, they were unwavering in their revelation of the danger that a seductively sentimental and floral aesthetic posed to the heroic and intrinsically homoerotic ethos which insists on men making men. Faulkner was, and to this day remains, the reader who was most aware that his prominent female predecessors, Wharton and Cather, had written influential novels about art that were masterpieces—clearly overdetermined masterworks—of misogyny.

If Faulkner was looking for himself in *Soldiers' Pay* (1926), his "lost generation" novel that placed him in Fitzgerald's and Hemingway's downstream, he discovered himself as he began writing under the influence of this female-dominated mainstream. Faulkner, cold sober, was drunk with words. From the cloyingly confessional "Elmer" and "Portrait of Elmer" (unpublished in his lifetime) that paint the portrait of the artist as a young man, to the tale of the imprisoned hack writer Wilbourne, who has been seduced into sculpting the pregnant female body with a knife in *The Wild Palms*, Faulkner's life story is the story of art. A river—not just a branch—of Faulkner's strongest fictions narrates the story of the artist (female as well as male) as a failed man. This failed man is defined, regardless of morphology, by a desire for masculine authority that leaves him dead or mad, mad or dead, convicted of having murdered a living woman into art. Faulkner found himself and the story of his art in compellingly didactic novels by Wharton and Cather,[7] in which male protagonists grieve over literally threatened, wounded, and feminized heads: signs (not just symbols) of the imminent castration of male narrators and writers. Wharton's unnamed narrator of *Ethan Frome* and Cather's Godfrey St. Peter of *The Professor's House* tell and write tales, respectively, that compel them to focus on the lives of sacrificial men. Their failed heroes are the protagonists of the story housed within the story, the tales of the protagonists' protagonists.

Finally, both *Ethan Frome* and *The Professor's House* tell the archetypal story of men who cannot escape the reproduction of death.

Marriage, in the well-known theatrical convention, brings down the curtain on a comedy. Pregnancy, in the traditional ballad of the United States, from Appalachia to the banks of the Ohio, leads to the murder of the unmarried woman whose body has begun to tell its tale. A melodramatic counter to the comic, this is the iconic story that Theodore Dreiser addressed in his masterpiece, *An American Tragedy* (1925). In the novels of William Faulkner, a pregnancy may be a prelude to comedy, to tragedy, or to both. Pregnancy often precipitates acts of suicide or some other form of death, such as life imprisonment, for the failed male artist. A pregnant woman returns at the close of Edith Wharton's *Summer* (1917), her sequel to *Ethan Frome*, and Cather's *The Professor's House* closes with a letter announcing the return of the professor's pregnant daughter along with his wife. For the professor, a writer who romanticizes history by dreaming of a past that is free from women and the domestic prison of materialism, this female threat is the return of the repressed.[8]

Survival trumps romance, as the male local color artist from the city—a historical preservationist who sketches houses—impregnates and abandons the rural girl who does not like to read in Wharton's *Summer*. Impregnated by the kindly Jewish climber, the florally named professor's daughter ushers in a more negative aspect as Cather's *The Professor's House* closes under the shadow of a feminized future in which female materialism will triumph over masculinity and the possibility of creating art. Faulkner's Dewey Dell Bundren, unable to find the abortion that her literary antecedent has decided against in *Summer*, is clearly part of this reigning paradigm of art. Indeed, the pregnant Dewey Dell does not represent hope. Like the pregnant Rosamond of *The Professor's House*, Dewey Dell embodies the emptiness of materialism in the penultimate section of Faulkner's *As I Lay Dying*. Aside from framing references to the disputed money, the final "Dewey Dell" section in *As I Lay Dying* takes place entirely in the spoken word. This dialogue between the increasingly triumphant father and the downcast daughter reveals the viscerally pregnant Dewey Dell as a figure of emptiness: she has been emptied entirely of the interiority that has made her a complex figure in her three earlier sections.

Dismissing what she called the "New England of fiction" in her 1922 "Author's Introduction" to *Ethan Frome* (1911), Wharton later castigated the New England local colorists for their "rose-coloured" visions that obscured what she saw as "still grim places, morally and physically" rife with "insanity, incest and slow mental and moral starvation . . . hidden away behind the paintless wooden house-fronts" (*Backward* 294).[9] Both the stalwart Wharton and her formidable (albeit younger) contemporary Cather appear to have feared that their success would be defined by what they perceived (their sentimental attachments to Sarah Orne Jewett aside)[10] as part of the feminine legacy of nineteenth-century local color. Wharton's *Ethan Frome* and Cather's *The Professor's House* are strongly gendered parables of art that articulate their authors' fears about the feminization of American literature.[11]

Significantly, Faulkner never mentioned Wharton in his lists of influential American authors. His acknowledgments, notably spare, named few men, fewer women, and no authors of color. Faulkner may have excluded Wharton because he placed her with Hawthorne and James, whom he classified as "not truly American writers. Their tradition was from Europe . . . They were not true Americans." To Faulkner, Twain and Whitman were the "indigenous American writers who were produced, nurtured by a culture" that was "completely American."[12] As she wrote an article criticizing her own first novel, Cather blamed the mistakes of young American writers on their misguided efforts to become followers of James and Wharton.[13] This generation had been misled by the idea that novels had to be about intelligent, witty people in drawing rooms. Cather did not acknowledge the fact that her first novel, *Alexander's Bridge* (1912), was actually a recasting of Wharton's *Ethan Frome*, published just a year earlier. Cather would rewrite *Ethan Frome* again and more generatively (particularly from the perspective of Faulkner's experimentally acute imagination) in *The Professor's House* (1925). In *Alexander's Bridge*, Cather had composed a prosaic version of *Ethan Frome* that like its predecessor focused on the trials of a cultured engineer as he literally fails to bridge a gap between two women (a New England Brahmin wife and an Irish actress mistress) and two countries (the United States and Canada). Faced with the enigma posed by Wharton's complexly framed and highly experimental *Ethan Frome*, the story that Cather heard and repeated in *Alexander's Bridge* is the tale that Wharton's engineer-narrator has projected onto his tale's protagonist, the silent Ethan. Stranded in snowbound mountains, Wharton's urbane narrator is obsessed with the fragments of tales that fail to explain Ethan Frome, an emasculated man wounded in a suicide manqué that has left him trapped in a living prison framed by complaining women: his elderly wife and her paralytic double (Ethan's broken former beloved with her witchlike stare).

Nearly four years before anyone could have cared, Faulkner dismissed Willa Cather in an admiring letter to Anita Loos dated "Febry [*sic*] Something 1926." Addressing the celebrated author of *Gentlemen Prefer Blondes* (1925), Faulkner baldly asserted: "I am still rather Victorian in my prejudice regarding the intelligence of women, despite Elinor Wylie and Willa Cather and all the balance of them."[14] Five years before his death, Faulkner responded relatively expansively to a question about the significance of women writers to his work. His list, characteristically short, included "Brontë, Willa Cather, Ellen Glasgow," before he framed these names with a sweeping gesture toward "any number of them . . . any number." Faulkner's Brontë, like Wharton's Brontë, was the Emily who wrote *Wuthering Heights*, the novel that spawns a line of descent that leads to *Ethan Frome* and *Absalom, Absalom!*[15] Two years before this pronouncement, Faulkner (repeatedly pressed for names of his antecedents during his Nobel Prize tour of 1955) listed Mark Twain, Herman Melville, and Theodore Dreiser as significant nineteenth-century figures before confessing that he had also been "influenced" by "a woman, Willa Cather—I think she is known in Japan."[16] Wharton, who had much to say about many, says a great deal by never mentioning Cather.[17] Yet Edith Wharton did privately admit a taste for Faulkner. Calling his work "masterful," Wharton complimented Faulkner's fiction as she panned another young writer's "trite" treatment of the theme of incest: Faulkner (coupled here with Céline) was praised for doing "it *nastier.*"[18]

The connections between Faulkner and Cather are evident and legion. Merrill Maguire Skaggs, struck by the specificity of the echoes found in Faulkner's early and bad novel about aesthetics, has concluded, "The list of Catherian items reappearing in Faulkner's *Mosquitoes* reads like a catalogue of stolen articles in a police report."[19] Yet, arguably on the deepest level, the Faulkner who was inspired to borrow or steal from Willa Cather's *The Professor's House* was most moved by the Cather who had chosen this very novel to place herself in productive dialogue with Edith Wharton. Cather's Wharton was, and to some extent always would be, the Wharton who wrote *Ethan Frome*. *The Professor's House*, Cather's own gendered narrative about aesthetics, constitutes an inspired conversation with Wharton at her most experimental. By 1925, Cather was alive to the experimentalism—the form rather than just the story—that Wharton had defensively explained in her newly theorized "Author's Introduction" to the recently republished *Ethan Frome* (1911, 1922).

Faulkner was profoundly influenced by Edith Wharton, despite the fact that he appears never to have spoken her name. This gifted literary mother, the sworn enemy of cubism, modernism, and what she understood as their context—the cacophony of post–World War I culture—can be said to have established the terms for the creation of William Faulkner. Indeed, Edith Wharton provoked his most radical experiment: the novel he repeatedly referred to as his "most splendid failure." In 1925, as he was preparing his first novel for publication, Faulkner was not only reading Wharton's fiction, he was reading her literary criticism. The most significant consequence of Wharton's only volume of literary criticism, *The Writing of Fiction* (1925), is a narrative sally that appears in one of her diatribes against modernism.[20] Shakespeare provided the inspiriting metaphor, but Wharton was clearly the narrative provocateur, as she threw down the gauntlet that provoked *The Sound and the Fury*. Condemning modernism, she chastised this literary fad for its fealty to a "pathological world where the action, taking place between people of abnormal psychology and not keeping with our normal human rhythms, becomes an idiot's tale, signifying nothing."[21]

Faulkner, like Cather, clearly felt the reverberations of Wharton's critical intelligence as she articulated the narrative theory behind *Ethan Frome*. In her 1922 "Author's Introduction," Wharton defended her realism in this 1911 novella by articulating a narrative theory based on the sculptural power of voice. Trying "to draw" characters known for their "deep-rooted reticence and inarticulateness," Wharton insisted that "the effect of 'roundness' (in the plastic sense) [could be] produced by letting their case be seen through [the] eyes" and heard in the voices of different informants (vii, ix). Using sculptural language to insist on the spatial dimensions of narrative, Wharton proposed a carving of the story that would gain dimensionality through the narrator's incorporation of the voices of multiple observers. A reprise of the multiperspectival theory of realism that Hamlin Garland had named "veritism,"[22] Wharton's "Author's Introduction" to *Ethan Frome* can be read as a formal template for Faulkner's *As I Lay Dying* as well as his other masterpieces of voice-based experimentalism. Featuring an elitist defense of her "sophisticated" narrator, Wharton's "I" mounts an unacknowledged assault on a positivism that cannot fulfill its own elitist claims for her narrator's superiority as the synthesizer of a single truth.[23] As Wharton's unnamed engineer initiates the novel's narrative, his perspective is positively Faulknerian: "I had the story bit by bit [and] . . . each time it was a different story" (3). Beneath the rural informant's facts, the engineer intuits "that the deeper story . . . was in the gaps" (7). In *As I Lay Dying*, fifteen named characters occupy the position of the first-person narrator, and each of these figures is threatened with the objectification of a progressive death as they "lay dying." Two-thirds of the way through the novel, in the single section that bears her name, the dead and rotting mother rails against the need to fill silence. Addie Bundren's unspoken assertion that words are "just a shape to fill a lack" argues for the active power of being and doing over the inadequacy of saying and, by implication, writing. Addie Bundren distinguishes between "the words [that] are the deeds, and the other words that are not deeds, that are just the gaps in people's lacks." In *As I Lay Dying*, the deeper story, like Addie's illegitimate son, Jewel, who constitutes the word made act, appears in "the gap" (174).

Through the fifty-nine sections comprised of spoken and unspoken thoughts, Faulkner's novel uses voice, audible and inaudible, to create a sculptural form in which words come up against things. Language in *As I Lay Dying* articulates the physical world through presence and absence, picturing sounds as literal and substantive as they abrupt against inanimate objects and animate beings to sculpt absence as well as presence. Describing the place where her virginity used to be, Addie Bundren pictures a word-shaped blank space. She can signify "nothing" only through the concept of negative space, as this absence ("the deeper . . . story [that lies] in the gaps" [Wharton, *Ethan* 7]) is both defined by and articulated through the inked-in presence of the surrounding words.

Defining the matricidal urge that is fundamental to this parable of modernism, Wharton's and Cather's novels are forceful replacement-narratives that are masterminded by the desires of narrating and writing men obsessed with exhuming and burying the body of the mother. Harbingers of Addie Bundren, these darkly promiscuous mountain mothers—the animal-like mother of Wharton's *Summer* (1917), said to be "like a dead dog in a ditch" and part of a "promiscuous herd," and Cather's Indian mother, whose ancient murder (fantasized as the fate of promiscuity) makes her the traditional sign of an annihilated race—are explicitly buried or boxed in novels that insist on the triumph of men. Those who undertake this act of burial, Wharton's and Cather's engineers, lawmakers, professors, and would-be anthropologists, are driven by their passions for heroic epics, scientific exploits, and other cerebral narratives of masculine desire. In many ways, the old and often gendered struggle that pits the mind against the body is explicitly replayed as Wharton's and Cather's heroes are threatened with death (creative and/or literal) and the related derailing of masculine pursuits by female materialists. *Ethan Frome* (republished with Wharton's prefatory defense of its form in 1922) and *The Professor's House* (1925) are not just writers' books; these works—appearing after their authors had won the Pulitzer Prize in 1921 and 1923, respectively—are clearly manifestoes about the making of art, intoned by women who had gained significant authority. Finally, it is no accident that *Ethan Frome* and *The Professor's House* are highly embodied books that with shocking directness address what it means for male narrators, as creators of accounts, to replace the mother's body with a book.

While Wharton's unnamed narrator fills the vacuum in his knowledge with a book-shaped "vision" (complete with numbered chapters) that constitutes a projection of his own psyche, the isolated men of Cather's novel commune with past epics: Professor Godfrey St. Peter writes prizewinning historical volumes on the Spanish conquistadors while Tom Outland reads Virgil's *Aeneid*. Cather's men of words literally position themselves in workspaces atop eviscerated domestic interiors, emptied of furniture and females. The most explicit version of this parable is narrated by Tom Outland, who later invents a device that in its very name offers a diagnosis and etiology of what is wrong with post–World War I America: the "Outland Vacuum" names the cultural emptiness at the center of the country. Excavating an Indian ruin that he sees as a "sculpture," Outland discovers three elderly bodies, a man and two women, formally sealed away behind the wall where they occupy a fallen platform, literally a story that has crashed into another story. In formal and thematic terms, this detail in Cather's novel is a direct, jokingly acute reference to *Ethan Frome*'s interior story. The psychic vision of Wharton's unnamed engineer that is projected to form the novel within the novel is an embedded and embodied book—calling attention to itself by shifting to third-person narration—an interior that purports to tell the story of three people:

an elderly man and two aged women essentially buried alive in a snowbound house. In her tripartite reversal of *Ethan Frome*, Cather's *The Professor's House* embeds the spoken tale of a first-person narrator in a center that is entitled "Tom Outland's Story." This character's autobiographical tale is surrounded by the story of the professor, which is told in traditional omniscient narration. Tom Outland is a dead man when he speaks, or more precisely (as Faulkner realized), he is already a dead man when he is heard.

In a precise inversion of *Ethan Frome*, *The Professor's House* has an oral narrative in the middle, but this oral narrative is itself a site of buried books. The narrator's book-shaped vision of *Ethan Frome* is found here in reference to form as well as content in Tom Outland's discovery of the bodies behind the wall. However, there is another more troubling body, the female "mummy" (this pun is as old as the word) discovered by Tom Outland and his collaborator. Not self-made, this dried Indian woman lies unburied, the mummified archetype of an originary man-made art, biblically identified by the rib that has violated her leathern skin. Dubbed "Mother Eve" by the priest who insists on her promiscuous past, this primal mountain-mother is linked by her violated head to the feminized men of Wharton's and Cather's novels as well as to her literary descendant, the adulterous mother, Addie Bundren. Cather's hero, Tom Outland, has replaced this dried mother with a book, a narrative that he has written in an account book that, among other things, contains the story of the discovery and removal of "Mother Eve." Tom Outland's book, which catalogs the discovery of objects, among them the prized and murdered mummy, is preserved by being given a ritualized, if temporary, burial, before being unearthed by the professor. This replacement narrative could not have been executed with more clarity as the hero chooses to seal his account, in a mock-up of a tribal burial, behind the wall of the very room where the unburied "Mother Eve" had lain drying for hundreds of years.

As these works embody stories within stories to foreground the experimental possibilities posed by first-person narration, *Ethan Frome*, *The Professor's House*, and *As I Lay Dying* are joined by their focus on the sculptural qualities of the threatened male head. Like Wharton's milked-out caretaker, Ethan Frome, who bears the feminizing mark of a "red gash" on his "forehead" (4), Cather's representative of a decorative and domestic aesthetic, Henry, is repeatedly said to be in danger of losing his head. When Henry is brought to the camp, the cattle boss warns the two cowboys: "he's got no head" (*Professor's* 176), and later, Tom Outland's partner, Roddy Blake, advises Henry about the dangers of swimming across the river: "You have to keep your head" (184). Clearly marked as a sacrificial figure, Henry does not lose his head in the water but rather after a snake has "struck him square in the forehead" as he is literally standing on the shoulders (becoming the head) of the masculine hero Tom Outland.

In this Edenic tragedy, Henry's forehead has been struck by a snake as he tries to ascend to the aerie distinguished for having once housed "Mother Eve." This phallicized madman with his engorged and purple head has had to be restrained from diving headfirst into the ravine, a desire that anticipates the fate of "Mother Eve," who escapes her berth in a German museum by falling to the bottom of the canyon. These feminized and wounded figures, female as well as male, embody warnings. Although they may not always preserve the lives of the narrating men who collaborate in the burial of mothers, these totemic women echo the protagonists' feared fate through their damaged heads. In terms of plot alone, the description in *The Professor's House* of bringing the desiccated "mummy," "Mother Eve," down from the mountainous mesa suggests that the connection between Cather's and Faulkner's novels is one of direct lineage. There is no doubt that Cather's Mother Eve, whose "box [has been made] extra wide" and who drags a mule named Jenny[24] to her death in her fall "to the bottom of Black Canyon" (221), is a direct antecedent of Faulkner's Addie Bundren and her precipitous descent in her own mule-killing and man-destroying box.

Wharton's and Cather's family romances of American literature, parables of art and the fate of the nation, brought William Faulkner face-to-face with the body of the cultural mother. These same works offered paeans to the sculptural qualities of the male head. In Wharton's *Ethan Frome*, the narrator pursues the eponymous hero, who, with his "red gash[ed]" head and truncated leg, provokes the narrator's vision of a feminizing region that entraps once virile men, while allowing the urban narrator to identify himself with "the smart ones [who] get away" (6). In the opening frame of *Ethan Frome*, as the narrator introduces his picturesque hero as "the most striking figure in Starkfield, though he was but the ruin of a man" (3), the silent Frome seems struck from a sculptural mold: "his brown seamed profile, under the helmet-like peak of the cap . . . like the bronze image of a hero" (14). To Cather's figure of the female artist who fails because she can only succeed in painting her own father's head, "the best thing" about the professor is "the modeling of his head between the top of his ear and his crown": "high, polished, hard as bronze," "[t]he mould of his head . . . was so individual and definite . . . that it was more like a statue's head than a man's" (*Professor's* 5). Her husband, the failed writer who makes a living penning jingles for the newspaper, seems moved to a lyrical phallicism as he describes his father-in-law's head. Seen as he swims with "his head and shoulders . . . out of the water," the professor wears a "vermillion" "rubber visor" that is said to be "like a continuation of his flesh . . . The visor was picturesque—his head looked sheathed and small and intensely alive, like the heads of the warriors on the Parthenon frieze in their tight, archaic helmets" (57). In *As I Lay Dying*, this mongrel image is worn but nevertheless recognizable as Darl, the head-obsessed artist figure, describes his own silent and hypermasculine brother Jewel as looking "through [his broken hat] like through the visor of a helmet" (94). Faulkner had already punctured Cather's adulatory image of this man's red "rubber," "sheathed" head by linking his rather distinctive sport's accessory to male loss. Long before the appearance of the toothless Anse Bundren, with his quest for masculinity objectified in the pursuit of "them teeth," Faulkner's fiction had mocked the professor's valorized head by insisting on the feminized character of Mr. Talliaferro in *Mosquitoes*, whose "red . . . bathing suit . . . giv[es] him a bizarre desiccated look, like a recently extracted tooth. He wore also a red rubber cap" (80).

Trying to make sense of the literary scene in the decades following the Great War, Wharton increasingly described an American literature rendered unstable by its focus on a localized past; and, as she looked forward, Wharton envisioned a literary landscape threatened by the assault of a similarly limited and (from her perspective) cacophonous modernism. Discouraged by what she saw as a downward turn in the nation's narrative pursuits, a literary compulsion gravitating toward the lower regions in more ways than one, Wharton argued that American literature was being taken over by writers who were obsessed with "the man with the dinner-pail" (*Backward* 21) and the mistaken sense of a "'real America,'" "as though the chief intellectual and moral resources of the country lay among the poor whites of the Appalachians" ("Tendencies" 173).[25] Paradoxically, as the author of *Ethan Frome*—an antiregional work that was by definition regional—Wharton herself was the author of a well-known work that in geographical terms was about "the poor whites of the Appalachians." Indeed, Wharton's Fromes inhabit the Berkshire hills, the northernmost ridges of the very range whose southernmost reaches would spew Faulkner's Bundrens down from their hill, putting them on the road to race in *As I Lay Dying* (1930).

Race is at the core of Faulkner's revision of this tradition of burying the regional mother, and Faulkner's knowledge of race is fundamental to his understanding of ritualized violence, which separates him and his work from that of his foremothers. This begins with Faulkner's racial revision of Wharton's and Cather's related parables of art. From the beginning, in his early composition of the "Father Abraham" stories, race was central to Faulkner's representation of class. Race, for Faulkner, was always more than blackness, or even blackness and whiteness; race, in historical as well as practical terms, embodied his region. Like the children of Faulkner's Mississippi Abraham, the upland Bundrens are locally colored, and in their descent the Bundrens foreground an aesthetic crossroads that acknowledges the attraction of death in the valleys, bodied forth in the seductive and prophetic embrace of a maternal muse. At the same time, *As I Lay Dying* understands the ritual necessity of this burial of the procreative body to the mystery of masculine conception, a burial that is increasingly marked by race in Faulkner's cubist novel.[26]

Carving Out a Man-Made Art

As I Lay Dying articulates the gendered drama between a regional culture and a national aesthetic with striking clarity. As Faulkner devotes an entire novel to the collaborative project of burying the mother, the elements he has reconfigured from the parables formulated by Wharton and Cather retain their archetypal power. Faulkner's *As I Lay Dying* both reads and revises Wharton's and Cather's parables of art by reveling in the excesses of parody. Comic and macabre, Faulkner's *As I Lay Dying* is feminist in its revision of the paradigms of art laid out in what I have called Wharton's and Cather's writer's books. While Wharton's and Cather's novels critique the threat that domesticity poses to epic heroes, Faulkner's novel, focusing on the delayed burial of a rotting mother, dramatizes the fear of embodiment and ultimately the terror of the loss of embodiment itself. Darl Bundren, a direct descendant of Quentin Compson, is the primary artist figure of *As I Lay Dying*. Like Wharton's Ethan Frome, Cather's Godfrey St. Peter, and Faulkner's Quentin, Darl dwells in the paradox of male creation as he experiments with what it means "to be or not to be," a state that is mediated through the presence and absence of the maternal body.

In *As I Lay Dying*, the motherless son is the madman artist who uses his sculptural vision to carve a masculine work of art. Darl Bundren's vision in itself emerges as a creative act of seeing in which the practical vocabulary of aesthetics results in his ability to create paintings out of woodchips and sculptures from living heads. Darl uses the act of description like an artist's knife: to thicken paintings and to carve his silent double, Jewel. From the novel's opening words, the silent Jewel emerges as a work of art being methodically carved into existence through Darl's sculpturally repetitive and thickening language. Darl's focus on Jewel's head emerges as an obsession in the opening paragraph of *As I Lay Dying*: Darl, walking "fifteen feet ahead of him," insists "anyone watching us from the cottonhouse can see Jewel's frayed and broken straw hat a full head above my own" (3). Moving from the circle, a worn path made by "feet in fading precision" (3), Jewel steps into this "square [through] the window," exiting the same way "in a single stride through the opposite window" (4). Imagined by Darl in this series of wooden frames, Jewel with his "full head" "ahead" is defined through the wooden quality of his face and eyes.

In this novel that insists on Darl's omniscient vision, the absent Darl details his carpenter brother's progress: "Cash bevels the edge . . . with the tedious and minute care of a jeweler" (79). If Cash is the figure Darl associates most often with painting and the painted, Darl himself, through his relentlessly sculptural vision, is the most obsessed "jeweler" of the work. Darl creates or, more precisely, shapes the multifaceted form of the near-silent Jewel. Lacking the clear boundaries of phallic masculinity, Darl is tutored in his vague bodily knowledge by Cash's faltering explanation of Jewel's sexuality. The inexperienced Darl has intuited the existence of a masculinity that is not unlike Vardaman's longed-for object, the shiny red train; this neophyte fantasy of masculine desire is for "something . . . new and hard and bright" (132). Darl repeatedly refers to Jewel solely by the word "he," a practice that becomes visible in Darl's sections, particularly in those where Jewel's name is withheld and he (Jewel) is revealed as the novel's iconic "he."

Indeed, the almost singular focus that Darl keeps on Jewel would threaten to replace the coffin itself for Darl, if Jewel himself were not so concerned with preserving what is repeatedly referred to as the "box."[27] Taunting Jewel about the mystery of his paternity (Jewel has been fathered by a potent evangelist whose name, "Whitfield,"[28] recalls that of the most powerful preacher in colonial America), Darl through his sculptural vision is not only a brother but a carver in words. Here, in the absence of a legitimate father, Darl attempts to establish himself as Jewel's narrator, his aesthetic creator. Describing Jewel as "no less than the signboard," Darl sees him repeatedly as "wooden-faced" and "wooden-backed" (94, 95, 108, 209), with his "wooden face," "wooden look" (181), "his pale eyes like wood set into his wooden face" (4), "his eyes like pale wooden eyes" (18), "eyes like pale wood in his high-blooded face" (17), "the pale rigidity of his eyes" (128), and later "[h]is eyes . . . pale as two bleached chips" (145). Like the paleness of Jewel's chiplike eyes, Darl's description of Jewel as "wooden-faced" and "wooden-backed" becomes part of a staidly obsessive and only gradually transformed sculptural portrait. In a vision pointedly excluding his brother's legs, Darl sees Jewel and his horse as "like two figures carved for a tableau savage in the sun" (12).

To Darl's eyes, the "wooden-backed, wooden-faced" Jewel assumes classical dimensions as "he looks through [his broken hat] like through the visor of a helmet" (94). Recalling the truncated sculpture of the female torso present in Faulkner's *Mosquitoes* (1927), a statue that is based directly on the black cotton dress form which serves as the historian Godfrey St. Peter's muse in *The Professor's House*, Darl has a vision of divided men. As Jewel is joined by their neighbor, Tull, in the flood-swollen river, Darl concludes: "they do not appear to violate the surface at all; it is as though it had severed them both at a single blow, the two torsos moving with infinitesimal and ludicrous care upon the surface" (163).

Significantly, Jewel, who is most associated with a carved and masculine shape, is divided as he looks for his brother's lost tools. This scene, which insists on Cash's loss of masculine prowess, suggests that his loss of the tools of production has consequences for his tools of reproduction. Having broken his leg in the uncontrollable flood, Cash is maimed as he loses his tools in his failed effort to hold on to the man-destroying female box. Although the hypermasculine Jewel remains the focal figure of Darl's sculptural vision, Darl's artist's eye also notes the inferior shaping of his own father. Pa (Anse) is said to look "like a figure carved clumsily from tough wood by a drunken caricaturist" (163); and it is significant that Pa (whom the neighbor Tull describes as looking like he is wearing Jewel's clothes) draws Darl's attention when he (Pa) is actually wearing Jewel's raincoat. In Darl's aesthetic critique, Pa in his roughly hewn form is seen as an explicit caricature of the family's Jewel, the manly man who is not Anse Bundren's son. To Darl, Pa's "face [appears] streaming slowly . . . as though upon a face carved by a savage caricaturist [a face where] a monstrous burlesque of all bereavement flowed" (78). Just as he has earlier described Pa's shoes as looking "as though they had been hacked with a blunt ax out of pig-iron" (11), Darl's similes describing Anse Bundren suggest that his father has been made with bad tools from base materials. In this scene as Anse (a piece of failed art) cross-dresses as a man in Jewel's clothing, Cash, already dragging his leg from a previous fall, seems confirmed in his own feminized fate by "wearing Mrs Tull's raincoat" (78).

"Pale Paint on a Black Canvas": Framing the Mother

While the increasingly feminized and mad Darl Bundren loses his head at the close of the novel—arguably because the female body is finally buried—the only children whom Addie Bundren claims in her last count, her sons Cash and Jewel, are pictured as wounded and transformed by their efforts to preserve the body of the mother. Indeed, these loyal sons are implicated in the most explicitly pictorial scenes of *As I Lay Dying*. In Darl's pictorial visions, Addie Bundren is framed at the center of pictures, which confirms the place of the mother flanked by sacrificial sons as the crucial tableaux in Faulkner's complexly gendered and, finally, racially coded family romance of art.

From Darl's perspective, as Cash brings together boards for Addie's coffin,

> He [Cash] looks up at the gaunt face framed by the window in the twilight. It is a composite picture of all time since he was a child. He drops the saw and lifts the board for her to see, watching the window in which the face has not moved . . . For a while still she looks down at him from the composite picture, neither with censure nor approbation. Then the face disappears. (48)

Here, Cash's act of making a container for the mother is described in the language of giving birth. Seeing his mother, Cash is said to be "laboring on toward darkness," "it [is] as though the [stroke] of the saw"—"the stroke" of the verb "to see" in the past tense—"illumined its own motion, board and saw engendered" (48). Although Addie Bundren dying appears "like a casting of fading bronze" (51), it is Cash's completion of the box that marks the "final juxtaposition" (48) of the son's art of preservation, a process that requires the death of the mother. After gazing from the window, framed in what Darl twice calls the "composite picture," Addie Bundren's "face disappears" (48). In this "picture" described omnisciently by the absent Darl, Addie's youngest child appears to have a "pale face fading into the dusk like a piece of paper pasted on a failing wall" (49); and, as the oldest son, Cash, focuses for a final time on his dying mother's face, he sees a "peaceful, rigid face fading into the dusk as though darkness were a precursor of the ultimate earth, until at last the face seems to float detached upon it, lightly as the reflection of a dead leaf" (50). These fading faces of the final progeny and the soon-to-be-dead mother are both associated with "pasted" paper and a "dead leaf," both past and dead. The detached face or head of the mother is likened to "the reflection of a dead leaf," a dead page in which characters who have generated other characters threaten to reveal their origins by returning to their elemental forms as dead and receding paper. While the dying Addie is framed as the "composite picture of all time," Cash seems to be making a painting "on a black canvas" as he builds a maternal box specifically designed to contain the "[a]nimal magnetism" (83) of the mother. Trying to tear materiality out of "the flat darkness," Cash's labor produces "[u]pon the dark ground the chips [that] look like random smears of soft pale paint on a black canvas. The boards look like long smooth tatters torn from the flat darkness and turned backside out" (75).

Later, in Darl's aesthetically structured view, Jewel assumes the position of Cash in the earlier scene. Here, Jewel himself becomes framed along with the maternal box at the center of what appears to be an excessively framed geometric picture:

> Against the dark doorway he [Jewel] seems to materialise out of darkness, lean as a race horse . . . in the beginning of the glare . . . He has seen me without even turning his head or his eyes in which the glare swims like two small torches . . . [H]e runs silver in the moonlight, then he springs out like a flat figure cut leanly from tin against an abrupt and soundless explosion . . . The front, the conical façade with the square orifice of doorway broken only by the square squat shape of the coffin on the sawhorses like a cubistic bug, comes into relief. (218–19)

To fulfill his role as the modern artist, Darl must try to burn this picture that insists on the mother's centrality to the scene of art. The coffin mounted on sawhorses appears (in the most infamous simile of the novel) "like a cubistic bug." As the barn begins to burn, Jewel (in Darl's words) springs "out like a flat figure cut leanly from tin [while] the square squat shape of the coffin on the sawhorses like a cubistic bug, comes into relief" (218–19). As the coffin threatens to emerge from the deceptive illusion of its pictorial flatness, this centerpiece is likened to the exoskeleton of an insect, which, like the cubist shapes of modern art, suggests that the dead and the flat may molt from exteriority back into life. Recalling Cash's struggle to transform the "flat darkness," Jewel (again from Darl's aesthetically driven view) emerges from flatness to roundness as he confronts the "stark naked" owner of the barn. To Darl's eye, Jewel and Gillespie are "like two figures in a Greek frieze, isolated out of all reality by the red glare" (221).

Darl uses the language of theater as he stands with the other spectators: "We watch through the dissolving proscenium of the doorway" that frames Jewel in a fiery curtain "like a portière of flaming beads" (221, 222). The coffin, said to "loom . . . unbelievably tall, hiding him," becomes the vertical frame that obscures Jewel before he is joined to the "upend[ed]" maternal box "gaining momentum" as it "crashes slowly forward and through the curtain." "[E]nclosed in a thin nimbus of fire" (222), the body of Jewel himself recalls the stroke that Darl has earlier ascribed to Cash's extravagantly phallic tool, the saw illumined by the "thin thread of fire" that repeatedly penetrates the paternal "silhouette":

> He saws again . . . a thin thread of fire running along the edge of the saw, lost and recovered at the top and bottom of each stroke in unbroken elongation, so that the saw appears to be six feet long, into and out of pa's shabby and aimless silhouette . . . [Cash] sweep[s] pa away with the long swinging gleam of the balanced board. (76)

"[T]he balanced board" with its "long swinging gleam" bears the light of Cash's still incomplete creation as this elongated beam seems to sweep away the father himself, who has already been diminished to a flattened outline, a "shabby and aimless silhouette." Amid the Zeus-like fecundity of a shower of gold, the connection between Jewel and Addie's box maintains its generative power: "sparks rain on it [the upright coffin] as though they engendered other sparks from the contact," "revealing Jewel and the sparks raining on him too in engendering gusts" (222). Backlit by the "red glare" of a barn burning rather than the illuminating nationalism of "the rocket's red glare," Jewel with his "thin smell of scorching meat" (222) is significantly blackened as he becomes a descendant of Melville's Ishmael.[29] Ishmael, the most distinguished illegitimate son of the Old Testament (the rejected son of Abraham exiled into the desert with his foreign mother, Hagar), becomes a patriarch, the founder of a race and religion in his own right, establishing the line that would lead to Mohammed. Never claimed by his blood father (a religious patriarch and hill-bred Abraham), Jewel is his mother's son. Like Melville's Ishmael of *Moby Dick*, Jewel (literally mounted astride the maternal box) rides a coffin to safety in a scene of grotesque rebirth (221–22).

In *As I Lay Dying*, as Jewel is burned in fire and Cash is crushed in the flood, these wounded men are marked as the novel's sacrificial sons. Dying and dead, Addie Bundren is the focal point in these two passages that comprise the most self-conscious and explicitly pictorial visions of the novel. Faithful to the female force who is seen as the "composite picture of all time,"[30] Cash and Jewel are blackened and feminized as a direct result of their efforts to preserve the body of the mother, which has been literally framed at the center of the scene of art.

Blackened Sons: Seeing Race in *As I Lay Dying*

Pointedly, the idiot-like youngest son, Vardaman, is the figure who sees the world in dissolution as elements are deconstructed (in the old sense of the term) into pieces and parts. It is Vardaman who envisions the world as it dissolves before his eyes in a type of reverse photographic emergence, and it is Vardaman who can see the racial elements in Faulkner's increasingly complex revision of Wharton's and Cather's male-centered paradigms of art. As the rotting mother of *As I Lay Dying* goes through flood and fire, the only sons Addie Bundren ultimately claims are physically blackened after they have been threatened with the loss of their legs as a direct result of their futile efforts to preserve their mother's body. To Vardaman's eyes, "Cash's leg and foot turned black. We held the lamp and looked at Cash's foot and leg where it was black" (224). Continuing, Vardaman insists on the racial specificity of his brother's blackened parts: "your foot looks like a nigger's foot, Cash" (224); and if Jewel (the iconographic American male who has earlier been described as "having the rigid gravity of a cigar store Indian" [4]) is initially reddened by the fire, race is increasingly at issue as Jewel is painted black by the mother to be. The pregnant Dewey Dell smears Jewel's back with butter and soot, turning "his back . . . black" (224). Color, castration, the female touch, and the man-destroying power of the female box are revealed in Vardaman's description of Addie's sons: "'Your back looks like a nigger's, Jewel' . . . Cash's foot and leg looked like a nigger's. Then they broke it off. Cash's leg bled" (224). In Darl's speech that follows, the maiming power of the maternal box is juxtaposed with the male leg: "We mount the wagon again where Cash lies on the box, the jagged shards of cement cracked about his leg" (227).

In *As I Lay Dying*, both the tool-wielding male sculptor, Cash, and the verbally sculpted and masculine art object, Jewel, have been blackened in terms of their damaged or lost legs—Cash's actual leg and Jewel's legs in the form of his horse. Both of these brothers are increasingly emasculated by their intimate association with the mother. Even before Jewel runs around "through the gap" (221) to save the body of the mother, even before he has been literally blackened, Vardaman positions Jewel not only in relation to Cash, but more specifically in relation to Cash's maimed leg: "Jewel came back . . . He was walking. Jewel hasn't got a horse anymore. Jewel is my brother. Cash is my brother. Cash has a broken leg . . . Cash is my brother. Jewel is my brother too, but he hasn't got a broken leg" (210). Finally, it is no accident that just after Jewel has been burned and recognized along with Cash as a racially marked figure, the stinking wagon passes "[t]hree negroes" (229).

While "white-eyed faces" peer from the darkened doorways of this rural settlement, these "negroes" on the road are the only characters of African American descent who make an obvious appearance in this upcountry novel.[31] Expressing their "shock and instinctive outrage" at the ripe smell of the rotting mother, the "negroes" ask, "Great God . . . what they got in that wagon?" And Jewel, "blind[ed]" by his anger, might be said to misfire racially as he turns to shout, "Son of a bitches" (229). Hearing this curse as directed at himself, the white man who is also on the road focuses on the singular "son" rather than the plural "bitches" in Jewel's insult aimed at the "three negroes." Fighting words (even as an acronym, s.o.b.) well into the twentieth century, Jewel's curse is an insult blaspheming mothers ("bitches" in the plural) by linking them to animal reproduction. Described as having become "slack-jawed" (229), this white man's response does not suggest slackness or passivity. Rather, to be "slack-jawed"[32] in the Mississippi slang of the early twentieth century is to assume an aggressive, impertinent expression. This "slack-jawed" man is ready to avenge what he has heard as Jewel's unprovoked insult to his own, "the white man['s]," mother. Preparing himself to fight, the whiteness of this man's masculinity is never in question as he is seen holding "the knife low against his flank" (230). According to the grammar of the sentence (although the pronoun retains an element of its classic Faulknerian ambiguity), it is Jewel who "leans above him, his [own] jaw muscles gone white" (230). Jewel with his characteristically "high-blooded face" (17) goes from being racially identified through his "black . . . back" to his "white" face, as he is threatened with an actual carving by this "white man['s]" knife. Yet, as this racially inflected passage suggests, "white" is indeed a color for this hill country son, a man of "high-blooded" color whose very face has been seen as too dark for his "bleached" eyes. In Darl's earlier vision, Jewel is bicolored and somehow "*wrong*": *"He had that wooden look on his face again; that bold, surly, high-colored rigid look like his face and eyes were two colors of wood, the wrong one pale and the wrong one dark"* (181).[33]

Immediately after the dark-faced Jewel is threatened with the white man's knife, the whitened and horseless Jewel is no longer walking. Instead, he is depicted as he is incorporated into the family's wagon. Even as "ahead . . . the square opens and the monument stands before the courthouse" (231), the blackened Jewel has been replaced as the monumental sculpture whose head "ahead" (3) has been dramatically positioned in wooden squares, most notably in Darl's window-inscribed vision that opens the novel and in Darl's account that frames Jewel with his mother's boxed corpse at the center of the cataclysmic barn-burning. Before he arrives at the town square, the burned Jewel becomes a squatting lower body framed by a circle: "he sets his foot on the turning hub of the rear wheel . . . the hub turning smoothly under his sole [as] he lifts the other foot and squats there, staring straight ahead, motionless, lean, wooden-backed, as though carved squatting out of the lean wood" (231).

In his geometric aesthetic, Darl has seen his siblings' mother as an encircling and binding frame as well as a central figure: "the red road lies like a spoke of which Addie Bundren is the rim" (108). The unwieldy mother (read in terms of the puns that structure so much of the novel) is the "rim" of "spokes," the container of what has been spoken; and this angry mother is the figure whose outrage against language will not be contained, primarily because her diatribe exists outside of the audible—the spoken—word. In the section that bears Addie's name, the quotation marks that demarcate the intrusion of words, which to her "are just the gaps in people's lacks," are found framing the conversations with Anse that have led to their marriage and their continued "chapping" (174). Surrounded by so much composition, Addie Bundren has become the activist advocate of an aesthetic of decomposition. Begotten "without the words" (27) or (to use Addie's more sophisticated version) by the "hearing [of] the dark voicelessness in which the words are the deeds" (174), the silent Jewel, a man of action, has become the circumscribed figure of the sacrificial son. As he reframes his wounded, blackened, and "wooden-backed" body at the center of Addie's maternal rim, Jewel has reentered the picture on different terms. No longer struggling to escape from flatness to roundness, nor trying to midwife the mother out of "the gap," Jewel has lost his edge to the knife of the "white man" as he becomes the maternally framed and receding sculpture of Darl's shifting vision. Encircled by the maternal rim, Jewel, like the rotting mother, threatens to return to the inanimacy of his origins. The axle turns beneath his static foot as Jewel remains "motionless . . . as though [he has been] carved squatting out of the lean wood" (231).

In *As I Lay Dying*, a major paradigm shift lies in the racial definition of masculinity achieved at the moment of the bodily sacrifice of sons. Amid the Faulknerian excess that defines the house of Addie, the chosen sons, blackened by their association with the mother's box, become visible in Vardaman's sections that flank the novel's dénouement: Darl's cubistic vision of the barn-burning scene. In Vardaman's section that immediately follows, this simple artist, whose rituals (albeit language driven) identify him as a descendant of the wordless artist figure Benjy of *The Sound and the Fury*, sees the "blackness" of his brothers' maimed parts as racial. In stark contrast, Darl, having lost his connection both to the unbounded, because unbirthed, femaleness that has allowed him to get on the inside of others, and his connection to the blackening maternal body that he himself has tried to burn, is depicted as "lying on [top of] her [Addie] . . . cry[ing]" (*AILD* 225). Vardaman in his section before the barn-burning thinks, "we will lie half in the white and half in the black, with the moonlight on our legs" (215–16). Speaking to Dewey Dell, the young boy declares, "Look . . . my legs look black. Your legs look black, too" (216). The same moonlight that has allowed Vardaman to see the blackened parts of his brothers and sister reveals only a "dappled" (post-Edenic, already "appled") Darl, unblackened as he lies crying, "lying [on top] of her" "under the apple tree." Vardaman, speaking about the barn-burning, says, "*And I saw something Dewey Dell told me not to tell nobody . . . And I saw something Dewey Dell told me not to tell nobody. It is not about pa and it is not about Cash and it is not about Jewel and it is not about Dewey Dell and it is not about me.*" (215). This "nobody" is the word that closes Vardaman's two sections that worry over the barn-burning. "Nobody" is the "something" that Vardaman has seen, and "nobody" is the "something" the sight of whom must remain a secret. Vardaman's omission of Darl clearly marks him as the missing man. Except for his memories that include the lifting of his shirt in the night to let the wind blow on his parts and his poignant recollection of animal-like fear as he recalls crouching next to Cash, Darl is disembodied.[34] Darl speaks out loud, sits in the wagon, and walks uphill, but despite repeated references to those "queer eyes of hisn" (125), his physicality remains almost as fleeting as the barely visible (but omnipresent) fact that Anse holds the reins during the entire journey across the land to Jefferson.[35] Disembodied, the brother that Vardaman calls "*nobody*" loses his ability to see "with those queer eyes of hisn" (125) into the minds and meanings of others. Like Quentin Compson, the motherless Darl Bundren from his very origins is a man of words. "[H]idden within a word like within a paper screen," which Addie feels has "struck [her] in the back," Darl's seminal origins suggest that his totemic surrogate is paternal, and that that paternal surrogate is the maternally maligned "word" (172).[36] The pictorial scenes of *As I Lay Dying* frame the mother at the center of the scene of art to insist on the place of race. If the increasing embodiment has colored Addie's masculine sons, then it is significant that Darl is not "of woman born" (*Macbeth* 4.1.80). Darl is neither blackened nor embodied by an association with the maternal body, neither that of Addie nor his sister Dewey Dell: Darl appears to be the only white Bundren.

In the effort to escape the embodied creation of female reproduction, the male artist may be seeking to lose himself in acts of abstraction and deconstructive or, more precisely, reconfigured cubist worldviews. But ultimately, Quentin as well as Darl cannot flee the knowledge that these wounded and, in Faulkner's schema, racialized bodies bear. Marked as sacrificial figures, these bodies (female as well as male) reveal the presence of race through their dark parts, becoming increasingly real through their capacity for death.

In the burial that is accomplished at the close of *As I Lay Dying*, the mother's body is disposed of in the vague brevity that merely refers to the filling in of a hole in the same sentence that details Darl's violent excision from the family: "But when we got it filled and covered and drove out the gate and turned into the lane where them fellows was waiting, when they come out and come on him and he jerked back, it was Dewey Dell that was on him before even Jewel could get at him" (237). The madman poet has once again been thrown out of the republic (in Mississippi, madmen and legislators are sent to Jackson). Having disposed of the artist, the father, continuing his past practice of "slavin" and "aslavin" the once living Addie and her children, has whited-up by filling his black-rimmed gums ("his face, slack-mouthed, the wet black rim of snuff plastered close along the base of his gums" [76]) with "them teeth." In his triumph of consumption that ends in the acquisition of the new "Mrs Bundren," Anse has taken the fruits of his children's labors to mastermind what *As I Lay Dying* has located as the masculinist and nationalist narrative of materialism. Money and the reproduction of "Mrs Bundren[s]" have come to replace the mystery of life and the mystery of art. As the pregnable woman becomes the mere vessel or rutted ditch of another man's "mire" (132), the mystery of female creation as a direct legacy of slavery—a grotesque, because visceral, anticipation of the assembly line—has been valued and therefore devalued. Without the pregnant woman as part of the aesthetic paradigm, the artist is condemned to a life regulated by a debased economy that insists on the sameness of men, the sameness of wagons, the sameness of death, and the sameness of exchange based on the grotesque equation of money and the reusable, "chapping" (173) female body.

"Sad Young [White] Man on a Train" or the United States of Incest

In his parting section, Darl at last sees Jewel revealed as a man "like any other man," a revelation that revises the moral of Wharton's and Cather's parables of art.[37] *As I Lay Dying* insists on the impotence of this head-obsessed narrative. With their resonant names, Cash and, to some extent, Jewel have come to embody a failure of generation and the failure (at least in the fiduciary sense) of the fiction of nationalism. Darl's nightmare vision of the square no longer focuses on Jewel's head. Instead, he sees "The wagon [that] stands on the square . . . It looks no different from a hundred other wagons there; Jewel standing beside it . . . looking up the street like any other man." Yet to Darl's eye, "there is something different, distinctive" (254) in his vision of sameness: the Bundren family, like Darl himself, is poised for departure. While Jewel is framed in the multitude of wooden boxes within "the square," Darl (himself at the opening of his internal multilogue) creates a framed picture of his own head in the window of the departing train (see fig. 9). In his final entry, Darl has replaced Jewel as the "he" with whom he (Darl), the self-divided man, is now obsessed. Two men himself, as he speaks to and of himself in the third person, the riven Darl has carried his omniscience to its mad conclusion. As he replaces Jewel as his own double, Darl addresses questions to himself as a separate character who exists in the third person as "him" while being talked about to himself in the second person, whom he addresses as "you." When Darl sees himself as a "he" foaming from a "cage," he assumes the pictorial position. Framed by the window, he has already entered the first-person plural through the possessive pronoun that includes him at the very moment that the family is excluding him; the unquoted, nonitalicized chorus chants in Darl's

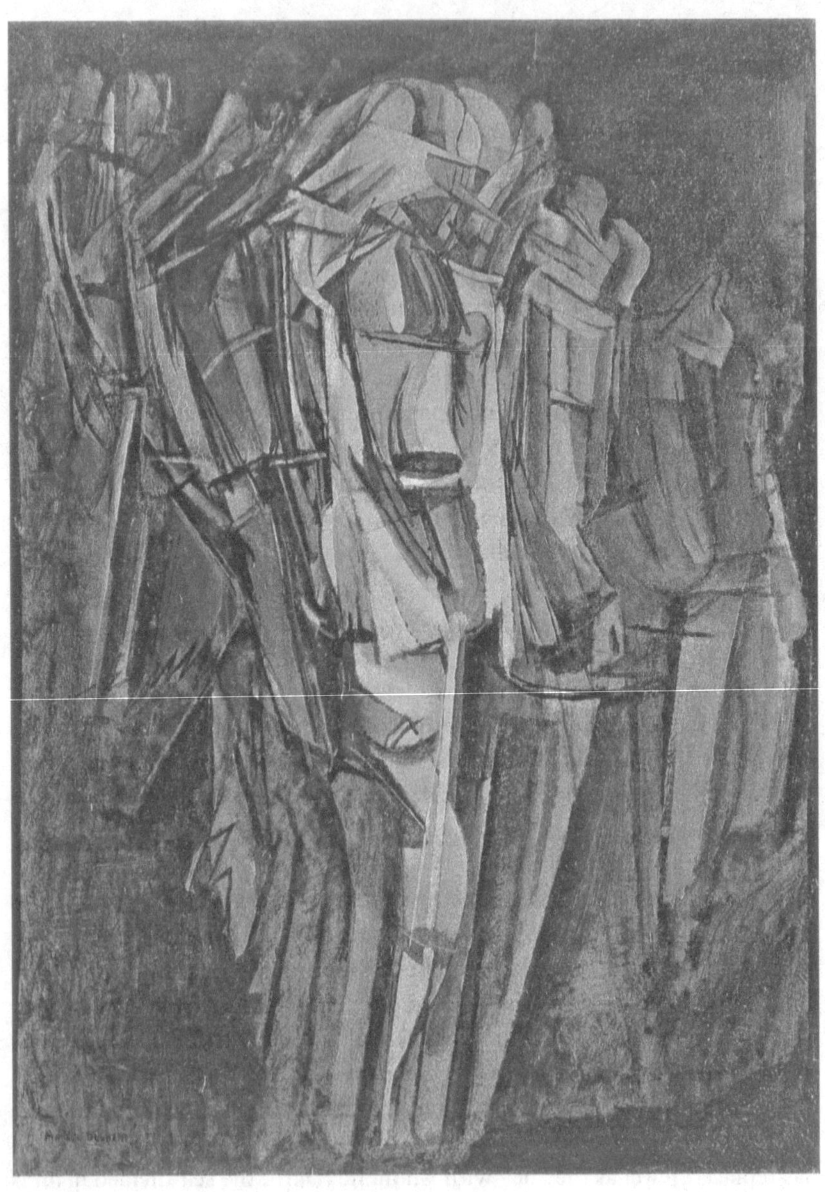

Figure 9. Marcel Duchamp, *Jeune homme triste dans un train / Sad Young Man on a Train*. © 2013 Artists Rights Society (ARS), New York / ADAGP, Paris / Succession Marcel Duchamp.

mind: "Darl is our brother, our brother Darl. Our brother Darl in a cage in Jackson where, his grimed hands lying light in the quiet interstices, looking out he foams" (254).

Excised from the family, Darl in his parting section has finally lost his head. He is a self-divided man who engages himself in a dialogue about the meaning of sameness and difference. Finally, it is Darl's vision of the sameness of the men who are taking him away to the insane asylum, a sameness he associates with heads—literally the heads and tails of coins—that exposes Darl's riddle about incest. There is an illicit potency associated with too much sameness. Questioning Darl's hysterical laughter, Darl asks himself whether the humor lies in the grotesqueness of joining represented by the picture at the end of a spyglass that he himself has brought home from the war in France. This spyglass, which features the beast with two backs (in this instance the back of a woman and the back of a pig), leads with ostensibly mad logic to Darl's other associations of animality and sex: the humor of conjoined coins is stamped onto the impossible nickel with its woman and buffalo.[38] He links this grotesque joining with the government-issued heads of the "[t]wo men":

> They pulled two seats together so Darl could sit by the window to laugh. One of them sat beside him, the other sat on the seat facing him, riding backward. One of them had to ride backward because the state's money has a face to each backside and a backside to each face, and they are riding on the state's money which is incest. (254)

These identically cut male heads, facing each other with bulging backsides, constitute a madman's riddle, a riddle that returns to the failure of generation associated with male heads, and the "heads and tails" of coins. In Darl's last section, two male heads of state with their obvious and suggestive protuberant guns face each other as they ride "on the state's money which is incest." Darl's much earlier description of Jewel's head, where he observes, "his neck is trimmed close, with a white line between hair and sunburn like a joint of a white bone" (39), is recognizable in his view of these matched government men: "[t]heir necks were shaved to a hairline, as though the recent and simultaneous barbers had had a chalk-line like Cash's" (253). Here, Darl's vision of sameness focuses on the saw-marked heads of two men whose pockets are "bulging" with "pistols" rather than with money or its genital counterpart—male interest.

There is too much sameness in sanity and nationalism. In this world of men making men, a world where men are obsessed with the heads of other men, Darl concludes in equally mad logic that sameness leads to a soiling insanity, the infertile intimacy of monetary incest. These men, like the debased coinage of the realm emblazoned with the severed heads of state (emblems of decapitation), are "riding on the state's money which is incest." "Incest" in this use of the term refers to Aristotle's pecuniary concept elaborated in the Middle

Ages that critiques usury as an illicit (because too close) relationship between money and money.[39] Monetary incest occurs when money is used to generate money without any recourse to the exogamy of productive work.

Like the leg of Wharton's Ethan Frome, Cash's leg has already been damaged by an accident, a fall; and like Ethan Frome, Cash's truncated leg suggests his impotence. Literally a fallen man, Cash cast in concrete is threatened with the loss of his leg through his family's crude parody of sculptural art. In this instance, the living male leg has been buried alive in a misguided effort at preservation. Cash's "circulation" has been cut off. This already maimed Bundren may not lose an "arm and a leg" in the stock market (shades of Jason Compson) but an actual limb in this cycle of grotesque exchange that suggests there is too much intimacy between money and art. There is, as Darl's provocatively mad riddle insists, an explicit economic allegory that must be heard in the fall of a character named Cash, who has the last word in this post-Crash novel. Seeing the horror of a living body made concrete, the farmer Gillespie (immediately after Vardaman has commented that Cash's "foot looks like a nigger's foot") replaces the standard expletive "damnation" (a curse that would have acknowledged Cash's black leg as the sign of a damned nation) with the more racially provocative (if less profane) slang: "tarnation" (224). In the vernacular of the novel, Cash has been damned by being blackened, touched with the tar brush, dammed by the rotting regional mother. Broken and blackened, Cash's leg "lies" dying atop what might be called the "Cash box." Cash's third crash suggests that he will perhaps lose more than his skin. This mother's son is severely maimed, and the future of his leg itself has been called into question in his fall from masculine and national power.

As the men discuss Cash's first fall, which has resulted in his truncated leg, Cash (in a seeming non sequitur) announces vehemently: "It's them durn women" (90); and later, when his complaint is repeated (although he appears to be angry about the women singing over his mother's dead body), there is the sense that women, even before he has broken his leg the second time in his effort to save the maternal box, have been the "durn," the damned and damming source of threats to the male leg and masculine potency. Loyal to the mother, Cash and Jewel are, in terms of the history of the nation and literary nationalism, the disloyal sons who have been emasculated as a result of their parental preference. These poor whites, colored by their class—classified and classed through their wounds and poverty as pale-blooded relatives of southern blacks—are among those who caused "the South" to become (in Roosevelt's famous observation) "the nation's economic problem number one." Upland southerners of color, these hill country men were never quite reconstructed after their collaborative efforts to sever the Union, to cut off the head of the father. A race apart, Faulkner's "poor whites," who are described elsewhere as "vermin" descending from their wild and warrened hills, had never been incorporated, a fact that makes reincorporation as unlikely as Reconstruction. These descendants of the hill country, particularly those whose iconoclastic ties tended toward confederation, had been briefly joined together with yeoman farmers of the Piedmont and the landed elites of the low country through a nationalist war fought for (among other things) the principle of divided states.

Matricidal Modernism

As I Lay Dying is a pivotal work in the transformation of this family romance of American literature. Insisting on the difficulty of burying the past embodied by a matrifocal literature, Faulkner took the measure of his own anxiety about the resilient presence of cultural mothers as he entered into explicit dialogues with the dominating voices of Wharton and Cather. In this engagement, he recast their definitions of America, which emerged during the contentious and generative decades of the early twentieth century. Taking the measure of Faulkner's anxiety about his cultural mothers (a maternal ancestry that in its mother-centered writing about the regions includes Sherwood Anderson and Jean Toomer), Faulkner chose to cast his family romance in terms of his own region, a South where questions of a reviled matriarchy had long been associated with the violent scene of failed nationalism, nostalgically narrated as the fall of white men.

Cash and Jewel, with their suggestive names, are sacrificial embodiments of female treasure: the mother's art of making sons and destroying men. Loyal to the centrality of the mother in this regionally resilient parable of art, these men, like the South and southern art itself, are blackened by the fertilizing richness of West African ethnicity. Colored by class, these sacrificial sons are colored by their devotion to the matrifocal art of regionalism. The salvation of the fecund and rotting body of the regional mother depends on a narrative of masculine sacrifice, a parable of art that insists on southern difference. Race, in terms of secrets of blood, rising tides of blackness associated with racial knowledge, and the centrality of black mothers, becomes increasingly important to Faulkner's fiction and to his literary accomplishments throughout the 1930s and 1940s.

In *As I Lay Dying*, race emerges as essential to Faulkner's parable of art as the coloring of class and sexuality becomes the generative source—the mother—of southern discomfort. The blackened Jewel, after avoiding the "white man['s]" knife, literally frames himself in what Darl has named the maternal "rim." Indeed, this is the last time Darl sees Jewel as a sculpted figure, and what he sees is equivocal: Jewel seems to be emerging carved out of the lean wood, but as he is encircled by the frame of the mother, this scene is neither of emergent creation or procreation. Following this framing, Jewel, seen by Darl as "like any other man," is boxed and ready for departure; all the boxes carry the "dying"; and all the roads ("spokes" and the way of all speaking) lead to death. Cash, with his wounded, broken, and blackened leg, is the most explicit figure of a castrated man in *As I Lay Dying*: his is the body that Addie recognizes as having broken the "circle of [her] aloneness."

Broken and burned in acts of intense embodiment, these racialized sons are not just "obverse reflection[s] of the white people" (*SF* 55) that surround them—the concept Quentin Compson uses to define race and to explain how, in what might be called the view from the mirror, he has become isolated as a "minstrel[-voiced]" "white fact" under a "microscope" (*SF* 76, 108). The blackness of these sacrificial sons, as well as the violent cleaning out of the befouled and once archetypal pregnant daughter, is a cubist cutting, a reconfiguration through abstraction that separates and juxtaposes to expose previously hidden parts of Faulkner's racially inflected and gendered parable of art. This cultural story is more than a mere structural act that attempts to signify meaning through rupture and arrangement; this narrative is a politically savvy, cultural collage that reifies acts of art even as Faulkner's artist protagonists kill themselves in rivers or more slowly through the maddening multiplicity of internalized voices that lead to formal acts of self-division. These madmen artists, the motherless sons of Faulkner's fictions—Quentin as well as Darl—are destroyed by what they lack as they pursue words, seduced by the disembodied aesthetic of a cerebral and ultimately matricidal modernism.

Coda. Vanquished and Vanished: Laying Away the Mother of the Locally Colored

> *She does not look at Anse at all. She looks at me, then at the boy. Beneath the quilt she is no more than a bundle of rotten sticks.*
> —Doc Peabody, in *As I Lay Dying*

> *[Granny] had collapsed, like she had been made out of a lot of little thin dry light sticks notched together and braced with cord, and now the cord had broken and all the little sticks had collapsed in a quiet heap on the floor, and somebody had spread a clean and faded calico dress over them.*
> —William Faulkner, *The Unvanquished*

> I could look across the grave and beyond the other headstones and monuments and see the dripping cedar grove full of mules with long black smears on their hips where Granny and Ringo had burned out the U.S. Brand.
> —William Faulkner, *The Unvanquished*

The most influential novel ever written for the United States nationalizes maternity: Harriet Beecher Stowe's *Uncle Tom's Cabin; or, Life Among the Lowly* (1852) lays claim to the antislavery home front, appealing twice to "[T]he Mothers of America" in this novel's concluding remarks. A half-century after this novel's publication, the popular lyrics for the hymn "Jesus Loves the Little Children" were written and sung to proclaim the unboundaried love promised in and by the sacrificial son. Sung to the tune of the 1864 military exhortation that proclaimed, "Tramp, tramp, tramp, the boys are marching,"[40] this Christian anthem for children was intrinsic to the world conceived of for the Sunday-school faithful by the Lottie Moon mission movement. These lyrics, published in 1898, raised questions for children in the Jim Crow South while consolidating the Christian destiny manifesting itself westward as a militarized nation cast its sights toward heathen Easts, singing of Jesus to soften the killing edge of a predestined imperialism:

> Jesus loves the little children.
> All the children of the world.
> Red and yellow, black and white,
> They are precious in his sight.
> Jesus loves the little children of the world.

Other verses of this song made a nostalgic storybook figure of the now non-threatening Indian boy with his "bow," made menacing "the big Filipino" (the U.S. enemy of choice in 1898), and diminished the stature (and threat level) of those other others, "the little Chinee."

In William Faulkner's 1938 story-cycle novel *The Unvanquished*, Granny Millard has an aestheticized funeral that ritually enacts the ending of an era. A redistributor of military resources, Granny Millard plies justice for the laboring class that is gained through restitution claims issuing from a fictional phalanx of elite-styled ladies. Seeking to address the real poverty during the last months of the Civil War, this socialist matriarch is a woman of the decade that saw her creation. Laid away in the mid-1930s along with Granny is any political hope that the economic crisis will lead to a redistribution of wealth or, more pointedly, a responsibility to feed the many colors of the hungry or give them the long-promised mules—much less the lie of the promised land of forty acres—to enable them to feed themselves.

Near the close of *As I Lay Dying*, the journey's end for the obscenely rotting body of the mother, who has been saved from flood and fire, merits a mere hole rather than a whole sentence. Here, Addie Bundren, the ostensible *primum mobile* of the novel, is merely "covered" over, subordinate to the exile of Darl—Faulkner's visually obsessed, madman poet—from the reformulated Bundrens. In contrast and in conjunction, the most beautiful funeral in Faulkner's fiction is the rain-painted burial of Granny Millard in *The Unvanquished*. Seen through the eyes of her grandson Bayard, Granny Millard's grave is a painting in which colors liquefy to soften the rawness of the earth's wound:

> [T]he rain [was] splashing slow and cold and gray on the umbrella and splashing slow on the yellow boards where Granny was and into the dark red dirt beside the red grave without splashing at all . . . Ringo and I stood there and

watched Granny going down into the earth with the quiet rain splashing on the yellow boards until they quit looking like boards and began to look like water with thin sunlight reflected in it, sinking away into the ground. Then the wet red dirt began to flow into the grave . . . The earth was loose and soft now, dark and red with rain, so that the rain didn't splash on Granny at all: it just dissolved slow and gray into the dark red mound, so that after a while the mound began to dissolve too without changing shape, like the soft yellow color of the boards had dissolved and stained up through the earth and mound and boards and rain were all melting into one vague quiet reddish gray. (*U* 156, 157, 158–59)

This funeral ritual is completed several months later with the same colors melting into autumnal oblivion despite the fullness of the Mississippi winter. The grave with its scarlet mound has settled into the ground, but the wound is remarked through the flagrant absence of the killing brute's burial when the dead mother's acolytes unwrap a severed limb from a blood-stained "square of . . . faded gray cloth," "fasten[ing]" the arm of the murderer to the grave marker of the slaughtered mother (*U* 184).

In *The Unvanquished*, two boys who have been joined from birth collaborate to become men by carving a man: a ritualized art of revenge for the murder of their primal mother,[41] Granny Millard. The villain that the white Bayard and the black Ringo kill is a war's end brigand who is himself paired with a writer whose spidery script ("in a hand neat and small and prettier than Granny's" [177]) conveys his effeminate sadism. Whereas Grumby leaves a crudely lettered note on "that dirty paper," a "woning [warning] not thret" to "children no children," the feminine addendum is bluntly elegant: "This is signed by others besides G., one of wh*m* in particular hav*ng* less scruples re children than he has. Nethless undersg*nd* desires to give both you and G. one more chance. Take it, and someday become a man. Refuse it, and cease even to be a child" (177–78). This last message about manhood and what it means to "become a man" comes from a killer who conveys that real men kill children as well as women. Warned of their impending death as children that will become in Grumby's resonant phrase "no children," the killer's message telegraphically points toward a series of possible consequences that in addition to negating their lives as children by ending their lives also enunciates the dictum that children who kill will no longer be children.

Rich in grandmothers—both Ringo and Bayard are said to call Granny Millard "Granny," while Louvinia, Ringo's actual grandmother, keeps an eye on them—both boys are motherless. Bayard's mother has died giving birth to him; Ringo (according to Bayard's father, the smartest and the tallest of the two) is provided with what might be called a preemptive or rumor-staunching father in the form of the manservant Simon who accompanies Bayard's short and larger-than-life father to the war. In addition to their sharing of Granny Millard, a bond that includes hiding together under her capacious skirts to avoid being nailed to the barn "like coon hides" after they have shot at a Yankee and killed a conscripted race horse, Ringo and Bayard are said to have nursed at "the same breast." Here, the black breast of slavery joins the boys through mother's milk, but whose mother's remains unsaid. This breast, unattached to any designated entity, both metonymy and synecdoche, stands for the body of a single woman and for the female body of nurturance that has succored the soul-sucking (whether seen as parasitic or vampiristic) institution of slavery. In practical terms of labor history, the source of this life force remains unknowable in an era when wet-nursing was a domestic work assignment, albeit one that was more specialized than the female job of milking cows. Amid the detailed genealogy that places Ringo among the Sartorian slaves—a father, a grandfather, a grandmother, an uncle, and an aunt—Ringo's mother is never mentioned, nor does her absence merit a breath of attention. As John T. Matthews has asserted (echoing Wharton's unnamed engineer narrator in *Ethan Frome*, who avers that "the deeper story was in the gaps"), "To glimpse historical reality, the reader must be prepared to look in the gaps that open in all texts. These pits of contradiction may be read as the points at which history has been given textual form without becoming wholly neutralized." If "[h]istory and its representation abide in dissonant relation," this black breast in conjunction with the absence of the black mother in what has been read as a profoundly (even sentimentally) matricentric text may not tell all, but this absence locates "the gap" that speaks volumes.[42]

Recalling the negrification—the racialized blackening—of the bodies of Addie Bundren's sacrificial sons that attend the extended burial cortege of the mother in *As I Lay Dying*, Faulkner's stories published in the premier Depression-era venue of *The Saturday Evening Post* conclude with the violent death of the boys' shared primal mother, which is itself framed by the sacrificial murder of black men. Before Granny is killed, "Grumby's Independents" are credited with burning a black man ("a negro") in his cabin and afterward, the brigands' messages to the boys are pinned onto what the narrator, Granny's grandson Bayard, sees as "the thing hanging over the middle of the road from a limb":

> It was an old negro man, with a rim of white hair and with his bare toes pointing down and his head on one side like he was thinking about something quiet. The note was pinned to him . . . It was a scrap of dirty paper, with big crude printed letters like a child might have made them. (177)

Whereas the mother-figure "bears," this sacrificial body of the black man in the literalized pun of Grumby's rough dialect is called "the barer": this "thing" is the bearer of the message that bares the long present, still pregnant, and incumbent violence that has seen this man, dead or living, as "a thing." This male writing, men making men through violence, a burning and a hanging, sends messages through the composite medium of ritualized lynchings.

Feminized masculinity (seen in Grumby's sadistic sidekick with "his little fine made boots . . . and his two hands on his knees as small as a woman's hands" [166]) like masculinized femininity is vicious in Faulkner's only novel set during the Civil War. The major purveyor of masculinized womanhood in *The Unvanquished* is the fatal Medusa, Drusilla Hawk, the unrepentant rebel soldier who is known for her bayonet-cut, spiky locks and her passion for violent death by continuing to advocate killing even in the post–Civil War South. Significantly, the Medusa-invoking sign appears to the boys and the elderly Uncle Buck in the absence of women. After months of searching in a circle described as no bigger than "a silver dollar" (164) on the geography book's map, a snake has emerged, tempted by false warmth, and its head has been caught, frozen in a hole in the skimming ice as if it had been "set into a mirror" (*U* 171), its phallus body lying exposed. Seeing the squirming body of Ab Snopes as "a moccasin" left behind by Grumby's gang (whom Ab himself calls "no better than a passel of rattlesnakes" [176]), they know they are looking for the "snake den" (173) of answerable death. Even among the males that are killing for the good, weapons in *The Unvanquished* tend to come from feminine sources. Long before the seductive stepmother Drusilla hands the man-grown Bayard the guns that illustrate the pointing malignity of her own breasts (their phallicism is illustrated in the drawing by Edward Shenton [see fig. 10]), the unarmed child seeks Uncle Buck's pistol to avenge the murder of "the mother." This old man reluctant to give up his power wears his "pistol on a loop of lace leather . . . stuck into his pants like a lady's watch" (166), a feminizing nuance that is underlined by a later allusion to the same pistol "hanging down his [Uncle Buck's] back like a girl's pigtail" (172).

In "Vendée," the *Post*'s final story of Faulkner's Civil War chronicle published early in December 1936, the body of the mother-murderer has been "pegged . . . like a coon hide" to the abandoned compress where the murder of Granny Millard has taken place some months earlier. This medium, Grumby's dismembered corpse, embodies a primal message: more of an announcement than a "woning" to the community, which is waiting for the posting that declares their loss has been avenged. The inspiration to bring Grumby's hand and arm itself to be attached to Granny's grave marker is more mannered and vexed, even though Ringo contends (as if the murdered matriarch waits and watches not from heaven but from her body's grave) that "[n]ow [Granny] can lay good and quiet" from knowing what this severed body part tells.[43] Ritually lynched by Bayard and Ringo, Grumby has been shot, dismembered, and then hanged. Bayard's first two shots are more seen than heard as they pulse brightly through the fabric of the murderer's gray coat. Cloaked in the narrative indirection which signals that this memory is too painful for him

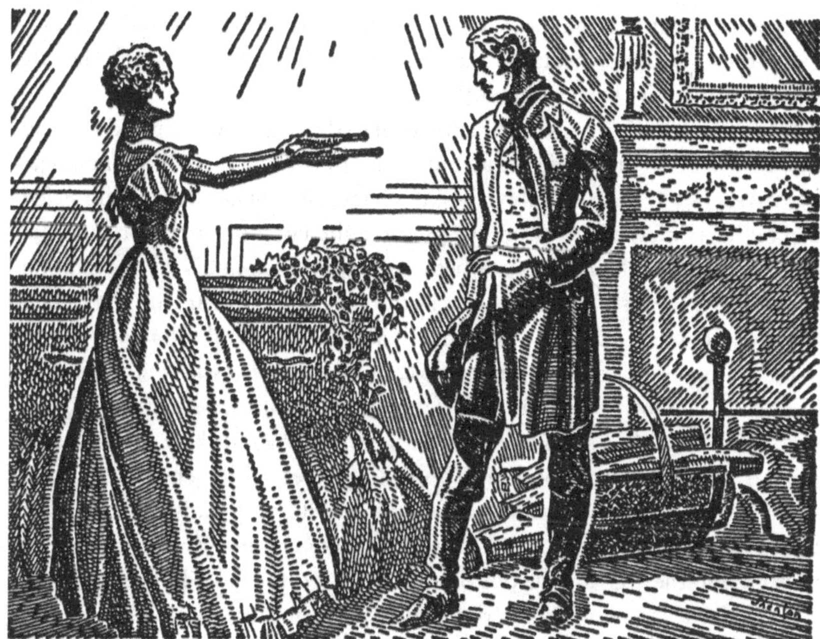

Figure 10. Engraving by Edward Shenton introducing "An Odor of Verbena" in William Faulkner, *The Unvanquished* (Random House, 1938). Reproduced here with gratitude for the consent of the Edward Shenton Family.

to picture, Bayard remembers the weight of the pistol when he shoots the bear-like killer in the back as the wounded Grumby tries to escape.

Before this final shot is fired, Ringo, who has been repeatedly described as holding and using his knife to notch wood, is seen by Bayard as "in the air, looking exactly like a frog, even to the eyes, with his mouth open too and his open pocket knife in his hand" (183). Already established as the Faulknerian artist, Ringo holds the tool that literally sculpts this man into a body that realizes, that records, this corpse's heinous act. Here, after Ringo's narration with the knife (accomplished off page), the body has been made to speak the story of the crime. Grumby's arm is troubling art as the medium becomes the message, cut to be hung on the community mother's grave. Meant as a direct testament to revenge, this arm joined to Granny's memorial creates a montage: the murderous limb juxtaposed with the grave marker re-creates the scene of the murder as always happening or as a conjunction that is permanently enjoined. Symbolically, the murdering arm, with its writing hand touching the exposed and inscribed memorial, recalls the moment when Granny's death was viscerally written and before it had been answered with another act of violence. Whatever story this arm may tell to the dead woman, for the boys this hand literalizes more than symbolic or even visceral revenge: this limb reaches back into the past before the deed and death have been done, commemorating both the instant of the murder and the moment in time when the murder could have been stopped.[44]

Set in the past of the Civil War and taken to the edge of ending and survival, these Depression-era stories echo and repeat the primal themes of Faulkner's 1930 *As I Lay Dying*. Notably, the artist figure is not blackened and negrified by hurts incurred in efforts to preserve the body of the rotting mother. Rather, the black Ringo has aesthetic gifts that, like his racial designation, are inborn as he rises to his position as the central artist figure in *The Unvanquished*. Here, the familiar story already pitched by Poe,[45] Wharton, Cather, and Faulkner himself features men who become obsessed with the art of making men, a violently pursued art that is made possible or, perhaps even necessary, by the burial of a woman. Indeed, here the brigands have murdered the mother who herself has been the driving force behind the emergence of the black artist. In describing the precipitating event[46] that leads to the mother-figure's conscription of Ringo's talents to make fictional documents for her venture into the vigilante justice of con-artistry, Granny Millard credits "the hand of God" (112) and, shortly afterward as he pitches a successful ruse that anticipates his role as a practical artist, Ringo fingering the familiar heresy queries: "Hah . . . [w]hose hand was that?" (114). Ringo, who has earlier refused to learn to write his name—literacy is not forbidden to the slaves owned by John Sartoris—becomes a master counterfeiter. This black boy, a realist artist, does not literally make money but rather performs an alchemy resonant for the practical as well as the sentimental Faulkner: Ringo turns writing into mules. After stealing U.S. stationery and ink, the still enslaved artist invents alphabetized fictions, asserting that he and Granny can turn to numbers for the names when they run out of letters. Countering Granny's proposed name of "Mrs Mary Harris," Ringo feels pride in his ability to provide a believable—because somehow unbelievable—moniker for his and Granny's next fictional claimant: "Miz Plurella Harris," in her resonant plurality, revels in the singularity made possible by given names.

It is not surprising that Faulkner's major artist figures from the mid- to late 1930s are concerned with the relationship between art and survival. Ringo of *The Unvanquished* (1938) and Charlotte Rittenmeyer of *The Wild Palms* (1939) turn to realist art in situations justified by the claims of survival. Charlotte Rittenmeyer, the sculptor who wants to convey motion rather than the mere structure of the animal she shapes, takes up charcoal and paper to speak in the visual vocabulary of social realism: her pictures warn the miners and their wives—who do not speak English—about the fate that awaits them and their children should they choose to winter in the mountain camp. Charlotte's drawings in charcoal, tacked to the wall for all to see, tell the story not just of not being paid, but of the starvation and death that will seize them in this isolated camp if they do not take this last train down from the mountain. Ringo's art, his con-artistry, is essential to the survival of the hill country folk: men, women, and children. Through the unsalable mules and the money from the mules that can be sold, he and Granny furnish these starving white people from the hill country with the means to scratch a living out of their difficult earth.

But Ringo also proposes another reason—justification, if you will—for representational art. Charlotte makes realist drawings in her effort to avoid catastrophe: she draws the future in the hope of using art to prevent her pictures from becoming reality. Surrounded by a resurgence of popular nostalgia for the Old South in films and novels catering to a market for "moonlight and magnolias," Faulkner allowed his fourteen-year-old artist Ringo to explain this obsession with the past as being less concerned with the real than with filling the emptiness of the loss. When the Yankee lieutenant riding through the still-standing gate questions the young slave's vision as he draws a house, the subject of the boy's picture suddenly becomes clear: "Oh . . . I see. You're drawing it like it used to be." To which Ringo sharply replies: "Co-rect . . . What I wanter draw hit like hit is now for? I can walk down here ten times a day and look at hit like hit is now. I can even ride in that gate on a horse and do that." The immense future prospects for the past, the absent, and the immolated as provocations for art become clear as the same officer, alluding to the burned Jefferson, quips: "When you get done here, you can move into town and keep busy all winter, cant you?" (*U* 141). Con-artistry and the precise art of counterfeiting aside, representational drawing is unnecessary and inadequate when it competes with the actual. Yet representational art and efforts at realism are justified when the artist, like Ringo, feels compelled to remember what has been destroyed, or when the artist like Charlotte, dead set on life, is driven to communicate, to picture a fatal future that can be prevented from becoming a past catastrophe. By recalling the past and warning of the future in these didactic scenes, realistic art paradoxically serves its highest, most instrumental purpose by picturing what is not there.

In the church scene that stages the most public performance between the community matriarch and her partner, the black artist, Ringo is told to "Bring the book": "It was a big blank account book; . . . they opened it on the reading desk, Granny and Ringo side by side, while Granny drew the tin can out of her dress and spread the money on the book." Granny calls names while Ringo is said to "read the names off the book" as well as the information about dates and money already recorded there. Earlier, Ringo has been asked to bring a book, and this is the book of dreams, a "cook book" from which they make imagined cakes. Here, "the book" that has replaced the prayer book and the Bible is carried from the slave gallery as the black artist stands alongside the socialist mother at the front of the church to face the segregated poor. As the mother and a black boy ascend to the place of power, even the preacher has been replaced in what Ann Douglas has analyzed as the alliance that shifted the balance of power to bring about "the feminization of American culture" that held sway during the mid-nineteenth century.[47]

The community mother and her artist partner have joined to save the poor whites, the locally colored denizens who have come down from the hills. Aside from Ab Snopes, the wily mule trader and slippery front man for Granny and Ringo's mule business, only women from this backwoods contingent speak. Ab Snopes's wife tries to throw the revenge-minded Bayard and Ringo off the scent by trying to send them toward Alabama (Uncle Buck translates this into the opposite direction), and a woman whose face has been cut by what seems to have been a metal stinger on the end of a whip urges the two boys and their elderly chaperone in the right direction, goading them onward with her parting words: "Kill them. Kill them" (164). Otherwise, these mountain people are present and silent even as they are said to give their accounts at the front of the church and later, at Granny Millard's funeral, to pay their respects. Covered by their croker sacks from the rain, these men who have ridden in for the funeral in carriages without tops (the folk idiom for being born outside of wedlock without the legitimating roof of a certified father)[48] are represented by their "borrowed" mules that no longer bear the national "brand" that reads "U.S." (156). This pronominal claim of an in-group is obscured by a black-on-black smear that erases but does not conceal these working animals' legitimate origins. The white elite have moved into the slave cabins, and the abandoned and "abolished" (*U* 199) former slaves, particularly those "who had lost their white people" (*U* 150), have been reduced to living like animals burrowed into caves and trees. Aside from Ringo, none of the dark faces that look down from the slave gallery during the novel's scene of distribution is seen to benefit or even to participate, except in the fact of being left out. (Significantly, the blacks now gathered at the Sartoris place are referred to—along with Bayard and his father—as having needs to be met, as Ab Snopes details what Granny has died trying to secure in her last, failed and fatal, deal.) Read unflinchingly,[49] Granny's nascent socialism anticipates the hell of the present (the descent into the worst of the Depression) as whites as well as blacks work with borrowed mules and are given limited "furnish" money in the replacement slavery of tenant farming and sharecropping. Even tenant slavery was being abolished in a climate of uncertainty in which, as Richard Godden notes, New Deal programs such as the 1933 Agricultural Adjustment Act turned the agricultural poor into wage laborers whose tasks were limited by subsidies that paid landowners not to plant. As the men from the mountains wait for their allocations from Granny, they look at her as if they were Bayard's father's "fox hounds" watching their master when he comes into the "dog-run," and when Ringo joins the matriarch behind "the reading desk" at the front of the church, this pack of men begins to look like the dogs when Loosh (Ringo's uncle) "would go in to feed them" (136). Meanwhile, Uncle Buck and Uncle Buddy's pre-war plan of their *slaves* working to buy themselves back is as honest and as revelatory as capitalism gets. John Sartoris's dream, as Drusilla contends, may be concerned with a better life for all, but that dream includes preserving the racial hierarchy by literally killing those who would support the ideals of political equality.

In *As I Lay Dying*, Addie Bundren's body, grotesquely reenacting pregnancy or the sexual act, fills an undescribed but nonetheless vacated hole. The violating and unviolated Drusilla Hawk is the daughter of an impregnable elite, a sport of war who like Athena prefers killing to fornication. Her proclivities suggest that she (who literally negates life by subtracting from the living) may embody an end in herself. From the perspective of a procreative imperative, the pants-wearing Drusilla—who is most intimately coupled with John Sartoris in their Reconstructive counterbid to birth a nation through killing—finally disappears by train whether into modernity or the West, a kind of unkind Huck venturing to the territories to escape the skirts of domesticity. With regard to the issue of birth, Drusilla deserts the home front, effectively joining the mother-murderers by favoring death over maternity. In contrast, Dewey Dell of *As I Lay Dying* confirms the coloring of class as she becomes the sacrificial daughter who gives the lie to the lie that has claimed whiteness as purity. Born to descend, to fall into her valley name, Dewey Dell's destination becomes her destiny. The childless Drusilla who prefers action over speech is the hardline harbinger of the already composed and decomposed Addie, while Dewey Dell, feminine in her passions, is the viscerally pregnant daughter who becomes the emotionally empty reproducer of a vacuous, thing-defined future.[50]

The Saturday Evening Post stopped short of an ending to their series in which a Phaedra-like incest plot ("An Odor of Verbena") critiques the ideal of a pure white southern womanhood, exposing the marriage plot as a cover for a maiden's malign, man-killing masculinity ("Skirmish at Sartoris"). Faulkner's fourth story to be published, "Skirmish at Sartoris," set amid race-motivated violence of the postwar era, found a less lucrative publisher in *Scribner's*. This story, which would become the penultimate story in *The Unvanquished*, features Drusilla Hawk's active participation in two murders to maintain white power, after which (in the same story) she is forced to go through with the mother-mandated marriage plot[51] that the female community demands. Indeed, murder trumps marriage, and seduction is at the core of the final story, "An Odor of Verbena." Whereas "Skirmish at Sartoris" features Drusilla's own mother condemning her in a letter for "flouting and outraging all Southern principles of purity and womanhood" (*U* 193) that have justified so many Confederate soldiers' deaths, the final story, through a critique of honor killing, continues this earlier narrative's work by further debunking the haloed fiction of female purity. Despite, or perhaps because of, his stepmother's seductive ploys, Bayard refuses to kill the killer of his father. Unsuitable for the magazines, "An Odor of Verbena" was written as an ending for *The Unvanquished* that, following his *Scribner's*-published "Skirmish at Sartoris," rescued Faulkner's story-cycle novel[52] from the local color conventions that had secured a loyal following for his series as it had appeared in the *Post*. Having developed the future that awaits Drusilla in the exiled story that had appeared in 1935 in the lower-paying *Scribner's*, Faulkner wrote the fourth and fifth installments that were deemed suitable for the *Post*, stories that laid a foundation for the feminized and—through Drusilla—already developed narrative of fatal female malice[53] that had seen print elsewhere the previous year. In these two stories that finished the series of five for the *Post*, Faulkner completed his parable of art. In his fourth, originally titled "The Unvanquished," Faulkner accomplished the rise of the artist and the death of the regional mother while using the fifth, "Vendée," to provide the by now *de rigueur* burial of the mother. Finally, this burial sets the stage for the male collaboration that ends in the edgy art of visceral dismemberment, already a prominent Faulknerian trope in his *As I Lay Dying*, *Sanctuary*, and *Light in August*. While the *Post* series ends by staking claim to a world where it may continue to be "the wrong season [for killing] women and children" (*U* 168), Faulkner's postwar stories, written fourth and seventh (the pieces that were not published in the *Post*), add a conclusion that insists on female violence while neutralizing and subordinating the most compelling character to emerge in his popularly received stories set during the Civil War. Ringo (with no ado) is summarily reduced to the role of a sidekick who remains in these postwar stories to provide first comic, then tragically practical relief after—to make a long story short—the killing is no longer good.[54]

Ringo may represent progress: he is the black artist who is not sacrificed—neither hanged nor burned—but he (and even his narrative diminution in *The Unvanquished*'s concluding stories set after the war) cannot be a revelatory surprise. Rather, given the reckoning of race and aesthetics and an aesthetics of race framed in the arc of the *Post*'s stories as they were read in the contemporary context, Ringo emerges as a man among the men and women who had already established the Harlem Renaissance as a cultural force. While this movement featured an infamous maternal patroness,[55] the most powerfully female and ameliorating patrons had been (to name a few) *The Atlantic*, *The Century*, *Scribner's*, and *The Saturday Evening Post*. Ringo, abetted by his boyhood partner in crime or justice, may be the only black boy of 1930s fiction in the United States who has cut off the extremity of a white man with impunity, receiving the equivalent of applause in a story published as holiday fare in a family focused venue. The *Post*, as its full name designates, locates Saturday evening as a time for reading in respectable homes whose denizens would be preparing for church and a day of more reading. During this decade in which ritualized lynching reached its highest point for the century, the claim of an interracial bond between a black male and even a maternal white female—if race is stressed and the scene is not distanced by history—bears an edge of danger.[56] Here, Granny, as she goes to her own death, acknowledges that Ringo (as well as Bayard) can be killed because these boys "look like men" (152). Faulkner's storyline of white maternal sacrifice idealizes the closeness of slavery by desexualizing the predatory power inherent in the institution that Harriet Jacobs called an "obscene cage of birds." Faulkner's *The Unvanquished* rewrites slavery as an idealized if not ideal past,[57] which when viewed as a threat to the color line in a contemporary context, contains the ingredients in which a misstep could result in the lynching of an ambitious, smart, and economically savvy man of color. Ringo, in a display of his powerful literacy, is called to this sanctuary's "reading desk" to look down on a congregation of poor whites.

In *The Unvanquished*, the preacher's eulogy ends in the traditional closure, "rest in . . . Peace," and Granny's avenged death is the RIP that tears and heals the war-torn fissure. Reverend Fortinbride (who "sprang right up out of the ground with the names and histories of all of the hill folks at his tongue's end" [136] yet is never confirmed as being one of them) concludes that this white matriarch may be dead, but her work remains undone as she is assigned to a needy and multiracial heaven: "God has already seen to it that there are men women and children, black white yellow or red, waiting for her to tend and worry over" (158). The majority of those who read this funeral oration in *The Saturday Evening Post* would have known the tune and the words to "Jesus Loves the Little Children," which designates "all the children of the world. Red and yellow, black and white," to insist "they are precious in His sight."

The Unvanquished conceives of a heaven, an afterlife, where the meek of the four colors will still be hungry and struggling, a Christian heaven that is in need of another mother. The singling out of the "red" by placing this color, political and racial, at the end, calls attention to the delicate parataxis: the absence of a comma-divided hierarchy between and among "men women and children . . . black white yellow or red," and, one would hope, old white ladies and young black boys. While efforts to remove this song from hymnals in the twenty-first century attest to the drive toward political correctness as well as the ongoing project of privatizing Jesus, the mother of local color and of the locally colored had returned in her full deification in Faulkner's fiction of the 1930s as he experimented with writing readable prose that was entirely saleable. Miss Daisy[58] may continue to be driven in the nostalgic possibility of partnerships of women past childbearing age with servants of color (shades of Miss Emily and her manservant, Tobe),[59] but in the heightened, race-based violence of the 1930s Harlem, these stories are nostalgic fictions that continue to market slavery. *The Unvanquished* accomplishes this dubious feat by removing black men. Ringo, a man before his time and certainly before the coming of age of his boyhood companion Bayard, has once again become Bayard's "boy" in "An Odor of Verbena." The enemy of this novel is not the freed blacks or the martyred, murdered Burdens who are killed in "Skirmish at Sartoris," but those who will not stop killing. As the color-coded burial of Granny Millard reveals, this narrative is among other things an expressionist painting in which yellow boards dissolve as the rain paints strokes of gray bleeding into red. Here, the rain

> splashing slow and cold and gray . . . on the yellow boards . . . [sinks] into the dark red dirt beside the red grave . . . Then the wet red dirt began to flow into the grave . . . The earth was . . . dark and red with rain . . . : it just dissolved slow and gray into the dark red mound . . . like the soft yellow color of the boards had dissolved and stained up through the earth and mound and boards and rain were all melting into one vague quiet reddish gray.

The enemy of the novel remains the unprincipled and vicious white man introduced and dispatched in the *Post* serial. As Bayard confirms at the end of *The Unvanquished*, the villain is not the lawyer named Redmond who has been provoked by Col. Sartoris but the disloyal white brigand in blood-stained gray who only fails because he has hesitated to kill children.

CHAPTER THREE

Dewey Dell, Dead Center

He [Anse] had a word, too. Love, he called it. But I had been used to words for a long time. I knew that that word was like the others: just a shape to fill a lack . . .
—William Faulkner, *As I Lay Dying*

Love set you going like a fat gold watch.
—Sylvia Plath, "Morning Song"

Things are in the saddle
—Ralph Waldo Emerson, "Ode to William H. Channing"

Claiming to have conceived of *As I Lay Dying* as his "*tour de force*," a novel by which he could "stand or fall if [he] never touched ink again," Faulkner in his own melodrama of loss complained that this work lacked the mystery of creation.[1] At a profound level, *As I Lay Dying* narrates the loss of mystery—not just the loss of the virgin mother as muse, but the loss of the dynamism of the Madonna herself, the inspiration that Faulkner's Fairchild of *Mosquitoes* celebrates as "a perversion that builds Chartres" (*M* 320). This Madonna had justified the obsession that called generation after generation of guildsmen, without hope of witnessing the cathedral's completion in their lifetime, to build a sacred place for the pregnant mother of God.[2] Section 30, Dewey Dell's third entry, lies at the dead center of *As I Lay Dying*'s fifty-nine parts. Quickened by words, section 30 uses signs to signal the violent end of Dewey Dell's thwarted quest as she ends her fertile multiplicity. Taking up the psychic knife, Dewey Dell cuts herself out of the heretical trinity that had long incorporated the pregnant daughter into this reigning paradigm of art. This misogynist paradigm or parable, insisting that art required the burial (if not murder) of the mother, is made manifest in narratives written by the most respected U.S. authors in 1929, Wharton and Cather.[3] Read in the context of this female-dominated masculinist tradition, Faulkner's *As I Lay Dying* offers a revelatory view of the consequences of burying the cultural mother and the matrifocal literature she had birthed and inhabited in the second half of the nineteenth century. This mother, presented by Faulkner through what is arguably the most difficult burial in the history of the English language, suggests the ways in which this cultural force continued to haunt the literary stream of the early twentieth century. By the close of the novel, the only Bundren daughter has cut herself out of this productive paradigm of art; not a figure of continued matriarchal power, Dewey Dell embodies the wages of materialism. In section 58, Dewey Dell's final chapter and the penultimate set piece in *As I Lay Dying*, Dewey Dell embodies the unreflective paradox of a pregnant emptiness.

In Faulkner's own reworking of this paradigm of art, masculinity is known at the moment of its loss through the blackening association with the maternal body. Sentimental maternity is laid to rest in *As I Lay Dying* as the outraged and obscenely rotting mother breaks the code of silence. The dead Addie Bundren, eloquent in her vengeful mastery (like an outraged God softened as He shifts testaments from a denied Ishmael to a chosen Jesus), declares that legitimacy be dammed—birthed—as she takes her tribute in a sacrificial daughter as well as in the blackened bodies of her sacrificial sons. In the end, *As I Lay Dying* insists on this loss of mystery, not just through the burial and replacement of the mother, but also through what has become the negative centrality of the pregnant daughter.

In a plot as old as Zeus's decision to devour his pregnant wife rather than be supplanted by a son, men have scripted and conscripted daughters by giving birth from the head.[4] *As I Lay Dying* is Faulkner's most explicit portrayal of the gendered battleground that places the visceral fact of procreative bodies and wombs (even empty wombs) in tension with the abstract and nation-breeding ideals of words and war. Downstream from Wharton and Cather, Faulkner's fifth published novel (the first to name Yoknapatawpha County) accomplishes the burial of the regional mother, cauterizing this matricentric story from the flank of an old and viscerally conceived world. The daughter of Faulkner's *As I Lay Dying* remains pregnant at the close of the novel, but Dewey Dell's condition is one of abjection and subjection. Despite the fact that her father, Anse, is a marginal landowner, Dewey Dell's pregnancy embodies the Bundren family's fall in the 1930s hill country of northern Mississippi.

Addie Bundren, who has only one section that bears her name, has garnered attention not just because she surprises the unwarned reader by speaking from the dead (to rephrase Quentin Compson, the dead mother speaks from "out of time"), but also because she is an acknowledged precursor to Lacan as well as the primary philosopher of language in all of Faulkner's fiction. Addie gives meaning to the composite word, cum emphatic placeholder or rhetorical tic, "in-deed." Indeed, Addie Bundren's place in the exegesis of *As I Lay Dying* is commensurate with her stature in readings of Faulkner's oeuvre as a whole. Marc Hewson, noting that "Addie is at the core of *As I Lay Dying*," associates this powerful mother with Caddy Compson and other "female characters" in Faulkner's fiction: "Addie functions as the almost absent center of the novel . . . Literally, she is centered by reason of her single monologue and its placement, though admittedly her chapter falls somewhat after the true midpoint and so does not neatly divide the book in two."[5] Diane Roberts rightly recognizes Addie as the "dynamic epicenter of the novel," while Roberts and Deborah Clarke join Hewson and other critics in both acknowledging and explaining Addie's centrality.[6] Clarke sees Faulkner as "gran[ting] greater powers to the physical" as he "plac[es] the mother's literal dead body rather than the mother's absence at the center of the text."[7] In language that leads to bodily speculations on sexual morphology and signifiers, Cleanth Brooks explicitly does not include Addie in his list of Faulkner's "masculinized women," but T. H. Adamowski (with less gentility) describes Addie as "a woman with a penis."[8] Presence and absence and presence through absence are key elements in Addie Bundren's critique of words as signs of emptiness or, more precisely, empty signs: "the gaps in people's lacks" that are countered by her own word-shaped blank space, her own generative "gap." According to Addie, giving birth has violated her "aloneness," making her "whole" again.[9]

Either not interesting enough (or perhaps too interesting) to have elicited much critical attention, Addie's daughter has been classified as simply pregnant and crazy or crazy and pregnant. But Dewey Dell is in trouble, and her being in trouble is because she is so forcefully "in time" (*SF* 48). Dewey Dell has been a troubling and often dismissed figure in the overworked and still fertile field of gender analysis in Faulkner studies. While Dewey Dell is analyzed in interesting ways by Clarke and Roberts, their work shares a pattern. Both *Robbing the Mother* and *Faulkner and Southern Womanhood* mention, but finally remain chary of, the narratively unsettling Dewey Dell of section 30. In terms of politically savvy and historicist readings of Faulkner's women, Diane Roberts's listing of Dewey Dell as an unwed and pregnant peasant woman who is equated with her rural kind, specifically Lena Grove of *Light in August* and Eula Varner of *The Hamlet*, recognizes a pattern that Anne Goodwyn Jones, with characteristic wit, has summarized as "the over-bodied and the under-worded" female character in Faulkner's fiction. While Roberts's book takes its point of origin in the use and usefulness of stereotypes, these rural and pregnant women, despite their relative silence and their extravagantly described and much looked-at bodies, come from very different class backgrounds. Classified through an agrarian determinism that takes cover in a body-based essentialism, Dewey Dell as a "country girl" (242) has remained unclassed or roughly shelved in the critical literature. Leslie Fiedler, following the masculinist tradition, does not go beyond good and evil as he, in an unusually punitive assessment, places Dewey Dell with Lena Grove and Eula Varner as one of the "great, sluggish, mindless daughters of peasants, whose fertility and allure are scarcely distinguishable from those of a beast in heat."[10] Roberts, recognizing the flamboyance of Fiedler's language, concurs with his identification, marking Dewey Dell, Eula, and Lena as peasant women "born to get pregnant."[11] No doubt sensing a flaw in this grouping, Jones is right in calling for a form of literary analysis that understands the differences in history as experienced by women in the South. Such a history necessitates an understanding of place that is cognizant of the fact that these pregnant women come from different class backgrounds. Pregnancy, even the unwed pregnancy of rural southern women, is not death. It is not the great leveler.

Neither laboring nor working class, Eula Varner of *The Hamlet* takes her own virginity by force, violating a man with a broken arm. Eula is inspired to carnal conquest by her bloodlust after conquering three of her five suitors with the handle of her buggy whip. While Eula has been described by numerous critics as an earth goddess, her beau McCarron does not violate the passive earth. Rather, as the novel makes clear, in a moment of forceful, male-violating agency, Eula chooses her consort. This self-preserving man, made drone, flees—takes flight—from this frightening woman to preserve his life. Eula Varner is the unleashed and ravenous female who has taken this man amid the blood and the bodies that lie in the wake of her conquering violence. Entomologically speaking, Eula, inanimate to the point of seeming like a queen bee being battened by royal jelly in the form of sweet potatoes, is the definition of inertia until her life force is let loose. In her only known literary reference and the only trace that her brother-enforced schooling appears to have left on her, Eula mixes her characters as she taunts the lust-mad schoolteacher Labove, calling him "[y]ou old headless horseman Ichabod Crane" (*H* 135). The reference to the Yankee schoolmaster, equating him with the headless horseman, reveals Eula's capacity for translating men into headless ghosts. Linked by her own frame of reference to Washington Irving, Eula appears to have drawn her own parallels between herself and the squire's buxom daughter, Katrina Van Tassel: Eula knows she is rural aristocracy. Eula's father has bought at least one plantation after the war, he has foreclosed and continues to foreclose on farms, and he is the respected healer of animals referred to familiarly as "Uncle Billy" in *As I Lay Dying*. Will Varner has gained his economic leverage by being the owner of a country store, the post–Civil War institution that C. Vann Woodward argues shifted class hierarchies in *The Origins of the New South, 1877–1913*. While it may be difficult to tell unmarried, pregnant women apart (particularly in novels set in the rural South in the first third of the twentieth century), Eula is closer in class to Caddy than she is to Lena or Dewey Dell.

Dewey Dell inhabits a body and a position that gains significance because her family occupies a class edge or ledge in the precipitant economics of 1930s Mississippi. The fact that Dewey Dell belongs to a family separates her with finality from Lena Grove. Unlike Dewey Dell, the Lena of *Light in August* is unconnected. There is no sense of family property hanging in the balance, no cows to be milked, no fish to be gutted, no mother to be buried. On the road pursuing the father of her child, Lena Grove depends on the kindness of men and the butter and "eggmoney" of their infuriated and contemning wives (*LA* 21). Lena, orphaned and extremely pregnant, has nothing to lose. Dewey Dell is different. Still pregnant at the novel's close, she will inevitably be seen as the source and cause of the Bundrens' lost honor. With Addie dead, Cash lame, Darl in the state asylum, and Anse married to a woman who, if not of easy virtue, is certainly easily married, the Bundrens are falling fast, and the exposure of Dewey Dell's pregnancy will be a final and fatal blow to whatever respectability the family has left. Socially abject, there is no reason for the Bundrens to jettison Dewey Dell, and they will use her instead for her labor. Unlike Lena, Dewey Dell is framed and trapped by her family, a captivity narrative that includes her body becoming her own dungeon, the mother herself.[12]

Female virtue and virginity are fundamental to the inflexible male Code of Honor touted by a chivalry-proud and gun-ready South; however, in Faulkner's fiction this question of honor applies even more to the southern and rural poor than to the region's libertine and moneyed aristocracy.[13] As his family falls, this property and propriety in the hymen rises to the level of an obsession for Quentin Compson in *The Sound and the Fury* of 1929 and the "Appendix Compson" to that novel, published in 1946. In her first section, Dewey Dell, who recounts asking her brother Darl "without the words" whether he plans to kill her lover Lafe, hears his single spoken word (audibly framed by quotation marks): "Why?" Darl, who elsewhere realizes that he has known about his mother's illegitimate child, Jewel, in the same way he has come to know the secret that Dewey Dell carries within, understands well before the family begins its funeral march that he has nothing to defend in terms of familial or other codes of honor. It is not just that the Bundrens are not aristocrats; they are poor whites who despite owning their land are economically destined to remain poor. Yet "honor," as sociologists working in the southern foothills of the 1930s assert, was based on an inflexible moral economy in which a single daughter pregnant out of wedlock predicated a family's fall from being merely "poor" to being classified as irredeemably "sorry."[14] What Darl in his sanity understands, with Jewel as his embodied evidence, is that the family's females have already fallen.

Her Long Row to Hoe

> I feel like a wet seed wild in the hot blind earth.
> —The final line, Dewey Dell's second section[15]

> The way I see it . . . this film studio work, it's like chopping cotton . . . ; you know damn well it's not painting the Sistine Chapel or winning the Kentucky Derby. But a man likes to feel some money in his pocket.
> —William Faulkner[16]

The strangest narrator in *As I Lay Dying* is not Faulkner's madman, Darl, but the Bundren daughter and sister, Dewey Dell. Dewey Dell has been seen, explained, ridiculed, commiserated with, and dismissed as being just pregnant and crazy. The Bundren daughter and sister is, in many ways, presented as a speaking body whose hysteria has become etymologically literalized as she bodies forth a "wandering womb." Prey to these dialectically escalating states of being pregnant and crazy, Dewey Dell in her four sections becomes a figure of extravagant embodiment who inhabits a radically changing narrative arc. Of the eight sections narrated by females in the fifty-nine that comprise *As I Lay Dying*, Dewey Dell's name stands at the head of four, Cora Tull's at three, and the powerful Addie needs only one. Cora Tull's first section, the second of the novel as a whole, like nearly all of the first nineteen sections, advances the action of the story. Cora's second section, as André Bleikasten has observed, is the only section among those of the opening third of the novel that is narrated outside of the sequence of events. Addie Bundren's section is by definition out of sequence. When the dead speak,[17] the narration may always be in conflict with orderly time. This means that aside from Cora's initial section, Dewey Dell is the female figure who inhabits linear time, and whose sections even as they recount experiences, memories, and dreams from the past are moving the action ineluctably forward. This may be because Dewey Dell's baby, like most babies in fiction, represents the impending future. But like the seemingly already dead baby of Ruby Lamar in the already written but not yet revised and not yet published *Sanctuary*, this particular baby and the future it represents is not an embodiment of hope. This is clearly a future that Dewey Dell would like to terminate.

Dewey Dell is a prominent presence in *As I Lay Dying*. Pregnant at the time of her mother's bodily death, this daughter is the first to throw herself on top of the mother's dead body. It is only later that her older brothers can enjoy an approximate intimacy as they ride or lie on top of Addie's coffin.[18] As Dewey Dell violently lays herself on the "bundle of sticks" that is Addie's corpse, she has already been embraced by the female narrative of biological determinism, a bodily journey punctuated by bloody birth that is destined to end in death. The bedroom (or the room of bedding), in history as well as in fiction, is the most common site of death for a childbearing woman or, reflecting the statistical record of female mortality, this room, in which the daughter becomes the mother, is the place of death waiting for a woman of childbearing age.

While she may not get pregnant in a bedroom, the Bundren daughter certainly does not get pregnant at the end of the row during cotton picking.[19] Nevertheless, Dewey Dell's section, which tells of her bag being filled by Lafe, is still a seminal scene, both harbinger and actual harvest. In *As I Lay Dying*, Dewey Dell and Lafe are inscribed in an agriculturally determined calendar: the time of sexual consummation and the moment of conception are auspicious. Revisiting the obsession that drives Quentin in *The Sound and the Fury*, the property of the maidenhead (Dewey Dell's virginity) is indeed harvested. While Dewey Dell's hymen is harvested along with the cotton, the Bundren daughter does not become productive until well after this initial planting of seeds. Rather, Dewey Dell is planted near the beginning of the most extended and back-straining season of cotton cultivation. In full knowledge of her state, the girl, by her own count, has missed two periods. Planted at the time of "chopping," Dewey Dell has been fertilized during this time of intense labor, the only phase of the cotton cycle (aside from picking) that necessitated the hiring of hands. Chopping occurs after the cotton plants have matured, and each row presents its own possibilities. Hoe in hand, the worker chops down, uproots, and turns under stalwart as well as spindly plants to establish the row: a spacing that provides sufficient earth and light for the chosen plants to thrive.[20] Read figuratively and literally, chopping is the time that the human eye determines the orderly progression essential to the success of the crop through selective slaughter. It is telling that Dewey Dell has been planted at this time of radical selection, what might with concision be called the season of abortion.

The horticultural roots mediating sex and death frame Anse's compliment for Addie's seasonal sensibility in the timing of her passing. As Addie's body waits to be planted in the earth, this woman, according to her own horticultural nihilism, has only been "planted" "to get ready to stay dead a long time" (170, 169). Anse asserts that his dead wife has waited until the crop has been "laid-by," adding she was "ever a thoughtful woman." Indeed, the Bundren cotton has been "laid-by," plowed a final time by the dirt-turning blade that reaffirms the mounds of the established rows before Addie Bundren has had time to go to bed to continue her act of dying. After the laying-by, Vardaman goes fishing. Darl and Jewel go logging and break an axle. The neighbor woman, Cora Tull, makes cakes. Significantly, Cora's husband, Vernon Tull, is seen as he completes his laying-by. Unplaced in the community of the novel, Lafe is a seasonally employed day laborer from a farm or a more populous settlement[21] that does not border that of the Bundrens and is not located along the road to Jefferson. Not a regular part of the family's common intercourse and concerns, Lafe enters the novel with no backstory: he is familiar enough to require no explanation. Aside from his presence in Dewey Dell's memories and her erotic fantasies in sections 7 and 14, respectively, no one besides Dewey Dell and the drugstore men gives a first thought to Lafe either by name or as a planter of acorns in female bellies. Aside from his hidden presence inside Dewey Dell, Lafe (who is there for the first missed period also during chopping) has obviously returned to check on the status of the second. Lafe has done his laying-by, and his effort to resolve the fact of his living residue in Dewey Dell's womb is evidenced by the ten dollars that she brings with her in her attempt to buy an abortifacient. As she offers them money, Dewey Dell exposes her condition to the drugstore men,[22] both of whom see the law as at least part of an answer. Moseley proposes a forced marriage, and MacGowan, less direct in his suggestion, advises the country girl to go to the courthouse even before he knows what her "female trouble" is.

As Dewey Dell recounts her initial sexual encounter with Lafe in her first section in the novel, this only daughter presents a strong narrative that joins fate and compulsivity.[23] Whatever her bag contains, whatever the amount that it takes for both of them to fill her sack by the end of the row, Dewey Dell's virginity has been brokered for significantly less than a quarter, bartered for a dime[24] that is not hers. As the novel details, Anse owns the labor of all the children in his household, including the night work that Jewel has stolen from him to acquire his "gaudy" spotted horse. While the symbolism of the sack is quite heavy and has been commented upon at length, Dewey Dell's relationship to the agricultural calendar has remained uncharted. Like the cotton, Dewey Dell is harvested: reaped at the end of the row. "Laid," the Bundren daughter has not been "laid by"; seeded at harvest, she has not been planted nor has her visceral sack been more than temporarily filled. In section 30, the Bundren neighbor, Vernon Tull, stands in a field of cotton. In the autograph version (copied over by Faulkner—no first draft could be so cleanly rowed), the solitary Tull is temporarily misplaced in the cotton calendar. As Dewey Dell observes, "We turn into Tull's lane. We pass the barn and go on past the green rows of cotton in the ~~mud~~ wild earth and then Vernon chopping. He sees us and lifts his hand as we pass and stands there looking after us for a long time." The published passage that begins "We turned into Tull's lane . . ." continues, "We pass the barn and go on, the wheels whispering in the mud, passing the green rows of cotton in the wild earth, and Vernon little across the field behind the plow" (122). While the excised "mud" has been reincorporated and the more distant figure of Vernon seems smaller, the crucial difference is that Vernon Tull "behind the plow" is not "chopping." The chopping has been accomplished; he is laying-by.

Despite the extended labor and the number of weeks required for the chopping of cotton, Vernon Tull cannot still be "chopping" in the thirtieth section, even though "chopping" is on Dewey Dell's mind. While as many as two months might pass between the beginning of the chopping of a field and the beginning or, as here, the completion of the laying-by, this estimate in relation to *As I Lay Dying* is determined by the female, rather than the cotton, cycle. Asked a direct question by Moseley, the Mottson druggist, Dewey Dell unknowingly reveals her repetition of her mother's illicit maternity, calculating the months for him, "It aint been but two." Like her mother who wakes up to discover "he is two months gone" (leaving it unclear whether she means her lover Whitfield or the progressing growth of her woods-begotten son), the Bundren daughter and sister knows she is pregnant. And Dewey Dell has been impregnated during chopping. *As I Lay Dying* is too calculated a work to have Anse's daughter impregnated at any other time.

"Govern[ing] the Female System"

> It will cure entirely the worst form of Female Complaints, all Ovarian troubles, Inflammation, Ulceration, Falling and Displacements of the Womb and the consequent Spinal Weakness and is particularly adapted to the Change of Life. It will dissolve and expel Tumors from the uterus in an early stage of development. The tendency of cancerous tumors there is checked very speedily by its use—That feeling of bearing down, causing pain[,] is always permanently cured by its use. It will at all times and under all circumstances act in harmony with the laws that govern the female system.
>
> —Lydia E. Pinkham's "Vegetable Compound"

In his second and worst (though possibly most pleasurably quotable) novel, *Mosquitoes* (1927), Faulkner, as he was establishing himself as an author whose works did not sell, featured an Australian man with a military title pitching a product that he feels reflects the consuming desires of an American public. As Major Ayers avers: "All Americans are constipated." The writer Fairchild (based on Sherwood Anderson) pictures a label decoration for this needed laxative that would feature an American flag with doves holding dollar signs in their beaks. "The semitic man" proposes a label that would include a recipe for beer and a formula for calculating interest, while the poet (named Frost) positing the problem of a gender-divided market ventures that the jar have a "bit of mirror," adding that what women want could be addressed directly by a label with instructions for contraception and a place for hiding hairpins. The entrepreneurial Major Ayers, repeating his assessment of the state of the nation's bowels, and possibly its business ethics, begins "All Americans are con—," before he is interrupted, leaving open whether his "con" will lead to con-artistry, constipation, or just a nation of consumers.

Not only does Dewey Dell's name appear at the heading of four of the novel's fifty-nine sections, this daughter is exposed as the most desperate and least successful consumer in the novel.[25] The pregnant Dewey Dell is featured in the role of consumer in the two sections rather extravagantly apportioned to drugstores. The harsh external view of the Bundren daughter provided by these mercantile figures provokes sympathy for Dewey Dell, but it also markets this country girl and her exposed secret as a type of public "fact." As Olga W. Vickery (summarizing decades of critical views) puts it, "Quite obviously, neither Moseley nor MacGowan is concerned with Dewey Dell as a person; they respond only to the fact that she is somewhat stupid, pregnant, and unmarried."[26] In these accounts, the single entries of Moseley, the druggist in Mottson, and MacGowan, a soda jerk masquerading as a druggist in Jefferson, Dewey Dell enters their stores looking for a "female remedy," a remedy for being female. Such female remedies, sold as "Woman's Friend," "Wine of Cardui," and "Wine of Life Root," promising to "act in harmony with the laws that govern the female system," were widely marketed to the female popu-

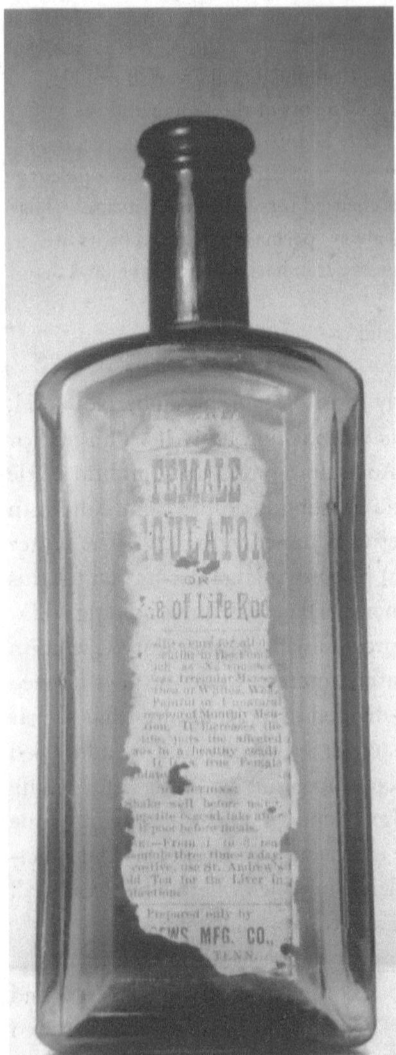

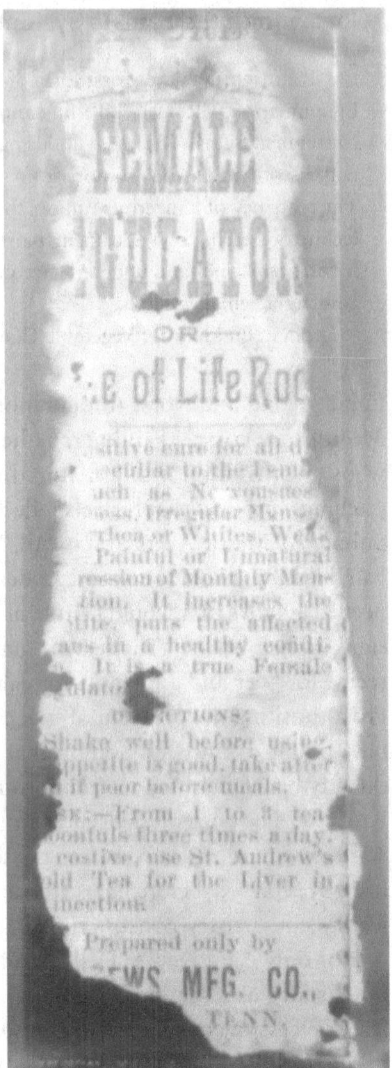

Figure 11. "Wine of Life Root" is one of several female remedies and regulators distilled in east Tennessee during the late nineteenth and early twentieth centuries. This amber glass bottle is from the St. Andrew's Manufacturing Company of Bristol, Tennessee, in operation from the 1870s to 1932. (Bristol is on the Tennessee–Virginia border, and through the years this patent medicine was at times being produced on streets located in Virginia.) The labels for these remedies sometimes used the grand acronym GFP, which promised that the product was a "General Female Panacea." The photograph of the bottle is by Dr. Richard Cannon, who has an extensive collection of early patent medicine bottles. The label for "St. Andrew's Wine of Life Root Female Regulator," featured alongside this historic bottle, has been digitally enhanced to increase its legibility. Among other more recognizable female problems, the "Whites" is listed as a condition to be cured by this root tincture. The "Whites" is preceded in this eroded label by the closing syllables of "leukorrhea"—the medical name for this condition. Luekorrhea is signaled by the whitish discharge associated with inflammation or congestion of the vaginal tissues.

lace in the late nineteenth and early twentieth centuries. Lydia Pinkham, who founded a patent medicine empire on what the drugstore owner in Mottson refers to as "female dope,"[27] had powerful "wine"-producing competitors in the mountains of east Tennessee whose products were also designed to induce the contractions of menstrual periods ("painful and unnatural suppression of monthly menstruation"),[28] flushing out the uterus of unwanted, if not cancerous, growths (see fig. 11). These elixirs with names that promised some of the power of the blood of Jesus in their claims to be the "Wine of Life" were sought by those who had "female complaints." However, in an acknowledgment that the ultimate female complaint might be the men that get them pregnant, Faulkner imagines male birth control as well. Near the close of *As I Lay Dying*, Doc Peabody jokes bitterly about the possibility of "spare legs," asking the beleaguered Cash why Anse, the Bundren patriarch, "didn't . . . carry you to the nearest sawmill and stick your leg in the saw? That would have cured it." This country physician conceives of a sawmill cure that could have prevented the whole family, halting the procession of men replicating themselves through the "chapping" bodies of a series of easily replicable and replicating Mrs. Bundrens.[29] Recognizing the problem embodied in Anse, Doc Peabody proposes decapitation as castration, birth control that would strike at the root: "[y]ou all could have stuck his [Anse's] head into the saw and cured a whole family . . .." (240; Faulkner's ellipses).

At the opening of his section, Skeet MacGowan locates himself in the drugstore "back of the prescription case, pouring up some chocolate sauce" (241). Giving "the chocolate" to his underling Jody, the jerk assumes masculine authority by taking "off [hi]s apron" to deal with the "hot mamma," that he sees as "[o]ne of them black eyed ones that look like she'd as soon put a knife in you as not if you two-timed her" (242). Neither the self-righteous druggist Moseley nor the lascivious soda jerk MacGowan offer Dewey Dell any of the female elixirs with euphemistic names. While Moseley classifies the entire genre as "female dope," MacGowan, who intimates that these formulas might work, names the consequences of such a remedy as "the penitentiary," and, with Jason Compson–like humor, he admits that if he loses this job he would have to go "to work."[30] Rife with suggestive references to consumption, Skeet MacGowan answers his lackey who has asked if he is not "going to give [him] no seconds on it" with a question: "'What the hell do you think this is?' I says; 'a stud-farm?'" (243). Claiming he "aint doing nothing but filling a prescription," MacGowan is driven by fantasies of filling with no risk of planting this "country girl" whose dell has already been rutted at the end of the row (244). Addressing her, MacGowan asks about the man who has planted his seed: "[t]he one that put the acorn in your belly" (243). In the Jefferson drugstore, as in the more sanctimonious Mottson establishment, Dewey Dell's ailment continues to be defined through bellies and bowels. MacGowan euphemistically explains to the inquisitive and prurient Jody, "[s]he's got a bad case of dysentery" (247).[31]

As part of her dinnertime visit, MacGowan has given Dewey Dell something to drink from an "unlabelled bottle" that smells "like turpentine" to both of them and, when she returns that night, he gives her a "box" containing the "six capsules" that he has already filled with "talcum powder," followed by his personal doctoring, the "operation" performed in the drugstore cellar (247, 248). Having earlier offered her "the hair of the dog" ("the hair of the dog that bit you"), "Skeet" is right in that whatever he pumps into Dewey Dell, this "hot mamma" cannot become more pregnant. It is clear that Dewey Dell understands that this concluding rite is a form of payment: "the same operation" that has gotten this girl in trouble can purchase what, in MacGowan's words, a "paltry sawbuck" (ten dollars) cannot buy (247, 246).

Whereas the girl's "complexion" is at issue in the Mottson drugstore (199), first with regard to makeup and later in the druggist's anticipation of the destructive side effects of taking "female dope," the unauthorized infusions served up in the courthouse town of Jefferson by Skeet (whose legitimate authority in the drugstore appears to be limited to cleaning-up floors and "pouring [. . .] chocolate"), if not precisely "poison" (247), represent dangerous hygiene. Turpentine, a pine product associated with medicinal resins (the black pitch long used in salves for boils), is a solvent that acts as a corrosive to thin or remove paint, while the perfumed toilet powder known as "talcum" is used primarily on the dampness of babies' bottoms and to dry and freshen sweating female flesh. The ground powder of talc has the noted side effect of not just soaking up excretions but also of whiting-up skin. Associated with whiting-up or removing color—exterior uses—these ingested products mock this "[c]ountry woman['s]" quest for a cleaning out of her class-colored interior. This whiting-up reveals that she has been blackened in a punitive social economy that has racialized sexuality itself (see figs. 12–15, pages 98–100).

The most explicit use of racially inflected language to describe desired toiletries appears in Moseley's section. Not knowing what Dewey Dell is seeking, Moseley, who later muses twice that her complexion will change for the worse with what she may be looking for in his drugstore, initially suspects that she wants something he thinks of as "nigger toilet water," offering to show her "some toilet things" (199). These narrators, white men who are faced with a body that bares and bears the story of illicit sexuality, respond to this difference through the coloring of class and the animalizing of female difference. In her second section, Dewey Dell herself expresses her envy of Doc Peabody's flatulent guts, introducing this pattern of explicitly scatological puns that reveal her desire to be a pee-body, a male body that cannot become pregnant. In the manuscript version, Faulkner revised Moseley's bowel-based comment to sharpen the humor through the double entendre explicit in his query about Dewey Dell's periods: "Are you too regular, or not regular enough?"

(201). MacGowan asks, "Have you got female troubles or do you want female troubles?" insisting that he is "the right doctor" for either condition (243). Feminizing excretion itself, masculine narcissism (otherwise known as point of view) maps the female reproductive system onto the male body. The dirtiness of the female body, whether in menstruation or pregnancy, is toilet oriented in these drugstore men's euphemistic allusions to "regularity" and "dysentery" as nature and consumption run their course. Still viscerally pregnant to the end, Dewey Dell, far removed from the mystery of the "*spreading entrails of time*," has lost the power that the pregnant woman, competitor or muse, despised or revered, has achieved in her role as a major character in what Faulkner's male artist figures embrace or flee as the defining dialectic of their aesthetics.[32]

In Faulkner's depiction of modernity, canned goods picture a world of mystery and the unattainable. Near the opening of *Light in August,* as Lena Grove asks to buy something in a can for a nickel, the pregnant and unmarried girl is told that she can get a can of shoe blacking. Recalling Dewey Dell, Lena Grove establishes the pattern of the pregnant and motherless daughter as a materially defined product on view in a store. Dewey Dell's condition is mocked by the products that whiten her up (the detail of the talcum powder in the capsules was added after the typescript was completed), just as the offer of shoe blacking as a food for Lena manages to intimate the same thing about her. If illicit sexuality blackens these girls, there is also a reason why these country girls are the only nubile female characters (aside from Bobbie the prostitute displayed as a waitress in *Light in August*) who are presented in a mercantile setting in either of these novels. It is significant that Dewey Dell is the only Bundren seen in a store and that she is the central character of Moseley's narrative—the only section that includes an account of the family's other mercantile adventure in Mottson. Moseley's assistant recounts that a Bundren son has entered a store to buy concrete to encase, to preserve, and possibly to destroy Cash's blackening leg. Echoing the town's fear that this wagon and potentially everything it holds might fall apart, Moseley himself concludes that "[i]t must have been like a piece of rotten cheese coming into an ant-hill" (203). While Dewey Dell remains the novel's major consumable, her mother, whom she tells Moseley is "out yonder in the wagon," is without question the most grotesque body, a stinking cheese in terms of imagined consumption.

A more ordinary (and therefore more disturbing) pattern frames women such as Narcissa of *Sartoris* (1929), Miss Quentin of *The Sound and the Fury* (1929), Lena Grove of *Light in August* (1932), Milly Jones of *Absalom, Absalom!* (1936), and Dewey Dell of *As I Lay Dying* (1930)—no matter whether they are pregnant or not—as objects of sexual consumption or objects meant to be consumed. These women and nubile girls are fodder for uncontrollable fantasies (most notably those inscribed by the letter writer, Byron Snopes) as

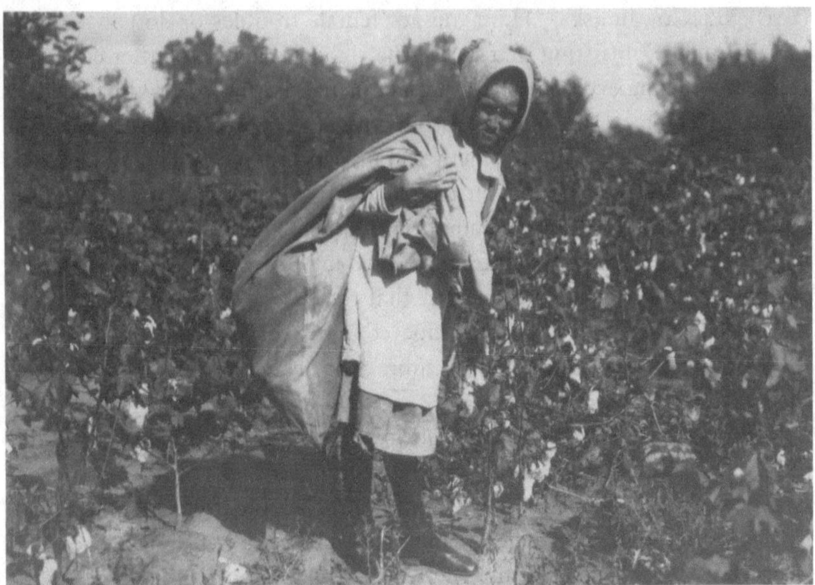

Figure 12. "Cleo Campbell, 9 years, picks 75 to 100 pounds of cotton a day. Expects to start school soon. Said: 'I'd ruther go to school and then I wouldn't have ter work.' Father said she and her sister begin about 6 A.M. and work until 6 or 7 P.M. with 1½ hours off at noon." Pottawatomie County, Oklahoma, 1916. Photograph by Lewis Hine, Child Labor Collection, Library of Congress.

A note on figures 12–15. All of these Lewis Hine photographs were published in the W. H. Swift Report. The individual portraits were posed. Certainly, these particular images of girls in cultivated nature, despite the captions describing hard labor, have a romanticized, even fairy-tale, quality when compared to Hine's photographs of the exposed and deformed bodies of children who are working in factories, mines, and fisheries. In addition to documenting girls' labor in cotton production, these photographs reveal an investment in whiteness and the class-based concept of preserving a "complexion" practiced by some female agricultural laborers. Cleo Campbell's face is darkened by the sun, but her hands (protected for practical reasons) shine at the end of her dark-brown arms, as if she is still wearing her work gloves (fig. 12). In contrast, her older sister Callie (figs. 13 and 14) is clearly committed to preserving her whiteness. As she is featured here in two photographs, her Mother Hubbard hat has protected her face while the thick black stockings on her arms, as well as her legs, protect her limbs from the leathering rays of the sun. Folk myths aside, this work is being done under a sun in which people of color, even those of the darkest hues, burn and blister. Little changed in the methods of chopping and picking cotton during the nearly fifteen-year period between Hine's taking of these photographs and the publication of *As I Lay Dying*. A fifty-pound bag could indeed be part of the harvest, but smaller bags and baskets, pulled along or strapped on the picker's neck, could be emptied into these larger sacks. While the shorter rows and uneven ground, characteristic of patch cotton, may have discouraged the use of the capacious, long, and slender bags so well suited to the mile-long rows of the Mississippi Delta, the bag shown here as it is hoisted by Callie Campbell would have been less practical for her to drag during active picking.

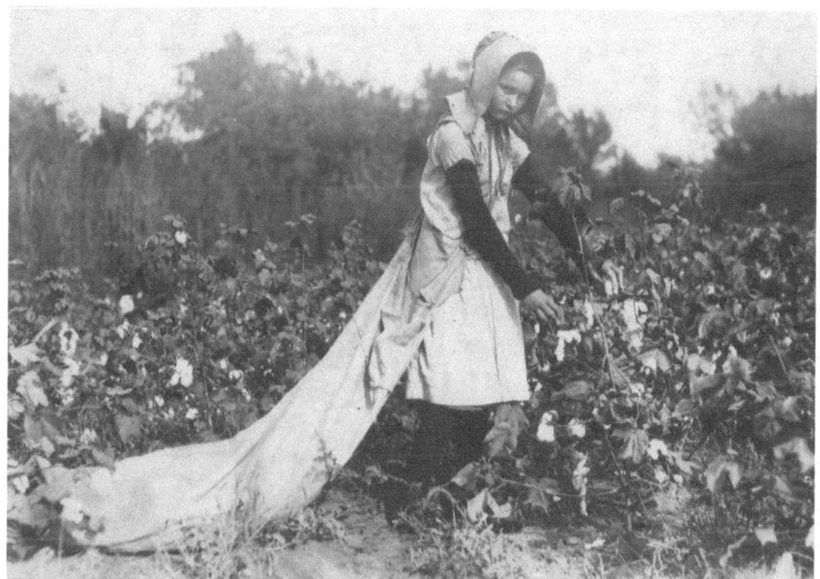

Figure 13. "Callie Campbell, 11 years old, picks 75 to 125 pounds of cotton a day, and totes 50 pounds of it when sack [*sic*] gets full. 'No, I don't like it very much.'" Pottawatomie County, Oklahoma, 1916. Photograph by Lewis Hine, Child Labor Collection, Library of Congress.

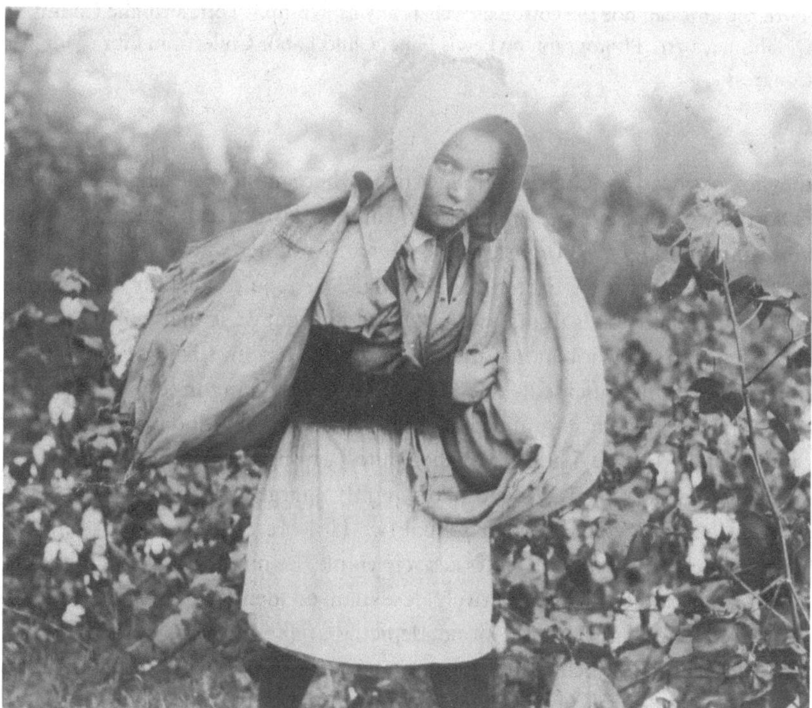

Figure 14. Callie Campbell, 11 years old. Pottawatomie County, Oklahoma, 1916. Photograph by Lewis Hine, Child Labor Collection, Library of Congress.

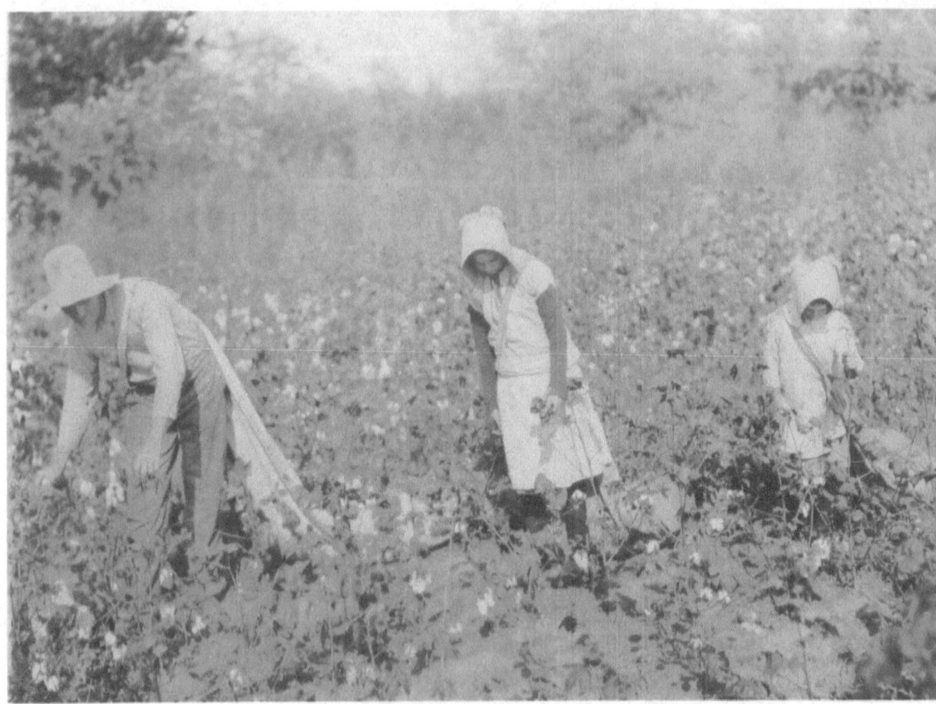

Figure 15. "Campbell family picking cotton. W. W. Campbell, Route 1, Box 64, Shawnee. Children go to Pioneer School, 7 miles northwest of Shawnee. Father said: 'Both the girls can hoe the cotton as well as any grown-up.'" Pottawatomie County, Oklahoma, 1916. Photograph by Lewis Hine, Child Labor Collection, Library of Congress.

they are exposed by entering public venues where money is exchanged. Aside from the women who are already prostitutes and procuresses such as Bobbie and Mame in *Light in August*, the women in Faulkner's novels who are used in the highest realm of barter are exchanged to acquire jobs for men. While Caddy's sexuality fails in maintaining her impotent or sexually disinterested brother Jason in his job at her already cuckolded groom's bank, Eula Varner, until she commits suicide, is the gift that keeps on giving in terms of her impotent husband Flem's advancement in her lover's bank. Linda Snopes, Eula's only child, is the one daughter of the South (among Faulkner's major female characters) who repeatedly enters the highly charged setting of a drugstore without being bartered for her sexuality.[33] However, the fact that some observers (including Linda herself) actively think she might be adds a mocking layer of tension to the provocatively desexualized identity of Gavin Stevens.[34] Of these female figures, Eula alone, depicted as she stands in a greasy apron cooking behind a lunch counter, is momentarily seen in a context where she is neither the desired nor the glorified meat. Indeed, this scene is genuinely startling as it ratchets up the realism in relation to Eula, the most celebrated female flesh, "galmeat," in all of Faulkner's fiction. Limited to human meat, the traded upon Eula does not have to compete with the pastoral majesty and beauty unaware of Ike Snopes's bovine beloved, the creature whose fate is to become rendered into hamburger and other unkind cuts in *The Hamlet*.[35]

"Coming Unalone Is Terrible": Female Being

Dewey Dell's encounter with the cow (as she feels that her own body's needs are more pressing than a full udder) has been understood as masturbatory, an argument that is supported by her rage when she assumes that the hidden Vardaman has been spying on her.[36] Onanism aside, Dewey Dell is clearly beside herself, and this desperate girl's encounter with the self is about not being alone. Erotic in its mode, her experience here doubles as an emotional anticipation of the motion of the feared quickening. Addie's view that pregnancy violates her aloneness is given immediacy in Dewey Dell's second section, as terror transforms orgasm into that quickening (the old name for the movement as the seed turns to come alive within): "I feel my body, my bones and flesh beginning to part and open upon the alone, and the process of coming unalone is terrible. Lafe. Lafe. 'Lafe' Lafe. Lafe" (61–62).

While Addie Bundren in section 40 adds (not in quotation marks and therefore still not viewed as articulated speech), "[i]t was not that I could not think of myself as no longer unvirgin, because I was three now" (173), she has already offered a disquisition on the condition of her "aloneness," thinking "not that my aloneness had to be violated over and over again each day, but that it had never been violated until Cash came. Not even by Anse in the nights . . . My aloneness had been violated and then made whole by the violation: time, Anse, love, what you will, outside the circle" (172). Dewey Dell's unspoken reverie, with its simple repetitive phrases confessing her ambivalence about being alone and her anticipation of becoming "unalone," insists that aloneness itself is a characteristic of female troubles and a paradoxical casualty of being "in trouble." In her second section, Dewey Dell worries: "It's because I am alone. If I could just feel it, it would be different, because I would not be alone. But if I were not alone, everybody would know it. And he [Doc Peabody] could do so much for me, and then I would not be alone. Then I could be all right alone" (58–59). What Dewey Dell imagines demands a second look: "I feel my body, my bones and flesh beginning to part and open upon the alone, and the process of coming unalone is terrible. Lafe. Lafe. 'Lafe' Lafe. Lafe." (61–62). The only voiced word, "Lafe"—surrounded by the doubled and unspoken words "Lafe. Lafe."—is telling in its missing period. Like Darl's closing assertion in section 12, "*Addie Bundren is dead*" (52), the absence of a period connotes the continuation of "Lafe" through the unwanted baby that gestates in Dewey Dell. Like death in *As I Lay Dying*, being born into being is a process. Deep South southerners can hear the dialect pun that resounds in the single spoken word "Lafe"[37] as it calls out and personifies "Life."

Speaking "Without the Words"

> Talk, talk, talk, the utter and heartbreaking stupidity of words.
> —William Faulkner, *Mosquitoes* (1927)

The dead Addie Bundren in unspoken derision damns the shiftless Anse: "He had a word for it, too. Love, he called it." The only words that Addie's account frames in quotation marks, indicating that these utterances have the hollow status of spoken words, are two conversations with Anse. The first is a spoken dialogue between Anse and Addie that constitutes their initial meeting as well as Anse's proposal of marriage. Here, Addie with her graveyard humor jokes that Anse may have difficulty asking permission from her relatives, all already buried in the Jefferson cemetery. The second quoted (spoken) interjection is a single assertion by Anse, who threatens the death-ready Addie by declaring: "you and me aint nigh done chapping yet" (quotation marks Faulkner's). It is significant that Addie's and Anse's words that lead to marriage, and later Anse's expressed intention to continue the reproduction of children, are spoken pronouncements, and in the act of being spoken prove their emptiness. According to Addie's philosophy of language, words spoken aloud prove their meaninglessness to the speaker who uses people through words in the stead of acts or to fill in for the absence of lived or actual experience. As *As I Lay Dying* underlines in its title, dying is a continuing condition—a social condition that must be played even as it already lies with the qualities of an object.

Dewey Dell's initial section anticipates Addie Bundren's sophisticated disquisition on the spoken and the unspoken as this pregnant daughter recounts the significance of a conversation she has had with Darl: "He said he knew without the words like he told me ma is going to die without the words, and I knew he knew because if he had said he knew with the words I would not have believed that he had been there and saw us" (27). Later, as Darl recounts his moment of realization about Addie Bundren's secret, it is not one of seeing, but of epiphanic knowing: "That night I found ma sitting beside the bed where he [Jewel] was sleeping, in the dark . . . [a]nd then I knew that I knew. I knew that as plain on that day as I knew about Dewey Dell on that day" (136). Unlike Anse's word "Love," the immanence of birth and the finality of death must be known "without the words."

Throughout the novel, the increasingly bodiless Darl is shown to have a particular closeness to women and their natal secrets.[38] While the paradigm of art explicated in this work emphasizes tension and conflict, it is a necessary tension and conflict that makes the madman artist and the fertile woman part of the same productive dialectic. Indeed, Darl is shown in cahoots with Addie Bundren in a double entendre that appears in the form of a repeatedly dangling modifier, dangled before the reader by the unconscious Anse who is aware that the goings-on in the wagon are somehow slipping out of his control. In Anse's second section, he describes Darl as "[s]etting back there on the plank seat with Cash, with his dead ma laying in her coffin at his feet, laughing." At the section's close, the location reserved for the most significant lines in the novel as a whole, Anse repeats his suggestive sentence: "And, Darl setting on the plank seat right above her where she was laying, laughing" (106). These estranged observations frame direct references to him, "laughing" and "Darl laughing" that clearly refer to this mad son's hysteria. But modifiers do not dangle, much less dangle twice, in the same way in Faulkner's prose without purpose or portent. To dangle after the highly significant word "laying" calculates the level at which Faulkner himself is enjoying playing the game. It should be Darl, but grammatically speaking, Addie is laughing. Just prior to section 30 (the mathematical middle of the novel), Darl and Addie appear to be having fun because of, rather than despite, the Bundren family's travails. While Darl later lies "crying" on top of the coffin he has tried to burn, Addie's and Darl's fates are closely intertwined: both are excised from the family in the same unceremonious sentence. Addie Bundren is disposed of, buried, as it were, in a dependent clause that does not mention her name, her body, or even her box, but rather a hole, an "it" that is "filled and buried" in a sentence that is devoted in large part to Dewey Dell's role in the ambushing of Darl as he is forcibly procured for the state mental asylum. Puzzling over the fact that Dewey Dell, like Darl, has had to be restrained bodily by the town's mob, Cash recalls what he had understood as their closeness: "I always kind of had a idea that him [Darl] and Dewey Dell kind of knowed things betwixt them" (237). This knowledge is the prelude to madness, precipitating Darl's "laughing," "laughing," "laughing," "laughing," "laughing" in his final section as he is being taken away to Shakespeare's "dark house."[39]

Dewey Dell: Dead Center

> *Dewey Dell*
>
> I dont know whether I can see it or not. *But I know that I am I and I know that it is it and that it is there because I saw it there, curving red away in to the pines. And if I see it and it is there, I see it. But if I don't see it, it is not there. And if it is not there, I am not I. And if I am I, then yesterday is not because I don't see it. But I don't know if I see it or not. So I don't know if yesterday was or not or whether I am or not. But yesterday was, that's why I must see it.*
>
> The signboard comes in sight. *And so it is yesterday. And beyond yesterday is the day before yesterday. And the day before that. And the day before that. That's why I must pass it. I heard that my mother died. I wish I had time to let her die.*

I wish I had time to wish I had. And the day before that is beyond the wild~~ness,~~ ~~us~~ in the cold ~~earth~~ and outraged earth too soon too soon too soon. Its not that I would not its too soon too soon too soon.
—Section 30, first extant version of *As I Lay Dying*, copied in Faulkner's hand[40]

Tomorrow, and tomorrow, and tomorrow,
Creeps in this petty pace from day to day
To the last syllable of recorded time,
And all our yesterdays have lighted fools
The way to dusty death. Out, out, brief candle!
—Shakespeare, *Macbeth*, act 5, scene 5

As the Bundren family approaches Jefferson, Darl is aware of the visual change. As the advertising increases, the distance diminishes: "We have been passing the signs for sometime now: the drugstores, the clothing stores, the patent medicine and the garages and cafés, and the mile-boards diminishing, becoming more starkly reaccruent: 3mi. 2mi." (226). Dewey Dell, a believer in signs, who in her first section knows what will happen at the end of the row if her sack is filled with cotton, and who in her second section knows that "God gave women a sign when something has happened bad" (58), opens her third section in the published text by obsessively anticipating a signboard that is not yet visible in the distance, thinking: "New Hope 3 mi. it will say. New Hope 3 mi. New Hope 3 mi. And then the road will begin, curving away into the trees, empty with waiting, saying New Hope three miles" (120). Noting she has "heard that my mother is dead" and wishing she "had time to let her die," Dewey Dell, aware that everything is "too soon too soon too soon . . . too soon too soon too soon" is interrupted by the sign itself: "Now it begins to say it. New Hope three miles. New Hope three miles" (121).[41] Here, the absence of the abbreviation calls attention to the sound of the actual lettering in the earlier renditions. As the resonant name of the church promising New Hope beckons, Dewey Dell sees Cash looking on with "his pale empty sad composed and questioning face follow[ing] the red and empty curve." This "red and empty curve," here a bodily sign, represents the paradox of "new hope" as it is feared and desired by a Dewey Dell who repeats to herself "3mi.": the paradoxically aural and sonorously oracular pun silently (and heretically) declares "three am I period." New Hope may lie in maintaining wholeness through suffering and violation, the monotheism achieved through the death of a son as three become one—a holy trinity—in a novel in which all three grown sons (including the denied Darl) are sacrificial sons. Nevertheless, as Dewey Dell's second section maintains, more than one man's hand stands to compete or collaborate with God in relation to her crowded interior. In her second section, Dewey Dell imagines other groupings of three: "I would let him [Doc Peabody] come in between me and Lafe, like Darl came in between me and Lafe," concluding enigmatically, "so Lafe is alone too" (59). Dewey

Dell imagines that by convincing the doctor to come "in between" that she, by becoming a different "three," can cease to be "two" and finally become "one" in possession of her own "little tub of guts." Without question, the wildest narrative in *As I Lay Dying* occupies the center of section 30. It is no accident that this, Dewey Dell's third section, is the segment of the novel that Faulkner revised the most. Just after this narrative excitement (which will be interrogated in due time), Dewey Dell establishes closure in relation to hope, new or otherwise. "Was" is the motive word here as Dewey Dell, now near the close of section 30, inhabits nonitalicized thoughts as she returns to the sign: "New Hope. Was 3 mi. Was 3 mi." (122). Significantly, she has no further use for italics in the novel as a whole, because she is no longer: "3 am I period." In the well-known mathematics of sexuality (leaving aside her sense of those crowding her interior and desired as interveners in her uterine terrors in her second section), one plus one equals three—only a "period" can counter this sum.

The two Bundrens whose minds mirror what the sign sounds: the "mi.," are the characters who are defined through their explicit multiplicity. Aside from the madman son, Darl, who lives the narrative life—or lie—of the omniscient narrator, Dewey Dell is the only other character who mentally pictures the "3 mi." or "three am I." Ostensibly referring to the wind, these markers are for Dewey Dell the "sad steady sound" that "blows cool out of the pines" (122). As the wagon later approaches Jefferson, Darl (who earlier was the first to anticipate "the white sign" reading "New Hope 3 mi.") has replaced Dewey Dell as the sign reader: "3mi. 2 mi." Clearly, his own multiplicity of being has been at stake from the outset. Darl questions whether he "is" or not, disclaiming Addie Bundren as his mother because he, in his multiplicity of shifting perspectives and provisional identities, requires the plural verb "are," and "'[*a*]*re* is too many for one woman to foal" (Faulkner's italics, 101). Here, Darl has become the man-made man, the madman and artist who frames himself outside of the story of female procreation, positioning himself through a plethora of pronominal possibilities that allow him in his final section to interrogate and answer himself.[42]

Dewey Dell's first three sections, erupting in outbursts of eroticism tempered by her terrifying internal concerns, reach a crescendo in her third section as she is taunted by a presence that enters her pages without quotation marks; in Dewey Dell's phrase from her first section, this voice speaks "without the words." Increasingly crowded with preoccupations, section 30 provides one of the most remarkable excavation sites for glimpsing the layers of complexity that Faulkner wrote into his multivocal masterpiece. There is a coy, feminine quality to the taunting narrative that at midsection begins to counter Dewey Dell's desire for an abortion by asserting power over a masculine figure:

> *Suppose I tell him to turn. He will do what I say. Dont you know he will do what I say?*

Instead of responding directly, Dewey Dell in nonitalicized, unspoken words (quotation marks mine) recalls "wak[ing] with a black void rushing under me." In Dewey Dell's countering thought, she sees "Vardaman rise and go to the window and strike the knife into the fish, the blood gushing, hissing like steam, but I could not see." The taunting voice continuing in italicized threat confidently reasserts itself over "the black void" and Dewey Dell's vision of the youngest Bundren with a knife:

> *He'll do as I say. He always does. I can persuade him to anything. You know I can. Suppose I say Turn here.*

Here Dewey Dell's nonitalicized thought makes a Caddy-like reference to orgasm as death, insisting: "That was when I died that time."[43] Then, the taunting voice continues:

> *Suppose I do. We'll go to New Hope. We wont have to go to town.*

As the unspeaking voice threatens to tell Anse to turn onto the road to the New Hope cemetery where Addie can be buried, this adversary asserts authorial power. This voice does nothing less than threaten to stop the book. Anse, amenable to suggestion as long as he is not required to exert himself, has never been shown to be under Darl's power. Addie, a former schoolteacher and an excellent baker, is the best candidate for a character who has had control over her shiftless, toothless husband.

As I Lay Dying is subtle in its depictions of power. Anse, pictured pulling at the reins only once, is clearly sitting in the driving seat with Dewey Dell sitting next to him filling the place once reserved for the matriarch who has heretofore directed Anse and the rest of the family. During the journey to Jefferson, Anse uses his holding of the reins as a means of passively masterminding the decreased mobility and social descent experienced by all his children.[44] In section 30, Dewey Dell takes up the psychic knife as the voice continues to threaten:

> *He will do what I say*

It is significant that the knife she holds is not clean. Indeed, the knife in her vision has just been used by her brother Vardaman on the fish that he himself believes with totemic certainty is his mother (in the shortest section of *As I Lay Dying*, Vardaman has earlier announced with conviction: "My mother is a fish").[45] The voice, using the loaded word "*We*," threatens to halt the family's journey to Jefferson. Dewey Dell responds with envisioned action: "I rose and took the knife from the streaming fish still hissing and I killed Darl" (121). What is shocking here is not just that Dewey Dell has killed Darl—cut him out of her body—but rather that she has killed him with an Orestian knife, still wet with the blood of the mother. In an abrupt turn, Dewey Dell's italics become her own. Her italicized fantasies of an annihilated self constitute her last eruption of internalized emotion in the novel. Indeed, this passage comprises her last italicized entry:

> *When I used to sleep with Vardaman I had a nightmare once I thought I was awake but I couldn't see and couldn't feel I couldn't feel the bed under me and I couldn't think what I was I couldn't think of my name I couldn't even think I am a girl I couldn't even think I nor even think I want to wake up nor remember what was opposite to awake so I could do that I knew that something was passing but I couldn't even think of time then all of a sudden I knew that something was it was wind blowing over me it was like the wind came and blew me back from where it was I was not blowing the room and Vardaman asleep and all of them back under me again and going on like a piece of cool silk dragging across my naked legs* (121–22)[46]

Having taken back her guts, Dewey Dell has cut herself out of a major cultural story. No longer the touchstone in the male artist's paradigm of art, Dewey Dell, once the figure whom Darl has seen "her leg coming long from beneath her tightening dress: that lever which moves the world; one of that caliper that measures the length and breadth of life" (104), has lost her position as a primal mother.

I could argue that it does not matter whether Darl and Addie speak the words that emerge in Dewey Dell's interior. These italicized interventions might, with some calisthenics, be read along the lines of the internalized voice of the father that provokes such forceful dialogues within the mind of Quentin Compson in *The Sound and the Fury*. However, this voice and the recognition of these voices mattered to William Faulkner. In the autograph copy as well as in the typescript, Faulkner resorted to punctuation to announce that this voice had clearly erupted. In the handwritten version, this entire passage including the words of the threatening speaker and Dewey Dell appear in italics, divided by double slash marks that are used to cue the radically alternating strands of voice. These slash marks were replaced by wide spaces in the typescript that had already been rendered less necessary by Faulkner's decision to alternate between roman and italic typefaces. Yet the width of these spaces in the typescript is interesting, as it indicates the writer's desire to emphasize this distance, to picture the sense of interruption and interjection. It is even more significant that Faulkner placed a single unanswered and unclosed pair of quotation marks in each version,[47] the handwritten and the typescript, notably in different places. On each occasion, these orphaned quotation marks insist on the eruption of speech itself as this vengeful voice taunts Dewey Dell with the proposal of a revenge burial.

Speech is undoubtedly signified in the handwritten version that actually contains the words "he says."[48] (Had this autograph copy said, "she says," the archivist would assume that this "she" referred to Dewey Dell, even though this marker of speech would have had Dewey Dell, shades of the Darl of section 58, speaking about herself in the third person.) In the autograph copy, Darl is obviously the taunting presence, speaking without the words as the wagon passes New Hope. Again, it is important to remember that section 30 was the part of *As I Lay Dying* that Faulkner changed the most. The first two paragraphs had to be replaced not just because Dewey Dell was on the verge of becoming the new self-conjugating Quentin Compson or Darl, and not just because it was essential that she focus on a sign rather than the red road to New Hope that fixates her in the earliest version. These paragraphs had to be changed because Dewey Dell was no longer the source of the italicized epiphany of the third paragraph: she ceased to be the point of origin for the most elegant assertion in the book when Faulkner altered the text from "the outraged entrails of things" to "the outraged entrails of events." Arguably, the alien voice had already begun to assert itself in the reference to a philosophical "they" that is concerned with "the womb of time." In the original version, Dewey Dell observes and intuits:

> The mule's ears are passing it; then it begins to curve away into the pines. *And so yesterday cannot be 2 things. That's what they mean by the womb of time; the agony and despair of ~~parting flesh and bones~~ spreading bones the hand pulls there in which ~~lies~~ lie the outraged entrails of ~~things~~ events.* Cash's head turns slowly as we approach, his pale, empty, composed face left the red and empty curve; at the wheel Jewel sits the horse, along straight ahead.

This is clearly Dewey Dell speaking because of the continued concern with "yesterday" that dominates the first two paragraphs opening the original version of section 30, which muse:

> *And if I am I, then yesterday is not because I don't see it. But I don't know if I see it or not. So I don't know if yesterday was or not or whether I am or not. But yesterday was, that's why I must see it.*
>
> The signboard comes in sight. *And so it is yesterday. And beyond yesterday is the day before yesterday. And the day before that. And the day before that.*

Finally, who else but Darl could speak in the word-drunk poetry, the confident profundity of a philosopher of aesthetics—answering the old desire, the womb envy expressed so vehemently by the sculptor of *Mosquitoes*, who wants to know what it is like to create life, to contain another life in the female loins? Darl, inside Dewey Dell speaking "without the words," experiences "the process" (62) (the quickening seen just before his narrative death) that offers artists this longed-for view from within the female interior:

> *That's what they mean by the womb of time: the agony and despair of spreading bones, the hard girdle in which lie the outraged entrails of events.* (121)

Darl was the adversary in the original version and remains a fine possibility for this spiteful character in the published novel. Darl violates Dewey Dell near the beginning of section 30: "Darl's eyes . . . swim to pinpoints. They begin at my feet and rise along my body to my face, and then my dress is gone: I sit naked on the seat above the unhurrying mules, above the travail" (121). However, Dewey Dell (like readers who condescend to Faulkner) may be just a bit slow on the uptake. It may go without saying, but *As I Lay Dying* is a work of art. "[L]aughing" (105–6) with Addie, Darl may have decided to join the mother in plotting a revenge burial or, taking his cue from her inspiringly vicious guile, he may be proposing a timely burial to take revenge against both the mother and this reluctant mother to be. This being said, the possibility that Addie herself has decided to reassert her control over the family's narrative is more plausible. Faulkner removed the crucial designation "he said" from the published novel. Addie is after all the novel's originator of the concept of the revenge burial, and if tone means anything, if diction means anything, these taunting words with their clipped quality have a sadistic edge that is recognizable. This tone, this clipped diction, this detailed engagement, is not characteristic of the strange but disinterested Darl. Finally, Darl lacks the authority in the family to brag that he is able to control anyone, much less the passive-aggressive and stubbornly self-serving Anse.

In her fourth and final narration in section 58, Dewey Dell speaks with no interiority at all. Insistently external, this section consists of words between the vacuous daughter and her equally empty father. Unrelenting and striking in its orality, section 58 is almost entirely in the reviled form of the spoken word. Section 58 bears, and, in many ways, can only be grasped by, being quoted in full:

> When he saw the money I said, "It's not my money, it doesn't belong to me."
>
> "Whose is it, then?"
>
> "It's Cora Tull's money. It's Mrs. Tull's. I sold the cakes for it."
>
> "Ten dollars for two cakes?"
>
> "Dont you touch it. It's not mine."
>
> "You never had them cakes. It's a lie. It was them Sunday clothes you had in that package."
>
> "Dont you touch it! If you take it you are a thief."
>
> "My own daughter accuses me of being a thief. My own daughter."
>
> "Pa. Pa."
>
> "I have fed you and sheltered you. I give you love and care, yet my own daughter, the daughter of my dead wife, calls me a thief over her mother's grave."
>
> "It's not mine, I tell you. If it was, God knows you could have it."
>
> "Where did you get ten dollars?"
>
> "Pa. Pa."
>
> "You wont tell me. Did you come by it so shameful you dare not?"
>
> "It's not mine, I tell you. Cant you understand it's not mine?"

"It's not like I wouldn't pay it back. But she calls her own father a thief."

"I cant, I tell you. I tell you it's not my money. God knows you could have it."

"I wouldn't take it. My own born daughter that has et my food for seventeen years, begrudges me the loan of ten dollars."

"It's not mine, I cant."

"Whose is it, then?"

"It was give to me. To buy something with."

"To buy what with?"

"Pa. Pa."

"It's just a loan. God knows, I hate for my blooden children to reproach me. But I give them what was mine without stint. Cheerful I give them, without stint. And now they deny me. Addie. It was lucky for you you died, Addie."

"Pa. Pa."

"God knows it is."

He took the money and went out. (255–57)

The only descriptive lines in the predominately spoken dialogue of section 58 concern the question of who will have the money Dewey Dell has been given to terminate her pregnancy. At the close, this disputed money is taken away from the desperate and increasingly pregnant daughter to put teeth in her paw's black-rimmed maw. Dewey Dell is neither married nor is she destined to be married, to say the words "I do." These words are, of course, the primary example of a speech act, words that, when they are spoken in a ritual and legal context, have the consequences of a major action.[49] The ending of the handwritten section 30, which opens with the mocking repetition of the unspoken words "I believe in God. I do I do I do," was edited, to leave its powerful closing referring repeatedly to her belief in God in a more powerful form. The published ending achieves the echo narration that this volume insists is the signal and sign of Quentin Compson's madness in *The Sound and the Fury* and would become the distinguishing formal characteristic of *Absalom, Absalom!*: "I believe in God, God. God, I believe in God." (This echo formation that gives a visual solidity to the spoken or written word is the primary subject of this volume's chapter 5, "Echoing Back to *Absalom*.") The repetition of "God" three times in sequence or, read another way, three times after the first call that takes the form of an apostrophe to "God," constitutes a call to a religious trinity after the aesthetic triumvirate (the mother, the artist son or consort, and the daughter as an embodiment of creation), the other "three am I," has been cut from Dewey Dell's gut. The pregnant Dewey Dell, unable to find the abortion that her literary antecedent has decided against in Edith Wharton's *Summer*, plays a role that disputes her place in this familiar paradigm of art. It bears saying again that the pregnant Dewey Dell and her baby do not represent hope. Like the pregnant Rosamond of Cather's *The Professor's House*, Dewey Dell by the penultimate section of *As I Lay Dy-*

ing has come to embody the future as a word-winded and empty materialism. A major difference is that Charity Royal of *Summer* and Rosamond of *The Professor's House* are destined to rule the houses to which they return, while Dewey Dell has been reduced to an empty object filled with words made even more meaningless by this vacuous fight over money. Her embodiment of hopelessness is compounded by the emotional vacuity that is paradoxically the hopelessness inherent in replication itself: replication without end or the reprieve from reproduction promised by what this novel savors—maternal mortality. In Cather's world, Professor Godfrey, possibly "God free," is the suicidal model for Quentin Compson or, more precisely, the jeweler he meets as he (Quentin) enters the watch repair shop to question time. In the post–World War I society that Cather's professor has inherited, female materialism will triumph over creation and procreation, precluding the possibility that even the most cleanly cut masculinity can be sacrificed to art.

In a crisp and shocking shift, Dewey Dell's section 58 is the only performance of pure dialogue in *As I Lay Dying*.[50] This exchange between the basely greedy and increasingly triumphant father and his downcast daughter exposes the pregnant Dewey Dell as empty. Dewey Dell has been emptied of any residue of the interiority that has made her a compelling figure in her three previous sections. Having been literally preoccupied by the voices of her brother and mother in the dead center of the book, Dewey Dell has cut herself out of the paradigm of art by speaking with the words and by speaking in the voice of her father. Her words here do not fill emptiness; they are the emptiness. Dialogue demarcates and fills "the gaps" in what remain her and her father's "lack[s]." No longer a girl of feeling, Dewey Dell has become a woman of words in an ending in which she uses and is used by words that articulate the fact of her narrative abortion.

By mentally taking up the already mother-bloodied "knife" to kill Darl in section 30, Dewey Dell severs her connection to this paradigm of art. No longer a vessel of mystery, the Bundren daughter has become the pregnant woman devoid of mystery. Finally, Dewey Dell is not the muse who either inspires or provokes the desires of the male artist, nor is she the caliper or fulcrum, the measure or means to move a world. By the penultimate section of the novel, Dewey Dell is no longer the richly contested figure caught between the madman artist and the demanding dead mother. Unable to remember in section 30 "*what was opposite to awake*," whether sleeping or lying dying, whether she is a negation or merely an object, the Dewey Dell of her last section has lost the content of her discontent that has made her sections interesting. What matters is that Dewey Dell takes the knife to Darl, killing the internalized voice that has tried to take over the mother's place as he speaks from his sister's womb in Faulkner's novel. What matters for Faulkner's paradigm of art is that Dewey Dell in her final section has not only lost her identity by killing the brother who has placed her in the matricentric dialectic, which has long decreed that the female's pregnant body is the site of masculine envy and aesthetic competition, but, by that same psychic act, has become vacuous. Dewey Dell's final section immediately follows Darl's last section, but Dewey Dell has already cut Darl out of female consciousness, cut Darl out of his bid to create an art out of either opposition to the mother or his matricidal bid to usurp the creative power of the mother.

Dewey Dell may begin in a seasonal economy, but her mother's death places her in the unforgiving linearity, defined not just by the need for sustenance or even subsistence, but by a relentless march toward consumption in which Dewey Dell becomes a thing to be consumed and bartered in the marketplace. Even as she recalls picking cotton in her first section and the compulsive inevitability of her sexual initiation, Dewey Dell does not inhabit an idyllic natural world; she and Lafe are inscribed in the row of a demanding cash crop. In terms of picking, chopping, and chapping, the labor expected from her is unrelenting. It is a long row to hoe. The novel closes with Cash's summary that reveals Anse Bundren's foray into the female market to discover that women, whether those taken from the schoolhouse or those acquired from a house of no repute at the edge of town, can all be "Mrs Bundren[s]."

No longer a point of contention between her philosophically and physically sadistic mother who reviles words and her artist brother (spawned by Anse "hidden within a word like within a paper screen") who exists only in words even when he is speaking "without the words," Dewey Dell has prostituted herself in an effort to empty her interior: she has become an object of exchange in the cellar of a tawdry marketplace. Reduced to a sign of materialism in spite of her pregnancy, Dewey Dell in this brutal parable is on the road to the end of a female-driven art that Faulkner lays, if not on the drugstore counter, then at the destructive door of male appetite. Finally, what is at stake in section 30, the dead center of this fifty-nine-section novel, is the disputed body of the pregnant daughter that exposes the conflict between the mother and this Faulknerian artist who (in Shakespeare's own plot turn) "is not of woman born." This turning point positioned at the mathematical center of *As I Lay Dying* exposes the function of the novel as the container of the contested pregnant daughter, in a revisionist paradigm of art that articulates Faulkner's high degree of self-consciousness about the paradox of creation. Faulkner's particular attention to revising Dewey Dell in *As I Lay Dying* reveals what can only be understood as a frightening level of intentionality.

CHAPTER FOUR

The Signifying Eye

Faulkner's Artists and the Engendering of Art

Flesh was the reason that oil paint was invented.
—Willem de Kooning

Life and death struggle in each detail: here there is a woman, there a statue, beyond that a cadaver. Your creation is incomplete.
—Critic responding to a painter's canvas in Balzac's "The Unknown Masterpiece"[1]

In 1910 William Faulkner, then thirteen years old, gave his mother a knife. In a letter signed "From your loving son, William," he noted that his gift was for her "to sharpen pencils with." Along with the knife, the note, and a piece of ribbon, Faulkner completed her birthday present by including an ink drawing that he had composed on a scrap of art paper (see fig. 16, page 115). The young Faulkner's composition depicts an older woman, rigid and stylized—her hair tightly drawn into a bun—sitting in a chair as she watches a short-legged child seen from the back with his legs dangling down from the height of his less formal perch. The woman shares the fire's warmth with this child who holds a slate board divided into rows to make a grid of rectangular drawing spaces, each of which seems designed to be about the size of the gift picture. Some are empty, but four contain the child's readable drawings: two roughly sawn log or board buildings, a four-legged creature (mule or dog), and another of a bird. If it were not part of a package of preserved and related presents, this drawing, even on its acid-eaten and fibrous paper, might seem to be a self-parodic salting of the autobiographical remains. In light of what Faulkner would later write, this drawing tells too much as it offers in retrospect a focused view, not just into the mind of the artist as a young man, but into the obsessions of an intelligence that some fifteen years later would impel his first experimental masterpiece, *The Sound and the Fury*, into print. Beneath the most dominant of the displayed things—the round and marked face of the clock sitting alongside a jug and other objects such as lines of elegantly stacked paper (possibly books) on the mantle—a young child's toys, including a rifle, harnessed wagon, and steam locomotive, are scattered on the floor. Yet what is finally on display is nothing less than the young William's decision to depict a child's developing sense of visual perspective. This accomplishment takes shape in a readable, notably uneven sequence of blocks that follows the progression of the alphabet. The keynote is "C," a middle "C" that positions the seer at the dead center. This "C" blocks in a simple square with no dimensional reach beyond the flatness of the page. In the alphabetic play on the right side, letters are unfolded as if the cube has been inverted or naïvely seen through to become, or at least to take the form of, an opened book. Except for "C," the beginning letters of the alphabet are seen as almost folding objects, blocks that lay booklike on their bellies, spread-eagled, facedown or left open to reveal a single inner letter, while later letters are laid out in a more orderly progression. Demonstrating the calculated mastery of three-dimensional space rapidly in the framing of the letters "H" and "I," the blocks stop at "J." In this sequence that pictures this child's innocence as well as his ambition, the thirteen-year-old Faulkner has begun his genre painting by scattering blocks on the right side of the paper, and as the space is filled with experimental containers, the letters on the left side achieve a structural progression as these signs march in sequence. The "J" in spatial terms provides a convenient end for this part of his design, but the significance of this block also serves as a culmination for the story being told about the pictured child's achievement: the drawing of the classical vectors of a well-rendered cube. This block, the "J," takes the drawing from flatness to depth, insisting on the artificiality and, at the same time, the visible vectors that emerge in looking at a flat drawing from a developed point of view.[2]

The major exception to the formal, inked-in, and stylized order in which the pubescent Faulkner alphabetizes and thereby narrates a child's progress toward the dimensionality of literal cubism takes shape in an eruption into liquidity. Here, this evenly curved and irregular shape literally gives the lie to perspectival claims, as it appears to be suspended without visible means of support. In what would have been the midground in a sophisticated work mediated by perspective, this thing, without weight or fathomable substance, resembles a flat puzzle piece. On the basis of shape alone, this outline that obscures the view of what might lie behind it suggests the idea of an outsized, cornucopia-like gourd that, despite its exterior line, is not a gourd or even a dipper made from a gourd. If this object were written, the shape would be a metaphor. Drawn flatly (impossibly hung in the air) framed by the formally controlled depiction of recognizable people and things, this deviation has remained a puzzle in this piece that is a drawing about drawing *for* the mother. Mysterious to those who have seen it in the archives, this shape in Faulkner's picture (like large expanses of yet to be colonized speech that characterize the mature author's riddling oeuvre) seems strange. What is strange and estranged in Faulkner's writing is often the ordinary. In Faulkner's fiction, things seen—really seen—evoke word pictures that are extraordinary.

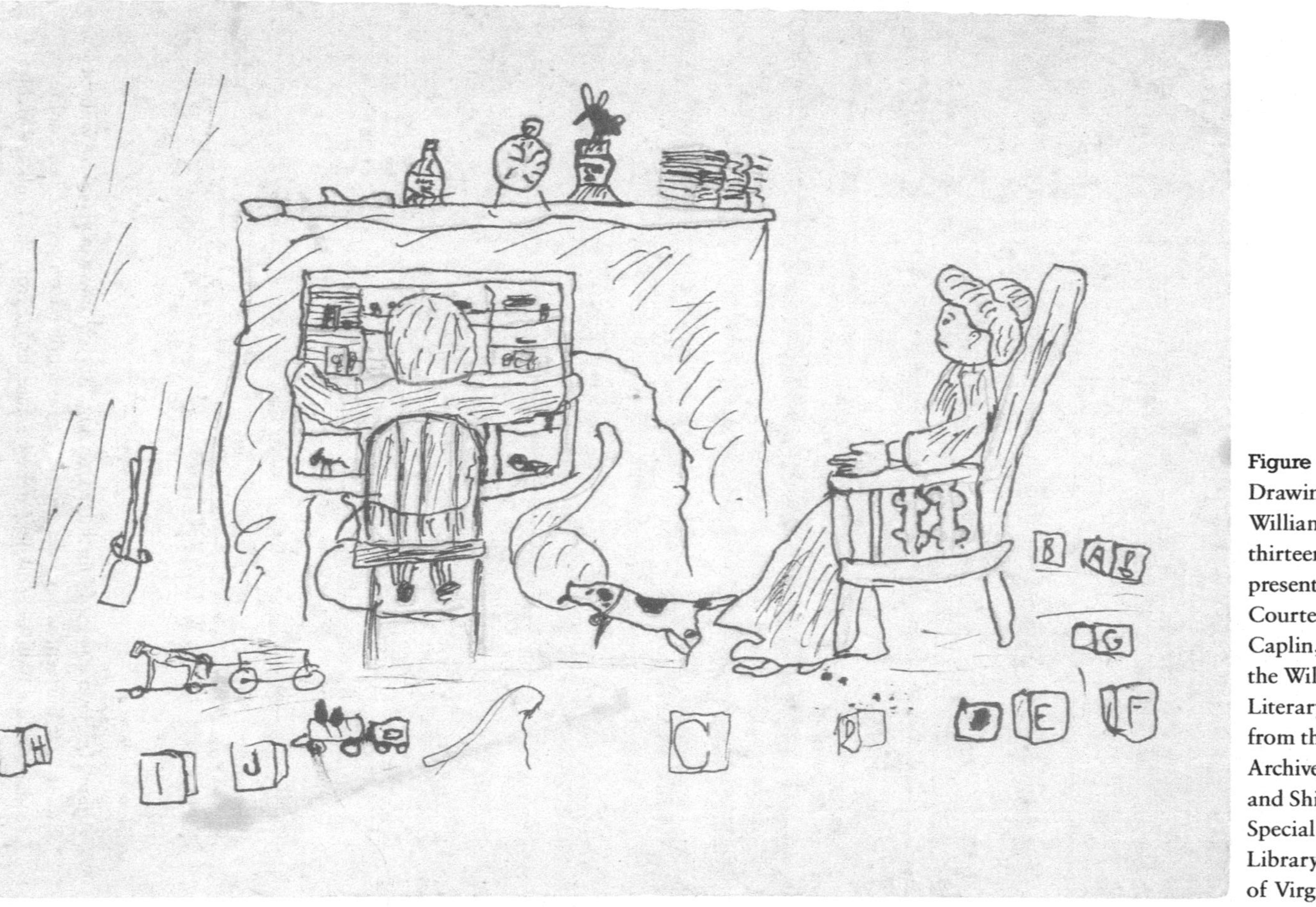

Figure 16. "Birthday Drawing" in ink by William Falkner, age thirteen, as part of a present for his mother. Courtesy of Lee Caplin, Producer of the William Faulkner Literary Estate. Image from the Faulkner Archives of the Albert and Shirley Small Special Collections Library, the University of Virginia.

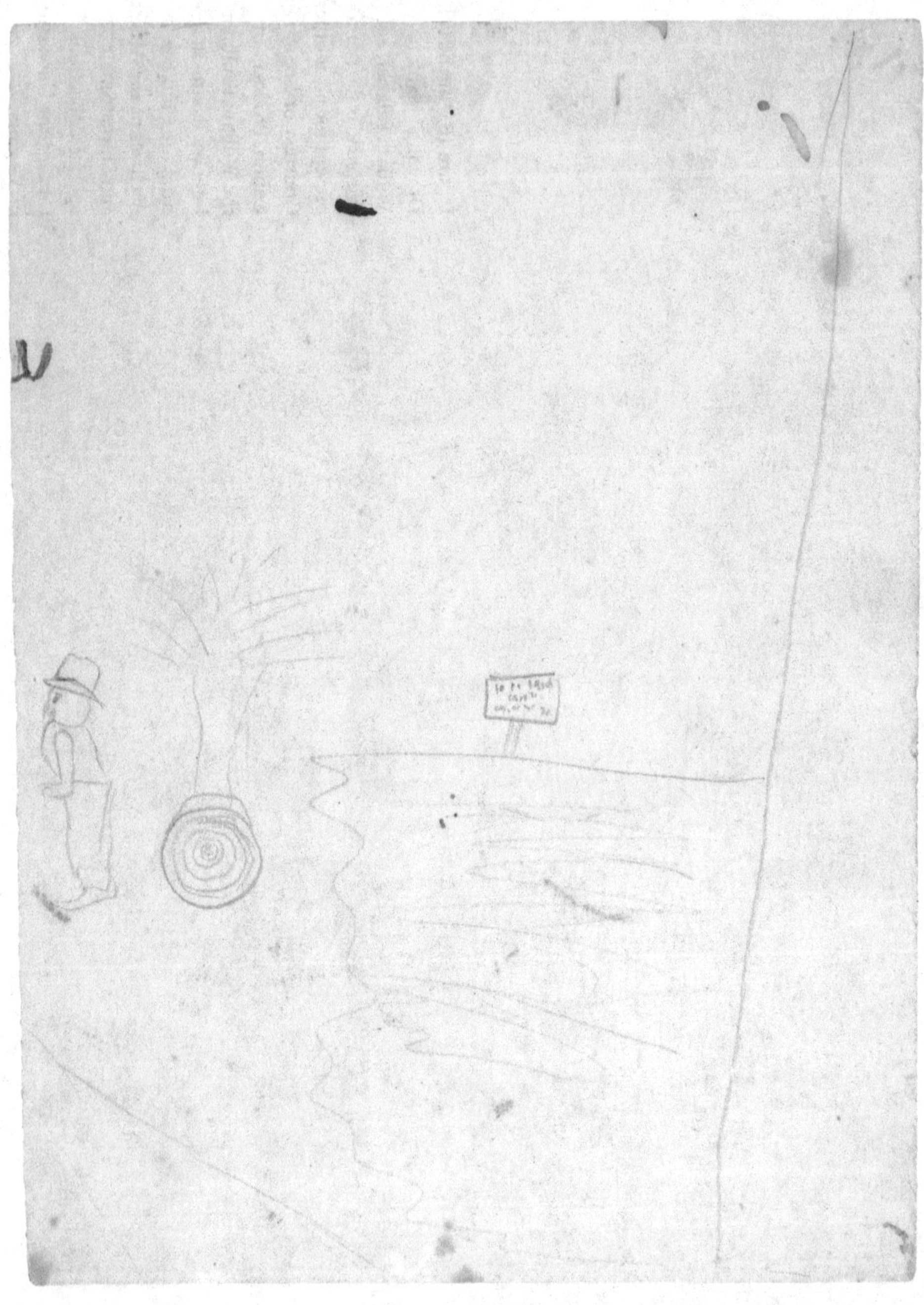

Figure 17a. Reverse side of "Birthday Drawing," sketch drawn in pencil by William Falkner, age thirteen, as part of a present for his mother. Courtesy of Lee Caplin, Producer of the William Faulkner Literary Estate. Image from the Faulkner Archives of the Albert and Shirley Small Special Collections Library, University of Virginia.

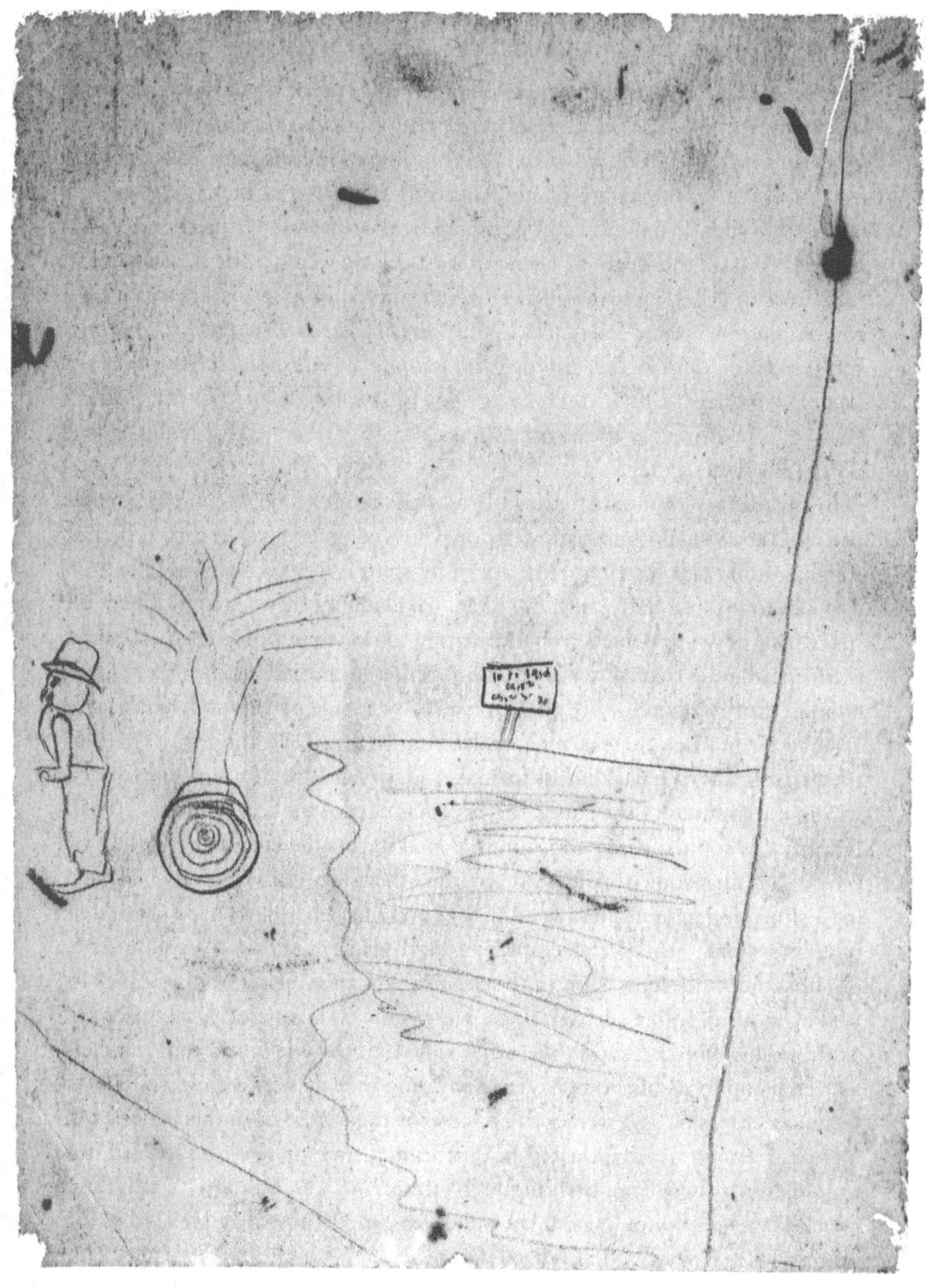

Figure 17b. Reverse side of "Birthday Drawing," digitally enhanced.

David Minter's succinct insight about *The Sound and the Fury* being "formally innovative and stylistically and thematically regressive" speaks to the connection between mundane acts of repetition and death. Known through repeated processes such as digestion, repetition has become mock-heroic in Quentin's meditation on his own adumbrating awareness that seeks an ending. Dwelling on the length of nights during the day that he has chosen for his death, Quentin's mind is preoccupied by thoughts of "[t]he corridor . . . still empty of all the feet in sad generations seeking water," a depressing quest that leads to "the pipes, the porcelain, the stained quiet walls, the throne of contemplation." Amid references to the "*invisible swan-throat . . . drumming cooling the metal the glass full overfull cooling the glass the fingers flushing sleep leaving the taste of dampened sleep in the long silence of the throat*" (*SF* 110), Quentin goes to the toilet in the elegance designed for male defecation in the Ivy League.

By far the most animate figure in Faulkner's rendering of a child's drawing *of* a child drawing is a small spotted dog whose tongue tells the story. Whether water or milk, this puzzling blot, not quite spilt, is lapped into liquidity as if it has been poured flatly onto the page. Challenging the meaning of time in space, this drawing depicts a child learning to sketch, reproduces the hearth, picturing the site that is most familiar to representational art. But there is yet another story drawn in this gift. On the reverse side of this stylized picture given to his mother, there is another drawing (see figs. 17a and 17b). This picture in pencil on the back is less formal, and yet because this sketch is framed within the confines of the paper, this sketch is part of the son's present as well. Indeed, this sophisticated addition in pencil makes the surprising gesture of the de Kooningesque puddle-vessel on the other side quite believable. Featuring a slouching man in a hat walking by a pond or lake—a realized space that has dimensions—this sketch employs a spare visual economy to evoke a sense of substance and depression in the man's demeanor, in his bodily stance as well as in his desolate surroundings. Here, time is, if anything, more central as the young William shows the other side—an outside world that parallels as well as opposes his homely genre painting that depicts a child ruled over by an older female and a clock. The sense of the temporal in this penciled-in picture is either already located in Quentinian time or working toward this time-driven conception. Strikingly "in time" (*SF* 48), Faulkner's sketch in pencil leaves no doubt as it stakes out a year; a partially illegible sign in the ground reads "1910." Less stylized and more archetypal, this sketch presents a montage, juxtaposing an avian-faced man whose posture indicates either advanced age, affliction, or depression in proximity to a cut tree with its bottom exposed, its freshness belying the absence of a truncated stump. What remains decisively unknowable in this drawing is the prior state of the tree. As the multiple limbs branch out to end without abutting, these bifurcating extremities remain parallel lines that literally conclude, abrupt, at the point of erasure, as if the upper limbs have faded, severed by a rounded frame that lies within the bounds of the paper. Faulkner's experiment with conveying perspective in the concluding development of blocks in his ink drawing has a striking counterpoint and analogue in the exposed bottom of the tree. As the seasons reel out in organic and necessarily irregular layers from a center of origins, the thickening boll at the bottom of the tree accretes, ring by concentric ring, to insinuate girth. These enfiladed shapes amplify and add a sense of dimension to the tree's stem as they go beyond the width of the upper trunk to tell the annually inscribed history of this sharply sawn and readable tree. Whether this leafless tree indicates the possibility that there will be "no . . . enduring branch," like Poe's line of Ushers, remains unknown.

What can be known is that this gifted teenager, fully capable of sentimental design, speculated on death in 1910. In retrospect, this pencil sketch must be read as partial source, whether seed memory or harbinger, of Quentin's suicidal leap that takes place off page at the close of "June Second, 1910," the title of the second section of *The Sound and the Fury*. The presence of the clock alone could identify these drawings as a *memento mori* insisting on the inevitability of death. Taken together, this grandmother figure backed by a montage picturing the male realization of death constructs a telling document. Numerically driven (choosing 1833 for the arrival of Sutpen in Jefferson, 2nd Samuel 18:33 reads: "Absalom, my son, my son, Absalom"), Faulkner's choice of the title "June Second, 1910" for the second section of *The Sound and the Fury* goes beyond the second in which "again" is proposed as "the saddest word" (*SF* 110). June 2 was a resonant date for the detail-conscious author. Faulkner's maternal grandmother, referred to intimately as Damuddy, had died on June 1, 1907. The death of the grandmother named Damuddy haunts the suicidal Quentin's consciousness in *The Sound and the Fury* as death becomes as inevitable as his association of Damuddy's funeral with Caddy's primal stain: female change signals lost innocence. Articulating the tragedy that mocks this artist figure's dream of an unchanging art, these childhood drawings with their intimations of mortality also focus on time: the moment before life is changed by the knowledge of death. Not yet Faulkner with the "u" in tow, "Falkner" was already Faulknerian as he struck deep, commemorating his mother's birthday by picturing not just the life but the death of her own mother. First, Quentin jumps off the bridge in *The Sound and the Fury* on "June Second," a likely day for the laying away of his grandmother.[3] If Faulkner's ink drawing depicts the child before he knows death, the pencil sketch functions as the pubescent adolescent's signature as it pictures his mature command of dimensional space by locating a lonely male body in violated nature where the felled tree narrates the finality of time-cut death exacted as an ending.

Portrait of the Artists and the Violation of Art

As the older and self-named Faulkner (his family eventually assumed his spelling of the name) chose to depict the relation between the artist and the work of art in his fiction, his work remained fraught with the tension of primal scenes that locate body-obsessed sites of aesthetic reproduction. Picturing rupture by interrupting words, the experimental Faulkner inserted graphic representations into his fiction. Sites of pictured absences and pictorial presences, these shapes on the page mark the crossroads of art and sexual generation that for Faulkner was found in the union of the visual and verbal. From Faulkner's first novel, *Soldiers' Pay* (1926), his earliest works (with varying dynamics) revealed an obsession that would continue to shape—literally to inform—his most experimental texts. Faulkner at his most creative chose to write about the mystery of creation: what makes artists and compels artists to the extremity of making art. The painter in his unfinished "Elmer," who is pictured in another fragmentary typescript entitled "Portrait of Elmer"; the sculptor, painters, and writers of *Mosquitoes* (a group that includes two female artists: a pathetic, love-hungry-seeking woman who paints portraits, and a sexually vital and gifted lesbian poet who seeks the amusement of muses along with the men); and the sister-worshiping glassblower of *Sartoris* are all troubled by female sexuality and fecundity—forces made flesh in the bodies of women. As Faulkner's artist figures attempt to incorporate these female forms and forces into their work, their art is in direct conflict with bodily time intimated through patterns of blood: the stains of menarche and the stale smell of menopause or "old female flesh." In both versions of "Elmer" and in *Mosquitoes*, Faulkner's artists (compelled by the spell of Swinburne) are drawn into the mysterious eroticism of *Hermaphroditus*.[4] Overdetermined to the point of exposing their author, Faulkner's early narratives gender the materials of art and the work of art itself as his artists, whether protagonists or supporting characters, describe the conception, genesis, and origins of their own art in strongly sexualized accounts of creation. In eroticized descriptions, Faulkner's artists revisit the profoundly familiar connection between creation and procreation, wallowing in their desire to create art. Faulkner's artists revel in compulsions forged in competition: preoccupied—haunted and lured—by living flesh realized in the female body.

Faulkner's interest in this story had become central as early as the mid-1920s as he continued his efforts to write longer fictions. "Elmer" and its equally scrappy kin, "Portrait of Elmer," portray the story of an adolescent whose vague yearnings are articulated through visual and tactile obsessions with smokestacks, cigars, drugstore jars filled with brightly colored liquids, and slender pipelike structures. Critics have speculated (and Faulkner himself inferred) that "Elmer" remained unfinished because Faulkner's account of this would-be artist became too intimate and, if not precisely autobiographical, too cloyingly confessional in tone. Elmer is a painter who as a child has enjoyed crayons (cylindrical shapes that leave their mark), and even as an adult, he approaches a "new unstained box of paints" with a painful awareness of the erotic valences inherent in the materials of art:

> To finger lasciviously smooth dull silver tubes virgin yet at the same time pregnant, comfortably heavy to the palm—such an immaculate mating of bulk and weight that it were a shame to violate them, innocent clean brushes slender and bristled to all sizes and interesting chubby bottles of oil . . . Elmer hovered over them with a brooding maternity, taking up one at the time those fat portentous tubes in which was yet wombed his heart's desire, the world itself—thick-bodied and female and at the same time phallic: hermaphroditic. He closed his eyes the better to savour its feel . . . (Faulkner's ellipses)[5]

Elmer savors the moment before creation, the moment before possibility is violated by the artist's actual efforts to conceive. For Elmer, the materials themselves are "portentous"; the paint tubes are not just containers but generatively conceived as the yet-to-be-opened place that holds "his heart's desire, the world itself," "wombed" and waiting.

Elmer dwells on the idea of a self-contained object experienced as complete in itself: "an immaculate mating of bulk and weight." "Thick bodied and female and at the same time phallic," the tubes are provocatively hermaphroditic from the outset; "virgin yet at the same time pregnant," these tubes of paint embody "an immaculate mating." In the hermaphroditic materials of his art—phallicized wombs of desire—Elmer intimates both the masculine and feminine forces of conception and creation. A transfer of fertility, this immaculate mating of virginity and pregnancy seeds the "brooding maternity" of the artist. Here, in generative paradox, the "innocent clean brushes" and the "immaculate mating" propose a virgin birth that removes art from carnal acts, notably the sexuality that threatens to taint both creation and procreation. Focusing on the moment before conception, the artist is closer to God's creation than to woman's procreation: his desire that lies "wombed" is nothing less than the "world itself." The images that charge the male artist's act of creation with gender and sexuality serve to distance this process from the sexual defilement that is part of the traditional story of female procreation.

In *Mosquitoes*, Faulkner's novel about Bohemian life in 1920s New Orleans, there are repeated conversations about the tensions between life and art that recall the concerns of "Elmer." Neither Mr. Talliaferro (an admirer of art and the female form and a sales clerk in the sensitive area of women's clothing) nor Mrs. Maurier (a self-styled patroness of the arts) is an artist. Yet when the two meet on the street carrying packages, each turns out to bear an icon that, like everything else in this novel, becomes the occasion for a meditation on art and artists. Mrs. Maurier's object is "a dull lead plaque from which in dim bas-relief of faded red and blue simpered a Madonna with an expression of infantile astonishment identical with that of Mrs. Maurier" (*M* 17). After she reveals the object she is carrying, the curious woman insists on finding out what is in Talliaferro's hidden parcel, forcing the discovery of a bottle of milk. With her own "breast heav[ing] with repression," she asks, "A bottle of milk? Have you turned artist, too?" Responding with "abortive heartiness," Talliaferro responds: "An artist? You flatter me, dear lady. I'm afraid my soul does not aspire so high." As Talliaferro tries to represent himself as a "Maecenas" (the classical figure who is credited with bringing the arts to Emperor Augustus), Mrs. Maurier's androgynous niece interrupts his assertion, "I am content to be merely a—" by completing his sentence with her own devastating word: "Milkman" (*M* 18).

Earlier, near the opening of *Mosquitoes*, the sculptor, Gordon, has sent Talliaferro out on a mundane errand to get milk. As he sets out, Talliaferro is already embarrassed by the empty bottle he has been asked to return. Walking past "two people indistinguishably kissing" in a "darkling corridor," the "unwashed milk bottle" he clutches in his hand feels "clammy" and "unbearably dirty." Hoping to conceal the increasingly humiliating object in a newspaper, in desperation he wraps it in "his immaculate linen handkerchief . . . thrusting the bottle beneath his coat" where "it bulged distressingly under his exploring hand." Embarrassingly phallic in this exposition of masturbatory imagery, the empty bottle bulging beneath his coat becomes an appendage that (like the mixed appellation "Milkman") is disturbingly hermaphroditic. In the embarrassed man's hands, this object is a dirty vessel that is as suggestively seminal as it has been innocently bovine. Described as "nursing his bottle" when it is both empty and full, he is greeted by the grocer who identifies the full milk bottle as feminine, agreeing to "make her in a parcel."[6] Mrs. Maurier's odd joke about the milk bottle identifying Talliaferro as an artist is consistent with the associations in "Elmer" that gender the materials of art in images that picture them as simultaneously phallic and maternal.[7]

The icons associated with art in *Mosquitoes*—the simpering face of the virgin mother on Mrs. Maurier's plaque and the milk bottle—are juxtaposed with the work of art that has been carved by the sculptor, Gordon. Described by him as "motionless and passionately eternal—the virginal breastless torso of a girl, headless, armless, legless, in marble temporarily caught and hushed yet passionate still for escape" (*M* 11), Gordon's statue embodies his "feminine ideal: a virgin with no legs to leave me, no arms to hold me, no head to talk to me" (*M* 26). This virgin is inviolable only because man (as Gordon concludes) has not found a way to defile marble. Female yet unmaternal, virginal yet not entirely sexless, Gordon's marble torso presages the vases that Horace Benbow blows from glass in Faulkner's third novel, *Sartoris*, vases that are also adored as idealized feminine figures. Emphasizing the purity of his art, Horace Benbow describes one of his early creations as "a small chaste shape in clear glass, . . . fragile as a silver lily and incomplete."[8] Like Gordon,

Horace is driven by the need to make a virginal woman; his other delicate vessel is described as an "almost perfect vase of clear amber, larger, more richly and chastely serene, which he always kept on his night table and called by his sister's name." If this nightly paean were recorded on the page, Horace Benbow's beloved vase would be called "Narcissa,"[9] a name for his work of art that indicates that this "chastely serene" object is not just an echo but rather a considerably more fatal reflection of the artist in a feminine form. Quoting a line from Keats's "Ode on a Grecian Urn," he addresses both his sister and the vase without distinction as "Thou still unravished bride of quietness" (*S* 154).

To Horace Benbow, the works of the glassblowers whom he watches in Europe are "[s]heerly and tragically beautiful, like preserved flowers . . . [m]acabre and inviolate" (*S* 147).[10] Unlike the foul and defiled urns that haunt Joe Christmas's imagination in *Light in August*, the cracked vessels distinguished by the "deathcolored" effulgence of what Faulkner's Quentin reviles as "periodic filth," and unlike Caddy Compson, who by the publication of Faulkner's 1946 appendix to that novel has become a "frail doomed vessel," these works of art are presented as "unravished," virginal and "chaste." Like Faulkner, who insisted that he began bent over the blank sheet, "unmarred" and "inviolate,"[11] as he initiated *The Sound and the Fury*, the author's artists are obsessed with the virginity and chastity of their works of art. Driven to create art that is modeled on the female form, Faulkner's artists are framed through heavily emblematic imagery: the pregnant virginity of paint tubes, painted icons of the Virgin Mary, dirty and embarrassing milk bottles, sculpted female torsos without breasts, chastely feminine vases, and virginal blank pages. Taken together, these objects assume an accreting significance as their materiality provokes and embodies Faulkner's artists' drives toward creation.

In the misogynist world of *Mosquitoes*, real artists are men (or lesbians such as the allegorically named Eva Wiseman) who are driven in their art (at least in part) by the desire for women. While the addiction to words is "like morphine," the most driven writer asserts, "the Thing is merely the symbol for the Word" (*M* 130), but nevertheless even these words and other forms of art continue to focus on women: "every word a writing man writes is put down" to impress "some woman . . . maybe she ain't always a flesh and blood creature. She may be only the symbol of a desire" (*M* 250). Drawing on literary sources, the sculptor in *Mosquitoes* tells about the character Cyrano, who has trapped the woman he loves in the pages of a book (a story that Mrs. Maurier's epicene niece sees as the sculptor's own narrative of his truncated girl arrested in the moment of her flight). Art is a way of "making" women in both senses of the verb. Not only is art a means of seduction—an aesthete from *Mosquitoes* feels the need to discount "the illusion that art is just a valid camouflage for rutting" (*M* 71)—art itself is seen as replacing women as both love objects and as procreators. To compensate for their inability to create life from flesh, to procreate from their loins, these artists are compelled to embody the female. Notably, this fetishized form is embodied in virginal suspension: unmarried and unmarred, without child, breasts, or maternal milk. These objects are objects, unchanging and inviolable. Just as Gordon prides himself on the purity of stone—confident that marble cannot be defiled, Elmer feels happiest when he approaches "a new unstained box of paints," and Horace Benbow can breathe his art into shapes because the "crucible and retorts" (elsewhere called "tubes") arrive "intact." Intact, untouched, and unstained, the materials of art reappear introduced by words that articulate a presexual and nubile innocence that lies waiting: erotic, generative, and provocatively procreative, compelling the hands of the potent (if appropriately wary) artist.

In a distinctly gendered argument about why men need to create, the most prominent writer in *Mosquitoes* reveals that making art is "getting into life, getting into it and wrapping it around you, becoming a part of it" (*M* 320):

> Women can do it without art—old biology takes care of that. But men, men . . . [Faulkner's ellipses] A woman conceives: does she care afterward whose seed it was? . . . And bears, and all the rest of her life—her young troubling years, that is—is filled. Of course the father can look at it occasionally. But in art, a man can create without any assistance at all. (*M* 320)

Fairchild (the character Faulkner based on Sherwood Anderson), calling his own observation a "perversion," continues, adding: "a perversion that builds Chartres and invents Lear is a pretty good thing." Raising the idea of "[c]reation, reproduction from within," Fairchild asks: "Is the dominating impulse in the world feminine . . . as aboriginal peoples believe?" Here, in a surprising turn, this writer recalls the female spider who devours her mate "during the act of conception" (*M* 320), but this is not seen as an example of female appetite or dominance. Rather the creating man is placed in the female arachnid's stead as this description is said to depict the voraciousness of the artist who paradoxically devours life as he stands apart from it with a notebook in hand. In these overdetermined images, artists are linked to the female force in nature, even as this particular spider recalls the women of *Mosquitoes* who threaten to devour men, artists, and the possibility of art in their vigorously imagined acts of conception. In their intense formulations, Faulkner's women are seen as sexual creatures whose erotic pull (like the female spider's) is a harbinger of death. Women in *Mosquitoes* are feared as all-consuming, threatening to devour man and his seed; it is "[a]s though the earth, the world, man and his very desires and impulses themselves, had been invented for the sole purpose of hushing their little hungry souls by filling their time through serving their biological ends . . ." (*M* 305; Faulkner's ellipses). The artist's drive to create not only imitates and rivals the female act of reproduction, it is locked in a death struggle, trying to devour the world before the artist himself is devoured by the omnivorous hungers of embodied reproduction.

In *Sartoris* (1929) and in its uncut manuscript version, *Flags in the Dust*, the creation of art is figured as a scene of procreation experienced by Horace Benbow as he journeys into the belly of the beast—or, more specifically, into the womb of a woman. Visiting a glass-blowing foundry in Europe, Horace Benbow discovers the primal scene of his art forged in a fired furnace lit by the shadows of a benign Inferno. Telling his sister, Narcissa, the initiate recalls his descent:

> They work in caves . . . down flights of stairs underground. You feel water seeping under your foot while you're reaching for the next step; and when you put your hand out to steady yourself against the wall, it's wet when you take it away. It feels just like blood . . . And 'way ahead you see the glow. All of a sudden the tunnel comes glimmering out of nothing; then you see the furnace, with things rising and falling before it, shutting off the light, and the walls go glimmering again. At first they're just shapeless things hunching about. Antic, with shadows on the bloody walls, red shadows. A glare, and black shapes like paper dolls weaving and rising and falling in front of it, like a magic-lantern shutter. And then a face comes out, blowing, and other faces sort of swell out of the red dark with faces like painted balloons. (*S* 146–47)[12]

This descent into a cave with "bloody walls" (in *Sartoris*) or wet walls that feel "like blood" (in both *Sartoris* and *Flags in the Dust*) details a descent into the human body. The "tunnel" that appears "all of a sudden" coming "out of nothing" marks a moment of origin. Like the newly born coming into light and life, the "face [that] comes out blowing" and the "other faces [that] swell out of the red dark like painted balloons" emerge from the "red dark" head first. In this underworld, the source of the light is the heated crucible of art in which the faces that appear "blowing" are those of the artists who breathe their wordless materials into shapes. These pristine vessels, viscerally exhaled from the artist's body, balloonlike, are articulated and made in his breathing image. Descending into this womblike interior, Horace finds a site of creation in which artists are born headfirst as they open their mouths to give birth to their works of art.

The "chaste" vases that Benbow creates, like the one that he "called by his sister's name" and addressed as a "still unravished bride," are feminine figures; even as they (like Gordon's statue) represent only part of a woman, these objects emphasize the female body as a potential container. For Faulkner, who later would call the "beautiful and tragic little girl" he was trying to make in *The Sound and the Fury* "a frail doomed vessel," and who referred to a woman he fancied at the time as "a lovely vase," virginal females are empty vases, while experienced women are vessels that are already filled—signified by stains of procreative potential, realized in Joe Christmas's vision of menstruation as the "foul" "deathcolored" liquid that oozes unincorporated from the "suavely shaped" and "cracked" urns in *Light in August* (189). Although Horace sees the balloon heads of the artists emerge as vases are made, neither his vases nor the fleeing marble torso carved by Gordon has a head. In *Light in*

August, before the castration and murder of Joe Christmas, Faulkner returns to a scene of female castration. In a detail that recalls Gordon's abbreviated statue and looks forward to the decapitation of an unacknowledged doe near the close of "Delta Autumn," Joanna Burden's head is found nearly severed from her body in an enactment of the traditional Western insistence on the severing of the mind to make the body female. While this recurring trope of the headless woman constructs a female body untroubled by the supposedly masculine part located in the head, the doe in "Delta Autumn" has her head removed because her dead body tells a story of signifying absence: the missing antlers that would prove this particular creature is forbidden game. By cutting off the does' heads, the hunters conceal the fact that they have not respected the laws against slaughtering females. Even with the liplike rim of Horace's vase, the part to be worn away with kissing, Horace's virginal vases are headless vessels representing women as incomplete in the truncated body of art.

It is Gordon, Faulkner's most serious artist, who realizes that there is something missing—but he locates this lack not in his breastless, armless, legless, and headless sculpture of a girl (defined by absence that abrogates the need for dismemberment), but in the head of an actual woman. Returning from the boat excursion on Lake Pontchartrain that he has joined to look at Mrs. Maurier's niece (the girl who resembles his statue so much that she might have been the model for it), Gordon molds a female head in clay. This female head does not have the masculine jaw of the young woman whose body resembles his marble girl; rather, this head is that of the aged virgin who has not escaped time by being frozen in stone:

> It was clay, yet damp, and from out its dull, dead grayness Mrs. Maurier looked at them . . . Her eyes were caverns thumbed with two motions into the dead familiar astonishment of her face; and . . . behind them, somewhere within those empty sockets, . . . there was something else—something that exposed her face for the mask it was, and still more a mask unaware. (*M* 322)

Speculating on her emptiness, one of *Mosquitoes'* aesthetes (recalling the story of Mrs. Maurier's youth being traded in through her marriage to a much older man) sees "something thwarted back of it all, something stifled, yet which won't quite die" (*M* 326). In a Sherwood Anderson–like story, Fairchild, the writer, declares: "A virgin . . . She missed something: her body told her so, insisted, forced her to try to remedy it and fill the vacuum. But now her body is old; it no longer remembers that it missed anything, and all she has left is a habit, the ghost of a need to rectify something the lack of which her body has long since forgotten about" (*M* 326). Once a muse in her own right who inspired painters with her cold "Dresden china" beauty, Mrs. Maurier is now a hollow woman who no longer tries "to fill the vacuum" or "to rectify . . . the lack." Gordon dismembers Mrs. Maurier at the neck, allowing her cavernous "thumbed" eyes and "empty sockets" to tell her story. Earlier, preoccupied with the body of the virginal niece, the living echo of his marble torso, the sculptor takes Mrs. Maurier's face in his hands and exclaims: "Why aren't you her mother, so you could tell me how conceiving her must have been, how carrying her in your loins must have been?" (*M* 154). This is the most explicit articulation of womb envy in all of Faulkner's work. The hollow and empty Mrs. Maurier cannot tell him what he longs to know because (from his perspective) she has missed what he has missed. Although he makes women out of marble, he cannot make them out of flesh: the novel's "real" artist cannot be a vessel for the origination of life.

In *Sartoris*, Horace witnesses the primal scene of his art in the bloody dungeon: "all at once a tunnel" comes "glimmering out of nothing." This description of the furnace stands for what is not described: the way in which the vases emerge from the breath of the blowing men as tunnels coming "out of nothing." Both the scene and the activity witnessed in it evoke a startling channel of birth. In *Mosquitoes*, the fog-shrouded shore is associated, in Faulkner's words, with a primal "first prehistoric morning of time itself; it might have been the very substance in which the seed of the beginning of things fecundated" (*M* 169). The trees that "might have been the first of living things" are described as "too recently born to know either fear or astonishment, dragging their sluggish umbilical cords from out the old miasmic womb of a nothingness latent and dreadful" (*M* 169). In this fantasy, as with Elmer's experience of his tubes of paint, the "whole world" lies "wombed"—or rather the whole world being birthed emerges "from the miasmic womb of a nothingness." Taking their seed for generation from Genesis, these pregnant scenes locate birth and creation in an originary nothing.

In a related passage, Mrs. Maurier's niece, the androgynous muse with the treelike body, masculine jaw, and "buttocks that . . . might well belong to a boy of fifteen," has a vision of a nothing at the center of the female body. The girl speculates on the difference between her body and that of Jenny, the other desired female in the novel, whose breath is "a little regular wind come recently from off fresh milk" and whose body features "the soft bulging rabbitlike things women used to have inside their clothes" (*M* 240). Fascinated with the shape of the uncovered body of this most feminine of forms, as "Jenny's angelic nakedness went beyond her vision" to disappear past a window, the boyish muse is struck by an Emersonian vision of nature. After looking at her naked female body, "suddenly she stared at nothing with a vague orifice vaguely in the center of it, and beyond the orifice a pale moonfilled sky" (*M* 140). Near the opening of *As I Lay Dying*, this vision is revisited as Darl dips his gourd into the cosmos. The Bundrens' water bucket, which (in shades of Benjy's Caddy) smells "like the hot July wind in cedar trees," conjures for Darl the blackness of "a round orifice in nothingness": "It would be black, the shelf black, the still surface of the water a round orifice in nothingness, where before I stirred it awake with the dipper I could see maybe a star or two in the bucket, and maybe in the dipper a star or two before I drank" (*AILD* 11). While Darl is clearly the Quentonian, sibling-obsessed madman artist of *As I Lay Dying*, this passage finds its antecedent in the vision of *Mosquitoes'* epicene girl musing on the more developed figure of her feminine counterpart. And, if this girl's vision echoes in Darl's reflection, in which he sees the universe mirrored in a dark bucket, Darl's sight recalls the epiphany of the drunken Temple as she peers outward from the whorehouse bed into the darkness to see "the cryptic depths of ordered chaos" in "the clock face" "a round orifice suspended in nothingness" (*S* 151) in the language of the as-yet-unpublished *Sanctuary*.

Much earlier, near the opening of *Mosquitoes*, when Mrs. Maurier's boyish niece sees Gordon's statue for the first time and recognizes it as being like herself, she has yet another insight into the connection between the female form and art. Looking at the torso, Mrs. Maurier asks, "What does it signify?" Her niece, an unlikely reader of Shakespeare, answers, "Nothing." Long before he had begun to fashion his "tale / Told by an idiot, full of sound and fury / Signifying nothing" and the novel that stands as a line-by-line explication of Macbeth's famous soliloquy, Faulkner—like Macbeth—was concerned with what it meant to be "of woman born." In *Mosquitoes*, Faulkner includes two visions of the naked female form "signifying nothing." Both of these muses in *Mosquitoes*, the woman associated with milk and fecundity who becomes an image of nothing with a hole in it and the boylike girl-woman linked to the dismembered torso that she has determined signifies "Nothing," represent the womb of nothingness from which art and men are born.

Even as Faulkner's early fictions are tied together by a series of images that connect the artist and the work of art to the female body, this contradictory series of associations complicates the conventional narrative of the artist as creator into charged sexual terms in which the act of creation as well as the materials of art are eroticized and dangerous. At the same time, the only seemingly contrary notion that the artistic process is either hermaphroditic or an immaculate conception (or both) recurs to deny the necessity for a consummated union. As male or masculine artists, defined by their desire for women, make works of art that are objects of their desire, these female figures are sculpted to be inviolable and fated to be broken. Made from hard materials like marble and glass, these sculptural forms are by design frozen in a state of virginal reluctance. Gordon's sculpture and Horace's fragile forms represent the female body and the ostensible site of the womb, but these objects are cut off from the threatening maturity of the maternal breast and the milk-ready temptation of a nurturance that threatens to consume manhood itself. In *Mosquitoes,* women are crudely circumscribed as "merely articulated genital organs," while men are depicted as the sacrificial materials for desire made flesh as their aesthetic longings are consumed in the unwavering female drive toward procreation (*M* 241).

Incorporating the language of procreation and birth, Faulkner's fiction discovers a womb envy that locates a body to house the artist's fears of being feminized by his act of creation: making art that puts the artist in God's or, more viscerally, in the woman's place. The emphasis on art as a way of bypassing women, the solitary act of creation that is called "a perversion," intimates the artist's fear as he ventures to take the place of a woman. These images, which are potentiated by terror, reveal the artist's desires to control, usurp, and deny female sexuality—to create, to become, and to nullify the woman through the creation of art. Preoccupied, Faulkner's artists occupy the center of an anxiety about origins. Like the world that is created out of the "miasmic womb of a nothingness latent and dreadful," the act of birth, even the moment of conception, is narrated as a terrifying creation from a female abyss. Meanwhile, the womb that creates is repeatedly figured as the site of absence. The work of art may seem idealized in the form of the virginal and chaste female body, but in its dismembered state, art is always the site of a telling absence—the provocative gap of a signifying nothing.

Signifying "I": The Wild Reprise

"The Wild Palms" contains Faulkner's most intimate and tender portrayal of the female body; the flesh-driven woman at the heart of the story is an artist. Published in 1939 along with alternating chapters of a story called "Old Man," the volume as a whole entitled *The Wild Palms* is wild. Comprised of these two ostensibly unrelated narratives that take place a decade apart in time, both of these plaited and syncopated story lines focus on, among other things, the haplessness of men as they try to escape the inevitability of female pregnancy and the ultimate destination of such men: actual imprisonment. "Old Man" tells the story of errant characters, including the "tall convict" and a tree-stranded pregnant woman, cut loose and forced to go into the catastrophic flow of the Mississippi in the legendary flood of 1927, while "The Wild Palms," in Faulkner's own abbreviated description, is "about the doctor who performed the abortion on his own sweetheart."[13] "The Wild Palms," like Faulkner's early fiction and *The Sound and the Fury*, is about art and sexuality, about the problem of writing and reproduction and the crisis of creation and procreation. Published a decade after *The Sound and the Fury*, "The Wild Palms" marks Faulkner's return to the explicit dramatization of his concerns about art, artists, and the effort to embody the female that forms the fertile matrix for so much of his early fiction.

In "The Wild Palms," an almost-doctor with the evocative name of Wilbourne becomes a hack writer, and through this turn, the story develops into a painful allegory about the relation between sexuality and art. Returning like a bad dream to the scenes and themes of Faulkner's early work, this telling narrative emerges as a culmination of Faulkner's past obsessions. "The Wild

Palms" dramatizes this crossroads, realizing pain as creation and procreation come into fatal conflict. Fleshing out Faulkner's own brief synopsis of his melodramatic tragedy, the plot of the "The Wild Palms" could with equal accuracy be described as the story of a male writer who performs an abortion on a female sculptor to kill the woman artist. Significantly, "The Wild Palms" depicts an artist who kills a living woman in his botched and literal effort to rob the mother. In a statement (among the most infamous and quoted of the writer's pronouncements about the sources of his art), Faulkner warned: "An artist will rob his own mother for his art. One 'Ode on a Grecian Urn' is worth any number of old ladies."[14]

Mosquitoes centers on questions about art and creation, speculating without much aesthetic relief about art and sexual desire. In "The Wild Palms," desire is consummated, and the making of art appears to have become almost as physical. In a tawdry hotel where the lovers meet to consummate their passion, Charlotte Rittenmeyer, the female artist, refuses to have sex with her chosen lover because she does not want their erotic union to begin in "back alleys." As Wilbourne stands over her, "holding her wrists," Charlotte abruptly justifies her refusal by evoking her art: "I told you how I wanted to make things, take the fine hard clean brass or stone and cut it, no matter how hard, how long it took, cut it into something fine, that you could be proud to show, that you could touch, hold, see the behind side of it and feel the fine solid weight."[15] In her peculiar interruption, Charlotte's assertion that the hardness of her materials brings purity to her work clearly recalls the sexual aesthetics advanced by Faulkner's other serious artist, the sculptor of *Mosquitoes* who praises the hardness and inviolability of his marble. Making love in "The Wild Palms" is closely related to the making of art. Charlotte repeatedly insists that she likes "bitching"—her raw word for sex—and "making things with [her] hands."

The narrative of "The Wild Palms" opens near the end of the lovers' story, circling back to relate the events of the year in which the young intern Wilbourne leaves New Orleans with the married Charlotte Rittenmeyer. The abortion has already taken place at the beginning of the book, and it casts a pall over the chapters that tell the story of the couple's lives before the narrative brings them back to the Gulf Coast and the scene of Charlotte's death. In the opening section of the book, the suspicious landlord (who is a trained physician) tries to understand which "organ" is causing Charlotte's apparent illness, and (like the reader) he looks for the truth of a living woman that he can glimpse only through a screen of leaves:

> It seemed to him that he saw the truth already, the shadowy indefinite shape of truth, as though he were separated from the truth only by a veil just as he was separated from the living woman by the screen of oleander leaves . . . *I will have plenty of time in which to learn just what organ it is she is listening to.* (W 6)

The landlord asks Wilbourne what he does, and his new tenant inexplicably tells him that he is "trying to be a painter." Explaining that he is not a house painter, Wilbourne adds, "I paint pictures . . . At least, I think I do" (*W* 15).[16] This claim is never explained, but the assertion that follows, declaring that the woman is "probably still bleeding," turns out to provide an ominous commentary on Wilbourne's art.

The second section of "The Wild Palms" recalls the initial scenes of *Mosquitoes*, as Charlotte Rittenmeyer and Harry Wilbourne meet for the first time in "French town" in an artist's studio filled with unframed paintings. Charlotte's assertion to the young intern that she is a painter reveals an echo in Wilbourne's surprising assertion (pitched to the inquiring landlord at the opening of the novel) that he is a painter. Before this art-viewing evening is over, Charlotte tells Wilbourne, "Listen. I lied to you. I dont paint. I work with clay, and some in brass, and once with a piece of stone, with a chisel and maul. Feel." Instead of handing him a piece of her art, Charlotte asks him to feel her hand. The female sculptor takes "his hand and drew his finger-tips along the base of her other palm—the broad, blunt, strong, supple-fingered hand . . . the skin at the base and lower joints of the fingers not calloused exactly but smoothly hardened and toughened like the heel of a foot" (*W* 35). Linked with passion, works of art, "transformed steadily and endlessly beneath [Charlotte's] deft untiring hands" (*W* 76), emerge from and are equated with the palms of the living woman. Having given him her palm, the part of her body that stands in for the sculpture and which has itself been toughened and sculpted by the act of shaping art, Charlotte explains the difference between sculpture and painting: "I make . . . something you can touch, pick up, something with weight in your hand that you can look at the behind side of, that displaces air and displaces water." Introducing a hierarchy of the arts, she insists this is not like painting, "[n]ot poking at a piece of cloth with a knife or a brush like you were trying to put together a jig saw puzzle with a rotten switch" (*W* 35–36). When Wilbourne comes to call himself "a painter" as well, his perverse claim confesses a hidden horror since Charlotte herself has been put in place of the work of art. The living woman has become the painter's "jig saw puzzle" to be "put together" by her lover "with a knife." Wilbourne's gratuitous lie that he is a painter becomes increasingly disturbing as the novel progresses, particularly when he advances from brushes to knives.

Notably, Wilbourne does make a significant painting in "The Wild Palms," but he appears most graphically as a writer. Fired from his low-level position at a hospital long after he and Charlotte have become unmoored from their past respectabilities, Wilbourne writes stories for "confession magazines" that begin with sentences such as "I had the body and desires of a woman yet in knowledge and experience of the world I was but a child" and "If I had only had a mother's love to guard me on that fatal day" (*W* 103). The failed doctor appears to fear the "respectability" that makes men into "chiropractors and clerks and bill posters and motormen and pulp writers"—the respectability that makes even sinning and writing pulp fiction seem routine; yet, like the author of sensationalist works such as *Sanctuary* and *The Wild Palms*, Wilbourne is confident that he can write to "make all the money [he and Charlotte] will need" because "there seems to be no limit to what I can invent on the theme of female sex troubles" (*W* 115). As his and Charlotte's first winter descends, Wilbourne sits "before an unfinished page in the typewriter, believing he was thinking of nothing, believing he was thinking only of the money" (*W* 107). Yet it is not only the money. There is an intensity that surrounds Wilbourne's frenzy of writing that reveals the uncertified doctor has become entangled in the process itself: "I had tied myself hand and foot in a little strip of inked ribbon, daily I watched myself getting more and more tangled in it like a roach in a spider web" (*W* 114). While the artist in *Mosquitoes* is likened to the female spider who devours her mate, Wilbourne seems to have become entrapped in the web. Characters travel light in both of the alternating narratives of *The Wild Palms*, but as Wilbourne admits near the close of section 3, he would not have dared to desert his typewriter any more "than I would my eyelashes" (*W* 114). Recalling Faulkner's own famous defense of his long sentences, his effort to get everything said "between one Cap and one period," Wilbourne, neglecting to eat, writes his stories "from the first capital to the last period in one sustained frenzied agonizing rush" (*W* 103).

The obsessiveness of the bland Wilbourne's writing of pulp fiction is clearly out of proportion—out of drawing—as if he has been invested with the intensity of Faulkner's own Herculean enterprise.[17] Wilbourne's most significant act of creation in "The Wild Palms" as a whole is not his fiction but rather the strange painting. In the same section of the novel, just before he becomes a writer, Wilbourne tries his hand at painting. Day after day he sits in a clearing near his and Charlotte's cabin in the woods with "his half of the sketch pad and his converted sardine can color-box intact and pristine beside him" (*W* 96). Then, bizarrely, he begins to paint a calendar. As Wilbourne unravels "one by one out of the wine-sharp and honey-still warp of tideless solitude the lost Tuesdays and Fridays and Sundays," he realizes "that he could prove his figures, establish mathematical truth out of the sunny and timeless void into which the individual days had vanished by the dates of and intervals between Charlotte's menstrual periods" (*W* 96–97). Recalling Elmer with his new and "unstained box" of paints and Horace Benbow with the "intact" tubes, crucible, and retorts that are the tools of his art, in a phrase echoing Elmer's idea of "immaculate mating," Wilbourne claims that his decision to paint time in the form of a calendar measured in relation to a woman's bodily cycles has come from an "innocently conceived" notion. Wilbourne's painting is shaped by the tidal flow that marks the absence of conception and paradoxically establishes "truth" from the midst of a "tideless solitude" and "timeless void." In this painting of days, Wilbourne initially constructs a six-week month as he tries to deny the coming of winter; this troubling month in terms of the narrative as a whole introduces the specter of pregnancy long before the moment of conception.

Charlotte, who returns from her own painting expedition to find that Wilbourne is uncharacteristically happy, presciently asks: "Have you painted a picture or have you discovered at last that the human race really doesn't have to even try to produce art—" (*W* 98). While her query and its air of significance remain unexplained, Wilbourne's painting does indeed frame a question about the "human race" and the drive "to produce art." This painting, like the torso sculpted by Gordon in *Mosquitoes*, is measured against the truth embodied by a living woman.[18] Wilbourne's calendar charting the absence of conception, even without its anomalous and predictive six-week month, carries a procreative potential. Wilbourne's art, articulated and measured by Charlotte's blood flow, calls attention to the other possibility, an absence of blood, the absence of a period that would demonstrate how completely Wilbourne's art and his painting of days can be supplanted by procreation, by creation in flesh and blood.

Charlotte Rittenmeyer has already created in flesh and blood; she is the mother of two daughters who have been left behind with her husband when she leaves New Orleans to run away with Wilbourne. From the opening of the novel, which finds the couple beached on the Gulf Coast at their relationship's end, the new landlord, who has a professional knowledge about bodies but who has never been blessed or cursed to know passion, realizes: "His wife would have noticed the faint mark of the absent wedding ring, but he, the doctor, saw more than that: *She has borne children . . . One, anyway; I would stake my degree on that*" (*W* 10). As a mother as well as sculptor, Charlotte Rittenmeyer bears the marks of her experience on her body. Wilbourne, too, inspirited by their passionate affair, also sees Charlotte as a mother. At the close of the third and most extensive section of "The Wild Palms," the portion of the book devoted to the description of artists and art, Wilbourne confesses to McCord, the journalist friend who first loaned him the fetishized typewriter, that "there is something in me [Charlotte] is not mistress to but mother"; and, with intensity, he adds: "there is something in me you and she parented between you, that you are father of" (*W* 119–20).[19] What has been born of Wilbourne remains mysterious, but his reference to Charlotte and McCord as parents reveals that he sees himself as the child of an artist and a writer. The intensity that surrounds Wilbourne's creation of what he calls his "moron's pap" intimates that there is something primal in the frenzied acts of writing in which he imagines "the body and desires of a woman" and "a mother's love."

After leaving her marriage and her family, Charlotte begins to make figures, some of which are said to be the size of "small children." Working with paper soaked in water as well as wire, paint, shellac, and wood fiber, Charlotte makes her first "collection of little figures—deer and wolfhounds and horses and men and women, lean epicene sophisticated and bizarre, with a quality fantastic and perverse" (*W* 74); and even after she tells Wilbourne that she is "not an artist" anymore, Charlotte is unable to stop creating. Faulkner, the author of a play called *The Marionettes,* which he illustrated with drawings, pictures his woman artist making "puppets, marionettes" to be used in photographs "for magazine covers and advertisements" and possibly even for use in "charades, tableaux [in a] hired hall." Modeled out of shaped paper among other things, Charlotte's art shifts from its earlier focus on shaping animals and humorous historical figures to modeling great figures from literature: "a Quixote with a gaunt mad dreamy uncoordinated face, a Falstaff with the worn face of a syphilitic barber and gross with meat, . . . Roxane with spit curls and a wad of gum . . . Cyrano with the face of a low-comedy Jew in vaudeville" (*W* 77–78). Whereas Wilbourne in his writing assumes the confessional voice of the fallen woman, following a tradition in the novel that extends from Moll Flanders and Clarissa to the unrepentant, though severely punished, sexually transgressive heroine of "The Wild Palms" itself, Charlotte Rittenmeyer's rendition of great figures of literature "almost as large as small children" insists on her creative and procreative potential, her status as a mother and a creator of works of art. A creator of bodies as both mother and artist, Charlotte here creates literary characters in figures that both parody and give life to these characters from books.

Charlotte's "fragile perverse and disturbing" figures, at first "lean" and "epicene," become caricatures of literary characters. Falstaff, "gross with meat," is described as

> a single figure, yet when [Wilbourne] looked at it he seemed to see two: the man and the gross flesh like a huge bear and its fragile consumptive keeper; it seemed to him that he could actually watch the man struggling with the mountain of entrails as the keeper might wrestle with the bear, not to overcome it but to pass it, escape it, like you do with the atavistic beasts in nightmare. (*W* 77–78)

Wilbourne seems to see in the fat of Falstaff the female form of body within a body. Indeed, the entrails and the fate of man and woman as bearers of flesh is the nightmare of "The Wild Palms," in which Charlotte goes beyond the pure essences represented in the "epicene" or androgynous figures of her earlier art to embody the fate of woman as the keeper of flesh. In a related realization in Chicago, Wilbourne glimpses the physicality of art and its representations of bodies when he visits Charlotte at her night job as a window dresser in a department store.[20] Waiting amidst the mannequins, "surrounded by jointless figures with suave organless bodies and serene almost incredible faces," Wilbourne watches as the women who clean the store on their knees move about like "another species just crawled molelike from some tunnel or orifice leading from the foundations of the earth itself" (*W* 102). In contrast to this graphic image of the animal-like women who seem to emerge from the earth's "orifice," the "organless bodies" (who, like Charlotte's puppets, are designed to perform in tableaux devoted to advertising art) have an unbelievable serenity, a more pristine form that is reminiscent of Gordon's sculpture.

Early in "The Wild Palms," in a bizarre and intensely self-reflective reverie, Wilbourne muses over what is wrong with the role of characters in books in relation to people like himself. "*Maybe I can read* he thought. Then he cursed, thinking, *That's it. It's all exactly backward. It should be the books, the people in the books inventing and reading about us—the Does and Roes and Wilbournes and Smiths—males and females but without the pricks or cunts*" (*W* 44–45). While it is not entirely clear here whether the readers or characters are organless, Wilbourne himself is, of course, also a character in a book. In Jonson's *Bartholomew Fair*, the Puppet Dionysius wins a debate with a Puritan by pointing out that "your old stale argument against the players" about wearing the clothes of the opposite sex will not hold because puppets "have neither male nor female amongst us."[21] Unlike the organless bodies of the manikins, the literary creations of "The Wild Palms" have genders and bodies, bodies that become too real. Wilbourne is a character in a book who becomes a writer of stories about "Wilbournes" and tales of women whose fate is not unlike that of the "Does," if not the Roes, who are the sacrificial figures of Faulkner's "Delta Autumn." By the end of Charlotte's story, it is clear to the doctor "*just what organ it is she is listening to.*" Like one of Wilbourne's characters with an unwanted pregnancy ("I was sixteen and an unwed mother"), the object of the writer's fantasies and speculations about the maternal body, Charlotte dies after becoming "two" in her "gross flesh." Although a literary character, a puppetlike figure, as artist and as mother Charlotte pays the price of making bodies and having a body.

Pointedly, "The Wild Palms" provides a culmination to Faulkner's earlier concerns with the source of art and the struggle between creation and procreation. The writer who composes melodramatic and confessional stories in the name of passion, if not art, performs an abortion on the woman who is both the sexually vital artist and the embodiment of the mother. As Charlotte dies in a hospital room, a policeman, who calls Wilbourne by the name of "Webster," as if alluding to this miscreant's association with words, tells him: "You played hell, didn't you. Using a knife. I'm old fashioned; the old way still suits me. I don't want variety" (*W* 251). Earlier, as Wilbourne prepares to perform the abortion, Charlotte herself makes the same bitter joke. In a remark that recalls Quentin's sexualized memory of the knife in *The Sound and the Fury*, Charlotte quips: "All right. We'll wait a minute. It's simple. It's funny. New, I mean. We've done this lots of ways but not with knives, have we? There. Now your hand has stopped" (*W* 185–86). In Charlotte's words that continue to recall the mad desires of Quentin Compson, this extreme version of a negative primal scene will mean it "will be us again forever and ever." Much later, after they have returned south to Mississippi, Wilbourne looks at Charlotte's dying body, sensing "a black wind" that fills "the room but coming from nothing . . . no croaching shadow of ineradicable blackness, no shape of death cuckolding him; nothing to see, yet it was there, he not permitted to watch his own cuckolding but only to look down upon the invisible pregnancy of his horning" (*W* 238–39). The abortion, repeatedly imaged as a knifing or in this instance as a horning, is presented as a novel and violent revision of the sexual act: the knife that replaces the phallus in this construction has already been implicated in "The Wild Palms" as one of the tools of a lesser art.

In a grotesque literalization of the early themes of his work, Faulkner has invented a writer who sees no end to the market for stories about the sex troubles of women; moreover, this writer who claims to be a painter takes his knife to life, "poking" at the body of the woman he loves, the figure of fecundity who is both mother and artist. With appropriateness, the woman who is in pain from Wilbourne's earlier horning with "the knife" seems to ask him to go beyond painting: "poking" at her as if she were "a piece of cloth." Asking Wilbourne to become a sculptor, to create a dead center, Charlotte begs him to carve her out: "take the knife and cut it out of me. All of it. Deep. So there wont be anything left but just a shell to hold the cold air" (*W* 240). Here, the woman, suffering from the abortive attempts of a writer as he assumes the role of a painter, asks to be freed from life by being made into a shell. Although she cannot by any means become the virginal vase, this woman artist desires to be emptied of her procreative organs and pleads for the death that will come from being an emptied container, a version of the idealized work of art which takes the female form in Faulkner's earlier works.

In *Mosquitoes*, the sufficiency of Gordon's ideal woman, the truncated and inviolable statue, "passionate and eternal," is called into question by the appearance of the young woman who in her flesh seems to mirror while miraculously transforming and translating the inadequacies of art. Preferring hard substances like marble, perhaps because it will not melt like wax to the shape of his touch, Gordon has no hope of becoming a Pygmalion whose work, infused with the heat of his desire, will turn into flesh. Faulkner's Gordon is haunted and temporarily lured away from his art by a living Galatea whose bodily presence as she stands in his studio mocks the marble limits of his "feminine ideal." The sculptor of *Mosquitoes* does not mate with the muse to produce art; instead, he seems troubled by his susceptibility to the siren call of woman. Seen in this light, his carved art appears to be an effort both to bypass sexuality and to replace the need for reproduction—to create female figures (on one occasion, a body, and on the other, a head) without reproductive organs. Although procreation seems to provide both the model and the impetus for the human need "to produce art," Faulkner reveals through Gordon another driving force in art: the artist's desire to create objects that erase the means of reproduction.

In *As I Lay Dying*, the absence of a period after Darl's sentence, "*Addie*

Bundren is dead," reveals a lack of closure in death itself as dying becomes an incomplete part of a social process. As Dewey Dell explains the next time she speaks, "God gave women a sign when something has happened bad."[22] The female sign of "something bad" is a sign of absence. This sign, a missing period, does not mean death;[23] instead, like the earlier missing period, it marks the initiation of a process—the beginning of a life that will lead to death. If Wilbourne's first painting with a brush is calibrated on the absence rather than just the alleged innocence of conception, his second and fatal "painting" with a knife is also based on the fact of the same bleeding woman; in his effort to thwart procreation with art, the failed painter tries to bring the blood that will signal the absence of conception. Wilbourne's art, like art born of William, and indeed all art when read against the natural world, can only be (as Eudora Welty's Audubon realizes) "a dead thing."

In "The Wild Palms," the woman artist is killed by the writer. As she lies dying and unconscious, Charlotte Rittenmeyer returns briefly to herself and becomes, as her name itself intones, a curiously written figure. Standing with his hand on the doorframe, Wilbourne sees "the eyes open full upon him though still profoundly empty of sentience. Then he saw it begin: the *I*. It was like watching a fish rise in water—a dot, a minnow, and still increasing; in a second there would be no more pool but all sentience" (*W* 239). As her lover repeatedly tells her to "go back," Charlotte hears him "from somewhere because at once the fish became the minnow again and then the dot; in another second the eyes would be empty again and blank." Finally, her eyes in a rapid transformation become "a vortex of cognizant pupil," and while he watches, "the black shadow" that has been linked with death is "not on the belly but in the eyes." The "*I*," of course, stands for her identity, but there is also a play between the eyes and the I in which Charlotte's sentience becomes visually alphabetic. In an image which describes the fishlike body and jump of the capital letter "I" in cursive writing (𝒥), this passage also acknowledges Charlotte's closeness to death as she (like Quentin Compson in his final moments of narration and life) is reduced from the signifying "*I*"—the fish—to the minnow and the dot, the fragile and diminished identity of the lowercase "i." The dot here, while alluding to the shape of a letter, also marks a point of origin, the beginning of what will be transformed from minnow to fish and back again before emerging in what is described as a "vortex of cognizant pupil." The minnow's dive from her living eye punctuates death not just as diminution, but as an upside-down and vanishing "¡," an exclamatory end: !

Pleading to be cleaned out, to be released from her abortive life, the body of Charlotte Rittenmeyer, whose identity and sentience is embodied through the eyes in the shape of letters and the shout of silent (pictorially animalized) exclamation, becomes flat. In death, Wilbourne sees "the shape of Charlotte's body just indicated and curiously flattened beneath the sheet" (*W* 256). Witnessing what appears to be the "collapsing of the entire body as undammed water collapses, . . . lower than the prone one of the little death called sleep, lower even than the paper-thin spurning sole," Wilbourne likens his love's body in death to "the flat earth itself and even this not low enough." The most forcefully embodied of all of Faulkner's female characters, Charlotte Rittenmeyer is herself paper-thin and destined to vanish with "no trace left above the insatiable dust." Dead, the sculptor has become the opposite of her sculptures. As Wilbourne sees: "There was no especial shape beneath the sheet now at all and it came onto the stretcher as if it had no weight either" (*W* 257). This flattened figure concealed by sheets, which cover the fact that her eyes have been drained of their alphabetic and exclamatory leaping into intensity, erases the troubling physicality of the female body, picturing a desire to go back to a point of origins before this woman was conceived and given shape, blood, breath, and finally murdered into writing.

An Eye, a Coffin, and an Upside-down Triangle

In 1946, when the Modern Library decided to reprint *The Sound and the Fury* and *As I Lay Dying* in a single volume, Faulkner expressed his disapproval, insisting that he "had never thought about his *Sound and the Fury* and *As I Lay Dying* in the same breath."[24] In Faulkner's view, *The Sound and the Fury* should have been paired with "The Wild Palms" strand of *The Wild Palms*. William Faulkner had indeed thought about these two works "in the same breath," even using some of the same language in "The Wild Palms" that he had used ten years earlier in *The Sound and the Fury*. Harry Wilbourne, as he muses philosophically in "The Wild Palms," recalls the concerns and the narrative voice of the Quentin Compson of *The Sound and the Fury*. In his most Quentin-like reverie, Wilbourne speculates about

> the current of time that runs through remembering, that exists only in relation to what little of reality . . . we know, else there is no such thing as time. You know: *I was not*. Then I *am*, and then time begins, retroactive, is was and will be. Then I *was* and so I am not and so time never existed. It was like the instant of virginity, it was the instant of virginity: that condition, fact, that does not actually exist except during the instant you know you are losing it. (*W* 116)

This Hamlet-like obsession that in Faulkner's fiction so famously conjugates being and not-being follows a direct itinerary from Quentin to Darl to Harry Wilbourne, and even briefly (in an unpublished form) had a female conjugator of the verb. Significantly, this questioner of what it means to be an "I" is the pregnant Dewey Dell musing on her multiplicity in the holographic manuscript of *As I Lay Dying*.[25]

Faulkner wrote the "Appendix Compson" to *The Sound and the Fury* for inclusion in *The Portable Faulkner*, edited by Malcolm Cowley. Cowley's influential work brought Faulkner into print again, precipitating New Directions' issuing of *Light in August*. Reinvented as an author whose books could be bought, Faulkner borrowed an image from "The Wild Palms" (1939) to describe the bodily signifier (the sign of presence and absence) that is the crucial site of origins in *The Sound and the Fury*. In this 1946 appendix that Faulkner sent to Cowley (designating it as the fifth section of his 1929 masterpiece), Quentin is said to have "loved not his sister's body but some concept of Compson honor precariously and (he knew well) only temporarily supported by the minute fragile membrane of her maidenhead as a miniature replica of all the whole vast globy earth may be poised on the nose of a trained seal."[26] "The Wild Palms" contains closely related lines that represent not virginity but rather the equally "fragile" and suggestively "intact" moment of physical union—the "joint life" of a man and a woman. Pictured in bed with Charlotte, as Wilbourne lies "still and relaxed in the darkness while she held him, not even bothering to be aware whether his eyes were open or not," he "see[s] their joint life as a fragile globe, a bubble, which she kept balanced and intact above disaster like a trained seal does its ball" (*W* 78–79). Both Charlotte and Caddy, two women whose prowess is associated with masculine verve, are described with the same evocative shape that indicates their sexual potency and erotic potential. To make the bawdy point that Faulkner did not hesitate to dot in his golf course opening for *The Sound and the Fury*, both Charlotte and Caddy are pictured with or seen through balls.[27] Just as Faulkner's Elmer Hodge's "world itself" lies "wombed" in the untouched—intact—materials of his art, the "fragile globe" and "whole vast globy earth," these balls associated with sexually active female figures (however precariously imagined as poised on the nose of seal) picture their worldly potential.

Although there is no artist portrayed in *The Sound and the Fury*, Faulkner clearly identifies his obsessions with aesthetics in the novel through the terms that he had used to represent the artist in his early fiction. In an often-cited passage that concludes an introduction to *The Sound and the Fury* drafted in the summer of 1933 but published only after his death, Faulkner describes his relation to and the creation of his novel. With an image that recalls the obsessions of Horace Benbow, Faulkner provides both a reading and a reformulation of his stories about the making of art:

> There is a story somewhere about an old Roman who kept at his bedside a Tyrrhenian vase which he loved and the rim of which he wore slowly away with kissing it. I had made myself a vase, but I suppose I knew all the time that I could not live forever inside of it, that perhaps to have it so that I too could lie in bed and look at it would be better; surely so when that day should come when not only the ecstasy of writing would be gone, but the unreluctance and the something worth saying too. (*SF* 232)

In a similar version of the introduction written around the same time, Faulkner describes himself thinking, "Now I can write. Now I can make myself a vase like that which the old Roman kept at his bedside and wore the rim slowly away with kissing it. So I, who had never had a sister and was fated to lose my daughter in infancy, set out to make myself a beautiful and tragic little girl" (*SF* 228). As David Minter notes, Faulkner alludes to a passage in Henryk Sienkiewicz's 1895 novel *Quo Vadis*.[28] Remarking that "every man has his preferences," before asking the young man (whom he himself desires) whether he writes verses or plays the lute and sings, Petronius remarks that Scaurus prefers "his Corinthian vase, which stands near his bed at night, and which he kisses when he cannot sleep. He has kissed the edge off already."[29] In Sienkiewicz's same chapter, evoking the erotically charged relationships that Faulkner represents between artists and their works of art, the men admire slave women "resembling noble statues of ebony." Here, a Grecian maiden, who puts "statuesque folds in the togas of the lords," pointedly embraces a statue that "represented Petronius as Hermes with a staff in his hand": "Eunice stood on the stool, and, finding herself at the level of the statue, cast her arms suddenly around its neck; . . . pressing her rosy body to the white marble, she pressed her lips with ecstasy to the cold lips of Petronius."[30] Explicitly comparing the writing of his novel to the making of a vase and a girl, Faulkner makes it clear in these two unused introductions for the early reprint that he has cast *The Sound and the Fury* in the role of the female container, the sexualized and idealized work of art that haunts his early fiction.

While Faulkner openly links himself here to Horace Benbow and the art of creating sisterly vases, the repeatedly crossed female thresholds of *The Sound and the Fury* represent a change from the earlier plots that valorize inviolable materials and works of art. In *The Sound and the Fury*, Faulkner realizes that the work of art will never be chaste. He understands, to borrow a line from David Lodge, that words are "never virgin: words come to the writer already violated by other men."[31] Endowing Quentin with his earlier artists' obsessions with chastity, Faulkner turns in this novel to the moment of conception. *The Sound and the Fury* repeatedly recalls and reenacts the juncture of male and female as a site of origins that is crucial to art. In this sexualized conjunction, Faulkner coded words as male, and his dramatic insertions of pictorial forms, including the literalized absence of a word (the word-shaped blank space in *As I Lay Dying*), are symbolic embodiments of the female organs of reproduction. Faulkner introduces these disjunctive pictorial forms into his published writings on three notorious occasions: the "eye" in *The Sound and the Fury*, the "coffin" in *As I Lay Dying*, and the upended "delta" (in the form of an upside-down pyramid) in *Go Down, Moses*. With shocking and characteristic awareness, Faulkner used these pictorial interventions to represent types of female containers, bodying forth sites of origin and transformation, of conception, birth, and death. These female sites of origin are mapped in Freud's essay "The Dream of the Three Caskets," as the analyst interpreted his own dream to chart the psychic sites of a man's (men's) sequential location in female bodies: in the womb of the mother, in the female box during coital joining, and in the final "box," the coffin displacing dirt to form the mounded belly of a maternal earth, pregnant with the death of a newly filled grave. With archetypal precision,[32] Faulkner's images fit into this schema; each is finally like the female vases and vessels that have obsessed Faulkner's fictional artists. In "The Wild Palms," Faulkner's Wilbourne reveals a related conception of the female body as he describes the *petite mort* of orgasm. Speaking of "that one second or two seconds you were present in space but not in time," he pictures "the thunder of solitude, the shock, the death, the moment when, stopped physically by the ponderable clay, you yet feel all your life rush out of you into the pervading immemorial blind receptive matrix, the hot fluid blind foundation—grave-womb or womb-grave, it's all one" (*W* 117).[33] The least obvious yet the most obsessively represented of these images in the symbolism of *The Sound and the Fury* is the eye; in this novel, the eye is not merely the window to the soul but the displaced gateway of the female body: the site of lost virginity and the site of human origin. (The following discussion refers to fig. 18 on page 144 and to figs. 19 and 20 on page 162.)

The Sound and the Fury, a book that returns again and again to the signifying eye, is obsessed with the moment of origin, the sexualized conjunction that is implicated in both the reproduction of offspring and the production of art. In this novel, Faulkner is obviously concerned with the virginity or chastity of his characters, but like the artists of his earlier works, he is also concerned with questions about the chastity of art. In *The Sound and the Fury*, Faulkner's suicidal Quentin focuses on the concept of purity as a lost ideal. Obsessed with the idea of loss, *The Sound and the Fury* turns repeatedly to the moment of conception, the site of a fertile breaking that marks a scene of origins. While these fertile ruptures conjoin to produce art and to discover a latent potency in words, the male Compsons (the first three narrators of *The Sound and the Fury*) are faced with the threat of impotence as they find themselves caught in and taunted by the sterile futility of "just words." Again and again, the Compson brothers tell stories in which they find themselves feminized by their experience of dangerous female thresholds; entrapped in their own narrative constructions, the Compson boys find themselves looking at or knowing their impotence in a world where women, whether sensed by odor or act, embody life and death.

If both of Faulkner's 1933 introductions written for *The Sound and the Fury* picture Caddy, like the novel, as an erotically cast vase, this "tragic little girl" is conceived (in Faulkner's words from the appendix) as a "frail doomed vessel." Revising the image of the vase kissed by the Roman to a vase that one could "look at" rather than "live forever inside of," Faulkner concludes, "It's fine to think that you will leave something behind you when you die, but it's better to have made something you can die with. Much better the muddy bottom of a little doomed girl climbing a blooming pear tree in April to look in the window at the funeral" (*SF* 232). Faulkner shifts from the erotic scene of artist and vase into an image focusing on the doomed sister as a site of origins associated with death. As Caddy, the female character onto whom Faulkner shifts the viewing of the primal scene, tries to understand what is happening, she sees a forbidden sight that reveals the death of Damuddy. The source for Caddy's eye as a symbol is already pictorially present in the official seal of the University of Mississippi (see fig. 19), which Faulkner would have seen repeatedly in Oxford—at the post office, on the campus of his hometown university, on official documents, as well as inscribed in stone. In the final decade of his life, Faulkner would have walked through the foyer of the university library over this modern seal, the university's signifying eye. This pictorial and word-based source for Caddy's hymen is imaged as a ball perched on the "nose of a trained seal" before she is pictured for the last time in a "seal coat" ("Appendix Compson" 207, 209). The Faulkner who drew the birthday drawings in 1910, in which a grandmother watches a child artist learn to draw, transposed this scene (which also pictures the male realization of death through the montage of the felled tree) onto the scene of the sister climbing a tree, looking through a window onto death to picture the visual point of origin for the novel itself.

Writing about the composition of *The Sound and the Fury*, Faulkner claimed that this scene of seeing Caddy in the tree looking in on the dead Damuddy while her brothers looked up at her muddied drawers was the originary germ of the novel. In the same introductions, Faulkner placed the origins of *Light in August* through a related vision of a woman "walking along a strange country road," naming the pregnant Lena Grove as the primal (the fertilizing) sight of that novel's origins. Faulkner's accounts of the conception of these novels may be actual memories, screen memories, or conscious fictions.[34] In any case, these primal visions focusing female fertility reveal the depth of his aesthetic brooding, associating eroticized scenes of creation in *Mosquitoes* (and other works in which he depicts artists making art) with the crucial scene of voyeurism in which Caddy is posed as both voyeur and spectacle. The scene of Caddy looking through a window onto a secret scene of death is not only an image of the novel's conception but also frames this novel's obsession with the visual, signifying, and seeing focus on the eye in *The Sound and the Fury*.

In an interview in 1957, Faulkner explained that Caddy "was the beautiful one, she was my heart's darling. That's what I wrote the book about and I used the tools which seemed to me the proper tools to try to tell, try to draw the picture of Caddy."[35] This pictorial image of Faulkner's artistic enterprise in *The Sound and the Fury* is significant because Caddy Compson embodies the source of vision in the novel; and this image of her as a picture begins to locate Faulkner's inscription of himself as an artist in the text. If *The Sound and the Fury* does not explicitly portray an artist, it recapitulates Faulkner's representation of the conceiving of art and stages Faulkner's own surprising and overdetermined entry into the graphic representation of the visual.

In the fourth section of *The Sound and the Fury*, part of the narrative's symbolic scheme and way of looking at the world is made visible in the form of a sign. At a crucial moment in the career of the fainting and bleeding Compson brothers, Jason sees a sign. Worried that his head is bleeding and threatened by a man with a hatchet who has been unable to find his butcher knife, Jason gives up his futile search for his missing niece, Caddy's daughter named Quentin. Nearly blind, Jason is led to an "empty platform" where "the grass grew rigidly in a plot bordered with rigid flowers," and he sees "a sign in electric lights: Keep your on Mottson, the gap filled by a human eye with an electric pupil" (*SF* 193; see fig. 18, page 144; see figs. 19 and 20, page 162). With its eye that recalls the one on the Great Seal of the United States, the "all-seeing" eye of Providence (only pictured on the dollar bill the year after Faulkner's death) and its slogan typical of New South boosterism, this sign is represented on the page in a startling and, in relation to Faulkner's literary work, unprecedented way. In this passage, Faulkner, who is reputed to have done some work as a sign painter, actually reproduces the sign on the page, breaking into the words of his text and filling "the gap" with a pictorial eye.[36] This sign of the visual is given a visual form that changes the way the words encoded in the sign are read.

Like much that is electric in Faulkner's work, this overdetermined sign signifies too much. This sign instructs the viewer to "Keep your on Mottson," replacing a word with a picture. On one level, Faulkner can be seen as indulging in the Joycean bilingual wordplay that appears elsewhere in the novel: as the word is eschewed for a picture, other words like the French word for "word"—*mot*—can be seen, presenting the sign as warning: "Keep your on Mot-son"—as if to say, "Keep your eye on the word, 'son'" (speaking the unspoken word that constitutes the vacuum which is the provocation for *Absalom, Absalom!*). Or, still focusing on French, the sign speaks to offer advice about a way of reading: "Keep your on Mot son"—"Keep your on the 'word' [French: *mot*] 'sound' [French: *son*],"[37] on the sound of the word that does not appear, "I." Whether one hears or sees this wordplay or not, this passage is crucial because it pictures the sound of a word (a word sound) and replaces a verbal sign with a pictorial symbol. This picture opens up and fills "a gap" in the text and dramatizes a graphic illustration that stands in the place of a word.[38]

To understand what it means for Faulkner to fill this gap with a picture rather than a word, it is necessary to speculate on the meaning of this particular picture in *The Sound and the Fury*: the signifying eye that must also be understood as "signifying nothing." Obsessed with incest and driven by Oedipal tensions, the novel is particularly concerned with eyes.[39] The placement of the sign of the eye "in a plot bordered with rigid flowers" returns to the beginning of the book, to one of the novel's many scenes of sexual displacement and the first allusion to Caddy's name (or rather to the sound of her name). Here, in the opening line of the novel, Benjy sees "between the curling flower spaces,"

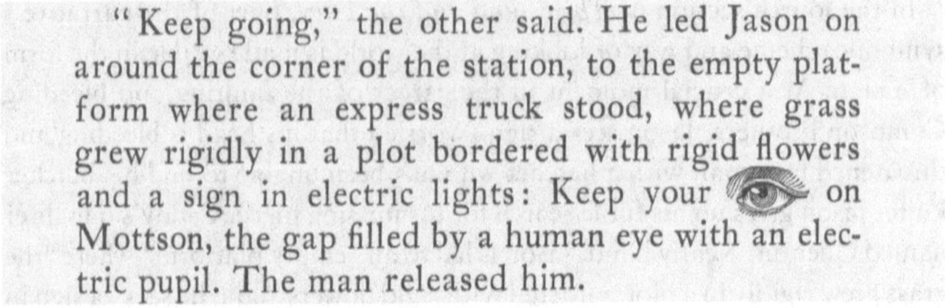

"Keep going," the other said. He led Jason on around the corner of the station, to the empty platform where an express truck stood, where grass grew rigidly in a plot bordered with rigid flowers and a sign in electric lights: Keep your on Mottson, the gap filled by a human eye with an electric pupil. The man released him.

Figure 18. The pictorial eye as it appears in the 1929 first edition of William Faulkner's *The Sound and the Fury.*

watching men hitting balls with sticks and calling their "caddies." The wordplay is obvious as Benjy and Luster look for lost balls. When Luster asks the young woman at the branch, "You all found any balls yet," he is told "Aint you talking biggity. I bet you better not let your grandmammy hear you talking like that" (*SF* 10); later the word itself has become unnecessary as Benjy looks down at himself and Luster tells him simply, "*Looking for them aint going to do no good. They're gone*" (*SF* 47). The inventory of symbols of and signs for castration in Faulkner's novels is well known, and I will not catalog the collations of one-handed men, one-armed straightjackets, one-handed clocks, or the biblical association of the Ethiopian queen Candace with eunuchs; but in this scene, which brings together "the curling flower spaces" and men with sticks, one might ask why Caddy looks for balls.

Throughout the novel, the eye is linked to the mystery of women's sexuality and the question of what sort of ball Caddy might have. Writing in the appendix to *The Sound and the Fury*, Faulkner insists on this female ball as he describes the "minute fragile membrane of [Caddy's] maidenhead" balanced like "a miniature replica of all the whole vast globy earth . . . poised on the nose of a trained seal." The language in this passage, which echoes the passage in "The Wild Palms," is also closely related to an even earlier description in *Sanctuary* that sees eyes as signifying lost virginity. In Horace Benbow's reverie that follows Temple Drake's story of her broken maidenhead, Horace imagines the annihilation of the central characters in *Sanctuary*, thinking of them as they are "all put into a single chamber, bare, lethal, immediate and profound." This fantasy of a lethal chamber echoes the entrapping walls of the maternal dungeon in *The Sound and the Fury* and, at the same time, visualizes the lawyer-artist's fantasy of erasing these figures through an act of writing, inking them out in a "single blotting instant." Horace's fantasy of death as "the only solution" for these characters is followed by an image of an abortion in which these figures are "[r]emoved, cauterised out of the old and tragic flank of the world." This reverie, precipitated by Temple Drake's description of her rape and the surprising flow from her ruptured maidenhead, closes as Horace Benbow remembers the eyes of a dead child: "two empty globes in which the motionless world lurked profoundly in miniature (*S* 221), a description that establishes the imagery for seeing Caddy's maidenhead in the 1946 "Appendix Compson" as "a miniature replica of all the whole vast globy earth." Seen together, these images reveal the profound connections between eyes and the female genitals as fundamental to a symbolic vocabulary that had been developed in *The Sound and the Fury*. Both Mrs. Compson and Benjy see the sign of Caddy's lost virginity in her eyes. Insisting that there is "no halfway ground . . . a woman is either a lady or not," Caddy's mother concludes, "I can look at her eyes and tell" (*SF* 66); and what might just be a cliché as it comes from this mother's mouth is supported by the recurring thoughts of her more insightful idiot son. Earlier, when Benjy sees Caddy on the swing with Charlie (probably kissing because it is the sight of kissing that precipitates this memory), he takes her into the kitchen, where she washes her mouth out with soap. In a later scene, the problem of Caddy's virginity is located as Benjy's focus shifts from the mouth to the eyes. As Benjy sees the scene, "Caddy came to the door and stood there, looking at Father and Mother. Her eyes flew at me, and away . . . Her eyes ran," and finally, "Her hand was against her mouth and I saw her eyes and I cried" (*SF* 44). Benjy drags his sister through the house again, but in Faulkner's morphology of houses the kitchen (associated with kissing, mouths, and eating) no longer provides appropriate cleansing; as Caddy tries to enter her bedroom, Benjy addresses the need to cleanse the body part in question by pulling her toward the bathroom.

In this displacement upward, Faulkner focuses on the eyes as the site of Caddy's lost virginity. Perhaps familiar with the vulgar nineteenth-century colloquialism for sexual intercourse, "to be poked in the blind eye," Faulkner (who explored every other valence of this female name in the novel, notably white light and the incandescence of the fire reflected in Caddy's eyes) extends his allusions to gesture toward other meanings of Caddy's formal name, "Candace," recognizing her as the one-eyed warrior queen of ancient Ethiopian legend.[40] The broken eyes and balls of *The Sound and the Fury* are signs of feminization. Yet the specter of Caddy's lost virginity also embodies potential generation and conception; this fertile breaking, which precedes the production of progeny, is also essential to the generation of meaning through the fertile ruptures characteristic of modernist discourse. Caddy's maidenhead, like a "miniature replica of all the whole vast globy earth . . . poised on the nose of a trained seal," is there to be broken; and although the loss or breaking of balls signals castration or impotence in men, in Caddy Compson and other women like her, this rupture is a fertile breaking that marks the beginning of female potency. When broken, Caddy's fragile maidenhead, her ball-like hymen, establishes her power as a sexual figure. If "purity is a negative state," as Quentin's internalized voice of the father avers, the loss of virginity opens the possibility for generation—the moment of conception that, in Faulkner's fiction, marks the beginning of time.

Writing "The Wild Palms," the work that, as we have seen, Faulkner considered closest to *The Sound and the Fury*, Faulkner returned to the bodily eye as an image associated not merely with virginity but also with the necessity of cutting or breaking to effect change, a severing that is linked to the cutting force of female sexuality. On the train leaving New Orleans, Charlotte speaks of severing her ties to her husband: "Only it's not finished . . . It's not finished. It will have to be cut." To Wilbourne's query, "Cut?" Charlotte with biblical backing replies, "'If thine eye offend thee, pluck it out, lad, and be whole.' That's it. Whole. Wholly lost—something. I've got to cut it. That drawing room back there was empty. Find the conductor and engage it to Jackson" (*W* 50). Charlotte's bid for wholeness depends on the cutting that will take place in an "empty" "drawing room." The cutting, an act of sexual consummation that will release her from the residual ties of her marriage, is likened to the plucking out of an offensive "eye." Adapting this well-known biblical injunction against adultery to her own adulterous purposes, Charlotte alludes to a passage that proposes plucking out eyes and severing right hands,[41] the cutting away of offensive parts of the body in a paradoxical effort to become whole.

In *Mosquitoes*, the authentic artist Gordon locates the problem with women somewhere about the eyes. Shaping the head of the aging and seemingly virginal Mrs. Maurier, Gordon emphasizes her vacuity, her failure to bear children, by focusing on her eyes: "Her eyes were caverns thumbed with two motions into the dead familiar astonishment of her face." Behind these eyes, "somewhere within those empty sockets," lies the story of her face as a mask and, by implication, her body and loins as another type of concealing clay. The "thumbed" eyes represent the artist's displacement of the procreative act as well as the emptiness of this woman with caverns and sockets. Gordon sculpts to reveal the emptiness of Mrs. Maurier's eyes; and in the words of Fairchild, the writer, Gordon's art has exposed "the vacuum" that this patroness of the arts no longer tries to fill, "the lack . . . her body has long since forgotten about" (*M* 326). In terms of the clay-shaped work of art, this last "lack" is made explicit in the absence of the body or, more precisely, in the displacement by which the head has become the body.

In a 1956 interview, Faulkner insisted that Caddy was the genesis of a novel that had been generated "to fill [the] vacuum" left by a missing woman, a lost sister. Combining the sexual and maternal, Caddy is the absence around whom Faulkner structures the entire novel. Entering the text with the power of metaphor (a kind of caddy in a novel that begins on a golf course), Caddy is the means of transporting meaning; she is the fertile figure who bears or carries meaning across the broken surface of a narrative comprised of shards of memory joined to fragments of immediate experience. Like an empty vessel, Caddy (whose name can also mean a small box to carry or to organize things) is filled, given shape by the words of her brothers, the narrators of the first three sections of the novel. The missing figure that each brother tries to reconstitute in both her being and meaning, Caddy is a silent sister, speaking directly in the first person only once in the novel, and here only in the ineffectual written words of a letter sent to Jason and read into the record of the novel. Paradoxically, as so many critics have understood, Caddy is the character who is most present in the novel.[42] Like the silent and maimed figure of the soldier in Faulkner's first novel, *Soldiers' Pay*, like the inanimate statue that cannot replace the real woman in *Mosquitoes*, like the dead twin who haunts the living one in *Sartoris*, Caddy is the generative vacuum at the center of *The Sound and the Fury*.[43] As a troubling maternal absence who anticipates the powerful presence of the dead and rotting Addie Bundren of *As I Lay Dying*, the figure of Caddy is a pregnant absence that provokes speech and drives the narrative of the novel forward, becoming to some degree like Addie Bundren: the very air that the remaining characters are left to breathe.

Like Addie, Caddy appears to occupy the dead center of the novel. *The Sound and the Fury* is not just a "tale told by an idiot," haunted by at least one death-seeking life that is just "a walking shadow"; the novel also calls "Out, out brief candle" as it worries with "sound and fury" over a "signifying nothing." The name of the missing heroine, Candace, with its etymological link to the word "candle," resonates with Macbeth's plea: "Out, out brief candle." This image of a candle to be blown out or snuffed underlines the association between Caddy's sexual initiation and death. In *As I Lay Dying*, Addie Bundren's dying eyes are "like two candles when you watch them gutter down into the sockets of iron candle-sticks" (*AILD* 8). While "Candace" means (among other things) "white fire," Benjy alone sees that Caddy's "hair was like fire, and little points of fire were in her eyes" (*SF* 46), and this moment captures their only flash of incandescence. Rather, Caddy's eyes, like Caddy herself, signify change in *The Sound and the Fury*; like her evanescent and temporal maidenhead, Caddy casts the light of a guttering or extinguished candle, appearing only in the transitory flashes that, as André Bleikasten observes, have come to represent her in the novel: "reflections, shadows, moonlight, a cloud, a breath, 'a long veil like shining wind.'"[44] Whether shadow or moonlight, Caddy simultaneously signifies death and the fertilizing light of creation.

The eyes are of crucial importance to Quentin as he recalls scenes from the past in which he symbolically loses possession of the phallus in the form of a knife and a gun.[45] In his most extensive interior monologue—the long reverie—Quentin recalls an erotically charged scene in which he and Caddy appear to have had a detailed, technical discussion about how to kill themselves. Ostensibly a scene of attempted suicide that is disrupted when Quentin drops his knife, the narrative reads as an embarrassingly detailed lesson in sexual intercourse or masturbatory technique:

> will you close your eyes
> no like this youll have to push it harder

touch your hand to it
but she didnt move her eyes were wide open. (*SF* 96)

Almost immediately Quentin evokes the primal scene of Caddy seeing; faced with her eyes, he pictures her muddy panties: "Caddy do you remember how Dilsey fussed at you because your drawers were muddy" (*SF* 96). A few lines earlier, he has disrupted memory by remembering this same interlude from the deeper past: "do you remember the day damuddy died when you sat down in the water in your drawers." This initial query itself has followed, seemingly provoked by another fertile conjunction of symbols: a knife and the rim of a woman's eyes. In a line that recalls the sticks and "the curling flower spaces" or plots surrounded by flowers and filled with eyes, Quentin says: "I could see a rim of white under her irises I opened my knife" (*SF* 96). After Quentin recalls that Caddy's "muscles gathered," the reverie-immersed Quentin concludes: "I dropped my knife." Although the causal relation is unclear here (Quentin may have already mislaid the knife), the loss of the knife is clearly linked to the force of Caddy's bodily presence. Like the muscular snake in Cather's *My Ántonia*, which is an emblem of power but not phallocentrism as it encircles Jim Burden's leg, Caddy's gathering muscles represent a literally disarming and potentially unmanning female potency.

In the related confrontation with his sister's first lover, Dalton Ames, which Quentin recalls as his reverie continues unbroken, Quentin refuses a gun that is presented to him "butt first" (*SF* 102). In terms of this face-off between men, Quentin refuses to assume the masculine position. As smoke streams from the barrel of Ames's gun in the same way as just moments before cigarette smoke has streamed from his nose, Quentin refuses the gun and faints. "[P]ass[ing] out like a girl," Quentin gives himself a bloody eye that allows him to look "at [Dalton Ames] through a piece of colored glass"[46] (*SF* 102). This detail of the bloody and broken eye confirms his feminization. Later, Quentin is aware that Caddy's lover has never really seen him, that Dalton Ames has only seen him through her—as if he is looking through "colored glass" (*SF* 111). Broken glass and bloody eyes appear here in a dense conjunction of images, which brings Quentin back to the present and memories of a more recent past. The pain from his punched eye ends his reverie by bringing him abruptly back to the present: his face feeling "cold and sort of dead, and my eye, and the cut place on my finger was smarting again" (*SF* 104).

Found once in its more common usage to describe the frames of a woman's "spectacles" (with their "neat gray rims . . . like a cash box in a store" [*SF* 79]), the unusual word "rim" is used twice by Quentin to describe the edges of Caddy's eyes. Quentin sees "a rim of white under her irises" as he opens his knife in the scene of attempted murder and/or suicide, and in the same scene he recalls that "she lifted her face then I saw she wasnt even looking at me at all I could see that white rim" (*SF* 99). In a telling usage, the word "rim" first appears much earlier in Quentin's narrative in another displacement of the sexual act that emphasizes the novel's obsession with dismemberment. Here, Quentin smashes the glass face of his watch, twists off its hands, and intently "cleaned the rest of the glass out of the rim" (*SF* 51). Wrenching off the hands, he slices his own hand and the cut finger leaves a "red smear" on what (later in this section) is called "the eye of the clock." This connection between eyes and the face of time reverberates from the beginning of the novel through a series of associations linking watching, the sound of chimes that tell time, and eyes. Just before Quentin breaks the glass of his watch, he observes a sparrow watching him with his "cocked . . . head . . . [h]is eye . . . round and bright. First he'd watch me with one eye, then flick! and it would be the other one, his throat pumping faster than any pulse. The hour began to strike. The sparrow quit swapping eyes and watched me steadily with the same one until the chimes ceased" (*SF* 50).

In a subsequent scene, still quite early in Quentin Compson's last day, the Harvard freshman enters an increasingly symbolic and temporally fatal world where watching and watches and, finally, eyes and watches are part of an elaborate sexual displacement that goes beyond the association of voyeurism with the concept of the penetrating gaze. After Quentin shatters the glass of his watch, he enters a jewelry shop with watches in the window to find a man wearing the eyepiece that is a tool of watch repair: "There was a glass in his eye—a metal tube screwed into his face . . . He looked at me again . . . and pushed the glass up onto his forehead. It left a red circle around his eye and when it was gone his whole face looked naked" (*SF* 53–54). The explicit description of a "tube screwed into [a] face," which leaves a "red circle" around the "eye" of a "face" that looks "naked," marks this hallucinatory account of eyes as a graphic scene of sexual conjunction. With "a glass in his eye," the jeweler is prepared to look at—to watch—watches. The threat to the eyes is emphasized as the jeweler shifts the tube (described elsewhere as "tunneled into his face") "onto his forehead"—recalling the singular and displaced eye of the Cyclops that is put out by the wily Odysseus, who has called himself "Nobody." Uniting the screwed phallic tube with the red circle on the naked face, the imprinted visage of the jeweler projects his omnipotent gaze unwary of the continuing threat of feminization through castration.

However, there is something even more troubling in this intense metonymic and synecdochal economy. Entering the jeweler's shop, Quentin hears a room "full of ticking . . . and I could hear a big clock on the wall above his head. He looked up, his eye big and blurred and rushing beyond the glass. I took mine out and handed it to him" (*SF* 53). Although Quentin then says, "I broke my watch," there is a momentary slippage here in which the "eye . . . rushing beyond the glass" becomes the focus of the thought. In one of Faulkner's characteristic elisions through indefinite pronouns, Quentin (like St. Lucy or the mythological sisters who share a single eye) seems to take his "out" and hand "it" to the man. From the beginning, Quentin seems destined to break both his watch and the eye for which the word "watch" stands; the connection between the two images is confirmed as they are brought together once again: "He held my watch on his palm and looked up at me with his blurred rushing eye" (*SF* 53). For Quentin, the watch with its glass and "rim" (like the vase "which the old Roman kept at his bedside and wore the rim slowly away with kissing it") is seen as a site of origins. Breaking the watch is part of his futile effort to stop time. This is Quentin's ritualized act meant to thwart conception: to stop time before it begins.

Paradoxically, although the hands of the watch can be twisted off, the breaking of glass takes Quentin into another more potent tradition (preserved in the rituals of fairy tales and Jewish weddings) in which the broken vessel signifies fertility.[47] The "red smear" across the face of the watch in Quentin's ritualized enactment of dismemberment is not simply the mark of a broken hymen; as Miss Rosa Coldfield warns in *Absalom, Absalom!*, "Blood can come from anywhere" (*AA* 123). The Quentin Compson of *The Sound and the Fury* is confused about blood in acts that involve men and women, tellingly musing, "Oh her blood or my blood Oh" (*SF* 85); and he is particularly confused about castration and sexual difference. In a telling juxtaposition of thoughts, as he recalls Verge's story about a man who actually castrates himself, "flinging them backward over his shoulder," Quentin immediately thinks of the female body and is stumped: "It's not not having them. It's never to have had them then I could say O That That's Chinese I dont know Chinese" (*SF* 73). In Quentin's meditation on the lack associated with women, the "O" is serious. This is an extremely rare moment in *The Sound and the Fury* in which the text articulates an "O" rather than an "Oh" (another rare appearance of the "O" is an apostrophe to Jesus outside of a Memphis brothel)—and in this context this simplified form clearly marks a turn to the alphabetic pictorial. (Faulkner had already used a pictorial "O" in *Mosquitoes* to depict the shape of the red circle of a woman's mouth: "Jenny's eyes were quite round and her mouth was a small red 'O.'") In *The Sound and the Fury*, this "O" stands as a picture of absence: a picture of what is there if you never "have had them," the zero, aught, or naught—what has been referred to in slang as "the divine monosyllable." Faced with the female as the source of generation, Quentin finds words to be inadequate, as if he is speaking in an unknown tongue. For Quentin, female difference is like Chinese: an unknown, a foreign language that is nonetheless more telling because of its foundation in pictographs. Meanwhile, the sounded "o"—which Quentin hears as "WhoOooo" in the hoot of an owl that warns of death as it questions "who" is responsible for Caddy's illicit pregnancy—echoes through the intense replication of this letter-sound, haunting and marking the scene of female reproduction: "WhoOoooo.   WhoOoooo.   WhoOooooooooooooooo. *Got to marry somebody*" (*SF* 73; long spaces, italics, and absence of period all Faulkner's).

In the fourth section of the novel, Jason is at the center of the nexus of symbols represented by the eye and glass, recalling the colored glass, the broken glass of the watch, the cut finger, and the twisted-off watch hands. Here, once again, Jason, who presents himself as obsessed with the future, finds himself caught in the past as he is caught with his hand in his pockets trying to rob the recesses of the maternal body in a scene that confirms his powerlessness in relation to women. Looking for the culprit to blame for a broken window in his bedroom, Jason realizes that his inner sanctum has been violated by a hand. Jason begins by saying, there is "a hole in the window you could stick your hand" through, but then is silenced: "his voice ceased, ebbed, left him staring at his mother with eyes that for an instant were quite empty of anything" (*SF* 174). In this pointed link to Quentin's feminization through bloody and broken eyes, Jason reveals his knowledge of loss as he faces the conjunction of broken glass and a hand. This loss recorded in "eyes . . . empty of anything" goes beyond the loss of the hoarded money and his niece Quentin, who has been the living hostage to his revenge.

Caddy's brother Quentin has had problems with knives and guns; before he is threatened with knives and hatchets, Jason is depicted here as having problems with keys. Having stolen and then been robbed of female treasure, Jason is shown trying to rob a female interior: the pockets of his own mother. In this shocking scene, unable to wait for his mother to give him the key to his niece Quentin's locked room, "[h]e fell to pawing at the pockets of the rusty black dressing sacque she wore." As she resists, "clutching her sacque about her" and calling Dilsey for help, Jason pulls from "her pocket . . . a huge bunch of rusted keys on an iron ring" (*SF* 175). From his childhood, Jason's greed is linked to his habit of keeping his hands in his pockets. If Benjy's hands (and ultimately in one of *The Sound and the Fury*'s most graphic literalization of symbols, his genitals) are threatened because of the dangers of a gate he associates with Caddy, Jason's hands are endangered by being caught in pockets and, particularly, by his futile efforts to rob maternal pockets.

After looking into the empty room that is "not a girl's room . . . not anybody's room," he goes to his own room to find that his hidden "box" has been broken into; and Jason is left holding what has become a useless key. Even before his cache has been stolen from him, the money Jason has stolen from Caddy's daughter Quentin has been an emblem of and substitute for his loss of power, the job (promised by Caddy's brief husband, the banker brother-in-law)[48] that has been lost as a result of his sister's sexual promiscuity:

> he had been outwitted by a woman, by a girl. If he could just believe it was the man who had robbed him. But to have been robbed of that which was to have compensated him for the lost job, which he had acquired through so much effort and risk, by the very symbol of the lost job itself, and worst of all, by a bitch of a girl. (*SF* 191)

Jason has been feminized not only by his loss of a promised job in a bank as a result of Caddy's illicit pregnancy but also, anticipating the feminist complaint of nearly half a century later, ended up with the baby instead of a job. Like the eunuch who is entrusted with Queen Candace's treasure in the Bible, Jason has been entrusted with Caddy's female treasure, but this twentieth-century eunuch has been robbed.

Left standing at the threshold of what had been a girl's room, Jason is aware of his own broken box. Both of these structures have been eviscerated and robbed of their female interiors: Caddy's money and her grown baby. Writing nearly ten years later in "The Wild Palms," Faulkner makes explicit this association of the money box with female sexual organs. Trying to understand his failure in performing an abortion on his lover, Wilbourne muses, "*I loved her . . . A miser would probably bungle the blowing of his own safe too. Should have called in a professional, a cracksman who didn't care, didn't love the very iron flanks that held the money*" (W 250). Anticipating Wilbourne, Jason is caught in a cycle of inevitable return to a scene of origins where in a parodic replaying of his own birth he tries to rob the pockets of the mother. Associated with violated and vacant female interiors, revealing his loss in his "empty" eyes, Jason suffers from a more primal sense of loss, some wound from the past. As he races toward Mottson where he is faced with the sign of the eye, he reads the change to better weather as a "cunning stroke on the part of the foe, the fresh battle toward which he was carrying ancient wounds" (*SF* 190). Jason is not merely feminized in these scenes; he robs the keys from his mother's body as he himself seems to stand in the position of the wounded mother. Confronted by broken glass, an empty room, an empty box, stolen money taken by his absent niece, Jason bears the wound of the female, the cutting of a "cunning stroke."

Signifying Nothing

> I love you dammit, the red hair the violet eyes the taste of your mouth the drop of ambrosia that lives in your navel the rich close patch of your delta with the sweet hole in the center of it.
>
> —William Faulkner in a letter to Joan Williams[49]

In *The Sound and the Fury*, words are linked to men, male sexuality, and ultimately to masculine impotence. When Benjy hears himself as "trying to say," running through the gate after the girl he associates with his absent sister, his gestures are interpreted as sexual and he is literally castrated. In the related scene in which Jason has been robbed, his impotence takes the form of words and feeds on the sound of his story of loss. Speaking to the sheriff, Jason feels a "sense of injury and impotence feeding upon its own sound . . . He repeated his story, harshly recapitulant, seeming to get an actual pleasure out of his outrage and impotence" (*SF* 188–89). Trying to think of something else, he imagines himself in bed beside Lorraine (his prostitute friend from Memphis), "only he was just lying beside her, pleading with her to help him, then he thought of the money again" (191). If Jason is rendered powerless by his relation to money, like Benjy he displays his impotence by "trying to say," trying to plead for help from the sheriff and from Lorraine (a sexually identified woman). Considering the other brother, Donald Kartiganer argues that Quentin, "[c]onfronted everywhere with his impotence, . . . is desperate to believe in the power of words alone." In his desire "to see words as the originator rather than the imitator of deeds," writes Kartiganer, Quentin tries "to convince Caddy of the reality of his fantasy, not that they have literally made love but that words have a substance more real than bodies."[50] In his raging interior monologue, Quentin insists: "*Ill tell you how it was Ill tell Father then itll have to be because you love Father . . . Ill make you say we did Im stronger than you Ill make you know we did you thought it was them but it was me listen I fooled you all the time it was me*" (*SF* 94). For Quentin, saying replaces doing; as in the cases of Benjy and Jason, saying for Quentin also sounds wounded potency as words stand in for a sexual act.[51]

Whereas words and "trying to say" dictate the terms of the impotence of the Compson brothers in *The Sound and the Fury*, the novel also offers a more redemptive possibility. The "dark twin" of the male Compsons' sterility is found in the vitality of the Gibson family—in particular, Dilsey, the powerful figure who is the reigning spirit of the narratively framed objective world that appears to be seen and made visible to the eye in the fourth section. In this section, signs take a physical form. In the final section, which is presented in third-person narration, Caddy is literally missing (her name is repeated on only one occasion as Luster taunts Benjy); and her daughter, her emotionally diminished substitute, is missing as well, but the stalwart Dilsey remains. The figure who stands in the open door at the beginning of this section has replaced the Caddy of Quentin's narrative as the woman who stands in the door.[52] Like Caddy, Dilsey is a monumental figure. With her "indomitable skeleton . . . left rising like a ruin or a landmark above the somnolent and impervious guts," Dilsey can be read as part of a divided deity (*SF* 165). As the "mammy" figure, Dilsey has been robbed of her erotic components, assuming the place of a sexually neutral caretaker for her white charges. Desexualized, Dilsey is joined with another figure who has been diminished by virtue of her sexuality—Caddy's daughter, Quentin, who has been pathetically reduced to her sexual qualities. Taken together, the strong housekeeper Dilsey and the petulant female Quentin stand in for Caddy, the absent female figure who is remembered as both maternal and sexual.[53]

In *The Sound and the Fury*, the black community, represented by Dilsey, forms the foundation upon which everything else is built. Like Dilsey, who knows how to compensate for the impotent Compson men and one-handed

Compson clocks, black labor provides the basis and the matrix for what otherwise would be missing in the Compsons' South. Although the words of white men in *The Sound and the Fury* are sterile, bearing impotence, Faulkner offers an alternative in the fourth section. Before we see the sign of the pictorial eye "where grass grew rigidly in a plot bordered with rigid flowers," Dilsey walks to church passing the cabins of the black settlement: "They were set in small grassless plots littered with broken things, bricks, planks, crockery" (*SF* 181). Instead of an eye, these grassless counterplots are filled with the signs of "broken things," broken structures, including the shards of once utilitarian vessels. Surrounded by "foul desiccation," the trees are said "to feed upon the rich and unmistakable smell of negroes in which they grew." This fecund site anticipates the fertile setting of the Easter service, in which words are transformed and ultimately transcend the limits of their human and bodily source.

In Dilsey's church, Reverend Shegog preaches a sermon about the sacrifice of the Son and the promise of "de ricklickshun en de Blood of de Lamb"; the sermon becomes especially moving for the congregation, as they picture the scene from the perspective of the "po mammy" (184). This visiting preacher, whose "wizened black face" looks "like a small, aged monkey" (182), is pictured after the first part of the sermon as "reft of all motion as a mummy or an emptied vessel" (*SF* 183). In Faulkner's iconography the "emptied vessel" would be enough to identify this preacher (already punningly "mummy"-like) with the mother. As he continues, the congregation witnesses a scene of transformation as the holy man's voice, at first like that of "a white man," becomes "as different as day from dark." Preaching beneath "the twisted paper,"

> [w]ith his body he seemed to feed the voice that, succubus like, had fleshed its teeth in him. And the congregation seemed to watch with its own eyes while the voice consumed him, until he was nothing and they were nothing and there was not even a voice but instead their hearts were speaking to one another in chanting measures beyond the need for words. (*SF* 183)

In this image of monstrous maternity, Rev. Shegog feeds a creature within himself, a voice that has gained flesh and teeth. As the "succubus like" voice consumes the preacher's body, he performs a priestly miracle; the believers are joined in a communion that brings them to signify "nothing" ("he was nothing and they were nothing") as their hearts are understood to speak to one another "beyond the need for words."

Unaware of when the preacher's "intonation, his pronunciation, became negroid," the congregation sways "as the voice took them into itself" (*SF* 184). An evocatively female figure (pregnant with "the voice that . . . had fleshed its teeth in him"), the black preacher goes beyond the legacy of the impotent voice bequeathed to him by the white men of the novel to embody, to intone, to sound the possibility of a spiritual redemption. As he imagines the "po mammy widout de salvations en de word of God," wordless sounds rise repeatedly from the congregation ("Mmmmmmmmmmmmmmmm!"); another voice rises "without words, like bubbles rising in water" (*SF* 184). Reverend Shegog partakes of the potency that has previously been the province of women in *The Sound and the Fury*, whether "mummy or an emptied vessel," consumed by a hungry inner voice that takes the congregants "into itself," the preacher becomes and incorporates others to a voiceless and wordless nothing. Preaching about the sorrows of the "po mammy," he goes beyond the impotence of the words that fail the Compson brothers and by implication even Faulkner himself. As Faulkner tries to imagine a site of fecundity and richness, a site of maternal plenitude for the world of his novel and narrative itself, he draws on the powerful oratorical tradition of the black community to imagine words that might go beyond language—a creation into rather than (as in *Absalom, Absalom!*) "out of the soundless Nothing." It is not for nothing that the speechless Benjy is the disruptive and ultimately soothed presence in the congregation during this sermon.

The dream of an art that could take readers, like believers, beyond the need for words can be seen in the pictorial images that occur at key junctures in Faulkner's texts. Like the pictorial eye in *The Sound and the Fury*, these shapes, these dramatic moments of representation, speak to Faulkner's continuing obsession with the gendering of art at the crossroads of the creative and procreative. The picture of the coffin that appears inserted between the words in *As I Lay Dying* has been seen by critics as a womb with the corpse upside down in the position for birth. The coffin represents a container for the body of the mother, herself a vessel for so many children. Unlike the "still unravish'd bride of quietness" apostrophized by Keats and Faulkner's vase-making Horace Benbow, Addie Bundren is a ravished bride in her wedding gown—her face bored with holes—as she returns to the earth. The coffin is said to be "clock-shaped," but the picture tells us that this clock is not like an eye (the "eye of the clock" [*SF* 76]) but rather shaped like a grandfather clock. By using the picture rather than the word, Faulkner avoids framing the process of generation in explicitly patrilineal terms. In an early revision of one of Darl's monologues, Faulkner replaced the word "coffin" with the more fundamental and evocative word "box." Elsewhere Jewel finds himself unable to say the word "coffin": "It's laying there, watching Cash whittle on that damn . . . ." [Faulkner's ellipses]. Jewel "says it harshly, savagely, but he does not say the word. Like a little boy in the dark to flail his courage and suddenly aghast into silence by his own noise" (*AILD* 18). Later in the same monologue, Jewel is heard to say: "With Cash all day long right under the window, hammering and sawing at that——" (*AILD* 19). Whereas the missing word "coffin" is replaced by extensive ellipses and a pictorially long dash, Vardaman turns to pronouns, but even then he has difficulty saying "it": "When they get it finished they are going to put her in it and then for a long time I couldn't say it. I saw the dark stand up and go whirling away and I said 'Are you going to nail her up in it, Cash? Cash? Cash?'" (*AILD* 65).[54] The pictorial coffin provides a shape for a word whose absence marks the site of ruptured speech in the novel and whose absence (at least in Jewel's words) is filled with signs signifying silence and broken speech.

Buried in the ground, the coffin is like the fecund, triangular wedge pictured in "Delta Autumn" in *Go Down, Moses* to represent a "∇-shaped section of earth." A funnel-like structure, "brooding" and "impenetrable," this figure points downward in the archetypal shape of the mound of Venus, the triangle of fertility or fertile triangle; it is also the Greek letter △ (delta) turned on its head—an abstract but evocatively direct pictorial depiction of the fertile flanks of the Mississippi Yazoo Delta (a physical place that is shaped like the letter which gives this landform its name). Like *The Sound and the Fury* and *As I Lay Dying, Go Down, Moses* draws part of its peculiar force from the intentional absence of white mothers. Certainly, this near absence (or quick laying away) of white mothers in *Go Down, Moses* is emphasized by the powerful presence of the black women who are maternal figures that go beyond being mere vessels of origination. The pictorial funnel, the last wedge of wilderness in "Delta Autumn," is associated with the tangled fertility and maternal richness of the black mothers who (along with the Native American, Sam Twofathers) are the powerful parental figures in Faulkner's story-cycle novel. Like the pictorial eye and coffin, this funnel-like triangular structure is a type of vessel associated with female sexuality. However, the phrase "∇-shaped" is a hybrid not just because it is hyphenated and contains a word that is in fact "shaped," but because the shape itself is also a letter. Like the pictorial "O" that Faulkner used in *Mosquitoes* and *The Sound and the Fury*, this upended Greek letter articulates a scene of origins in which letters themselves are potential vessels. Like the "O," this "∇" pictures not only a female site of origin but also the potential of letters themselves to signify as pictures.

Like the of *The Sound and the Fury*, which is associated with "the eye of the clock" and the broken watch crystal, and like the "clock-shaped" 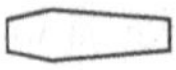 of *As I Lay Dying*, the upside-down △ tells time. Built up from the sand and earth that floods the alluvial plain, this piece of earth shapes the upper half of an hourglass; and, in "Delta Autumn," this "∇-shaped" earth with its dense growth is all that remains of a past world which is being eaten away like the sands of time. There is a palpable sense of diminution as this wedge of wild earth is gradually eroded by an encroaching civilization.[55] These pictorial containers are visible signs of Faulkner's emphasis on female sexuality as an embodiment of beginnings, the initial locus of life and time. In one of the most powerful images in Faulkner's work, Addie Bundren's pregnant daughter provides the vessel for the artist's voice, which explains what it means to experience the mystery of pregnancy: "*That's what they mean by the womb of time: the agony and the despair of spreading bones, the hard girdle in which lie the outraged entrails of events*" (AILD 121).[56] The idea of the "womb of time"—👁 ▭ ▽—recalls another meditation by a violated woman in Faulkner's work during the time in which he was revising *The Sound and the Fury*. The fact that the female box or container is a "ball" that tells time by containing the future is most clearly articulated in *Sanctuary*. As the defiled Temple Drake lies in her bed at Miss Reba's whorehouse in Memphis, she sees that the clock itself has become the focal point of an originary story:

> She watched the final light condense into the clock face, and the dial change from a round orifice in the darkness to a disc suspended in nothingness, the original chaos, and change in turn to a crystal ball holding in its still and cryptic depths the ordered chaos of the intricate and shadowy world upon whose scarred flanks the old wounds whirl onward at a dizzy speed into the darkness. (*S* 151)

A "crystal ball" that holds the shadowy forms of the future, the "clock face" locates a beginning, recalling the "miasmic womb of . . . nothingness" in *Mosquitoes*, here "a round orifice" that is transformed "to a disc suspended in nothingness."

In *As I Lay Dying*, in addition to the coffin, Faulkner also pictures a blank space,[57] an actual gap between words that provides a picture of absence. Addie Bundren speaks of Anse's "name"—"I could see the word as a shape, a vessel"—and "a significant shape profoundly without life like an empty door frame." She describes herself thinking: "The shape of my body where I used to be a virgin is in the shape of a   ." Faulkner leaves a blank space on the page to picture the place where Addie Bundren's virginity used to be. This absence is anticipated in *Flags in the Dust* in Horace Benbow's fantasy about the pinkness of unnamed female parts, which leads to the single word "unchaste" followed by a word-sized blank space and a question mark: "Unchaste   ?" For the writers in Faulkner's *Mosquitoes* and for Addie Bundren in *As I Lay Dying*, words are instruments of masculine desire, but Addie Bundren has learned to despise the words that from her husband's mouth are "just a shape to fill a lack." Addie, experiencing unmediated life, hears "the dark voicelessness in which the words are the deeds, and the other words that are not deeds, that are just the gaps in people's lacks" (*AILD* 174). Bleikasten concludes that "the novels written in [the early] years, especially *The Sound and the Fury* and *As I Lay Dying*, are novels about lack and loss, in which desire is always intimately bound up with grief and death. And it is clear too that they have sprung out of a deep sense of lack and loss—texts spun around a primal gap."[58] The lack and loss in both of these novels centers on the omnipresence of a missing mother or maternal figure, but as Faulkner's enraged maternal philosopher makes clear in *As I Lay Dying*, it is the gap that men try in their impotence to fill with words—"the gaps" in other people's "lacks." When Addie learns that she is pregnant with Darl, she thinks of her husband: "It was as though he had tricked me, hidden within a word like within a paper screen and struck me in the back through it" (*AILD* 172). If words signal the male contribution to procreation, a signifying absence marks the female site of origination. This gap for Addie Bundren is represented by the word-shaped blank space where her virginity used to be. In *The Sound and the Fury*, as the text opens up to reproduce a picture rather than a word, Faulkner explains that "the gap [is] filled by a human eye"; and, as if the picture has revealed too signifying a gap, the gap is filled once again by words that name the "eye" as "human."

Each of these pictorial images might be said to signify nothing: not only the actual gaps or blank spaces on the page, but also the pictorial interventions that stand for an eye, a coffin, and the fertile triangle of diminishing earth. Like the eye that stands as a symbol of the sexual presence and absence at the center of the woman, these figures evoke female sexuality: both its terrifying embodiment of the "nothing," which in the slang of Shakespeare's time named the female genitals, and the signifying nothing that for Faulkner articulates the transformative power of the female. These pictorial markers represent nothing and what comes from nothing. Faulkner's magnificent oeuvre consists of obsessed narration generated by speakers who are driven to fill the gaps in their own, as well as other people's, lacks with words. In *The Sound and the Fury*, Faulkner—openly casting himself in the role of one of his artist figures—interjects the pictures that in fertile conjunction with words signify the absence of language and the genesis of the artist's creation.

Signifying William

> [S]he had asked him if he had a knife, until she fumbled in the pocket of the shrunken tunic (it had a darker double vee on one cuff and a darker blotch on one shoulder where service stripes and a divisional emblem had been ripped off but this meant nothing to him).
>
> —Unnamed woman about to give birth in "Old Man," *The Wild Palms*[59]

In addition to the signifying eruption of the pictorial eye, there is another picture in *The Sound and the Fury* that embodies the threat of female potency. Fearing the generative power of woman, the Quentin Compson of *The Sound and the Fury* dreads all forms of conception. Recalling Horace Benbow, who, after his return to Jefferson, first makes his chaste and feminine vases in the "dungeon" (*S* 154) of the family home, Quentin pictures his mother as a "dungeon" (*SF* 109), a dangerous and entrapping originary space.[60] Driven by a desire to negate primal scenes, Quentin recalls a picture in one of his childhood books that shows two people trapped in a "dark place into which a single weak ray of light came slanting upon two faces lifted out of the shadow." Quentin sees this picture as his parents, and as he imagines himself and his siblings in the darkness below, he begins to see his mother herself as the "dungeon," a bodily room that will trap them into life. It is as if he is captivated by the horror of generation. Quentin describes himself as caught in an obsessive cycle of rereading: "I'd have to turn back to it until the dungeon was Mother herself she and Father upward into weak light holding hands and us lost somewhere below even them without even a ray of light" (*SF* 109–10). Below light and life, the Compson children wait to experience their fate, to be called into the dim light of this upper world. In his Manichean fantasy, Quentin sees himself and his siblings before birth as they are about to be imprisoned through conception: the joining of their parents, who are pictured as "holding hands." Quentin's dreaded book, like mothers and the maternal dungeon located within the female body, is a site of entrapment. In an act that shows her potency, Caddy, who was "never a queen or a fairy" but "always a king or a giant a general," is said to declare that if she were a king she would "break that place open"; and then we read that the page of the book "was torn out, jagged out" (109). In an explicit demonstration of the female power to remove the hymen that anticipates Quentin's self-wounding as he breaks the glass from the watch rim, the fierce Caddy tears the page and breaks open her brother's book-inscribed prison, removing the picture that for him bears the burden of his unattainable desire to not be—to never have been. This drawing pictures the moment to which Quentin, a creature of compulsions, feels compelled to return, seeking the stasis of an earlier page that exists before his and his sister's conception.

The awareness that time begins at conception causes the obsessed Quentin to return to this moment before conception. Early in his narrative, in a fantasy about the power of women to prevent generation, Quentin imagines himself as Dalton Ames's mother refusing to lie with her husband, an act that would have prevented the birth of Caddy's seducer: "If I could have been his mother lying with open body lifted laughing, holding his father with my hand refraining, seeing, watching him die before he lived" (*SF* 51). Quentin has equally desperate fantasies in which he intimates his desire to rewrite the fiction he inhabits so that he can antedate his own father and thereby preclude his and Caddy's very existence. As John Irwin contends, basing his insight, for the most part, on the Quentin Compson of *Absalom, Absalom!*, Quentin tries to use language to gain priority, to become his own father by taking control of the story.[61] Long before Caddy is recalled as tearing out the troubling page, in his desire to thwart conception (whether by mothers or artists), Quentin breaks frame to acknowledge that he has been trapped into life not so much by his mother as by an author who has imprisoned him in the pages of a book. In his plea for nonexistence, acknowledging his status as a character, Quentin turns to the artist rather than the mother to make his plea for his own nullification.

In the most difficult passage of a work that critics have damned from its inception as intentionally difficult and unnecessarily obscure, Quentin abruptly shifts from a present—amid the fishing boys—to an interior thought: "*Say it to Father will you I will am my father's Progenitive I invented him created I him Say it to him it will not be for he will say I was not then you and I since philoprogenitive*" (Faulkner's italics; *SF* 78). In his address to "you," Quentin ostensibly speaks to Caddy, who is not present, proposing a philosophical method for his and her annihilation or, rather, the more absolute and desired nonbeing of never having been. Again, this passage is driven, if not by the desire for narrative vengeance, then by a fantasy of priority, a revised account in which by insisting on becoming one's own father or one's "father's Progenitive," the moment of coming conception can be anticipated and stopped.

In this passage concerned with issues of paternal generation, creation through words, and the power of narrative authority, Faulkner acknowledges his authorial presence. On one level, this passage may be read as an imperative statement, insisting that an announcement be made to Father: "*I will am.*" Quentin shifts course in midphrase, what is in the context of this text a highly unusual mental stuttering that juxtaposes verbs, replacing "I will" with "I am." However, the syntax (in the absence of formal capitalization and other conventions of grammar) makes way for the reading of the word "will" in "I will am" as a noun, a name that stands in apposition to the "I," asserting the existence of Will in a Cartesian self-declaration: I Will am, or I, Will, am—I am Will and I am. This declaration of existence "I will am" inscribes Faulkner's presence in this passage through the inclusion of this anagram of his given name, William. In *Sanctuary*, Horace Benbow sees a letter and looks "at the superscription, at the small disfigurations which held a name, a juxtaposition of letters which did not move him at all, scrawled there by a hand that had no actual relation to his life" (*S* 219–20). Here, in the awkward juxtaposition of letters that spell "I will am," the text offers an encryption or disfiguration of Faulkner's name. This constitutes an authorial signature that simultaneously declares Quentin's—and Faulkner's—obsession with the complex relation of time to paternity.

As Will seems to be commanded to speak to the father (Say it to Father, Will), this name also names a literary father—a Father Will—famous for writing sonnets that play on his name. This father gave Faulkner his title for this novel, and, as this analysis details, this William provided Faulkner with a formal model for his radical experiment that appeared in 1929. Following line for line from Macbeth's famous speech, from "out, out brief candle" to his conclusion that arrives at a "signifying nothing," Faulkner's *Sound and the Fury* uses this soliloquy in act 5, scene 5, as an outline for the symbolic obsessions and even the outrage narrated in his novel. Indeed, this passage (the most difficult and obscure in Faulkner's novel as a whole) addresses a greater father than "Father," the biological progenitor of the Compson children. By appealing directly to Father Will, Quentin calls upon his creator, William Faulkner, to stand up to his own literary progenitor: Shakespeare. Quentin's advice, advice from the mind of a madman, insists with Borgesian certainty that Faulkner is the ultimate father and the site of origination. At the same time, with more urgency, the troubled character Quentin makes an explicit plea for his own nonexistence. Turning to address Father Will, or William, the author of the novel, Quentin proposes a change in the script, an alteration of ancestry that would erase Quentin and in the same bold gesture free Quentin's author from his own necessity to exist. It is after all the creation of characters like Quentin that compels the writer to continue to write, to become an author. In this densely layered passage, the "you" who is addressed may be Quentin himself, the psychically divided character who will be is referred to as "the two Quentins" in *Absalom, Absalom!* However, framed within this narrative, as he makes his plea to prevent conception, Quentin appeals to the mother and, at the same time, to the artist. This interior raging is ostensibly directed to the fertile Caddy who turns out to be the source of yet another Quentin, and it is also addressed to Will Faulkner by name, as the mad character speaks directly to the driven progenitor of *The Sound and the Fury* (the book Faulkner affectionately claimed as a "real son of bitch"), the work that has conceived and trapped Quentin into being.

Haunted by scenes of conception, the seconds of sexualized conjunction that threaten to generate meaning from art or life, *The Sound and the Fury* is obsessed with origins. Words, awkwardly joined on the page, call out with a nascent identity as letters inscribe the name "will" between the assertion of existence—the primal statement of being—and the fact of identity, both articulated in the words "I am." Like the fishlike "I" of *The Wild Palms* that jumps up in the dying woman's eyes, and like the minnow's dot of sentience that begins in this dying artist's pupils, letters (and punctuation marks) are pregnant with meaning. These inscriptions (like the "O" or, more precisely, the act of being able to "say 'O'" in *The Sound and the Fury*) picture the body through their very shapes. Immediately following this scene in *The Sound and the Fury* that comments on female difference as being like a different language, the text returns to a discussion of the significance of "virginity" and the limits of what Quentin's disdains as "just words." While the "Appendix Compson" offers the image of a maidenhead that is balanced like a "miniature replica of the whole vast globy earth" (recalling Elmer's uninitiated art in which "the whole world lies wombed"), Faulkner insists that virginity only has meaning in the moment of its loss, in its absence. Even as the idealized work of art in Faulkner's early fiction is based on the virginal female body, Faulkner (like his fragmented Elmer) was moved by the "dark shape" at the back of the mind. Neither male nor female, whether coital or maternal, this fecund darkness represents the forces of generation that drive the artist to go beyond purity to replicate the female and to erase the means of reproduction. Staging the robbing of the mother and picturing artists being feminized as they try to create ex nihilo, *The Sound and the Fury* locates origins: the significance in the face, the box, and hourglass of time as these images signify absence through the pictorially glyphed portals of the female body. These female and embodied timepieces are literal signs that picture the writer's dream of being outside of time: the word-soiled hope of signifying nothing.

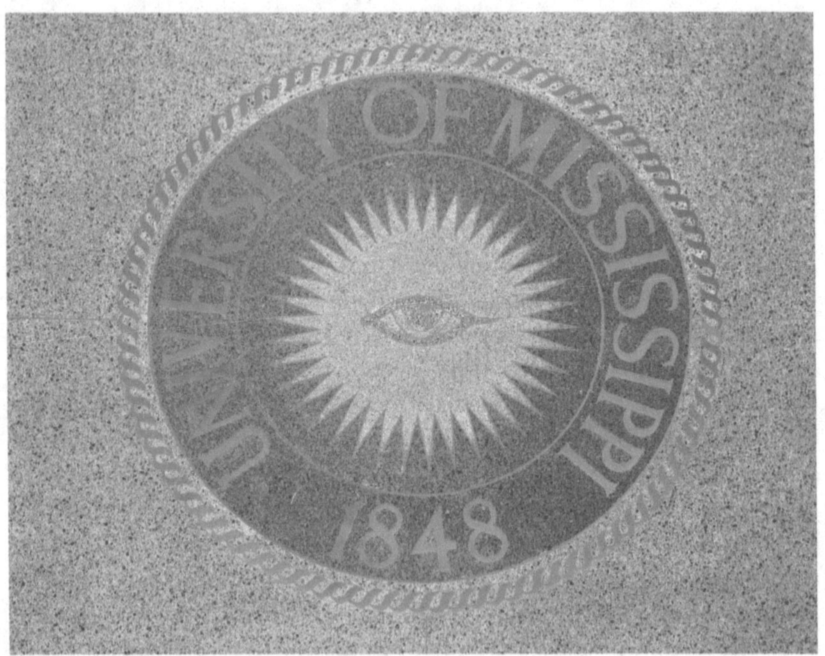

Figure 19. Official seal of the University of Mississippi as it appears set in stone and metal into the main library floor. Photograph by Robert Jordon, courtesy of UM Photographic Services.

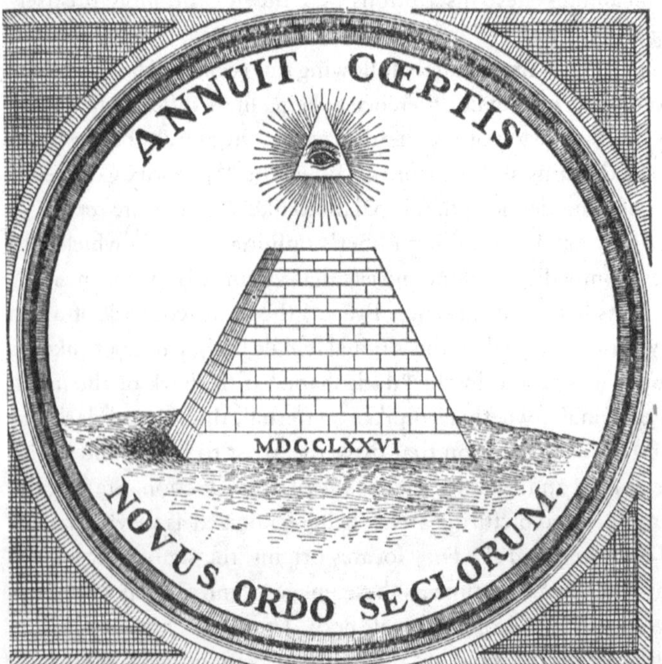

Figure 20. Reverse side of the Great Seal of the United States designed in 1782. This now ubiquitous emblem did not appear on the back of the dollar bill until 1963, one year after Faulkner's death.

CHAPTER FIVE

Echoing Back to *Absalom*

Quentin's Reverie in *The Sound and the Fury*

After great pain a formal feeling comes—
—Emily Dickinson

"Yes," Quentin said. "The two children" thinking *Yes. Maybe we are both Father. Maybe nothing ever happens once and is finished. Maybe happen is never once but like ripples maybe on water after the pebble sinks, the ripples moving on, spreading, the pool attached by a narrow umbilical water-cord to the next pool which the first pool feeds, has fed, did feed, let this second pool contain a different temperature of water, a different molecularity of having seen, felt, remembered, reflect in a different tone the infinite unchanging sky, it doesn't matter: that pebble's watery echo whose fall it did not even see moves across the surface too at the original ripple-space, to the old ineradicable rhythm* thinking *Yes, we are both Father. Or maybe Father and I are both Shreve, maybe it took Father and me both to make Shreve or Shreve and me both to make Father or maybe Thomas Sutpen to make all of us.*
—William Faulkner, *Absalom, Absalom!*

yes Yes Yes yes
—William Faulkner, *The Sound and the Fury*

In the periodless period that constitutes Quentin's longest reverie into the past, he bears once again what is unbearable. Indeed, this ten-page reverie near the end of "June Second, 1910" that manifests his obsessions bears a great deal;[1] and, in formal terms, this interlude must be recognized as the progenitor (in retrospect) of the recognizable Quentin of *The Sound and the Fury* (1929), whose obsession with repetition is integral to the long reach of the past realized in *Absalom, Absalom!* (1936).[2] Just as Faulkner becomes the author who writes like Faulkner in *The Sound and the Fury*, *Absalom, Absalom!* becomes *Absalom, Absalom!* through the echoing fatality that is irrevocably identified with the Quentin Compson of the reverie. Arguably, the reverie itself, as it insists on the formal structure of this ritualized echo, is what allowed William Faulkner to realize that "Evangeline," his rejected short story of 1931 that concerned the Sutpens (Henry, Judith, and their dark half-sister),[3] and circled around the unexplained murder of Judith's husband, Charles Bon, by her brother, Henry, was going to become a narrative about Quentin Compson. In fact, *Absalom, Absalom!* announces its genealogical connection to Quentin Compson in the very first of that book's italicized echoes, as Quentin—silent listener and voluble hearer—exposes the shape of his hidden reflections as he incorporates Miss Rosa Coldfield's narration into his mirroring mind.

This highly formal passage, introducing the intimacy of the echo form, was consciously deleted from the first chapter of *Absalom, Absalom!* when it appeared in *The American Mercury* just months before the publication of the novel. While Quentin's unspoken thoughts rise briefly to the surface in italics in this circulated venue, his role as the echoing listener who identifies with ghosts—female as well as male, living as well as dead—has been left out because it introduces the jarring textual strangeness that signals Quentin's madness in both *The Sound and the Fury* and *Absalom, Absalom!* Like the dueling voices of the twins' account in the plantation journal that was deleted from the novella "The Bear"—the same journal entry whose presence in "The Bear" transforms *Go Down, Moses* from a collection of related stories into a novel—the reverberating echo form that was excised when the first chapter of *Absalom, Absalom!* appeared in *The American Mercury* is what makes *Absalom, Absalom!* into the novel that it is: a literally provocative masterpiece of modernist narrative.

In the published novel as a whole, this echo formation demonstrates the erasure of boundaries between characters and insists on an almost incestuous intimacy of dialogue that emerges on the second page of the novel, as Quentin Compson of *Absalom, Absalom!* is joined to Miss Rosa. Rising to the level of a psychic signature, this silent inscription of echoing dialogue is not the sign of the resisting reader but that of the active writer, as reading becomes writing: the composing of a composite self into existence. It is no accident that Quentin Compson enters into this ritualized form of echoing voice just before Miss Rosa articulates her fantasy that the young man before her may be destined to become a professional writer. This juxtaposition, linking Quentin's narrative madness found in the italicized echoing of his interiority (deemed unfriendly for publication in an actual magazine) to the production of magazine copy, is instructive:

> *It seems that this demon—his name was Sutpen—(Colonel Sutpen)—Colonel Sutpen . . .* [came] *and built a plantation—(Tore violently a plantation, Miss Rosa Coldfield says)—tore violently . . . (Without gentleness begot, Miss Rosa Coldfield says)—without gentleness . . . (Only they destroyed him or something or he destroyed them or something. And died)—and died. Without regret, Miss Rosa Coldfield says—(Save by her) Yes, save by her. (And by Quentin Compson) Yes. And by Quentin Compson.*

> "Because you are going away to attend the college at Harvard they tell me," she said. "So I dont imagine you will ever come back here and settle down as a country lawyer in a little town like Jefferson since Northern people have already seen to it that there is little left in the South for a young man. So maybe you will enter the literary profession as so many Southern gentlemen and gentlewomen too are doing now and maybe some day you will remember this and write about it. You will be married then I expect and perhaps your wife will want a new gown or a new chair for the house and you can write this and submit it to the magazines." (*AA!* 5)

Rereading Quentin's Longest Reverie

Like the much-discussed water-splashing scene of the Benjy section, Quentin's longest reverie, contained and self-contained, can be read as a microcosm of *The Sound and the Fury* as a whole.[4] Preoccupied by the past, the events that will bear Quentin to his death occupy a type of uterine penumbra that is permeable to, yet finally ruptured from, a present or even a past that would lead to an imagined or imaginable future. Precipitated by a tellingly brief break into italics that interrupts Shreve's bizarre list of gentlemanly accoutrements for Gerald Bland's picnic basket of behaviors ("*did you love them Caddy did you love them When they touched me I died*" [94; quotation marks added]), Quentin's longest reverie in *The Sound and the Fury* has its genesis in the unbearable image of a woman standing at a threshold that has already been crossed. Here, the bellowing voice of outrage is sounded by the idiot brother who can "smell" death and who is able to scent a primal change in his sister Caddy's eyes.

Gerald Bland, the ruling misogynist of the second section of *The Sound and the Fury*, is the invisible yet physically present presence in the long reverie. Part of Faulkner's experimental project becomes visible in the emergence of multiple layers, as the text insists on divisions and junctures between levels of mental and physical consciousness. After the long reverie, the wound Quentin receives while he is moving between these layers of consciousness must be explained to Quentin himself.[5] In retrospect, Gerald Bland is revealed as the pugilist source of Quentin's bloodied eye.[6] It is this maiming, the pain that finally brings Quentin back to the present, that insists on the reality of the body behind the thronging and enthroned language of reverie.

Quentin's longest reverie into the past serves as a narrative screen that conceals the ongoing experience of the violent encounter with Gerald Bland. Artfully incorporating his present wound, Quentin relives his humiliating experience of seeing the world through the broken and bloody eye of his past. Covered by the mesmerizing and parallel scenes of pasts within the past, the language of Quentin's actual (what we might call his consummated) fight with Gerald bleeds through, as he relives his earlier encounter with his sister's lover, Dalton Ames—the fainting rather than fighting that has broken Quentin's eye the first time. The Quentin immersed in the reverie queries:

> did you ever have a sister did you no but theyre all bitches. (102; absence of quotation marks Faulkner's)

Shreve and Spoade affirm to Quentin that he himself has begun the fight with Gerald Bland after "jump[ing] up" asking, "'Did you ever have a sister? did you?' and when he said No, you hit him" (105; selective capitalization Faulkner's). The word "bitch" in its various forms is relatively rare in *The Sound and the Fury*. Suggesting a selectivity of the heard and unheard, the word "bitch" that does not appear at all in Benjy's section appears in Quentin's section only in conjunction with the actual presence of or allusion to the presence of Gerald Bland or Gerald Bland's mother (save for Deacon's passing reference to his son-in-law). On the surface, it might seem that the appearance of the word "bitches" in Quentin's reverie would be the exception to this pattern, but I am arguing here that it is not. Indeed, this very word constitutes evidence of Gerald Bland's presence rather than his absence.

This obscene reference, a word that becomes Jason's misogynist mantra, "Once a bitch always a bitch," appears only in the frame to his section of the novel. While Jason is the only character to use the word "bitch" even in its "b______" form in the fourth section, notably in the second section of the novel, Quentin's intervening life has added this crude term to the language through which he hears and sees the scenes of his traumatic past. Aside from Jason, Shreve is the character to whom this word is most often attributed, and his use of it with regard to the Blands (repeatedly calling Gerald a "son of a bitch") is a direct reference to Gerald's mother, whom Shreve identifies as a "woman [with] more ways like a bitch than any lady in these sovereign states and dominions" (68). The novel's "son of a bitch" (105, 105, 106), Gerald Bland, becomes the figure who provides Quentin with a model to develop a more brutal vocabulary for his memory of Dalton Ames. While Gerald Bland is not explicitly quoted in Spoade's and Shreve's account as saying "theyre all bitches," the animality this seducer ascribes to women as he brags about his prowess suggestively fills this narrative gap. Following up with a braggartly story of a female who might said to be "in heat" for him, Gerald relishes his animalistic memory of a woman (in Shreve's words) "waiting . . . without him there to give her what she wanted . . . Leda lurking in the bushes, whimpering and moaning for the swan, see" (106). Aside from Shreve, who defines himself as "a Canadian" "not a gentleman" and defends Quentin as having more sense than to mess with those he (Shreve) classifies as "the little dirty sluts" (50), this corrupt (and Bland) southern "gentleman," and by implication his lady-bitch of a mother, join Jason Compson as the most visible characters in the novel who revel in fantasies of female sexual desire. In Quentin's narrative, a Dalton Ames bent on asking, "I want to know if shes all right have they been / bothering her up there" suggests the retrospective contamination of memory when viewed through the misogynist presence of Gerald Bland (101). The echoing name of "Dalton Ames" ("Dalton Ames. Dalton Ames. Dalton Ames.") (51), a name that to Quentin's ear "just missed gentility," does not connote a figure who would blandly conclude "no but theyre all bitches" (59, 102). Indeed, Dalton Ames, like Quentin's own father, appears in the role of a worldly man whose words and acts insist on the inevitability as well as the necessity—whether biological or social—of female sexuality.[7]

Focusing on a series of increasingly ritualized encounters that link female change to masculine loss, the long reverie ends as Quentin's physical bleeding brings him back to the exteriority of the moment known as the present: he is ruptured back into this present by his body in pain. This sharp turn is a return that with grammatical as well as thematic specificity insists on Quentin's feminization: his curse is marked in blood by a female period. This return to periods begins with the displaced sexual conjunction of Quentin's bloody eye and his cut thumb: "It kept on running for a long time, but my face felt cold and sort of dead, and my eye, and the cut place on my finger was smarting again" (104).[8] As this Narcissus with his broken eye tries to see "[his] face in" the framed water, the basin shows "a round blob of twilight wobbling in it, with a yellow edge like a fading balloon, then my reflection." As he dips the "rag again, breaking the balloon," we read: "[t]he rag stained the water" (104).[9] Father's description of menstruation (infused for Quentin with "the saddest odor of all"—honeysuckle) has already surfaced in Quentin's mind as he is pursued by an errant sister, the little Italian girl:

> Delicate equilibrium of periodical filth between two moons balanced. Moons he said full and yellow as harvest moons her hips thighs . . . Yellow . . . Liquid putrefaction like drowned things floating like pale rubber flabbily filled getting the odor of honeysuckle all mixed up. (81)[10]

Distinguished as the longest interval without periods (capitalization only remains for proper names and the first-person singular pronoun), Quentin's reverie echoes an earlier passage in his section of *The Sound and the Fury* that also lacks punctuation and also concerns his failed confrontation with a male interloper, Herbert Head, the cheating banker-bridegroom who has come to marry Quentin's already-deflowered sister.[11] Although Quentin's refusal of Dalton Ames's gun will be narrated in the long reverie, a fragment associated with shooting Herbert Head surfaces early in "June Second, 1910." This emergent fragment—"*Quentin has shot*" (67); "*shot him through the*" (68); "*Shot his voice through the*" (71)—preoccupies Quentin's consciousness with only slight variations. These interjections articulate and echo Quentin's unfulfilled fantasy that twice rises to the level of a completed thought: "*Quentin has shot Herbert Head he shot his voice through the floor of Caddy's room*" (67), and the more directed and inclusive version, "*Quentin has shot all of their voices through the floor of Caddy's room*" (71). The ambiguous possessive pronoun in the phrase "*his voice*" alludes to Quentin's voice as a weapon and, at the same time, this voice ("*his voice*") is the sound of Herbert Head and the object *cum* target of Quentin's violent fantasy. While the crossover is characteristic of what has come to be known as the Faulknerian "he" (a building of interrelationships through the very ambiguity inherent in pronouns), Quentin's fantasy of shooting "voices" remains stable because—whether Quentin shoots with his own voice or he aims at that from Herbert's head—Quentin (a man of words) is gunning for male power.

Linked by more than the fact that they center on scenes of triangulation that involve a gun, these two reveries (featuring Quentin, Caddy, and Herbert Head and Quentin, Caddy, and Dalton Ames) are connected by parallel sentences in which Quentin refuses each of these interlopers' offers of masculine power. Overtaken by mesmeric memory, Quentin shouts in his head to Herbert Head: "To hell with your money" (70); and, as memory believes, Quentin relives his refusal of Dalton Ames's gun offered to him "butt first," shouting to Ames: "to hell with your gun" (102). In "June Second, 1910," Hell is the desired destination. The reason that Quentin gives for not killing Caddy's first lover is that then there would be three of them: "That's why I didn't [shoot him]. He would be there and she would and I would" (51).[12] He wants hell to themselves.[13]

Strange periods erupt amid Quentin's vacation from punctuation as he is revisited by his confrontation with Herbert Head. Unnecessary for Quentin's stream-of-consciousness (his unspoken but mentally replayed) narration, these periods mark Quentin's sister's refusal to see Doc Peabody. In the resonant country that will be named Yoknapatawpha, Doc Peabody rises to the level of a speaking character in Faulkner's 1930 *As I Lay Dying*, the novel where he is associated with an unmarried sister's inability to ask him for an abortion. *As I Lay Dying*'s Dewey Dell insists, "God gave women a sign when something has happened bad" (58), and this very sign has already been introduced as an absence—the missing period at the close of her own mad brother's most recent and proximate section. Darl's famously open-ended closing line insists: "*Addie Bundren is dead*" (52). In Faulkner's biology of grammar, mothers do not *die*, they are replaced and reconstituted through the births that follow missing periods. The word "period" here is more than a pun, it is a spot that insists on closure itself, whether that of death or bloody unproductiveness.[14] Seen in this light, the eruption of periods in Quentin's reverie about Caddy and Herbert Head can be read as wishful signs. Instead of an ostentatiously missing period, the periods that erupt twice in Quentin's traumatic reverie about his sister's forced marriage frame Caddy's words about her pregnancy: "I'm just sick**.** I cant ask**.**" (71; emphasis of enlarged periods added).

This parallel reverie—I am referring here to the passage about Herbert Head that prefigures Quentin's longest reverie, which features Dalton Ames—

is precipitated by Shreve. Periods disappear in the course of the introductory paragraph that bridges the gap between the lived present and the relived past that closes with Shreve's retailing of one of Gerald Bland's mother's tall tales about her son's sexual exploits: "the sawmill husband came to the kitchen door with a shotgun Gerald went down and bit the gun in two" (68).[15] This staple of "Bland" family lore, featuring a man's mouth and a man's gun consummating a confrontation over a woman, calls attention to crucial junctures between thematic and formal obsessions in these related reveries in *The Sound and the Fury*. Indeed, versions of these confrontations between men, resounding in *Absalom, Absalom!* where they appear in what I will be calling the formula of the echo, are made even clearer in *The Sound and the Fury* by their reverberations in the intensely rendered scenes between brother and sister that follow these very encounters. Indicated by italics, these narratives hinging and echoing backward also swing forward to sound still other reverberations. Significant in themselves, these echo formations signal and embody crucial junctures, connections within *The Sound and the Fury* as well as between the Quentin of this early masterpiece and *Absalom, Absalom!*, *The Sound and the Fury*'s paradoxical predecessor that would appear seven years later. Performing their roles as equations, these narrative echoes resound in this recognizable series of dialogic plays designed to carry the meaning, to bear the mystery, of *Absalom, Absalom!*

While Quentin's longest reverie is both a thematic and formal point of origin for *Absalom, Absalom!*, there are notable differences between the two texts. Unlike *Absalom, Absalom!*, this crucial passage about masculine loss and lost masculinity that paves Quentin's progress toward his suicidal ending, the sentences are not four pages in length. In contrast, Quentin's longest reverie recounts what is unbearable without recourse to sentences at all. Arranged as if it were dialogic blank verse, interspersed with unspoken thoughts and observations, it is not possible at key junctures in the reverie to know whose internalized voice is speaking. The fact that the reverie itself is not in italics insists on the status of this interlude as the reigning reality that constitutes Quentin's life in the present. Significantly, the brief, hysterically rendered italics that precede the reverie insist on the contrast between Quentin's experience of raw trauma and the honed memories that have been framed in the confident art of painful associations, events of the past that have become more real than the present through the radical juxtapositions of the reverie.

It is Quentin who sees Caddy at the threshold in the reverie's beginning: "one minute she was standing there" (94). This opening line insists on the status of the reverie as a microcosm echoing the formal past of the literal text. In the manuscript version, this very image originally stood as the opening line, the planned threshold into Quentin's mind that was to have been the precise point of entry into "June Second, 1910." As one of the phrases that marks a mnemonic of obsessive and traumatic return, this recurring line situates this threshold as a ritually resonant location. In "June Second, 1910," this repeated scene that features the idiot brother's horror at change insists on the significance of Caddy being seen in the postvirginal moment. As Benjy pulls at her dress, Caddy is backed up against a door that must be seen as opening onto a heavily symbolic threshold: her entry into a place of washing rather than of bedding. In the morphology of houses, readers of Benjy and his section know that Caddy washes her mouth out with soap in the kitchen after her offensive act of kissing, and that later the bedroom is an insufficient location to clean up what the idiot brother has seen in "her eyes." What Caddy has been doing requires a type of cleansing that Benjy associates with the bathroom. Quentin's reverie begins with his own memory of this crucial scene as Benjy is seen "shoving at her up the stairs to the bathroom door and stop[ping] her back against the door" (94). Immediately thereafter, Quentin describes Caddy as he has witnessed her in what is clearly an earlier act of ritual ablution: "she was lying in the water her head on the sand spit the water flowing about her hips . . . her skirt half saturated flopped along her flanks to the water's motion" (94).

This event followed by Quentin's embedded recollections of pasts within the past—returning repeatedly to his memory of Caddy's stained drawers from the critically celebrated water-splashing scene of the Compson children's early childhood (discussed here in chapter 1, "Envisioning Faulkner and Southern Literature," where it is read in terms of the primacy of its visual and aural components)—is glossed in the description of another creek-side ritual described in Faulkner's 1934 story, "There Was a Queen."[16] *Flags in the Dust*, soon to be cut and published as *Sartoris* (1929), was already written when Faulkner was completing *The Sound and the Fury*. *Sartoris*'s Narcissa has already developed her narcissistic habit of reading too much Byron (Snopes, that is). In Faulkner's short story, Byron Snopes, the "book-keeper" embezzler who has stolen back his "anonymous love letters" (739) from Narcissa's underwear drawer, has mislaid these letters that turn out to have been found and secretly possessed for twelve years by a government investigator. Narcissa's ablutions—a recognizable version of Caddy's sodden skirts at the water's edge—follow this widow in white's (Narcissa's) prostitution of herself in Memphis, where she has traded her body to this U.S. government "Yankee" and "Jew" in order to procure these salacious letters. After her mysterious overnight trip to Memphis, Narcissa has her son join her as she immerses herself in water. As Narcissa's son tells his great aunt, Jenny: "We been in the creek . . . Not swimming, though. Just sitting in the water . . . We just sat in the water with our clothes on. All evening. She wanted to do it" (737). By having carnal relations in Memphis, Narcissa performs in the character in which she has been imagined in Byron's letters with a man who has shared the promiscuity that the obsessive and secret reading of the letters (by Narcissa's own report) had once awakened in her. As this narrative linking prostitution and publication suggests, the perverse relation between money and art or writing for money remains a troubling and explicit theme in Faulkner's life and his fiction.[17] In seeming paradox, Narcissa's self-serving promiscuity and Quentin's suicidal chastity are close kin in that they suggest radical ways of refusing to publish hidden stories.

Anticipating his brother Jason as a fainting and bleeding Compson boy, Quentin looking through his own smashed "watch-face" sees Dalton Ames through the wash of his own blood, "like . . . through a piece of colored glass" (102). Close to the end of "June Second, 1910," in an italicized thought that reflects back on this encounter with Dalton Ames that has appeared in the longest reverie, Quentin realizes that he has been seen "not as potential source of harm" in the failed standoff but rather as a version of Caddy: Dalton Ames "was thinking of her when he looked at me was looking at me through her like through a piece of colored glass" (111; quotation marks added). In the reverie itself, Quentin is the one who suggests meeting Dalton Ames in his "room . . . at the hotel" (100), which raises the question of who is replacing whom when Dalton Ames holds Quentin's arms behind him, and Quentin, echoing this physicality, almost immediately recalls himself as restraining Caddy in the same way. Such a reading leads to a less obvious (but nonetheless present) layer of meaning through cross-identification, as Caddy asks Quentin what he plans to do and he answers, "none of your business whore whore" (101). Uttered as a demeaning epithet, the words "whore whore" are jarring here. Read prosaically, the term serves as a surprisingly crude noun (preceded by the same word that can be read as an exclamatory verb) to accuse a still beloved, if fallen, sister. Repeated, the words "whore whore" can state what should be "none of [Caddy's] business" and what at the same time has become part of Quentin's own pointedly feminized form of lost honor. Driven by compulsion, Quentin's revulsion comes from his masculine failure that has made repetition itself a soiling act. As he is haunted by the idea of "Again. Saddest of all. Again," Quentin is "whoring," to use a word that Faulkner used to describe the act of writing for money, in the mire of memory. Quentin may answer Caddy's question by declaring *his* intentions to go whoring or to become a whore himself. In full paradox, he may be telling the whore that in his continuing protection of her lost virtue he himself is whoring for honor. The words "whore whore," like the interjection that "theyre [women are] all bitches," are provocative because such words seem out of tone, out of place, or, perhaps, just misplaced, even given the deranged arrangement of Quentin's psyche.

Whether driven by the logic of a madman or merely some naturalist drive endemic to human maturation, Quentin is seeking initiation that ends in violation. Bent on sharing or canceling the meaning of his sister's bodily experience, Quentin tries to own, to participate in, Caddy's wound. In his repeated fantasy of having committed incest, Quentin has preserved the family honor or the "concept of Compson honor"[18] by claiming to possess (to own through having taken) the maidenhead that he has failed to protect or preserve. Notably, as the Quentin of the reverie refuses the gun that Dalton Ames offers to him "butt first," he resists assuming the male or the female position. Instead, Quentin keeps returning to the memory of a stain that cannot be washed away. There are two versions of his sister's soiling that Quentin maps onto his deeper memory of Caddy's muddy bottom. The black matriarch, Dilsey, is the witness who is recalled as seeing Caddy's soiled bottom, the stained flesh that is harbinger of the death of innocence and death itself. The past-obsessed Quentin who asks, "do you remember the day damuddy died when you sat down in the water / in your drawers" interrupts his own stream of consciousness with a follow-up question: "Caddy do you remember how Dilsey fussed at you because your drawers / were muddy" (96). If Damuddy's death itself has made the day of Caddy's soiling so memorable and so highly symbolic, a similar death marks the fact of an actual female fall in "There Was a Queen." In this story, the queen that becomes past is the stately Civil War Aunt, Jenny DuPre, who dies alone and regal at the window just after Narcissa has matter-of-factly explained the justification of her overnight whoring for letters in Memphis. "There Was a Queen" also includes a morally superior woman of color, Elnora (shades of Dilsey's role as a witness to Caddy's stained bottom), who with excoriating insight identifies Narcissa's sexual corruption by classifying this widow in white as "trash. Town trash" (729).

In some ways, Quentin's recollection and his juxtaposition of memories that return to scenes of failed initiations must be read as his lived aversion to the repetitions that might release him into the possibilities of art. As we have seen, Miss Rosa of *Absalom, Absalom!* from the outset has imagined Quentin's future as a publishing writer, a practitioner of "the literary profession" (5). There is desire revealed in Quentin's glances that take in Shreve's rosy, "rubicund" (*AA!* 147) nakedness that is somewhat troublingly feminized by "his glasses," which are said to look "like small yellow moons" (*SF* 106). Shreve's reflective, moonlike glasses are linked to the symbolism of menstruation established in *The Sound and the Fury*, imagery that bleeds through into descriptions of Shreve that appear in *Absalom, Absalom!* Quentin's ambivalent attraction to the body of his Canadian roommate rises to consciousness and is heard in the taunt of another Harvard boy: "[c]alling Shreve my husband" (*SF* 50). It is significant that Quentin's desire surfaces most purely, if briefly, in his aesthetic awareness of Dalton Ames, his shirts making "his face so brown his eyes so blue." His very name, "Dalton Ames," is said to have "just missed gentility" (59). As the 1946 "Appendix Compson" concludes, Quentin "loved not his sister's body" but "death above all, who loved only death, loved and lived in a deliberate and almost perverted anticipation of death as a lover loves" (207–8). And from this vantage point, his fleeting glimpse of the aesthetics of Dalton Ames's beauty is moving because it underlines the stark absence in the past or the present of a philosopher or fool that can offer Quentin a compelling focus for his desire *or* for emulation.[19] Here, Narcissus drowns himself not out of self-love, but to escape Echo. Aestheticized by association with the fragile beauty of a water-rotted leaf, death has become the destination of Quentin's desire. Again, "again" is "the saddest of all," and Quentin clearly fears the living death that he would experience in repetition. The obsessive reflection of the reverie locates him as a prisoner of the past and as the doorman of a threshold that has already been irrevocably crossed.

Scholars have long referred to the internalized dialogue between Quentin and Caddy featuring a knife that appears near the opening of Quentin's long reverie as the murder/suicide scene. And while this encounter does parallel and stage the symbolism of Quentin's suicide, his assumed last act as he refuses to cross the bridge into a future that would necessitate leaving the past as past, this scene with the knife is didactically onanistic:

> it wont take but a second just a second then I can do mine I can do mine then
> all right can you do yours by yourself
> . . .
> will you close your eyes
> no like this youll have to push it harder
> touch your hand to it
> . . .
> push it are you going to
> do you want me to
> yes push it
> touch your hand to it. (96)

Sequence becomes of consequence as Quentin recalls: "her muscles gathered I sat up / its my knife I dropped it." We do not know which internalized voice asks: "what time is it?" We cannot know whether a male or female voice marks this version of a postvirginal moment that is not death (or the "little death") by answering "I dont know" (96). The most famous antecedent of these gathering, leg-threatening, and therefore female muscles is found in Willa Cather's looping snake that makes the letter "W" in *My Ántonia*.[20] This frighteningly muscular snake that encircles Jim Burden's leg in *My Ántonia* links Cather's Jim—along with Cather's Henry of *The Professor's House*—to Twain's Jim of *Huckleberry Finn*. The folk-schooled Jim of *Huckleberry Finn* knows that in such an encounter either the man's head or the snake's head will have to be sacrificed.

Losing and refusing weapons, the Quentin of the reverie cannot accept either a masculine or a feminine position. He is a "gentleman" with all of that word's oxymoronic tensions. With one gun, all that can happen is a murder and/or a suicide or a displaced skills contest proving who might have killed whom. In the gendered mayhem of the twentieth century, forensic science places wives with knives in the kitchen and husbands with guns in the bedroom. The knife and the wound-opening gun in the modern era are not just extensions of the masculine; they are euphemisms for the male organ of generation. In terms of phallic displacements, Herbert Head—associated with money, cigars, and cars—is clearly a debased figure. Knives (in the form of swords) and guns (both part of the weaponry of choice in duels staged on the nineteenth- and twentieth-century fields of honor) are crucial to masculine ways of dying: suicide as well as murder. Knives and guns are the ways by which Quentin does not die here. Instead, Quentin (in more ways than one) chooses a female death. Lacking the masculine verve of a Lucrece, Quentin in his overdetermined jump has eschewed the knife and gun, choosing instead the two favored female forms of death: death by leaping and death by drowning.[21] In classical tragedy, death by air is chosen by pursued women who escape ravishment by jumping off cliffs. I should add that even hanging constitutes a form of death by leaping, a death by air.

Pursued by the terrifying state of female availability ("i was afraid to i was afraid she might" [*SF* 112]), Quentin flees the accommodating women whose voices call to him from the honeysuckle. Quentin flees the sexual violation that cannot put him in the honored place of a Lucrece, who ultimately violates her violated self with a sword. Like the legendary Lucrece, Quentin kills himself and has left a note, but as a man he is charged with honoring female rather than male chastity. His own chastity is a matter of shame, not honor. Quentin's father belabors the point in Quentin's internalized version of their dialogue:

> In the South you are ashamed of being a virgin. Boys. Men. They lie about it. Because it means less to women, Father said. He said it was men invented virginity not women. Father said it's like death: only a state in which the others are left and I said, But to believe it doesn't matter and he said, That's what's so sad about anything: not only virginity and I said, Why couldn't it have been me and not her who is unvirgin and he said, That's why that's sad too; nothing is even worth the changing of it. (50)

Recognized as one of Leslie Fiedler's gothic maidens who has lost his "moral home," Quentin (nasty Natalie aside) has failed at or has refused to engage in either homo- or hetero-erotic initiation. Finally assuming the female position, Quentin (albeit off the page) accomplishes a classical female death through air and water. Both forms of death are linked to strangulation; both focus on the loss of air that is the end of breath; both of these deaths call attention to the silence that marks the end or compels the beginning of art. It is telling that both the Dalton Ames and the Caddy of the reverie threaten to recede into art: the gunlike Ames is likened to "bronze" while Caddy is seen, near the close of the reverie, as she sees Quentin: "she looked at me then everything emptied out of her eyes and they looked / like the eyes in statues blank unseeing and serene" (104; quotation marks added).[22]

Located on what itself might be seen as an exaggerated threshold, the dénouement of the reverie takes place on a bridge. An obvious prologue to Quentin's final leap into the water from a Boston bridge, this scene emphasizes the story of triangulated desire, which underlines the fact that the reverie of *The Sound and the Fury* is a prologue to *Absalom, Absalom!* Faulkner's *Absalom, Absalom!* features repeated accounts of confrontations between men who are fighting over questions of male honor that dispute the meaning of race in relation to class and class in relation to race and caste, as these dialectics chart the arenas of masculine violence. Ostensibly a desired or rejected woman, the object in dispute may be the broken or preserved hymen or the embodied threshold of class repeatedly located in the concept of the front door. Such rights of entry, like the formal rules regulating duels, require that both parties acknowledge that they are on an equal footing. The duel that does not occur and the murder that does not take place on the bridge of the reverie plots the past that preoccupies the Quentin Compson of *Absalom, Absalom!* The fictional chronology, one of the conclusions appended to *Absalom, Absalom!*, places the actual confrontation with Dalton Ames deep in the summer of 1909; and these events clearly infuse the ways that Quentin creates his own fiction in concert with Miss Rosa's history of Sutpen's Hundred.[23]

In *Absalom, Absalom!*, Quentin's emotional avatar, Henry Sutpen, gains heft by murdering a sybaritic male, a soldier, an unarmed officer who, like Dalton Ames, is known for wearing silk. The murder that replaces the duel in *Absalom, Absalom!* signals that Charles Bon (despite his aristocratic demeanor) is not acknowledged as his "country brother['s]" equal (*AA!* 74). Disputes over social class, race, or a history of dishonor (such as cheating and being expelled from Harvard) are all "honorable" reasons for shooting down in cold blood a man who wants to marry one's sister.[24] This tale of two men, with one drawing a line at a gate or forbidden threshold that leads to a contested woman or a feminized structure of a door to be stormed, is an old story. Indeed, the lines drawn to signify male territory are not always about marking trees with lifted legs or preserving the property in the maidenhead. I can even imagine that it might in some cases not be necessary to think about the "epistemology of the closet,"[25] just not in any of the narratives of cross-gender triangles that I have met. No longer the nihilist philosopher that haunts Quentin's mind in *The Sound and the Fury*, Quentin's father in *Absalom, Absalom!* has become the explicator of complex passions, exploring the pleasures of protection and predation as he enjoys an extended fantasy about the ritualized love—the protecting as well as the secret owning—of dark-blooded and light-skinned women (a woman "with a face like a tragic magnolia, the eternal female, the eternal Who-suffers" [91]) in a lengthy disquisition on the institution of plaçage. Speaking in the voice of Bon, Quentin's father says:

> Not whore. Dont say that. In fact, never refer to one of them by that name in New Orleans: otherwise you may be forced to purchase that privilege with some of your blood from probably a thousand men . . . Not whores. And not whores because of us, the thousand. We—the thousand, the white men—made them, created and produced them; we even made the laws which declare that one eighth of a specified kind of blood shall outweigh seven eighths of another kind. I admit that. But that same white race would have made them slaves too, laborers, cooks, maybe even field hands, if it were not for this thousand, these few men like myself without principles or honor either, perhaps you will say. We cannot, perhaps we do not even want to, save all of them; perhaps the thousand we save are not one in a thousand. But we save that one. God may mark every sparrow, but we do not pretend to be God, you see. Perhaps we do not even want to be God, since no man would want but one of these sparrows. (91–92)

Through his description of the desires that drive his characterization of Bon, Mr. Compson offers the most complete analysis of the triangulated identity that his son, Quentin, suffers in the more mysterious (because less explained) desire for his sister Caddy in *The Sound and the Fury*. Speaking to a Quentin who just shortly before (according to the retrospective dialogues that fill his consciousness in *The Sound and the Fury*) has been insistently haranguing his father about his (Quentin's) incestuous fantasies,[26] Mr. Compson assumes Henry's point of view to provide Quentin with a mirror for his soul that would explicate the complexities of such desire. Father explains:

> In fact, perhaps this is the pure and perfect incest: the brother realising that the sister's virginity must be destroyed in order to have existed at all, taking that virginity in the person of the brother-in-law, the man whom he would be if he could become, metamorphose into, the lover, the husband; by whom he would be despoiled, choose for despoiler, if he could become, metamorphose into the sister, the mistress, the bride. Perhaps that is what went on, not in Henry's mind but in his soul. (*AA!* 77)

Brother Echoing Brother: Faulkner's *Cane*

While the narrative staging of male territoriality has become archetypal, with one figure storming and one figure guarding the female gate, the formula for Faulkner has a more direct rhetorical and visual source in the epiphanic equations that most pointedly mark the territory of manhood and identity in Jean Toomer's *Cane* (1923).[27] I am referring here to two specific equations that are pivotally placed near the ending of stories that themselves mark crescendos in the formal thirds of the "broken circle" that comprises the tripartite structure of Toomer's modernist masterpiecc. Leaving aside the suggestively menstrual and racial connotations of Shreve's description of Quentin as "mooning" around, Toomer's "moony"[28] Paul at the close of "Bona and Paul" refuses to pass either in terms of covering his racial identity or his erotic passion. Choosing to return to the "uniformed black man" that he has "passed" on his way out of the "Crimson Gardens" while strangers exchange knowing looks, the "moony" Paul speaks to the "doorman":

"Youre wrong."

"Yassur."

"Brother, youre wrong." (77)

The pivotal affirmation of "yassur"—the elided dialect word "sur" for "sir" that appears in both of Toomer's equations—insists on the announced distance of race joined to class; yet the interjection of the word "brother" on the part of the light-skinned Paul insists on a level of identity that goes beyond the surface color of skin as well as the divisive uniform of service that designates the separation of class. Homoerotics are paramount for this "moony" young man involved in several triangles, including a triangulated parable of aesthetics. We read, "He loves Art," and immediately thereafter Paul wonders: "But is it not queer, this pale purple facsimile of a red-blooded Norwegian friend of his?" (73). If "[h]e loves Art," Art who is drawn to Paul has a more superficial attachment to a "puffy yellow[-haired]" female named "Helen." Helen, a nominal descendant of the legendary woman whose beauty launched a thousand ships and a direct descendant of *Winesburg, Ohio*'s Helen White, is the white Helen who is jealous of Art's attraction to his dark, "moony," and mysterious male friend. Toomer's allegorically named "Bona," specifically identified as being "Southern" with "black-hair curled staccato" (73), is the embodiment of the desired and dark feminine. Bona is also a possible source, through her vaguely Italianate name, for the French last name said to have been created by Sutpen for Faulkner's Charles Bon, the mysterious and darkly feminine bridegroom who has been murdered by his brother in *Absalom, Absalom!*[29]

The other precisely placed epiphanic equation appears near the close of *Cane*'s "Blood-Burning Moon," a story that parallels "Bona and Paul" in formal and thematic terms, and that itself also marks one of the formal junctures in the tripartite structure of Toomer's prose/poem cycle. Notably, "Blood-Burning Moon" is the piece that closes the "Southern" section, indicating a sense of provisional closure that is marked throughout *Cane* by a blank space bearing the pictorial inscription of what Toomer described as a broken circle. Here, this broken circle is inscribed in an arc (a single line in a spherically calibrated rainbow arch) that occupies the right side of an essentially blank double-page spread.[30] Called "the marks *Cane*"—Toomer's homophonic intent surfaces in a letter in which he refers to this work as "Cain"—these pictorial forms literally mark crucial moments of transition. "Blood-Burning Moon," the final story of the "initial" third of *Cane*, centers on a love triangle that leads to a lynching. This is the violent killing of the black Tom Burwell as he insists on his manhood and his role as the protector of a black woman's virtue. This figure of sacrificial manhood makes his point despite or because of his knife-cut throat as he is burned alive as a phallic martyr and monument: he dies "[o]nly his head, erect, lean, like a blackened stone" (37). In a story pendant with racial equations and questions of balance, Louisa is the woman in contention who has two men who love her: "[h]is [Tom Burwell's] black balanced, and pulled against, the white of [Bob] Stone" (31). In a confrontation that is short and epiphanic, the black Tom Burwell confronts Bob Stone in what (through reading Toomer) I have learned to recognize as a narrative equation:

> "Whats y want?"
> "I'm Bob Stone."
> "Yassur—an I'm Tom Burwell. Whats y want?" (36)

It should be clear that I am approaching Peter Brooks and his epiphany about the almost "palindrome" that appears near the close of *Absalom, Absalom!* This vacuum, filled by the echo that paradoxically articulates its emptiness, gives voice to the mystery that draws this novel forward narratively into the complexity of its being. Faulkner's almost "palindrome" that begins "You are Henry Sutpen" hinges on the words:

> *To die. Yes.*
> *To die?*
> *Yes. To die.* (298)[31]

The narrative of the echoing, hinging whole may be said to hold the key to this narrative form:

> *And you are———?*
> *Henry Sutpen.*
> *And you have been here———?*
> *Four years.*
> *And you came home———?*
> *To die. Yes.*
> *To die?*
> *Yes. To die.*
> *And you have been here———?*
> *Four years.*
> *And you are Henry Sutpen———?*
> *Henry Sutpen.* (*AA!* 298)

This provocatively strange, because empty, narrative might be imagined as looping back to repeat itself in perpetuity, refusing to answer the question of what Quentin knew after he had "seen Clytie." *Absalom, Absalom!* enacts a principle of gossip or story-making, which demonstrates that narrative, like nature (as Thoreau understood), "abhors a vacuum," and that a narrative absence or mystery must be filled. Brooks has found this passage to be the emptiness that fills while configuring emptiness itself through repetition. In Brooks's words, this italicized passage serves as a "concave mirror."[32] A carefully worded conversation that signifies nothing, this passage is the most elaborate visual and aural manifestation in Faulkner's work of what I am arguing is the psychic sign of Quentin's interiority, the haunting echo that signals his madness. Quentin's reveries return to a formula that turns—hinges—on the single word: "yes." Based on repetition itself to form a recognizable language pattern, the hinging, echoing words follow the affirmative turn, the literally enunciated "yes," to locate the fold in the reflective moment. Like the literal fold in father's language-evoking letter that tells of Miss Rosa's death, or like the emerging and disappearing stream of Miss Rosa's voice, these echoes that surface and resurface call attention to this narcissistic fold: the particular junctures where language turns back to echo, to reflect, to mirror, to repeat itself . . . again.[33]

In many ways, Toomer's identifying focus on the "I am" ("Ah'm [I'm] Tom Burwell") as his dark hero insists on his equal value, invokes the counterbalancing or weighing-in of black manhood. At the same time, this assertion of identity calls attention to the Latin *Sum* [*I am*] (*SF* 110) that sums it up for Quentin's internalized father: "Man [is] the sum of his climactic experiences" (*SF* 78). In thematic terms, Toomer's triangles, particularly this violent encounter between the figures who fit the categories of white predator and black protector in a story that takes place under both the title and the celestial omen of a "Blood-Burning Moon," is closely related to Quentin's lunar obsessions.[34] However, the most telling feature that joins Faulkner to Toomer in terms of form and content is stamped with specificity into the echoing dialogue of Quentin's reverie. Virtually the same words spoken by Tom Burwell, words that are narrated in the same reflective and reflexively formal structure, appear in the longest reverie of *The Sound and the Fury*. Faulkner begins this exchange with a classic formulation:

> I dont know yes I dont know (94)

Quentin's interior dialogue continues in full echo of the equation birthed in "Blood-Burning Moon." In Quentin's reverie, Caddy questions Quentin following his failed confrontation with Dalton Ames. Removing the contextual observations (descriptions of setting and what might be called stage directions), Quentin's internalized dialogue echoes the very words of Tom Burwell and Bob Stone in Toomer's *Cane*:

> Quentin . . .
> what do you want . . .
> come here
> what do you want
> come here Quentin (98)

There is no "yes" or "*yes Yes Yes yes*" (94), but the twice-repeated language of "com[ing]" into the "here" now forms the affirmative pivot. This act of affirmation, the "yes" or "yassur," constitutes the folding back of language, spoken and written, the echo that is the narrative equivalent of Narcissus's elusive and ungraspable reflected face.

Echoing Forward to *Absalom, Absalom!*

> . . . and talking in that grim haggard amazed voice until at last listening would renege and hearing-sense self-confound and the long-dead object of her impotent yet indomitable frustration would appear . . .
>
> —William Faulkner, *Absalom, Absalom!*

Versions of this form or formula, often pivoting around or framed by the word "yes," and occasionally folding around the word "no," appear repeatedly in *Absalom, Absalom!* Beginning with the conclusion of the very first italicized segment, the intruding italics signal that Quentin's unspoken thoughts have taken over. From the outset, Quentin listening and "not listening" is actively linked in his mind to the "outraged recapitulation" of the female ghost, Miss Rosa Coldfield. Reverie as well as relationship is encoded in the echoing lines that appear as early as the close of the second page of this linguistically gargantuan and complex novel. "[T]he two separate Quentins now talking to one another in the long silence of notpeople in notlanguage" introduce the dialogic echo—what I am calling the narcissistic fold—that characterizes the formal structure of Quentin's memory-obsessed interiority:

> *It seems that this demon—his name was Sutpen—(Colonel Sutpen)—Colonel Sutpen . . .* [came] *and built a plantation—(Tore violently a plantation, Miss Rosa Coldfield says)—tore violently . . . (Without gentleness begot, Miss Rosa Coldfield says)—without gentleness . . . (Only they destroyed him or something or he destroyed them or something. And died)—and died. Without regret, Miss Rosa Coldfield says—(Save by her) Yes, save by her. (And by Quentin Compson) Yes. And by Quentin Compson.* (5)

While gestures toward such a narrative equation emerge as a tendency in Quentin's interiority before the reverie in "June Second, 1910," this formal device becomes identified as the structure that defines Quentin's madness when it develops into a recognizable form in the reverie. This form conveys a sense of content as its construction with its resonant echo goes beyond repetition to insist on the fold that reflects language narcissistically back into itself. Already a drowned man looking for his shadow that has been "watching for him in the water all the time" (*SF* 57), the Quentin of the reverie is shadowed by repeated reflections, shadows that register his embodiment, while introducing a form of narrative onanism that foreshadows death.

Read in relation to the cataclysmic dénouement of *Absalom, Absalom!*, Quentin's interlude becomes "the prologue to a suttee" (*SF* 64). Near the close of *Absalom, Absalom!*, Clytie sets the fire that burns her and her unwed brother, Henry. Once again, Quentin's reverie, both in formal and thematic terms, rises to a heated pitch that insists on this echoing equation as the defining characteristic of *Absalom, Absalom!* Like Quentin's long reverie, *Absalom, Absalom!*—unquestionably dominated by the longest of all of Quentin's reveries—is written to come before. While *Absalom, Absalom!* provides a literal history, a temporal past that is itself obsessed with the past, this novel was also written by William Faulkner in full consciousness that he was creating a fiction that would stand as a formal past for Quentin Compson.

The vacuum ("that vacuum of crickets"), introduced at the beginning of the longest reverie of *The Sound and the Fury*, is signified and given visibility through the description of a "breath traveling across a mirror" (*SF* 94). This visible breath, the traditional method of determining whether a seemingly dead body might still be living (just as the breath-clouded mirror of my southern girlhood could tell on a menstruating woman) also alludes to the emptiness of the mirrored breath, the tragedy of Echo. Caddy arrives to confront Quentin in the reverie because she has heard the shot; Miss Rosa's fate is to live life listening Cassandra-like at a door that she (like Quentin) cannot pass: "*I heard an echo, but not the shot; I saw a closed door but I did not enter it*" (*AA!* 121). As Quentin in italicized reverie interrupts Mr. Compson's version of the Sutpens' tale, his unvoiced thoughts take shape as the unspoken dialogue of Thomas Sutpen speaking to himself, what might in the terms of *Absalom, Absalom!* be called "the two Thomas Sutpens." Echoing the "two Quentin Compsons" that Miss Rosa's voice has already provoked, Quentin stops listening to his father as he invents an interior dialogue for the young Thomas Sutpen. As Quentin's imagined Sutpen puzzles over whether he should kill the owner of the slave who has forced him to go around to the back of the house, this mountain boy already knows that the dark, "balloon fac[ed]" keeper of doors and guardian of elite thresholds is just a doorman. Quentin's Sutpen argues with himself in an extended echo—a repeated question that follows a repeated answer—that turns on the word "No":

> *But I can shoot him:* and the other: No. *That wouldn't do no good:* and the first: *What shall we do then?*: and the other: *I dont know:*[35] and the first: *But I can shoot him. I could slip right up there through them bushes and lay there until he come out to lay in the hammock and shoot him:* and the other: No. *That wouldn't do no good:* and the first: *Then what shall we do?* and the other: *I dont know . . . But I can kill him—No. That wouldn't do no good—Then what shall we do about it?—I dont know . . .* (*AA!* 190, 191)

Seen as seeing all at once that he and his kind are considered lower than the slaves, Mr. Compson's Thomas Sutpen imagines the plantation owner seeing his family and other poor whites as useless: "cattle, creatures heavy and without grace, brutely evacuated into a world without hope or purpose for them" (*AA!* 190).

The Quentin of *Absalom, Absalom!* is succinct as he returns to his own mind to enter a sharply active phase of "not listening" that ruptures him from and preserves the long, italicized voice that has occupied all but the final page of *Absalom, Absalom!*'s chapter 5. This italicized voice that preoccupies the middle of the novel (chapter 5 out of nine) remains seemingly uninterrupted because it could be read as narrative devourment, as Miss Rosa appears to be swallowed whole by Quentin Compson. Now, actively "not listening," Quentin takes over and begins to describe his own consciousness while losing consciousness as he himself is taken over once again by his need to create voices for the past. Indeed, the peculiar chapter 5 might be said to constitute Miss Rosa being heard rather than Miss Rosa speaking. As he "hears" Miss Rosa, Quentin remains enthralled in the strongly voiced but nevertheless interiorized[36] account that does not waver in its italicized form. The pronouns indicate moments of distancing: Miss Rosa is heard primarily in first-person narration, but Quentin (still inhabiting the emphatic *frisson* indicated by these italics) distances himself from Miss Rosa's voice as her words become the fiction that has possessed his mind. Without explanation, Miss Rosa becomes a figure who is spoken of as a "she" rather than continuing to appear to be just speaking in this narrative that masquerades as an unbroken account delivered in the first person. Returning to conscious awareness and his more active form of "not listening," a not listening that finally blocks his hearing of Miss Rosa, Quentin "abrupt[s]" himself into consciousness as the italics precipitously disappear on the final page of chapter 5. This abrupt return to the present allows Quentin to revert to his own interiority, to script what for him is the most cataclysmic scene of the Sutpens' imagined past: a dramatic dialogue between a brother and a sister, between Henry and Judith.

On the final page of *Absalom, Absalom!*'s chapter 5, italics cease as Quentin is brought back to himself by something he calls "that door"—"something that he too could not pass." And it is striking that Quentin consciously takes over the narration when Miss Rosa's tale has entered the very form and structure of the echo. The italicized narrative (whether we see it as *spoken* by Miss Rosa or *heard* by the unlistening Quentin Compson) concludes: "*'Dead?' I cried. 'Dead? You? You lie; you're not dead; heaven cannot, and hell dare not, have you!*'" (139). As Quentin passively hears her words, he does not interrupt their italicized flow with his own italics because these words (potentially extending backward through the preceding enormity of the novel's fifth chapter) are already (with close to Benjy-like accuracy) imprinted on his brain. As

Quentin interrupts, returning to the roman type that signals his "not listening," this rupture indicates that he has come up against another door. This barrier forces him into his compulsively rendered private fictions that compel him to script a dialogue for the dead or absent. Indeed, Bon's lengthy letter that occupies all save the final page of the close of chapter 4 can be read as an instructive prologue to chapter 5. Just over two pages in length, this letter allows Bon to assume the status of a first-person narrator through an inscribed document in which a "dead tongue speak[s]" (102). Anticipating and confirming the strangeness of what many readers have accepted as Miss Rosa's voice narrating the novel, Bon's missive, as it is read silently into the record of the novel, appears in italicized type without quotation marks. Holding Bon's letter, Quentin is even said to "hear . . . without having to listen as he read the faint spidery script not like something impressed upon the paper by a once living hand but like a shadow cast upon it" (102). In other words, the Quentin of chapter 5 is *not* "not listening." Chapter 5, like Bon's letter, proceeds at length without the narrative ruptures that signal Quentin's active form of "not listening." If Miss Rosa's words can be imagined as swallowed whole in a type of consumption that amounts to narrative incorporation or aural pregnancy on Quentin's part, her voice in chapter 5 is rendered strange by its return in its non-italicized form as Quentin at the close of the chapter asks her to repeat some words that he admits he has not heard.

Miss Rosa's announcement of the gothic presence of "Something living in it . . . living hidden in that house" (140) gives her the final words spoken in chapter 5. At the point Miss Rosa refuses to believe that her adversary has been killed—what we have seen as her echoing refusal to believe in the demon's death—Quentin cuts to the displaced scene of his own failure to uphold the "concept of Compson honor" ("Appendix Compson," *SF* 207). This is the story of preserved honor that Quentin has successfully relocated in the mysterious tale of the Sutpen family's past:

> But Quentin was not listening, because there was also something which he too could not pass—that door, the running feet on the stairs beyond it almost a continuation of the faint shot . . . as the door crashed in and the brother stood there . . . [in] his patched and faded gray tunic, the pistol still hanging against his flank. (*AA!* 139)

A version of the "two Quentins" or Quentin's "two Sutpens" in conversation with their own divided selves, Quentin conceives of what he calls

> the two of them, brother and sister, curiously alike as if the difference in sex had merely sharpened the common blood to a terrific, an almost unbearable, similarity, speaking to one another in short brief staccato sentences like slaps, as if they stood breast to breast striking one another in turn, neither making any attempt to guard against the blows . . . (*AA!* 139)

Heard in the context of the echo form, the narcissistic fold, developed in the longest reverie in *The Sound and the Fury*, the Quentin of *Absalom, Absalom!* introduces the formal echoes that appear as italicized interventions throughout the novel. Notably, Quentin's dialogue that erupts once again into italics at the close of chapter 5 deviates from this established pattern by introducing a note of serious emotional dissonance: an absence that sounds a painful and profound joke. Since all but the final page of chapter 5 is in italics and Quentin's "not listening" is ruptured (established in retrospect) by the willful and precipitant appearance of unaccentuated roman type that indicates psychic presence in the present, Quentin may be said to interrupt himself as he imagines this longed-for, if ritually formulaic and italicized, conversation between a brother and a sister. Quentin's truncated version of this conversation is an unanswered echo. Here, the expected echo has been replaced by the finality of the sentence that proclaims: "*I killed him.*" Quentin's imagined dialogue insists on the radical cutting-off—a homicide in form as well as content—that murders the necessity of (or could even be said to kill the possibility of) the expected echo. In other words, the narcissistic fold literally turns to the question of death ("*Dead?*" Judith queries) and the reverie is silenced after the affirmation, "*Yes*": "*Yes. I killed him.*" Here, Quentin's Judith is silenced by the finality of death. Giving voice to this unspoken reverie serves as a vicarious and possibly painful pleasure for Quentin as his imagined dialogue depicts Henry as having shot the man who has come for *his* sister. This verbal confrontation at the gate is cut short by the violent act that abrogates the necessity for repetition, narrative or otherwise:

> *Now you cant marry him.*
> *Why cant I marry him?*
> *Because he's dead.*
> *Dead?*
> *Yes. I killed him.*
> He [Quentin] couldn't pass that. (*AA!* 139–40)

This truncated echo of Quentin's imagined, italicized confrontation between Judith and Henry that erupts in the final two pages of chapter 5 is framed, as it were, by the echoing "no"s of a preliminary (imagined and italicized) dialogue that takes place precisely three chapters later within two pages of the close of chapter 8. Just as the "no" in "no, no" and "no, no, no" can become the affirmation of the double negative as well as the negation of an inappropriate act, what might be called a "no-no," the "no" is an aural pun that raises the epistemological quandary of what it means to "know" at all, as well as insisting on the biblical sense of what it means to "know"—to have carnal knowledge. The threat of touching is also a threat of teaching.[37] This confrontation that imagines Henry forbidding Bon to marry or, perhaps more pointedly, forbidding him to bed his sister insists on the ritualized form of the echo:

—No! Henry cries.—No! No! I will—I'll—

[. . .]

—No, Henry says.—No. No.

—I cannot?

—You shall not.

—Who will stop me, Henry?

—No, Henry says.—No. No. No. (*AA!* 285)[38]

What does punctuation mean when it appears in purely invented dialogue? Is it more pure because it is "said" without the words? This series of "no"s goes from the exclamatory call back to the title that itself laments the sacrifice of sons and sexually violated and rejected sisters (the biblical Tamar as well as Caddy). What do negated "periods" mean in imagined, unspoken dialogue? The exclamation "*No. No. No.*" in this echo formation can function as an emphatically stated "Yes," with the concluding "*No.*" confirming that there will indeed be "*No. No.*"

Thomas Sutpen's murder told in the echoing challenge of male confronting male clearly repeats the young Sutpen's earlier quandary in which he (in Quentin's invented dialogue) argues with himself, finally deciding not to kill the owner of the Tidewater plantation. Yet, as John Irwin has argued, in the fatal repetition of this scene with the father and grandfather figure, Wash Jones, Sutpen has once again assumed the place of the son who is faced with death for having violated the rule of the father. Ironically, as Irwin also points out, Sutpen has just stood in the place of the father rejecting a "son" (as Shreve and the reader must be told) because the child is not a son but a daughter. Repeated the second time by Quentin Compson, the scene of confrontation between Sutpen and Wash is not generated from Quentin's dialogue-driven mind. Indeed, Sutpen's and Wash's words, overheard as a challenge that follows the moment of birth, gain their importance because they precipitate violent death. These words that result in three murders and a virtual suicide have the sacredness of all last words, whether uttered from the gallows or from the head of a dying man on a pillow. The black female witness, the midwife, has heard "Sutpen say, 'Stand back, Wash. Dont you touch me': and then Wash, his voice soft and hardly loud enough to reach her: 'I'm going to tech you, Kernel': and Sutpen again; 'Stand back Wash!'" (*AA!* 229). As Quentin repeats this exchange, he does so with the precision traditional to deathbed narratives, and we are fully aware that his very words echo those of the actual witness: "'Stand back. Don't you touch me' [. . .] 'I'm going to tech you, Kernel' and Sutpen said 'Stand back, Wash'" (*AA!* 231). As critics have pointed out, the word "touch" in Wash Jones's repetition has become the dialect word "tech"—a word that depending on the pronunciation can transform the echoed "touch" into "teach," aurally marking this as a scene of violent pedagogy. In other words, as the father kills the son, Quentin repeats the narrative act of repetition in a confrontation between men. This is framed as an actual historical event (heard by the midwife) and could be understood as a site of narrative origins that has grandfathered-in (so to speak) the formal and enfolding echo which has come to define the Quentin Compson of both novels.

In terms of claims for the fiction of the historically real, four years before Wash kills Sutpen, there is already a documented appearance of this narrative echo that surfaces as a mere trace in Bon's letter to Judith. I should add for the record that this letter, Bon's last words, has the status of a deathbed narrative, as do the words spoken by Judith when she bequeaths this letter to Quentin's grandmother. Judith's words, inherited by Quentin Compson from his grandmother, have rare documentary weight in the tenuous reality of this metafiction made up of convincing tales. Judith's account has become a legacy, attached to and made real as part of the extended aura of a physical object (Bon's letter) that continues to speak as well as to bear the narrative that has framed its portentous exchange. Despite Judith's tone of eulogy, there is no sermonic distance as she offers an evocative deathbed speech for this letter and letters in the broader sense of the term:

> Read it if you like or dont read it if you like. Because you make so little impression, you see . . . And so maybe you could go to someone, the stranger the better, and give them something—a scrap of paper—something, anything, it not to mean anything in itself and them not even to read it or keep it, not even bother to throw it away or destroy it, at least it would be something just because it would have happened, be remembered even if only from passing from one hand to another, one mind to another, and it would be at least a scratch, something, something that might make a mark on something that *was* once for the reason that it can die someday, while the block of stone cant be *is* because it never can become *was* because it cant ever die or perish. . . . . . . (100–101)

Bon's letter with its inscribed trace of an echo captures the camaraderie of men mired together in a lost cause: "*How we laughed. Yes, we laughed*" (103). Faulkner's use of this formal device as a defining characteristic of Quentin's interiority may have begun in the realm of authorial transcendence, but this form has become a conscious device in the writing of *Absalom, Absalom!* Two pages into chapter 6, the novel calculates this very form as a verbal confrontation based on a strict economy of words: "the two of them slashing at one another with twelve or fourteen words and most of these the same words repeated two or three times so that when you boiled it down they did it with eight or ten" (142). This is a direct reference to Quentin's invented dialogue between Henry and Judith that has just appeared on the concluding page of chapter 5. Before the echo is truncated, stopped by the finality of the announcement attributed to Henry, "I killed him," Faulkner's text actually uses "fourteen words" "boiled" "down [to] ten." An exact counting here, this formula calibrates the economy of the echo form throughout Faulkner's fiction. Significantly, had the echo form continued to echo in Quentin's truncated fantasy, the formula still would have been "boiled" down to "eight or ten" repeating words.

"Evangeline, Evangeline!"

Faulkner's short story "Evangeline" hearkens back to at least 1929 and the publication of *The Sound and the Fury*, and looks forward to the past rendered for that novel's Quentin Compson in *Absalom, Absalom!* (1936). The emergence of this echo formula in "Evangeline" strongly suggests a formal genealogy that told Faulkner *Absalom, Absalom!* was meant to be a retrospective narrative about Quentin Compson. While "Evangeline" was rejected for publication in 1931, the completed story itself (or some of its earlier versions) could have been written before or even at the same time that Faulkner was writing *The Sound and the Fury*. This crucial claim of genealogy is not based on temporal sequence but rather on Faulkner's acts of reading and rereading his own work. What I am insisting on here is a moment of recognition that allowed William Faulkner to realize that his unnamed narrator in "Evangeline" *was* Quentin Compson. Whether this story or its earlier variants was written before or after *The Sound and the Fury*, the rejected "Evangeline" mirrors Quentin's psychic signature, the ritualized echo form that in its reverberation displays his madness and insists (at the end of the day—"June Second, 1910") on the role of the reverie as a narrative prelude to Quentin's suicide, as well as providing a prologue to Quentin Compson's echoing past that would emerge in *Absalom, Absalom!*

"Evangeline" begins with dueling narrators who argue tongue-in-cheek over what flower—the writer interrupts proposing "Azalea" then "Syringa"—will name Sutpen's "jewel," the daughter who is actually named "Judith" (*Uncollected Stories* 584). Looking forward to David's lament, condensed from the second book of Samuel to become the title of *Absalom, Absalom!* by removing the internal and intervening echo "my son, my son," the former slaves of "Evangeline" entering the hall after Judith's death hear a primal call for silence: "[A]ll that day the house seemed to be whispering: 'Shhhhhh. Miss Judith. Miss Judith. Shhhhhh'" (592). And whether by this admonition or by authorial design (death is not only the great leveler but, in practical terms, somewhat of a silencer), Judith Sutpen and her "coffee-colored" sister, Clytie, are known for their silence in *Absalom, Absalom!*

In Faulkner's "Evangeline," the women of color on the Sutpen place are the informants who speak to the "painter" and the "writer." The "Clytie" figure of "Evangeline," Raby, is the watchdog: she is the Cerberus figure, the ultimate doorkeeper who along with a purebred German shepherd dog (shades of canine and Teutonic eugenics) guards against intrusions into the Sutpen mansion. In a frightening turn of events, the invasive reporter, who identifies himself to the female doorkeeper as "[a] man that writes pieces for the newspapers and such," is forced by Raby to come upstairs to see the dying figure of "Henry Sutpen" (595). Hoping to see the female ghost promised by his friend in the ten-word telegram that has brought him to this small town in Mississippi, the writer expects to see a living Judith Sutpen who (as the local, suspicion-laden story goes) had been put into her coffin by Raby alone. Following the trope that sees the Civil War as a family dispute, a war between brothers and, here, brothers-in-law, "Evangeline" turns on echoing narration that frames a family murder.[39]

The echo formation appears as Henry and Judith speak in "Evangeline." As the man who will later introduce himself to Raby as a newspaper reporter presents the dialogue, it begins with Judith speaking to the returning Henry:

> "'Yes?' she says. 'Yes?'"

Henry may be imagined here as echoing Judith's questioning "Yes?" since the conversation concludes as a responsive dialogue:

> "Oh," she says. . . . . "Was—was the journey hard on him?"
> "It was not hard on him."
> "Oh," she says. "Yes. Yes. Of course. There must have been a last . . . last shot, so that it could end. Yes." (591; Faulkner's ellipses)

The first echo is framed by Judith's speaking of the "Yes," the next by her apostrophe, the repeated phrase "'Oh,' she says" that frames an internal pattern of repetition before the echoing refrain returns to Judith's affirming "Yes." This dialogue hinging on the repeated word "last . . . last" has been separated by Faulkner's ellipses or, more precisely, the grammatical signal that indicates a catch in Judith's voice, a momentary silence. In terms of the prospects of its documentary status, this dialogue has the sanctity of a deathbed narrative and is spoken within earshot, so to speak, of an array of black witnesses. These unnamed figures, whom Judith is pointedly said to refer to by name when she calls to them to bring the dead "Mr Charles"[40] into the house, are the heirs to the Sutpen story. Raby, once the source of powerful stories, as "the grandmother" (Raby's daughter) tells the painter, has long since ceased to speak about the past. Speaking to the writer, the painter explains

> how the old woman [Raby] used to talk a lot, telling the stories over and over, until about forty years ago. Then she quit talking, telling the stories . . . [T]he old woman would get mad and say such and such a thing never happened at all and tell them to hush their mouths and get out of the house. But she said that before that she [Raby's daughter] had heard the stories so much that now she never could remember whether she had seen something or just heard it told. (586)

In the fifth section of "Evangeline," the self-described writer hears mockingbirds, "two of them, answering one another, brief, quiring, risinginflectioned." As "the insects and birds became one peaceful sound bowled inside the skull in monotonous miniature," the unnamed "newspaper writer" imagines "the earth . . . contracted and reduced to the dimensions of a baseball" (605). Like a speaking version of a magic lantern, the shades of the dead become the "shapes, fading, emerged fading and faded emerging." Again, the echoing dialogue that immediately follows has been introduced by this shorter echo, but this time the fading shapes of the dead "emerge" to be interviewed by the reporter in a dialogue with the dead that reads like a legal deposition:

> "And you were killed by the last shot fired in the war?"
> "I was so killed. Yes."
> "Who fired the last shot fired in the war?"
> "Was it the last shot you fired in the war, Henry?"
> "I fired a last shot in the war; yes." (606)

The echo begins before the framing word "yes" emerges, but the echo here is found in the shot, the peculiar status established in the earlier exchange in which Judith insists on the necessity of a "last . . . last shot," concluding without interruption: "so it could end" (591). This writer's thoughts parallel the mirrorlike passage that contains Quentin's formulaic echoing and self-erasingly reflective conversation with the dying Henry Sutpen in *Absalom, Absalom!* who has "come home" "*To die? / Yes. To die.*" And, as in *Absalom, Absalom!*, where Miss Rosa famously imagines Quentin becoming a writer and selling her story to sate his wife's material desires, the writer in "Evangeline," as he hears "the sound bowled inside [his] skull," has assumed the prerogatives of an author.

Reverie does not just allow reflection; it is arguably the favored form of conversation with the dead. Bon has been killed, but those who died or who became ghosts when this "last . . . last shot" was fired constitute a more inclusive category. The writer in "Evangeline" understands the concept of the living dead after he sees the sleeping, the dying, Henry. Having spent forty years hiding in the house of Sutpen, Henry, in effect, has killed himself when he kills Bon. As the writer figure continues to question Henry and Raby in his dialogic soliloquy, he generates an interview that is clearly a composite fiction that has been invoked under the sign of repeaters: the conversation of mockingbirds. There is no "vacuum of crickets" (*SF* 94) here as the figure of the writer is whelmed by the voices coming from his skull, emerging once again into a strict and then modified echo form:

> "Yes."
> "Yes what?"
> "Yes."

"Oh. And you have lived hidden here for forty years."

"I have lived here forty years."

"Were you at peace?"

"I was tired."

"That's the same thing, isn't it? For you and Raby too."

Here, as the unnamed writer recalls Raby speaking, the Clytie figure of "Evangeline" seems to echo his narrative of sameness, literally voiced as repeating the writer figure's phrase by saying the "same thing":

"Same thing. Same as me. I tired too."

"Why did you do all of this for Henry Sutpen?"

"He was my brother." (606)

Before her voice answers, "He was my brother," Raby intervenes in the writer's recalled or invented dialogue—the shapes "fading" and "emerging" from his "bowled . . . skull"—to point out her role of sameness in the narrative equation: "Same thing. Same as me. I tired too." As part of the conversation of mockingbirds, these words echo Raby's earlier repetition of what Judith has been heard to say to this same brother as she lies dying:

"Henry. Henry, I'm tired. I'm so tired, Henry" (604).

While the sources for the echoing voices of the writer's dialogue with the dead, like Judith's overheard conversation with her murderous brother, remain unsubstantiated, the words attributed to Raby are based closely on her actual statements in section 4 of "Evangeline": "I going soon too. Because I tired as Judith, too" (604). Speaking "her voice not waisthigh, level, quiet," Raby tells the reporter: "Henry Sutpen is my brother," and what have been presented as her actual words are only slightly rearranged in the fifth section, as her brother's name becomes part of the writer's created (or re-created) dialogue: "Why did you do all of this for Henry Sutpen?" / "He is my brother."

The ultimately echoing images are the framed faces of women of color who do not speak, but manage in their faces themselves to bear the last word. "[A] shade darker than the mother . . . still the Indian, faintly; still the Sutpen, in her face" (608), "the grandmother" (Raby's daughter) wears a "mudstained khaki army overcoat" (609) as she walks with the writer amid the "unfallen chimneys and the charred wood" (608) in a scene that could be the ruins of a war. Raby's parting visage echoes the pictorial framings of Addie Bundren, while the unnamed first bride of Bon speaks through the features of her photographed head to evoke the literary tradition of the tragic mulatta.[41] Found in the smoldering ashes, this pictured woman's words inscribed to the man she refers to as "*mon mari*" remain legible: "*Toujours*," literally "all days," meaning "always" (609). This long-concealed face, hammered shut into the "book"-like metal case some fifty years earlier, speaks to the writer figure of a wife who is not the blonde and virginal Judith. Earlier the writer has opened another "door" to discover another figure who is not Judith but the dying Henry Sutpen laid out on "yellowish" sheets (598). In a culture that has procured its identity through a fetishization of pure-white southern womanhood, Judith is the expected yet absent figure. While Raby, the Clytie figure of "Evangeline," echoes back to the pictures of her hill country sister, Addie Bundren,[42] the face of Raby forms a jarring echo, a pictorial counterpoint, to the sensual face of the other "white" woman of color that has been hidden in the violently closed picture's "book." Charles Bon's imagined photograph (in one of the two references to mirrors that appear in this object-rich and intently reflective novel) is what Miss Rosa would "*invent*" "*if* [she] *were God*":

> *something (a machine perhaps) which would adorn the barren mirror altars of every plain girl that breathes with such as this* [. . .]*—this pictured face. It would not even need a skull behind it . . .* (*AA!* 118)

Bon's photographed visage is the unseen face that for Miss Rosa can exist "*in some shadow realm of make-believe.—A picture seen by stealth*" (118). Bon's face in *Absalom, Absalom!* is the face that does not reflect. Bon, alone among Thomas Sutpen's putative progeny, is never said to have a "Sutpen" face. The secret female face of "Evangeline," the hidden photograph, bears the story of race as a fatal reflection. This "light picture"[43] of Bon's first wife in "Evangeline," with her "doomed and passionate face," is described by the writer-narrator:

> the mouth rich, full, a little loose, the hot, slumberous, secretive eyes, the inklike hair with its faint but unmistakable wiriness—all the ineradicable and tragic stamp of negro blood. (608)

Unlike the Quentin of *Absalom, Absalom!*, neither of the dueling and collaborative tellers, neither the painter nor the reporter of "Evangeline," search for themselves in the living ghosts of the Sutpen legacy.[44] The final faces that are framed are those of the women of color who, speaking or silent, serve as the informants to the "amateur painter" and the newspaper writer. Raby breaks her silence after forty years, forcing the writer to hear and see the partial story that must be imagined as versions of the mesmerically real stories she has told to her daughter. This unnamed woman in the daguerreotype is the echo that does not echo. The tragic mulatta of "Evangeline" is the wire-haired Medusa unaware: "the face which had unawares [*sic*] destroyed three lives" (609).

There is no Shreve figure in "Evangeline"; there is only the "*rêve*," the reverie, the dream that such a figure represents in the divided consciousness which brings together the characters of a painter and a writer to pursue a story of living ghosts. The Quentin of *Absalom, Absalom!* is clearly both the painter and the writer. As he interrupts his listening and his hearing with literalized visions, intently pictured people and doors that he is unable to pass, Quentin the fiction-maker and inventor of dialogues first sees the characters of his fancy in visual forms. To borrow a phrase from the classical philosopher Horace,[45] whose pages (along with liquor) occupy Quentin's father's waking hours, Quentin suffers from "*ut pictura poesis.*"[46] According to this idealized aesthetic theory (an actual, practical experience in the lives of some men and women), words on the page succeed as art only insofar as they are able to invoke actual pictures in the mind's eye. Quentin in his madness is haunted by the ritualized echoes that he hears when he remembers or imagines verbal confrontations. But as he listens to the tales of others, Quentin Compson is interrupted by his picture-making compulsion that so often evokes the echoing voices which preoccupy his present. For Faulkner's Quentin Compson "the representation compulsion" is close kin to "the repetition compulsion." Quentin Compson is both male and female, both writer and painter: the visual image in his divided consciousness both precedes and is provoked by the echoing word.

Unable to stop the echo that his sister is incarnating in her fatherless daughter that will bear his name, the Narcissus-like Quentin can only escape the pursuit of repetition and the formal haunting of the echo by embracing his reflection, which waits on the waiter. The door that cannot be passed is "the dark tall place on the wall" that is "like a door, only it wasn't a door": the dark, unfaded place that once held Benjy's beloved mirror (*SF* 39). In his last glance, Quentin sees his broken eye in the mirror: we do not. Ending with the closed "bag" (113) required by the conventions of autobiography, Quentin leaves letters that speak beyond the grave. Turning to Quentin's early words of *Absalom, Absalom!*, the suicide that takes place beyond the ending of *The Sound and the Fury* allows Quentin to cease to be an occupied—largely a preoccupied—body: "his very body" is no longer "an empty hall echoing with sonorous defeated names" (*AA!* 7). The reflective moment in the dark mirror must be read through Faulkner's ultimate reverie, *Absalom, Absalom!*, a novel that echoes the attractions of death for the Quentin of *The Sound and the Fury*. Quentin's ending takes place off of any page save those of critics' imaginations that see him trying to end echoing words by choosing the dark embrace of a river named Charles.

Coda. Textual Intimacies in the Frame of History

> "Now I want you to tell me just one thing more. Why do you hate the South?"
>
> "I dont hate it," Quentin said, quickly, at once, immediately; "I dont hate it," he said. *I dont hate it* he thought, panting in the cold air, the iron New England dark: *I dont. I dont! I dont hate it! I dont hate it!*
>
> —Quentin's final echo, *Absalom, Absalom!*

As it narrates the end of Quentin Compson, *The Sound and the Fury* paradoxically looks forward to the past that has almost conquered the Quentin of *Absalom, Absalom!* Certainly, the emergence of this reverberating echo charts a formal genealogy, which underlines the fact that Faulkner designed *Absalom, Absalom!* as a retrospective narrative integral to the story of Quentin Compson. The recognizable signature of Quentin's madness, articulated in this reflective formula, rises to the level of a haunting in his longest reverie in "June Second, 1910," to establish this periodless period as a signifying place of narrative origins. Using "slow reading,"[47] Richard Godden's term for a type of close reading that is alive to history, I would like to return to Quentin Compson's reverie as a provocation to what might be called a larger frame. It is necessary to ask what this masculine allegory of confrontation that takes the emasculating form of a swallowing echo might mean by revisiting the threshold that appears at the opening of Quentin's longest reverie in *The Sound and the Fury*. This threshold is morphological and irrevocable, and it comes before Caddy's wedding that is, in itself, neither an entry into nor an exit from paradise. Herbert Head with his bank cannot hoover[48] the Compsons into an appropriate vacuum. Caddy, like Herbert Head himself, is guilty of cheating on a "mid-term" project: he does not know that she is already pregnant when she meets him in French Lick, Indiana.[49] This passage's "vacuum of crickets like a breath traveling across a mirror" leads to the scene of ablution, but Caddy cannot be washed clean to an empty "nothing." The pregnant sister cannot signify the intact "nothing" that wreaked such havoc and "much ado" in the resonant slang of Shakespeare's world.

The Civil War with its violated boundaries has taken place, and Caddy cannot embody the clean slate of a female South that will marry the banks and Herbert Hoover's nation to offer a pure bloodline and an untainted descent that would avoid the Depression. (Of course, in a Faulknerian economy, the word "depression" should be imagined here as appearing both with and without capitalization.) Caddy has been broken in by the "khaki"-clad Dalton Ames, the signifier of the Spanish-American War and the repatriation of a militarized South.[50] The Thomas Sutpen who rides into *Absalom, Absalom!*'s Jefferson in 1833, a year that originates in the biblical notation for David's lament in 2 Samuel 18:33 ("O my son Absalom! my son, my son, Absalom! . . . O Absalom, my son, my son!"), designs history. Acquiring class and history by means of his get on the body of a respectable Methodist daughter, his unequal—dominating—partnership with Wash Jones in the country store is part of the rise of the mercantile class that C. Van Woodward identified in *The Origins of the New South*.[51] Woodward saw a class rise based on change rather than continuity, as figures like Flem Snopes and Thomas Sutpen rose to positions of power during the postbellum years by owning and operating the small stores that provided the staples for newly freed blacks as well as whites of all classes. Whereas Sutpen has decided not to kill the plantation owner who has ordained that his (Sutpen's) kind will be forever turned away from the front door reserved for class equals who call to court or even just to visit, the Wash Jones of 1869 stands with his scythe as the "Grim Reaper." He is a primal doorkeeper who is both very old and edgily new. A member of the generation some twenty years too early for the populism that would, in its most visionary reach, imagine class as the great uniter for those at the bottom, Wash Jones has not envisioned the rise of poor southerners across racial lines in a revolt that would insist on fundamental change rather than mere reversals of hierarchies. Yet Faulkner's choice of his character's name is clearly provocative here. The name Wash Jones is based on that of George Washington Jones, a prominent populist candidate for the U.S. Congress in the east Texas of the 1890s. This nominal tie frames a formerly feudal figure, naming his highly symbolic, practical, and ultimately futile violence as a harbinger of the most magnificent failure in the history of southern class revolts.[52]

At the close of *Absalom, Absalom!*, Sutpen's mixed-blood grandchild, the idiot Jim Bond, haunts the sooty prowling ground of Sutpen's Hundred. This ash heap with its lone howling idiot is all that remains of the House of Sutpen, and there is equality in the fact that the House of Jones has been slaughtered by the grandfather in a confrontation of old men. What remains is Jones's daughter, who inhabits another type of mansion of men's tawdry dreams in a Memphis that is not heaven. Finally, as Melissa Meek's magazine photograph drawn folded from her purse shows, there are worse fates than that of whoring in Memphis; there are worse fates than Faulkner's self-described "whoring" to the magazines as he offered short stories—his letters—in exchange for money. The worst fate of a fallen South is pictured not in the body of the fallen daughter of a defeated nation but in the reappearance of that very woman as an accessory to another defeated nation: the Reich on the rise. Caddy Compson is last seen in the librarian's photograph "from a slick magazine" as she stands next to "an open powerful expensive chromiumtrimmed sports car" and a "German staffgeneral" ("Appendix Compson" 209, 210).

Echoing himself as he anticipates his own suicide as a folding of his body into its waiting shadow or reflection, Quentin's death is a form of failed initiation. As Quentin imagines his sentimental version of heaven in *Absalom, Absalom!*, the celestial hill is already occupied in ranked order by dead heroes, identified as the waiting figures of Colonel Sartoris and "grandfather" (General Compson). Drawn, however briefly, to the phallicized figure of Dalton Ames, Quentin finally eschews the fetishized masculinity that would allow him to join Caddy's first lover and the other brown-shirted "heroes"[53] that stand across the bridge leading into twentieth-century Nazism, Fascism, and the Cult of Masculinity so attractive to the male children of the defeated. Self-absorbed and reflective, Quentin pursues his flight from sexuality as he seeks chastity in death, choosing suicide over the more patriotic and nationalist pastime of organized homicide. In "Evangeline," the early manuscript that would in retrospect become a seed-story for *Absalom, Absalom!*, Judith Sutpen sees what she refers to as "the ending" in her brother Henry's killing of Charles Bon. Amid the full presence of the echo structure with its formal folding back into itself and the notable absence of Quentin Compson, Judith focuses with significance on what she calls a "last . . . last shot" in the war: the formal necessity of declaring "the ending" that demarcates and constitutes an unechoing boundary beyond which killing once again can become murder.

CHAPTER SIX

Bonfires of the Masculinities

Wharton and Faulkner in the Glare of Whistler's *Falling Rocket*

If ever mortal painted an idea, that mortal was Roderick Usher.
—Edgar Allan Poe, "The Fall of the House of Usher"

It loomed, bulked, square and enormous, with jagged half-toppled chimneys, its roofline sagging a little; for an instant as they moved, hurried, toward it Quentin saw completely through it a ragged segment of sky with three hot stars in it as if the house were of one dimension, painted on a canvas curtain in which there was a tear; now, almost beneath it, the dead furnace-breath of air in which they moved seemed to reek in slow and protracted violence with a smell of desolation and decay as if the wood of which it was built were flesh.
—William Faulkner, *Absalom, Absalom!*[1]

In a profound engagement with the meaning of Addie Bundren, Doreen Fowler has argued (building on the critique advanced by Luce Irigaray) that the primal tale of the son killing the father has functioned as an androcentric cover story that has itself concealed (repressed) the "founding myth of Western culture": the murder of the mother. Hers is the dead body over whom the patriarchy lords its primacy (48–49).[2] This murdered mother (or violated wife or virgin who stands in her place) appears early and often in Faulkner's fiction. The original manuscript of *Sanctuary*, rejected for publication before Faulkner completed *As I Lay Dying*, opens with an incarcerated black artist—"de bes ba'ytone singer in nawth Mississippi" (115). This "negro murderer," the admired baritone who draws a chorus as he continues to sing, awaits his hanging for having "slashed [his wife's] throat with a razor so that" "her whole head toss[ed] . . . backward from the bloody regurgitation" (114). In this once originary scene (later tellingly buried at the opening of chapter 16 in the published *Sanctuary*), the dismembered woman, said to have continued to run "up the quiet moonlit lane" (114). This troubled couple lacks the metonym for burning flesh, the gasoline that signals the seemingly inevitable lynching which awaits the incarcerated black man, Lucas Beauchamp, in Faulkner's overtly political *Intruder in the Dust* (1948). However, as this strange (because seemingly nonessential) side story in *Sanctuary* reveals, the racial directive that links sculpted bodies to Faulkner's parables of art had already been formulated before he began to blacken his Bundrens in *As I Lay Dying*.[3] Race, leaving the concern with skin color aside, is foregrounded in this early version as the male artist who, having killed a woman, is sentenced to a hanging. Applying Fowler's sense of the "founding myth[s]" of Western culture, Faulkner offers a feminist revision: a man will be killed for having killed a woman or, more pointedly, a male artist has been condemned to die because he has sculpted his woman into a headless body. Yet this is not just a feminist retelling of the male art of violence as it gives the lie to Freud's version of the origins of Western culture. By telling the story that lies before, the tale that has been masked by the replacement narrative, this account of a cutting and a hanging in the 1920s South joins male and female depradations to compose a ritualized lynching, a fatal story of art that has become too embodied.

As I Lay Dying is not only the first novel to mention Yoknapatawpha County; this work holds the status of being Faulkner's first published novel to focus primarily on race.[4] This being said, Faulkner's attentiveness to race as crucial to his parable of art precedes even the bloody opening gambit composed for the original typescript of *Sanctuary*. The "only real artist" in Faulkner's *Mosquitoes* is the white sculptor who is called "black": an "autogethsemane carved darkly out of pure space," and this same bad novel about aesthetics details the story of yet another white anomaly who may be an artist: a "little black man" met in a bookstore (25, 48). His name is not "Walker," not "Foster," it is "Faulkner" spelled with a *u*. While the Whartonian Faulkner was being catalytically thrust into his wildly controlled experimentalism, he, like the Wharton who wrote *Ethan Frome*, inherited what would remain for both of them the explicitly gendered story of abstract art found in the mother of all head games: Edgar Allan Poe's "The Fall of the House of Usher."

Poe's proto-Jungian, pre–Civil War parable of art narrates a return to a lost state of wholeness. "The Fall of the House of Usher" follows a first-person narrator as he ostensibly goes to visit the decaying, tarn-mirrored ancestral home of his "boon companion [. . .]," Roderick Usher. Once there, he comes to find the inhabitants of the structure, Roderick and his twin sister, Madeline, to be worse off than the house itself. Roderick regales the narrator with descriptions of his mental and physical deterioration and later devotes himself to art: playing dirges on the guitar, extemporizing complex analogues for the family fate in an elegant poem, painting light, and reading aloud from a tome of medieval terrors to accompany the sublime music of nature—a loud and light-filled electric storm. After the narrator has only seen her alive once and before this frenzy of art erupts, Madeline appears to die, and the narrator helps install her body in an impregnable, metal-reinforced chamber beneath the house. However, in typical Poe fashion, Roderick Usher's twin sister is not quite dead and claws her way out of this tomb to reunite with her male half, scaring both the brother and his blood-streaked risen sister to death. Having found the deferred wholeness in their final and fatal embrace, brother and sister, male and female, are swallowed by the black and miasmic tarn that ends art by eradicating the distance which (in the Lacanian view) has rendered words necessary in the first place. Anticipating Samuel Beckett's postnuclear drama *Endgame*, Poe chose to set his prophetic story of the origins of abstract art in a human skull—a morphological house with "vacant eye-like windows" and an interior door of "ebony jaws" (318, 335).[5] As my own earlier work has recognized, chiming along with that of many others, Poe's most famous story, a direct and primary antecedent to Wharton's *Ethan Frome*, is also a clear antecedent to important cataclysmic scenes in Faulkner's fiction, in particular the gothic realm located in his "Dark House[s]."[6] Faulkner chose this phrase (most famous as the description of the madhouse in Shakespeare's *Twelfth Night*) as his working title for both *Absalom, Absalom!* and *Light in August*, his most detailed philosophical accounts of the social construction of race.[7] The relationship between Poe's "Fall of the House of Usher" and its modernist progeny is formal as well as thematic. Like *Absalom, Absalom!*, Cather's *The Professor's House*, Wharton's *Ethan Frome*, and others, "The Fall of the House of Usher" contains a "book within the book," a story within the story, in this case an extemporaneous poem. Sung by its madman creator, "The Haunted Palace" foretells the "fall" of the Usher house and ancestral line in a narrative that is a direct harbinger of the grotesque fate of Addie Bundren. The final stanza summarizes the way of all flesh. Here, death is depicted as liquefaction as what was once living pours out of what appears to be a tooth-bared skull: "While, like a rapid ghastly river, / Through the pale door, / A hideous throng rush out forever, / And laugh—but smile no more" (327).

This poem with its generic sense of the fall of a kingdom and a family that comes down to the dark house of the rotting human body is finally less moving than another story within the story that takes the form of a painting. The obsessed Roderick Usher has created a picture of a tunnel-like enclosure, articulated through "a flood of intense rays of light roll[ing] throughout, and bath[ing] the whole in a ghastly and inappropriate splendor" (325). This man, whose head and creations continue to be the subject of the narrator's focused view, has made a painting of terrifyingly liquid light. Roderick Usher's painting of trapped light, contained in a deep place with no exit, pictures the power of abstraction to go beyond representational art. The narrator has already averred: "If ever mortal painted an idea, that mortal was Roderick Usher" (324). This painting of "an idea" said to be "partaking not so much of the rigid spirit of abstraction" anticipates the potency of abstract art to tell a more primal tale. If the light itself signifies life unburdened by flesh, this contained space clearly pictures the suppressed story, the story of a laid-away body that drives Poe's tale. Such art is possible, arguably rendered necessary, because two men, the narrator and the artist, have collaborated in the burial of a woman. Indeed, this burial of the woman, the only potential mother in the story necessitates the veritable glut of art produced as the story explodes toward an ending. This uncontainable light is the life force of death that radiates outward as the source of Poe's story as well as the wellspring of the grand succession of morphological houses of fiction that have fallen in its wake. If art must be produced to make the burial bearable, to make the "sound of it . . . as though it never had been" (*SF* 112),[8] abstraction depends on getting rid of the mother's body.[9]

What is at stake in Poe's sounding of the archetype is the peace that comes from the ultimate erasure of representational art. There is nothing left after the "rushing asunder" as the dark water closes "sullenly and silently over the fragments of the '*House of Usher*'" (335, 336; Poe's italics and quotation marks). Lit in the glare of exploding "orbs" of light, the "House of Usher" (the place, family, and the quotation-framed title of the story that has headed the tale) has been swallowed like art, silencing the need for narrative itself. The "House," whether the morphological structure or the family that the word is said to encompass, is the subject that has folded into its reflected and inverted representation. Art, as Lacan intuits of language, has no reason to exist as both the representation and what has been represented disappear in a return to the primordial womb, a prelingual intimacy that leaves only a dark mirror untroubled by reflection. Finally, "The House of Usher" may reflect the end of reflection, the peace which covers the fear that the woman may not always return and that a man might learn "at last that the human race really doesn't have to even try to produce art" (*WP* 98).[10]

Faulkner's Wharton and Wharton's Whistler

The most pictorial scenes of *As I Lay Dying* consciously frame a picture of the dying and rotting mother at the center of the scene of art. Made visible in their wounded bodies, Addie Bundren's increasingly feminized sons have become blackened men (the adjective "nigger" defines their damaged parts) as they risk their skins to preserve the mother despite her death. These "pictures" are crucial to the reading of race as it emerges in *As I Lay Dying*, and to the development of Faulkner's regionally revised parable of art. Meanwhile, these explicitly pictorial scenes in *As I Lay Dying* are directly based on crucially relevant passages from Edith Wharton's novels *The Age of Innocence* (1920) and *Twilight Sleep* (1927). As Cash looks up at "the gaunt face framed by the window in the twilight," Darl concludes: "It is [for Cash] a composite picture of all time . . . [Cash's mother, Addie] looks down at him from the composite picture, neither with censure nor approbation. Then the face disappears"

(48). As Wharton's Newland Archer muses at his "writing table" in the final chapter of *The Age of Innocence*, the narrator explains: "When he thought of Ellen Olenska it was abstractly, serenely, as one might think of some imaginary beloved in a book or a picture: she had become the composite vision of all that he had missed."[11] This picturing of the renounced love of his life is immediately followed by the story of the death of his wife, the mother who has died saving one of their sons.

Wharton's "composite vision" of an "abstractly" present "imaginary beloved in a book or picture," as it is juxtaposed with the fact of the dead mother, is significant when read in relation to what Faulkner's Darl sees as "the composite picture of all time" in *As I Lay Dying*. Wharton's *Twilight Sleep* (1927), a novel about irresponsible mothers and the sacrifice of daughters, takes its name from an anesthesia developed for amputations during the Civil War that continued to be used through the 1960s to blunt the pain of childbirth. In *Twilight Sleep*, Wharton's "cubist" decorator "unbosom[s] himself to a devotee [by holding] up a guttering church-candle to a canvas which simulated a window open on a geometrical representation of brick walls, fire escapes and back-yards" (88–89). Wharton's decorator, unable to tolerate the original view from his window because it has been repeatedly seen as a "Whistler nocturne," has covered this window with a painting of a "simulated . . . window" that opens onto "a geometrical representation" of urban forms. Addie Bundren's eyes, "like two candles when you watch them gutter down into the sockets of iron candle-sticks" (8), form just one of the strokes of her visage as a "composite picture," a picture that is being composed through Faulkner's portrayal—a portrait of Addie Bundren, the unmaternal mother who is a reigning figure here and elsewhere in Faulkner's fiction. Significantly, the painting chosen by Wharton's cubist decorator of *Twilight Sleep* specifically anticipates Darl's "cubist" vision in *As I Lay Dying:*

> Against the dark doorway he [Jewel] seems to materialise out of darkness, lean as a race horse . . . in the beginning of the glare . . . He has seen me without even turning his head or his eyes in which the glare swims like two small torches . . . The front, the conical façade with the square orifice of doorway broken only by the square squat shape of the coffin on the sawhorses like a cubistic bug, comes into relief. (218–19)

Watson Branch has defined the aesthetic of this obsessively framed scene:

> Darl [not only] makes an explicit verbal allusion to Cubism, he also creates a Cubist painting by reducing the three-dimensional barn to geometric shapes—conical and square—flattened to the two-dimensional surface of the façade with the coffin and sawhorses brought up to the plane of the empty doorway. (117)[12]

The novel will potentially end here, because Darl, for reasons in addition to those that Cash speculates on at length near the close of the novel, has set the barn containing Addie's body on fire. But Jewel, becoming burned and blackened in the process, extends the novel by saving Addie's dead body. In Darl's "cubist" vision of the scene of conflagration, Jewel's torchlike eyes have replaced Addie's candlelike eyes described earlier as they "gutter down into the sockets." Darl's painterly configuration in *As I Lay Dying* includes multiple "fire escapes," as Wharton's noun—"fire escape"—gains the action of a verb. Jewel is the son who rides his mother's coffin to escape from (to borrow a key phrase from *Twilight Sleep*) the "geometrical representation[s]" as he preserves the mother by going out in flames. These "geometric shapes," to use the term introduced by Branch, frame and reframe the strangest simile in the novel that sees the coffin as being "like a cubistic bug." As he replaces Wharton's fiction of a canvas with a painting of his own, Faulkner was sparked by *Twilight Sleep*'s condescending allusion to modern art found in her "cubist decorator['s]" antirealist manifesto that favors adulterous aesthetics:

> It [the window] looked out on that stupid old "night piece" of Brooklyn Bridge and the East River. Everybody who came here said: "A Whistler nocturne!" and I got so bored. Besides it was *really there:* and I hate things that are really where you think they are . . . Everything in art should be false. Everything in life should be art. *Ergo*, everything in life should be false: complexions, teeth, hair, wives . . . specially wives. (89)

In the fiery dénouement of *As I Lay Dying*, Faulkner gave his distinguished literary mother, Edith Wharton, or more precisely her maligned cubist decorator, an encoded art history lesson. Aware of himself as an innovator, and conscious of the controversies that had marked the advent of aesthetic movements in painting as well as in literature, the author of *As I Lay Dying* realized the explosive possibilities of what might be meant by Wharton's "cubist decorator'[s]" reference to a "Whistler Nocturne." Faulkner's inspired response to this reference in *Twilight Sleep* took Whistler's work from the province of composed mothers and peaceful bridges in twilight to recall Whistler's own explosive nocturne. Certainly, Whistler's most famous painting remains his *Arrangement in Black and Grey: Portrait of the Painter's Mother*, commonly known as "Whistler's Mother." Long before 1934, when Whistler's painting achieved iconic status by appearing on a U.S. postage stamp dedicated "To the Memory of the Mothers of America," Whistler's preferred title for the painting of his own mother remained the pointedly abstract: she was *Arrangement in Black and Gray, No. 1*.[13] In stark contrast to the sentimentality attached by generations of viewers to this painting of his mother, Whistler's most infamous painting, his *Nocturne in Black and Gold, The Falling Rocket*, assured his place in the history of painting as an originator of abstract art (see plate 4).

Baiting Whistler in his journal *Fors Clavigera* (1877), John Ruskin ridiculed *The Falling Rocket*: "I have seen, and heard, much of Cockney impudence before now; but never expected to hear a coxcomb ask two hundred guineas for flinging a pot of paint in the public's face" (qtd. in Pennell and Pennell 170).[14] Whistler was not just classed by the British Ruskin as an impudent "Cockney" and a preening "coxcomb" (he was posing as a Tidewater gentleman), he was a foreign nuisance: an American painter contaminated with French ideas.[15] Whistler sued the prominent Ruskin for libel, claiming that his black nocturne, meant to be evocative, was not designed to be a realistic representation of a fireworks display. If aesthetic disputes (in familiar parlance) were not deemed to be "worth a single farthing," the judge in *Whistler v. Ruskin* corrected this view by finding in Whistler's favor, awarding the painter that proverbial farthing. The libeled Whistler, already vulnerable financially, fell into bankruptcy, a fall that condemned him to an extended sentence as an engraver. Inherent in the judge's devastating finding, abstract art flying in the face of representable facts continued to lose in the court of public opinion. Whether this incident added to or diminished the legend of the painter was of little consequence to the growing group of admirers who recognized his work. Whistler, by Faulkner's birth in 1897, had become a household name. His reputation as a painter of note was assumed among those who professed any acquaintance with high culture, and much more with those directly concerned with the history of painting. His work would have been known in Faulkner's childhood home, particularly because he grew up in a household run by a dedicated reader and painter like Maud Butler Falkner. As Faulkner included such terms as "futurist" and "vorticist" in letters to his mother from the Paris of 1925, he clearly felt that both the history of painting and the ongoing developments in modern art were something to write home about.[16]

Whistler's *Falling Rocket* could serve without alteration as an illustration of Darl's vision of the burning barn in *As I Lay Dying*. In language and image, Darl's "Cubist painting" is a response to the passage in Wharton's *Twilight Sleep* that immediately precedes the most racist scene Edith Wharton ever wrote. I should add that while Wharton's classism (her inherited sense of propriety and privilege that was much more complex than a merely moneyed sense of elitism) was at times acute, her racism—in the private documents that speak for her life as well as in her extensive literary oeuvre—was unexceptional and mundane. Wharton's manuscript versions of *The House of Mirth* (1905) reveal that that work's calculated use of anti-Semitism, along with the increasingly developed storyline of a fallen and uplifted working girl, was a late addition; clearly both changes were part of her decision to rewrite her novel to project a more radically inclusive social critique.[17] Based on an examination of her over fifty books—fiction and nonfiction, her extant personal letters, versions of both published and unpublished documents in the largest collection of Wharton's narrative remains—the racism of this passage from *Twilight Sleep* is not only unusual in terms of Wharton's words, it is ultimately significant because this outrageous interlude drew the imagination of the young Faulkner. Race was becoming increasingly central to Faulkner's conception of art.

Referring to the changes in "fads and fetishes and frivolities" (211) and new social movements, Wharton's Pulitzer Prize–winning novel *The Age of Innocence* closes with the fin-de-siècle young expressing their desire for the latest scores of Debussy and advising their elders to attend the new plays at Grand-Guignol (without mention of or apology for this venue's reputation for performances featuring sexual violence). For Newland's son, his father's long ago beloved, the Countess Olenska herself, completes the list of the necessary sights as he ventures to expose his "old-fashioned" father to this shockingly modern and modernist-tinged Parisian world. By contrast, *Twilight Sleep*, Wharton's novel that blames the mother for what has gone wrong in the mores of the United States, trashes new age fads, hobbies, and self-indulgent social missions that have distracted women from their moral and ethical responsibility to sacrifice themselves to preserve family and society. Among the diabolic subplots threatening to seduce the young women of *Twilight Sleep*, who in turn are threatening to seduce older men (including an incestuous bid at a step-father-in-law), is the insinuating beat of jazz played in a club with the oxymoronic name the "Cubist Cabaret." The language of *Twilight Sleep* becomes vicious as Wharton applies popular and racist eugenics, on the rise in the 1920s, to her novel's ugly critique of what is presented as a degenerate and grotesquely mongrelized modern art. Wharton's rabid and fast-paced critique of a mongrel Manhattan and a sex-crazed Hollywood in *Twilight Sleep* must have been riveting to the pre–Warner Brothers Faulkner, as he himself was writing *Mosquitoes*, his own offensive and bad novel about aesthetics published in the same year.[18]

Mosquitoes, with a few exceptions, takes place in an almost all-white world with a peculiarly Faulknerian iteration of race that is already being articulated as variously experienced sexualities. The artists in *Mosquitoes* (acknowledging what Freud elsewhere identified as the "polymorphously perverse") are evocatively described by the writer figure: "Maybe we have different ideas of sex, like all races do . . . Maybe us three sitting here are racially unrelated to each other, as regards sex" (*M* 239).[19] Yet by 1927, the year Faulkner published *Mosquitoes* and Wharton published *Twilight Sleep*, Faulkner had already begun to recast himself as the modernist whose own oeuvre was in some profound way destined to be about race, racial miscegenation, emasculation, and feminization as well as the formal impact of these cultural constructions on the meaning of an art known through embodiment.[20] Wharton's crude fictional foray in *Twilight Sleep* was clearly one of the visions of violence that Faulkner was responding to in his developing propensity for gendering art and race. Undoubtedly, Faulkner was aware that these violent fires lit by Wharton and Whistler marked the contested space of modern art. This debate over representation led Faulkner to imagine his own highly pictorial scenes of sacrifice that transform the bodies of sons and daughters and sisters and mothers in *As I Lay Dying*, *Light in August*, and in his short story "Evangeline," the long-unpublished seed-story for *Absalom, Absalom!* While *Twilight Sleep* is about failed and irresponsible mothers and daughter sacrifice, the novel moves from droll ridicule to vicious, racist cant in a resurgent strand that posits a bodily or, more precisely, a "blooded" connection between racial degeneracy and degenerate art. The cubist decorator of *Twilight Sleep*, with his "falsetto" voice, his "snaky head and too square shoulders," is likened to "a cross between a Japanese waiter and a full-page advertisement for silk underwear." The "octoroon pianist" (whose last name, Keiler, means "wild boar" in German) "assemble[s] a series of sausage arms and bolster legs" before her "tiny hands like blueish mice dart . . . out at the keyboard from the end of her bludgeon arms" (89, 90).

As this jazz-playing "octoroon" (stuffed mixed meat and furniture limbs) pretends to be mistaken for a "mislaid" wife, it is significant that the husband of this sought-after wife is alluded to throughout the novel (shades of Twain) as "the poor boy" and "poor old Jim." Without getting too far into Wharton's wild foray into what might be called regional eugenics, Jim appears to have been tacitly placed as a mixed-blood figure because he has been born of a union between a father from the elite of old New York and a mother from the nouveau riche, car-manufacturing Midwest. This region produces people who are grotesquely modern in the cyborgean sense, an amalgamation of man and machine articulated in the mother's more recent Midwestern husband's telling last name, "Manford." The nickname of Jim's elite father, "Exhibit A," emphasizes the fact that Jim's half-sister, the younger Nona Manford, born of two Midwestern parents (in Wharton's subtle—one is tempted to say Faulknerian—joke), is literally "Nona": "Non-A." Non-aristocratic.

Harlem remains unnamed in *Twilight Sleep*. In its stead, New York jazz, embodied by the stuffed octoroon, is linked to the debased cacophony of Hollywood film, embodied by a Jewish filmmaker aggressively named "Klawhammer." This figure (called "the dirty Jew"[21] by "Exhibit A") is described here as "[a] short man with a deceptively blond head, thick lips under a stubby blond moustache, and eyes like needles behind tortoiseshell-rimmed glasses." Said to have "a voice like melted butter, a few drops of which seemed to trickle down his lips and be licked back at intervals" (89–90), Klawhammer, joining the carpenter's tool to animal claws and ham, suggests that something is not kosher here. The slender, stylized, and Orientalized decorator with his high voice—a "falsetto" figure who, by his own declaration, favors female falseness—is a cavorting stereotype. This mock-up of an effeminate homosexual male, the overly stuffed, overly processed, mixed-race woman of color, and the "deceptively blond" Jew are tellingly unctuous, whether snaky, porcine, or dairy slimed. Details, such as the decorator's squareness of shoulders, the octoroon pianist's "bludgeon arms," and the filmmaker Klawhammer's name itself, identify these figures as tools of destruction. Taken together, these characters body forth Wharton's most rabid rant on the cultural consequences of gender crossovers and racial mixing, as her grotesquely amalgamated characters are further defined through their practice of degenerate arts:[22] interior decoration,[23] jazz, and flesh-flashing films.

In *Twilight Sleep*, the "Mahatma," an Orientalized spiritual leader also referred to as "the nigger chap," runs an ashram that is depicted as a type of harem where debutantes trailing translucent veils appear exposed, dancing "naked" in newspaper photographs. What is shocking is that the "mislaid" wife of Jim believes that she can get a leading role in a film by merely showing Klawhammer this revealing photograph of her body that has been published in a scandal sheet. What theoretically should be a preposterous idea—that a still photograph can convey cinematic talent—is confirmed in this vicious scene that damns the new medium in which looking good and a willingness to expose the body in a still photograph is enough to satisfy the demands of silent film. As Nona (looking for her half-brother Jim's wife) is asked unceremoniously to "take off [her] togs" to audition for the proposed film, *Herodias*, it becomes clear that Klawhammer, the "dirty Jew,"[24] may be searching for a celluloid Salomé who will dance (at her mother Herodias's request) to exact the price of a man's head on a platter.

Faulkner, who had gone to Europe before his first novel was published, spent the autumn of 1925 in Paris on a street close to galleries that were exhibiting paintings by some of the most experimental and influential artists of the twentieth century. Fluent in the terminology of his times, Faulkner wrote to his mother about seeing "paintings [by] the more-or-less moderns, like Degas, Manet and Chavannes." While Faulkner reported having seen privately owned paintings by Picasso and Matisse, he was clearly most moved by the art of Cézanne, the painter whom he described as having "dipped his brush in light" (Lind 138, 139, 141). Wharton, too, was visiting galleries in this Paris, the city that had been her place of permanent residence since 1909. Separated by age and taste as they established positions on opposing sides of the post–World War I abyss, Wharton and Faulkner in their obsessions with the visual and plastic arts were incorporating the worlds they saw and, to some extent, shared into their fictions. Highly conscious and allusive writers whose fictions were marked by their almost painful visual acuity, Wharton and Faulkner, in the full paradox of their divergent origins, must be seen as complex fish swimming in what by 1927 was the same water. If one believes in the film savvy of the avant-garde-obsessed and clearly edgy young Faulkner, it follows that he would have known that Wharton's reference in *Twilight Sleep* to a cinematic project entitled *Herodias* was to a particular film: the famed 1923 production of Oscar Wilde's *Salome*, nominally directed by Charles Bryant, who is said to have taken his direction from Alla Nazimov (the leading lady who was also his openly lesbian wife) and Natacha Rambova (author of the screenplay and in charge of art direction and costumes, who was also Rudolf Valentino's wife). Rumored to have had an all-gay cast in honor of Wilde, this silent film features characters who are clearly in drag. Known for its famously stylized and highly artificial sets in black and white, this silent film was staged as an homage to Beardsley's well-known illustrations of Wilde's one-act play. Indeed, the words of Wilde's *Salome* (first composed in French) are much less shocking than Beardsley's engravings. Beardsley's stylized line drawings convey a decadence that is meant to shock conventional viewers. While female navels and nipples (fantastically articulated as eyes) are extraordinary, undraped genitals in the drawings for *Salome* are male and ordinary. His illustrations may depict characters with breasts, but even in the presence of these breasts, the genitals of all the undraped figures are articulated as male.[25]

The film's star (as well as its unacknowledged director), the well-known political actress Alla Nazimov, celebrated for her starring roles in 1920s films based on Ibsen's feminist plays, would have come to Wharton's attention as early as 1905 when she first arrived in the United States as part of a Russian troupe, playing the lead in *The Chosen People*. A widely publicized political event in the New York of 1905 (Emma Goldman attended every performance, and her Long Island collective actually took the actors in when they became stranded), *The Chosen People* was written and performed in Russia, London, and the United States in an effort to expose the ongoing anti-Semitism of the pogroms taking place in Russia and along its borders in eastern Europe. While Wharton did not see the film,[26] she, like Faulkner (who actually owned a copy of the Beardsley-illustrated *Salome*), would have been amused by stories about the modernist sets of *Salomé*, which were radically designed in black and white to create the first completely faux world made expressly for filming indoors. Wharton's embellished plotline, introducing a Jewish film mogul scouting for a film called *Herodias* (the name of Salomé's mother), points directly to this film as the source for Wharton's idea of the stark cubist interiors designed by her "cubist decorator." Most notably, the boudoir of the aspiring Salomé of *Twilight Sleep* is newly decorated in all black. The focal point of this black room is a well-lighted bowl where—in a critique of publicity, film, and the film industry that is far from subtle—fish swim madly toward what is surmised as their sleepless death from constant exposure.

Beardsley's Cistern: Painting Black

> As from the bottom of a thick black pit he saw himself enclosed . . . as if the black life, the black breathing had compounded the substance of breath so that not only voices but moving bodies and light itself must become fluid . . .
>
> On all sides even within him, the bodiless fecundmellow voices of negro women murmured. It was as though he and all other manshaped life about him has been returned to the lightless hot wet primogenative Female.
>
> —William Faulkner, *Light in August* (114–15)

In their intersecting life cycles, Joanna Burden and Joe Christmas of Faulkner's *Light in August* pass through a "sister stage" that threatens to drown them both in the black liquidity of bodily fusion:

> [H]e stayed, watching the two creatures that struggled in the one body like two moongleamed shapes struggling drowning in alternate throes upon the surface of a thick black pool . . . [One] impervious and impregnable . . . the other . . . in furious denial of that impregnability strove to drown in the black abyss of its own creating . . . Now and then they would come to the black surface, locked like sisters. (260–61)[27]

This violently fluid eroticism places the sexually indeterminate Joanna as a morphological female in relation to Joe as well as to herself. Here, in "the thick black pool . . . the black abyss" as "the two creatures" with their "one body . . . come to the black surface," Joe assumes the position of a blackened and tabooed sexual sister to Joanna. Striking erotic attitudes that are likened to a "Beardsley of the time of Petronius," Joanna is like the Medusa "with her wild hair, each strand of which would seem to come alive like octopus tentacles."[28] With monstrous *politesse*, she breathes out the repeated word that is meant to color and pique her tabooed passion: "Negro! Negro! Negro!" (260).

By specifying "the time of Petronius" (Petronius was Nero's *arbiter elegantiae*, the official advisor in matters of style and luxury for the most excessive ruler in the history of the Roman Empire), the narrative imagines a stylized sexual aesthetic that would go beyond that of Beardsley's most decadent and genitally excessive drawings. Indeed, Rambova's script and costume designs for the influential film version of Wilde's *Salome* drew from an even more shocking Beardsley drawing that might be said to define Greco-Roman decadence rather than the more mannered and eroticized Orientalism of Beardsley's illustrations drawn for Wilde's Judeo-Roman drama. The twin black pygmylike characters whose headdresses allow them to appear initially as potted plants in the silent film of *Salome* are modeled on Beardsley's drawing, "The Lacedaemonian Ambassador," an illustration for *Lysistrata* in which a small man from Sparta sports an exposed penis that competes in size with the rest of his body (see fig. 21, page 209).[29] Faulkner's reference to

"Petronius" suggests a wider knowledge of Beardsley, which would have allowed him to parse the visually rendered racial nuances of the film. And as the theatrical poses of his sexually voracious Joanna Burden as the Medusa only begin to suggest, Faulkner drew inspiration from Beardsley's illustrations drawn for Wilde's one-act play *Salome*. However, Faulkner's depiction of this erotic baptism is deeper and becomes even more racially marked as he incorporated what was for him the most influential of Beardsley's drawings as a determining illustration for the imagery of *Light in August*. This Beardsley drawing showing the snakelike locks of John the Baptist depicts the prophet's head held high by the hair-pocked arm of a figure the stage directions name as "*the Executioner*." Extending upward from a black pool that is named a "*cistern*,"[30] this "huge black" arm is grotesque because it is a visually ambiguous haunch that rises from the ink-black liquidity, a visually dismembered body part holding a dismembered part of a body (see fig. 22, page 210).[31] In Beardsley's two illustrations that depict the severed head of John the Baptist, the story of the Medusa is told not just in the violent fact of the dismembered head, but also in the serpentine form of this head's wild locks (see fig. 23, page 211).[32] Joanna Burden is Faulkner's wild-haired Medusa of *Light in August*, and the "parchmentcolored" man who kills her by nearly cutting off her head is cast in the role of Wilde's "*Executioner*." However, what appears to have been most blackening in this narrative of sexual seduction and dismemberment is the reappearing visual element of the cistern: the fecal and fatal liquidity that haunts *Light in August* in the allusions to the racialized "black tide creeping up his [Joe's] legs" (339).

Nocturnal Musings

In a characteristically specific reference, Wharton's allusion in *Twilight Sleep* to the "cubist decorator['s]" decision to cover up a window that frames what to him is an unacceptably picturesque sight of the "Brooklyn Bridge and the East River" is designed to replace the framed view of the composition recognizable as that of a particular painting: Whistler's much-admired, twilight portrayal called *Nocturne in Blue and Gold—Old Battersea Bridge* (see plate 5). The "cubist decorator['s]" replacement for this offensively painterly view from the actual window, his canvas *cum* window treatment, is construed through the urban geometry of man-made shapes, configured in a painting. This painting on canvas forms a geometric palimpsest meant not just to replace, but also to obscure, the scenes of natural beauty that unavoidably border islanded cities such as Manhattan. In its most obvious function, this canvas in *Twilight Sleep* is meant to replace a view that already looks like a representational painting. However, as the decorator's abstract painting and its geometric aesthetic are incorporated into Darl's pictorial vision, Wharton's "geometric shape[s]" have been transmogrified into the frames within frames that in

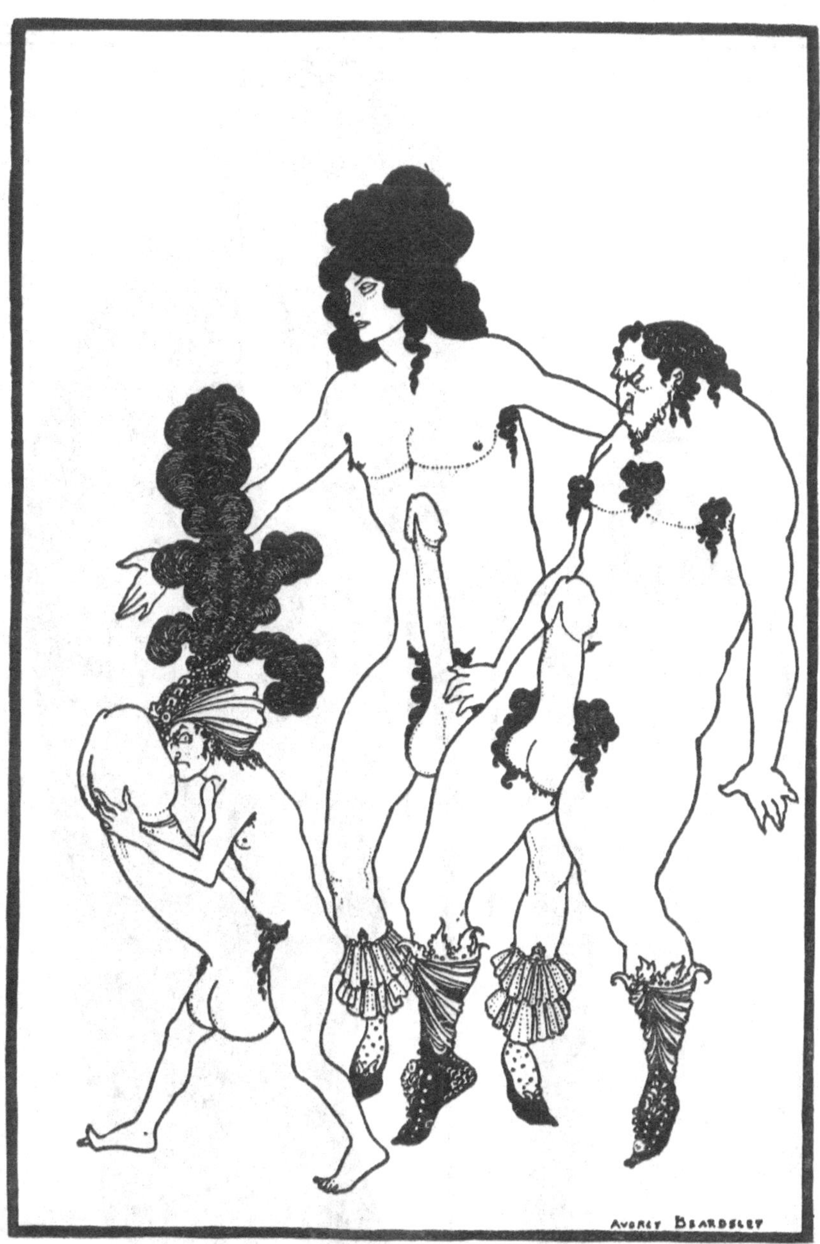

Figure 21. Aubrey Beardsley, "The Lacedaemonian Ambassador." Illustration in ink, Aristophanes, *Lysistrata*, 1896. In addition to pointing toward the model for the racially designated pygmies of the silent film *Salomé*, this drawing—considered to be a particularly offensive work drawn by Beardsley—suggests what Faulkner's reference to a "Beardsley of the time of Petronius" (*LA* 260) might convey. What does it mean to out-Beardsley Beardsley—to be (as Petronius himself threatened to be) more decadent than Nero himself?

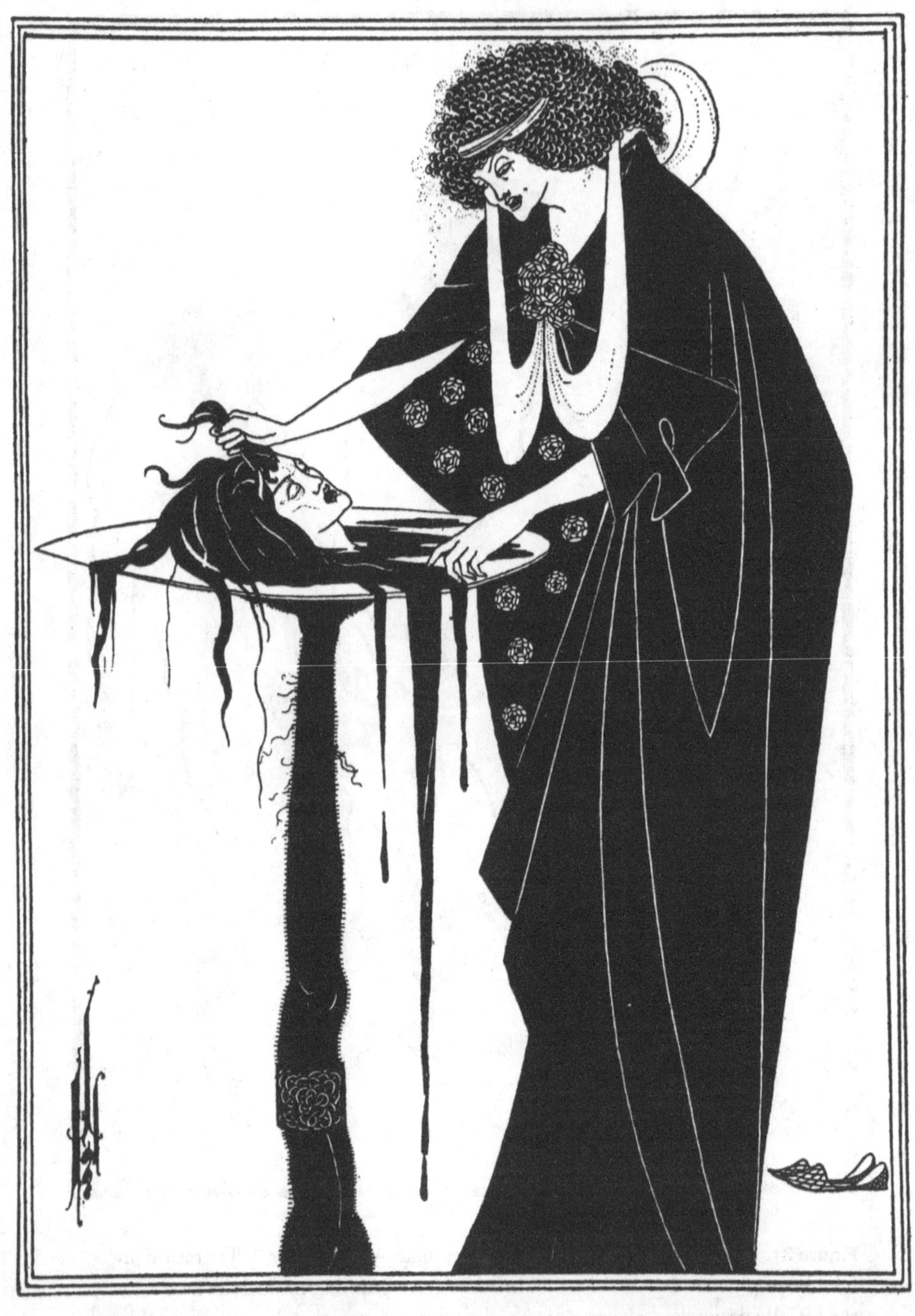

Figure 22. Aubrey Beardsley, "The Dancer's Reward." Illustration in ink for Oscar Wilde, *Salome: A Tragedy in One Act*, 1894.

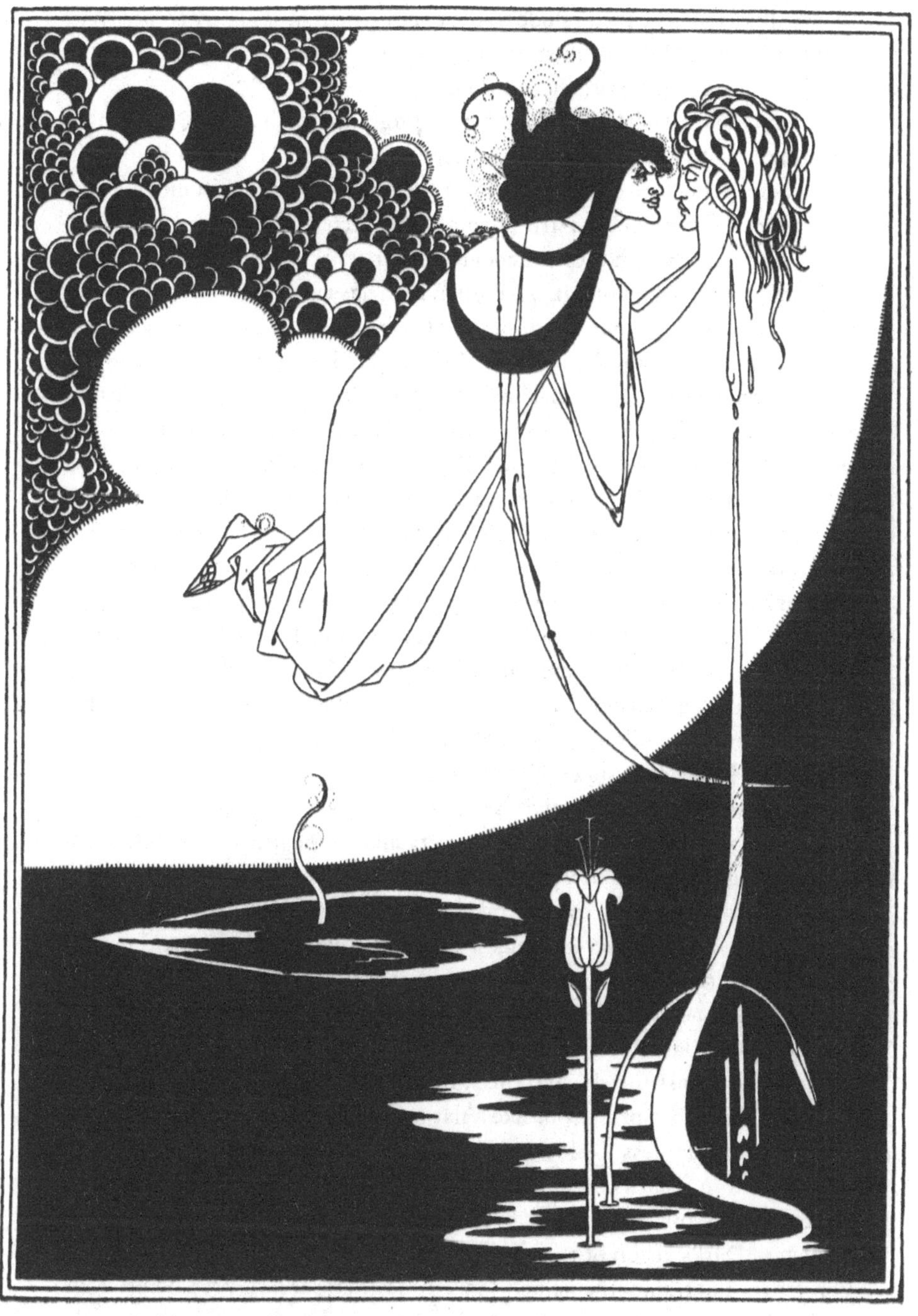

Figure 23. Aubrey Beardsley, "The Climax." Illustration in ink for Oscar Wilde, *Salome: A Tragedy in One Act*, 1894.

their stillness picture the prelude to the dénouement of *As I Lay Dying*. With pointed impact, "Darl's cubist painting" (to use Branch's term) must still be seen as the painting before the painting.

In Faulkner's *As I Lay Dying*, the photographic fixity of "Darl's cubist painting," composed of "geometric representations" (*TS* 89), pictures the scene before this artist's incendiary act creates a dynamic and moving conflagration. The cinematic barn-burning, in which "sparks rain . . . in scattering bursts as though they engendered other sparks," constitutes a theatrically staged moving picture (222). Earlier, Darl has visually composed abstract paintings as he, some miles distant, sees Cash's progress in sculpting the box being made to contain the mother: "[u]pon the dark ground the chips look like random smears of soft pale paint on a black canvas" (75). This abstract painting on black is directly juxtaposed to his window-framed vision of Addie Bundren, described by the absent Darl as "a composite picture of all time" (48). Going beyond the stasis of color on canvas, Whistler's *Nocturne in Black and Gold* becomes an action painting in the second half of its title. *The Falling Rocket* alludes to the dynamically rising gold that depicts movement in this fiery spray across a nocturnal sky, a rising of color that precedes and joins with the "falling." In Darl's vision of the geometrically boxed and darkening shapes that evocatively frame and reframe Addie's coffin, the mother's box atop the wooden "sawhorses" is seen as being "like a cubistic bug." The fire, with its rising and falling sparks, animates the inanimate as the flat planes of this cubist-like canvas stage the potential animacy of the nested and temporarily still shapes. Here, the night's stillness gives way to the curtaining flames that frame the scene of this literally spectacular—theatrically as well as cinematically moving—disaster.

As sparks fly up from the central conflagration to light the black night in *As I Lay Dying*, Faulkner's youngest Bundren could be describing the visual continuity between the Whistlerian stars that scatter across the painter's more genteel nocturnes as well as Whistler's painting of rising sparks in *The Falling Rocket*. As Vardaman observes, "red went swirling up . . . swirling up in little red pieces, against the sky and the stars so that the stars moved backward" (223). Jewel, who "springs out like a flat figure cut leanly from tin against an abrupt and soundless explosion" (218), enters the tableau of this Whistler painting more fully as he fights with Gillespie "like two figures in a Greek frieze, isolated out of all reality by the red glare" (221). Reversing Wharton's sequence, Darl's vision of the stylized geometrical shapes within shapes both constructs and frames the named "cubist" aesthetic at its center, before being replaced by the wildest of "Whistler nocturne[s]." To his intellectual credit, the author of *As I Lay Dying* realized the explosive possibilities of what might be meant by Wharton's "cubist decorator['s]" condescending reference to "A Whistler nocturne!" As the "red glare" (221) ricochets in from the lyrics of the "Star-Spangled Banner" to insist on the presence of *The Falling Rocket*,

Whistler's infamous painting sparked Faulkner's own famous night piece, the barn-burning of *As I Lay Dying*. This fire links *As I Lay Dying* (as well as the obsessive return to culminations in scenes of fire in novels and short stories by Faulkner) to the incendiary confrontation made public by Whistler and Ruskin, as they took the argument about whether art must be representational out of the studio and into the court-room.

What is finally most disturbing about this conflagration in *As I Lay Dying* is Faulkner's determination that fire will be the sign of a racialized narrative. This fire-marked and explosive scene joins Addie Bundren's illegitimate and blackened son Jewel to the illegitimate and long racially indeterminate (but increasingly blackened) orphan Joe Christmas of *Light in August*. As Joe Christmas is carved with a knife into a legible body, this scene of sacrifice in diction and theme alludes directly to Whistler's *Falling Rocket*. Whistler's nocturne as a fiery night scene calls attention to the pictorial connection that would link Faulkner's dark scenes of male sacrifice in *As I Lay Dying* and *Light in August* even if Whistler had never flung his infamous "pot of paint." Yet, significantly, Joe Christmas is seen as "a rising rocket" in the precipitous liquidity of his castration:

> Then his face, body, all, seemed to collapse, to fall in upon itself, and from out of the slashed garments about his hips and loins the pent black blood seemed to rush like a released breath. It seemed to rush out of his pale body like the rush of sparks from a rising rocket; upon that black blast the man seemed to rise soaring into their memories forever and ever. (465)

In *Light in August*, the imagery that paints Joe Christmas into racial fixity is not merely the desperately invoked "rising tide" of blackness—the imagery of the sewer of soiling sexuality defined through a female and black liquidity—but rather the rocketing of his released "black blood" that becomes the scene of seeing that can never be erased.[33] Joined by more than the conflagration of "engender[ing] . . . sparks" (*AILD* 222) and the "glare and glitter" (*LA* 463), "the rush of sparks from a rising [and falling] rocket" (*LA* 465), these ejaculatory dénouements expose the direct connection between the illegitimate and finally emasculated sons in *As I Lay Dying* and *Light in August*. Addie's Jewel and Joanna's Joe are colored by their rocketing rises that result in the physical blackening of flesh and blood (respectively) as they are burned and cut (respectively) to become racialized bodies. In their falls from hypermasculinity, Jewel and Joe become blackened and domesticated—filially mired in the maternal fold.

Blackened Sons and the Sisterhood of Burning Mothers

Imagining that she is pregnant when her menstrual periods stop, the menopausal Joanna tries to seize parental authority by another route. As Joanna proposes that Joe become what he calls "a nigger lawyer," Joanna Burden assumes the role of a cultural father who with her "cap-and-ball revolver" speaks for God. Joanna has taken on a position of masculine authority, proposing a design that depends on his [Joe's] declaration of a racial identity that will position him socially as what was known then as a "race man."[34] Whether one accepts this life-cycle narrative as coming into play or not is less important than the gender and racial ramifications in scenes where misfired and unfired guns give way to razors and knives that inscribe bodies,[35] sculpting them into racial types. In their final meeting, Joanna Burden stands briefly as the failed and castrated father before she passes into the stage of being a mother. Emasculated by her severed head, she waxes by waning maternal in the feminizing light of what has previously been seen as "moongleamed shapes." Joanna Burden as she dies births Joe into blackness by becoming the fictive embodiment of the violated white woman. Ritually lynched (cut before she is found dead in her burning house), Joanna Burden has finally become a woman. When Joe divides her masculine head from her now sexed and fixedly feminized body, this former enigma has become a literalization of the mind/body split. Placed racially by his use of a razor, Joe has positioned himself to be carved into a fixed racial identity by Faulkner's proto-Nazi's knife.[36] These acts of female and male castration (beheadings) complete the ritual of lynching as both Joe and Joanna form and perform roles in a sequence of two related *tableaux morts*. Each *tableau* fixes Joe Christmas as black, and each tableau insists on Joanna Burden's new status as a violated body that stands for southern white womanhood.[37]

Described as inhabiting the center of a wheel as paths "like spokes" converge on her house, Joanna Burden initially appears as a childless Addie Bundren. Yet, despite her biological childlessness, Joanna Burden, who has replaced her now-dead father as a dispenser of advice and succor to the blacks who live in the deep woods around her house, has occupied a more central position than Addie Bundren: Joanna is the axle while "Addie Bundren is the rim" (*AILD* 108). In his labor-based analysis of the Bundrens, Marc Baldwin has identified Addie Bundren as a "slave mother," the mother of those who are born to labor in the fields.[38] Addie Bundren, an activist proponent of decomposition who narrates a largely unspoken diatribe against words, argues that words like spider's spittle are only necessary for those who have never had the experience. "Mother" is one of the words that Addie Bundren does not need to say. Like her textual sister Joanna, Addie cannot be violated sexually (by her husband "Anse in the nights" [172]), but only by the bloody breach of birthing her ultimately blackened, firstborn son, Cash.

Said by Anse to be "slavin" and "aslavin," Addie labors in more than just the breeding that produces laborers for the family's fields. Addie has gone from being a violent schoolmarm to being an outraged, wildly passionate as well as coldly philosophical, mother. Unmaternal mothers with a taste for forbidden men, Addie Bundren and Joanna Burden—both of whose corpses have violated heads before their dead bodies are framed by fire—are catalysts for dramas that unfold after their deaths. Through their deaths, these thwarted women in fierce retribution take their tributes in sacrificial men, as they birth their chosen sons into blackness.

As I Lay Dying and *Light in August* are both (to use Randy Schiff's phrase) "epistemologies of race," teaching narratives that call knowledge itself into question to ignite the series of fictions that lead to Faulkner's epistemology of all epistemologies: *Absalom, Absalom!* Faulkner wrote a great deal of short fiction during the 1920s and '30s as he was trying to raise enough income from publication in magazines to support his family in Mississippi.[39] His long-unpublished short story, "Evangeline" (written sometime around 1931), is a warm-up for *Absalom, Absalom!* that includes a Clytie figure (a white woman of color) who burns herself alive with the body of her brother—technically her half-brother—Henry Sutpen.

The Henry Sutpen of "Evangeline" has been hidden in the house for forty years (not the less extravagant four claimed for the Henry Sutpen of *Absalom, Absalom!*) after killing his virginal sister Judith's husband, Charles Bon. As the Clytie-figure of "Evangeline," Raby, comes to the window of the Sutpen house that she herself has set afire, the mixed-blood Sutpen sister (on the formal level of the sentence as well as through the thematic suggestions of words and images) is a composite portrait of Addie Bundren. Rather than a burning barn, Faulkner's Raby inhabits a burning and falling house:

> Then the whole house seemed to collapse, to fold in upon itself, melting . . . We stood there and watched the house dissolve and liquefy and rush upward in silent and furious scarlet, licking and leaping among the wild and blazing branches of the cedars, so that, blazing, melting too, against the soft, mild-starred sky of summer they too wildly tossed and swirled. ("Evangeline" 607–8)

Clearly Usher-like, the fall of the house of Sutpen in "Evangeline" suffers an implosion that is almost identical to that of the castrated body of Joe Christmas: "Then his face, body, all, seemed to collapse, to fall in upon itself" (*LA* 465).

Like Clytie of *Absalom, Absalom!*, Raby of Faulkner's "Evangeline" is depicted as rock-firm, long-silent, and seemingly sexless. However, unlike Clytie, Raby is not childless: she herself has been a slave as well as a slave mother. Blood is important in "Evangeline." "Indian," "Sutpen," and "Negroid" become the categories in this story that begins with a local color painter, who has focused on the heads of people of color, announcing from the outset that there is a difference between the "heads" of "hill niggers" and "those of the lowlands [and] the cities." Raby (said to look as if "she had been nine years old when God was born") rules a female world of four generations with "[n]ot a man over eleven years old" ("Evangeline" 585).

Emphatically parodic, "Evangeline" displays an obsession with German bloodlines[40] that serves as a prelude to, as well as a critique of, what will become Thomas Sutpen's racially driven obsession to use the last shots in his aging cannon to try to fire or, more precisely, to seed a son in *Absalom, Absalom!*[41] In Faulkner's "Evangeline," Sutpen's son, the "white" Henry Sutpen, is "yellow": his skin is yellow, his waist-length beard is "yellow," his pillow is "yellow," and he is framed, as it were, between "yellow" sheets. This German bloodline or breed is so important to the childless Henry that Raby has had to make the final trip in the stead of her invalid brother to acquire what she tells the writer is the "last dog." This series of dogs (seeming to outsiders to proliferate in "Evangeline" "like plums on a bush" [593]) guards the gate to hell or the "closed doors" of secreted Sutpens.[42] Springing into the flames, this dog referred to as a "son," along with the "yellow" Henry Sutpen, joins the sexless mother Raby, to become this story's requisite offering of loyal and blackened "son[s]" ("Evangeline" 593).

Like the famous threshold scenes of *Ethan Frome*, there is the startling appearance of a woman behind a door in "Evangeline" in the ghostly face of a woman whose visage has the power of destruction.[43] In what approaches an exact transcription of the Whartonian formulation that repeatedly interjects the warning word "Then" in *Ethan Frome* to signal an unexpected barrier (often in Wharton's gothic tale, this man-maiming barrier is the face of a woman), Faulkner's unnamed writer of "Evangeline" notes: "Then we saw the woman in the house" (607).[44] After Addie Bundren appears in the window as a "composite picture of all time," we read, "Then the face disappears" (*AILD* 48). Window after window is consumed in "Evangeline" before Raby—described previously as "white," the color of "pale coffee," and specifically said to lack "negroid features"—becomes racially fixed as she assumes the pictorial position. Framed as a figure "no bigger than a doll [and] as impervious as an effigy of bronze," Raby is the maternal muse "musing" as she passes through the progenitive stages of art. Forged in finality, she becomes "the old negress [in] the window upstairs": "She came through fire and she leaned for a moment in the window, her hands on the burning ledge, looking no bigger than a doll, as impervious as an effigy of bronze, serene, dynamic, musing in the foreground of Holocaust. Then the whole house seemed to collapse, to fold in upon itself" (607).

Faulkner's "Evangeline," from the opening frame spoken by the unnamed writer to the series of doors that must be forced open to reveal the hidden story, is Faulkner's closest and most detailed rewriting of *Ethan Frome* and Poe's "Fall of the House of Usher." This revision, still recognizable in the extravagant narratives that comprise *Absalom, Absalom!*, closes with the discovery of a metal book, a photograph case that has to have its hinged and locked door forced open:

> The picture was intact . . . Then I came awake, alive. I looked quietly at the face: the smooth, oval, unblemished face, the mouth rich, full, a little loose, the hot, slumbrous, secretive eyes, the inklike hair with its faint but unmistakable wiriness—all the ineradicable and tragic stamp of negro blood. (608)[45]

Faced with the face that belongs in an old and once highly popular genre, "Evangeline" has introduced Mr. Compson's obsession with the "tragic mulatta" that is so productive because it does not quite obscure the hidden story of race which it is meant to bear and to hide in *Absalom, Absalom!* Faulkner's obsessive trope of the book buried within the book is central to this paradigm of art—the textual pregnancy—that he inherits from Cather's *The Professor's House* and Wharton's *Ethan Frome*.[46]

Analyzing the appearance of the white Sutpens of color, Faulkner's painter "of heads" is obsessed with Raby's color. Near the opening of "Evangeline," the painter concludes: "[s]he's pretty near whiter than she is black; a regular empress maybe because she is white." Described earlier by the painter as "looking no bigger than one of these half lifesize dolls-of-all-nations in the church bazaar" (585), Raby, seen as a doll by both the painter and the writer, goes through a series of sculptural transformations that link her to the works of art worshipped and reviled in the artist-infested world of Faulkner's *Mosquitoes*. The "white" Raby of "Evangeline" has a "torso" that has acquired the flat darkness of a "silhouette" with a face "like a mask in which the eyesockets had been savagely thumbed and the eyes themselves forgotten" (595). Raby's "hill-country" head, in image after specific image, echoes the framed features of *As I Lay Dying*'s Addie Bundren.[47]

Whether Raby was conceived before or after Addie Bundren begins rotting in her burdensome liquidity cannot be known. And sequence, in relation to the creation of Addie and Raby as well as with regard to other characters created by Faulkner, is less important than the consequence of connection. These "hill-country" women, Addie and Raby, who are themselves blackened along with their increasingly blackened and racially marked progeny, are textual sisters. Even as Joanna Burden is joined to Addie Bundren by her shared blackening through her own embrace of black liquidity, Joanna Burden is also linked to Raby and Addie as all three "white" figures are forged into blackness by the fires that threaten to burn and, in the case of Raby, succeed in burning their bodies.

Raby, with her female descendants, daughters of daughters, darkening "like stairsteps" with each generation, is racially darkened by the fire that burns her father's only son (it remains unknown whether her literally "yellow" and dying brother Henry is burned dead or alive), along with the loyal progeny that the story "Evangeline" identifies specifically as the "son." This "German shepherd," part of a series of parodically pure and certifiably pedigreed sons (shades of the young Thomas Sutpen in the defining episode of his life in *Absalom, Absalom!*), repeatedly flings himself at the blocked front door before leaping into the backside of the fire-consumed Sutpen mansion. "Evangeline," composed and rejected for publication in the early 1930s, reveals a racially aware and politically savvy Faulkner. Alongside the casual racist cant in which characters of artists describe the physiognomy of a mixed-blood woman as well as the nostalgic and slumberous sexuality seen in the photograph of a "tragic mulatta," "Evangeline" reveals and reviles the racial politics of the rising Reich by offering a canine-based eugenics that in retrospect reads as a parody of Thomas Sutpen's race-based design that drives *Absalom, Absalom!* Significantly, the sacrificial son of "Evangeline" who cannot gain entry through the front door, is a literal son-of-a-bitch: a self-immolating, pure and pedigreed German shepherd.

Indeed, the lesser-known Raby of Faulkner's "Evangeline" casts heat and light on a destructive pantheon of Faulkner's maternal muses, whether they are "musing in the foreground" or the background in stories of burnt offerings named here for what they are: a "Holocaust." A harbinger of the sexless and childless "Clytie" of *Absalom, Absalom!*, the "negress" Raby of "Evangeline" (the lighter of a Sutpen suttee) burns herself alive with her father's son along with the pure, purchased, and replaceable "son." Coloring in her dead and fire-shrouded textual sisters, the slave mother of "Evangeline," a muse without mercy, joins Addie Bundren and Joanna Burden to uncover this telling pattern in Faulkner's fiction that pictures burning mothers flanked by art realized through blackened sons.

CHAPTER SEVEN

De Kooning's Faulkner Trilogy

Light in August, *Black Friday*, and *Black Untitled*

Heard melodies are sweet, but those unheard
  Are sweeter; therefore, ye soft pipes, play on;
Not to the sensual ear, but, more endeared,
  Pipe to the spirit ditties of no tone.
—John Keats, "Ode on a Grecian Urn"

Kandinsky understood "form" as a form, like an object in the real world;
and an object, he said, was a narrative—and so, of course, he disapproved of it.
He wanted "his music without words."
—Willem de Kooning, Museum of Modern Art, February 5, 1951

Having the story always adds value to an object.
—Article of Faith, *Antiques Roadshow*

In 1948 Elaine de Kooning and her husband arrived for the summer at Black Mountain College (a haven in the mountains of North Carolina for intellectual and creative émigrés who had fled Hitler's Europe) alive with fears of entering "Faulkner's South"[1] (see fig. 24). During the middle of what I identify as his Faulkner period, Willem de Kooning dedicated his entire summer to working on a notably small Picasso- and Gorky-influenced painting,[2] which he completed that autumn in New York by scrawling the word "Ashville"[3] across its back. At Black Mountain, de Kooning enjoyed his talks with Buckminster Fuller and later recalled his pleasure of being among writers, "not because they are more intelligent or better speakers than artists," but because he found "their conversation very stimulating." For de Kooning, as for Faulkner and for Quentin Compson (the suicidal character with whom Faulkner confessed his closest filiation), words had incantatory power. De Kooning remembered his "gratitude because [these writers'] talk, the words they used, made a picture in my mind." An early

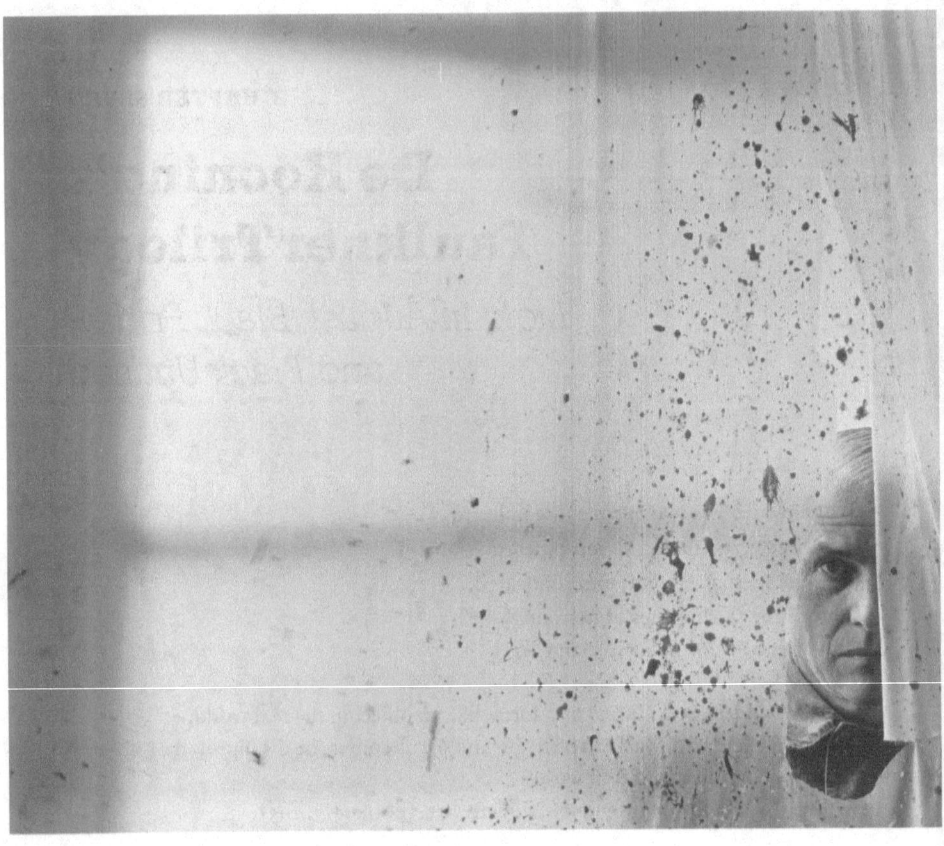

Figure 24. Arnold Newman, photographic portrait of Willem de Kooning peeking through plastic in homage to the painter's great black and whites. Like Newman's photograph of Stravinsky that is dominated by the starkly abstract lifted and curvilinear top of a grand piano, this photograph provides a reading of de Kooning's art signed by the painter's countenance. Backed by the classic window shapes (a defining element of some of de Kooning's major works including *Black Friday*), the painter's face peers out in startling clarity through a tear in the water-flecked, opaque and translucent surface that is framed in the photograph. Newman's photograph is striking because it itself approaches an ekphrastic act of criticism. De Kooning's black-and-whites, as well as his other abstracts, eerily have a face peeking from them: looking back at the viewer. Library of Congress, Prints & Photographs Division, Arnold Newman, photographer. Rights permitted by Getty Images.

aesthetic mentor, Bernard Romein, under whom de Kooning had worked at a Rotterdam department store, advised the young artist to read Dostoevsky,[4] the Russian whose novels spoke so powerfully to de Kooning's art. Known to have read Dostoevsky and Stein, Kierkegaard and Wittgenstein, de Kooning turned to Faulkner and to Faulkner's Keats to find his verbal muses in America. Reading and listening, de Kooning, who celebrated rather than denied the beauty of influence, complimented himself in an understatement: "[s]ometimes I could say of myself that I painted with a good ear."[5] While Dostoevsky included only a few famous paintings in his fiction, his work is darkened and shaded in with what might be called his own great black and whites, his negative-like engraved grays of scenes seen in the distance. Dostoevsky is a painter's writer. Faulkner wrote in color, but blood in his 1932 novel *Light in August* is black and white, flowing in "parchmentcolored" skin (*LA* 120, 123, 277).[6]

Art historians have located de Kooning's interest in Faulkner through the character of Joe Christmas, a rootless man of unknowable racial heritage who violently seeks a race-based identity that eludes him until he sculpts and is sculpted into a fixed identity. What de Kooning might have felt or seen as he read about the castration of Joe Christmas that appeared in an excerpt from *Light in August* entitled "Percy Grimm," published in Malcolm Cowley's 1946 *Portable Faulkner*, cannot be known. But de Kooning's story of stowing away and jumping ship when the S.S. *Shelley* docked in Newport News, Virginia, has been recorded. De Kooning's expectations of America had been shaped by the dark Dutch street performer Black Max, who declaimed Whitman's "Song of Myself" into the air of Rotterdam, but the wily artist would also later claim that he came to the United States to get rich. Instead, de Kooning, as he jumped ship, found himself in the unreconstructed South: "When Leo Cohan [his friend] and some sailors took him to a barber shop, the barber recounted with great relish the details of a lynching" (Stevens and Swann 61). In 1926, as the South entered the Depression (the bottom had fallen out of the cotton market) and the outrage of lynching rose toward its statistical peak for the twentieth century, Virginia had the lowest recorded number of lynchings of the southern states. De Kooning's memory can be linked to a specific incident that remained part of his account of the terror that attended his illegal entry into the United States. On August 15, 1926, just over two weeks after the *Shelley* docked in Newport News, Raymond Bird, a black farmhand was murdered in Wytheville, Virginia: his head was bludgeoned, his body was dragged for miles, and he was hanged from a tree, after which he was shot numerous times. This news was reported in regional, and eventually national, newspapers and magazines. Bird was alleged to have had carnal relations with two white sisters, one of whom had exposed the issue by bearing a mixed-race child on July 23, while the other was then revealed to be pregnant.[7] Whatever he knew of this lynching and its context, de Kooning's feeling of terror was an experience he recalled throughout his life. For de Kooning, the barber's story, first sounded and then translated, would have made "a picture." De Kooning became de Kooning because this expression, "ma[king] a picture," was more than a figure of speech: it was the way that he, coming to consciousness, had lived on the earth.

De Kooning, a gamer in language and a player in pictures, described the relationship of his often word-interested art to word-based forms. Declaring to Harold Rosenberg that "[a] novel is different from a painting," he found himself thinking about form as well as scope: "I have said that I am more like a novelist in painting than a poet. But this is a vague comparison because there is no plot in painting."[8] In his most insightful classification of the miscreant and representational de Kooning, Clement Greenberg—primary author and enforcer of the rigid catechism mandating abstraction—opined that this painter had "even more Luciferian pride behind [his] ambition" than Picasso himself.[9] From the outset, de Kooning's place as a leader in the post–World War II avant-garde embodied multiple paradoxes, not least of which was his unrelenting devotion to an art that was concerned with flesh and the human figure. The intensity of what was at stake in de Kooning's decision to remain outside the ranks was addressed by Jackson Pollock (quite drunk and direct) outside the 1953 gallery opening that featured *Woman I* (1950–52) along with her five more frightening-than-life sisters: "Bill, you betrayed it. You're doing the figure, you're still doing the same goddamn thing. You know you never got out of being a figure painter." In a sign that this confrontation had taken place over half a century before, Richard Schiff ventures a note to express his strong doubts that de Kooning's work had ever been divorced from the figural: "I nevertheless believe that nearly all of de Kooning's 'abstractions' either began with a reference to the human figure or incorporated figural elements along the way."[10]

In the period of apocalyptic optimism immediately following World War II, Faulkner was de Kooning's writer. Picasso had broken bodies, reassembling their parts to great effect. Faulkner's work, as it spoke through collations of objects, presented the human form as construction work, narrated through violated bodies and the wholeness made possible by dismemberment. Gallery owner Allan Stone, describing de Kooning's role in the history of art, credited his friend with having accomplished "the liquefaction of cubism."[11] There may not be a better phrase for describing what happens as a result of the focus on the visceral and rotting body of the mother in *As I Lay Dying*. Addie Bundren is an embodiment of decomposition, and in her "Animal magnetism" poses an infinite challenge to the best beveled box ever made to contain a woman.[12] Identifying this work as Faulkner's "cubist novel," Panthea Reid has argued that *As I Lay Dying* is so formidably formal that its very structure may interfere with the conveying of its theme-laden story.[13] Faulkner's work as a whole is like entering into a modernist field/space drawing that pulls simultaneously toward two visions, as the forces of composition and theory compete for dominance with theme and content: the energy of the binary is palpable as each constructs the other in fertile dialectic.

In the crucible of the postwar years, de Kooning read Faulkner, and as *Light in August*, *Black Friday*, and *Black Untitled*—de Kooning's Faulkner trilogy—illustrate, the painter's act of reading was so intense that Faulkner's work might be said to have read de Kooning. More than Sartre and Camus, more than Cowley or even Ben Wasson, de Kooning was the best reader of William Faulkner to emerge in the first half of the twentieth century. An interpretive masterwork, de Kooning's *Light in August* committed one of the most detailed and synthesizing acts of ekphrasis in all of twentieth-century art.[14] The de Kooning that Faulkner precipitated was an intellectually perceptive and concept-driven painter who went beyond descriptive interiors or representational exteriors to discover what Whitman had identified as the "inherences of things." For a painter like de Kooning, interested in parables of art, the visual play of metamorphoses, and the problem of stillness caught forever in pursuit around an Attic vase, Faulkner was a painter's writer. In the crucial transformative period that saw de Kooning's apotheosis in the art world through his startling black and whites, Faulkner joined select company to become de Kooning's painter as well. As Randall S. Wilhelm points out with regard to Faulkner, theorists of the visual have understood that artists who work in one medium develop aesthetic practices (creative gestures and vocabularies) that influence their work when they turn to a new medium or genre. Since Faulkner continued to work seriously on his drawing with an eye toward a possible career in the visual arts well through his twenties, this theory of cross-fertilizing aesthetics provides grounds for speculating on the textural ingredients and patterns that drew de Kooning to Faulkner, what caused him to attempt to draw some of the profoundly visual narratives and formal structures found in Faulkner's difficult fiction.

The de Kooning of the late 1940s had not seen Faulkner's own early forays into the visual arts. De Kooning could not have seen Faulkner's pen-and-ink drawings in his handmade book, *The Marionettes: A Play in One Act* (1920),[15] including "The Apotheosis of Marietta" (see fig. 1, p. 4)—a picture that exposes the female figure's breasts as eyes, making a simian-comic face that locates her navel as its mouth; "The Kiss" (see fig. 2, p. 5), an actual field/space drawing that articulates a phallus,[16] in a shape that doubles as a long-dressed, small-headed figure of the mother; or Faulkner's frontispiece (see fig. 5, p. 10), which in the original version exposes the blackened leg of Marietta with an Afro-napped black ball placed at the top of her slit skirt to form the naked figure of an Africanist sculpture. This stylized albeit hidden black female dances toward the poet-seducer as the rest of Marietta's virginal body seems to demur (resisting coyly), pulling away from Pierrot's grasping of her hand. The most experimental visual performance by the drawings of *The Marionettes* takes place in the palimpsest created by facing drawings depicting Pierrot's dream across from his counterposing reality in "Pierrot's Two

Visions" (see fig. 7, p. 14, and fig. 8, p. 15). The signal that these two drawings are meant to be read (attended to) when they are overlapped is given by the strongly curved vertical vectors of the poplars that cross to make a clear "V" when the pages are closed. Indeed, these drawings become one as the double-page spread closes, picturing the poet-seducer as he is throwing his arm around Marietta to remain in permanent embrace within the physical confines and intimacy of the unopened book. The fact that these facing drawings when laid on top of each other form a complex collage—a sliced torso picturing buttocks when seen through the front blank page and a giant breast with a marked aureole visible through the closed and blank back—reveals Faulkner's visual sophistication that plots intimacy and intimates artful obscenity despite the narrative-challenging stillness of the drawn image. While de Kooning never saw Faulkner's drawings, he appears to have sensed the energy of their compositional tension in the visually volatile verbal play of Faulkner's fiction. Even before de Kooning read Faulkner, before he in his signifying act spelled out his connection with the great author by creating and naming a breakthrough painting *Light in August*, de Kooning had drawn parables of art that contained hidden stories waiting to be recognized and exposed through visual enactments of metamorphoses. De Kooning's use of the female body to make faces with breasts depicted as eyes is well known, as is his mouth/cunt conundrum,[17] underlined by his bawdy comment that "a woman has two mouths, one is the sex."[18] The more subtle of de Kooning's drawings (a mixed-media form that sometimes included charcoal, pastels, oil, and water colors as well as ink and pencil), field/space works that require a full shift of vision on the viewer's part, provide an introduction to de Kooning's own obsession with parables of art.[19] This obsession is part of what attracted him to Faulkner and explains why the pattern of collaged metamorphoses is more prominent in de Kooning's highly narrated Faulkner paintings than anywhere else in the painter's oeuvre. While de Kooning's "purely pictorial idiom" was not entirely unsullied by referents, Renée Arb's review of de Kooning's first single-artist show in 1948 was acute in observing that his "virtuosity [is] disguised by voluptuousness [as] the process of painting becomes the end," and that de Kooning's great "subject seems to be the crucial intensity of the creative process itself."[20]

De Kooning's *Light in August*

> Joe Christmas is an abstraction seeking to become a human being.
> —Alfred Kazin, "The Stillness of [Faulkner's] *Light in August*"[21]

> Repeating geometric designs—lines and circles, verticals and horizontals—Faulkner actually facets, like a cubist painter . . .
> —Panthea Reid Broughton on Faulkner's "design" of *As I Lay Dying*[22]

Recognized as a point of origin that led to his first one-man show, de Kooning's *Light in August* (1946–47) is a noted painting in the history of the midcentury movement that would come to be known as Abstract Expressionism, action painting, or, more parochially, "the New York School" (see plate 1). This painting, distinguished by its lushness in detail, ushered in the radical series of black-and-white paintings that appeared in de Kooning's gallery opening, an event in the history of art that announced the United States' entry into the abstraction of emotive motion that would define and redefine the modernism of post–World War II art. In her review that announced de Kooning's arrival onto the New York art scene as his milieu began to speak to, not just back to, the innovators in France, Renée Arb understood the significance of these new paintings: "his subject seems to be . . . the creative process itself which de Kooning has translated into a new and purely pictorial idiom." Insisting on the use of white as a color, *Light in August* was one of de Kooning's surprising black-and-white paintings that challenged the eye to relegate either the light of darkness or the darkness of light to foreground or background. With the exception of *Sanctuary* (1931), Faulkner's carefully revised potboiler that linked the violence of male impotence to the unstaunchable blood of female evil, none of William Faulkner's novels had managed to remain in print through 1946, when Malcolm Cowley published *The Portable Faulkner*. Comprised of short stories and pieces cut from longer works to collate a temporally ordered "history" of Faulkner's fictional Mississippi county, Cowley's anthology brought Faulkner and his Yoknapatawpha back from obscurity to secure this highly experimental author's place among the great unread.

De Kooning's *Light in August* is startlingly readable if you come knowing the language. What is not in question is that the Willem de Kooning of 1946 knew the language of Faulkner's art as he painted his *Light in August*. De Kooning's plot, like Faulkner's plot, is based on the superimposing of images and acts of repetition in which the flow and direction of the narrative is determined by being overdetermined. Writing about de Kooning's white-and-black paintings, Thomas Hess seems to understand de Kooning's work as a collage, noting the interconnectedness in which forms construct other forms:

> The white cuts out a shape in the black; the black in the white . . . There are no spaces between shapes. The plane of the picture becomes filled and seamless; illusions are contradicted as the "line" that evokes them becomes, in turn, legible as a negative of the shape it defines and then as a shape of its own.[23]

De Kooning's interest in Faulkner, which had begun with *Sanctuary* (widely acknowledged to be Faulkner's most shocking book), continued in the artist's best-known engagement with Faulkner's fiction: the painting he named *Light in August*. De Kooning's fascination with Faulkner's *Sanctuary* and *Light in August* has been seen as an extension of his taste for the lurid, which drew him through much of his life to read the tabloids for their crude tales of violence. Elaine de Kooning recalled that de Kooning along with their coterie read Raymond Chandler and other detective fiction, in the same way that they played tennis, for leisure and for pleasure.[24]

As de Kooning's wife of forty years—although not in the same household for most of them—recounted in an interview for the Smithsonian:

> Well, he [de Kooning] read *Light in August*. He adored Faulkner and he loved Faulkner's endless sentences. He just was lost in admiration over how much would happen in one sentence. He talked of a sentence where a man was failing and then there was a great deal of memory involved before Faulkner got to the end of the sentence, and Bill just loves that. His way of reading is to become totally immersed in an author, and back then, in the late '40s and the early '50s, he was very much involved with Faulkner. In his adolescence it was [Fyodor] Dostoevsky.[25]

De Kooning not only read Faulkner's *Light in August*, he appears to have read this novel on the level of the sentence. As Charles F. Stuckey initially questioned de Kooning's acts of reading (a perennial concern raised in the scant criticism, which acknowledges that the painter could and did read deeply), he speculated on the strong visual prompting that de Kooning might have received from Alvin Lustig's dust jacket design for the 1946 edition of Faulkner's *Light in August* (see fig. 25). Were there no evidence that the painter had read Faulkner's novel, in Stuckey's view, Lustig's explosive dust jacket would have been enough to prompt de Kooning's experiment in black and white.[26] Yet, like de Kooning's painting, Lustig's drawing erupts from the content of Faulkner's novel: Lustig himself had made an invertible drawing that depicts the Klan through a burning cross, an evocative vision that appears before the work is turned right-side up (the direction in which it would be published). Lustig's stick protagonist, as he appears on the righted cover, has a stylized double head rather than the pictorially specific testicles that accompany the fiery cross in the upended view of this drawing that so graphically remembers Percy Grimm's castration of Joe Christmas.

In his essay connecting de Kooning's *Light in August* to Faulkner's *Light in August*, Stuckey concludes:

> Like Faulkner, de Kooning appreciates ambiguous visual metaphors, shapes and images which look like many things at once. Rather than indicating his interest in some episode or setting of Faulkner's novel, de Kooning's choice of *Light in August* for a title suggests that the artist shared Faulkner's concern for what he and "no one else will know."[27]

In de Kooning's often-quoted warning against efforts to interpret his work, he confessed to Harold Rosenberg: "That's what fascinates me—to make something I can never be sure of, and that no one else can either. I will never know

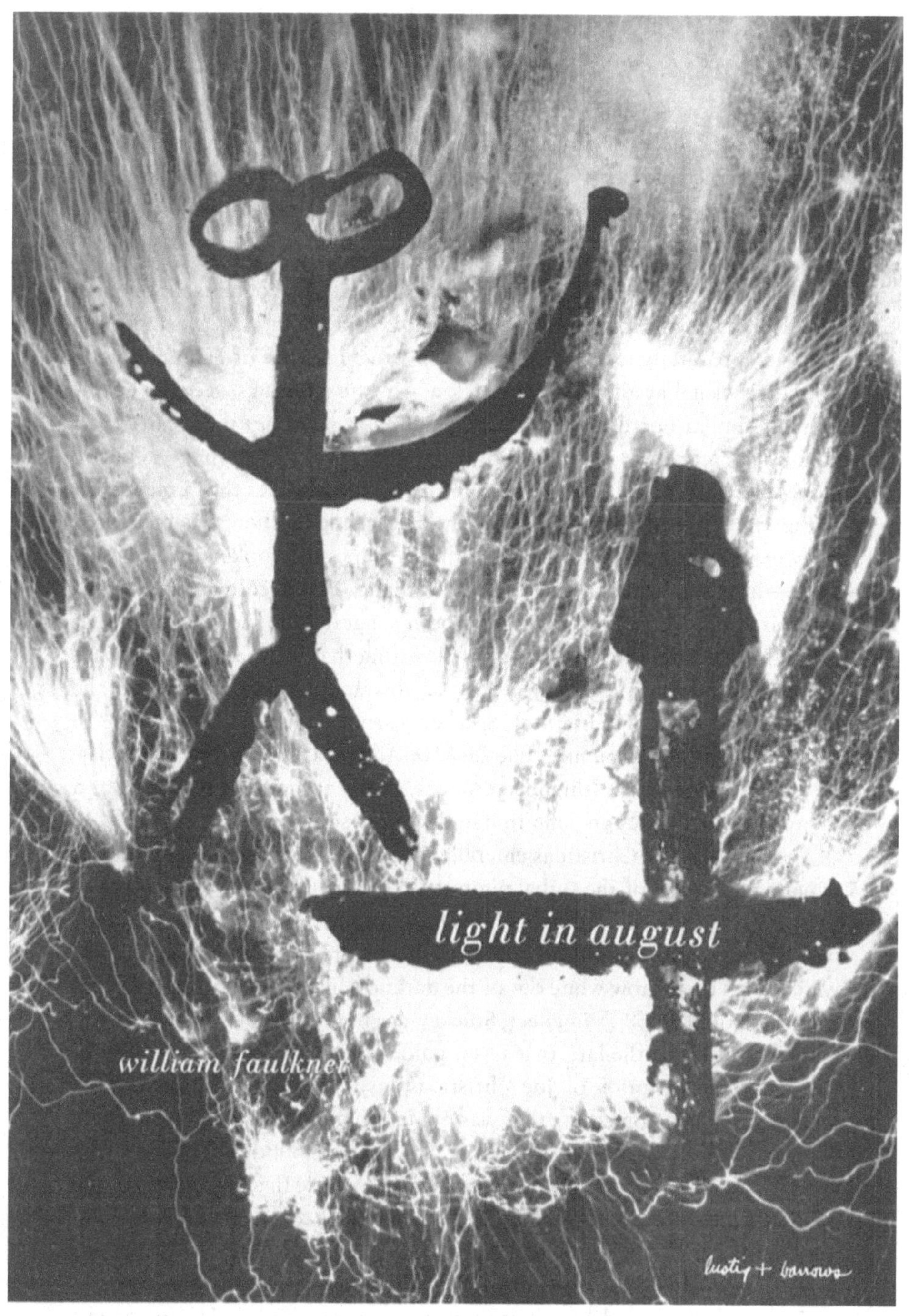

Figure 25. Alvin Lustig, dust jacket design for William Faulkner, *Light in August* (New Directions, 1946). Courtesy of the Alvin Lustig Foundation.

and no one else will ever know." Alive to the visual, Stuckey quotes passages from Faulkner's *Light in August* that he recognizes as

> analogous to de Kooning's paintings. They present imagistic equivalents for Joe's reaction to tension-fraught situations in which he tries to overcome the torment of not knowing which world [black or white] he belongs to. Faulkner emphasizes turbulent, shadowy movements accented by flickers of darkness and light in liquid and active spaces.[28]

What is brilliant about Stuckey's observation is that he recognizes the remarkable degree to which Faulkner used words as a medium as well as a means to create a painterly text. Stuckey, analyzing the influence of Faulkner on de Kooning's visual aesthetic in the black-and-white paintings, sees the evocation of "similar nocturnal townscape[s]" in later paintings that "call . . . to mind *Town Square* or *Night Square* (1950–51)." Speculating that Faulkner's influence can be found in other paintings, Stuckey observes that a piece such as *Painting*—a work that was part of the field-changing show which featured *Light in August* and *Black Friday*—with its "shapes that look like curvy body parts—hips and breasts vivisected, charred and scrambled helter-skelter" is comprised of "forms that might have been suggested by the violent murder in Faulkner's novel [*Light in August*]." Insisting that de Kooning remain unreadable (what is at stake is the power of abstraction that is violated by the mere thought of representation), Stuckey warns against the temptation "to read the long drips in pictures like *Light in August* as the 'octopus tentacles' of Joanna's hair, or the 'thighdeep' weeds, or the at first illegible forms of a photograph as it takes on definition in developer solution."[29]

The figure of Joe Christmas emerging as a naked torso is one of the most dynamically visual of the verbal photographs in Faulkner's *Light in August*: "He stood with his hands on his hips, naked, thighdeep in the dusty weeds, while the car came over the hill and approached, the lights full upon him. He watched his body grow white out of the darkness like a kodak print emerging from the liquid" (108).[30] In effect, Stuckey has used de Kooning's black-and-white paintings of the late 1940s as a guide to Faulkner's *Light in August*. Reading the description of Joe Christmas "as if he were running headfirst and laughing into something that was obliterating him like a picture in chalk being erased from a blackboard" (208), Stuckey has found the Faulkner who spoke to de Kooning, the Faulkner who helped to write this influential version of the painter into existence. Picturing paintings of torsos as well as narrating the tonal and enfiladed aesthetic of surprise, de Kooning saw Faulkner's word-pictures and created paintings that sharpened the edge of the new art.

Chary of the forced search for representations, the looking for figures among the chimeras of abstract forms, Stuckey imagines the disappointment of de Kooning (who was aware of the emotional power as well as the celebrated indecipherability of his black-and-white paintings) were he to have known what the "original owner" of *Light in August*, most likely Charles Egan, saw in his painting. Egan or possibly his wife of the period (Stuckey out of generosity does not identify his source) wrote of the piece: "the title was derived from Faulkner's story 'Light in August' which I think was about a boy who went to a circus or a country fair. You can see this in the painting. There is a balloon, some objects that slightly resemble animals and other oddities suggesting a circus."[31] This fantasy about Faulkner's fiction reveals the dangers of not reading (or not even knowing the plot of an implicated work), but the first owner, unbiased by a knowledge of Faulkner (and apparently unfettered by the edicts of Abstract Expressionism), was significantly able to see a story. Alongside the traditional accounts of dismembered bodies, "biomorphic" fragments, and things seen to litter de Kooning's work, the original owner's proposition (seen as risible) is finally among the most insightful views of this painting. His interpretation understands that de Kooning's *Light in August* is linked to Faulkner's *Light in August*, and that whether through a circus or its circles, whether through balloons filled with air or balloons inscribing fragmented bodies, de Kooning's painting is indeed trying to say something.

In addition to the crescent moon, some of the most realistically rendered objects in the painting include a frying pan, a carved wooden chair, and a milk stool that doubles as a black oval or pool that seems to be absorbing a female torso from above. Harry Gaugh, offering the most complete catalog of symbols in de Kooning's *Light in August*, lists: a crescent moon, a balloon or repeating circles, and a closed gate or Mosaic tablet. In works such as *Light in August*, "shapes as semi-autonomous units were dismantled and piled up"; in Gaugh's words, "de Kooning seemed to be rummaging through a junkyard at night."[32] Extrapolating from his impression of *Light in August* and the other dark canvasses, Gaugh concludes that these "were largely black works in which white didn't have much of a chance." Rather, as he sees it, these de Koonings were the "shape-infested forebears of Ad Reinhardt's all-black canvasses of the 1950s and '60s."[33]

There is a great deal going on in de Kooning's *Light in August* as it creates a dynamic sense of motion in terms of the interplay between dark and light. Stuckey argues that "the internal shapes interlock so completely that neither black nor white can be accurately described as figure or ground."[34] Indeed, the formal intensity, more than the idea of order—the enactment of order in *Light in August*—begins with de Kooning's known practice of dividing the canvas into windowlike rectangles. The center of this painting, the crossing of diagonals, marks the center of a rectangle, the inner point at which four equal rectangles meet. In *Light in August*, the juncture of the "X" is marked by the crossing of curved white lines that constitute the cantilevered and broken (partially obliterated) figure "8." De Kooning, ridiculed for his highly developed mastery of technique, did not, as some have argued, abandon his draftsman's skills in *Light in August*. This geometric center extended to the left side of the canvas marks the position of what appears to be a recognizable object in the painting, the carved top of a wooden chair. There is a substantial vertical line bisecting the painting, a medial marker that descends from the stumpy area of whiteness at the top, changing at intervals from black to white as it passes downward through this center toward the bottom of the painting. Touching the right side of the crescent moon along the way, this line cleaves the canvas in half. In *Light in August*, this tipping bowl of a moon either pours out black liquidity toward the painting's largest circle of whiteness, or, seen from below, this moon is being broached by a column of phallic blackness that moves upward, finishing in a white tip that does not touch but could be the ejaculatory source of the whiteness that the moon-bowl holds. Geometrically, de Kooning's *Light in August* (despite its carefully mapped quadrants) is dominated by circles and marked by smaller triangles that take the shape of a closed number—the Roman numeral "V" as well as open-ended and jagged "vees" that articulate breasts and other parts of the torsos, notably the rounded but fierce upward points, double triangles that form the neckline of what appears to be a freestanding evening dress.

Declared as abstract, *Light in August* has been seen as a painting that radically addresses color and hierarchy and by direct implication the constructed quality of race through the significant interplay of ground, foreground, and background to question and confound a hierarchy based on color. De Kooning entered *Light in August* through Cowley's *Portable Faulkner*. This means that de Kooning's point of visual entry into Faulkner's long out-of-print novel was focused on the castration of Joe Christmas. It is no accident that the works from Cowley's collection that drew de Kooning's eye are those that focused on the violence of racism and the violation of the earth: narratives of threatening razors, the beheadings of female and feminized figures, the feared phallus of the black man, and the erosion haunting once-peaceful valleys, carving away the delta of a diminishing wilderness.[35]

If the temporal act of reading, if not looking, at a painting must begin somewhere, de Kooning's *Light in August* with its series of circles, marked and demarcated, offers a point of origin in the lower right-hand corner. This encoded legend, a type of signature to the right of the artist's name, points to the idea that this canvas has directional components. This legend in the corner is a nearly blank circle with visible white hash marks slicing with precision into the blackness at twelve and six o'clock. Wearing blackface, this circle is a clock with "one hand" ("Dilsey," *PF*, 410), a somewhat rounded, fleshed limb—a fairly figured human arm—pointing with a decentered confidence to eight o'clock.[36] In the edited version of "April Eighth 1928" that appeared as "Dilsey" in *The Portable Faulkner*, Dilsey, with her "indomitable skeleton . . . rising like a ruin or a landmark above [her] somnolent and impervious guts," knows what time it is:

> On the wall above a cupboard, invisible save at night, by lamplight and even then evincing an enigmatic profundity because it had but one hand, a cabinet clock ticked, then with a preliminary sound as if it had cleared its throat, struck five times.
>
> "Eight o'clock," Dilsey said. (*PF* 410)

Inscribed to the left above the clock, the Roman numeral "V" echoes the chimes' "five times" while the clock itself points toward the missing "8" that sounds and resounds in the section's title: "April Eighth 1928." In de Kooning's *Light in August*, the missing "8" has been only partially blacked out, enabling it to become part of a series of echoing busts or outlined heads that initially seem to dominate the painting, as they rotate clockwise to become a white-edged shape of science fiction's classic rocket ship or a pawn piece from chess. The point of crossing in the figure eight occupies a juncture that is at the precise middle of the painting. For the vertical rectangle that is *Light in August*, this is the juncture where two diagonal vectors would intersect, the juncture that would mark the inner corners of the equal quadrants that comprise the painting. This crossing at what remains of the left-leaning 8 is the dead center of the painting. The imaginary line shared by the upper-left quadrant and the lower-left quadrant marks the top of the carved wooden chair (a large object for the painting), while the division between the two upper rectangles emerges in the clearly visible, vertical line of whiteness that exits quite near the midpoint of the upper edge of the canvas. The mathematical play and punning become evident in the top portion of this figure "**8**," to note what is "ate" or eaten by the balloonlike head of the number. Cantilevering to the left, this "**8**" has a tiny pie-shaped piece cut or eaten into its circular side, while the top of the "**8**" as a whole contains a large rendering of the Greek letter "π" (pi), a letter that stands for the number that is essential for calculating the area or circumference of a circle. The number "**8**" turning back on itself has long been the sign of the infinite. Here, this symbol for infinity has been broken or erased—"pi" has been inscribed, insisting through the combination of a number and a letter and a letter that is a number that signs (like "**8**" and "π") are sounds (homophones) as well as signals.

Known for wielding his handmade sign painter's brush with the precision of a draftsman's pencil, de Kooning, educated at the Rotterdam Academy of Fine Arts and Techniques (with an eye toward a future in advertising),[37] had been required to devote a year to the study of the alphabet and the art of painting letters. Both he and Faulkner were obsessed with the experimentally provocative vision (a reality known in ancient Egypt and China) that primal pictures could be articulated through abstract forms such as letters. In his expression of abstraction, looking for a starting point, a place of beginning, de Kooning in noted instances followed the inspirational practice of the surrealist painters who used the physical shapes of letters as origins for animals and objects, incorporating his looping and dripping signifiers as they were freed to express the meaning latent—waiting, the fatalists and psychoanalysts might argue—in their material shapes. The small piece of pie that de Kooning cut from the leftward arced top of the figure "**8**" is the actual Phoenician letter for "pi," which signifies the word "mouth."[38] He also would have known that the simple circle, or the "O," stood for the word "eye" in the Phoenician system.[39]

If de Kooning had not read Faulkner's *Light in August* in its entirety earlier, he read this work after it was reissued with its electrifying cover by Lustig in 1946, and after he had been introduced to this work (as well as other of Faulkner's narratives that turn on dismemberment)[40] that appeared in the excerpted and edited version condensed by Cowley for *The Portable Faulkner*. De Kooning's *Light in August* is haunted by Faulknerian excess found in the novel's repeating elements of ink and blood, liquid excrescences of blackness: cisterns of sexual entanglements, rising tides of race sensed as the feared pollution of blood—the tainting of race, and the soiling, feminizing power of menstrual fluids.[41] This female soiling is seen in a vision of leaking vessels that haunts a cave in the young Joe Christmas's imagination: "he seemed to see a diminishing row of suavely shaped urns in moonlight, blanched. And not one was perfect. Each one was cracked and from each crack there issued something liquid, deathcoloured, and foul" (*LA* 189).

Time in de Kooning's *Light in August* is inscribed through circles drawn from two pieces that Cowley chose for *The Portable Faulkner*, two separate narratives that depict *The Sound and the Fury*'s Dilsey as a figure of stability and order. In addition to the clock in the lower right, the upper-left corner of the painting is inscribed with a partial circle that radiates ribbons of light streaming downward. There is an inside and an outside to this painting, and the outside is seen through the lucent space of what must be a window to reveal the naïve and recognizable trope of a child's art, the cornered sun. In this instance, the "evening sun" (an allusion to "That Evening Sun," an originary story for *The Sound and the Fury*), placed in the west of de Kooning's *Light in August*, is "going down." Here, the late-descending dark of Mississippi summer underlines this painting's obsessions with celestial light, the miracle of math, and the Faulknerian trope that locates time through women. While the light of evening in the eighth month of the year is late, the clock from "April Eighth, 1928" can be used to signify evening as well as morning in this painting that refers so specifically to the story that Faulkner wrote as he was developing his families—the Compsons and the Gibsons—for *The Sound and the Fury*. The light in de Kooning's *Light in August* is not from the dissipating rays of the sun but from the strong lightness that ribbons and streams next to the darkness. Whiteness or lightness provides the lines that link shapes and, most pointedly, circumscribe the thickly brushed circles of white paint. These circles, one located in the upper-right corner and the other a larger circle located in the lower center, are both connected (the lower most clearly and emphatically to the vaginal crescent moon). This lower circle is connected by a curving vein of blackness descending from above, structuring the presence of umbilical ties in the physiology of the painting. The thicker white swipe on the right side of this lower circle provides perspective to the black, optically ovoid shape that is not just the center of an eye but a deeply contemplative eye that imagistically reflects. Like the man in the moon, this shimmering circle of the legible illegibility holds a long-limbed headless man flailing in flight, a body that seen from another angle suggests the macabre profile of a face. Abstract Expressionists, committed to realizing the two-dimensional flatness of the canvas, often added a distinct point of visual entry, a window, a door, an opening into deeper interiority, and de Kooning's reflective (his retinal) portal recalls the vague specificity of the bodies of Adam and Eve, whose limbs are escaping the primal triangle positioned at the center of the eye of David Davidovich Burliuk's radiant vision in his painting *The Eye of God* (1923–25; see cover and frontispiece). The calibrated sense of depth accomplished by de Kooning's surrounding white stroke conceals the fact that this shape, despite its uneven outer rim, is an actual circle. And this lower circle itself is centered, clearly aiming at equidistance from each side of the painting.

The circle has been and continues to be seen as central to the formal and thematic construction of Faulkner's *Light in August*. In terms of the plotline and narrative trajectories of the novel's multiple protagonists, the narrative form of Faulkner's *Light in August* has been convincingly described in the critical commentary as a series of circles looping backward from the present of the novel to incorporate detailed accounts of each individual's past before coming forward to the crisis that locates them in the immediacy of a present. The first chapter closes with a rising "yellow column" of smoke from a burning house, and the more permanent exhaling monument of a factory's smokestack. For Lena Grove and Gail Hightower, the impending culmination is the scene of a birth, the rewriting of a past scene for Reverend Hightower, who has previously delivered the stillborn child of a black woman. The crisis for Joanna Burden and Joe Christmas is fatal as their bodies—Joanna Burden's neck and Joe Christmas's genitals—are carved into death. After her dismemberment by Joe Christmas, Joanna Burden is left at her house, which her lover, refusing her as patron or father, has set afire. The castration of Joe Christmas culminates in the emotionally moving psalmlike shift into the voice of prayer that describes the inability of those who watch (including the resistant and impotent Hightower) to forget this sacrifice of a man named Christmas:

> For a long moment he looked up at them with peaceful and unfathomable and unbearable eyes. Then his face, body, all, seemed to collapse, to fall in upon itself, and from out the slashed garments about his hips and loins the pent black blood seemed to rush like a released breath. It seemed to rush out of his

> pale body like the rush of sparks from a rising rocket; upon that black blast the man seemed to rise soaring into their memories forever and ever. They are not to lose it, in whatever peaceful valleys, beside whatever placid and reassuring streams of old age, in the mirroring face of whatever children they will contemplate old disasters and newer hopes. (*LA* 423)

This is the indelible printing of Joe Christmas looking back that does not "fad[e]" and remains forever "of itself alone serene, of itself alone triumphant."

De Kooning entered (possibly reentered) *Light in August* through this scene in which Percy Grimm takes a knife to black masculinity, a scene that focuses on the still living and conscious eyes of the castrated man. Cowley chose to include the castration of Joe Christmas, the only literal castration that takes place on the page in Faulkner's fiction, because this was the piece that he felt could be excised as the most complete story from *Light in August*. As Cowley's title for the piece, "Percy Grimm," conveys, this section is more a portrait of the violator than of his victim. Meanwhile, Joe Christmas and his life's trajectory constitute the primary narrative of the novel. Critics, most notably Charles Stuckey and David Craven, have discussed the relationship between de Kooning's painting and the novel from which it takes its name, noting the power of the tonality of the black-and-white paint that conveys Joe Christmas's own ambiguity about his racial identity. Some twenty years after painting *Light in August*, de Kooning described a painting to an interviewer sent by *Newsweek*, pointing out two men in the foreground before naming the shadowy and less distinct figure of a watcher as "that half-breed Joe Christmas dressed in . . . a kind of zoot suit." He added, "I'd like to paint Joe Christmas one of these days."[42] De Kooning's *Light in August* is only a portrait of Joe Christmas insofar as it portrays the violent feminization of women as well as men through a narrative of dismemberment and sacrifice. While it is not a portrait of Joe Christmas, de Kooning's *Light in August* is a masterful synthesis of Faulkner's violent parables of art refracted with particular power through cataclysmic references to the life of Joe Christmas.

Sartorial Sculptures

The most aggressively pursued figure in de Kooning's *Light in August* is what might be called the sartorial torso. Clothed or unclothed, there is a sense that these truncated body-shapes are wearing flesh. Indicated by necklines, the sharp articulation of the double "vee" pictures where the missing dress might be on the first body in the upper-left quadrant. The waist of this first female figure with her downward-etched breasts is shaped in her nakedness from the right by the fabric-covered breast of the second torso (hers are the breasts which appear to be the triangular peaks [pinnacles] of a stand-alone dress).

Here, the breast on the right side of the second figure has a textured nipple that comes forward through the thin fabric of this dramatic bodice, and in its very roundness articulates the waist of the diminutive inset of another torso recognizable by the scoop-neckline of her flesh, and by her evocative smear of black pubic hair. This tiny headless torso resting on top of the truncated figure "**8**" emerges in her whiteness like a badge that signifies the color of the flesh beneath the black dress that wears her. Identifiable through her distinguishing mammalian features, this first torso (located to the left of the "dress" in the upper-left quadrant of the painting) is accomplished as a beautifully fluid figure ruptured by these gouged, white-lined "vees," her sharply carved breasts that place her in the aesthetic of African sculpture. The curved calf of her backlit leg seems to be melting into or emerging from a pool, an elliptical shape of blackness with legs that allow it to double as a milking stool. Like the diminutive torso that is superimposed onto the dominant torso of the painting, the first and second figures are identified as female by the articulation of their genitals. The dot that marks the navel of the first (black and Africanist) torso is somewhat high, but the clarity of the heart-shape that intimates a vagina secures her identity. As she shapes the waist of this svelte figure, the dominant torso (or second figure), with her enormous breasts, seems too fully sartorial. In her garish full-breasted gown that peaks upward toward strapless vacuity, this seemingly bodiless diva has a body that seems altogether too present. This dress becomes physically embodied by her crescent moon that has a strong umbilical line flowing downward into the largest circle near the bottom of the painting. Aside from the triangle, the heart and the crescent moon are the best known of the archetypal and pictorial symbols for the female genital.

The most visible sartorial torso of a male is circumscribed in the white circle in the upper-right corner of de Kooning's *Light in August*. This circle, taken for a balloon by the painting's first owner, evokes a mental space, as if it were a thought balloon rising above the characters below in the already long-established tradition of cartoon narration. This male torso does not contain the thought; rather, he is the thought. The truncated male body in the upper circle seems to have an arm that has been torn away from the ragged sleeve, which signals an absent limb that is then countered by the sartorial sign of a tie which (defying gravity) goes up to his missing neck. This torso encircled in the upper-right corner is male not just because he does not have breasts, but because he has a dangling signifier. His torn suit of whiteness, seen from either upside-down or right-side up, articulates the same torso, as the suspended tie and the phallus reverse to signify male morphology. Viewed from either end, there are symmetrical indentations that mark the descent of the organ between or, rather, toward the missing legs. While conclusive in their statement, neither of these markers of maleness at either end of this suit of whiteness is particularly enunciated. What this male torso contributes to the formal and thematic narrative of the painting is the depiction of a hole in his whiteness; a tiny black tear in this already ragged fabric of flesh, leaks—spurts—white light or liquid, violating the circle.

As Percy Grimm castrates the living Joe Christmas, "the pent black blood seem[s] to rush like a released breath. It seem[s] to rush out of his pale body like the rush of sparks from a rising rocket" (*LA* 465). This blood described as "black" is analyzed by the novel's Harvard-educated lawyer, Gavin Stevens, who offers a eugenic analysis of black and white. Seen as dynamically opposed and distinct fluids, Stevens describes the "black blood" and the "white blood" that drive Joe Christmas during the final days of his life:

> [T]he black blood drove him first to the negro cabin. And then the white blood drove him out of there, as it was the black blood which snatched up the pistol and the white blood which would not let him fire it. And it was the white blood which sent him to the minister, which rising in him for the last and final time, sent him against all reason and all reality, into the embrace of a chimaera, a blind faith in something read in a printed Book. (449)

While the tiny idealized female inscribed on the bust of the dominant female torso conceivably marks the figure in the black dress as white, de Kooning's male torsos—to state the obvious—envision Joe Christmas. Articulated in the painting as a dismembered body, Joe Christmas has been framed off by the circles of whiteness in what is clearly the most cerebral and detailed masculine torso in the painting, and more enigmatically in the feminized, umbilically attached circle centered at the lower edge of the work. These circles, mind-womb, womb-mind ("all one"),[43] constitute a culturally circumscribed whiteness that frames and contains this severed man's light skin, his "parchment-colored" flesh. As art historian Sally Yard has observed, white is not white in de Kooning's *Light in August*; rather, this color is tempered by what she has identified as a "tincture of flesh."[44] Percy Grimm is the martinet-like vigilante who castrates Joe Christmas with a butcher knife, carving this scene "into [the watchers'] memories forever." Recalling the circularity that structures not only Joe Christmas's narrative but the novel as a whole, the castration of Joe Christmas dooms Reverend Hightower and all who witness this cutting to see this death for the rest of their lives.

De Kooning's repeated circles more than recall; they allude to and depict the novel's description of the roads and streets that the racially indeterminate Joe Christmas has been on for thirty years. This road, repeatedly described as "a circle," "the street [that] ran on: catlike, one place . . . the same as another to him," leads Joe Christmas at the age of thirty-three to Joanna Burden's house. In terms of female figures, this white woman who "aint old. Aint young neither" (*LA* 227) is enfiladed (in the novel as well as the painting), layered next to Christmas's previous lover, the black woman who resembles "an ebony carving":

> He now lived as man and wife with a woman who resembled an ebony carving. At night he would lie in bed beside her, sleepless, beginning to breathe deep and hard. He would do it deliberately, feeling, even watching, his white chest arch deeper and deeper within his ribcage, trying to breathe into himself the dark odor, the dark and inscrutable thinking and being of negroes, with each suspiration trying to expel from himself the white blood and the white thinking and being. And all the while his nostrils at the odor which he was trying to make his own would whiten and tauten, his whole being writhe and strain with physical outrage and spiritual denial. (225–26)

These are the only women in the novel with whom Joe Christmas has established domestic as well as carnal relations. Joe arrives at the mill in Jefferson in what will remain his signature garment, the "soiled white shirt" that will eventually be washed and worn with a tie both before and after he enters into the final stage of his relationship with the woman whom he imagines he will marry, but instead takes a razor to her neck.

Stuckey remained adamant that de Kooning's *Light in August* contained no recognizable "props" (his word for representational references) to Faulkner's *Light in August*, a critical view that has remained ubiquitous among de Kooning scholars. With few exceptions, the art historical line from Clement Greenberg forward has been concerned with policing the purity of the "purely pictorial idiom" of de Kooning's black-and-white abstracts. This has been to save paintings, such as *Light in August*, from the fate of being read and perused by naïve readers who might claim one-to-one correspondences on the basis of a shirt color or sharply carved ebon-colored breasts. Nevertheless, time and female procreation or the relation of time to masculine impotence is a major theme in Faulkner's fiction that de Kooning brings together in his narration of the castration of Joe Christmas by the vigilante and proto-Nazi Percy Grimm. Obviously observing that Grimm is the "Grim Reaper," de Kooning included this iconic, skull-faced figure of death, bending leftward over the severed figure of infinity, the broken figure "8." Properly sized to occupy the canvas with the diminutive white female torso that sits on the "8," the hooded and intent Grim Reaper oversees the center of the painting. His reaping scythe, here a potential tool for art, disappears into the same ink-black milk stool that seems to be absorbing or generating the beautiful Africanist torso which occupies the left side of the painting.

Following the medial line that extends upward from the center point of the painting to the top of the canvas, there is another surprising "prop" or representational reference in de Kooning's *Light in August*. As this line passes upward through the white stump or stalk, there is the nearly severed neck and the outraged lower half of a face that has been literally cut off by the edge of the painting just above her bleeding mouth. This is de Kooning's portrait of the carved head of Joanna Burden. Whether "the ebony statue" to the left alludes to the black woman with whom Joe Christmas has lived for two years or not, the dominating sartorial torso next to her, the black dress, is Joanna Burden. This character not only has a body, she has had a head that features her bleeding mouth, which drips black blood from her razor-sculpted neck authored by Joe Christmas.

Finally, Joanna Burden's head (her neck, lower jaw, and contorted mouth) floating atop her big-breasted dress is not the last female portrait in de Kooning's *Light in August*. Another major visage (recalling the eyes looking from the dark cabin doors of the black settlement in *As I Lay Dying*) peers out from the blackness beneath Joanna Burden's dripping head. This other head framed by clumped hair consists of a face made visible by the slight bulging of two white dots (her eyes) and a mouth articulated by a small nest of white glints, an opening into the site of her mangled teeth. Readers of Cowley's *Portable Faulkner* know that Dilsey and the Compson children of *The Sound and the Fury* are characters with a past. This past includes a connection to an impoverished black washerwoman and occasional prostitute named Nancy, who serves as the Compson family housekeeper at a time when Dilsey is temporarily indisposed. Faulkner's "That Evening Sun" (1931) tells of the fearful Nancy, who has sought protection from her violent husband by trying to remain with the Compson family after her services are no longer needed. In this story Nancy's eyes are repeatedly pictured. Said to be "like cat's eyes . . . like a big cat against the wall, watching us," Nancy often looks at the children and, from Caddy's perspective, "[Nancy's] eyes went fast like she was afraid there wasn't time to look, without hardly moving at all" (296, 298–99).[45] After Caddy sees Nancy's eyes on "the stairs," the young girl feels that she "had looked so hard at [Nancy's] eyes . . . that they had got printed on my eyeballs, like the sun does when you have closed your eyes and there is no sun" (296). Terrified for her life, Nancy's eyes convey her fear of the jealous husband who has said he "can cut down the vine" (to castrate or kill the man) who has planted "the watermelon that Nancy had under her dress" (292). Nancy's husband's scar from a previous cutting ("his razor scar on his black face [looking] like a piece of dirty string" [292]) is linked to "that razor in his mouth. That razor on that string down his back, inside his shirt" (295). "That Evening Sun," the work that in proportional terms contains the most references to cuttings and dismemberment in all of Faulkner's fiction, is a story in which passion cuts both ways. As Mr. Compson comforts Nancy by telling her that "it's all right now. He's probably in St. Louis now. Probably got another wife by now and forgot all about you," Nancy adds: "I'd stand there right over them, and every time he wropped her, I'd cut that arm off. I'd cut his head off and I'd slit her belly and I'd shove—" (295). Her passionate fantasy is broken off as she is hushed by the children's father. As the "evening sun goes down," Nancy tells the children that she has got the sign that she will be cut and killed; her husband has left a message on her table, "a hog bone, with blood meat still on it" (307).

Nancy's face in de Kooning's *Light in August* (articulated by Joanna Burden's tenuously severed head as it threatens to fall from above) emerges from the blackness through its bulging eyes that even in their shadowed subtlety evoke the racial stereotype that defines minstrel show mockery. While it was Faulkner who wrote this story that depicts a woman whose eyes shine her fear in the dark and who has had teeth kicked out by a customer whom she publicly accuses of refusing to pay for his use of her body, de Kooning told his own story as he juxtaposed Faulkner's wounded and racialized bodies into a newly collaged narrative. Rooted in the nineteenth-century pictorial form popularized by Thomas Nast in magazines such as *Harper's*, de Kooning's collage is a modernist panorama, a form of visual narration that is actually older than the sequential depictions of the Stations of the Cross. Finally, the question raised by his *Light in August* (a question de Kooning himself seems to have asked and answered in a later painting) is not whether he accomplished his narrative goal but whether de Kooning can be forgiven for what he himself did to Faulkner's Nancy in his own blatant act of representation.

Black Friday

> I love my man like a schoolboy loves his pie,
> Like a Kentucky Colonel loves his rocker and rye,
> I'll love my man until the day I die, Lord, Lord . . .
> I hate to see that evening sun go down.
> —W. C. Handy, "St. Louis Blues" (1914)

Nancy's distinctive head from de Kooning's *Light in August*—with its recognizable hair (in fashion-slang, dreds gone wrong)—is resituated in his *Black Friday*. Noting the visual power of the description of Joanna Burden's wild hair as she is in her fits of erotic mayhem, Stuckey (in his analysis of *Light in August*) joked about the temptation to overread, to see this white woman's tentacled hair in the drips that appear in de Kooning's painting. This image did speak to de Kooning, but it did not appear until he returned to Faulkner in a slightly later work. In *Black Friday* (see fig. 26, page 241), the white dots, markers of eyes, appear in roughly the position held by Nancy's abbreviated, albeit terrified, stare from the darkness under Joanna Burden's head in de Kooning's *Light in August*. But in this second painting of de Kooning's Faulkner series, the monstrous threat of gripping does more than drip from above: these eyes locate an octopus-like monster whose downward and snaky arms drape, with one culminating in the realized flesh of a penetrating human finger. In a positioning that repeats the narrative seen in de Kooning's *Light in August*, Nancy is once again placed under the ominous liquidity of Joanna Burden. Yet in *Black Friday*, this masculine white woman has been replaced by her sexualized animal totem. Faulkner's white woman in the woods is a dark monster with a taste for dark blood: "[s]he would be wild then, in the close, breathing halfdark without walls, with her wild hair, each strand of which would seem to come alive like octopus tentacles, and her wild hands and her breathing: 'Negro! Negro! Negro!'" (*LA* 260).

In *Black Friday*, the polite animality of Joanna Burden remains a pendant force of ominous ink. Coloring sex itself, this totem contaminates what might be, if not pure love between a black man and woman, then at least a connection less tainted than Joanna's racially charged paroxysms of pleasure as she chants the forbidden: "Negro! Negro! Negro!" The proximate and intimate placement of Nancy under the malignant and maligned Joanna Burden (head-severed or octopus-avatared) effects a cross-painting critique of the racializing of sexuality: the cultural blackening of sexual passion that associates bodily love with race and evil. Recalling the Mrs. Compson of "That Evening Sun" as well as her similarly narcissistic character in *The Sound and the Fury*, Joanna Burden, even as she arranges her Beardsleyesque trysts in the bushes, sees her own sexuality as a forbidden animal drive experienced in her ecstatic passions piqued by her racial classification of Joe Christmas. Black, Nancy is classed by her passion as well as by her public outing of the white man who has used her body three times without paying and has given her the glimmering of broken teeth that emerges from the shadows of de Kooning's *Light in August*. Nancy is only used by the Compsons (and her "Johns") when it suits them. In dramatic contrast, Dilsey runs the Compson household with authority in both "That Evening Sun" and *The Sound and the Fury* because she is desexualized.

The other threatening figure in de Kooning's *Black Friday*, aside from the black-fingered "wild hands" of a white woman's animalized and tentacled lust, is literally a hatchet-faced man. This hatchet head, with his blade facing inward from the middle of the right edge of the painting, is recognizable as a man or even as human because he, like the two other male figures in the painting, wears a distinctive black tie. Like the octopus, the hatchet man, with his evil shape and his threat of cutting (abetted by a threatening phallic and tentacle-like leg that arcs above him), portends over the joined figures of Nancy and her husband. Inhabiting the mental place above Nancy's head, he is, or rather represents, the most threatening male figure in "That Evening Sun." In de Kooning's *Black Friday*, neither Nancy nor her husband appears to anticipate the violence of this potentially murderous man (the razor-wielding husband who will lie in wait) or the tentacles of the maleficent octopus, as both forces are poised above them in the painting, waiting to destroy the dream of love. I say the dream of love because as Nancy and her husband's heads curve to touch, the painting depicts another version of this couple as faceless, black balloon heads nested and hidden in the space between them. This nested couple, a realized abstraction, comprises a simulacrum of the happy pair dressed for the evening. Ready for a night on the town, Nancy with her distinctive hair wears a dress with the suggestion of a collar punctu-

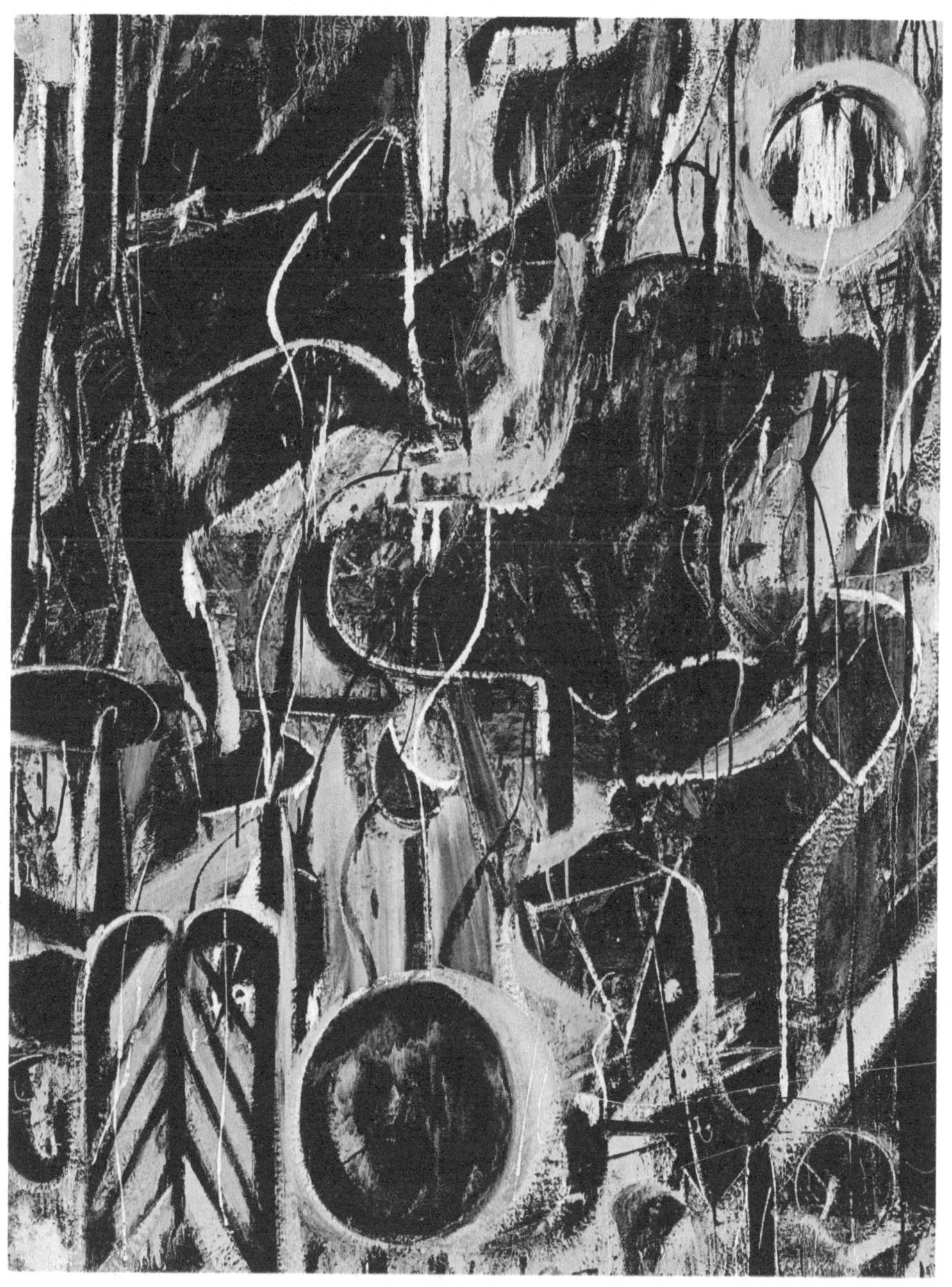

Plate 1. Willem de Kooning, *Light in August*, 1946. Oil and enamel on canvas, 55 1/8 in. × 41 9/16 in. (140 × 105.5 cm). The only high-resolution image of *Light in August* available for reproduction, this photograph does not include the entire painting, notably omitting de Kooning's signature. For a smaller—but more complete—photograph of the painting, see appendix 2 (page 293). Tehran Museum of Contemporary Art. © 2013 The Willem de Kooning Foundation / Artists Rights Society (ARS), New York.

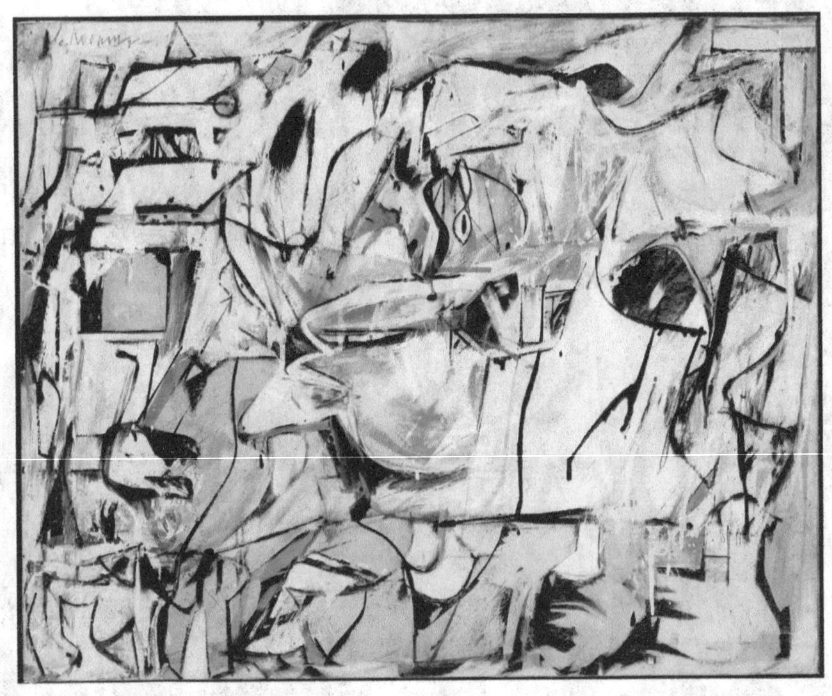

Plate 2. Willem de Kooning, *Asheville*, 1948. Oil and enamel on cardboard, $25\frac{9}{16} \times 31\frac{7}{8}$ in. (64.9×81 cm). Courtesy of the Phillips Collection, Washington, D.C. © 2013 The Willem de Kooning Foundation / Artists Rights Society (ARS), New York.

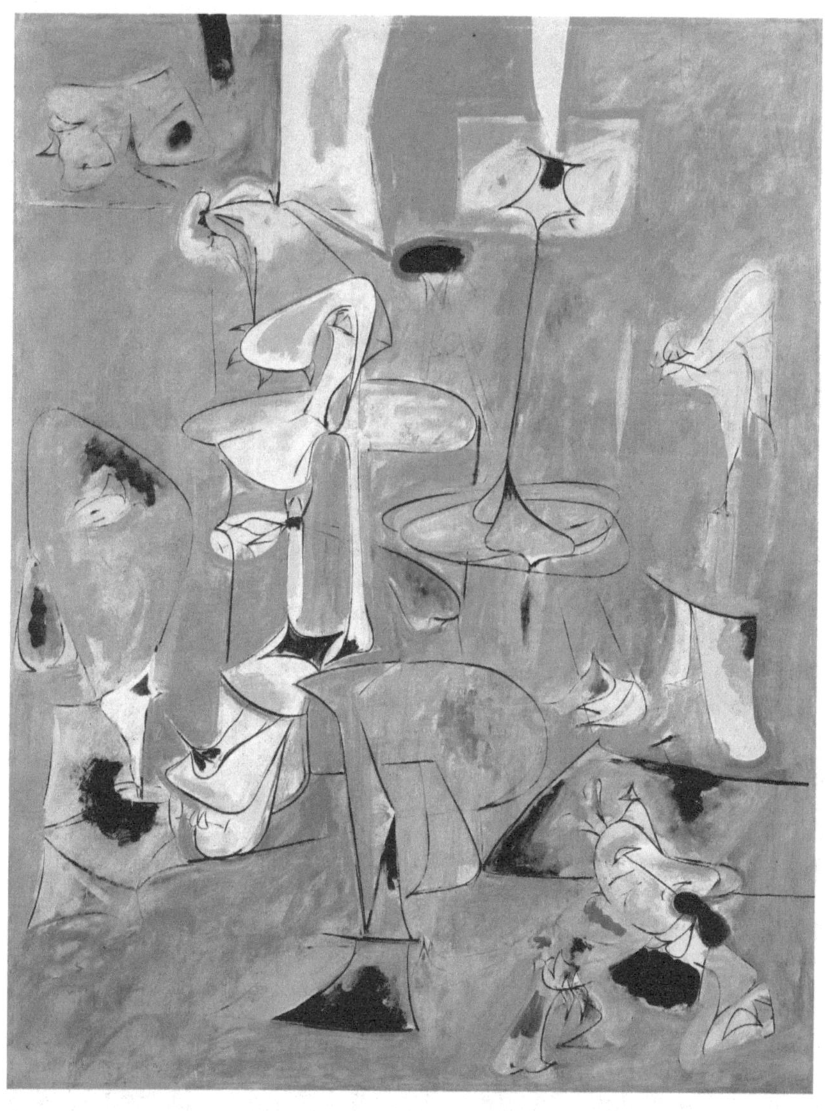

Plate 3. Arshile Gorky, *Betrothal I*, 1947. Oil on paper, 51 × 40 in. (129.5 × 101.6 cm). The Museum of Contemporary Art, Los Angeles, the Rita and Taft Schreiber Collection, Given in loving memory of her husband Taft Schreiber by Rita Schreiber.

Plate 4. James Abbott McNeill Whistler (1834–1903), *Nocturne in Black and Gold, The Falling Rocket*, 1875 (oil on panel). Courtesy of Detroit Institute of the Arts, Gift of Dexter M. Ferry, Jr.

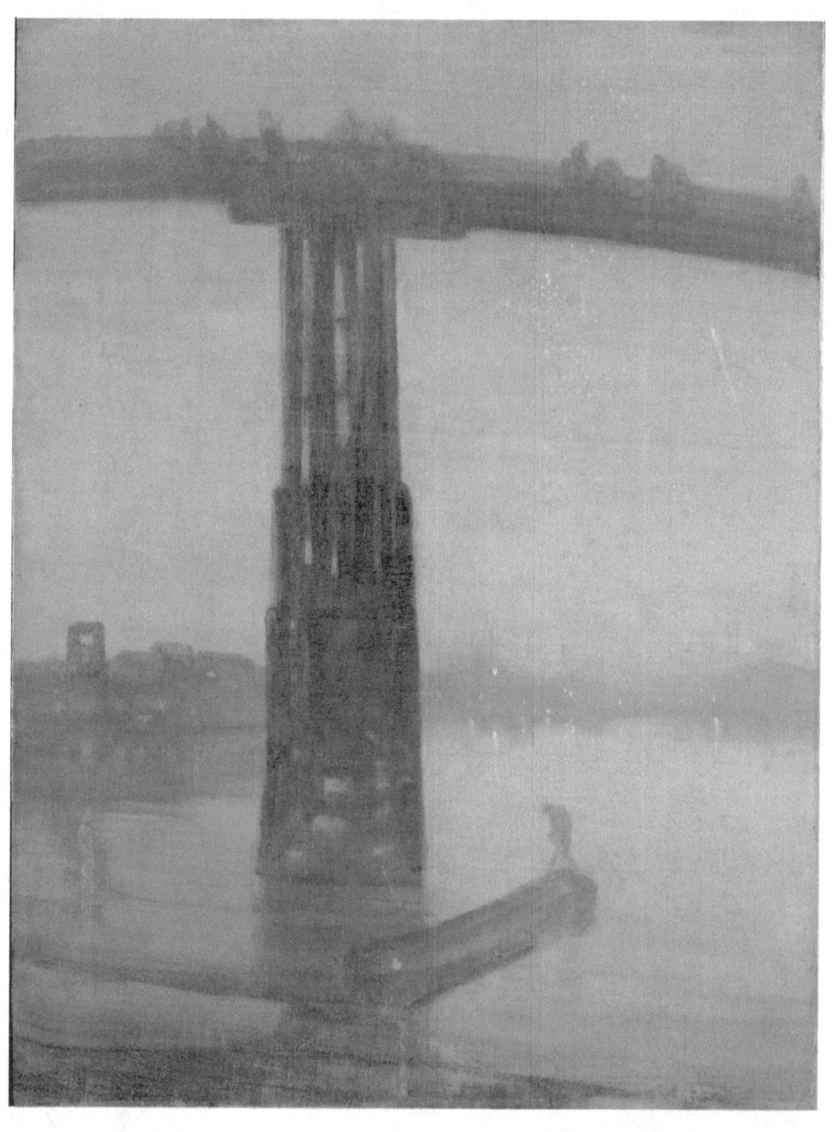

Plate 5. James Abbott McNeill Whistler, *Nocturne in Blue and Gold—Old Battersea Bridge*, 1872–75. Oil on panel. Courtesy of the Tate Gallery, London.

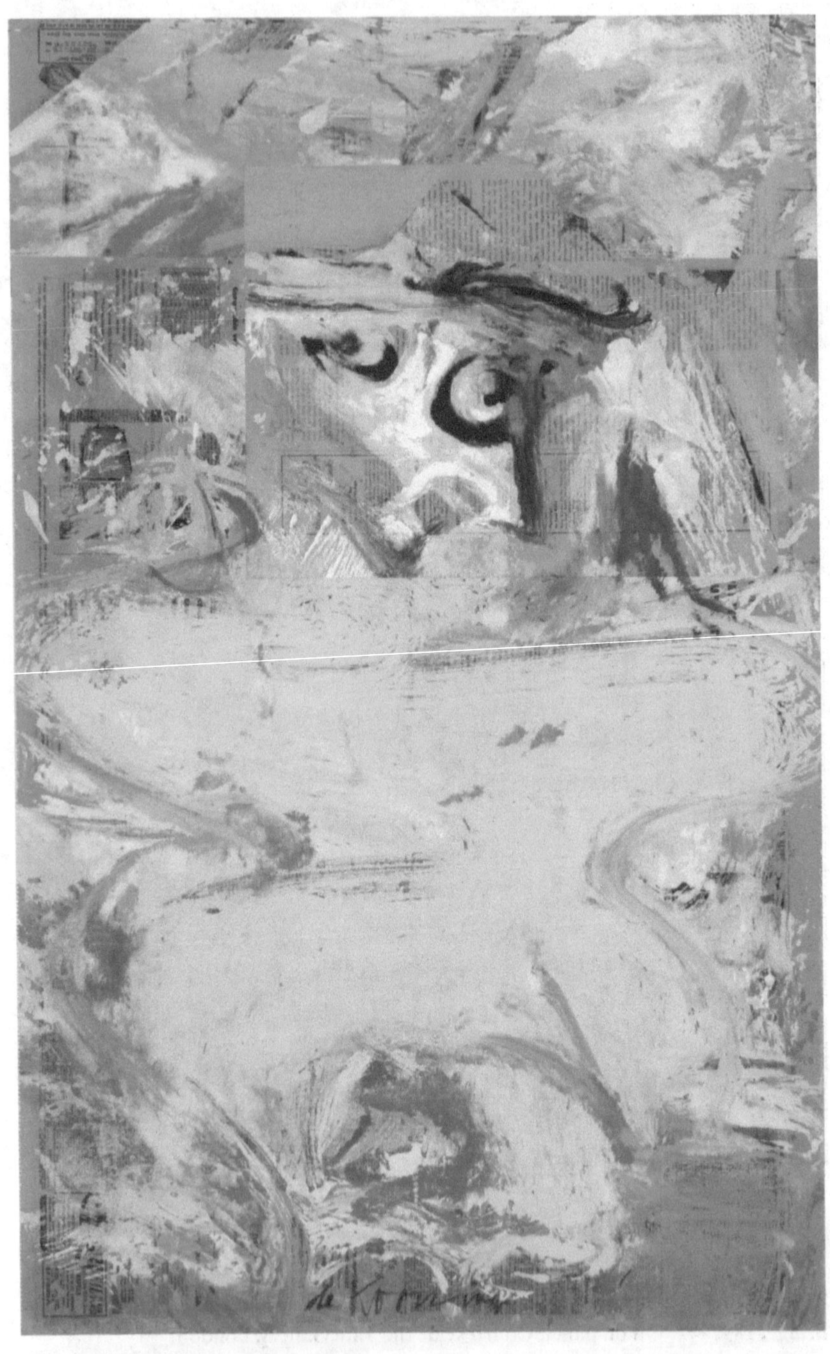

Plate 6. Willem de Kooning, *Weil Plaza*, 1964. Oil and newspaper on Masonite panel, 23⅜ × 36⅞ in. Courtesy of the Syracuse University Art Collection. © 2013 The Willem de Kooning Foundation / Artists Rights Society (ARS), New York.

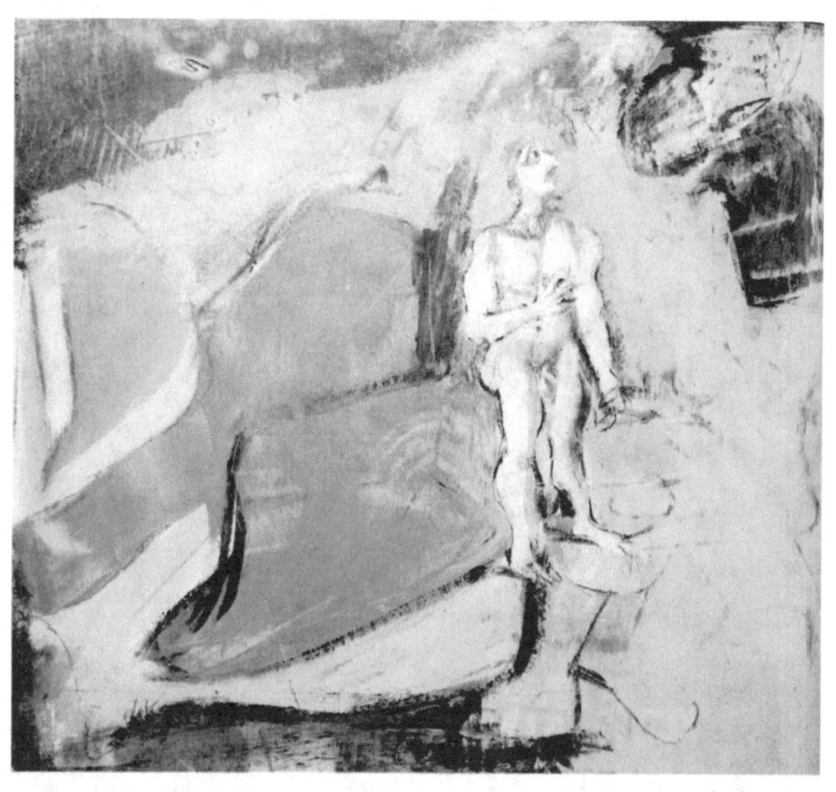

Plate 7. Willem de Kooning, *Untitled* ("Man"), 1949, 26 × 29 in.

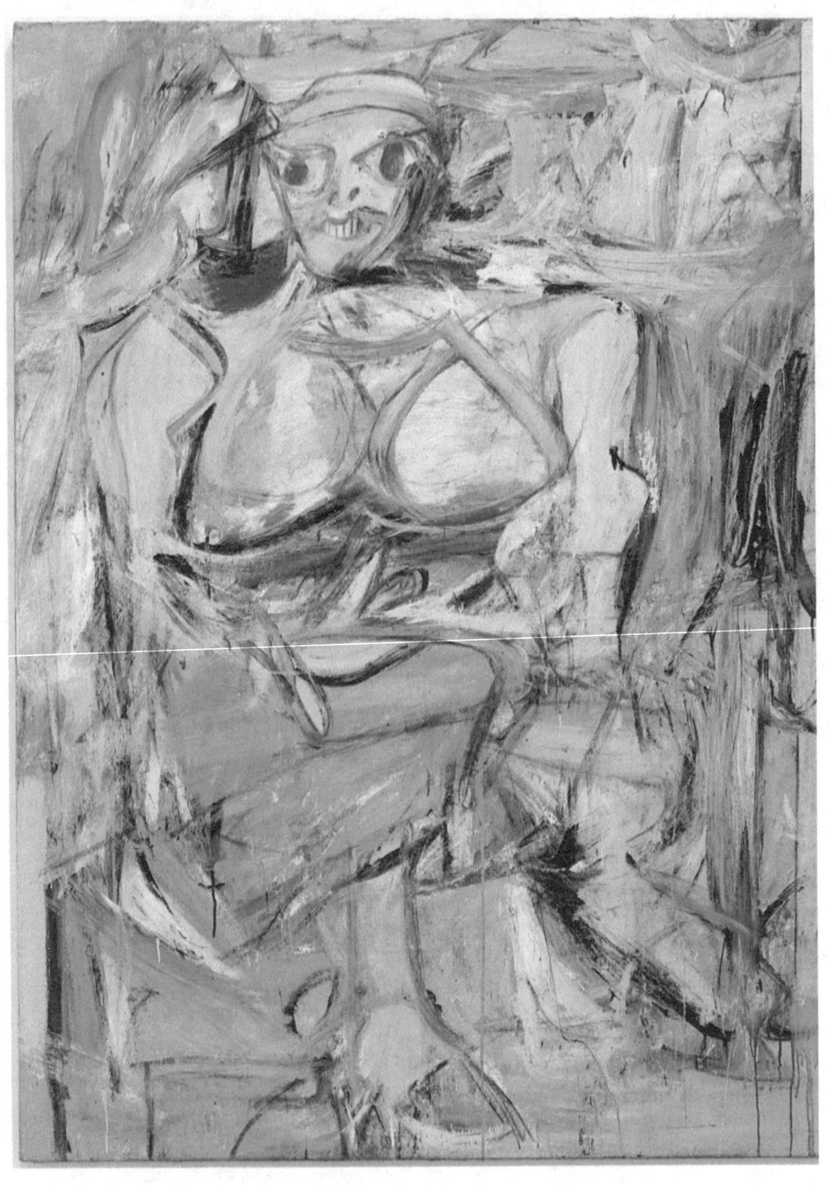

Plate 8. Willem de Kooning, *Woman I*, 1950–52. Oil, enamel, and charcoal on canvas, 6 ft. 3 ⅞ in. × 58 in. (192.7 × 147.3 cm). Courtesy of the Museum of Modern Art. © 2013 The Willem de Kooning Foundation / Artists Rights Society (ARS), New York.

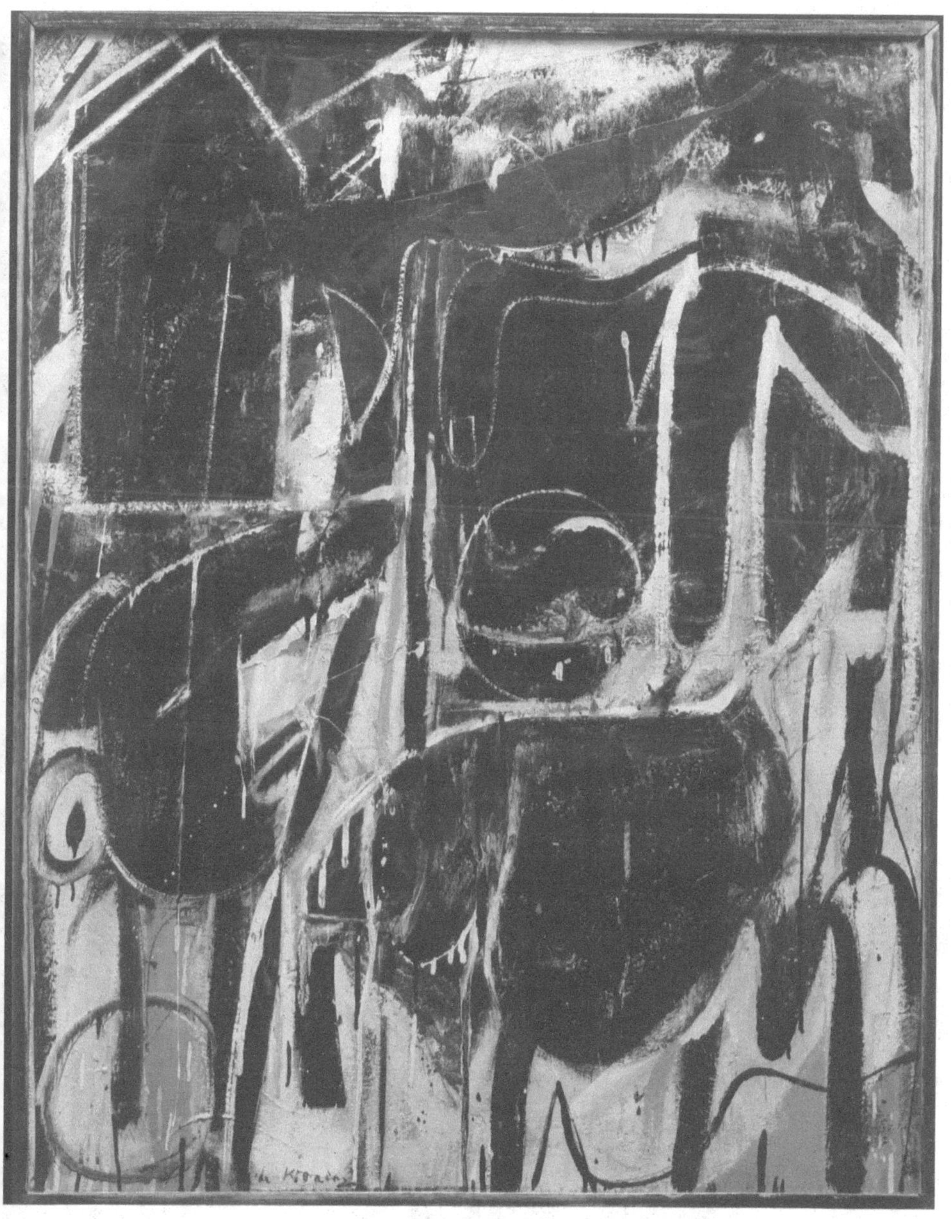

Figure 26. Willem de Kooning, *Black Friday*, 1948. Oil and enamel on pressed wood panel, $49\frac{3}{16} \times 39$ in. (125.0×99.0 cm). Largely black with strongly painted whites and few fully gray areas, this painting has a small green vertical near the center and pops of color, green as well as a brick-red located in the lower-right corner. Princeton University Art Museum. Gift of H. Gates Lloyd, Class of 1923, and Mrs. Lloyd in honor of the Class of 1923, 1976-44. Photo: Bruce M. White. © 2013 The Willem de Kooning Foundation / Artists Rights Society (ARS), New York.

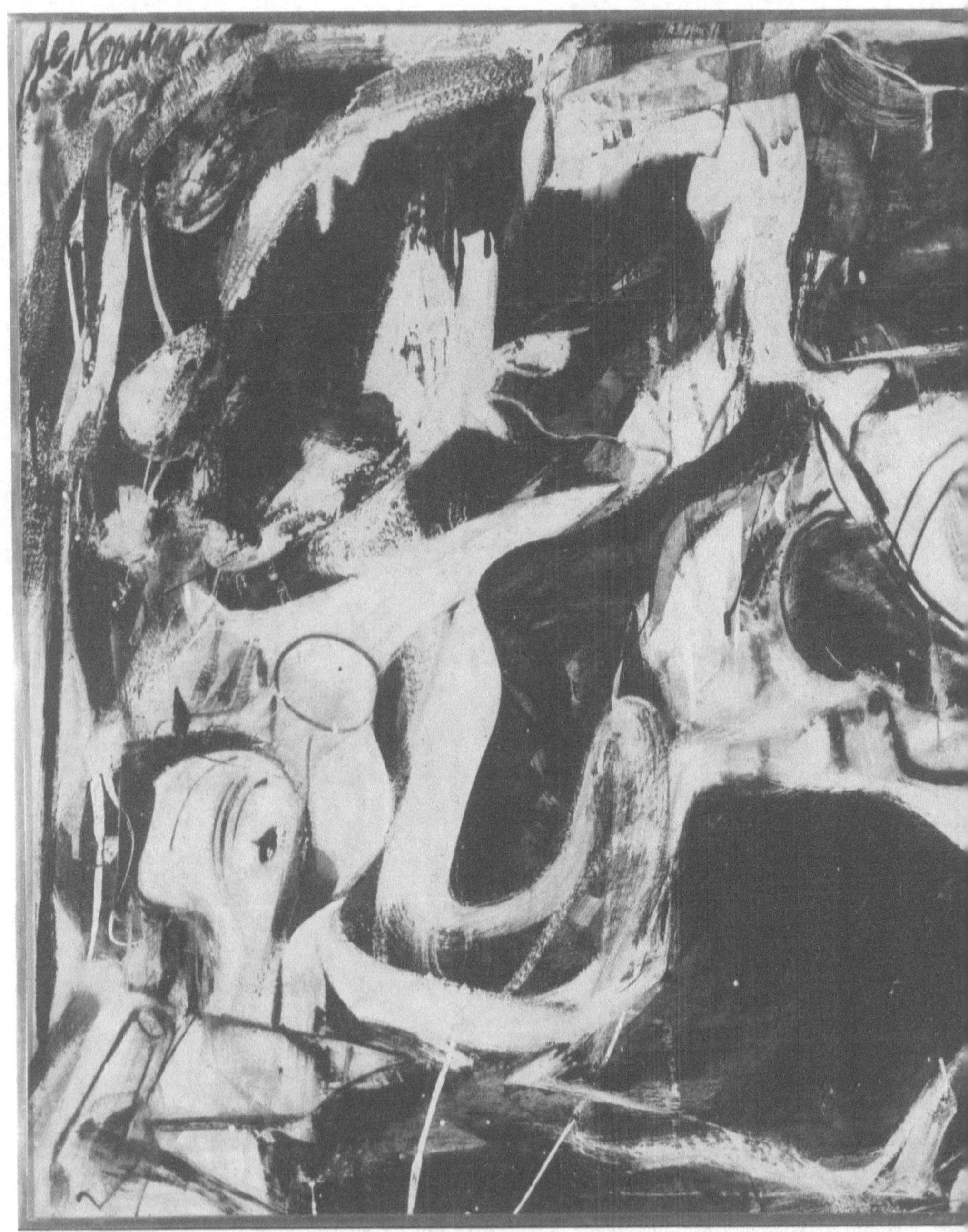

Figure 27. Willem de Kooning, *Black Untitled*, 1948. Oil and enamel on paper, mounted on wood, 29⅞ × 40¼ in. (75.9 × 102.2 cm). In addition to the shades of blacks, whites, and textured grays, there are several subtle gestures of an orange, dusty pink that are present in this painting. For the image complete on a single page, see fig. 34, page 295. Courtesy of the Metropolitan Museum, New York. From the Collection of Thomas B. Hess. Gift of the heirs of Thomas B. Hess. © 2013 The Willem de Kooning Foundation / Artists Rights Society (ARS), New York.

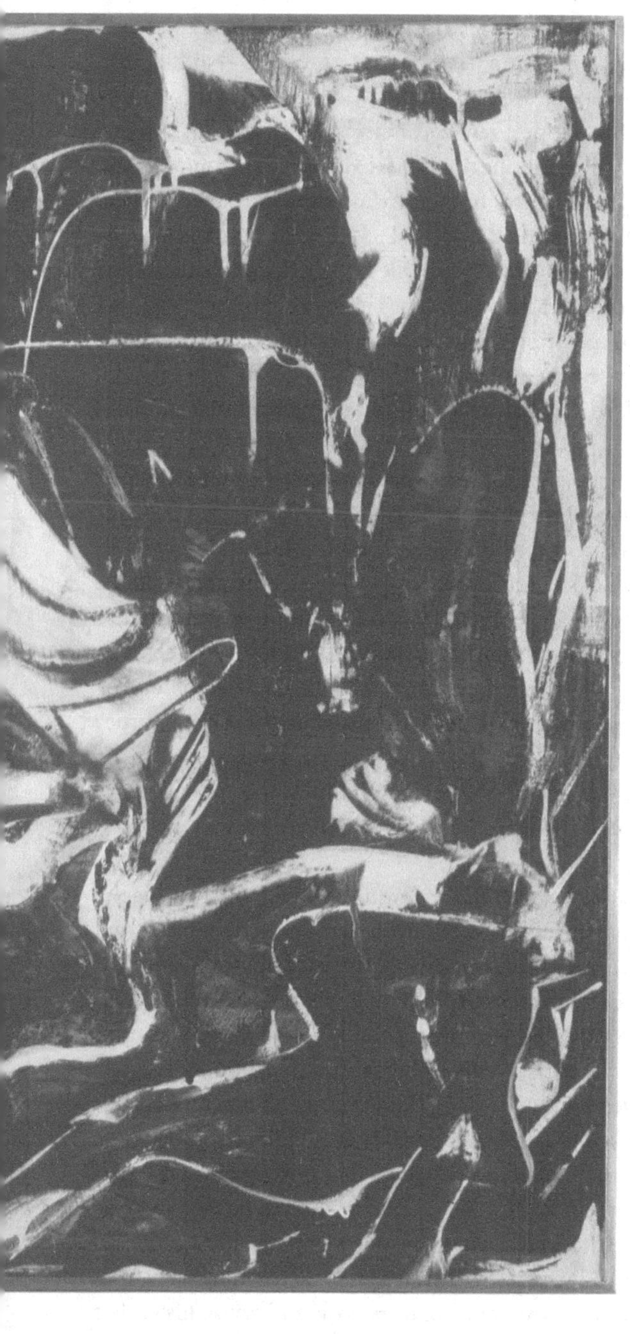

ated from beneath by two vertically placed dots, buttons. And here, Nancy's husband (to the left) with his coffee-cup head and his peach ear—split across the very pit (a fruit that doubles as the cup's handle)—completes this banjo-bodied torso of a man. This dapper, stylized man and his woman protect and frame the balloon-headed, symbolically rendered couple that models the idea of a deeper intimacy. These figures in their loving simulacrum echo their referents with the male balloon marked by the black tie that signifies masculinity and the female figure that is distinguishable by her balloon's definitive point, which repeats that found above in Nancy's chin. Locating the tie and the pointed chin is essential to seeing this idealized coupling of abstract, but clearly reflective, forms. These tiny ovoid and blank faces are made visible by looking for the lines that bleed drips of white liquidity—paint—that threaten to obscure both figures.

Along with biomorphic shapes of hips and breasts vaguely acknowledged and located in its lower half and the distinctive and large human finger piercing the canvas from the right side, the elements most commonly noted in *Black Friday* are the houselike structures that appear in the distance outside the window that forms the upper-left quadrant. A diminutive white figure sits on the sill: this woman in the moon that is fuller than a crescent seems to pose no danger as she dangles a single foot down into the coffee-cup head of Nancy's man. Whether these buildings suggest the possibility for urban order or not, de Kooning may be picturing and hearing the "St. Louis Blues" as he (who knew his W. C. Handy, "hat[ing] to see that evenin' sun go down") gave Nancy *Black Friday*, painting her into a last night on the town with her husband, Jesus.

Like de Kooning's *Light in August*, *Black Friday* was one of the "black" paintings comprising his transformative exhibition that focused on black and white. And, like *Light in August*, *Black Friday* is about race or, more precisely, about race and violence through the lens of William Faulkner's fiction. As Willem and Elaine de Kooning gathered with Egan, the gallery owner, to choose titles for the paintings for the artist's impending show, de Kooning himself named *Light in August*. Despite the hearsay claim advanced much later that Elaine de Kooning had chosen the title *Black Friday* as a high-sounding name that evoked the gravitas of the Crucifixion, Willem de Kooning himself either named *Black Friday* or put the name on the table. This had to be true since de Kooning was the only one who knew what this painting was about, or even that *Black Friday* was inspired by Faulkner's Jesus. Only de Kooning knew that he had created yet another narrative painting to rework and revise his earlier translation of the image of Nancy that he had hidden and incorporated in his *Light in August*. De Kooning used his painter's prerogative to paint the past, to imagine the fierce love that precedes and precipitates the violent passion which drives Faulkner's "That Evening Sun" and hangs pendant in the simulacrum nested, between Jesus and Nancy, in de Kooning's own *Black Friday*.[46]

Black Untitled

> *Black Untitled* of 1948 is a prime example of the allover compositions he produced that cohesively integrate positive and negative spaces, without representational allusions. Like his friend Franz Kline, de Kooning used both black and white paint, rather than letting the white of the paper show through. Sweeping white rivers of paint rush across the dark black ground, creating writhing intertwining shapes that suggest figures in a landscape setting, but without any specificity whatsoever.
> —Heilbrunn Timeline of Art History, Metropolitan Museum of Art

> A picture to me is not geometric—it has a face.
> —Willem de Kooning

As she was being interviewed about Rothko in 1981, Elaine de Kooning recalled her husband's "Faulkner connection," locating its beginning in the fall of 1948. After the summer spent at Black Mountain College, the "black and white" "huge canvas" that Elaine de Kooning recalls as having been painted in the fall of 1948 may have grown larger in memory. (Relatively speaking, this work was large when juxtaposed to de Kooning's previous painting, the considerably smaller *Asheville.*) Although Willem de Kooning was famous for destroying more paintings than he kept (destruction was one of the ways he worked on a canvas as he removed the "rottenness" of drying paint), the painting Elaine de Kooning describes in 1981 is too close to the culminating work in de Kooning's Faulkner series to doubt that she is speaking of *Black Untitled:*

> But the Faulkner connection occurred the following year [the fall following the summer of 1948], when Bill was working on a huge canvas. It was black and white. And I said to him, "It's very curious." You know, I came into the studio. I had my separate studio and I walked in and I said, "It's very curious. There are no treelike shapes in that painting. The forms are all like animals more or less and organic shapes that don't resemble the forest at all, but I get the feeling of a Faulkner forest from that painting." Bill said, "That's extraordinary." And he went over and lifted up a pile of papers and underneath was a book by Faulkner.[47]

Elaine de Kooning's recollection proves her husband's textual intimacy with William Faulkner as well as her own understanding of the sources of her husband's art. While she went on to misspeak about the timing of de Kooning's signature Faulkner painting, *Light in August*, placing this work's creation after the painting she described as a "Faulkner forest" (after *Light in August* had already made a sensation at the Egan Gallery in the spring of 1948), Elaine de Kooning makes clear that there was more than one Faulkner painting conceived in the late 1940s. The fact of this slippage has heretofore helped to conceal the identity of the third Faulkner painting, which was indeed a work completed in the fall of 1948: *Black Untitled* (see fig. 27, p. 242–43, and fig. 34, p. 295).

Through "specificity" of figures and "representational allusions,"[48] *Black Untitled*, the final painting of de Kooning's Faulkner trilogy, returns to the scene not just of his painting inspired by Faulkner's *Light in August* and other Faulkner works but to the elements of his own painting, *Light in August*, which refers with particularity to Faulkner's novel of the same name. *Black Untitled* belongs with *Light in August* and *Black Friday* as a major work that comments directly on de Kooning's understanding of the significance of race to the history of art, an understanding that he conceptualized and realized in response to Faulkner's fiction. As de Kooning read his own *Light in August*, using that painting to return once again to Faulkner's *Light in August*, he found himself moved to narrate in black and white his racially routed, ink-based and Picasso-instructed story of the history of art.[49]

Black Untitled is a painting that directs the eye to a point of entry. Signed in the upper left-hand corner, the lower corner on the left side speaks to the painting's origins. This corner is furnished with tools of the draftsman's, woodsman's, or murderer's art: the compass, pickax, and hatchet. In addition to these tools of production, this assemblage alludes to the underlying sound-based as well as material foundation of the work. De Kooning's practical inclusion of the coffee cup with a feminine handle (of practical use in mixing paint) offers a partial catalog of this lesser-known painting's collation of tools. As the compass for drawing circles initiates the sense of cartographic flow, this tool is shown to have a more practical function as it draws the line of a gigantic (outsized) bird talon that is demarcated through a downward arc. This fierce talon points toward its human cognate, the only piece of realistically rendered flesh in the whole painting, a finger that pushing upward is cut by a white slicing shape which is itself limned by the neck of a swan. This direct line, an arc that extends from the humanoid arm of the compass, is echoed in the form of another ovoid shape tied to a stringlike line that reaches upward to articulate the head of a pudgy white penis. This bad pun—a manifestation of de Kooning's pleasures in painting language—uses the rounded tip of this organ (dotted near the center for practical purposes) to double as a monocle-like eyepiece forming the round eye of yet another bird in this avian-obsessed, bird-beset painting. More lingual than ornithological, these details depict an owl whose identity is announced by the exaggeration of his distinguishing feature. As de Kooning insists on the erectile potential in names, he pictures this horned bird (with an exaggerated right peak) as a "horny" owl. The fact that this is a conscious joke that the viewer is meant to get is confirmed by the presence of the line that connects this bawdy witticism to the compass below, the painting's most explicit picturing of a tool for drawing. *Black Untitled* is a painting that uses pointers in the form of direct lines or even the inclusion of a tiny caret to direct the eye to set pieces that speak within its frame.

The sweep of *Black Untitled* follows the direction of the pointing talon from left to right across the lower third of the painting through a series of reversible animal and humanoid bodies. Dotted with signifying eyes, these spots indicate points of view or, more precisely, points for viewing. The most fertile (progenitive) area of metamorphoses is located in the large dark area near the center, close to the bottom of the painting. This substantial dark space plays on one of the most famous reversible images in the history of visual ambiguity. Second in prominence only to the Rorschachian staple of the field/space drawing, in which the vase in the foreground shifts to reveal that this vessel has been formed by two faces addressing each other in profile, is Wittgenstein's favorite: the animal silhouette that superimposes rabbit and duck. Here, the rabbit/duck incorporates dynamically shifting points of view to reveal this shape as one shared by different animals. De Kooning's version of this well-known image modifies the classic heads to offer a shape-shifting black blot that is a veritable bestiary of metamorphoses. This dark shape shifts into full bodies as well as heads of creatures that include a rabbit, more than one duck, and the flat head of a chicken or an enormous cardinal with a large beak. Visually flexible, rotating this same dark shape will reveal the silhouette of a cow's head with its tongue extended. In the interest of brevity, I will cut to the whale. The whale in this dark shape is particularly discernible because of the cuttings: seams made visible through an underlying structure, three connected lines, one of which seems to function as a reverse suture that blunts the face of the leftward-swimming mammal. Visually, this cutting off of the beak or tail to reveal the whale underlines the visual motion that commands the eye to follow the multiplicity of meanings, to add or delete distinguishing features such as tongues, tails, and bills that mediate and determine this remarkable sequence of animals. These pictured animals emerge through rotating the canvas or rotating the imagination of the eye of the beholder.

De Kooning's interest in metamorphoses in which whole bodies reconfigure from their latency to form canvas-filling faces, reveals the painter's fascination with shape-shifting parables of art as intrinsically generative. These gaming paintings can be found both prior to and after de Kooning's intense midcentury period, comprised of his signature black-and-white show of 1948 followed by his signifying *Woman* series shown in 1953. In his 1942–45 painting *Untitled* ("Still Life with Matches"), copulating bodies with disarranged parts produce a canvas from between a woman's legs in a work that morphs to reveal the leering face of a piratelike clown with a round nose and a sutured eye that opens into emptiness (see fig. 28). His later painting *Weil Plaza* (1964; see plate 6) attests to his continued commitment to metamorphic play, presenting the smooth swipes in soft pink that add hourglass curves to a Venus of Willendorf topped by a floating and diminutive African mask that stands for her head. As this body (the commonly seen figure in this painting) becomes a face, this mask is incorporated into a patterned turban of Africanist cloth and her mouth (the sex in the full-bodied painting) mirrors the sensual lips of de Kooning's famous portrait of Mae West.[50]

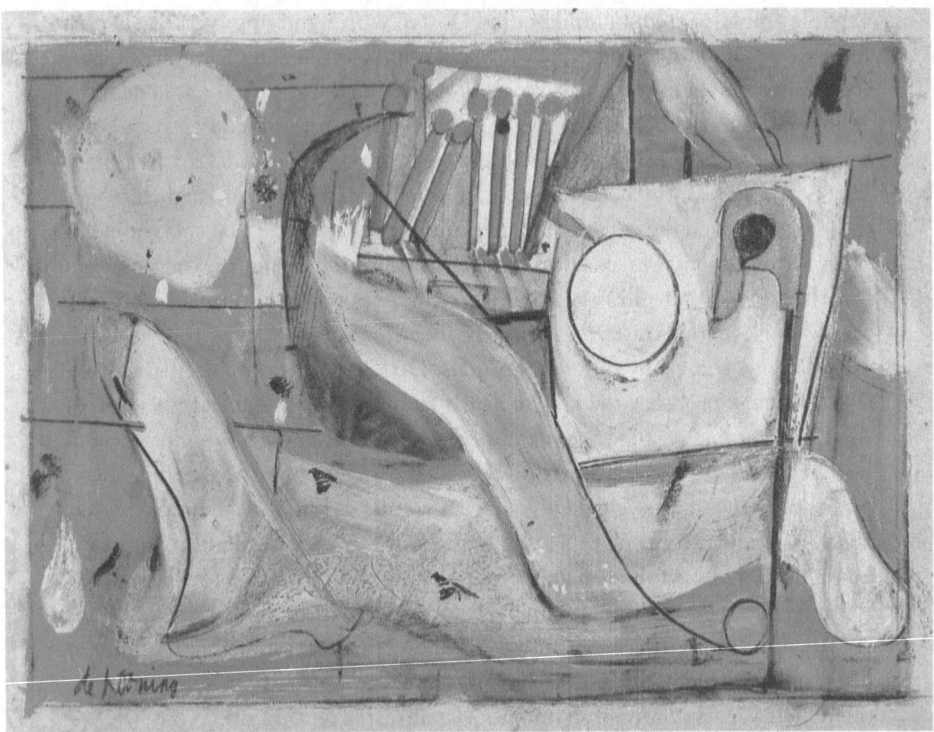

Figure 28. Willem de Kooning, *Untitled* ("Still Life with Matches"), ca. 1942–45. Oil and pencil on paper laid down on cardboard 5¾ × 7¾ in. (14.6 × 19.7 cm). (This is a vibrant work with the sense of a line drawing under and on top of bright colors: reddish-oranges, yellows, grays, pinks, blacks, and whites.)

Black Untitled is intensively concerned with metamorphoses: animals become other animals. Most intently, birds become other birds or even morph into parts of other birds. Along the bottom edge of the painting, moving laterally toward the right corner, *Black Untitled* seems particularly liquid as reversible humanoid bodies, from head to foot and from male to female, are either diving into or up from the inky pool. Just above, this painting's dedication to the grotesque is confirmed by the shapes, interleaving dark and light in narratives of field/space exchange that both join and superimpose animal heads on female bodies. I say female because in silhouette the sense of a fulsome breast predominates, but this favored feature in de Kooning's work remains ambiguous here because the upthrust shape is also potentially formed by a propped elbow.

From the tools of production found in the left-hand corner, to the larger blot that accomplishes the animal metamorphoses in the mid- and lower portion of the work, to the interplay of animal and human bodies that preoccupy the lower-right quadrant, *Black Untitled*—through the intersections of species as well as multiple media—initiates a narrative that links reproduction to the creative potential of art. The intimation that this is indeed a story of art is underlined by the formal statement made by an elegant and sculpturally stylized Africanist head. This head—prominently cornered in the painting's lower-right sector—is demarcated through an unsourced light illuminating the striking left side.[51] Positioned as the possible progeny of the reversible body below, this head insists on its separation as the painting's most compellingly formed work of art; its clean lines and rectitude separate it from the ornamented neckline of the black and comely—shapely and headless—female torso that rises vertically into the columnar blackness above. The horizontal torso (near the bottom of the painting) whether with her extravagant breast or propped elbow is contiguous to the large dark shape, extending from the nose of the rabbit or (as you might have it) the head of the duck. Here, this evocation of a supine human body shadows forth the bust of a lioness that itself doubles as a small-headed, extravagantly tailed, and fully profiled house cat; this shared feline silhouette in its lower curve in turn articulates the distinctive head of a lamb—as lion and lamb lie down together.

In a more dynamic reading of the painting, this horizontal torso may be using its elbowed arm to pull the African head from between the legs of the reversible body below. There are strong white lines that function as a loincloth concealing the organs that would be the orienting markers toward a human head (heads or tails is the joke). These lines are too firmly inscribed not to have meaning.[52] Turning his painting upside-down, de Kooning (who rotated his paintings in every way to see what was going on in the space of the canvas) insists on the emergence of a surprising sartorial pattern. This fleeting image, a realization of the potency of the visual flash that de Kooning (a player in language) celebrated as a "slipping glimpse," reveals costumes for a dancing scene reminiscent of the gravity-defying exuberance of characters in paintings by Jackson Pollock's teacher, the visual mythographer and noted muralist Thomas Hart Benton. This loincloth, seen from the perspective of the upended painting, reveals that these strong lines have become a human neck attached to the body of a calypso dancer whose putative head lies beyond the edge of the canvas.[53] This island sailor with his well-defined shirt and what are technically referred to as "calypso pants" is positioned in relation to a large-breasted (seemingly unoccupied) dress with defined hips that square off into the active knees of a dancing garment. There is an actual caret here that serves a dual purpose, providing the vaginal "vee" for this female figure even as this tiny pointer directs the gaze of the viewer upward to another site. Right-side up again, shades of de Kooning's own *Light in August*, this upper-right quadrant contains the shapely black torso of a woman with an out-of-drawing, seemingly unrelated dress above a dramatically rounded sleeve or breast.

De Kooning, who (in a meteorological mood) described his ideal painting to the poet Edwin Denby as the creation of "one wind blowing through the entire picture," achieved this wind with greatest clarity in *Black Untitled*.[54] This movement is personified in the upper reaches of the painting, creating a sense of direction through more than an intuited wind. Within the rectangular frame of *Black Untitled*, the circular sweep counters the clock in a motion that is at once cartographic and visible: the personified wind near the center of the top of the painting is a black, snaggletoothed deity embodying the unpredictable fury of winds that prevail in a physical form reminiscent of the impish puffed-cheek demons depicted on ancient maps.[55] The wind continues the counterclockwise circuit of this painting (which at the top is from right to left) as figures are blown from their moorings across the upper reaches of this painting. In *Black Untitled*, de Kooning succeeded in painting the wind as well as what might be called the winds of art. This circuit of unity ("one wind") is pictured through the telling fragments that bear the story—a Picasso-troubled Keatsian narrative of aesthetics—as iconic elements of the past have miscegenated the new art, growing strong through aesthetic contact with West African and Mississippi art. The lower-right and the upper-left corners are dominated by African imagery, sculptural and animal, while the upper-right corner and lower-left corner contain specific references to white characters from Faulkner's *Light in August* that echo portraits of these white figures found in de Kooning's *Light in August*.

De Kooning's sense of wind becomes highly visible as this world's breath creates the most islanded shape in his painting as a whole: the head of a Grecian woman. Located in the upper-left quadrant, this classical head (surrounded by a sea of black) is being blown across this dark shape—more precisely, the "dark continent." In this painting of richly layered animals depicted in the process of metamorphoses, this head's classically classical Greek profile has been de-vased and debased, marred by the cigarette that hangs from her mouth. In de Kooning's work the specificity of the marring, the necessity of the mark, signals this Grecian head's metamorphic content. Greek and female, her head is literally grotesque, masking and unmasking her animal potential. Rotated and reversed, this distinctive fragment of classical statuary, potentially a shard of a painting blown off an Attic vase, becomes the wrong end of a satyr, the head of a bearded goat, the animal totem for the indiscriminate appetites of randy sexuality. This classical head, blown from her vase, set loose from her body or her other moorings, is chased across the canvas by a comically rendered, large-nosed knight holding a shield. Together, blown by time, prevailing winds, or an art market, these figures both allude to and counter Keats's evocation of stillness in his "Ode on a Grecian Urn."

Keats (in particular the Keats who wrote this ode) was the patron poet for both Faulkner and de Kooning. Faulkner's attraction to Keats and to this very ode is well known, as he quotes from and alludes to "Ode on a Grecian Urn" prominently in his fiction and in his personal musings. De Kooning also left a specific record of his interest in the poet. After visiting Keats's grave in Rome during the early 1960s, de Kooning made a painting memorializing Keats, using Keats's epitaph as the title that speaks to a dead artist's wavering chance of immortality through the word. Keats had himself buried under the epithet, declaring that he was "he whose name was writ on water." While letters of Keats's name swim in never fully materialized possibility in the painting, the narratively driven de Kooning chose not to sign this work in any traditional way on the front of the canvas.[56] Rather, in his rendering of an artist's epitaph, there is only one clearly defined object in this painting: a portly bluish-gray arrow in the upper-left quadrant containing a scalpel-like scrawl—a small letter "d" along with a capital "K" and a plausible "o"—"writ" as if "on [or washed away by] water." Likely signed on the back, de Kooning with narrative intent washed away the beginnings of his own name in this painting that eulogized the fate of the artist, painter or poet.[57]

Certainly, Faulkner, who had already acknowledged Keats by alluding to the "unravished bride of quietness" in his third novel, *Sartoris* (1929), continued to return to Keats. Most pointedly, Faulkner's *Light in August* revisits lines and themes drawn from Keats's "Ode on a Grecian Urn" to picture characters driven in circles or doomed to fates of perpetual longing. Seemingly unmoving, *Light in August*'s Lena Grove embodies the narrative of Keats's poem: "she advanced in identical and anonymous and deliberate wagons as though through a succession of creakwheeled and limpeared avatars, like something moving forever and without progress across an urn" (7). This desire that lies in the perpetual absence of consummation, the stillness that depicts motion caught forever in the circuit of pursuit (seemingly a fact of drying paint, printed ink, and everyday life), was important to Faulkner and de Kooning. This woman on "an urn," Lena Grove, with her dryadic name, is herself the seeker and the sought; she is the female vase, whose flesh, initially pregnant and at last newly maternal (enclosing the novel in its opening and concluding chapters) provides the container for the violence that resides within *Light in August*.[58] This pregnant woman, reproducer of life, frames the sculpted bodies of Joanna Burden and Joe Christmas that, taken together in their cut flesh, both haunt and define the novel's interior narrative, making it one that joins race and art.

With more immediacy than that afforded by a novel, a story, or even a paragraph, it is possible to see a painting as a gestalt, a composition of "form solidity color" (*M* 340) in which the immediate and fragmented vision can be willed away, allowing another picture to appear as a discernible visual subject that has the capacity to dominate the confines of the canvas. This narrative of field/space images depends on the parataxical vision that gives way to alternate hierarchies—the moving and motive process of metamorphoses. The process of metamorphosis depends on the active eye of the spectator to reveal varieties of order between and among pieces and parts that allow multiple versions of a single painting to fall into place, to be read as a meaningful collage or collation. Just as Faulkner wrote neatly in blue ink on the back of a typescript page of *As I Lay Dying*, "This is really important" (striking out this sharply readable sentence with three crisp lines), de Kooning pointed to what was important through the repetition of forms.

De Kooning's *Black Untitled* is clearly marked by the "pictorial idioms" developed in his first solo exhibition that opened in 1948. The signature of this continuity is found in the explicit references to his *Light in August* as well as to Faulkner's *Light in August* through the stumplike neck and the blood-dripping mouth of Joanna Burden. Contorted in the violence of her death, de Kooning's version of Joanna Burden's violated face is recognizable as it reappears in *Black Untitled*. This pained visage is knowable because of its specific features as well as its echoing placement near the top right corner of the painting. She does not precisely bleed off the edge of the canvas, but again the top of her head in this more wavering form is severed just above the mouth by the frame of art. While Joanna Burden's head still has the "vee-necked" bodice of de Kooning's *Light in August*, here the sartorial torso is merely the top of a dress with a plunging décolletage—the campy bust-line of the earlier figure is missing.[59] But, as in his *Light in August*, de Kooning's depiction of a seemingly orphaned or bodiless dress (discernible in *Black Untitled*'s upper-right corner) does indeed have a head.

De Kooning's *Light in August* draws from Faulkner's fiction to configure, to plumb the narrative of race in black and white. De Kooning's painting portrays wombs of unconscious thought pictured through circles and cycles that advance a narrative of striking lushness, beauty, and literary, as well as social and political, exegesis. *Black Friday* fills in the picture by correcting de Kooning's own mocking of a black woman's fears, even as he mirrors this woman's terror exposed by Faulkner in "That Evening Sun." As he painted *Black Friday*, de Kooning revealed that he had an understanding of the meaning of the days of the week from the perspective of the poor, the exuberance of the "eagle flying" (Friday's money for the week's work). *Black Untitled* is a work of intellectual complexity insisting on the place of his own *Light in August* as a reading of Faulkner's *Light in August* while locating both works instructively, tellingly in a sequence of symbolic exchange that narrates an itinerary for the Picassoid—the Africanist-emanating—story of modern art in the twentieth century. Wavering off the upper edge of the canvas (near the right corner, quite close to where the image had been placed in his *Light in August*), the grimacing lower jaw of Joanna Burden threatens to disappear like smoke.[60] Here, the partial face of her identically severed head (whether "writ on water" or dissolving like smoke) features a mouth that bleeds white rather than the dripping black blood of de Kooning's original rendering. The other specific reference that *Black Untitled* makes to de Kooning's *Light in August* is a reprise and redefinition of Percy Grimm as the Grim Reaper who oversees the broken "8" at the center of de Kooning's *Light in August*. In *Black Untitled*, the bird talon in the lower-left corner that cuts toward the human finger insists on death as a consequence or destination of art. Here, the scythe-wielding hairdryer (the largest tool in the collation of instruments grouped in the left corner) is clearly a repeated (strangely comic) reference to the Grim Reaper. This hairdryer reaper, distinguished by his face with its single eye-shaped hole, signifies an artificial wind that can dry or kill art into a stillness that can only be broken, made motive by the metamorphoses set into motion by the viewer's catalytic eye.

De Kooning, demonstrating (to use Greenberg's phrase) his "Luciferian pride," set out in *Black Untitled* to narrate a particular history of twentieth-century art. Even as he was acknowledging the great fact of Picasso in this painting, de Kooning was also anticipating the poet Frank O'Hara's mid-century Manifesto: "Africa is on the way."[61] Indeed, for Faulkner's Mississippi, Africa had already come. *Black Untitled*, with its Africanist, sculptural presence and its emphasis on the birth of a stately African head, reasserts a point that is already stated in the shape of the signifying continent that dominates the upper-left quadrant of this painting. There is a wind blowing from Africa, but the lower wind from the cyborgean Reaper (albeit pointing downward to favor its humanoid shape) still contributes to the flow—counterclockwise, from left to right sweeping across and circling through African images and blowing back from right to left across the top of the painting through Africa itself in *Black Untitled*. This hairdryer embodies a cutting, withering, moisture-wicking, and sapping modernity that not only threatens human flesh (the realistic finger) but has the grim power to castrate art in this, de Kooning's most moving—literally set into visual motion—parable of art. This painting remains in motion through a nascent and eruptive quality, latent and resurgent in the viewer's capacity to experience this work's potential for metamorphoses. This, the big picture in *Black Untitled*, aspires to provide a reading of Faulkner's reading of the parable of art in his great novel *Light in August* that takes the indeterminacy of race as its catalytic subject.

Black Untitled, distinguished by its elegant acts of synthesis, continues to draw the eye into its shifting patterns of metamorphoses. In *Orestes*, a "white" painting from the original ten hung in Charles Egan's gallery in 1948, de Kooning included the suggestive black shape of a Scottie dog with a perspectival focus on its distinctive head. The biggest picture in *Black Untitled* is a collage formed by disparate components of the painting to picture the head of a Scottish terrier. With its pointed ears pricked up (see the upper-left side of the painting), this dog's squared jaw of its muzzle, tongue hanging out, occupies the full center of *Black Untitled*. De Kooning's surprising decision to create the portrait of the head of a dog is a testament to his *jouissance*, his pleasure in putting shapes in motion as abstract elements coalesce to become representational creatures before the viewer's willing eye. This dog is not easily seen, but once disclosed, this final animal portrait lays to rest any residual hopes for an absence of intentionality on de Kooning's part. Finally, motion is essential to the visual metamorphoses that continue to defy fixity in *Black Untitled*.

Certainly, de Kooning played with paint as he layed it, surprised at what his canvases were revealing to him: he of all painters was alive to possibility. It is a matter of more rather than less significance that few of his works resolve themselves into narrative portraits. This being acknowledged, there is also a big picture in de Kooning's *Light in August*. De Kooning's big picture, like Cowley's cutting from Faulkner, depicts a collaged portrait of a man who is not Joe Christmas. Less difficult to see than the Scottie dog, the dominant portrait in de Kooning's *Light in August* nevertheless requires a shift of vision. Arcing with clarity and sharing a boundary with the dismembered figure "8" is a white line that is finally too definitive not to contain meaning. This strongest white line in the painting articulates the head of a man in profile with his Aryan nose demarcated by the right top of the chair that continues leftward off the edge of the painting. (There is the leftward shadowing of a knight's mask and visor that imagistically echoes this profiled face, cantilevered and echoing the nose in the dark space that is cut off by the same chair as this object meets the edge of the canvas.) Grimm's backstory, as it were, is told by his symbol-filled cranium. This man with his notably squared shoulders repositions the largest and most mysterious symbol in the painting: the structure seen by Gaugh as a Mosaic tablet or a gate. This louvered object on the left side of the painting once it is recognized and positioned as the shoulder of a man indicates that these slats are a martial ornament, a descending epaulette of military stripes. Percy Grimm, the proto-Nazi of Faulkner's novel, wears a version of this conferred authority in his "insignatory brass"; "his bars" (pictured here as dramatic chevrons) denote his rank as a "captain in the State national guard" (*LA* 449–50). Percy Grimm, whom Faulkner (in a 1945 letter to Cowley) identified as "the Fascist galahad [*sic*] who saved the white race by murdering Christmas" (adding "I created a Nazi . . . before [Hitler] did"),[62] has a brain that is filled with the vaginal heart of a black woman, the Grim Reaper armed with the scythe of death, and the mathematical symbol "π." Grimm, recalling the portraits of Arshile Gorky's pensive man whose nose faces left in the lower-left quadrant of Gorky's *Betrothal* series (see plate 3), follows Gorky's lead into the articulation of this white man's burden, as this errant knight (shades of Gorky's pensive groom) is cut at the neck by the beheaded white woman's—Joanna Burden's—vaginal moon.[63] In this viewing of *Light in August*, the diminutive torso of the idealized white woman lounges naked just outside this castrating man's brain. De Kooning's portrait of Percy Grimm is formed by strong areas of black as well as white, and there is a disturbing appropriateness to the shape of darkness that makes a circular swath across this head's symbol-filled brain. This, the largest dark area in de Kooning's *Light in August*, initially appearing to be a series of sculpted busts and the rocket shape or pawn in chess, becomes a shockingly explicit alternate portrait as the painting is rotated.[64] The largest black thing in the painting is a silhouette of severed testicles that doubles as a frighteningly recognizable signifier of origins. Ultimately, Percy Grimm of de Kooning's *Light in August* has been pictured with a mind preoccupied by a dark shape, by sacrificial manhood, in what is revealed to be the testicular shape of the continent of Africa, severed at the Sinai peninsula.

Midcentury Masculine Hysteria

> The forms of *Night* are rich with suggestion. Some vaguely resemble human anatomy, while others recall architecture. These ambiguous shapes seem to float and jostle on the canvas. *Night* belongs to a series of abstract black-and-white paintings—inspired by de Kooning's late-night walks in New York—that express the spirit and texture of the modern metropolis. The broken brushwork and areas of scraping and reworking suggest the nervous energy of urban life—or the inner turmoil of the artist.
>
> —Minneapolis Institute of Art's caption for de Kooning's *Night*

De Kooning painted *Black Friday* in 1948 as he finished work for his first show, and this painting, along with his breakthrough masterpiece of the black and whites—*Light in August*—continued to be on view through the fall of 1948. During the summer of 1948, during what would be de Kooning's only trip back to the South after he jumped ship at Newport News, he returned to the painterly journey he had made in the violated bodies that invade and surround the collage portrait of Percy Grimm. While de Kooning's *Light in August* illustrates that he has read Faulkner's novel in its entirety, it bears repeating that his decision to create a collage portrait of Percy Grimm may also recall his familiarity with this work through Cowley's *Portable Faulkner*. This profile of Grimm with his nose facing toward the left edge of the painting is inspired by Arshile Gorky's *Betrothal*: the signature of de Kooning's tie to his Armenian-born friend and mentor is found in the crescent moon that marks the throat of de Kooning's Grimm and what I call "the pensive man" of Gorky's celebrated *Betrothal* series.

De Kooning's most dedicated collage portrait, the work in which a man's head dominates the center of the painting, is *Asheville*, his small piece that remained incomplete when he and Elaine returned to Manhattan from their southern summer at Black Mountain (see plate 2). The flame-colored oranges and strong blacks, amid recognizable elements from Picasso's *Guernica*, have been identified by Martin Ries, who articulates the potential narrative connection of the painting to Zelda Fitzgerald's death in a fire at an Asheville mental institution in the spring of 1948. Ries also speculates that the colors and the clearly punning title might have referred to the 1946 fire in Gorky's studio that had burned so many of his paintings.[65] Gorky's reasons for committing suicide two years later in the summer of 1948 were complex. Himself already cut and broken, Gorky had had a colostomy, and then had had his neck broken and his painting arm shattered and partially paralyzed in an automobile accident. De Kooning, whether through letters sent south or through the personal accounts of his friends who felt implicated as a result of their failed efforts to stop the tragedy, would have been told (among other things) that Arshile Gorky's self-lynched body had been found by Malcolm Cowley, the figure whom de Kooning and the rest of the English-reading world would have most associated with Faulkner's return to print.

Asheville, completed in the fall of 1948, may not be a portrait of Gorky, but it is a portrait of Gorky's pensive man from his *Betrothal* series. *Asheville* features a perspective-challenging version that reveals a man's head seen from the top, a cranium that contains among other things the recognizable visages of two African masks, one face-forward in the place of an ear and another floating sideways in the brain with one eye opened and the other closed. More tragic than comic, this stunning collage portrait is not "the large red form in the center that forms the bottom half of a silhouetted face, with lips cracked to reveal the top row of teeth";[66] rather, this row of teeth is the eye of a man's head seen somewhat frontally from the left, in partial profile. De Kooning was so committed to this long unseen reading of his painting that he drew an arrow pointing to the dotted pupil of this head's left eye. (Seen from the top, navigating from what is the red chin of the partial face seen by critics, this reddened area demarcates the top of an opened mouth with a white chin jutting outward from below. The slitted eyes of this figure are on either side of his large white and down-pointing nose.) By painting another version of Gorky's pensive man, a version that follows his display of his portrait of Percy Grimm in *Light in August* in the spring of 1948, de Kooning honors Gorky and Gorky's paintings, and also establishes the distinctly Faulknerian terms for his own series of paintings about male panic.

If de Kooning's *Night* (1948) locates a "modern metropolis" (see fig. 29, page 258), its setting is closer to a violent food chain served up as a naturalist allegory that has its gritty urban soul in a circus at the edges of a jungle. Like *Asheville*, *Night* speaks to de Kooning's brutally destroyed friend, Arshile Gorky, by alluding through its title, its puppy, and its repeated puzzle piece to its pictorial source in Gorky's *Nighttime, Enigma, and Nostalgia* (1931–32; see fig. 30, page 259).[67] More melodramatic than nostalgic, de Kooning's painting stages an allegory of the midcentury crisis in masculinity. The shapes in *Night* do not "vaguely resemble human anatomy": *Night* frames the torso and head of a dismembered man. This dead man's eyes, his mustache, his flattened nose and upthrust chin, like his carefully dimensional nipples, are realized features that present a body that has been surgically cut, divided into sliced segments, apparently by the claws or the visibly bared and pointed teeth of the creature who snarls and thrusts his long (out-of-drawing) leg vertically (from left to right) above the victim. This animal poised with its limbs in sweeping motion has the bearish and menacing grimace of a wild beast that also contains an alternate visage: the right-side face of a placid puppy in profile who, as he looks away, seems unaware of the scene of violence below. This puppy is identified as comic by being self-consciously drawn with a cartoonish circle marking the corner of its mouth. Through this stylized circle, the domesticated dog is echoed in the severed head of another male figure that lies in the shadowed darkness beyond and behind the violently dismembered man. This smaller male head (to the right of the body's head and much deeper in the perspective of the painting) alludes directly to the face of the puppy, by sporting an identical cartoonish circle at the corner of his mouth. This coy repetition may be art's version of a man: a painted face on the head of a doll. Killed by a wildness made blatant in a literally two-faced and deceptive domesticity, the allegory in *Night* features a more animated and less abstract version of Gorky's puzzle piece that dances in de Kooning's painting below the head of the dead man. This evocative shape, stepping out on two legs, exposing bones that are in the shape of human femurs, has become recognizable. This white piece of the puzzle is a pictorial statement that insists on a dancing death—a recognizable bone with a life of its own. What has deceived the eye of viewers in this explicit narrative painting is the work's play with size and perspective. Gorky's puzzle piece has morphed into an idiom. Unable to restrain the animality of this undomesticated—dual-faced—totemic creature, this man has "lost his backbone."

Among de Kooning's paintings of men (relatively rare by the late 1940s), his 1949 *Untitled* ("Man") has been seen as a painting framed by mysterious unreadable symbols, notably a distant snake and a piece of fence in the background (see plate 7). Like *Night*, *Untitled* ("Man") is an explicit allegory of threatened masculinity. Sitting atop an enormous crocodile whose clawed foot recalls that of the beast's deadly paw in *Night*, the naked man in *Untitled* ("Man") is clearly worried as he looks over his left shoulder. Indeed, this man has a reason to be worried. The de Kooning criticism, short on plot summary, has ignored this naked figure's plight: this man's disproportionally long, but anatomically correct and extremely detailed, penis hangs by shreds of flesh between his strangely rendered legs. Initially appearing as more of a statement than an allegory, this painting depicts a damaged and dismembered man as he perches on the leg of a large (out-of-drawing) African predator whose clawed foot is visible under the translucent green of the surrounding water. Yet this stark circumstance, placing man in violent and violating nature, is in the context of the late 1940s both cartographic and Faulknerian, recalling the recognizable shape of the dark continent in de Kooning's *Black Untitled* and

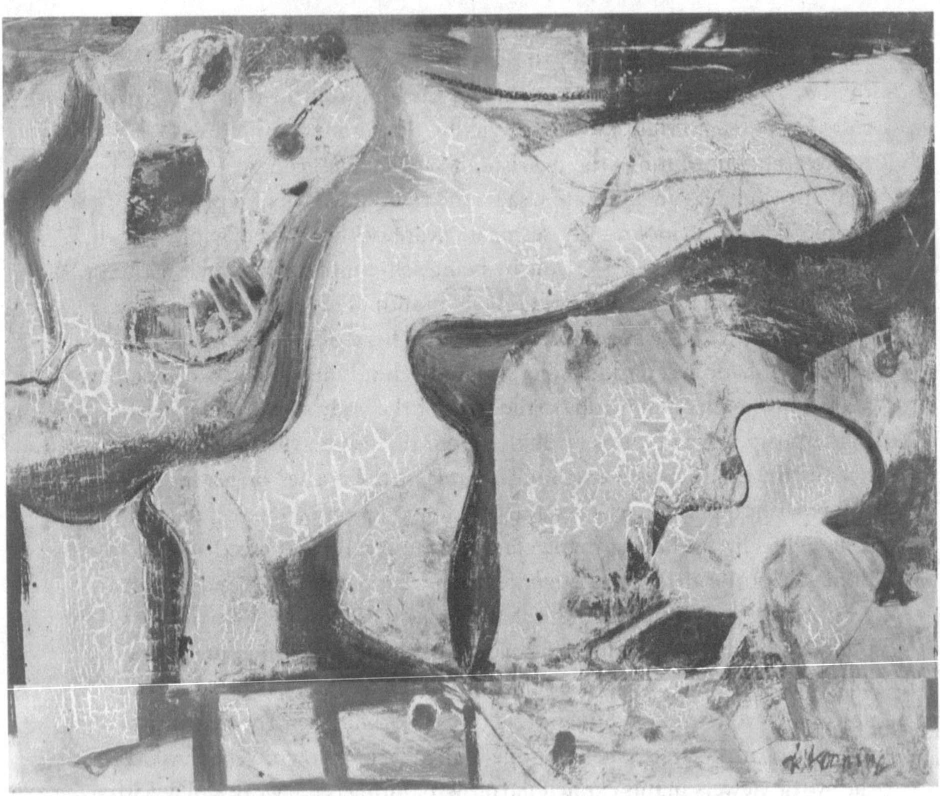

Figure 29. Willem de Kooning, *Night*, 1948. Oil on board, 22 × 28¾ in. (55.9 × 73 cm). Minneapolis Institute of Arts, the John R. Van Derlip Fund and the Ethel Morrison Van Derlip Fund. © 2013 The Willem de Kooning Foundation / Artists Rights Society (ARS), New York. (A richly painted work with subtle shadings, in pasty off-colored whites sometimes tinged with yellow and pink, *Night* has strong blacks and grays with a tiny eruption of slate blue and pink in the upper-left corner.)

his *Light in August*. Here, the castrated man gazes toward the upper-right corner of the painting to see the cloud-shrouded but clearly visible continent of Africa. Because de Kooning had not only read but translated and illustrated the narratives of race and dismemberment from Faulkner's fiction into paintings about pain and violent loss, this man is tellingly ambiguous. In the post–Joe Christmas world peopled by "half-breed[s],"[68] "parchmentcolored" (*LA* 120) men, the figure in *Untitled* ("Man") cannot be essentialized, colored, or identified in racial terms. This being said, his masculinity (or rather a prime piece of it) hangs by mere shreds as his troubled gaze is turned toward the dark and receding continent of Africa. Whether accusatory or mournful (for a world he has lost, or a race-based, castrating world he has inherited), *Untitled* ("Man") tells a story of a devastating hurt, depicting the vulnerability of masculinity in a painting that uses the male body to narrate a primal

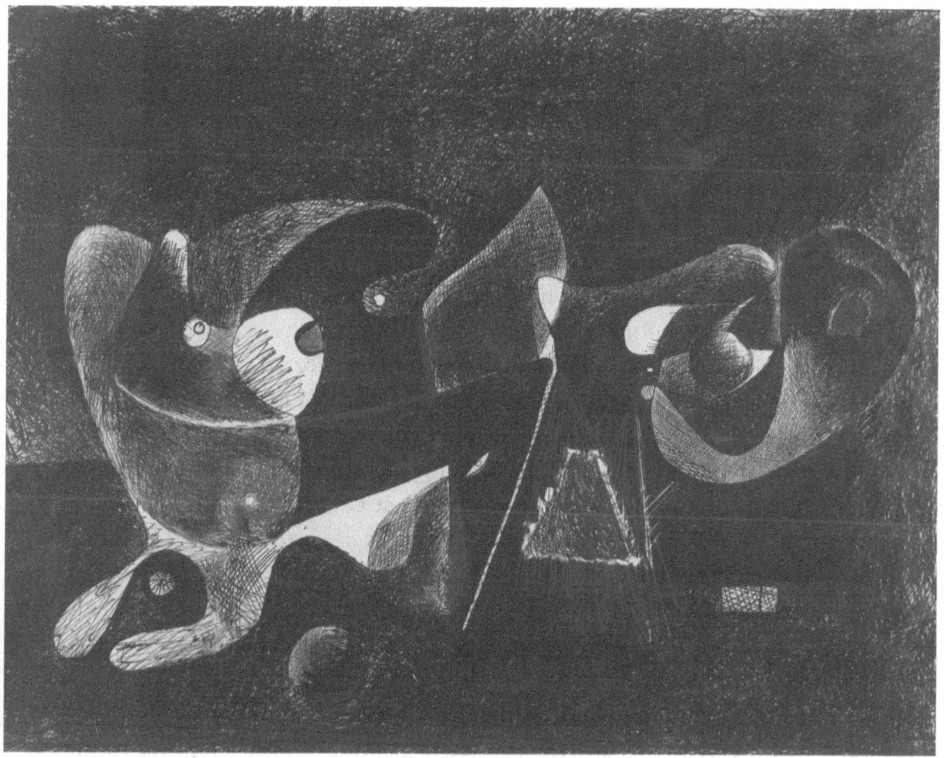

Figure 30. Arshile Gorky, *Nighttime, Enigma, Nostalgia*, Alisa Mellon Bruce Fund and Andrew W. Mellon Fund. Image courtesy of the National Gallery of Art, Washington, D.C. ca. 1932–34, pen and black and brown inks over graphite on wove paper overall: 22 × 28⅜ in. (59.9 × 72 cm). © 2013 The Arshile Gorky Foundation / Artists Rights Society (ARS), New York.

loss. What is clear in the de Koonings of the late 1940s is that Africa repeats itself.

In terms of de Kooning's "pictorial idiom[s]" of damaged masculinity, the dancing backbone from *Night*, the vertebrae released into its dance of death over the eviscerated and deboned male victim, could not be more significant in the history of de Kooning's art. This slightly elongated bone (still recognizable as a version of the repeated puzzle-piece from Gorky's *Nighttime, Enigma, and Nostalgia*) is the bought, borrowed, or stolen prosthesis from de Kooning's *Night* that has been incorporated as the veritable right arm of female materialism in *Woman I* (see plate 8). Classified variously as a painting that reveals misogyny or, at the very least, depicts male fear, the presence of this recognizable bone as an integral part of her body offers an instructive genealogy for *Woman I*. Her long and painful incarnation is directly linked to de Kooning's continuing narration of emasculation through female consumerism, a sexual materialism that could devour and castrate even wary men. De Kooning insists that he had seen *Woman I*, witnessing her rapacity in the eyes of female customers who fought over goods in the bargain basements of New York's department stores. De Kooning's women of the 1950s are more articulate than those that inhabit Philip Wylie's mother-maligning critique that denounced a *Generation of Vipers* (1942). Known for their bared teeth and their aggressive (eyelike or even eye-inscribed) breasts and grinning mouths that are worn like mock crescent moons on throats, de Kooning's women recall the face-based displacement of Quentin's vision of his sexually voracious sister Caddy, whom he imagines with "*eyes unseeing clenched like teeth*" (*SF* 110). De Kooning's *Woman* series of 1953 addresses the viewer with a carnivorous violence, an unbridled and undomesticated appetite in which the female figure exposes herself, revealing a power that is not made palatable by a puppy- or doll-like veneer of sentimentalized domesticity.

Light had already changed for de Kooning before he began his turn to black and white in 1946, before he painted his most explicit narrative of race in America by translating the obsessions of Faulkner's fiction into the painting he called *Light in August*. The fierce light de Kooning saw and began to paint in 1946 was beyond the diminishing light of late summer—the light Faulkner's novel had seen as "Augusttremulous" (*LA* 116). This autumnal light still burning from August 1945 illuminated a descending sun in the human universe. Speaking at a symposium at the Museum of Modern Art in 1951, de Kooning addressed the terror of light itself. Asked to answer the question posed by the title of his talk, to explain "What Abstract Art Means to Me," de Kooning reflected: "Today, some people think that the light of the atom bomb will change the concept of painting once and for all. The eyes that actually saw the light melted out of sheer ecstasy. For one instant everybody was the same color. It made angels out of everybody. A truly Christian light, painful but forgiving."[69] Seeing the erasure of race in the melting of the flesh of eyes, de Kooning spoke of the "ecstasy" of what might be called an atomic rapture. De Kooning's work and his philosophical concerns, the narrative impact of his black paintings, initiated in the canvas he called *Light in August*, were always a story hidden in plain sight. More hurtful than a "rummaging" after symbols "through a junkyard at night,"[70] de Kooning's paintings—drawn by the depths of Faulkner's fiction—reveal a pained and profoundly wounded masculinity where a scarred Jesus returns to cut his woman after the evening sun has gone down.

EPILOGUE

Collateral Damage, Collating Strange

Canned Death, Collage Portraits, and Uncanny and Uncannable Beauty in *Intruder in the Dust* and *The Town*

How do our lives ravel out into the no-wind, no-sound, the weary gestures wearily recapitulant: echoes of old compulsions with no-hand on no-strings: in sunset we fall into furious attitudes, dead gestures of dolls.
—William Faulkner, *As I Lay Dying*[1]

Monday night [in which] the sky's dark bowl cupped as though in a vacuum like the old bride's bouquet under its glass bell the town, the Square which was more than dead: abandoned: because he had gone on to look at it . . . [Chick] ringing his footfalls deliberate and unsecret into the hollow silence . . . himself not potent but at least the vessel of a potency like the actor looking from wings or perhaps empty balcony down upon the waiting stage vacant yet garnished and empty yet, nevertheless where in a moment now he will walk and posture in the last act's absolute cynosure, himself in himself nothing and maybe no world-beater of a play either but at least his to finish it, round it and put it away intact and unassailable, complete: and so onto the dark and empty Square stopping as soon as he could perceive at effortless once that whole dark lifeless rectangle . . .
—William Faulkner, *Intruder in the Dust*[2]

Dough, rubber, leather, pig iron, coal, tar, and ash as well as rigid wood, stamped tin, melted wax, and sawdust-bleeding limbs are just some of the ingredients of the eye-marked flesh that walks, stands rotting, or lays dying in William Faulkner's fiction. Samuel Beckett, hired to explain the dimensionality of Joyce's long forthcoming *Finnegans Wake*, could have been explicating the difficulty of seeing the lists of things that articulate Faulkner's art: "This writing you find so obscure is a quintessential extraction of language and painting, and gesture, with all the inevitable clarity of the old articulation. Here is the savage economy of hieroglyphics."[3] Drifts of words wash up in Faulkner's fiction, as if in eddies, just before or after the wake. These collations, whether constructing ideas or making the faces of composed and decomposing beings, are generative. Paradoxically, these accretions generate the inevitability of degeneration recounted in the engraved earth and its textual analogue, the composited word. Patterns, firm or fleeting—seeming just beyond the reach of meaning—characterize layers of deep consciousness and connection, collating the intentionality that forms and informs Faulkner's Yoknapatawpha.

Collage portraits are made through the juxtaposition and overlaying of constitutive elements. The strike of meaning through montage,[4] an associative ordering older than Eisenstein's recognition, offers a pictorial vocabulary that does not ask to be translated. Faulkner writes, as the de Kooning of the late 1940s sometimes chose to paint, in the narrative form of an accreting idiom. Developed in his prose through the turns and returns, strophe and antistrophe, Faulkner's use of simple montage along with a retinue of repeated objects collates to potentiate prose whose very gestures are hieroglyphics: this is a visual language that includes the solidity and materiality of alphabetic shape, word meanings, and the added meaning heard in the sounds of the spoken word. While adjectives modifying each other in mismodification in Faulkner's prose can gather the motive force of verbs, making descriptive qualities (thought of as static) active, these objects are content-laden, and whether they are preserved or degenerative, these words standing as objects become the descriptive strokes that make, color, and shape thing-portraits of people, places, and concepts. Created by laying syllabically laden words, these manifold objects make pictures and meaning on the page. Sketching and, in some instances, articulating worldviews, these portraits can collide to locate a moral or historical crossroads, a literalized juncture. In Faulkner's prose, these objects-turned-hieroglyphs are briefly concretized as they collate a glimpse, a backward glance at an appearing, because it is a disappearing, past.

There is an erotic component to the striking of meaning through montage and a slower accreting of pleasure that comes through the development of a Faulknerian conceit. These word-portraits are much more than piles of symbols: they are set pieces that are like the concluding fireworks arranged as culminations for early-twentieth-century pyrotechnic displays. In Faulkner's most incendiary montage, the medium is the message, and this imagining of a literalized missive makes a fire in its sender's brain. Here, in *The Hamlet* (1940), Flem Snopes's potency comes from an event that does not take place, a message that is not sent, and a barn that is not burned. This montage, conceived of by Jody Varner as a message, tells the Varners' new tenant, Ab Snopes, that his history as an unindicted barn-burner is known: it is fantasized as a single match on a shingle. This missive to be sent after the crop has been made, but before the family has been paid, becomes the message that the would-be exploiter sends to himself. As the clerk in his father's store can only briefly enjoy this montage, his thought of a match on a shingle signifies an incendiary coupling in which the past predicates or, more precisely, ignites the barn-burning threat of a foreseeable future. This preservation of the barn as a storehouse leads to the trade in which both Flem and the father of Eula Varner (albeit somewhat later) acquire respectability. After he gets Jody's job, Flem gets the Old Frenchman Place in trade for taking the obviously used "galmeat" ("too much of leg, too much of breast, too much of buttock; too much of mammalian female meat" [*H* 111]) that he has no desire or use for. And, for a brief period, Flem is coupled in a parallel montage that threatens to become a collage as he rides about with his father-in-law, Will Varner, in a showy, red-wheeled carriage pulled by what is elsewhere classified as a "mismatched team" ("the fat white horse and the roan"). The lusty Will and the toadlike Flem are joined not by Eula, but in "outrageous paradox" through their shared concupiscence for the land of others seen in the fiscal light of imminent foreclosure.

Perhaps the most formally arranged collage of an idea is sent as a homovindictive message between men in *The Town* (1957), the second volume of the Snopes Trilogy, the novel in which Faulkner most indulges his post–World War II stylistic obsession with collage. This collage uses materials that themselves encode violated virginity, efforts at feminizing men, and the conspicuous display of semen that has not been used for the purpose of reproduction. As Gavin Stevens opens a box that has obviously been sent to him by Manfred de Spain, the floral war fought through the sending of corsages to the ladies of the town for the Cotillion Ball is reprised. Too young to know what it means even after he is old enough to be told, Chick Mallison recalls the contents of the strange gift:

> It was the rake-head, with two flowers like a bouquet, all bound together with a band or strip of something that Gowan knew was thin rubber but it was another year or two until he was a good deal bigger and older that he knew what the thing was; and at the same time he realized what it was, he said he knew it had already been used; and at the same time he knew at least how Uncle Gavin was supposed to believe it had been used, which was the reason Mr de Spain sent it to him: that whether Uncle Gavin was right or not about how it had been used, he would never be sure and so forever afterward would have no peace about it. (*The Town* 71–72)

In this devastating collage, "the rake-head" that Gowan has buried in the road has punctured the tubes of de Spain's car (an opened can of sorts in which the metal exhaust pipe has been "cut-out" to increase the speed and the loudness of the sound that broadcasts his exploits with Eula). This punctured rubber tube is not just a violated air-filled vessel but a direct reference to Faulkner's material vocabulary, recalling Temple Drake's description of her rape and the seemingly unstaunchable blood of her ruptured hymen as a "little rubber tube" that breaking makes "a kind of plopping sound." As early as *The Sound and the Fury*, Jason's "impotence" that he feeds upon in his complaint to the sheriff has been precipitated not just by broken glass and his broken cash box but by the fact that even earlier his niece Quentin and the drummer have immobilized him (as he notes, not by puncturing rubber) but by merely letting the air out of his tires. Rubber has already been coded as a female substance in the suicidal Quentin's visions of rubbery yellow flesh, in particular the yellow balloon of the reflected moon that signifies back to the "periodic filth" when this yellow blob reappears stained with the bloody rag, implicating Caddy's brother's eye in the debased materiality of menstruating flesh. Instead of de Spain's masculinity being violated in the tires of his feminized car, this notorious "rake" sends an actual rubber, a used condom that states his case more explicitly than his previous message sent by the spewing of sound. Here as a rubber holds the "two flowers like a bouquet," the message is more than that of a deflowering, either of his car or of Eula: it is a sign of carnal incorporation and his refusal to incarnate. This floral coupling—in which the rubber vessel signals both the joining and the refusal to join that insists on Eula's having been used and de Spain's virility conserved—is finally not just raucously punning. This corsage is a raunchy set piece that signifies bodies while giving the lie to severed floral emblems, which signify death and the doomed in Faulkner's fiction. Neither a rose for Emily nor a sprig of verbena for Bayard is something that someone acquainted with "odors" in Faulkner's prose would willingly accept. Among other things in Faulkner's material vocabulary, cut flowers signify bodies, dead bodies, and long-dead bodies.

A collated set piece that can be read in sequence with everything on the mantle and the walls in Miss Reba's pink-accented room in Memphis demonstrates the ways in which collage portraits accrete, sometimes using the proximate to speak its piece through montage. The "wax lily beneath a bell jar" is already a montage as it displays the artifice of sacrificial purity framed by the art of preservation: a shrine to the ideal of southern womanhood served up in Miss Reba's house of some repute. This lily of purity (waxen like the melted chin of the deformed Popeye and wax like the plug used by the mortician to fill the hole shot by Popeye into Red's head), framed by the portrait of a "meek" "man" draped in "black," signals that these objects, taken together, constitute a shrine to the dead that reigns over the implausible preservation of the soon-to-be deflowered. Bell jars (like the "old bride's bouquet" preserved in the "vacuum" of a "glass bell" invoked in *Intruder in the Dust*) can only delay decay. Broken glass, both in the past—known through fairy tale and Faulkner and in the present—through joyous rituals of breaking, is a sign of fertility. Meaning comes out of the breaking of feminized vessels, creation is born of destruction: broken watch faces, hymens, glass panes, and the Thrush Girl's jugs. This being said, Miss Reba is an artist who works directly in the grotesque realm of lucrative bodies, the sex trades, and heteronormativity. Hearing the sound in the name, insisting that what has "been" will "be," the portly procuress (the widowed Mrs. "Binby") has added animal totems to the mix.

The conceit of the enshrined dead husband and the deceased legitimacy of the "wax lily" that their business, their trafficking in women, has battened on is extended in Miss Reba's obscenely alive and digestive "worm-like" dogs that she has named for herself and "Mr Binby." These creatures are distinguished not by their nether organs but by their pink and blue ribbons that echo in Miss Reba's bedroom "littered" with "toilet-articles tied in pink satin bows" (*Sanctuary* 222). In *The Sound and the Fury*, the rigid grass plot that surrounds the sign of the pictorial eye in Mottson, anticipated as Dilsey goes to church by the "grassless plots filled with broken things" (signaling the fertility of the black community), has a corollary in the obscene filth of Miss Reba's abbreviated yard:

> In the grimy grassplot before it two of those small, woolly, white, worm-like dogs, one with a pink, the other with a blue, ribbon about its neck, moved about with an air of sluggish and obscene paradox. In the sunlight their coats looked as though they had been cleaned with gasoline.

From Temple Drake's perspective, the connubial dogs are

> hear[d] outside her door, whimpering and scuffing, or, rushing thickly in when the negro maid opened the door, climbing and sprawling onto the bed and into Miss Reba's lap with wheezy, flatulent sounds, billowing into the rich pneumasis of her breast and tonguing along the metal tankard which she waved in one ringed hand as she talked. (*Sanctuary* 149)

These "small, wooly, wormlike" dogs occupy a "grimy grassplot" when they are not "tonguing" their mistress's "metal tankard" in unchecked promiscuity, and, at the same time, these animals allude to the absence of preservation, whether in bell jars or sealed cans. "[W]heezy, flatulant" totems of past married bliss, these dogs are digestively dirty as they "billow . . . into the rich pneumasis of [Miss Reba's] breast." Whether they convey the filth of bodies on other bodies, or whether they actually have been "cleaned with gasoline," the canine and color-coded "Mr and Miss Binby" signify "an air of sluggish and obscene paradox." Miss Reba's penchant for "obscene paradox" opens a can of worms that crosses the boundaries of animal and human, using the grotesque to critique fictions of purity when this state, married or not, infers flatulent, toilet-smelling bodies.

Montage, immediate and conclusive, is a more sharply defined narrative gesture than the full-blown and raucously punning conceits imbricated in collage. Collage is favored as a defining characteristic of Faulknerian humor in two of his finest post–World War II novels. Rising to prominence in his 1948 work, *Intruder in the Dust*, this form constructed of a series of related set pieces culminates in Faulkner's 1957 masterwork of collation, *The Town*. *Intruder in the Dust*, narrated from the point of view of the young Chick Mallison ("himself not potent but at least the vessel of a potency" [*ID* 206]), is recognized as Faulkner's most specific letter to the world (if not the Nobel Prize committee) narrating the story of manhood though the violence of racial identity in the Mississippi and South of the early twentieth century. Of the three narrators whose worldviews provide the syncopated perspective of *The Town*, Chick Mallison is the teller who sees and hears the other narrators, Gavin Stevens and V. K. Ratliff, with the most clarity and acuity, allowing these narrators to become more multidimensional as they are seen and heard in an adolescent boy's bemused struggle to understand. In *Intruder in the Dust*, Chick is haunted by memories that lie just outside of his reach. The Yoknapatawpha that forms the background for Chick in his coming-of-age narrative lies in the background of Lucas and Molly Beauchamp in Faulkner's 1942 story-cycle novel, *Go Down, Moses*. This never-repeated, yet alluded to and strongly present, backstory challenges those who would aspire to understand the context of *Intruder in the Dust*, a reservoir of events available to those willing to remember the past stories of Black Yoknapatawpha. Chick's retrieved and irretrievable past can be filled in by going back six years to Faulkner's previous novel, a work about race and paternal as well as maternal bonds, published during World War II. While the pattern of drawing on his earlier narratives about the Snopes clan was integral to the rewriting and incorporation of short stories about this notorious family into his 1940 novel, *The Hamlet*, this practice is what comes to distinguish the strongest work of this postwar period. These narratives of painfully wrought modernity describe a different world, but this world continues to maintain its deep connection to Faulkner's earlier narratives that are refashioned, retold, and reheard in the two final volumes of the Snopes Trilogy, *The Town* and *The Mansion*, as well as in *Intruder in the Dust*, the novel that preceded the publication of the second volume of the trilogy. Chick Mallison, recognized by scholars as an analogue for Quentin Compson (already dead by his own leap), provides an adolescent view that reports with some of the aural and visual accuracy of the idiot man-child, Benjy Compson of *The Sound and the Fury*, and the grief-struck and repetitive describer of inconceivable events, the child Vardaman of *As I Lay Dying*.

Things Intruding in the Dirt and Dust

> He stood . . . and heard the first clod strike the pine box. [He] restored the hand to the moving shovel, flinging the dirt with that effortless fury so that the mound seemed to be rising of its own volition, not built up from above but thrusting visibly upward out of the earth itself, until at last the grave, save for its rawness, resembled any other marked off without order about the barren plot by shards of pottery and

broken bottles and old brick and other objects insignificant to sight but actually of profound meaning and fatal to touch, which no white man could have read.
—Rider buries his beloved wife, Mannie, in Faulkner's "Pantaloon in Black."[5]

After an extravagant description of "chewed rubber and . . . bottles and cans" in a landscape "empty, vacant of any movement and any life" that has "not seen one in going on forty-eight hours," Chick Mallison ends his list by declaring that he has seen "one," the missing thing:

> [N]o smoke rose [from "the farmhouses"] because breakfast was long over by now and no dinner to be cooked where none would be home to eat it, the paintless Negro cabins where on Monday morning in the dust of the grassless treeless yards halfnaked children should have been crawling and scrabbling after broken cultivator wheels and wornout automobile tires and empty snuff-bottles and tin cans and in the backyards smoke-blackened iron pots should have been bubbling over wood fires beside the sagging fences of vegetable patches and chickenruns which by nightfall would be gaudy with drying overalls and aprons and towels and unionsuits: but not this morning, not now; the wheels and the giant-doughnuts of chewed rubber and the bottles and cans lying scattered and deserted in the dust since that moment Saturday afternoon when the first voice shouted from inside the house, and in the back yards the pots sitting empty and cold among last Monday's ashes among the empty clotheslines and as the car flashed past the blank and vacant doors he would catch one faint gleam of fire on hearth and no more see but only sense among the shadows the still white roll of eyes; but most of all, the empty fields themselves in each of which on this day at this hour on the second Monday in May there should have been fixed in monotonous repetition the land's living symbol—a formal group of ritual almost mystic significance identical and monotonous as milestones tying the county-seat to the county's ultimate rim as milestones would: the beast the plow and the man integrated in one foundationed into the frozen wave of their furrow tremendous with effort yet at the same time vacant of progress, ponderable immovable and immobile like groups of wrestling statuary set against the land's immensity—until suddenly (they were eight miles from town; already the blue-green lift of the hills was in sight) he said with an incredulous and almost shocked amazement who except for Paralee and Aleck Sander and Lucas had not seen one in going on forty-eight hours:
>
> "There's a nigger." (*ID* 144–45; see fig. 31)

What has been missing is "the land's living symbol—a formal group of ritual almost mystical significance identical and monotonous as milestones tying the county seat to the county's ultimate rim as milestones would: the beast the plow and the man integrated in one . . . like groups of wrestling statuary set against the land's immensity." As "the beast the plow and the man inte-

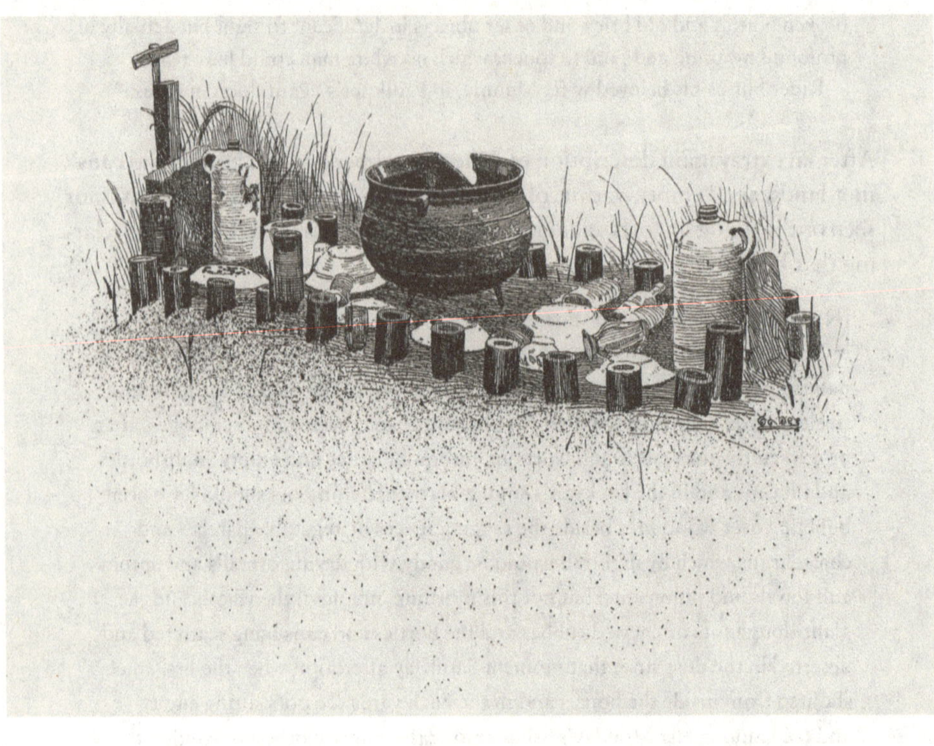

Figure 31. "A Congo Chieftain's Grave, Illustrated After Sketches by the Author," by E. J. Glave. Claiming authenticity in his authorial title as "One of Stanley's Pioneer Officers," Glave's article, "Fetishism in Congo Land," appeared in *The Century Illustrated Monthly*, April 1891. Although this depiction of grave decoration claims to be based on an actual African burial site, this image resonates with nineteenth- and twentieth-century traditional practices in African American decoration of graves and yards. Whereas the Beauchamp household features the orderly beauty of used cans and containers in Faulkner's *Intruder in the Dust*, the "broken things" that categorize the environs of the black community in the final section of *The Sound and the Fury* recall the "grassless plot[s]," graves that well into the twentieth century were incised with and bordered by broken vessels, headlights of cars, mirrors, and collations of other decorative objects. See grave described in epigraph as Rider buries Mannie (266). Image courtesy of Davidson Library, Special Collections, University of California, Santa Barbara.

grated in one," "the man," seen as "one" and as "one" of them, has become the missing thing. This characteristically long sentence serves as an archive of thrown-away materiality; yet amid this collation of inanimacy, something hidden looks back. This "still white roll of eyes" not "see[n] but only sense[d] among the shadows" is understood to be present as Chick "catch[es] one faint gleam of fire on the hearth."[6] Chick's obsessive listing of trash seemingly vacant of life or even imitations of life, in the form of composite "statuary" "wrestling" with the land, has a structural counterpoint that appears earlier in the novel. Chick's declaration, "There's a nigger," figures the whole problem of the book, Lucas Beauchamp's refusal to act "like a nigger" (*ID* 47): his refusal to say "Mister" like he means it frames the struggle in which he uses things, composing himself as a portrait of a man to become more than a thing. Called "You goddamn biggity stiffnecked stinking burrheaded Edmonds sonofabitch" as he eats "a five-cent carton of gingersnaps" in the store, Lucas only responds to the assertion that he is an "Edmonds sonofabitch": "I aint a Edmonds. I dont belong to these new folks. I belongs to the old lot. I'm a McCaslin" (*ID* 19). It is the female part of "Edmonds sonofabitch" rather than the female and animal implications of "bitch" that Lucas Beauchamp contests. Lucas is by his own proud assertion a "man-made" McCaslin (*GDM* 52). Saved by the proprietor's son from being hit by a "sawmill" man who is swinging "a plow singletree" that is there for sale, Lucas, by the intervention of a store clerk, avoids being killed in this "crossroads store four miles from Edmonds' place" (*ID* 18).

Deeded a "postage stamp" of land in his grandfather's plantation, Lucas and Molly become the figures who construct and valorize the idea of a column. This collated set piece recasts the story of "throwaway bodies" and discarded trash. Chick Mallison goes through a baptism of water (falling in first, he then goes under the ice a second time to retrieve his lost masculinity in the form of his hunting rifle) before stripping down to the skin that exposes his treasured whiteness, becoming the unwilling and beholden guest at Lucas and Molly's hearth. Like Darl carving Jewel into existence, Chick Mallison becomes aware of his obsession that links manhood with whiteness as he repeatedly faces the most manly man in Faulkner's fiction. Seeing Lucas Beauchamp, Chick constructs him out of what Daniel Pecchenino has termed "objects of pride":

> [T]he man in the gum boots and the faded overalls of a Negro but with a heavy gold watch-chain looping across the bib of the overalls and shortly after they entered the room he had been conscious of the man turning and taking something from the cluttered mantel and putting it into his mouth and later he had seen what it was: a gold toothpick such as his own grandfather had used: and the hat was a worn handmade beaver such as his grandfather had paid thirty and forty dollars apiece for, not set but raked slightly above the face pigmented

> like a Negro's but with a nose high in the bridge and even hooked a little and what looked out through it or from behind it not black nor white either, not arrogant at all and not even scornful: just intolerant inflexible and composed. (*ID* 12–13)

With the addition of a description of his pigment and the physiognomy of his nose, these framing appurtenances, lacking only the dressed-up elements of the frock coat and a copper button in the shape of a snake, form the collage portrait that Lucas has "composed." Again and again, he appears with his hat, a gold toothpick, the spectacular button that replaces a tie, a frock coat, and notably a Colt pistol (the latter worn only on Saturday, as his white grandfather had always done). Lucas is able to be framed for murder because of his ritual of wearing this gun, but, as Chick observes, Lucas Beauchamp appears increasingly vulnerable as items of his collated presence disappear. These missing objects whose absences terrify Chick become part of a decomposition, which is central to the plot that leads to Lucas's near lynching. The anticipated end is a burning alive that is designed not just to kill but, rather, to define Lucas as less than human, to transform him into what he has refused to be: "a nigger" (18, 22, 25). This is a word that is more spoken than thought by characters in Faulkner's work: this epithet is (to my knowledge) rarely if ever used in the commentary or observations of an omniscient narrator. As the freezing and wet Chick is led to Lucas and Molly's hearth, his descriptive powers as a narrator achieve an early crescendo. Chick sees their "paintless" home as a culmination of mindful composition over trash-evacuating modernity: a progression of order that he links to the aesthetic heights of classical antiquity.

Lucas and Molly Beauchamp's yard (their last name means "beautiful field" in French) follows the African practice of making the house safe from snakes:

> It would have been grassless even in summer . . . completely bare . . . , the dust each morning swept by some of Lucas' womenfolks with a broom made of willow switches . . . into an intricate series of whorls and overlapping loops which as the day advanced would be gradually and slowly defaced by the droppings and the cryptic three-toed prints of chickens like (remembering it now at sixteen) a terrain in miniature out of the age of the great lizards. (*ID* 8–9)

This single (almost page-long) Faulknerian sentence continues to recall the "grassless plot" filled with broken things that configure the black community below as Benjy and Dilsey walk toward the Easter service in *The Sound and the Fury*. Lucas and the soaked Chick and Aleck and another black boy are said to

> walk . . . in what was less than walk because its surface was dirt too yet more than path, the footpacked strip running plumbline straight between two borders of tin cans and empty bottles and shards of china and earthenware set into the ground, up to the paintless steps and paintless gallery along whose edge sat

> more cans but larger—empty gallon buckets which had once contained molasses or perhaps paint and wornout water or milk pails and one five-gallon can for kerosene with its top cut off and half of what had once been somebody's (Edmonds' without doubt) kitchen hot water tank sliced longways like a banana—out of which flowers had grown last summer and from which the dead stalks and the dried and brittle tendrils still leaned and drooped, and beyond this the house itself, gray and weathered and not so much paintless as independent and intractable to paint so that the house was not only the one possible continuation of the stern untended road but was its crown too as the carven ailanthus leaves are the Greek column's capital. (*ID* 9)

The Beauchamps are not trash, and trash is not trash in their "grassless" yard but rather a demarcation of order. They do not have hot water and, in the early and mid-1940s, such a rural dwelling would not have had indoor plumbing. While the road is untended and the "droppings . . . of chickens" mark the not so "cryptic" progression toward future meals and the extravagances afforded by "eggmoney" (*LA* 21), this house has a regal bearing. It is the "crown" that provides the finial top, the conclusion to the road that is ultimately finished by the tended straightness of what is in their control: the "plumbline" directive of this walk that is "more than [a] path." Seen as the "crown," "as the carven ailanthus leaves are the Greek column's capital," this structural support places Lucas and Molly at the top rather than the bottom of this classical icon of the Old South.[7]

Self-made or man-made, Lucas understands construction, and he has earned his status. Pigmented as black but colored in his absence of darkness, Lucas is definitively human and clearly a man. As Chick thinks the words "his grandfather," it is at times unclear whether he means his own grandfather or Lucas's grandfather: both grandfathers are white and both represent a past that (if "not dead") is at least increasingly distant. In a self-conscious act of changing iconography for posterity, Lucas Beauchamp controls the way that he and Molly will be seen. "Lucas's doins'" include altering the "picture" preserved in the photographic record; Lucas, in Molly's words, has refused to have a "field nigger picture" in the house. In this instant of viewing as Chick realizes that something is wrong with this gilt-framed picture on an easel, this glassed-in image is grotesque because "[Molly] had hair; it was like looking at an embalmed corpse through the hermetic glass lid of a coffin" (*ID* 14–15). The sense of something dead, something "embalmed," has violated the accuracy associated with the photographer's tool: "retouch[ing]" the image, the unknown artist has introduced the artificiality of painting over the actual, introducing a head of hair for Molly because Lucas has commanded a change of racial iconography. Lucas, the purchaser of the portrait, insists that art be applied to master the past. As Willem de Kooning and others have noted, hair is notoriously difficult to represent, and this is exacerbated in the case of Molly who (like Dilsey) prefers to dress up with a headcloth topped by a hat. The result, representing a problem component in picturing this woman of color's covered head as hair, strikes Chick as "ghastly, almost intolerably wrong":

> It had been retouched obviously; from behind the round faintly prismatic glass dome as out of a seer's crystal ball there looked back at him again the calm intolerant face beneath the swaggering rake of the hat, a tieless starched collar clipped to a white starched shirt with a collarbutton shaped like a snake's head and almost as large, the watch-chain looped now across a broadcloth vest inside a broadcloth coat and only the toothpick missing, and beside him the tiny doll-like woman in another painted straw hat and a shawl; that is it must have been the woman though it looked like nobody he had ever seen before and then he realized it was more than that: there was something ghastly, almost intolerably wrong about it or her. (*ID* 14)

This "hermetic glass lid[ded] . . . coffin" of a portrait, meant to be an act of preservation, doubles as "the prismatic glass dome . . . of a seer's crystal ball" for seeing the future of a past that never was. Lucas has failed in his design to collate Molly into his selectively composed picture. There is a strangeness here that goes beyond the patron's demand that art be used to alter photographic claims of reality. The head-rag, originally serving as a cloth designed to catch sweat, has become part of Molly's sense of sartorial neatness while the glass and the removal of this wrapping record his undressing, more precisely his re-dressing, as an act of violation.

In many ways, Flem Snopes is also a self-made, sartorially constructed character, but unlike Lucas Beauchamp he is not concerned with framing himself in a remastered history. Flem is a point of origin who in the end uses his capacity to buy wholesale as a way of replicating his earliest uniform of respectability: a simple black string tie and a black coat (identical in its cut) that are worn through and then replaced. Flem, with his established brand, changes less than the eroticized Coca-Colas in their sveltely sweating shapes that Mink Snopes (after his forty-eight-year stint in Parchman Prison) insists on paying more for in *The Mansion* than the bottles actually cost. Mink's monetary recognition is a paean to the displacement of the desire for the female body onto the shapely packaging chosen by the "pop" manufacturer in 1915. Flem Snopes as he chooses the uniformity of respectability is not unlike Andy Warhol's posters of sameness, exact replication, and canned plenty celebrated in his iconic work picturing repeated rows of Campbell's soup cans with their identical labels. The face of Marilyn Monroe (not the svelte bottle that makes her invention necessary) as it appears like other objects in ranked and even rows would become integral to Warhol's series about the concept of the serial itself. In the trilogy, Flem is his own recognizable brand as his personal packaging appears in pieces and parts: Flem is a sartorial ghost whose fabricated elements are sold and resold so that at twilight, disintegrated things from his costume of respectability have become apparitions. Here, clothes (rather than inherited meat encased in cloth) appear as ever-fading revenants sifting their way down through the echelons of race and class. Flem, who is conscious of his bodily fluids and who builds through acquisition, becomes a materially dispersed ghost whose incomplete uniform is met in fading precision walking down roads to diminished destinations. From the outset, *The Town* (Jefferson's water tank) poses the question of whether Flem's big can of water is a "monument" or a historical marker, a "footprint" that indicates his arrival and predicts his material propensity for erection and rise.

Eck and Eula

> She whirled again and without a break in her stride and still watching the old man, she ran right off the porch and fetched up on hands and knees in a litter of ashes and tin cans and bleached bones . . .
>
> —Temple Drake on the trash heap, William Faulkner, *Sanctuary* (43)

> But tonight the street was empty . . . But tonight they passed only one man, and he was not walking but standing just inside the front gate to a small neat shoebox of a house built last year between two other houses already close enough together to hear one another's toilets flush (his uncle had explained that: "When you were born and raised and lived all your life where you can't hear anything but owls at night and roosters at dawn . . . you like to live where you can hear and smell people on either side of you every time they flush a drain or open a can of salmon or of soup.,") . . .
>
> —Cans and being on the can in Faulkner's *Intruder in the Dust* (46)

Unlike many of his kinfolk, who are frequently cast as animals or half-baked or even "pie-face-ted" creatures molded from dough (*Sanctuary* 208), Eck Snopes is initially described as a "a young, well-made, muscle-bound man who, turning, revealed an open equable face beginning less than an inch below his hairline" (*The Hamlet* 69). Eck (physiognomically marked for less than remarkable intellect) reappears in *The Town* as an odd double for Eula, becoming the canned sacrifice in contrast to Eula's uncanny (irreplicable and irreplaceable) beauty. Finally, it is Eula who articulates the signifying absence that must be filled by art. Both Eula and Eck arrive in Jefferson—Eula with Flem and her daughter, Eck with his wife and their son—to live in what appears to be the same tent behind the lunch-counter business. Like Eula before him, Eck is seen as he moves meat on a grease-encrusted griddle. Eula's appearance in this position at the beginning of *The Town* is so uncanny that it functions as a tether, jerking the reader abruptly from myth to a realism that focuses on the necessities of the flesh. This scene of being seen insists on Eula's fall from early indolence and static consumption in *The Hamlet* to having to earn a living in *The Town*. Although the context is mercantile, Eula in this brief glimpse of her daily visibility is not eroticized. Her back is merely her back as she moves "tough pieces of steak on the grease-crusted kerosene griddle" (*The Town* 9).

There is syllabic play in the breaking off of the "n" that is anticipated in the naming of "Eck" and his fate to be first broken and then disintegrated. Like a nursery rhyme, his story begins: "That was his name: Eck. The one with the broken neck." Said to have "brought it [his broken neck] to town when he moved in as Flem's immediate successor," Eck arrives already bitted: "rigid in a steel brace and leather harness." Eck's body, broken to save the life of a black man, defines him from the outset as "[n]ever in the world a Snopes." Ratliff adds: "even his family—Flem—knew he was not a Snopes." Basing his argument on the claim that there is no grift in a sawmill (the Gowrie murders in *Intruder in the Dust* aside),[8] "where even the owner must be a financial genius to avoid bankruptcy" and where "to embezzle a wagonload of planks is . . . like embezzling an iron safe or a—yes: that dammed water tank itself," Ratliff tells Eck's story as a triumph of metal over flesh, over the visceral connection between meat and man.[9] Like Flem, Eula, and Linda, Eck and his wife and son live in "the tent behind the restaurant." Here, Eck is identified by his "greasy apron and steel-and-leather neck harness." Said later to be "like a post," Eck, unable to look down, announces the scandal of the mystery meat that he can only smell: "Aint we supposed to be selling beef in these here hamburgers? I don't know jest what this is yet but it aint no beef." Hampered by his sense of smell from being complicit as a shyster cook, the hapless Eck (according to Ratliff) is better suited for his next job of watching the industrial container of oil: "He won't need to look up to see whether the tank's still there or not, he can jest walk up and feel the bottom of it" (*The Town* 31–34). Beginning with "feeling the bottom of it," Eck's job becomes increasingly and obscenely scatological in a collage portrait that leads to disintegration and death. Eck whose "office" is said to be "about the size of a privy" has been charged with decanting cans and barrels of oil from the tank as well as opening the "man-hole" to release noxious fumes. In this over-determined collation, the tragedy occurs as Eck brings a lantern to search for a missing child that he believes has gone in through the "man-hole" and died in the can he has been assigned to watch. Ultimately, it is Eck rather than the child (who is playing in a different, more concrete container) who becomes the canned man. Eck's job is finally too visceral to deny its obscene implications. When he leaves his "privy"-sized office, Eck is assigned "to open the manhole" to "drive the gas out." The scene of Eck's life and death in *The Town* articulates a collage portrait about the dangers of being canned, a scatological narrative that links male digestion with the fatal consequences of male pregnancy, a condition of consumption that leads to defecation or death. Trying to save or recover a child whom he fears has been canned, Eck Snopes ceases to be flesh and cannot be found even as minced meat:

> But they never did find Mr Snopes until the next morning . . . in the telegraph wires about two hundred yards from where the tank had been and . . . [the "fireman" found] Mr Snopes's steel neck-brace though none of the leather was left.
>
> But they never did find anything of Mr Snopes. (*The Town* 109–10)

The question of whether there is a body in the coffin is, as Robert Dale Parker has argued, part of the experience of reading Faulkner. The structure of the work is there, but the question of the body, the thematic content, remains: is there anything there, present or absent, inside the box? Burying a piece of metal that stands for this man's sacrificial regard for others becomes part of the corporate ritual of bodiless coffins that had already risen to the level of a central motif in *Intruder in the Dust.* And the Masons (containing a direct allusion to home-canning—the standard reusable jars were inscribed "Ball Perfect Mason"—in their storied name) assume the fraternal responsibility of burying a man who no longer is "anything": "they buried the neck-brace anyway, in a coffin all regular . . . they buried what they did have of him; there was the Baptist preacher too, and the Masons in their aprons dropping a pinch of dirt into the grave and saying 'Alas my brother,' and covered the raw red dirt with the flowers (one of the flower pieces had the Mason signs worked into it)" (*The Town* 110; see fig. 32). As the Masons put this can-opened man, or rather his metal remainder, into a box, the obliterated Eck is symbolically contained while all of his fleshly components, including the leather part of his brace, have exploded into nothing.

Eula, Uncontained

Just as Eck is said to have brought "his neck" into *The Town*, there is a corporeally dismantling feature of applied art that Gavin sees in Eula on the evening before she commits suicide:

> Though it was enough to see her hair, that she had been to the beauty parlor: who according to Maggie had never been to one, the hair not bobbed of course, not waved, but something, I don't know what it was except that she had been to the beauty parlor that afternoon . . . no makeup, lips or nails either: just her hair that had been to the beauty shop. (*The Town* 319–20)

Asking himself why she has gone to a beauty shop for the first time in her life, Gavin finally settles on the perversely specific idea that this Olympian beauty had at the very least taken "her hair" to this establishment, clarifying that Eula has done nothing permanent: neither a wave nor a bob. Eula with equal accuracy has been preparing for the immediate future as it concerns, not her hair, but her soon-to-be violated head. Choosing to kill herself with a pistol, Eula's visit points toward an attempt at preserving her looks through the feminine

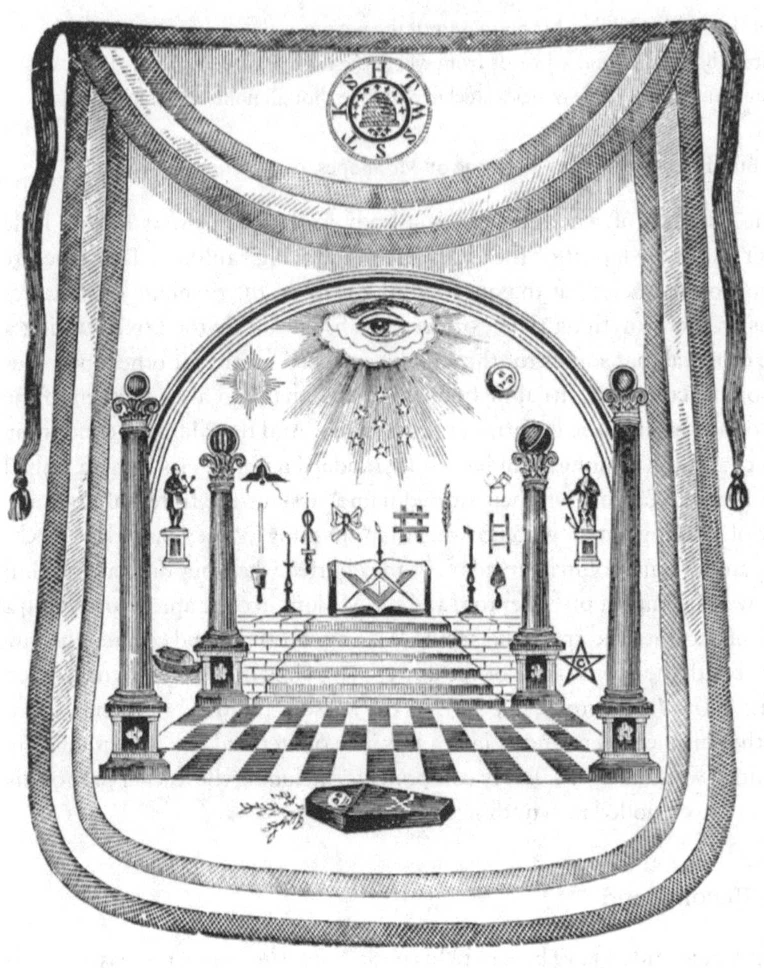

Figure 32. Engraving of George Washington's Masonic apron. Aside from the intersecting triangles of the compass and the square, the most common feature of the Masonic apron was the "All Seeing Eye," which was embroidered or stamped on the flap that formed the top of this traditional ritual vestment. While masonic emblems were worked into floral arrangements, a practice that reached its height at the turn into the twentieth century, these compositions were modeled on the intersecting triangles of the compass and square. Washington's apron with its eye, coffin, and triangles as well as its candlelit altar centering on an opened book could serve as a collated illustration of Faulkner's most dramatic uses of the pictorial form in his novels. See chapter 4 in this volume.

arts despite the fact she has already chosen a violent (male-favored, looks-spoiling) method for her suicide. While Chick (asking his mother) gleans the uncommented upon detail of Eula's use of a pistol, Gavin, Ratliff, the town, and *The Town* are notably silent about Eula's body and the disfiguring violence unavoidable in her method of suicide.

Finally, the construction of Eula's monument, and the obsessive focus that this memorial generates, speaks. While the state of her suicided and buried body is never broached by a single word, this monument stands in place of the dead Eula. In the aftermath of the burial, Gavin Stevens's exactions reveal the difficulty of his epic loss as he struggles to bring a work of art into existence. Near the opening of *The Town*, just after she is literalized frying "tough" cuts of meat behind a counter, Eula's image shifts entirely as she is imagined by the child narrator as wearing clothes that might fall off her body at any moment. Challenged, Chick tries to describe the unattainable and uncontainable Eula:

> She wasn't too big, heroic, what they call Junoesque. It was that there was just too much of what she was for any one human female package to contain, and hold: too much of white, too much of female, too much of maybe just glory, I dont know: so that at first sight of her you felt a kind of shock of gratitude just for being alive and being male at the same instant with her in space and time, and then in the next second and forever after a kind of despair because you knew that there never would be enough of any one male to match and hold and deserve her; grief forever after because forever after nothing less would ever do. (*The Town* 6)

The tension between myth and meat: the physical reality of Eula that reveals her as "too much of what she was for any one human female package" underlines the fact that she cannot be canned, boxed, or contained in life or in death. Her impact on male sanity and satiety is emphasized by Gavin's observations on the night in which she offers herself to him sexually and he refuses: "*Why, she can't be this small, this little*, apparently standing only inches short of my own six feet, yet small, little; too small to have displaced enough of my peace to contain this much unsleep, to have disarranged this much of what I had at least thought was peace" (*The Town* 90). Eula is a "loose-girdled bucolic Lilith" (*The Town* 319). Unable to be contained by stays or society, like the precursor to Eve, the gorgon or a goddess, she is also meant to be experienced from a distance as one looks at a work of art. Again, as with Ringo's observations in *The Unvanquished*,[10] realism is only made necessary by loss. And, once again, when art is in question, the reality framed by photographs confirms the loss that (unlike the distance of desire) decreases the realm in which the unconfined living flesh is larger than life. Faulkner's Eula is more than art, and this woman is more than the sum of her parts. As an embodiment of desire, like Lilith, who is mentioned only once in God's book and, in the annals of the gods, Eula is identified as Yoknapatawpha's singular figure of "Olympian" excess: "seed of the spendthrift Olympian ejaculation" (164).

Photographs have not been able to capture Eula: Linda searches assiduously for a visage of her mother that can even gesture toward the woman that Gavin Stevens has lost, to picture the missing figure that the bereaved lover who has refused to consummate his desire with her in life is driven to seek through funerary art. As Gavin turns to sculptural art to replace what he has lost and has chosen never to have, he is unable to be satisfied with photographic realism. Photographs with their flat, factual claims document and diminish the physical presence of the living woman. Such pictures with pretense to the real frame the challenge that faces the unnamed Italian sculptor, who after multiple attempts succeeds in making a drawing that Gavin Stevens concedes to be acceptable. And what follows is yet another act of translation that challenges and exposes the inadequacies of art itself. This artist has used the suggestiveness of drawing to go beyond the limits of the chosen photograph and carved a more evocative face in marble. Italian sculptors for millennia have been devoted to making stone goddesses, but Gavin (even as he avails himself of all the arts) cannot recall Eurydice or Eula; he cannot bring back a living woman from the dead, much less William Faulkner's woman of all women. A fastidious lover, Gavin Stevens has assumed responsibility for the problem of overseeing the representation of a beauty that like its bearer's "innocen[ce]" and her powers of evocation are finally not representable in visual or moral economies (*The Town* 339). This process of memorial in which Gavin tries to answer unconsummated love and consummated loss with art concludes with the arrival of a "marble medallion." Like the face on money, Eula's head has been taken: she is decapitated and circumscribed in her funeral visage. While Eula's boxed exit, like her self-violated head, remains unseen, this long-negotiated thing arrives packed in straw, encoffined, "nailed up in a wooden box" (*The Town* 352). Eula's tribute in marble is so heavy that it requires two black freight-men as pallbearers. Unlike the rituals that distinguish the violently canned man Eck Snopes, as his coffin is featured in a bodiless funeral constructed within the fraternal signs and rituals of the Masons, Eula's actual funeral does not present a coffin; rather, it reveals the rawness of the gouged earth, covered by the floral attempts at euphemistic eulogy. "[T]he graveyard and the new lot" are thought by Chick to look "empty except for the one raw excavation and even that not long, hidden quickly, rapidly beneath the massed flowers, themselves already doomed in the emblem-shapes—wreaths and harps and urns—of the mortality which they de-stingered, euphemised" (*The Town* 344). When Eula's stone is finally erected, "the marble—whiter than white itself in the warm October sun against the bright yellow and red and dark red hickories and sumacs and gums and oaks like splashes of fire itself among the dark green cedars" (*The Town* 354), the autumnal specificity recalls the rainy burial of the other woman from Beat Four whose funeral has marked the ending of another age. Granny Millard is the community mother and Eula is the singular Lilith who antedates Eve herself as the primal mother before she is divided from her sexual radiance. While one stands for survival of each hill man according to his needs and the deserts of his work and the other threatens men with death, both die as relatively small, larger than life, women. And both Granny Millard and Eula (who has birthed Linda) die as mothers and as precursors to an idealized communism.

This "whiter than white" sculpture, overseen by Gavin and paid for by Flem, does not initially look like this woman who has been seen as a goddess or even as the creatrix that comes before even Eve: the legendary forces of first life located in "Semiramus" and "Lilith." Eula from her early girlhood is seen as uncanny and somehow uncannable. "[L]oose girdled," she is ungirdled, and stay-defying. To the untutored and chastely adolescent eyes of Chick near the opening of *The Town*, Eula's ("Mrs Snopes['s]") clothes have the potential to reveal her nakedness at any time as she crosses the Jefferson square, an awareness that recalls the violence of Eula's brother Jody Varner's grabbing at the eleven-year-old nymphet[11] to try to enforce the undergirding of garments engineered to restrain the excess of this man-conquering girl. Faulkner's cultural critic, who understands art in Frenchman's Bend and appreciates nonrepresentational—abstract—sculpture in Greenwich Village, has come to know Eula intimately. V. K. Ratliff recognizes the accomplishment of this funerary sculpture. In his summary of this object's power as a work of art, Ratliff describes the translated power of Eula. Part of the power of this woman lies in the fact that Eula's daughter Linda refuses to look at this memorial while all the men that have ever seen the living woman (monument or no monument) are unable to forget her. As Ratliff recounts, Eula's daughter Linda

> not once not never once ever look[ed] at that stone monument with that marble medallion face that Lawyer had picked out and selected that never looked like Eula a-tall you thought at first, never looked like nobody nowhere you thought at first, until you were wrong because it never looked like all women because what it looked like was one woman that ever man that was lucky enough to have been a man would say. "Yes, that's her. I knowed her five years ago or ten years ago or fifty years ago and you would a thought that by now I would a earned the right not to have remembered her any more." (*The Town* 355)

Eula's monument takes a female head in the form of a marble medallion and places it atop a column, critiquing and reifying the ideal of the southern white woman who is placed on a pedestal. This is finally just one of the monuments that Flem erects celebrating devourment, dismemberment, and death. As Linda sits beside Flem, she is not only "still and straight as a post . . . not looking at nothing," but Eula's daughter is distinguished by the power and rage shown in her hands of manhood: "them two white balls of her fists on her lap." In obscene pairing rather than paradox, Eula (with her name that is short for Eulalia) has been memorialized atop her own post by men who lack her own daughter's "white balls." Finally, it is not just Flem's words carved in stone but the monument itself that flies in the visage of what must be commemorated as a class-belabored fiction of white female chastity based on an always already fallen South. Flem has chosen a column to memorialize "[a] Virtuous Wife" and leaves open whether he will be "[c]rown[ed]" or horned in the annals of posterity.

Reprising the conclusion to Chopin's *The Awakening*, an archetypal ending that considers the limited possibilities available for acceptable female identity, Eula kills herself as a mother rather than besmirching her child's life by making Linda the daughter of an exiled whore. Eula, dead and made into a monument, is put on top of a pedestal. Flem's monument in *The Town* begins with a water tank filled with dismembered and water-buried brass, and closes with a series of columns. Unrestrained by the taste of Sutpen's captured French architect, the Flem of his *Mansion* will inhabit a post–*Gone with the Wind* Tara theme park framed by popular fictions of the plantation romance. In a withering parenthetical, Faulkner's astute cultural critic Ratliff categorizes the genre of Flem's "new house": "(it was going to have colyums across the front now, I mean the extry big ones so even a feller that never seen colyums before wouldn't have no doubt a-tall what they was, like in the photographs where the Confedrit sweetheart in a hoop skirt and a magnolia is saying good-bye to her Confedrit beau jest before he rides off tending to General Grant)" (*The Town* 352). In the final volume of the trilogy, respectable houses of the historic elite (Flem's wife's lover's ancestral home), as well as those such as Mellisandre Backus's perfectly respectable family farmhouse that has been remodeled into the stage set for a New England horse farm, are devoured and repackaged to frame a taste-driven and tastelessly fake aristocracy.

The Sound and the Fury: Seeing Patterns

> The idea is amusing because they are moulds. And moulds to what? Gas. That is, gas is introduced into the moulds where it takes the shape of the soldier, the department-store delivery boy, the curraisier, the policeman, the priest, the station master, etc., which are inscribed on my drawing. Each is built on a common horizontal plane, where lines intersect at the point of their sex. All that helped me realize the glass entitled "Nine Malic Moulds" . . . The mould side was invisible. I always avoided doing something tangible, but with a mould it doesn't matter, because it's the inside I didn't want to show.
>
> —Marcel Duchamp describing "Nine Malic Moulds," his art piece between "Cemetery of Liveries and Uniforms" and the "Bachelors" of *The Bride Stripped Bare by Her Bachelors, Even* (see *Boîte-en-valise*, fig. 33)[12]

It is ultimately telling that the Jason Compson of "April Sixth, 1928" is Faulkner's first point man on whores and hoarding. After he explains his philosophy about gifts in exchange for favors, sexual or not, in relation to his prostitute friend Lorraine, Jason offers a brief disquisition on the value of

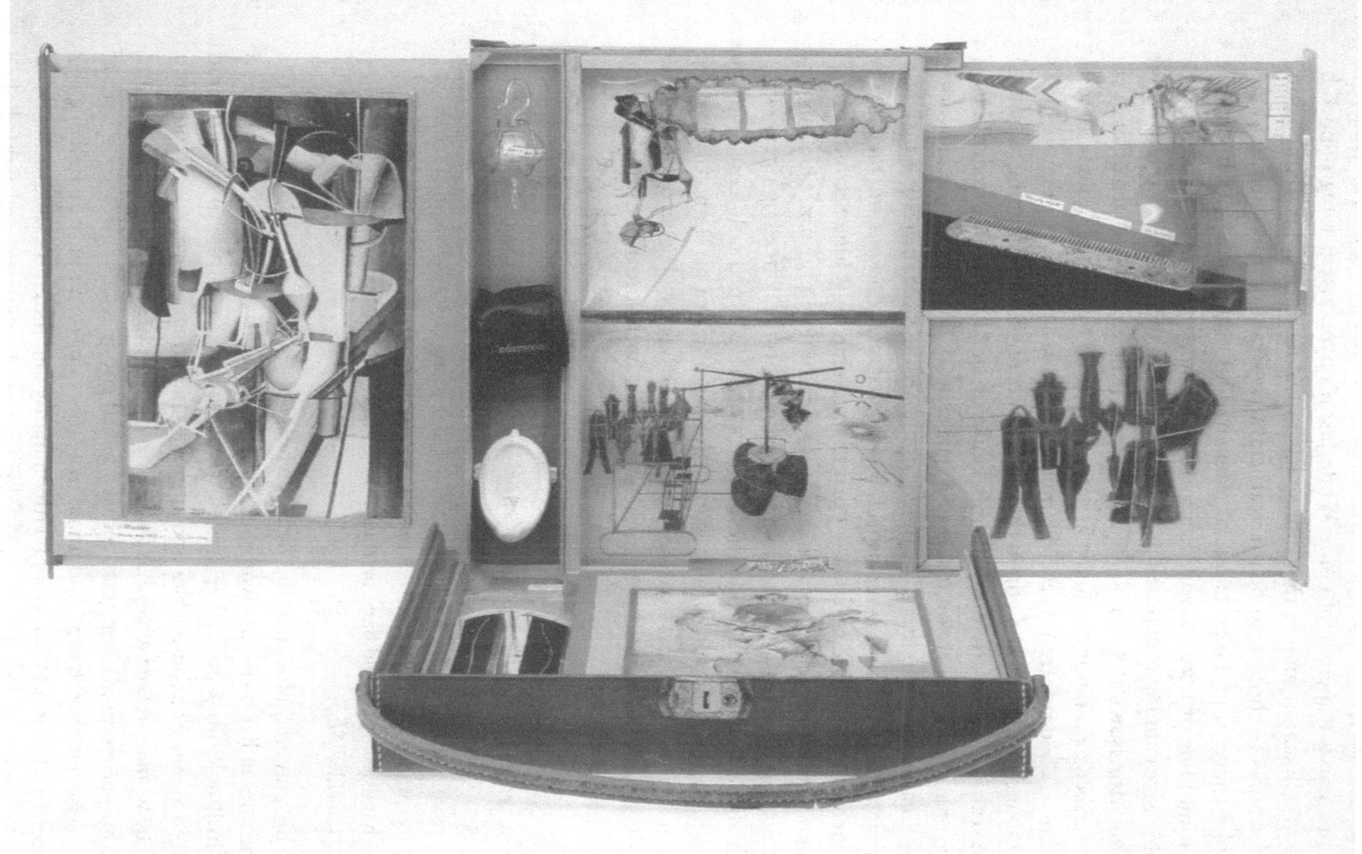

Figure 33. Marcel Duchamp, *Boîte-en-valise / Box in a Suitcase*, 1935–41. © 2013 Artists Rights Society (ARS), New York / ADAGP, Paris / Succession Marcel Duchamp.

money that critiques a storeowner for hoarding. This unnamed hoarder lives over his store, where he cooks for himself and makes his living by selling inferior goods to people of color. While Jason's hypocrisy is foregrounded by his intelligent argument that money has no value in itself, his juxtaposition of whores to those who hoard is crucial to a strain of Faulknerian philosophy concerning the exchange of women. This argument critiquing female withholding of sexual favors as a form of hermetic purity practiced through obsessive canning is exposed as integral to Hannah Peace's life and death in Toni Morrison's 1973 novel, *Sula*. Just after "[t]he greedy" women of 1923 are described as canning "as many as forty-two [jars] a day even though some of them . . . had jars from 1920," Hannah, who gives away sex to other women's husbands while standing up in the pantry, is canned while canning—"seared to sealing" as she attempts to can a cauldron of "Kentucky Wonder" beans (75–76). While Morrison just over a half-century later brings the idea home by creating her own literally canned, nonhoarding woman, Jason's insight is itself anticipated and, in retrospect, interpreted in *The Sound and the Fury* by Quentin's rare spate of collage portraits presented in "June Second, 1910." Significantly conceived in a bakery located in outlying Boston, Quentin pictures and opposes a canned, hoarding woman to the coffee-cup openness of the little Italian girl. While these figures of stereotyped ethnicities may be revealed in Quentin's nativist summation of America as "Land of the kike home of the wop," the hoarding woman in the bakery (Jewish or not) is presented with the metallic containment and cold enclosure of a canned woman as she is seen

> [a]bove the counter where the ranks of crisp shapes behind the glass her neat gray face her hair tight and sparse from her neat gray skull, spectacles in neat gray rims riding approaching like something on a wire, like a cash box in a store. She looked like a librarian. Something among dusty shelves in ordered certitudes long divorced from reality . . . Watching the bread, the neat gray hands, a broad gold band on the left forefinger, knuckled there by a blue knuckle. (*SF* 79)

This gray and blue metallic figure, who is likened to a "cash box" and ties pennies in her own skirt while accusing the little girl of having "pockets" and "hid[ing] things under her dress," stands in direct contrast to the girl-child seen as made of comestibles and animal—including maternal—components. The woman in the bakery has belled the door, set her metal-rimmed eyes, and continues to police her glass-encased baked goods.

Associated with food and found in a store, a bakery, this little Italian girl is seen by Quentin as associated with animality and the edible. Like other desirable females in Faulkner's work, this unnamed coffee-skinned girl is linked to a container that ties her to a yet to be determined nothing that is itself identified as "emptiness": "Her face was like a cup of milk dashed with coffee in the sweet warm emptiness" (79). Depicted as having white and maternal characteristics through the milk, the silent girl is diluted (and substantially warmed) by the dash of caffeinated color that echoes the earth on her face. Her attractions are evident in Quentin's description of her as "a little dirty child with eyes like a toy bear's and two patent-leather pigtails." Increasingly edible, "the little girl" is seen to "watch . . . with still unwinking eyes like two currants floating motionless in a cup of weak coffee" (79).

In an exchange that is racialized in Faulkner's post–World War II works such as *Intruder in the Dust* and the final volume of the trilogy, this ethnic communion between the hoarding woman and the hungry girl is framed by consumption in his modernist breakthrough of 1929. After Quentin has bought a roll for the girl and before he takes her to get ice cream at that Faulknerian den of iniquity, the common drugstore, the hoarding woman returns with "a funny looking thing in her hand," which she "carried . . . sort of like it might have been a pet dead rat . . . Here . . . It just looks peculiar. I calculate you wont know the difference when you eat it" (81). This cake is the pastry of assimilation. Her brother Julio's fear that his hungry and errant sister will be stolen prophesies her fate as a female to become a consuming and consumed American.

Dilsey Seeing, Seeing Dilsey

> I've seed de first en de last[;] . . . I seed de beginnin, en now I sees de endin.
> —Dilsey riffs on Revelation 22:13 in Faulkner's *The Sound and the Fury*

At the beginning of the end of Faulkner's "most splendid failure," his most radical experiment to date in 1929, Dilsey moving into action is the fabled red hen. On this Easter morning she rises, she gets the wood, she makes the fire to bake the bread, the biscuit that is prepared for those who do not help. Regal and only the filler of a "red rubber" vessel (likened to a "dead red hen") to heat a cold and "blobby" white woman, Dilsey has already opened the doorway of her cabin to initiate "April Eighth, 1928," the fourth and final section of *The Sound and the Fury*. Introduced as the moisture needles "laterally into her flesh, precipitating . . . a substance partaking of the quality of thin, not quite congealed oil," Dilsey

> wore a stiff black straw hat perched upon her turban, and a maroon velvet cape with a border of mangy and anonymous fur above a dress of purple silk, and she stood in the door for a while with her myriad and sunken face lifted to the weather, and one gaunt hand flac-soled as the belly of a fish, then she moved the cape aside and examined the bosom of her gown.
>
> The gown fell gauntly from her shoulders, across her fallen breasts, then tightened upon her paunch and fell again, ballooning a little above the nether

> garments which she would remove layer by layer as the spring accomplished and the warm days, in color regal and moribund. She had been a big woman once but now her skeleton rose, draped loosely in unpadded skin that tightened again upon a paunch almost dropsical, as though muscle and tissue had been courage or fortitude which the days or the years had consumed until only the indomitable skeleton was left rising like a ruin or a landmark above the somnolent and impervious guts, and above that the collapsed face that gave the impression of the bones themselves being outside the flesh, lifted into the driving day with an expression at once fatalistic and of a child's astonished disappointment, until she turned and entered the house again and closed the door. (165)

Articulated through layer after layer of garments and flesh, nether and otherwise, in which types of skin and external covering compete with the structural indomitability of her very bones, Dilsey stands as the structural figure of the always falling who never falls. She is a monument ("rising like a ruin or a landmark") to indomitability itself, finally driven from the Compson house by no longer having anyone to protect from Jason. In this accreting portrait, her internal being, her eternal presence, has become the external, and she becomes the rare example of an embodied figure whose dynamic form stands for the synthesis of inner and outer, content and structure, theory and theme, that allows Dilsey to stand as a figure for Faulkner's narrative art. Like Reverend Shegog, Dilsey is pictured as having been "consumed," but even in her multiple falls of "dropsical" flesh she stands as a monument to what neither sound nor fury can weather away. Dilsey framed in her cabin's doorway is the most stately and powerful of Faulkner's collage portraits. Shortly thereafter, she emerges again, not dressed for Easter, but readied in a man's hat and the rough clothes that precede her later transformation seen in the church scene as the iconic mother in the tableau vivant of the *Pietà* as she holds the sacrificial son—not dead but forever without speech. Acknowledged for her penetrating eyes (she sees beyond walls in *The Sound and the Fury*), Dilsey's face remains a type of mask: her eyes become the part of her face that like those of the gorgon are not to be looked upon or seen. Magnificently portrayed, the Dilsey of Faulkner's final account uses her last breath to invite the librarian and the reader to look into her eyes, eyes that, like those of her deified and eroticized white counterpart, Eula, are never seen. It is finally no accident that the last words Dilsey is heard to speak in Faulkner's narrative are addressed to the librarian in the "Appendix Compson: 1699–1945" published in 1946. Here, this monumental and falling (but not fallen) woman refuses to look at a glossy magazine picture of Caddy: "the woman's face hatless between a rich scarf and a seal coat, ageless and beautiful, cold serene and damned" (209). Dilsey, identified as "the old Negress," challenges the hysterical librarian Melissa Meek: "Look at my eyes . . . How can I see that picture?" before concluding, "My eyes aint any good anymore . . . I cant see it" (211).

The Art of Not Seeing Quentin

> But I was not there. I was not there to see . . .
> —Miss Rosa, Faulkner's *Absalom, Absalom!* (22)

While Horace Benbow appears in Faulkner's novels narrated from the third-person omniscient point of view, omniscience itself is limited, subtly and almost invisibly shaded and shaped. Indeed, when Horace, Quentin, Father Compson, Shreve, Temple, Chick, Gavin, or Ratliff is present as a center of consciousness, characters emerge visually in much greater clarity. As James G. Watson has observed, "Quentin's pictorial imagination is as acute as his creator's, often tormentingly so."[13] Quentin Compson, the most visually driven of Faulkner's characters, makes paintings of people and scenes, even those that he has never actually seen: he is moved to transform what he hears into detailed demons whose very beards "reek" of "sulphur" (*AA!* 4). As Horace sees Popeye rather than himself in the fractal light that shatters the spring, this scene that opens *Sanctuary* is a revision of what Quentin does not see: his fantasy that his face ("my face") is to be superimposed with "his face" (Shreve's face) in the windows of passing trolleys: "*then my face his face for an instant from the crashing when out of darkness two lighted windows in rigid fleeing crash gone his face and mine just I see saw did I see*" (*SF* 172). Even Quentin's fantasy here of reflective intimacy in which Shreve goes toward life (or at least Harvard), and Quentin is already on the tracks to the bridge and his planned death, is interrupted by his past act of seeing in which the briefly opposing, passing window has been occupied by the reflection of an unknown woman whose hat has a "broken feather" (*SF* 169, 172). Earlier, as Quentin looks to try to see his hurt eye, he does not see his reflection in the bucket of water. Instead, Quentin sees blood from a rag and the yellow wobbly thing that he has earlier envisioned as the "pale rubber" "[y]ellow," "[l]iquid putrifaction" of the "periodical filth" of menstruating and foul femaleness. These moments of seeing have been read and reread as related, but they are finally more important than merely connected scenes of disintegrating clots alluding to menstrual materiality, more significant than primal ingredients that are part of a larger collage portrait which accretes to form a critique of modernity in the rotten rubberiness of female flesh.

Here, Quentin looks for his reflection in the bucket, but he does not see himself. Glimpsed briefly early in chapter 8 of *Absalom, Absalom!*, Quentin sits "hunched in his chair, his hands thrust into his pockets as if he were trying to hug himself warm between his arms, looking somehow fragile and even wan" (235–36). Quentin persists in being the ghost that *Absalom, Absalom!* presents him as in the opening chapter of the novel. Shreve, who speaks aloud to equate "the hats and pants and shoes" to the "rubbish and refuse" "which you drag through the world," reprises this shrouded vision of his roommate:

"He just sat as before, his hands in his trousers pockets, his shoulders hugged inward and hunched, his face lowered and he looking somehow curiously smaller than he actually was because of his actual height and spareness—that quality of delicacy about the bones, articulation, which even at twenty still had something about it, some last echo about it, of adolescence" (259). These portraits of the "hunched" figure's "hands," "arms," "shoulders," "face lowered," with a "delicacy about the bones," making him "smaller than he . . . was," portray a Quentin who is a "last echo" in more ways than one. Unlike Shreve (his "more or less than twin"), who is repeatedly pictured by Quentin in eroticized portraits focusing on the rubicund vitality of his bare chest and his moonlike spectacles, Quentin remains a list of body parts hidden and hunched, "face lowered," in the shadows. Structurally most visible in the "delicacy about the bones," Quentin exists in his fullness of voice and his layers of interiority, but this paradoxical caster of shadows is visually absent: he is never given a collage portrait in *The Sound and the Fury* or *Absalom, Absalom!* Even though his eye is bleeding and broken toward the end of his final day of life in "June Second 1910" and he is there to be seen, his reflection has been displaced by a drowned and disintegrating female shape: the yellowness of a reflected light or the early moon. Quentin is not seen by himself or even by others except in shadowy and "hunched" vagueness. Echoing Cathy shouting from the wuthering heights, "I am Heathcliff," Faulkner once intimated, "I am Quentin." Faulkner's most deeply reflective character does not see his reflection even as his blood stains the water of the bucket, nor is he ever made visible to us by those who look at him. The Quentin Compson of *The Sound and the Fury* and *Absalom, Absalom!* is not seen. Ultimately, Quentin Compson cannot be seen because he is the eye of art in Faulkner's fiction.

Recognition of a pattern in Faulkner's fiction, seeing William Faulkner's art, is to find the place where obsession meets intentionality or where either obsession or intentionality trumps or even orchestrates transcendence.[14] To argue that description, in particular portraits of characters, has been consciously drawn and that, on telling occasions, details have been withheld by Faulkner is no mystery. Faulkner's acute awareness as a reader is evidenced in his spoken praise for Tolstoy's restraint. As Faulkner was aware, the character of Anna Karenina is pictured only as "beautiful and [as a woman who could] see in the dark like a cat," further qualifying his observation by concluding that "every man has a different idea of what is beautiful. And it is best to take the gesture, the shadow of the branch and let the mind create the tree."[15] *The Signifying Eye* is finally not a book about eyes, but rather a work that looks closely to see larger patterns in the cruel radiance and the definitive closeness of detail. Finding patterns is not to say that other patterns do not exist. These patterns with their visual and aural play, grotesque joinings of boxed human meat as well as other efforts at canning and preservation, whether in bell jars or art, are literary accretions, layerings of humor turned humus: what anthropologists call "thick description." These layers can be seen through a glass darkly while the eye behind it all refuses the translucence. The mystery of art, more than the sum of its patterns and parts, remains.[16] Faulkner's eye, like David Davidovich Burliuk's *Eye of God*,[17] signifies and radiates, but as with the eye of God and human fictions of omniscience, so much remains to be seen.

APPENDIX 1

Willem de Kooning's Parables of Art

Untitled ("Still Life with Matches"), *Weil Plaza*, and *Woman, Sag Harbor*

If the picture has a countenance I keep it. If it hasn't, I throw it away.
—Willem de Kooning[1]

In his 1942 *Untitled* ("Still Life with Matches") (see fig. 28, page 248), a painting seen as a matchbook, a safety pin, a circle on a rectangular canvas—trash wadded in an artist's studio—de Kooning reveals his fascination with parables of art realized through the generative act of visual epiphanies. Here, de Kooning uses a collation of things simultaneously to construct and to conceal a parable of art based on two copulating bodies. The balloon head of the male figure may refer to an airhead or even an egghead, but this form insists on the presence of a face: there is another egg-shaped head with the diminutive features of a face that occupies the position at which a more fully furnished head might project an ear. These bodies join to create rather than procreate, and the recognizable drawing of a canvas appears to be held (if not to spring) from between the legs of the figure whose face is masked. Her morphological identity is marked by the shadow of a crease that indicates a rising breast, which remains hidden behind the blank canvas that is not in fact blank; rather, it signifies blankness in an empty "o," a circle or a zero. It does not take Freud or even Freud's Dora to diagnose that the foot flicking the flame into life, causing the match to cast a smudgelike shadow on the figures below, suggests the friction and heat of a masturbatory act. The superimposed, surreally large safety pin with its ducklike head asserts the blackness and depth of no canvas beneath, while at the same time the turn at the bottom of the pin encircles the wooden rod, making it into the penis that forms a foundation which supports the couple's joining. *Untitled* ("Still Life with Matches") depicts the old parable linking creation to procreation, appearing to generate a nearly blank picture—the canvas at the center—that depicts a signifying nothing.

But there is another picture here, a sense of motion in a visual metamorphosis that calls on the eye of the beholder to see a big picture: the viewer shifting perspective can see the features of a grotesque face that forms a collage portrait occupying most of the space of the drawing. The rectangle of the canvas is not the one inscribed within; rather, it is demarcated by the outer edges of de Kooning's painting as a whole. With the epiphanic rush of viewing a field/space drawing, the matchbook is seen to open into one sutured and fluttering eye, with the matches as lashes as this aperture's lid opens into the space of nothingness beneath. The head of the safety pin locates the other eye, the circle (once a drawing on a canvas) provides the roundness of a clown's nose, and the crooked mouth (with its ominous slit of a down-turning scar, the mark that in the other perspective suggested the crease of the hidden breast) completes the carnivalesque and leering face of a representational art that ghoulishly mocks abstraction. These narratives of a drawing that is either all frightening face placed atop bones or an oddly headed and an oddly headless body, bodies joining to make the squarish rectangle of an artist's canvas bearing only the drawing of a single cipher that signifies either nothing or a nose, insist on the persistence of the emergent human form.

Proclaiming that "even abstract shapes must have a likeness" and referring to what he called the "countenance" of a painting, de Kooning argued with Clement Greenberg, Abstract Expressionism's most rigid formalist. After Greenberg announced, "In today's world, it is impossible to paint a face," de Kooning replied, "Yes. That's right. And it is impossible not to."[2] *Untitled* ("Still Life with Matches") makes de Kooning's point through a drawing that demonstrates that even bodies (or particularly bodies) will make a face. De Kooning's interest in metamorphoses in which faces map onto bodies and bodies map onto faces to become parables of art and generation resurfaced over twenty years later in a lesser-known work from the 1960s. *Weil Plaza* (1964; see plate 6), easily classified as one of the artist's fertility goddess figures, has a power that is expressed through the intensity of broad pink strokes that are less detailed and less fierce than his woman paintings of the 1950s. This iconic woman with her hourglass contours is rendered strange by a band of patterned Africanist cloth in a print that includes a face in the form of a stylized mask that completes the formal and evocative requisites of a body by providing this woman with a tiny, ritualized head. The key that more is going on, waiting to meet the eye, lies in the provocative shape of her vaginal lips that encompass a tiny penis with a specified head. This organ, pictured as pendant from but not part of this body, calls attention to the fact that a generative shift in visual focus is there in field/space potential waiting to reveal itself to the viewer. In this epiphanic revelation (precipitating a complete metamorphosis), the curves of the waist mark the indentation at the eye (between the brow and the fullness of this female figure's facial cheeks) to reveal a countenance. As the Africanist cloth becomes a stylish turban, the tiny penis as clue has become an anatomically correct cigarette that is positioned burning end outward, framed hanging from the lips of the highly sensual mouth of this face. For those familiar with de Kooning's celebrity portraits—*Marilyn Monroe, Reclining Man* (John F. Kennedy), and the more abstract *Minnie Mouse*—this mouth (cum vagina) is immediately recognizable as the lush and loosely curling come-hither lips of this artist's most evocative portrayal of female personation: these are the lips of his *Mae West* (1964).

The metamorphic play of *Weil Plaza* with its puzzling title finally has a great deal to say about the wicked humor of a narratively bent de Kooning. In the summer of 1948, if not before, de Kooning met the painter Susan Weil, who had come to Black Mountain College with Robert Rauschenberg, the man who would briefly be her husband. While both Weil and Rauschenberg studied with the color-obsessed Josep Alpers, Rauschenberg by 1953 had begun to work on what might be called "conscious absence," erasing his own work to produce a textured bareness. Armed with a bottle of Jack Daniel's (by his own account), Rauschenberg went to visit de Kooning at his New York studio to acquire what his failed project needed in 1953: a real work of art to be erased. Even as de Kooning claimed to understand what the younger artist was doing, the experience was emotionally complex and ultimately provoked a long-held resentment in the mature artist. De Kooning searched to find a really good multimedia (pencil, charcoal, ink, and paint) drawing that took the aspiring Rauschenberg close to a month to erase. The result formally entitled "Erased de Kooning Drawing" remains one of Rauschenberg's most famous and controversial works. The fact that this work is referred to familiarly as "Erased de Kooning" says a great deal about anxiety of influence as it meets a conscious artist's expectations: anxiety of annihilation. Rauschenberg erased "de Kooning" in 1953, the year of his divorce from Susan Weil and the time in which his sexual preference was becoming well known through his high-profile relationships with Cy Twombly and later with Jasper Johns. Just over a decade later, de Kooning, who enjoyed the puns native to his accent that caused him to pronounce his *w*'s as *v*'s (he delighted in the fact that the word "word" pronounced from his mouth sounded as "void"), depicted a diminutive masculine organ that could not fill the female space of *Weil Plaza* or, in his pronunciation, the "vile" plaza or "vile" place. This small painting that is close to the size of Rauschenberg's "Erased de Kooning" sounds like an inside joke. Painted in the first-person penis[3] of a less than hung Rauschenberg (not a physiological fact, but rather a synecdoche that vengefully pictures the man who has tried to erase him as less than potent through visual metonymy), this painting's title insisting on point of view critiques a Rauschenberg who rejects the lush pinkness of his former wife, Susan Weil, as a "vile" place.

BIRTHING ART: *WOMAN, SAG HARBOR*

As he was developing his catalog of visual symbols, de Kooning was trying to shape his own parable of art that used fire, the element that destroys as it creates, to illuminate, to illustrate, to expose his vision of the role of the female body in the creation—and in what might well be called the procreation—of art. While the paintings above reveal de Kooning's fascination with the body/face narrative of hidden metamorphoses (in paintings such as *Asheville*, he painted a collage portrait of a head busy with thought-provoked collations of things), *Woman, Sag Harbor* (1964) is interesting for its portrayal of art originating as pieces and parts leaking from the creative crevice of an older female. *Woman, Sag Harbor* with her estrogenous flesh, full and fallen, takes this geographic place name and embodies it as a procreative flow. This evocative figure, painted in the same year as *Weil Plaza* (and *Mae West*), distinguished by her sagging cheeks of liplike breasts and paunched thighs, is a fleshy pink violently marked by red, a gulled and gullied harboring of genitalia. *Woman, Sag Harbor* articulates the sagging harbors of an inclusive welcome, but her slightly open legs stand in the possibility of dissolution: she may be a painting of a reflection or a painting in water. What is telling about *Woman, Sag Harbor* may not be its name but rather the detailed narrative that extrudes downward in a Klimt-like column of excrescence from between her legs. This flow, which has ended (begun) with the diminutive image of a fully dressed woman in a shift amid varied pink fragments of afterbirth that stream from between this large woman's wavering legs, features the birthing (at the top of the stream) of a drawn figure, lines that suggest the profile—the dome and nose—of a man's head. This head, like the more fully developed collage portrait of Percy Grimm in de Kooning's *Light in August* (see plate 1), is reminiscent of the symbol-filled perspective from above that looks down on the male head which occupies the lower-left side of Gorky's *Betrothal Series* (see plate 3). (In the *Betrothal Series*, this outline of a male head might be thought of as a groom figure who is potentially the source of the suggestively drawn objects cum thoughts—some organically floral and others crafted things—that fill the remaining space in these closely related Gorky paintings.) In de Kooning's gendered parable of art, *Woman, Sag Harbor* in her own liquidity disgorges the detritus of life. Extending the conceit recognizable in *Untitled* ("Still Life with Matches") (a work painted over twenty years earlier), this painting calls attention to the fact that this is not just an outline of a male head: this black extrusion is an explicit drawing of a drawing. This woman, who may have finally birthed and separated from a soigné and prim earlier self, modeled in her conservative and curve-concealing shift-dress, has in her earlier extrusion given birth to a piece of art in the form of a drawing of a male head. This head, a simple domed line and nose, recalls the birth-eye perspective that de Kooning used to portray his collaged portrait of his thinking man, his Gorky-inspired *Asheville* (see plate 2).

APPENDIX 2

Willem de Kooning, *Light in August*, 1946

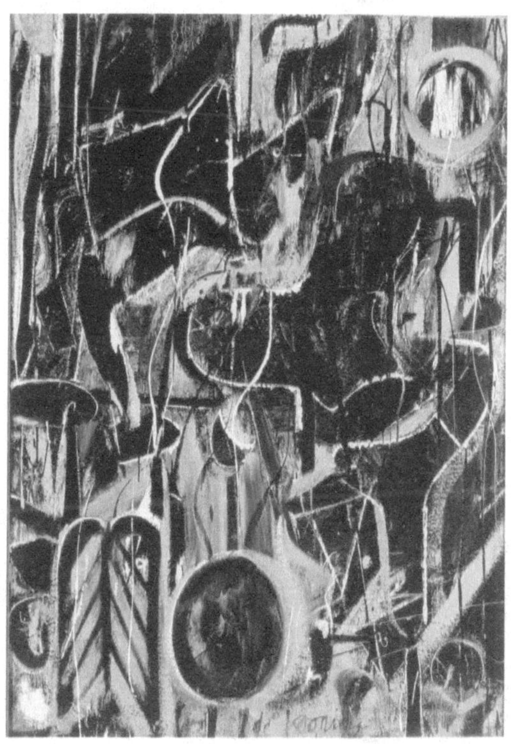

Figure 34. This low-resolution photograph is a more complete copy of the painting—including the artist's signature—than the high-resolution photograph reproduced in plate 1.

APPENDIX 3

Willem de Kooning, *Black Untitled,* 1948

Figure 36. For a larger version of this image, see fig. 27 (pp. 242–43). Oil and enamel on paper, mounted on wood, 29⅞ × 40¼ in. (75.9 × 102.2 cm). Courtesy of the Metropolitan Museum, New York. From the Collection of Thomas B. Hess. Gift of the heirs of Thomas B. Hess.

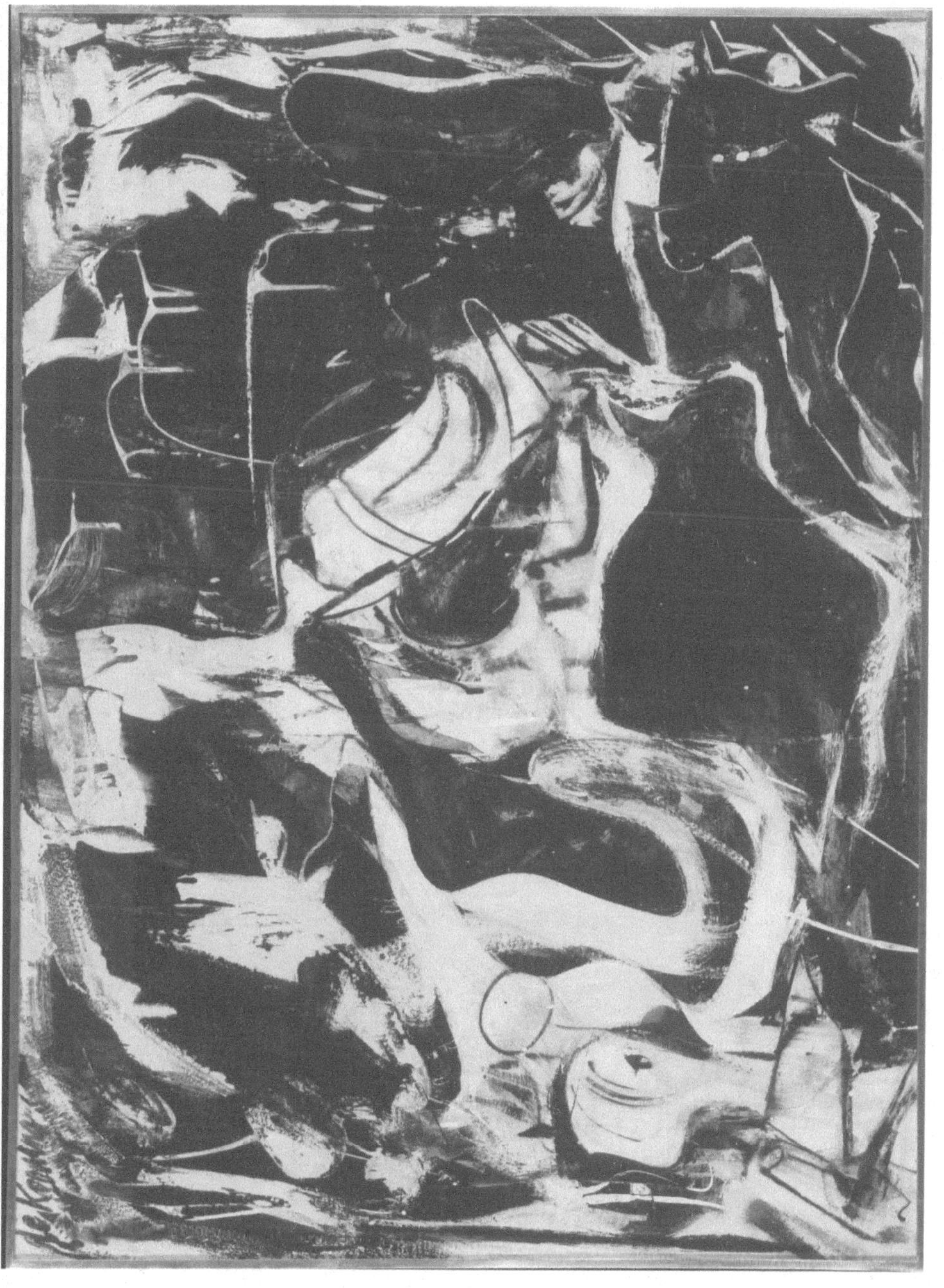

Notes

INTRODUCTION. *THE MARIONETTES*

1. Judith Sensibar, "Faulkner's Real and Imaginary Photos of Desire," *Faulkner and Popular Culture: Faulkner & Yoknapatawpha, 1988* (Jackson: University Press of Mississippi, 1990), 117. This article is the best exploration of Faulkner's creation of the visually conceived portrait or image as a particular container for emotional content.

2. William Faulkner, *The Sound and the Fury*, ed. David Minter, 2nd ed. (New York: Norton, 1994).

3. Of the four extant copies, the original is housed in the Faulkner Collection at the University of Virginia. This edition with its variant illustrations is dedicated to Ben Wasson. Of the three other nearly identical copies, two are located in the Ransom Collection at the University of Texas, and the other is housed in the special collections at the University of Mississippi. *The Marionettes* became available to the reading public in an edition edited by Noel Polk in 1977, for which Polk also wrote an introduction (Charlottesville: University Press of Virginia). My reading was made possible by Polk's decision to publish the variant images in the appendix to that edition. What distinguishes Polk's work, aside from making the text available to the public, are his "Textual Appendixes" (91–105), which compare Faulkner's work as it should be compared, on the level of the comma, noting major textual shifts as well as variations in spelling. Through this Herculean act, Polk shows the differences between and among all four of the copies, proving that the UVA text is the original. That version is marked as the original because of the distinctive differences in its drawings, but also because the lines of script are less planned, less justified and anticipated than those in the other three versions. As Polk notes in what remains the most comprehensive reading of the play, scholars have been unable to identify a sequence of composition for the other (almost identical) copies of the play. While some scholars have suggested that practicality influenced Faulkner's decision to simplify the drawings—noting Wasson's idea of using the proceeds from sales for the purchase of whiskey—I believe this a misreading of Faulkner and his relationship to art. As Daniel Pecchenino points out, Faulkner was able to produce on demand as long as the piper was paid; he succeeded in working in Hollywood as part of groups making successful films for popular audiences. In an

enterprise as personal as these hand-lettered and drawn books, his reason for simplifying lines is aesthetic. Faulkner's joking elements, which were removed from the elegant illustrations, like most jokes reveal a cultural edge, and in this case, his elisions reveal that these pictorial illustrations were conscious. Even though the hidden pictures—the woman-sized phallus as well as the severed breast in the second hidden palimpsest were not removed, they are tellingly marked by the specificity of the allusions to their content in the text itself. Hence, these images were conceived and left in as a conscious act on Faulkner's part.

4. Some fifteen years later, a female "wing-walker" recalls the dominatrix elements of the strapping costume worn by Marietta in "The Apotheosis." Laverne Schumann as she hurtles bare-bottomed toward the spectators below is "not merely naked but clothed in the very traditional symbology—the ruined dress with which she was trying wildly to cover her loins, and the parachute harness—of female bondage." William Faulkner, *Pylon* (New York: Random House, 1935, 1962), 196–97.

5. Here, there is a comic visage that mocks the primal fear most deeply associated with the exposure of the female genitals. This identified trauma—the response Ernst Gombrich classified as the "apotropaic"—is associated with the visual terror W. J. T. Mitchell identified as characteristic of "multistable images of face, genitalia, and dangerous animals, all summed up in the snaky locks of Medusa." For more on this, see W. J. T. Mitchell's *Picture Theory: Essays on Verbal and Visual Representation* (Chicago: University of Chicago Press, 1995).

6. For a developed reading, see Randall Wilhelm's "Faulkner's Big Picture Book: Word and Image in *The Marionettes*," *The Faulkner Journal* 19, no. 2 (Spring 2004). Wilhelm's articles answer Thomas McHaney's call for more work to be done on Faulkner's early picture books. What is striking about Wilhelm's work is his visual literacy and his ability to analyze Faulkner's image from an art historical perspective. The term "herm" refers to a boundary marker in ancient Greece. This vertical structure is not only unquestionably phallic, comprised of a squared post topped by a sculpted head, these stone structures are marked as if they are male bodies by carved phalluses with testicles. In many ways, the structure that Eula's grave marker most resembles in *The Town* is a classical herm. Obviously, Eula's stone does not have the phallus carved on, naming and echoing, the phallic structure of her columnar stone. Instead, her stone is marked by the impotence of words that Flem has chosen from the Bible. See the epilogue of this volume for a reading of Eula's daughter's body that serves to complete her mother's monument as a "herm."

7. For a reading that understands Pierrot's performance in "whiteface" and the racial role of the "Shade of Pierrot" pictured as a "little black man," see John N. Duvall's "'A Strange Nigger': Faulkner and the Minstrel Performance of Whiteness" in *The Faulkner Journal* 22, nos. 1/2 (Fall 2006): 106–21. For an analysis of race, the artist/outsider as black, and Pierrot as a figure in "whiteface," see Yamashita Naoto's "Drawing a Rough Sketch of Pierrot: The Transition of the Artist Figure in William Faulkner's Fiction," *The Faulkner Journal of Japan*, no. 5 (Sept. 2003).

8. This double-page spread that presents a blank page on the right side of the opened book to the reader before the images are displayed is read here as being seen through the blank front and the blank back of the two drawings folded together. John N. Duvall has noted that Faulkner's Pierrot framed by the moon in "Marietta

and the Statue" (fig. 5, page 10) is "perspectively a little black man" who anticipates this motif in Faulkner's fiction. See his "Faulkner's Black Sexualities," in *Faulkner's Sexualities: Faulkner and Yoknapatawpha, 2007*, ed. Annette Trefzer and Ann J. Abadie (Jackson: University Press of Mississippi, 2010), 134. Called the "tall clown" by Duvall and recognized as a phallic overstatement in the criticism in general, "Pierrot Standing" features an outsized drawing of Pierrot with his head coming out of the foreskin ruff of his clown's collar (see fig. 36, page 302). Positioned to be seen first through the translucence of a blank page as seen here through page 301, "Pierrot Standing" from this perspective emphasizes the blackness from the back as the poplar tree and the road form a vaginal "vee" (to use a Faulkner word) at the lower right side, a structure that threatens to scissor-in, forcepslike, to reclaim or claim this phallicized Pierrot.

9. For an influential and insightful analysis of Faulkner's earliest work, including his drawings for the University of Mississippi student newspaper and yearbook, see Lothar Hönnighausen's *William Faulkner: The Art of Stylization in His Early Graphic and Literary Work* (New York: Cambridge University Press, 1987).

10. For more on the role of the artistic women in Faulkner's life—notably the influence of his wife, Estelle Oldham, in her early stories and her vocation as a painter later in life—see Judith Sensibar's *Faulkner and Love: The Women Who Shaped His Art* (New Haven: Yale University Press, 2009).

11. Brigitte Peucker's conversations about the "sister arts" became integral to my ways of thinking about my own work at this project's inception. Her book that appeared later, *Incorporating Images: Film and the Rival Arts* (Princeton: Princeton University Press, 1994), even as it focuses on film, remains a model for interdisciplinary analysis between and among the arts.

12. *Mayday* was published in 1978 and features an introduction by Carvel Collins (Notre Dame: University of Notre Dame Press).

13. Faulkner's return visit to New Haven in 1921 deepened his ties to Yale (and to the nearby Italian-settled village of Fair Haven), providing the setting for the Harvard of *The Sound and the Fury*. While his name identifies him with the patron saint of the drowned, Faulkner demonstrates his early attention to the concept of syllabic destiny: Quentin would have taken the trolley that ran down the major thoroughfare of Quinnipiac Avenue to this ethnic and industrial settlement, jumping into the Quinnipiac rather than the Charles River at the close of his day in *The Sound and the Fury*.

14. See James W. Webb, "John Wesley Faulkner III," in *Southern Writers: A Biographical Dictionary*, ed. Robert Bain, Joseph M. Flora, and Louis D. Rubin, Jr. (Baton Rouge and London: Louisiana State University Press, 1979), 149–50.

15. Robert Penn Warren, "Introduction: Faulkner: Past and Future," in *Faulkner: A Collection of Critical Essays*, ed. Robert Penn Warren (Englewood Cliffs, N.J.: Prentice-Hall, 1966), 2.

16. See Arthur F. Kinney, *Faulkner's Narrative Poetics: Style as Vision* (Amherst: University of Massachusetts Press, 1978), for an important critical analysis that questions the distinction between "seeing" and "thinking" as these are practiced by Faulkner's characters. Kinney draws on the work of Rudolf Arnheim and his concept of "visual thinking" as bridging the artificial gap that has divided the "cognitive" from "perceptual" ways of knowing (17). Kinney drives this point home as he recognizes the connections between and among seeing, remembering, and believing to the more difficult

prospect of "knowing" in Faulkner's *Light in August*. "The subtle shift from image to concept" that emerges at the opening of the second chapter of *Light in August* is contrasted by Kinney to the "more radical segmentation of perceptions and conceptions" in *The Sound and the Fury* and *As I Lay Dying* (30).

17. Robert Cantwell, "The Faulkners: Recollections of a Gifted Family" (1938), in *Conversations with William Faulkner,* ed. M. Thomas Inge (Jackson: University Press of Mississippi, 1999), 35.

18. See Sundquist, "Death, Grief, Analogous Form: *As I Lay Dying,*" in *Philosophical Approaches to Literature: New Essays on Nineteenth- and Twentieth-Century Literary Texts*, ed. William E. Cain (Cranbury, N.J.: Associated University Presses, 1984), 288.

19. I was trained as a social and labor historian. The method of chapter 5 follows Richard Godden's definition of "slow reading," close reading that is aware of the link between formal constructions and political content in a literary text. Quentin suffers from an aesthetic compulsion, what Horace called *ut pictura poesis*, as pictures (initially visions of a "sulphur"-reeking demon who "abrupts upon a scene peaceful and decorous as a school prize water-color") interrupt the spoken word. Significantly, here the female poet's words disrupt Faulkner's suicidal artist figure's ability to listen, or hear, as Miss Rosa's words erupt into and are blocked by a series of compulsively present, visually driven hallucinations.

20. I should add for the record that art historians have persistently denied that there is any direct reference to what they dismissively call "props" referring directly to Faulkner's *Light in August* in de Kooning's painting of the same name. As recently as 2011–12, in MOMA's mounting of their major de Kooning retrospective, critics have chosen not just to see the circuit of patterns that rise to the level of meaningful narrative content; art historians have refused to see any reference besides the abstract equating of grounds that tends to flatten black and white into being a conceptualization of race. (When referring to Faulkner's fiction, art historians have gravitated toward Joe Christmas's killing of his adoptive father—an unsubstantiated claim made by Christmas himself that resides in a side plot. This archetypal, "Orestian" theme is an acceptable crisis of male creativity that is consecrated by Freud and Harold Bloom.) See Clement Greenberg for the heightened critical stakes of such a denial. If abstract art is itself a pure medium, the crisis surrounding de Kooning's inclusion of the figure in his paintings becomes a violation that is tantamount to conservative views opposed to miscegenation. The problem with objects that are not random is that such these narrating things take painting into the defiling realm of literature.

CHAPTER ONE. ENVISIONING FAULKNER AND SOUTHERN LITERATURE

1. H. L. Mencken, "The Sahara of the Bozart," in *Prejudices* (1920), originally published as a newspaper article in 1917. According to Richard Wright, Mencken's *Prejudices* taught him the use of published words as weapons.

2. When Mencken published "The Sahara of the Bozart," Ellen Glasgow, considered to be the preeminent southern novelist, had written eight of her seventeen novels, which would culminate with her Pulitzer Prize–winning *In This Our Life* (1941).

3. Howard Odum, *Rainbow Round My Shoulder: The Blue Trail of the Black*

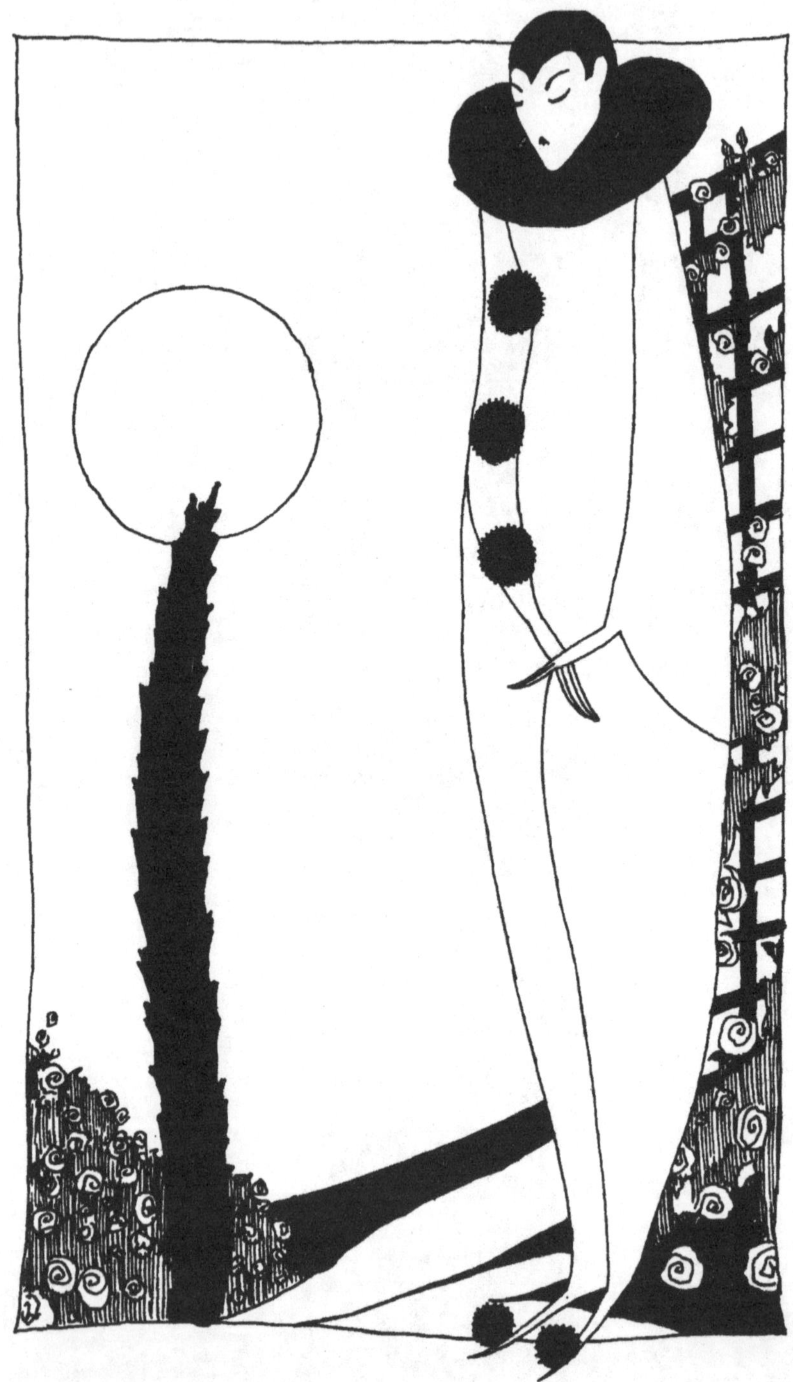

Figure 36. "Pierrot Standing," from William Faulkner, *The Marionettes: A Play in One Act*. Used by permission of W. W. Norton & Company, Inc. Original in Albert and Shirley Small Special Collections Library, University of Virginia.

Ulysses (New York: Bobbs-Merrill, 1928). This was the first of three volumes of folklore published by the University of North Carolina sociologist that were based on the exploits and tales of an actual black laborer whom Odum dubbed the "Black Ulysses."

4. See Margaret Jarman Hagood's *Mothers of the South: Portraiture of the White Tenant Farm Woman* (Chapel Hill: University of North Carolina Press, 1939) for a particularly good example of portraiture in the sociology of the South, pioneered by Howard C. Odum and his colleagues at *Social Forces.*

5. See Hurston's *Moses, Man of the Mountain* (New York: J. B. Lippincott, 1939).

6. In "The Uses of History in Fiction," an article based on a "panel discussion at the thirty-fourth annual meeting of the Southern Historical Association" moderated by C. Van Woodward that featured remarks by Ralph Ellison, William Styron, and Robert Penn Warren, Ellison says: "If you want to know something about the dynamics of the South, of interpersonal relationships in the South from, roughly, 1874 until today, you don't go to historians; not even to Negro historians. You go to William Faulkner and Robert Penn Warren" (64). The rest of the article can be found in *The Southern Literary Journal* 1, no 2 (Spring 1969).

7. Thomas McHaney speculates (in conversation) that Faulkner may have gotten in to see Gertrude Stein's collection, which the author left open in her absence on selected Sundays for viewing by those who had shown particular interest.

8. Mark Stevens and Annalyn Swan, *De Kooning: An American Master* (New York: Knopf, 2007), 280.

9. Lind, the strongest advocate for defining *As I Lay Dying* as an expressionist work, sees Faulkner's focus on intense color as outweighing the formal dedication to flatness and layered structures characteristic of cubism. For an extensive discussion of this novel as Faulkner's "cubist novel," see the work of Watson Branch and Panthea Reid Broughton, as well as my discussion of their work and Faulkner's play with these ideas in his writing of *As I Lay Dying* in chapter 6 of this volume. See also chapters 2, 3, and 7 for arguments concerning Faulkner's pivotal role in transforming cubism and inspiring development in expressionism that would be identified as "Abstract."

10. Musil quoted in Elizabeth Margaret Kerr, *William Faulkner's Yoknapatawpha: "A Kind of Keystone in the Universe"* (New York: Fordham University Press, 1983), 31. For detailed proof that Faulkner not only drew from spoken tales but also from actual written records that were the models for the account book entries that served as diaries, see Sally Wolf-King's *Ledgers of History: William Faulkner, an Almost Forgotten Friendship, and an Antebellum Plantation Diary* (Baton Rouge: Louisiana State University Press, 2010).

11. A great deal has been written on the phenomena of southern literature and the particularized role of culture in the region's dynamic history of aesthetic productions. For analyses speculating on this literary emergence, see Allen Tate's "The Profession of Letters in the South," *Virginia Quarterly Review* 11 (1935): 161–76; C. Vann Woodward's "Why the Southern Renaissance?" *Virginia Quarterly Review* (Spring 1975): 222–39; Cleanth Brooks's "Southern Literature: The Wellsprings of Its Vitality," *Georgia Review* 16 (1962): 238–53; Flannery O'Connor's *Mystery and Manners: Occasional Prose* (New York: Farrar, Straus and Giroux, 1969); Eudora Welty's *The Eye of the Story* (New York: Random House, 1978); Fred Hobson's *Tell About the South: The Southern Rage to Explain* (Baton Rouge: Louisiana State Uni-

versity Press, 1983); Daniel Joseph Singal's *The War Within: From Victorian to Modernist Thought in the South, 1919–1945* (Chapel Hill: University of North Carolina Press, 1982); and Ralph Ellison's *Shadow and Act* (New York: Random House, 1964). For works on cultural sources, in particular oral traditions that distinguish southern literature, see Henry Louis Gates's *The Signifying Monkey: A Theory of African American Literary Criticism* (New York: Oxford University Press, 1989); Lawrence Levine's *Black Culture and Black Consciousness: Afro-American Folk Thought from Slavery to Freedom* (New York: Oxford University Press, 1977); Albert Murray's *The Omni-Americans: New Perspectives on Black Experience and American Culture* (New York: Outerbridge and Dienstfrey, 1970) as well as his *The Hero and the Blues* (Columbia: University of Missouri Press, 1973). For histories of the South and regions within the region, see C. Vann Woodward, *The Burden of Southern History* (Baton Rouge: Louisiana State University Press, 1960), and Woodward's *The Origins of the New South, 1877–1913* (Baton Rouge: Louisiana State University Press, 1951). For background to the twentieth century, see John Hope Franklin's *From Slavery to Freedom: A History of Negro Americans* (New York: Knopf, 1947) as well as Franklin's *Race and History: Selected Essays 1938–1988* (Baton Rouge: Louisiana State University Press, 1989); Leon Litwack's *Been in the Storm So Long: The Aftermath of Slavery* (New York: Knopf, 1979); Richard Gray's *A Web of Words: The Great Dialogue of Southern Literature* (Athens: University of Georgia Press, 2007); and Jennifer Greeson's *Our South: Region, Nation, and World in U.S. Literature* (Harvard University Press, 2010). While the solid South is traditionally located in the Deep South or Slave South, other major regions include the Piedmont and Appalachia. For insight on the distinctiveness of the Piedmont, see Wilbur J. Cash's *The Mind of the South* (New York: Knopf, 1941); Liston Pope's *Millhands and Preachers: A Study of Gastonia* (New York: Oxford University Press, 1942); and Allen Tullos's *Habits of Industry: White Culture and the Transformation of the Carolina Piedmont* (Chapel Hill: University of North Carolina Press, 1989). For texts approaching the challenging grounds of Appalachia, see Horace Kephart's *Our Southern Highlanders* (New York: Outing, 1913) and David Whisnant's *All That Is Native and Fine: The Politics of Culture in an American Region* (Chapel Hill: University of North Carolina Press, 1983). For comprehensive approaches to the racial and sexual impact of the narratives of politics and the politics of narrative in the region, see Margaret Jarman Hagood's *Mothers of the South: Portraiture of the White Tenant Farm Women* (Chapel Hill: University of North Carolina Press, 1969); Anne Goodwyn Jones's *Tomorrow Is Another Day: The Woman Writer in the South, 1859–1936* (Baton Rouge: Louisiana State University Press, 1981); Trudier Harris's *From Mammies to Militants: Domestics in Black American Literature* (Philadelphia: Temple University Press, 1982); Diane Roberts's *The Myth of Aunt Jemima: Representations of Race and Region* (New York: Routledge, 1994); Patricia Yeager's *Dirt and Desire: Reconstructing Southern Women's Writing, 1930–1990* (Chicago: University of Chicago Press, 2000); Eric Sundquist's *To Wake the Nations: Race in the Making of American Literature* (Cambridge: Belknap Press of Harvard University Press, 1993); John Edgerton's *Speak Now Against the Day: The Generation Before the Civil Rights Movement in the South* (New York: Knopf, 1994); Fred Hobson's *But Now I See: The White Southern Racial Conversion Narrative* (Baton Rouge: Louisiana State University Press, 1999);

Orlando Patterson's *Rituals of Blood: Consequences of Slavery in Two American Centuries* (New York: Basic Civitas Books, 1998); and Michael Kreyling's *The South That Wasn't There: Postsouthern Memory and History* (Baton Rouge: Louisiana State University Press, 2010).

12. Thadious M. Davis, "From Jazz Syncopation to Blues Elegy: Faulkner's Development of Black Characterizations," in *Faulkner and Race: Faulkner and Yoknapatawpha, 1986*, ed. Doreen Fowler and Ann J. Abadie (Jackson: University Press of Mississippi, 1987), 70–72.

13. Born in Columbus, Georgia, Chattanooga, Tennessee, and Philadelphia, Pennsylvania, respectively, all these artists were major figures in defining secular music that had its roots in the South. (The baby who would become Billie Holiday was born of a thirteen-year-old mother who had been thrown out of her family's home in Baltimore for being unmarried and pregnant. Kept by family in Baltimore during her early years, Holiday herself is on record as having occasionally claimed Baltimore as the city of her birth.) Meanwhile, other major figures, like Mamie Smith, born in Cincinnati, Ohio (just across the river from Southgate, Kentucky), and Trixie Smith, a university-educated blues great born into a middle-class home in Atlanta, suggest some of the borders crossed in this period of cultural transformation.

14. For a discussion of the Sophie Newcomb arts and crafts movement and other pottery-based art forms, see Susan Donaldson's "Cracked Urns: Faulkner, Gender, and Art in the South," in *Faulkner and the Artist: Faulkner and Yoknapatawpha, 1993* (Jackson: University Press of Mississippi, 1996). For a discussion of the nineteenth-century Carolina Piedmont tradition and the emergence of folk pottery forms, see Charles G. Zug III, *Turners and Burners: The Folk Potters of North Carolina* (Chapel Hill: University of North Carolina Press, 1986).

15. Davis, "From Jazz Syncopation to Blues Elegy," 71–72.

16. C. Vann Woodward, "Why the Southern Renaissance?" *Virginia Quarterly Review* (Spring 1975): 222–39.

17. Louis Rubin, "The Dixie Special: William Faulkner and the Southern Literary Renascence" [1982], in *The Mockingbird in the Gum Tree: A Literary Gallimaufry* (Baton Rouge: Louisiana State University Press, 1991), 39.

18. A list partial and incomplete would include James Agee, Dorothy Allison, Raymond Andrews, Maya Angelou, Harriette Arnow, Doris Betts, Arna Bontemps, Olive Ann Burns, George Washington Cable, Erskine Caldwell, Truman Capote, Fred Chappell, Charles Chesnutt, Kate Chopin, Pat Conroy, Hubert Creekmore, Harry Crews, James Dickey, Ellen Douglas, Alice Dunbar-Nelson, Ralph Ellison, Fannie Flagg, Shelby Foote, Ernest Gaines, Tim Gautreaux, Ellen Glasgow, Caroline Gordon, Shirley Ann Grau, Barry Hannah, John Wylie Henderson, Mary Hood, William Bradford Huie, Zora Neale Hurston, James Weldon Johnson, Randall Keenan, Barbara Kingsolver, Harper Lee, Andrew Lytle, Bobbie Ann Mason, Jill McCorkle, Carson McCullers, Margaret Mitchell, Gurney Norman, Flannery O'Connor, John Kennedy O'Toole, Breece D'J Pancake, Walker Percy, William Alexander Percy, Katherine Anne Porter, Reynolds Price, Ron Rash, Ishmael Reed, Elise Sanguinetti, Evelyn Scott, Mary Lee Settle, Lee Smith, Elizabeth Spencer, William Styron, Allen Tate, Peter Taylor, Jean Toomer, Alice Walker, Margaret Walker, Robert Penn Warren, Eudora Welty, Thomas Wolfe, and Richard Wright.

19. Elizabeth Ammons, *Conflicting Stories: American Women Writers at the Turn into the Twentieth Century* (New York: Oxford University Press, 1992), 125.

20. For more on collage in African American art, see Rachel Farebrother's *The Collage Aesthetic in the Harlem Renaissance* (London: Ashgate, 2009).

21. For more on racial identity in Toomer's life and work, see Rudolph P. Byrd and Henry Louis Gates Jr.'s essay "'Song of the Son': The Emergence and Passing of Jean Toomer" in the 2011 Norton critical edition of *Cane*.

22. Alice Walker, "Beyond the Peacock: The Reconstruction of Flannery O'Connor," in *In Search of Our Mothers' Gardens* (New York: Harcourt Brace Jovanovich, 1983), 43. While Walker does not identify herself as "southern," she also does not cede ground. I well recall her response to a speaker's assertion that "we" "lost the [Civil] War," Walker with clipped irony asked, "What do you mean 'we'?" (The added address to the female speaker as "white man" is of course implied here.) Walker's critique of Faulkner's fiction using his public pronouncements in advocating gradualism in relation to change in racist policies as a lens for critique is well known. For insight into this view as well as others in the complex history of "Afro-American" writers' responses to Faulkner's provocations, see Craig Werner's excellent analysis, "Minstrel Nightmares: Black Dreams of Faulkner's Dreams of Blacks," in *Faulkner and Race: Faulkner and Yoknapatawpha, 1986*, ed. Doreen Fowler and Ann J. Abadie (Jackson: University Press of Mississippi, 1987).

23. Styron quoted in Tony Horwitz, "Untrue Confessions," *New Yorker*, December 13, 1999, 84.

24. Anne McKnight, "Crypticism, or Nakagami Kenji's Transplanted Faulkner: Plants, Saga, and Sabetsu," *Faulkner Journal of Japan* 1 (May 1999).

25. Werner, "Minstrel Nightmares." In this still relevant essay from a quarter of a century ago, Werner predicts cycles and finds patterns in the varied African American creative as well as critical riffs on Faulkner's fiction. Questions of female voice and queries concerning ways that race and history have forged definitions of class distinguish Werner's essay as a prescient work of cultural interpretation. The defining episode for the poor white's realization of race and class continues to be Sutpen's epiphany in *Absalom, Absalom!* after he is turned away, pointedly classified, by the well-dressed doorkeeper of a Tidewater residence and sent to the back door. See note 37 to chapter 5 in this volume.

26. For important recent work that analyzes race and class through the transformative lens of the affections, see Carina Evan's book manuscript in progress, *Loving Blackness: The Neo-Slave Slave Narrative and Contemporary Revisions of Slavery*, completed as a dissertation in the English Department of the University of California, Santa Barbara, 2009. It was my privilege not just to read Evan's work but also to have extensive conversations with her as she was developing her thesis.

27. André Bleikasten, *The Ink of Melancholy: Faulkner's Novels from* The Sound and the Fury *to* Light in August (Bloomington: Indiana University Press, 1990), 280. As Bleikasten continues, "even though the poet speaks to the urn and allows the urn to speak in the final two lines, Keats' ode is *on*, not *to*, a Grecian urn. Like Homer's famous description of the shield of Achilles, it is an *ekphrasis*, a verbal transposition of a plastic work of art, a word-shaper's tribute to a sculptor of marble in the *ut pictura poesis* tradition" (280).

28. For more on Hollywood's deployment of the trope of the "Old South," see Ida Jeter's "*Jezebel* and the Emergence of the Hollywood Tradition of a Decadent South," *The Southern Quarterly: A Journal of the Arts in the South* 19, nos. 3–4 (Spring–Summer 1981), 31–46.

29. Faulkner's *As I Lay Dying* (1931) was compared unfavorably to Erskine Caldwell's salaciously saleable depiction of southern poverty in *Tobacco Road* (1932), which devoted part of its mélange to the potential uplift for blacks and well as whites in the form of agricultural cooperatives. Caldwell, author of some twenty-five novels, only five of which were published in the 1930s, produced twenty novels in the 1940s.

30. At the 1998 Faulkner and Yoknapatawpha Conference ("Faulkner in America"), Trudier Harris gave a talk on Andrew's trilogy and his creation of an African American Yoknapatawpha in Georgia.

31. For a telling article that considers ethnicity and race in relation to "Southern Literature" as a concept, see Goto Kazuhko, "William Faulkner and Southern Literature in the Postmodern Era," *Faulkner Journal of Japan* 1 (May 1999). As Goto argues in relation to southern identity: "This intense historical sensitivity of the Southerners has formulated what is more than a regional peculiarity; it is something very close to 'ethnicity.'" Linking the multiple narrators of Gaines's *A Gathering of Old Men* to Faulkner's fifteen narrators of *As I Lay Dying*, Goto underlines the bonds forged by men (Gaines's characters) who "have shared the same fate." In Goto's view, Gaines's novel reveals a "literature of the ethnic solidarity bred through the history of oppression and discrimination, supported by the network of the traditional manners knitting up each and every niche of life and always reminding the members of the community of its historical fate [that] should be discussed not in the context of Southern literature but in that of the African American literature." Goto acknowledges the fact that "this novel by Gaines freely exploits . . . Faulkner's methods with success." The most extensive analysis linking Gaines's fictional world to Faulkner's Yoknapatawpha is Michel Fabre's "Bayonne or the Yoknapatawpha of Ernest Gaines," *Callaloo* 1 (1978): 110–24. Outside of the interest (antipathetic and otherwise) shown in the Americas, French and Japanese intellectuals have developed the most insightful critical communities concerned with and contributing to the growth of Faulkner studies.

32. For innovative and insightful work comparing these fictional worlds created in English, Spanish, and Brazilian Portuguese, see Paulo da-Luz-Moreira, *Regionalism and Modernism in the Short Stories of William Faulkner, João Guimarães Rosa, and Juan Rulfo*, University of California, Santa Barbara, PhD diss., 2007. My conversations with da-Luz-Moreira have proved invaluable in understanding the place of dialect, class, and race in relation to the diverse but deeply historically, culturally, and aesthetically connected inland modernisms of the Americas. As Rodrigo Bauer has emphasized in his conversations with me, whatever else this text may convey, a translation of *As I Lay Dying* that does not include the shifts into italics cannot have begun to understand the novel's shifts of time and levels in unconsciousness thought, much less the even more subtle alterations in who is speaking that are a primary focus of this volume's chapter 3.

33. While this word is used in English, its use is not considered acceptable in modern Japan. The Burakumin are thought of as village or rural people who have inherited a caste condition that is deeply reviled and entrenched through their families' inherited

fate to deal with death, the dead, and the dying. This group includes those in charge of killing in executions as well as those charged with the laying away of the dead, slaughtering animals for meat, and processing animal skins for leather. Nakagami gained access to literacy as a result of the post–World War II law that required that all Japanese children be educated.

34. For this and other important insights, see Kato Yuji, "'The Luxuriating South,' William Faulkner and Gabriel García Márquez: Voices, Narrations, and the Place of Existence," *Faulkner Journal of Japan* 1 (May 1999).

35. For a revelatory and detailed analysis that is only summarized here, see Anne McKnight, "Crypticism, or Nakagami Kenji's Transplanted Faulkner: Plants, Saga, and Sabetsu," *Faulkner Journal of Japan* 1 (May 1999).

36. While *Requiem for a Nun* was written as a play by Faulkner with his protégée, Joan Williams, this work's extravagant stage directions push the boundaries of this form toward the expanded definition of the novel insisted upon by Jean Toomer in *Cane* (1923), a prose-poem cycle that incorporates the alternating dialogue of a play as part of its experimental form.

37. Faulkner quoted in Thadious Davis, *Games of Property: Law, Race, Gender, and Faulkner's* Go Down, Moses (Durham: Duke University Press, 2003), 241.

38. Faulkner, who appears not to have cared whether or not his name was listed as a contributing writer, received credit for his work on *Today We Live* (1933), *The Road to Glory* (1936), *Slave Ship* (1937), *Gunga Din* (1939), *To Have and Have Not* (1940), *The Big Sleep* (1946), and *Land of the Pharaohs* (1955). Unlike F. Scott Fitzgerald and Katherine Anne Porter, Faulkner was able to pound out passable dialogue without investing his authorial self in the medium.

39. Joseph Urgo has gone against this commonly held view by pointing out that *Absalom, Absalom!*, composed during his tedious tenure as a scriptwriter, can be seen as a narrative form that was enriched by Faulkner's participation in the storyboard phase of film production that consists of the meeting of a group of writers who propose alternate and additional plot lines for shaping the narrative of a film. Urgo's point is not undercut by the fact that this communal creation exists as a form of recreation in an oral culture, a storyboard of versions in which narratives compete for what John Irwin has identified as "priority." See Irwin's *Doubling and Incest / Repetition and Revenge: A Speculative Reading of Faulkner*, the best psychological interpretation of Faulkner's long novel. Also, for more on Faulkner and film, see Peter Lurie's *Vision's Immanence: Faulkner, Film, and the Popular Imagination* (Baltimore: Johns Hopkins University Press, 2004) and Sarah Gleeson-White's article "William Faulkner, Screenwriter: 'Sutter's Gold' and 'Drums Along the Mohawk,'" *Mississippi Quarterly* 62, nos. 3–4 (2009): 427–42.

40. Daniel Pecchenino, "Incorrigibly and Invincibly Bachelor: The Unmarried Man and the Isolation of Individualism in Mid-Twentieth-Century U.S. Fiction," PhD diss., University of California, Santa Barbara, 2011.

41. J. M. Coetzee, "The Making of William Faulkner," *New York Review of Books*, April 7, 2005.

42. *Lion in the Garden*, ed. James B. Meriwether and Michael Millgate (Lincoln: University of Nebraska Press, 1980), 255.

43. David Minter, *William Faulkner: His Life and Work* (Baltimore: Johns Hopkins University Press, 1980), 94.

44. See Tom Lutz's "Cather and the Regional Imagination," in *The Cambridge History of the American Novel* (New York: Cambridge University Press, 2011). In the revised and posted version of his essay, Lutz insists on the cosmopolitanism of Faulkner and other regionalist authors who, in his reading, "assume specifically local mores and folkways [that] are significant frames for their characters' understanding of the world and each other," while also "taking for granted that elsewhere people and their doings are understood [as] somewhat dissimilar." Significantly, both Sarah Orne Jewett and Cather (writers to whom he alludes in this claim of contrast) also focused on the similarities in domestic cultures that were by definition devoted to fulfilling basic human needs. These prominent female regionalists from the nineteenth and twentieth centuries wrote about the relationship of localism, of regionalism, to an internationalism that crosses the boundaries of national literatures and national enmities based on the artificiality of politically mandated borders.

45. Outland is a precursor for the Quentin Compson of *The Sound and the Fury* as well as for the Addie Bundren of *As I Lay Dying*. Like Outland, Quentin speaks directly despite his death in a narrative that is somehow both embedded and literally outside of time. For more on this connection, see chapter 5 in this volume.

46. Edith Wharton, *The Writing of Fiction* (New York: Scribner's, 1925), 27–28. For a full discussion of Faulkner's connection to Edith Wharton and Willa Cather, see chapters 2 and 6 of this volume.

47. Arthur F. Kinney, "*Flags in the Dust* and the Birth of a Poetics," in *Faulkner and Formalism: The Returns of the Text*, ed. Annette Trefzer and Ann J. Abadie (Jackson: University Press of Mississippi, 2012), 3–19.

48. Joseph Blotner, *William Faulkner: A Biography* (Jackson: University Press of Mississippi, 2005), 222. This line was recalled to my mind by Arthur Kinney in his talk that formed the foundation for his essay listed above.

49. Eric J. Sundquist, *Faulkner: The House Divided* (Baltimore: Johns Hopkins University Press, 1983).

50. *Faulkner in the University*, ed. Frederick L. Gwynn, Joseph Blotner, and Douglas Day (Charlottesville: University Press of Virginia, 1959), 1.

51. See Roman Jakobson, "Why 'mama' and 'papa?'" in *Phonological Studies*, vol. 1 of *Selected Writings* (The Hague: Mouton, 1962), 538–45; and Maurice N. Walsh, "Explosives and Spirants: Primitive Sounds in Cathected Words," *Psychoanalytic Quarterly* 37 (1968): 199–211, for respective discussions of these sounds. While linguists have long been concerned with speculations about primal language and have come to some consensus on the "Mmmmmmmmmmmmmmmm" sound, Faulkner's use of these sounds in *The Sound and the Fury* demonstrates his concern with sound and his own theories of primal speech as early as 1928. Attuned to sound and repetition, Hortense Spillers has discussed the importance of the word "hush" in *The Sound and the Fury*. Spillers advises: "We need another name for this aural image that appears in so great a quantity of replication that it obtains a different *quality* and valence of the repeated." Spillers makes the point that Dilsey says this word the most, to which this reading would venture to add that this word is the most communicative word sound for and to Benjy. See Spillers, "Faulkner Adds Up: Reading *Absalom, Absalom!* and *The Sound and the Fury*," in *Faulkner in America: Faulkner and Yoknapatawpha, 1998*, ed. Joseph R. Urgo and Ann J. Abadie (Jackson: University Press of Mississippi, 2001), 35–36.

52. Eric J. Sundquist, *Faulkner: A House Divided* (Baltimore: Johns Hopkins University Press, 1983), 3.

53. Sundquist, *A House Divided*, 3.

54. Louis Rubin, "The High Sheriff of Yoknapatawpha County: A Study in the Genius of Place" [1990], in *The Mockingbird in the Gum Tree: A Literary Gallimaufry* (Baton Rouge: Louisiana State University Press, 1991), 80. Rubin would conclude, "The distance between the assorted local-color blacks in *Flags in the Dust* and the characterization of Dilsey in *The Sound and the Fury* is stunning to contemplate."

55. See Nancy Bentley's *The Ethnography of Manners: Hawthorne, James, Wharton* (New York: Cambridge University Press, 1995).

56. See Katherine Berry Frye's "'Washed Up and Wiped Out': Addie Bundren," delivered at "Backwoods, Backwater: Bartering Social Identities in Faulkner's South," University of California, Santa Barbara, 2008. The concept of "throwaway bodies" comes from Patricia Yeager's *Dirt and Desire: Reconstructing Southern Women's Writing, 1930–1990* (Chicago: University of Chicago Press, 2000), 11.

57. Philip Fisher, *Hard Facts: Setting and Form in the American Novel* (New York: Oxford University Press, 1985). A type of fiction that had been limited in the U.S. to the elite studied by Wharton and James had become grounds for study in the thwarted dreams of Sherwood Anderson's grotesques in *Winesburg, Ohio* and the denizens of coastal and inland Maine in Sarah Orne Jewett's *Country of the Pointed Firs*.

58. For important treatments and complex analyses of race in Faulkner's fiction, see Thadious Davis's *Games of Property: Law, Race, and Gender in Faulkner's* Go Down, Moses (Durham: Duke, 2003); Laura Doyle's "The Body Against Itself in Faulkner's Phenomenology of Race," *American Literature* 73, no. 2, (June 2001); Edouard Glissant's *Faulkner, Mississippi* (Chicago: University of Chicago Press, 2000); Richard Godden's *Fictions of Labor: William Faulkner and the South's Long Revolution* (New York: Cambridge University Press, 1997); Barbara Ladd's *Nationalism and the Color Line in George W. Cable, Mark Twain, and William Faulkner* (Baton Rouge: Louisiana State University Press, 1996); Walter Benn Michaels's *Our America: Nativism, Modernism, and Pluralism* (Berkeley: University of California Press, 1995); James Snead's *Figures of Division: William Faulkner's Major Novels* (New York: Methuen, 1986); Hortense Spillers's "Faulkner Adds Up: Reading *Absalom, Absalom!* and *The Sound and the Fury*," in *Faulkner and America* (Jackson: Mississippi, 2001); Eric Sundquist's *Faulkner: A House Divided* (Baltimore: Johns Hopkins University Press, 1983); Theresa Towner's *Faulkner and the Color Line: The Later Novels* (Jackson: University Press of Mississippi, 2000); Jay Watson's *Forensic Fictions: The Lawyer Figure in Faulkner* (Athens: University of Georgia Press, 1993); and Karl F. Zender's *Faulkner and the Politics of Reading* (Baton Rouge: Louisiana State University Press, 2002).

59. See Jay Watson's article "Writing Blood: The Art of the Literal in *Light in August*," in *Faulkner and the Natural World*, ed. Donald M. Kartiganer and Ann J. Abadie (Jackson: University Press of Mississippi, 1999), 66–96.

60. Robert Stepto, *From Behind the Veil: A Study of Afro-American Narrative* (Urbana: University of Illinois Press, 1979). My argument here was shaped and influenced by conversations with Robert Stepto and R. W. B. Lewis soon after this definitive work was published.

61. For a more detailed discussion of this, see chapter 2 in this volume.

62. The six stories that comprise the story cycle *The Old Order* were published individually in the 1930s and 1940s, and were first published together in a psychological rather than chronological sequence in *The Leaning Tower and Other Stories* (1944). See Jane Krause DeMouy's *Katherine Anne Porter's Women: The Eye of Her Fiction* (Austin: University of Texas Press, 1979), 115.

63. Mississippi-born Stark Young's *So Red the Rose* was the most prominent plantation novel until it was supplanted two years later by Margaret Mitchell's epic that established the type of the genre, *Gone with the Wind* (1936).

64. These works were published under the title *Pale Horse, Pale Rider: Three Short Novels* (1939).

65. Two of the major volumes treating the relationship between Faulkner's and Morrison's fiction are *Unflinching Gaze: Morrison and Faulkner Re-envisioned*, edited by Carol A. Kolmerten, Stephen M. Ross, and Judith Bryant Wittenberg (Jackson: University Press of Mississippi, 1997), and *What Else But Love? The Ordeal of Race in Faulkner and Morrison,* by Philip M. Weinstein (New York: Columbia University Press, 1996).

66. For what remains the most riveting analysis of sisters, aunts, and the location of a female plot in *Absalom, Absalom!*, see Carolyn Porter, "Symbolic Fathers and Dead Mothers: A Feminist Approach to Faulkner," in *Faulkner and Psychology: Faulkner and Yoknapatawpha, 1991*, ed. Donald M. Kartiganer and Ann J. Abadie (Jackson: University of Mississippi Press, 1994).

67. Words such as "stertorious," describing the deep and resonant lowing of the bovine, and "amoniac" to describe the specificity of the smell of animal urine, both of which appear in *As I Lay Dying*, articulate a knowledge of the senses that is not limited by knowing the words. Smells, recognizable, are not dependent on vocabulary to name their olfactoral specificity. People love, hate, and smell without being confined to their class backgrounds and without the aid of an internalized thesaurus. The vocabulary of Faulkner's novels is nevertheless stunning in its accuracy and its intimate detail. Faulkner's fiction reveals his archival knowledge of nineteenth-century domesticity that includes the genteel concept of the "cup towel," a distinctive and bygone term among the more lowly appurtenances of dish rags and drying cloths.

68. Allen Tate, "The Profession of Letters in the South," *Virginia Quarterly Review* 11 (April 1935): 161–76.

69. Eugene Genovese, *Roll, Jordan Roll: The World the Slaves Made* (New York: Vintage, 1974).

70. Joseph Blotner, *Faulkner: A Biography* (New York: Random House, 1974) 2: 1457. This was an undated letter from Faulkner to Joan Williams written in the spring of 1954.

CHAPTER TWO. BURYING THE REGIONAL MOTHER

1. This project began as talks for the Yoknapatawpha Conference "Faulkner in America" in 1998 and for the Society for the Study of Southern Literature in 2004. Versions of this essay in progress (part of a manuscript called "Mating with the Maternal Muse: William Faulkner's Parables of Art") were read and commented on by Donald Kartiganer, Joseph Urgo, Michael Zeitlin, and Jon Glover. Parts of this essay

appeared in my portion of an essay written with Claire Colquitt entitled "Toward a Modernist Aesthetic: The Literary Legacy of Edith Wharton," and my much longer essay, "Burying the Regional Mother: Faulkner's Road to Race through the Visual Arts," which first appeared in the 2007 *Faulkner Journal*. This is not the essay published there under the same title. In addition to alterations throughout, the final half of this chapter has been replaced by an extensive reading of Faulkner's 1938 story-cycle novel, *The Unvanquished*.

2. Ammons argues with force that Fitzgerald and Hemingway were "the most famous [authors] who found people like Wharton and Cather, and Stein, far more than any other literary 'father' of Harold Bloom's imagination, the real giants against whom they needed to define themselves." She goes on to make the important point that Faulkner along with Alain Locke joined these male writers in their "fear of female dominance" (viii). Ammons cites the survey of some two hundred literary critics in 1929 in which the respondents placed Wharton and Cather at the top of their lists. See Elizabeth Ammons, *Conflicting Stories: American Women Writers at the Turn into the Twentieth Century* (New York: Oxford University Press, 1991). See Greeson's book *Our South: Geographic Fantasy and the Rise of National Literature* (2010) for an important and relevant analysis of the local color movement's discovery of the American South as a project of racially defined conquest that was literally connected to the imperialist travelogues of Stanley in search of Livingstone in Africa.

3. For one of the major interventions discussing Faulkner in relation to the female arts, including art pottery and china painting, see Susan Donaldson's essay "Cracked Urns: Faulkner, Gender, and Art in the South" in *Faulkner and the Artist* (Jackson: University Press of Mississippi, 1996), 53.

4. Edith Wharton, "The Great American Novel," *Yale Review*, 16 (July 1927), 648.

5. This phrase is drawn from W. L. Courtney's *The Feminine Note in Fiction* (1904), which assesses the gendered state of U.S. fiction.

6. Cather's review begins, "A Creole Bovary is this little novel of Miss Chopin's" (697). This essay is included in the early criticism section of the Norton Critical edition of *The Awakening*, edited by Margo Culley (1993).

7. Cather had never heard of Faulkner when she invented a character that appears to mirror the type of character that Faulkner was performing on his return to post–World War I Oxford, Mississippi. There is a short, drunken, woman-driven air pilot with a strong component of Faulknerian cynicism and humor (and an English accent) in Cather's 1922 war novel, *One of Ours*. For an analysis of Faulkner's performance as the character of "Count-No Count" and his use of fictional masks as a form of self-fashioning himself as a man and as an artist, see Sensibar's *The Origins of Faulkner's Art* (Austin: University of Texas Press, 1984) and Lothar Hönnighausen's *Faulkner: Masks and Metaphors* (Jackson: University Press of Mississippi, 1997). For an important analysis of Faulkner's history of creating personal fictions, see James G. Watson's *William Faulkner: Self-Presentation and Performance* (Austin: University of Texas Press, 2000).

8. For a field-defining discussion on Freud's concept of the "return of the repressed," see René Girard's *Violence and the Sacred*, trans. Patrick Gregory (Baltimore: Johns Hopkins University Press, 1972). For the most complete study of this concept in rela-

tion to Faulkner's work, see Doreen Fowler's *Faulkner: The Return of the Repressed* (Charlottesville: University of Virginia Press, 1997).

9. For an extensive discussion of Wharton's anxious relationship to femininity and to the work of the female local colorists, particularly Mary Wilkins Freeman, see "Wharton and Wilkins: Rereading the Mother" in Waid, *Edith Wharton's Letters from the Underworld: Fictions of Women and Writing* (Chapel Hill: University of North Carolina Press, 1991).

10. Cather was close friends with Jewett as well as with Jewett's partner in life, Annie Ticknor Fields. Cather famously placed Jewett's story-cycle novel, *The Country of the Pointed Firs*, with *The Scarlet Letter* and *The Adventures of Huckleberry Finn*, as the three American works most likely to have a lasting impact. Edith Wharton and Henry James, in a pilgrimage of sorts, stopped by at Jewett's home in South Berwick, Maine, to discover that the elderly author was not home.

11. See Douglas's *The Feminization of American Culture* (New York: Farrar, Straus and Giroux, 1977), which argues that ministers and women had gained political control of American culture, feminizing national policy by insisting on the centrality of moral concerns—most notably in terms of high-ground issues with economic and martial consequences, such as slavery.

12. *Lion in the Garden: Interviews with William Faulkner, 1926–1962*, ed. James B. Meriwether and Michael Millgate (Lincoln: University of Nebraska Press, 1980), 167–68.

13. Fryer cites Cather's own critique of her first novel, published in 1912, *Alexander's Bridge* (204). Cather's essay "My First Novels (There Were Two)" offers a frank account of a young writer's quandaries in relation to established authors. For her part, Cather openly coupled Wharton with James, locating both of these figures as leaders of an elite, past, and class-based tradition that had limited the realm of fiction for their less interesting and less talented followers.

14. *Selected Letters of William Faulkner*, ed. Joseph Blotner (New York: Random House, 1977), 32.

15. See Judith B. Wittenberg for an early and detailed accounting of evidence that Faulkner read and drew from fiction by relatively obscure as well as prominent women writers: "Faulkner and Women Writers," in *Faulkner and Women: Faulkner and Yoknapatawpha, 1985*, ed. Doreen Fowler and Ann J. Abadie (Jackson: University Press of Mississippi, 1986), 287–96. Wharton is rarely acknowledged as having any serious relation to Faulkner's work (see Waid and Colquitt; and Waid, *Edith Wharton's Letters from the Underworld: Fictions of Women and Writing*). Seldom glimpsed as a modernist herself, Wharton, in terms of formal innovations as well as thematic, is one of Faulkner's most influential, modernist precursors. As others, notably Michael Zeitlin, have proven, James Joyce was a major influence on Faulkner's fiction. While *Ulysses* is referred to repeatedly in form and content, *Finnegans Wake*, which was appearing in suggestive fragments as a work in progress with its vigorous style of word collage and collation, continued to be important through Faulkner's late life as he was writing the Snopes trilogy.

16. *Lion in the Garden*, 167–68. Faulkner may have been in the same room with Cather in New York in 1931. According to Blotner, the crime novelist Dashiell Hammett and Faulkner had finagled an invitation to a Knopf dinner through Bennett Cerf. In-

ebriated beyond the likelihood of conversation, Faulkner was at least present part of the time. For an account of Faulkner's acknowledgments of Cather, see Zettsu Tomoyuki, "Faulkner's Mexican Connections: The Presence of Willa Cather in *Light in August*," *Faulkner Journal of Japan* 2 (June 2000). Zettsu summarizes the traditional view that sees Faulkner as outside of the realm of female influence: "Faulkner's lofty manliness or patriarchal isolation—whichever way one sees it—has been reinforced by the critical commonplace that Faulkner was too original an author to be inspired by any female precursors or contemporaries, even if he was indebted to such male precursors as Keats and Shakespeare. Nevertheless, Faulkner's own remarks make it clear that he read a number of women writers . . . Faulkner referred to Cather as a great writer at least on five occasions in his lifetime." As Zettsu notes, Faulkner mentioned Cather during "a period of more than thirty years," locating instances in 1926, 1932, 1947, 1955, and 1957.

17. See Woodress for Cather's views on modern art and its relationship to trends in U.S. culture. While Cather (unlike Wharton) did not devote full-blown essays to her own disparaging view of social and literary modernism, as Woodress writes, the Cather who "deplored Prohibition, the Jazz Age, the flapper, the relaxation of moral standards, the deterioration of taste, the scramble for money" did not "like cubism," nor could she "take Gertrude Stein or Ezra Pound seriously." James Woodress, *Willa Cather: A Literary Life* (Lincoln: University of Nebraska Press, 1987), 476.

18. Quoted in R.W. B. Lewis and Nancy Lewis's *The Letters of Edith Wharton* (New York: Scribner, 1988), 589, from a letter to Bernard Berenson dated August 14, 1935. The Italian novelist Alberto Moravia was being put in his place by Wharton, who was particularly competitive in relation to this particular topic, adding that she "had an incest donnee up [her] sleeve that wd make them all look like nursery-rhymes." Actually, she did. See Wharton's "Beatrice Palmato Fragment," in R.W. B. Lewis, *Edith Wharton: A Biography* (New York: Harper & Row, 1975).

19. Merrill Maguire Skaggs, "Thefts and Conversation: Cather and Faulkner," *Cather Studies* 3 (Lincoln: University of Nebraska Press, 1996), 120.

20. See Frederick Wegener, "Form, 'Selection,' and Ideology in Edith Wharton's Anti-Modernist Aesthetic," in *A Forward Glance: New Essays on Edith Wharton*, ed. Clare Colquitt, Susan Goodman, and Candace Waid (Newark: University of Delaware Press, 1999).

21. Edith Wharton, *The Writing of Fiction* (New York: Charles Scribner's Sons, 1925), 27–28. As both a Wharton and a Faulkner scholar, I have long cited this comment. The weight of textual evidence that links Faulkner to Wharton is too heavy to doubt the role of her work in sparking his fiction, or that this comment provoked the young Faulkner to make his experimental breakthrough. In his analysis of Wharton's notorious antimodernism, Wegener quotes the same evocative passage to argue that "Wharton almost seems to envision the celebrated experiment of a writer like Faulkner . . ." (124). Wegener accepts Wharton as a woman of her word as he presents her as an antimodernist. This argument does not dispute Wegener's claims; rather, as I argue, Wharton was a modernist *malgré lui*. See chapters 2, 3, and 4 of Waid, *Edith Wharton's Letters from the Underworld: Fictions of Women and Writing.*

22. See Bernard R. Bowron Jr., "Realism in America," *Comparative Literature* 3, no. 3 (1951): 279.

23. For an excellent discussion of veritism and the varieties of realism, see Bow-

ron. Carolyn Porter in a revelatory insight has linked art theory's understanding of cubism (drawing on the work of John Berger) to Faulkner's fiction: cubist painting "radically redefines the epistemological relationship between perceiving subject and perceived object as interaction rather than confrontation. The detached viewer of an illusionist space in the Renaissance painting becomes the active participant in a process of vision inaugurated by the cubist." See Porter's *Seeing and Being: The Plight of the Participant Observer in Emerson, James, Adams, and Faulkner* (Middletown, CT: Wesleyan University Press, 1981), 32. Also see Broughton, who sees *As I Lay Dying* as a whole like a cubist painting: the "quintessential cubist novel" (93). Panthea Reid Broughton, "Faulkner's Cubist Novels," in *"A Cosmos of My Own": Faulkner and Yoknapatawpha, 1980*, ed. Doreen Fowler and Ann Abadie (Jackson: University Press of Mississippi, 1981).

24. This may have been a private joke on Faulkner's part as he mused on the fate of Cather's Mother Eve and her penchant for diving into ravines when, two years later, he created the lesbian poet Eva Wiseman of *Mosquitoes* (1927), who has designs in that work on a girl named "Jenny." Willa Cather was one of the most well-known, if intensely private, lesbian artists of her time.

25. Both *A Backward Glance* and "Tendencies in Modern Fiction" (1934) reflect Wharton's critique of the rising fortunes of the proletarian novel and of the seemingly lurid obsession with rural poverty. The "poor whites" that have risen to such literary prominence are the backwoods and rural peoples depicted in Faulkner's *As I Lay Dying* (1930), *Sanctuary* (1931), and *Light in August* (1932), and in the more scandalous portrayals of Erskine Caldwell's *Bastard* (1929), *Poor Fool* (1930), *Tobacco Road* (1932), and *God's Little Acre* (1933).

26. For more for on the role of cubism in Faulkner's work, see chapters 6 and 7 of this volume, which note the works of Watson Branch, Panthea Reid Broughton, and Ilsa Dusoir Lind.

27. Garrett notes Faulkner's removal of the word "coffin," which was sometimes replaced by the cruder and more suggestive word "box" (George Palmer Garrett, "Some Revisions in *As I Lay Dying*," *Modern Language Notes* 73, no. 6 [1958]: 414–17). See Bleikasten for a more detailed account of Faulkner's attention on the level of the word in this novel: *Faulkner's* As I Lay Dying (Bloomington: Indiana University Press, 1973).

28. The Rev. George Whitefield is recognized as the most famous revivalist of the eighteenth century. A figure known for his oratorical power, Whitefield inspired the scientific and personal interest of Benjamin Franklin, who actually tried to calculate the range of this famed minister's voice as a way of estimating whether he could have spoken to crowds as large as his supporters claimed. Mentioned in Olaudah Equiano's slave narrative, this same figure is important to the history of African American poetry because the first poem published by the slave poet Phyllis Wheatley was "On the Death of the Rev. Mr. George Whitefield, 1770." Ultimately, the name "Whitefield" would have provided too much of a racial marker in *As I Lay Dying*.

29. Ishmael, the illegitimate son of Abraham and Hagar, is cast out in the book of Genesis by his father along with his "foreign" mother into the desert. This is the primal split that, according to the delegitimizing narrative claim of the Hebrew Bible, constitutes the origins of the Muslim people. This biblical narrative recounts the mixing of bloods that is settled by a formal bifurcation of Abraham's sons.

30. See chapter 6, "Bonfires of the Masculinities: Wharton and Faulkner in the Glare of Whistler's 'Falling Rocket,'" for an extensive discussion that details the ways in which these particular scenes from *As I Lay Dying* are based on language drawn from actual passages in Wharton's novels. These specific scenes, detailed in language and provocative in content, are found in *Age of Innocence* (1920) and *Twilight Sleep* (1927).

31. Theresa Towner offers a brief reading of this rarely noticed passage that notes how quickly Jewel's ire shifts from the "negroes" to the "white man," how "quickly the scene slides out of the racial arena and into conflict between country folk and town fellows" (126). See Theresa M. Towner, "Black Matters on the Dixie Limited: *As I Lay Dying* and *The Bluest Eye*," in *Unflinching Gaze: Morrison and Faulkner Re-Envisioned*, ed. Carol A. Kolmerten, Stephen M. Ross, and Judith Bryant Wittenberg (Jackson: University Press of Mississippi, 1997). For the best article on migration within and among the regions during the historical period of the novel, see Cheryl Lester's "As They Lay Dying: Rural Depopulation and Social Dislocation as a Structure of Feeling," *Faulkner Journal* 21, nos. 1–2 (2005, 2006). Lester notes that as the Bundrens "get . . . closer to town," they become racially marked and lowered as they are displaced from their rural environs. As Lester points out, readings of these passages have become much more common in recent years. Towner's mention above was still groundbreaking when I delivered my paper on the blackening of the Bundrens and race at the 1998 Yoknapatawpha Conference on "Faulkner and America."

32. Pa is depicted as "slack-faced" earlier in the novel when he expresses outrage at what he sees as Darl's inappropriate behavior in the presence of the coffin that contains the dead and rotting mother.

33. Recalling the reference to the hypermasculine hero of Cather's *The Professor's House,* whom the pastel-defined and florally named mother, Lillian, describes critically as "highly coloured" (38), Faulkner's Jewel is said here to have a look which is "high colored." "[H]igh-colored" (unlike the concept of high-color) is an odd phrase that in the context of the twentieth-century South evokes the chromatics of the color line with its closest hyphenated cognate being the historically familiar term "high-yellow." The mother's insight in Cather's novel is that the dead Tom Outland as a cowboy hero is a figure who himself fits into a local color aesthetic, albeit a masculine one.

34. See Deborah Clarke's *Robbing the Mother: Women in Faulkner* (Jackson: University Press of Mississippi, 2006). Clarke's transformative work on the mother in Faulkner is engaged in more detail in the following chapter, "Dewey Dell, Dead Center."

35. Anse only gives up the reins when the wagon goes from solid earth to the dangerous (life-threatening) crossing of the flooded river.

36. In Addie's section, Anse strikes, impregnates, and violates her with a word. In this same section, Addie describes Anse as a vessel into which words are poured to gain solidity. The bodiless Darl enters into the bodily vessels of others, but he, as this argument suggests, often dwells in the bodiless, unspoken, yet violating word. Clarke, in discussing the association of the mother with embodiment and the literal, argues that Darl seems to be disembodied.

37. Marcel Duchamp's *Sad Young Man on a Train*, a cubist work painted in 1911–12, could be seen as describing the consciousness of Darl as he literally (in both senses of the word) "departs" for the asylum in a scene of self-division that recalls the an-

ticipated journey of Quentin Compson, his literary antecedent, who will escape madness by taking a trolley to his death in *The Sound and the Fury*. The mad Quentin, like the mad Darl, is a "Sad Young Man on a Train." By the mid-1920s, Faulkner was familiar with Duchamp's work and the humor of his art. Merrill Horton links an image from Faulkner's *The Hamlet* in which the bilked husband of Mrs. Tull is said to look like "a portrait of a child saint . . . defaced by a vicious and idle boy" to Balzac's *Comédie*'s "The Maranas." As Horton points out, in Balzac's influential image, "a mustache graces the portrait of a Virgin well before Duchamp edited the *Mona Lisa*." See Horton, *Hunting the Sun: Faulkner's Appropriations of Balzac's Writings* (New York: Peter Lang, 2010), 189. Meanwhile, Faulkner referred directly to Duchamp's *L.H.O.O.Q.* (his mass-produced print of da Vinci's *Mona Lisa* refaced by simply penciling in a mustache and a goatee) when an early character, the painter Elmer, draws a mustache on Joan of Arc. The joke, as painter Carly Day Andrews pointed out to me in conversation, is heard in the sound of "Ark" in the text that refers to the postmark to Jonesboro, Ark.—Arkansas. Elmer is said to have made the female saint "into a man." In his well-known joke, Duchamp's bawdy humor is still audible as the alphabetic title of his mustached masterpiece, which, when pronounced quickly in French, proclaims: "Elle a chaud au cul" (She's hot in the ass).

38. See the unpublished paper by Andrew Kalaidjian, who investigates the coin ostensibly being described here to discover that the buffalo and the woman inhabit two different nickels. This is the proverbial "two nickels to rub together" that a poor man might lack, because the coins described are not from the same mintings, but two separate strikings.

39. As Chip Badley points out, this is a familiar concept, as seen in *The Merchant of Venice* when Shylock remarks, "I make it breed as fast" (1.3.104).

40. The next line from "Tramp, tramp, tramp, the boys are marching," "Cheer up comrades, they will come," echoes eerily with the use of this tune as one of two Christian hymns known to have been employed in the forwarding of the comrades in Mao's Long March, an event that was taking place at the time that Faulkner was composing and publishing the stories that would become *The Unvanquished*. Instead of the Civil War lyrics, Mao's peasant army would have been replacing the lyrics to the well-known "Jesus Loves the Little Children" as they sang "Kill, kill, kill, until the world runs with blood."

41. For my development of the argument that sees carving as part of the art of men making men, see earlier portions of this chapter, which this reading of *The Unvanquished* supplements as a coda. For the most complete analysis of modernism and matricidal revenge in relation to *The Unvanquished* as well as other works in Faulkner's oeuvre, see Doreen Fowler, who analyses this obsession and its cultural and local etiology, expanding to include a compelling reading of Faulkner's own family history (*Faulkner* xvi, 25). Speculating on *The Unvanquished*, Fowler recalls Faulkner's grandfather's decision not to kill the killer of his own father, the model for Colonel Sartoris. As Fowler and the most sophisticated and thoughtful critics have understood this conundrum, by killing the killer of the father, the son is still killing the father. See Irwin for the most complete discussion of the desire for narrative priority and its complex connection to the killing of the father in Faulkner's fiction.

42. John T. Matthews, "The Rhetoric of Containment in Faulkner," in *Faulkner's*

Discourse: An International Symposium, ed. Lothar Hönnighausen (Tübingen: M. Niemeyer Verlag, 1989), 59.

43. Trophies of body parts were taken as prizes from ritualized lynchings of black men in the South before and during the decade of the 1930s when lynching rose to its highest point in the U.S. South. Faulkner was aware of the manhunt and the obscenity of masculine sport that is the violence of lynching. Certainly, the acquisition of animal trophies preceded the sixteenth-century arts that elevated taxidermy into a profession while the corporeal preservation of the relics of saints was left to God. This ritualized cutting, a more manageable form of *habeas corpus* to provide proof of a kill or killing, is as old in the English literary record as Grendel's arm being hung from the rafters in Mead Hall, and as ancient and visceral as the bodily specific justice of Shiite law. Perhaps the closest analogue to Ringo and Bayard's severing of Grumby's arm as a completion of the burial ritual for their murdered Granny still hangs from the dome of St. James Cathedral in Prague. Ragged and mummified after four hundred years of warning about what happens when a man messes with the Mother, this remnant is what remains of the man who was literally caught trying to steal the jewels from the statue of the Virgin. As the legend contends, the priests cut off the would-be thief's grip the next morning because they could not detach him from the Virgin's hold.

44. In *The Unvanquished*, it is repeatedly asserted that men will not kill "a woman . . . Even Yankees will not kill a woman." Yet Granny Millard is in command, and after the Union officer, who realizes the enormity of her accomplishments in the mule business, pleads for a precise number of beasts, he asks this woman to speak to him "enemy to enemy," before altering his request to the telling equality of "man to man."

45. For an extensive reading of this pattern of female burial and its necessity to the making of art as it plays itself out in Poe's story "The Fall of the House of Usher," see chapter 6 in this volume.

46. This claim that become the first false document is based on Col. Dick and his army scribe's mishearing of Granny's words. Granny Millard, in another one of the telling human and animal equations that betray the meaning of slavery, names the two slaves, Loosh and Philadephy, who are missing, and she specifically also names the two mules: "Old Hundred and Tinney" (*U* 109). "Old Hundred" is the folk name for Psalm 100, which begins "Praise God from whom all blessings flow." This doxology that forms a liturgical step in formal Protestant services signals the flow of blessing in the form of mules from the Union Army. These mule names (anticipating Ringo's unconscious witticism about using numbers as names when he and Granny have finished going through the alphabet) are heard as numbers: the claim reads as requisition for 110 mules.

47. In *The Feminization of American Culture*, Ann Douglas argues that the joining of women and ministers as they took the high ground in the antislavery movement, which led to the Civil War and its consequences, constituted a shift in power in which women and their feminized minions (of, by definition, emasculated preachers) accomplished the threatening "feminization" of the United States. This scene penned by Faulkner in the mid-1930s anticipates Douglas's argument and provides an even more potent scene of usurpation when the matriarch in charge is joined at the front of the church at a pulpit (called "the reading desk") by a literate black artist. Together,

Granny and Ringo resolve the problem as white men—represented as having the eager pack mentality and unsatisfied hunger of dogs—sit below them in a church.

48. This is a statement about class and origins that in the funeral scene names what separates the townspeople of Jefferson from the hill country folk. Emphasizing the contrast between the two gathered groups, Brother Fortinbride reminds the Jeffersonians of their legitimacy and their protected lives: "Some of you aint come far and you came that distance in carriages with tops" (*U* 158). The mountain people have come on mules with their own bodies protected from the rain by croker sacks. They are without carriages, much less the protection provided by these structures' "tops."

49. While six out of the seven chapters of *The Unvanquished* were published in the mid-1930s and the novel as a whole in 1938, this novel, without its focus on color and the locally colored figures who are colored by class and repeated references to their doglike fealty, has elements of appeal that, if seen as focused on white solidarity, can neither be celebrated as socialism or praised or appraised as populism. The blacks, the former slaves in the gallery, are never given anything except roadside assistance meant to get them back to their former owners (with an assumption of *noblesse oblige* being the most positive version), urging these displaced people to find the white people who know them. Even in the earlier installments for the *Post*, the North is not offered to freed blacks as a place of refuge. The Union Army, described as retreating, commits a clear act of racial separatism as they blow up a bridge being crossed by a massive group of slaves who believe that they are trying to cross over into Jordan. Reading *The Unvanquished* as a whole with its lost war marked by the killing of the Mother and the racial violence that accompanies the land-based and preservationist drive of John Sartoris, it is impossible not to remember the coeval German definition of what was left after World War I: "Blood and Soil" (*Blut und Boden*). This movement was fundamental to the Reich's racist ideal of purity and the heightened value of a blood-defined and annihilating nation. Locally colored, the people who come down from the mountains for Granny Millard's help are white, but they have been colored by class and animalized by scarcity of resources. *The Unvanquished* closes with killings for the preservation of white power in a penultimate chapter that dissects and debunks any residual ideals of southern white womanhood and the fetishization of purity. This appearance of purity is embodied by the murder-prone, if virginal, seductress who gives piquancy to the narrating protagonist's decision to end the practice of killing in the name of honor, female or otherwise. For a further connection to Faulkner's fiction's problem with the concept of honor and killing as linked to contemporary crises in the Germany of the late 1920s as it rose to the Reich, see the analysis of Quentin Compson's preoccupation with bridges in *The Sound and the Fury*, which is discussed in detail at the close of chapter 4 in this volume.

50. See chapter 3, "Dewey Dell, Dead Center," for a detailed explication of this concept.

51. Peter Nicolaisen argues for an increased complexity achieved in *The Unvanquished* through the narrative strangeness that Faulkner chose to maintain when he republished the stories as the novel while still insisting on pairing a major comic episode with a profound or tragic concern. This pairing appears in "Skirmish at Sartoris" as Col. Sartoris kills the two Burdens who are actively advocating suffrage for blacks in the same story in which he and Drusilla are forced into marriage by the women of

Jefferson who see this legalized union as essential to their ideals of respectability. See Nicolaisen, "'Because We Were Forever Free': Slavery and Emancipation in *The Unvanquished*," *Faulkner Journal* 10, no. 2, (1995).

52. Faulkner's 1942 story-cycle novel, *Go Down, Moses*, is made up of significantly disturbing or baffling stories, a number of which were not readily publishable in magazines. Dead white mothers who in their absence foreground the need for the black breast and maternal care by women of color such as Molly Beauchamp abound in this book in which the dead mother consists of a violated and diminishing wilderness. The headless mother in "Delta Autumn," the penultimate story in *Go Down, Moses,* is the beheaded doe who has been slaughtered out of season. Traditionally, does were not killed by hunters, and the occasion of doe season is called by the Fishing and Hunting Commission only in times of severe overcrowding and inadequate food for the animal population. The pattern of maternal death in the story-cycle novel that is a *künstlerroman* is seen in Sherwood Anderson's influential *Winesburg, Ohio* (1919) and may be said to have culminated in Eudora Welty's 1949 masterpiece, *The Golden Apples*, in which the female artist (unlike Anderson's George Willard) chooses the life of the body over the life of formal art. When Faulkner went back to write his final two installments that suited the *Post*, he seems to have been aware of the female- and mother-centered genre of the story-cycle novel. In "The Unvanquished" (later retitled as "Riposte in Tertio") and "Vendée," Faulkner leaves two clues that he may have read the most significant story-cycle novel to come out of the United Sates in the nineteenth century, Sarah Orne Jewett's 1897 *The Country of the Pointed Firs*. Mary Harris, the name Granny proposes and Ringo decides against as a name to be used in one of his counterfeit documents, is the mysteriously disliked caretaker of Captain Littlepage in Jewett's classic work. This minor character in Jewett's work, whose name carries a rare note of dissension with it, is spelled "Mari' Harris." The gratuitous appearance of Matt Bowden as one of Grumby's brigands handing him over to the boys provides another possible pointer. "Bowden" is the family name in Jewett's matricentric novel in which the mother is presented as an undying figure who inhabits a place of renewal named "Green Island." Mari' Harris is mentioned four times (she is said to look like a "Chinee") in gossip during the chapter near the close of *The Country of the Pointed Firs* called "The Bowden Reunion." What I am suggesting here is the possibility that a highly print-savvy and market-aware Faulkner (sharpened by his experience in Hollywood) may have been looking at endings of classic story cycles for and about women that had been successful. In her 1926 edition of this work, Cather famously placed *The Country of the Pointed Firs* along with the *Scarlet Letter* and *The Adventures of Huckleberry Finn* as one of three lasting works in American fiction.

53. For an important analysis of the role of this prominent magazine and its readers' expectations as they shaped and defined the tenor of these stories, see Susan V. Donaldson's "Dismantling the *Saturday Evening Post* Reader: *The Unvanquished* and Changing 'Horizons of Expectations,'" in *Faulkner and Popular Culture: Faulkner and Yoknapatawpha 1988*, ed. Doreen Fowler and Ann J. Abadie (Jackson: University Press of Mississippi, 1990), 179–95.

54. Ringo rises to prominence in the arc of the five stories Faulkner was able to publish lucratively for the wide readership of the *Post*. As this black artist heralds the

already established fact of the Harlem Literary Renaissance (the great aesthetic fact of the 1920s and 1930s), Ringo's radical diminution from full partner completes *The Unvanquished*, exposes the historical reality of John Sartoris's postwar killing of men to prevent the former slaves from voting for Ringo's cousin, who is a candidate for office during Reconstruction. While Drusilla is named by Col. Sartoris as temporary officer in charge of the ballot box, this vindictive and (I believe) virginal woman warrior loses as she is forced to marry the source of her temporary power. This withholding of the vote, juxtaposed with the demand by the elite mothers who insist on marriage rather than the vote, confirms old definitions of power while anticipating that this violence will continue even as it is replaced by the equally cruel rule of law. The book ("the Coke") that Bayard, leaving Ringo behind, has been delegated to study at the university is the locus of the new power. Acknowledged repeatedly as being taller and smarter—intrinsically older from his experience as Granny's accomplished accomplice as an artist and mule getter—Ringo is reabsorbed into a subordinate role.

55. See chapter 6 in this volume. Even the partnership of the black artist and the mother had been given critical notice and attention: both Langston Hughes and Zora Neale Hurston were criticized because of their support by an older white patroness, Mary Osgood Mason, who insisted that these major literary figures address her as "godmother." To be sure, the word "patronized" carries with it a sense of being compromised and condescended to by one who assumes a superior vantage point.

56. Rigidly enforced binaries are enforced because of the fear that they have and will continue to be crossed. Human friendship and bonds forged in conditions of survival have always joined men and women, women and children, women and women, and men and men. Connections have always existed among those who can and do love as well as among those who can and do practice hatred. See note 6 in chapter 7 for the circumstances surrounding the 1926 lynching in Virginia that led to antilynching legislation in that state.

57. While the scholarship has documented Faulkner's inclusion of more passages about the relationships between blacks and whites as the stories were rewritten to be published as a novel, Philip M. Weinstein's "Diving into the Wreck: Faulknerian Practice and the Imagination of Slavery," *Faulkner Journal* 10 [1995]: 23–53, concludes that *The Unvanquished* is a regressive work that remains uncritical in its comic and unrepentant representations of race and race relations.

58. The play *Driving Miss Daisy*, by Alfred Uhry, is best known as the popular 1989 film of the same name that starred Jessica Tandy and Morgan Freeman. Miss Daisy is southern and Jewish.

59. Faulkner's well-known story "A Rose for Emily" (1930) was his first to be published in a national venue, the renamed *Century*. While any collaboration between Miss Emily and her manservant remains silent in the published story, Faulkner had drafted a fifth segment that focuses on a conversation between the two in which she supports his idea of going away by train after his responsibility for her is finished. Tobe is so old and tired by this point that he just goes out to watch a train. This portion, which damages the effect of this shocking story with its punch revealing Miss Emily's loyal necrophilia, humanizes Miss Emily and Tobe by reporting a man's simple aspirations. In the published story, the black manservant Tobe remains the keeper of possible secrets as the only living person besides Miss Emily who has lived in the house.

CHAPTER THREE. DEWEY DELL, DEAD CENTER

1. See Gail Mortimer's *Faulkner's Rhetoric of Loss: A Study of Perception and Meaning* (Austin: University of Texas Press, 1983), an early work that understands that absence is associated with femaleness, an important crossroads in the study of Faulkner and gender.

2. For the influential enunciation of the paradigm of culture to which I believe Faulkner's character Fairchild alludes, see "The Virgin and the Dynamo," in Henry Adams, *The Education of Henry Adams* (1914).

3. For a detailed presentation and analysis of this thesis, see "Burying the Regional Mother," chapter 2 of this volume. While they can be read separately, chapters 2 and 3 form the arc of an argument that moves from sacrificial sons to the sacrificial daughter to complete this reading of *As I Lay Dying*.

4. See Margaret Homans's seminal work, *Bearing the Word*, for a discussion of this classical paradigm and its consequences for ways of looking at the female body as a site of narrative literalism and literalization that female writers return to explicate (*Bearing the Word: Language and Female Experience in Nineteenth-Century Women's Writing* [Chicago: University of Chicago Press, 1986]). Homans shapes her well-known and influential argument by discovering a pattern in major works that prove her assertion that female voice is associated with the literal while male voice is accorded the privilege of figurative language, thereby employing and being associated with the power of the Lacanian-defined symbolic. For an analysis of Homans's use of Lacan and the applicability of both to the works of William Faulkner, see Doreen Fowler's "Matricide and the Mother's Revenge: *As I Lay Dying*," *Faulkner Journal* 4, nos. 1–2 (Fall 1988/Spring 1989). For a discussion of the ways in which this powerful narrative plays out in many of Faulkner's major novels, see Fowler's book *Faulkner: The Return of the Repressed* (Charlottesville: University of Virginia Press, 1997). Deborah Clarke offers a case-by-case analysis of this formulation in relation to the mother in many of Faulkner's major works. Clarke's work, like the intervention of Minrose Gwin in her groundbreaking *The Feminine and Faulkner*, looks at the cross-gendering of voice in Faulkner's work through the lens of French feminist critiques, particularly those of Hélène Cixous and Luce Irigaray. In many ways, the fact that Dewey Dell does not appear in Gwin's seminal work suggests that the Bundren daughter has been a problem character or, more precisely, that Dewey Dell may have seemed less interesting in that she is not seen as a problem, which may explain why Dewey Dell has not yet elicited or required what Gwin calls "bisexual" reading. This being said, Gwin's intervention in *The Feminine and Faulkner* introduced French feminist theory to Faulkner, providing an important treatise and foundation for rejecting the intrinsically masculinist form of binary opposition.

5. Marc Hewson, "'My children were of me alone': Maternal Influence in Faulkner's *As I Lay Dying*," *Mississippi Quarterly* 53, no. 4 (2000): 551–52. While women have been seen as the central absence, Martin Kreiswirth makes a crucial point with regard to race as he contends, "Charles Bon is at the center of the racial uncanny in *Absalom, Absalom!* Yet, like other characters in Faulkner's texts, Bon remains an empty center—projected as much by what he is as by what he is not. Or, more accurately Bon hovers between the two: awaiting the secret when what has been seen and not seen is re-

vealed." See Kreiswirth, "Faulkner's Dark House: The Uncanny Inheritance of Race," *Faulkner's Inheritance: Faulkner and Yoknapatawpha, 2005*, ed. Joseph R. Urgo and Ann J. Abadie (Jackson: University of Mississippi Press, 2007), 128. Kreiswirth's concept of the "empty center" is obviously important to my reading of Dewey Dell. Meanwhile, Bon, in his extensive letter near the close of chapter 4 in *Absalom, Absalom!*, achieves more of an actual narrative presence than most of the absent presences that provoke narrative in Faulkner's fiction. See chapter 5 in this volume for a reading of Bon's letter as a provocation for female speech, Judith Sutpen's as well as Rosa Coldfield's. In contrast, even though the dead Addie Bundren is given a full piece in *As I Lay Dying*, the parts that are quoted as spoken or heard in her section 40 are quite spare.

6. Diane Roberts, *Faulkner and Southern Womanhood* (Athens: University of Georgia Press, 1994), 197.

7. Deborah Clarke, *Robbing the Mother: Women in Faulkner* (Jackson: University Press of Mississippi, 2006), 35–36.

8. Cleanth Brooks, *William Faulkner: The Yoknapatawpha Country* (Baton Rouge: Louisiana State University Press, 1963), 148; T. H. Adamowski, "Meet Mrs. Bundren: *As I Lay Dying*—Gentility, Tact, and Psychoanalysis," *University of Toronto Quarterly* 49 (Spring 1980): 225.

9. Minrose Gwin, in one of the most powerful (and often quoted) theoretical positions articulated in her field-altering *Faulkner and the Feminine: Reading (Beyond) Sexual Difference* (Knoxville: University of Tennessee Press, 1990), "rethinks subjectivity as a female space" to speculate on "woman's voice and woman's desire that emerges from that space." Gwin sees this literalized absence in the line of Addie's words, the space or "place" where Addie's "virginity used to be," as signifying resistance to "the image of the phallus, the language of the Father and its appropriative gesture, the symbolic power of the word" (154).

10. It is instructive to see Fiedler's binary assessment of Faulkner's young women (quoted in part in the body of this chapter) in the lushness of its entirety: "Pubescent or nubile women, for Faulkner, fall into two classes . . . both are terrifying: great, sluggish, mindless daughters of peasants, whose fertility and allure are scarcely distinguishable from those of a beast in heat; and the febrile, almost fleshless but sexually insatiable daughters of the aristocracy. Not the women he observes but those he dreams inhabit Faulkner's novels, myths of masculine protest: the peasant wench as earth goddess (Lena Grove in *Light In August*, Dewey Dell in *As I Lay Dying*, Eula Varner in *The Hamlet*), or the coed as nymphomaniac Venus (Cecily of *Soldiers' Pay*, Patricia in *Mosquitoes*, Temple Drake in *Sanctuary*). Their very names tend toward allegory, 'Dewy Dell' [*sic*], for instance, suggesting both a natural setting and woman's sex, her sex as a fact of nature, while 'Temple Drake' evokes both a ruined sanctuary and the sense of unnatural usurpation: woman become a sexual aggressor—more drake than duck" (Leslie Fiedler, *Love and Death in the American Novel* [Champaign, Ill.: Dalkey Archive Press, 1966], 321).

11. Roberts, *Faulkner and Southern Womanhood*, 203.

12. Among the major articles on Faulkner and the mother are Philip Weinstein's "'If I Could Say Mother': Construing the Unsayable about Faulknerian Maternity," in *Faulkner's Discourse: An International Symposium*, ed. Lothar Hönnighausen (Tübingen: Max Niemeyer Verlag, 1989), 3–15, and Noel Polk's "'The Dungeon Was Mother

Herself': William Faulkner, 1927–1931" in *New Directions in Faulkner Studies*, ed. Doreen Fowler and Ann J. Abadie (Jackson: University Press of Mississippi, 1984), 61–93. As Weinstein argues in relation to the particularly "punitive" treatment of Caroline Compson in *The Sound and the Fury*, Mrs. Compson "is the jailor, but she is also the jail and the inmate." With acute insight, he goes on to explain that "she is the prisoner of her own womb. The dungeon is not mother, but motherhood" (13).

13. Honor killing in Faulkner's fiction has an unsurprising pattern that nonetheless goes against critics' purchase, which is largely a wholesale buying in to the code of chivalry that claims to sanctify female virtue. Successful honor killings in Faulkner, both real and imagined, primarily concern lower-class and mixed-race women, not the worried-over and fetishized daughters of the aristocracy. The first honor-style killing is reported in the backstory Ruby Lamar of *Sanctuary* (sent off in 1929 and published in a revised form in 1931) offers for herself. Ruby Lamar's father is a realistic depiction of the working- or laboring-class man who calls his daughter "whore," banishing her to a life on the streets while asserting his "honor" by killing Ruby's lover, Frank. In terms of histories of race and class, Lee Goodwin of *Sanctuary* is known to have been court-martialed and imprisoned (worse that a dishonorable discharge) for his murder of another soldier over a Filipino native classified simply as a "nigger woman." While the narrative re-creation of Henry's murder of Bon before he crosses the threshold (the gate) into Sutpen's Hundred and the morphological gate of the virginal sister is present as one of the major mysteries within *Absalom, Absalom!* itself, the honor killing with by far the most carnage begins with Wash Jones's killing of the self-made master, Thomas Sutpen. This killing is followed by Wash's slaughter of his granddaughter and the just-born and rejected female get of Sutpen. Mr. Compson's most detailed sexual fantasy reveling in the warmth and attractions of the women of color who were sequestered and preserved by men in the institution of *plaçage* locates his only concern with honor killing as he recalls that these beloved, mixed-blood beauties were not to be insulted at the cost of the speaker's life. Poor women and mixed-race women are killed over; grandmothers are killed over. The rape of Temple Drake and the death of Joanna Burden lead to ritualized lynchings enacted by the community of a mob or that mob's vigilante representative. In *Go Down, Moses*, the white black man Lucas Beauchamp almost enacts an honor killing over the purloining of his wife, Molly, as a wet-nurse for the child of his white cousin: the trigger is pulled but the gun fails to fire. In many ways, the most deviantly exciting variant on an honor killing is exacted by the politically acute Linda Snopes, who takes revenge for her mother's suicide by aiding Mink Snopes in his clan-based honor killing of Flem Snopes (her own cruelly legitimizing unbiological banker father). Quentin and Shreve have figured out the story (in Peter Brooks's concise formulation) that is precipitated by too much difference rather than too much sameness: the miscegenation, not the incest. Race and class figure largely in most of these narratives. Aside from Milly, who would have been offered a stable if she had foaled a mare rather than given birth to a female child, Miss Rosa, who is asked to breed to see if she will produce a son for Sutpen, is the most insulted figure in Faulkner's fiction. No one defends Miss Rosa except perhaps Rosa, who declares, "I hold no brief for myself" (*AA!* 13). In Faulkner's final novel, *The Reivers* (1962), Lucius Priest, the runaway boy of a fine family follows directly in the path of Don Quixote as he defends the honor of a Memphis prostitute, Corinthia Everbe. (This woman,

more commonly known as Miss Corrie, is being pursued by the mixed-race reprobate Boon Hoggenbeck, whose Indian blood on the distaff side is seen as a locus for his debasement in *Go Down, Moses* [1942].) Questions of female honor in Faulkner, whether tragically or comically quixotic or both, are depicted as unwinnable battles, but the fact that these skirmishes are fought most often over the violation of lower-class women and women of color, and that they end almost as often in the sacrifice of women as in the sacrifice of men, is not only telling; this catalog of honor-driven plot elements is instructive and provides grounds for Dewey Dell's concern that Darl might kill Lafe. For more on the code of honor as it is traditionally understood and functions between and among elite parties as well as their inferiors in claims to class, see Bertram Wyatt-Brown's *Southern Honor: Ethics and Behavior in the Old South* (New York: Oxford University Press, 1982).

14. For an explication of these terms and the most relevant social commentary on the community ethos and forces at work in Dewey Dell's world, see Margaret Jarman Hagood's *Mothers of the South* (1937). If the illegitimate Milly in *Absalom, Absalom!* (a violated daughter whose unmarried mother has gone to Memphis) is already in prospective retrospect positioned as the harbinger of Caddy's illegitimate daughter, Quentin, the violent slaughter of daughter and granddaughter by the grandfather ends the Jones family's descent. This is a legacy that in the absence of property follows the fate of daughters who bear the unchanging family name as a family is transformed from being poor to being placed at the considerably diminished status of being "sorry." In slave society, children were legally determined to follow the condition of the mother. This was a law designed to regulate ownership in the reproduction of human property that rendered questions of paternity of less concern, as Sutpen makes clear, than that brought to the siring of thoroughbred horses.

15. As the autograph copy shows, Faulkner reworked this line, changing words until he achieved this lyrical apotheosis. When completed, he moved this line to its present place at the end of the section. The final sectional lines in *As I Lay Dying* contain some of the strongest, most suggestive, and lyrical prose in the novel.

16. Interview with Steve Langstreet in Inge, ed., *Conversations with William Faulkner*, 53.

17. The revelation of *As I Lay Dying* is not that the dead and rotting mother, Addie Bundren, speaks. The dead often speak in dreams, plays, novels, and daily life, returning to offer warnings, helpful advice, advising sons about a murderous mother's infidelities ("something is rotten in the state of Denmark"), or even to remind the living of what Wharton elsewhere called "long unsatisfied hates."

18. The single exception, Vardaman, the youngest child, listens for life inside the box, auguring holes in the coffin to violate the mother's head to insist on Addie Bundren's emasculation. This joins her with feminized characters, Wharton's Ethan Frome and Cather's Henry, while maintaining her connection to the fatal female power of Cather's murdered (and supposedly adulterous) "Mother Eve." Addie wears her nuptial garment as her shroud, but because of Vardaman's drilling to allow her to breathe, the mosquito net veil has been added to intensify the sense of her wedding, emphasizing wedding itself as a form of death. As Toni Morrison's one-legged Eva Peace in *Sula* (1973) reminds us about the interpretation of dreams: the dream of a wedding always means a death.

19. The number of respected critics and attentive students of Faulkner who assume Dewey Dell gets pregnant at the end of the row during her encounter recalled in her initial entry, section 7, is finally too large not to have meaning. The fairy-tale—literally fabulous—quality of *As I Lay Dying* has caused the work to be repeatedly defined as a mock-heroic quest or epic. Part of what this belief belies is readers' refusal to acknowledge that what we know from the fifty-nine sections is finally only a partial story. Had Dewey Dell been impregnated during cotton picking (typically done in late September and early October), she would be in her ninth or tenth month of pregnancy by the time of Addie's death in July or August, and her condition would have been visible to Addie Bundren, Doc Peabody, the drugstore men, and everyone in the novel who sees her. The tenth month of pregnancy does exist and is more common for first-time mothers, but the Dewey Dell of *As I Lay Dying* still harbors her secret. When questioned by Moseley, she directly acknowledges having missed two periods. However one does the math, the bottom line is that she would be more than showing if she had been impregnated at harvest.

20. Cotton was planted in the hills of northern Mississippi in the spring—after the last frost, and usually after Easter. While the planting of some crops followed moon signs and were even said to grow better if sown by the light of the full moon, cotton was a cash crop and, as such, was planted according to stable organic signs. Farmers, according to their elevation, would observe the switch-hickory trees, watching for their leaves to become the size of a squirrel's ear. After harrowing the fields in March, the earth was smoothed by dragging two cross ties joined in tandem over the land. Rows were then sighted and laid out before being strewn with a line of guano (bat or cormorant manure) distributed by the turning wheel of a mule-pulled machine known as a "guano-knocker." Then, a fifty-pound bag of soda with a hole torn in it was carried on the back of a mule, being beaten rhythmically with a stick to sift the powder onto the row. Cotton seeds were deposited by a rolling planter in the shape of a hopper and immediately covered over by the rear action of the implement's smoothing arm. Almost a week after the seeds had sprouted, when the plants were three inches tall, chopping was begun. The first chopping was the width of the hoe (an implement called a "one-eyed John" that got its name from a hole in its handle). This accomplished the thinning of the seedlings. While a field might be worked with the hoe as many as three or four times, the second chopping, the most severe and critical, established which plants were chosen to survive. Designed to favor the strongest plants, this chopping (called siding or mounding) piled deeper dirt around the selected plants as other cotton plants were chopped out and turned under with the errant weeds. Here, even strong plants were removed to ensure the productivity of the cotton crop. Depending on the rain, bolls (the tight-fisted buds called "squares") then began to appear on a maturing plant; these bloomed into flowers before the seed pods formed, hardened, blackened, and finally broke into the quadrants that exposed the desired spills of white wool. Even in the foothills of the Appalachians and high rolling hills of the lower Piedmont, a few bolls mature as early as late August, but school calendars along the cotton-growing uplands of north Mississippi and Alabama reflected the need for family labor, declaring weeks of recess in early October that were called "cotton picking." This detailed account of cotton cultivation in the uplands of 1930 Mississippi and Alabama is based on oral accounts from Rolf Tullos, J. T. Rodgers, and Donald C. Waid. This account docu-

ments the production of cotton as it would have been practiced on farms that paralleled those tilled by the fictional Bundrens and Tulls.

21. See Lester, "As They Lay Dying: Rural Depopulation and Social Dislocation as a Structure of Feeling," *Faulkner Journal* 21, nos. 1–2 (Fall 2005/2006), for more on Dewey Dell's association of Lafe with town people in which Dewey Dell "reflects on her sexual liaison with Lafe and futilely seeks to resolve its undesirable consequences by wishing that it had never happened: 'I don't see why he didn't stay in town. We are country people, not as good as town people'" (44).

22. As Shin Moonsu contends, "Townspeople like Moseley and MacGowan are not exceptions: Moseley's self-righteous indignation at Dewey Dell's request for pills or MacGowan's wily trick on her innocence all shows the typical urban prejudices against the countryfolk like the Bundrens." In Shin's analysis, the vectors here are not South versus North but rather more rooted in Raymond Williams's categories that counterpose the "city" and the "country." See "*As I Lay Dying:* Emergence of Faulkner the Southern Modernist," *Faulkner Journal of Japan* 5 (September 2003).

23. Whatever its length, Dewey Dell and Lafe's row is not the two-mile (money-producing) variety found in the Delta. And, finally, whether Dewey Dell is picking on the family's crop or not, her bag (likely stiffened by tar at its dragging bottom) is not the nine- or even the seven-foot-long variety. This is a cotton patch: this upland field is a way of getting by. With picked cotton garnering piece-work wages for day laborers between 25 cents (in the up country) and 75 cents (on plantation lands) per hundred pounds, the difference between Yoknapatawpha and the Delta, between the early and the late 1930s, is significant but small. The average day laborer in the fields could expect wages of around 35 cents a day. As a high-hormoned man (less skilled that the legendary male slaves of the Delta who picked 600 pounds in a good day), Lafe is likely above average. In a decade in which cotton was selling for 4 cents a pound, 4 dollars for a hundred pounds, the picker who made a dollar a day was considered to be at the top of the scale. It is not possible to know how full Dewey Dell's sack already is. Her traditional croker sack with its small mouth and short neck strap can only be imagined by those who picked cotton as breast-intensive foreplay—albeit before Darl observes his pregnant sister's breasts as "mammalian ludicrosties."

24. The idea of "a dime" that is not her own is based on the idiom of doing things on your "own dime." I believe that what Lafe contributes to the Bundren daughter's cotton sack may be less than a dime's worth of raw cotton. In the best of years for pickers, it could be a little more. This assessment is based on the low price per pound for cotton as well as the limited length of rows in the small patch fields of the hill country of Mississippi and Alabama.

25. This seems obvious to me, and I believe it will be obvious to those who know the book, but I have been told by one unidentified reader that it is not. Aside from Dewey Dell's efforts to buy an abortifacient, the only narrative of a purchase is the story recounted of Jewel's purchase in a dry goods or hardware store of concrete to encase Cash's broken leg. Cash's desire for a "graphophone" comes as a by-product of Anse's purchase of the new teeth that allow him to acquire a wife who has this appliance as her major accessory. Dewey Dell's successful purchase of bananas takes place off page, but this exotic fruit is seen as a palliative for Vardaman's hopes for the toy train. Neither Jewel nor Darl is trying to buy anything, but the account of their experi-

ences amounts to the loss of freedom and independent mobility that is not a function of mercantile consumption but life-limiting acts of barter. While he will be curtailed by the forced trade of his hard-earned horse, Jewel's relation to town has been and will continue to be entirely different from that of Anse's children. Jewel's recent visit to town and the barber is marked by the white line at the base of his head bone.

26. Olga W. Vickery, "The Dimensions of Consciousness," in *As I Lay Dying, William Faulkner: Three Decades of Criticism*, ed. Frederick J. Hoffman and Olga W. Vickery (New York: Harcourt, Brace & World, 1963), 245.

27. For a discussion of the historical and social grounds for Pinkham's as well as other business ventures addressing female health, see Sarah Stage, *Female Complaints: Lydia Pinkham and the Business of Women's Health* (New York: W. W. Norton, 1979).

28. Responding to a report from the Secretary of Agriculture, the District Court of the United States for the Eastern District of Tennessee fined the Andrews Manufacturing Company of Bristol $50 in March 1916 for mislabeling. Andrews's "Wine of Life," marketed to women as a "female regulator," was fined for being "falsely and fraudulently represented as a remedy for all diseases peculiar to the female sex." The alcohol content of this product was duly measured for relabeling at 14.9 percent. The word "unnatural" as applied to "suppressed" periods both denies and alludes to this product's possible use as an over-the-counter abortion tonic.

29. Any walk through a rural cemetery provides more than anecdotal evidence that a successful country patriarch could, and often did, use up three bearing-aged women. Serial procreation abetted by fatal parturition made forty the median age for U.S. women at the turn into the twentieth century. This age of maternal death remained lower in the South not just because of poor health care and poverty, but because of higher fertility rates in an economy in which children married earlier and produced more children to be farmworkers. Children became financial liabilities in a vastly shifting economy that provided opportunities for workers in factories and service positions in the North at the same time that cotton cultivation was being progressively mechanized. While the romance of the machine has long been a central trope in works of labor history, it is extremely important in terms of race to recognize the agency of southern blacks as the primary impetus for the mechanization of cotton production. The machines had become more necessary because of the dearth of labor in the wake of massive northern migrations by white as well as black agricultural workers. The machines filled in for the 60 percent shortage in the workforce, while the entry of these same machines displaced the 40 percent of the workers who had planned to spend their lives working in the fields. In terms of families such as the Bundrens and the Tulls, much of the manual labor in the cultivation of cotton was finally rendered unnecessary as machines such as the cotton picker began to be used even on the small upland farms by the late 1960s. For the most complete record on the northern migration, see the *In Motion African-American Migration Experience: The Northern Migration* website (www.inmotionaame.org). Also, see Cheryl Lester's excellent article, "As They Lay Dying: Rural Depopulation and Social Dislocation as a Structure of Feeling," *Faulkner Journal* 21, nos. 1–2 (Fall 2005/2006), 28. Lester's analysis, along with the careful and revisionary work of Richard Godden in his field-altering books *William Faulkner: An Economy of Complex Words* (Princeton: Princeton University Press, 2002) and *Fictions of Labor: Faulkner and the South's Long Revolution* (Cambridge: Cambridge

University Press, 2007), constitute a long overdue sea change in Faulkner scholarship concerning the historically specific depredations of black labor and the romance of the machine. Lester mentions the advent of the machine but wisely does not make a claim for its role as the singular force in the decision of blacks (or whites) to move north to other pursuits. As Lester concludes, "From World War I to the 1960s, the years in which Faulkner flourished as a writer, rural depopulation, agricultural mechanization, and black migration confronted millions with the shock of social and spatial dislocation" (32). Machines that worked early and well in the mile-long rows of the Delta and between the California plants engineered to be the perfect height for mechanical cultivation were quite late in becoming cost-effective for small upland farms with their cotton patches on uneven and sometimes hilly land. Cotton in the uplands of Mississippi continued to be worked by hand.

30. MacGowan initially tells his lackey, Jody, to "Send her to the courthouse . . . Tell her all the doctors have gone to Memphis to a Barbers' Convention." This piece of prescient advice may suggest that legal marriage is the solution to the country girl's problem, but it also recalls the historical roles of barbers as surgeons, a professional sideline that recognized their skill with sharp, cutting tools. While MacGowan presciently suggests that what the as yet unseen girl may need is to be found at the courthouse—legal marriage and its authorization of sexual congress—his wisecrack about "Barbers' Convention" also suggests that she cannot get the surgery he does not yet know she seeks. For a strong and detailed analysis of the theme of abortion in Faulkner's novels in the 1930s that places this issue in a social context and describes the access to abortion and products proposing to be abortifacients that were advertised in the public press, see Janet Carey Elred, "Faulkner's Still Life: Art and Abortion in *The Wild Palms*," *Faulkner Journal* 4, nos. 1–2 (Fall 1988/Spring 1989): 139–58. Katherine Henninger joins the experience of Dewey Dell Bundren to that of Charlotte Rittenmeyer to understand the place of women in relation to access to abortion as a way of addressing larger issues concerning bodily control in national and international movements during these decades as a whole. In an argument that strains somewhat, this essay separates Moseley from his tone of offended morality and references to God's role by insisting on the shift of ideology that locates community as part of a masculine prerogative. Henninger identifies Moseley's effort at control to the rise of interest in controlling women's bodies being promulgated by groups of men such as those who were following and making public guidelines through the American Medical Association. In a discussion that includes the changing view toward maternity taken by the Communist Party, Henningsen "politiciz[es] Dewey Dell by exposing these public experiences as encounters with 'male ideology'" ("'It's an Outrage': Pregnancy and Abortion in Faulkner's Fiction of the Thirties," *Faulkner Journal* 12, no. 1 [Fall 1996]: 23–41). For work that places Faulkner's fiction concerning abortion in a tellingly national context, see Yamshita Noboru, "Faulkner's 'The Scarlet Letter': *If I Forget Thee, Jerusalem* as an Abortion Novel," *Faulkner Journal of Japan* 4 (September 2002). Yamshita focuses on Faulkner's problem novel on the tabooed subject of abortion, which is analyzed as a locus of rising concern because of the necessity of women's work outside the home during the Great Depression. Citing detailed Japanese research into U.S. practices concerning birth control and abortion, Yamshita's essay contends that puritanical sexual repression resulted in a widespread lack of knowledge among

American doctors about the workings of the female reproductive process, in particular the mysteries of the menstrual cycle. Linking the failed intern Harry Wilbourne's efforts to purchase an abortion pill in *The Wild Palms* (1939) with those of the more justifiably ignorant Dewey Dell, Yamshita reports that 14 percent of all deaths in pregnancy during the 1930s were attributable to "failed abortions which rose to 15,000 a year." Written to provide a social, historical, and literary context for "The Wild Palms" strand of Faulkner's 1939 novel, this essay speaks to the situation faced by Dewey Dell in the rural Mississippi of his 1930 *As I Lay Dying*.

31. "Dysentery," a term for severe diarrhea, an infection that includes the fecal passing of blood and mucus, gets its name from the Greek words for "bad intestines." While a streak of lasciviousness, prurience, and/or misogyny becomes a pattern in Faulkner's fiction among men who are not owners but clerks who meet the public, these men's responses to female incursions into their domains vary. *Sartoris*'s Byron Snopes, the bank clerk who writes obscene letters to a lady customer (Narcissa Benbow), remains mysterious while figures such as *The Sound and the Fury*'s Jason Compson and *As I Lay Dying*'s Skeet MacGowan speak the same language while having vastly different ways of enjoying the degradation of women.

32. For an extensive discussion of this aesthetic paradigm and the obsessions shared by Faulkner's artist figures and their idealized conception of the work of art and its threatened violation, see chapter 4 in this volume.

33. Miss Emily Grierson enters a drugstore in order to buy poison to preserve a lover, and she wants the best poison. Although money changes hands, she is clearly in control of any possible romantic potential in this transaction.

34. For more on the mysteries of Gavin Stevens's sexual identity, see Daniel Pecchenino's dissertation "'Incorrigibly and Invincibly Bachelor': The Unmarried Man and the Isolation of Individualism in Mid-20th-Century U.S. Fiction" (2011). Among the notable cameo appearances of women in stores are Mrs. Armstid, who is offered a bag of cheap candy—what Flem calls "sweetnin' for the chaps"—in exchange for the money that represents her life's arduous labor. The former prostitute Ruby Lamar is thrown out of a hotel because she is seen by others as exchanging sexual favors for legal assistance, an economy so well established that even she herself imagines this is the commodity she owes to her husband's lawyer, Horace Benbow. William Faulkner's joking sense of his relation to women exposed in the marketplace includes an encounter that Jenny from *Mosquitoes* recalls as taking place in a bookstore, where she is beset by a peculiar little man described as "black" in demeanor whose name turns out to be "Faulkner."

35. After being purchased in an arrangement justified by Flem, who calculates the amount of respectability by the pound, giving the lion's share of financial responsibility to the Snopes family with the most children, the bovine beloved is meted out ritually. In another remedy based on the "hair of the dog," Reverend Whitfield (reprised in a more respectable role than that of his earlier appearance as the speaker with his heavy adulterous secret in section 41 of *As I Lay Dying*) has declared that the only cure for such an amorous attachment to a specific beast is that the meat of this beloved must be consumed by her lover.

36. For a full analysis detailing the arguments that this is a masturbatory scene, see Charles Chappell, "The Sexual Fantasy of Dewey Dell Bundren," in *Notes on Mississippi Writers*, 85–90. Chappell supports his claims by an incisive reference in a

note to another encounter in a Faulkner story, "Miss Zilphia Grant," which appears in *The Uncollected Stories of William Faulkner*. It reads: "or, rousing, furious, her hands clenched at her sides, the covers flying back and her opened thighs tossing, she would violate her ineradicable virginity again and again with something evoked out of the darkness immemorial and philoprogenitive. 'I will conceive! I'll make myself conceive!'" (*US* 379).

37. Deborah Clarke, without reference to the sound of dialect pronunciation, also hears the homosonic hum, the play of the pun, linking "Lafe" to "Life" ("all this pro-life and pro-Lafe rhetoric" [45]).

38. See chapter 2 of this volume for a detailed analysis of Darl's progressive loss of a bodily presence in *As I Lay Dying*. See also Deborah Clarke, *Robbing the Mother*, for an analysis that observes the novel's insistence on Darl's bodilessness as it is complexly opposed to the literal physicality of mothers and others in this novel.

39. A favored work title of Faulkner's, "The Dark House," was the proposed name for *Light in August*, *Absalom, Absalom!*, and several shorter works. See Shakespeare's *Twelfth Night* for the most famous use of this phrase in reference to an insane asylum.

40. This autograph copy is housed in the Special Collections Library at the University of Virginia. Following tradition, Faulkner used underlining to indicate italics.

41. As they pass the road to New Hope for the first time, Darl sees "a white signboard with faded lettering: New Hope Church. 3 mi. It wheels up like a motionless hand lifted above the profound desolation of the ocean; beyond it the red road lies like a spoke of which Addie Bundren is the rim." Here in section 27, "Dewey Dell looks at the road too, . . . her eyes watchful and repudiant" (108). Dewey Dell's section 30 opens as she anticipates seeing this same sign. In the first extant version of *As I Lay Dying* (48), as the "entrails of things" become "the entrails of events," a "hand" is said to "pull [. . .]" in relation to these entrails. See page 108 in *The Signifying Eye* for a full transcription of this passage.

42. After being forcibly put on the train bound for Jackson and the state mental institution, Darl speaks of himself and to himself in the third person as "Darl" and "him," and "them." Occupying the first person as an "I," Darl addresses and again interrogates the Darl who in his hysterical laughter has begun to occupy the second-person position as the "you" before he metamorphoses into the exterior yet strangely inclusive perspective of the first-person plural possessive pronoun: "Darl is our brother, our brother Darl. Our brother Darl in a cage in Jackson . . . looking out he foams." Beyond being literally possessed at the moment he is excluded by his family, Darl begins to use the pronoun "he" to refer to himself. As Jewel becomes "the man who looks like any other man," Darl has replaced Jewel as the person whom he (Darl) refers to simply as "he." For an extensive discussion of Darl's final section, section 57, see chapter 4 of *The Signifying Eye*. ("She" is the missing pronoun.)

43. In the autograph version of the novel, Dewey Dell asks: ["]was I dead["] (quotation marks added). The statement about "when I died that time" is a vastly transformed form (an established Faulknerian trope for female orgasm) as it has been revised for the published novel. This statement in any form had been deleted at the typescript stage of the publication process before being added back into the published book.

44. The most obvious of these concerns Jewel, the child that he does not know is not his own. Jewel's loss of independent mobility is underlined by the bartering of

his horse for a team of mules and is reinforced as he tries to be part of the Bundren family by getting in the wagon, only to be ordered by Anse to join the already walking Darl, Dewey Dell, and Vardaman, relieving the wagon of its burdens as it challenges a substantial hill.

45. See Doreen Fowler's excellent analysis of animal totems and other maternal surrogates in *As I Lay Dying:* Vardaman's "mother is a fish"; Jewel's "mother is a horse"; and Cash's mother is the coffin (*Faulkner: The Return of the Repressed* [Charlottesville: University Press of Virginia, 1997]).

46. It is quite interesting that this long passage was not italicized until the published version.

47. To see where this orphaned (solitary, unanswered, and unframed) quotation mark appears (as well as to consider the presence of the phrase "// he says//" treated in the discussion below), see note 48 for the transcription of this entire passage from the handwritten version.

48. This is a transcription of this passage as it appears in the autograph version housed in the Special Collections of the Smart Library at the University of Virginia:

The land runs out of Darl's eyes; they swim to pin points. *They begin at my feet and rise up my body to my face and then my dress is gone. I sit naked on the seat above the mules, above the travail.* ~~Suppose~~ *"Suppose I tell him to turn. //he says/He will do what I say. // Once I waked with a black void rushing under me. I could not see. I saw Vardaman rise and go to the window and strike the knife into the fish, the blood gushing hissing like steam but I could not see.// He'll do as I say. He always does. I could persuade him to anything. You know I can.// Was I dead now?//Suppose I do. We'll go to New Hope. We wont have to go to town.//I rose took the knife from the streaming fish still hissing I killed Darl.* (Orphaned quotation marks in original.)

49. J. L. Austin, *How to Do Things with Words* (Oxford: Oxford University Press, 1962).

50. For an instructive discussion of narrative in *As I Lay Dying*, see Dorothy J. Hale, "*As I Lay Dying*'s Heterogeneous Discourse," *Novel: A Forum on Fiction* 23, no. 1 (Autumn 1989): 5–23. Hale, in an extensive note, distinguishes between Dewey Dell's private discourse and the sense of public usurpation in the dialogue that constitutes Dewey Dell's fourth section: "Dewey Dell's monologues chart a progression that is superficially similar to Cash's development; brother and sister both move from 'unsayable' private discourse to wholly sayable public discourse. Yet the extremity of Dewey Dell's final monologue—the fact that after the initial first-person introductory phrase her consciousness is represented entirely by recorded dialogue—suggests the public's complete usurpation of her rich private consciousness. She may ostensibly be a survivor like Cash, but with Anse's final victimization of her, with her loss of the economic resources that she needs to control her fate, she becomes like Darl, unable to bridge the gap between public and private discourses" (20–21).

CHAPTER FOUR. THE SIGNIFYING EYE

1. Honoré de Balzac, "Le Chef-d'œuvre inconnu," in *Le Chef-d'œuvre inconnu; Gambara; Massimilla Doni* (Paris: Flammarion, 1981), 47.

2. This drawing and letter are in the archives at the University of Virginia. See Blotner's biography for a brief listing of these objects, both in their role as birthday gifts and as an indication of the types of things housed in the richly layered Faulkner Collection in the Small Library at the University of Virginia in Charlottesville.

3. Early June is late spring for much of the United States, but as many school calendars acknowledge, this is a summer month. More relevant to *As I Lay Dying* as well as 1907 Mississippi (even in a cold spring) is the fact that an unembalmed body begins to turn color and to smell within the first twenty-four hours, even in the age of 67-degree air-conditioning.

4. "Hermaphroditus" is the title of a poem attributed to the character Eva Wiseman in *Mosquitoes*. Faulkner himself published virtually the same poem under the same title in *The Green Bough*, the collection of his early poems.

5. William Faulkner, *"Elmer"; and, "A Portrait of Elmer": The Typescripts, Manuscripts, and Miscellaneous Pages*, vol. 1 of the William Faulkner Manuscripts, introduced and arranged by Thomas L. McHaney (New York: Garland Publishing, 1987), 3–4. Further citations from this text will refer to this edition.

6. William Faulkner, *Mosquitoes* (New York: Liveright, 1997), 13–18. Further citations from this text will refer to this edition.

7. There are several interesting readings of this scene that discusses the milk bottle as a fetishized object that has strong sexual and erotic connotations. See Michael Zeitlin's discussion of this object as linked to the phallicism of this milk bottle as embodying the Freudian concept of castration anxiety. An early form of this essay benefited from conversations with Zeitlin on the possible interpretations of this fetishized object. Zeitlin's reading is developed in full in his "Faulkner in Nighttown: *Mosquitoes* and the 'Circe' Episode," *Mississippi Quarterly* 42 (Summer 1989). For his compelling analyses of Freudian structures and roots of identity formation in Faulkner's early fiction, see Zeitlin, "Faulkner and Psychoanalysis: The 'Elmer' Case," in *Faulkner and Psychology: Faulkner and Yoknapatawpha, 1991*, ed. Donald M. Kartiganer and Ann J. Abadie (Jackson: University Press of Mississippi, 1994), 219–41. See also Minrose C. Gwin, "Did Ernest Like Gordon? Faulkner's *Mosquitoes* and the Bite of 'Gender Trouble,'" *Faulkner and Gender: Faulkner and Yoknapatawpha, 1995*, ed. Donald M. Kartiganer and Ann J. Abadie (Jackson: University Press of Mississippi, 1996). Gwin's essay remains one of the most insightful readings of the painful positioning of Taliaferro in relation not just to this milk bottle but also in the context of hertero-normativity, which locates marriage as a shelter for celibacy and continued repression of desire in this novel.

8. William Faulkner, *Sartoris* (1929; reprint, New York: New American Library Signet Classics, 1964), 146. Further citations from this text will refer to this edition. See David Minter, *William Faulkner: His Life and His Work* (Baltimore: Johns Hopkins University Press, 1980), 99–103. In an insightful comment, Minter distinguishes among Faulkner's early artist figures: "Elmer and Horace work in their art toward a female figure that is actual; they make art a substitute for love of a real woman. Gordon, on the other hand, makes art a way of approaching an ideal whose identity remains vague" (101). Minter's work has been important to the conception of this project, especially his discussions of Faulkner's obsession with the feminine vase and the way this figure informs Faulkner's understanding of the relationship between sexuality and art. See

"Faulkner, Childhood, and the Making of *The Sound and the Fury*," in *The Sound and the Fury*, ed. David Minter, 2nd ed. (New York: Norton, 1994), 343–58.

9. For a riveting reading and rereading of the implications of the myth for understanding Horace Benbow, see John Irwin's "Horace Benbow and the Myth of Narcissa," which analyzes a version of the Narcissus story featuring incestuous desire of a brother for a sister as the inconsolable male grieves for the loss of his dead female twin, in *Faulkner and Psychology: Faulkner and Yoknapatawpha, 1991*, ed. Donald M. Kartiganer and Ann J. Abadie (Jackson: University Press of Mississippi, 1994).

10. William Faulkner, *Flags in the Dust* (New York: Random House, 1973), 153. *Flags in the Dust* was the original manuscript that in a cut and edited form appeared as *Sartoris*.

11. William Faulkner, "An Introduction to *The Sound and the Fury*," in *The Sound and the Fury*, ed. David Minter, 2nd ed. (New York: Norton, 1994), 226. Written by Faulkner for a 1933 edition of the novel, the two versions of the introductions printed in Minter's volume were not published in Faulkner's lifetime.

12. In *Flags in the Dust*, the "shapeless things" are said to be "Antic, with shadows on the wet walls, red shadows; a dull red gleam, and black shapes like cardboard cut-outs rising and falling like a magic-lantern shutter" (153). The spectacle of a magic-lantern show suggested by Faulkner's original representation of "the card board cut-outs" casting black shadows and the "red shadows" of the furnace are revised in *Sartoris* to focus on "paper dolls," which suggest the creations of the literary artist.

13. *Selected Letters of William Faulkner*, ed. Joseph Blotner (New York: Random House, 1977), 228.

14. For the most extensive understanding of this phenomenon in the criticism, see Deborah Clarke's *Robbing the Mother* (Jackson: University Press of Mississippi, 2006).

15. William Faulkner, *The Wild Palms* (1939; New York: Random House, 1990), 40. Further references to this text refer to this edition.

16. Wilbourne's reference to himself as a painter has baffled readers. Referring to Wilbourne's claim to be a painter in the opening chapter, Michael Millgate concludes: "There is much about *The Wild Palms* which does not seem wholly explicable in terms of the thematic patterns of the book or the psychology of the characters. It is, indeed, in many ways a strange and uncomfortable book" (*The Achievement of William Faulkner* [New York: Random House, 1966], 178–79).

17. Millgate speculates that there seems to be "some kind of autobiographical or peculiarly personal significance" for *The Wild Palms*. He bases this view on the "curious personal quality of many of its incidents and allusions" and "the almost masochistic intensity of Wilbourne's agony" (179). This novel has been seen by many as Faulkner's written response to the emotions he was facing after his relationship with his favored lover, Meta Carpenter.

18. There are few critical comments about this painting. Thomas L. McHaney suggests that "Charlotte's sexuality in its most basic, purely biological terms brings Harry back to an awareness of time" (*William Faulkner's* The Wild Palms: *A Study* [Jackson: University Press of Mississippi, 1975], 91–92).

19. McHaney calls this "one of the most cryptic passages in the novel." Speculating that the source is autobiographical, he reads this passage as a "blending of references to a romantic disappointment with references to [Sherwood] Anderson's art" (22).

20. Charlotte's job here reflects Faulkner's knowledge of labor history, particularly the ways in which actual artists made their livings in urban America during the 1930s. See chapter 7 in this volume for a brief discussion of the significance of Willem de Kooning's stint as a window dresser during his youth in Holland. This history is detailed in Mark Stevens and Annalyn Swan, *De Kooning: An American Master* (New York: Alfred A. Knopf, 2007). Three chapters in Stevens and Swan (81–122) demonstrate that this was indeed a day job for artists from the 1920s through the Depression in major cities of the United States. De Kooning left a high-paying job at A. S. Beck, a major department store chain in New York, to devote himself full-time to his art by attaining a position in the WPA. Meanwhile, de Kooning's talent for advertising and display is suggested by the fact that A. S. Beck offered to double his salary to keep him in their employ in 1935, a year not known for raises in pay.

21. Ben Jonson, *Bartholomew Fair*, ed. Edward B. Partridge (Lincoln: University of Nebraska Press, 1969), v, 90–97.

22. William Faulkner, *As I Lay Dying* (New York: Random House, 1990), 58. Further citations from this text will refer to this edition.

23. I am grateful to my former student Jarret Sonta and other students in numerous seminars for their insights into the connections between the missing periods and other formal codes in *As I Lay Dying*.

24. Quoted by Donald Kartiganer in *The Fragile Thread: The Meaning of Form in Faulkner's Novels* (Amherst: University of Massachusetts Press, 1979), 3.

25. For an extensive discussion of these manuscript changes to Dewey Dell's narrative in section 30 of *As I Lay Dying*, see the preceding chapter in this volume, "Dewey Dell, Dead Center."

26. William Faulkner, *The Sound and the Fury*, ed. David Minter (New York: Norton, 1994), 207. Further citations from this text will refer to this edition.

27. However anxiety-provoking this may be for readers, this reference to the interior female genital, the hymen, as a globy or earthlike ball is finally Faulkner's metaphor—not my own. Faulkner repeatedly emphasizes this common concept of the female body as a container, balloon, ball, or blood-filled inner tube that can be punctured, smashed, or otherwise broken. Faulkner's sense of the globular quality of hymenic tissue is one in which the biologically understood or drumlike flatness has become round in his fiction's vocabulary for embodiment. I make this point here by linking this passage from "The Wild Palms" to his later written "Appendix Compson" to *The Sound and the Fury*. Also, Temple Drake's excessively bleeding hymen is described as making a sound like a ruptured rubber tube in *Sanctuary*, and the violated tube of De Spain's car assaulted by a "rake" provides the complex material and lingual pun when adorned with a used condom and a discarded corsage in Faulkner's 1957 novel *The Town*.

28. See *The Sound and the Fury*, ed. Minter, 227.

29. Petronius is a historical figure who was in charge of excess and style during the reign of the Roman emperor Nero. Faulkner's 1932 novel *Light in August* refers to sexual poses as being "like Beardsley in the time of Petronius." This image is discussed fully along with Faulkner's use of the imagery from Beardsley's drawings in chapter 6 of this work.

30. Henryk Sienkiewicz, *Quo Vadis*, trans. Jeremiah Curtin (London: J. M. Dent, 1900), 6, 11–12.

31. David Lodge, *Language of Fiction* (New York: Columbia University Press, 1966), 47 (quoted by Susan Gubar in "The Blank Page," *in Writing and Sexual Difference*, ed. Elizabeth Abel [Chicago: University of Chicago Press, 1982], 77).

32. While Michael Zeitlin does not discuss Freud's "Three Caskets," his work has been invaluable in its nuanced discussions of the significance of Freud's understanding of archetypal structures and Joyce's crucial and troubling tropes as influential groundings for Faulkner's fiction. For particularly relevant interventions, see Zeitlin, "Faulkner, Joyce, and the Problem of Influence in *The Sound and the Fury*," *Faulkner Studies* 2 (1994): 1–25, and his "Returning to Freud and *The Sound and the Fury*," *Faulkner Journal* 13, nos. 1–2 (Fall 1997): 57–77.

33. From the female perspective, the pregnant Dewey Dell of *As I Lay Dying* concludes: "I feel like a wet seed wild in the hot blind earth" (58).

34. In an interesting discussion, Eric J. Sundquist insists that Faulkner's comments on *The Sound and the Fury* are part of his retrospective mythologizing of this novel. In particular, Sundquist speculates that the scene of looking up at Caddy's drawers is not actually the founding image of the novel. Putting aside the vexed question about whether anyone can truthfully describe the origins of a work of art, for my purposes here, it is important that Faulkner persisted in telling what was for him already an old story about works of art and women and vases, and that (even in retrospect) he focuses on the image of Caddy looking into the window onto death. See Sundquist, *Faulkner: The House Divided* (Baltimore: Johns Hopkins University Press, 1983), 3–27.

35. Gary Lee Stonum, commenting on Faulkner's return to the terms of "his earlier, image-based art" to explain the "gestation of the novel," notes that in this description "Faulkner abandons a narrative term, 'tell,' for a pictorial one." Faulkner's use of the pictorial term is interesting, but this language also contains an echo of the original question asked by the interviewer. Indeed, this question is the source of Faulkner's specific allusion to the visual arts. Yet while the answer echoes the question, the question itself is apt and inspired by a genuine insight into Caddy's figuring of the visual and plastic arts in the novel. See *Faulkner's Career: An Internal Literary History* (Ithaca: Cornell University Press, 1979), 76.

36. In a letter to his Aunt Bama written in the fall of 1927, Faulkner mentions that he has "a job of work" for "this month. Painting signs" (*The Sound and the Fury*, ed. Minter, 218).

37. *Son* in French is also the masculine possessive singular "his." The word for "word," *mot*, is gendered as masculine: his "word" and the word "his" are in play.

38. In the appendix to the novel, we learn that Ikkemotubbe was called "L'Homme" by the French, a name that was shortened to "Doom." Throughout the novel, there are plays on the Latin word *sum* ("I am") and the English word "sum." I am grateful to Heather O'Donnell for pointing out the striking use of a bilingual pun in the Quentin section as one of the Italian women who lives near the river keeps saying "si" as a polite affirmation while Quentin, hearing the word, thinks that she is saying "see."

39. For what might be seen as a companion piece to parts of this essay, see Michel Gresset's nuanced and influential reading of the violating and phallic gaze in *Fascination: Faulkner's Fiction, 1919–1936* (Durham: Duke University Press, 1989). As Gresset confirmed in personal conversation in Taylor, Mississippi, in 1993, he had not ever thought of the vaginal eye, but he was of course immediately able to see it in the

pictorial eye as it was described to him as a labial, layered, hair-rimmed oval opening into interior depths.

40. A historical figure (approximately 40 BCE–10 BCE) who attempted to overturn the Roman presence in Egypt following the death of Cleopatra.

41. McHaney offers a gloss of this biblical quotation from Matthew 5:29 and the verse that follows: "And if thy right hand offend thee, cut it off and cast it from thee." As McHaney explains, "Matthew 5:27–31 is an admonition against adultery—either through covetousness or divorce. Charlotte has turned the meaning of it upside down to justify adultery. The connection to Faulkner's original title is plain." The original title from Psalm 137:5, which reads "If I Forget Thee Jerusalem," continues with the phrase, "let my right hand forget her cunning." McHaney makes the point that "when [Charlotte] has conceived a child that will 'offend' the continuation of the idealized love affair which she has never actually created, she will want to pluck that out too by cutting" (58). Millgate also links the failed abortion with the other half of this psalm (171).

42. For discussions of this phenomenon, see John T. Matthews, *The Play of Faulkner's Language* (Ithaca: Cornell University Press, 1982). I am grateful to Donald Kartiganer, who had an extensive discussion with me about this paradox at the 1993 Faulkner and Yoknapatawpha conference in Oxford, Mississippi.

43. See André Bleikasten, *The Most Splendid Failure: Faulkner's* The Sound and the Fury (Bloomington: Indiana University Press, 1976), 20.

44. André Bleikasten, *The Ink of Melancholy: Faulkner's Novels from* The Sound and the Fury *to* Light in August (Bloomington: Indiana University Press, 1990), 51.

45. For the most extensive discussion of Quentin's "longest reveries" in *The Sound and the Fury* and its formal relationship to *Absalom, Absalom!*, see chapter 5 in this volume.

46. Near the close of the second section, Caddy is figured as a type of glass that transforms the way her lover sees Quentin. Here Quentin faces the fact that Dalton Ames did not think of him "at all as a potential source of harm but was thinking of her when he was looking at me through her like through a piece of colored glass" (*SF* 111).

47. This is seen in the Jewish tradition, which calls for the groom to break a glass under his foot as part of the wedding ritual to assure a fruitful union. This is a common theme in traditional stories like the fairy tale "The Thrush Girl," which features the smashing of numerous pots to signal the theme of female transformation. See my *Edith Wharton's Letters from the Underworld: Fictions of Women and Writing* (Chapel Hill: University of North Carolina Press, 1991) for a discussion of Wharton's use in *Ethan Frome* of the symbolism of broken glass and broken bodies to tell a story about thwarted fertility.

48. Like a 1970s feminist, Jason has lost the job he has been promised by Caddy's pre-cuckolded husband, Herbert Head, and has been given a baby in its stead. After her disgrace and banishment from the family, Caddy sends money monthly for Quentin's needs, money that Jason secretly hoards in his room.

49. *Los Angeles Review of Books*, quoted by Glen David Gold in "The Dial" (November 29, 2011). *William Faulkner and Joan Williams: The Romance of Two Writers,* by Lisa C. Hickman (Jefferson, N.C.: McFarland, 2006), collects a selection of their letters and offers insight into the details of their collaborative work on *Requiem for a Nun*.

50. Donald Kartiganer, *The Fragile Thread: The Meaning of Form in Faulkner's Novels* (Amherst: University of Massachusetts Press, 1979), 334. Kartiganer uses the quotation that follows to substantiate his claim.

51. Faulkner has Fairchild, his writer from *Mosquitoes*, speculate about "Words" as "a kind of sterility . . . You begin to substitute words for things and deeds, like the withered cuckold husband that took the Decameron to bed with him every night, and pretty soon the thing or the deed becomes just a kind of shadow of a certain sound you make by shaping your mouth a certain way" (*M* 210). The writer acknowledges that there is also "a confusion": "I don't claim that words have life in themselves. But words brought into a happy conjunction produce something that lives, just as soil and climate and an acorn in proper conjunction will produce a tree. Words are like acorns" (*M* 210). Elsewhere in *Mosquitoes*, Fairchild listens as one of his aesthetic cronies concludes that words are part of a mysterious process of procreation and replication in which a "book is the writer's secret life, the dark twin of a man" (*M* 251). In *As I Lay Dying*, Addie Bundren also conceives of words as a dark twin, the trace that remains of a negated life, in which words and talk have taken the place of actual experience. She thinks that "sin and love and fear are just sounds that people who never sinned nor loved nor feared have for what they never had and cannot have until they forget the words" (*AILD* 173–74).

52. See in particular the manuscript version of *The Sound and the Fury,* which opens with Caddy standing in the door framed like Dilsey is at the opening of "April Eighth, 1928." The threshold represents Caddy's loss of virginity as she is pulled by Benjy to the bathroom. The image of Caddy standing in the door and on the threshold is returned to again and again and commonly carries with it the idea of bodily change, which is associated with the rituals of wedding. Caddy crosses out of Benjy's life and is banned from the Compson household for having her threshold crossed illicitly.

53. Stonum notes that "Caddy becomes less important in each successive part of the novel. But her decreasing centrality does not necessarily compromise the centrality of the ideal" (77). I am grateful to my student Zuwena Packer for her insights about the relationship between Caddy and Dilsey in the fourth section, in particular the role that Dilsey plays as a replacement figure for the missing Caddy.

54. I owe this insight about Faulkner's anxiety over the use of the word "coffin" to my student Jarret Sonta. In a related insight, André Bleikasten notes Faulkner's reluctance to use the word "coffin" and his decision to change the word in Darl's monologue from "coffin" to "box."

55. For another interpretation that also acknowledges the vaginal quality of this symbol, see Richard Godden's "Bear, Man, and Black: Hunting the Hidden in Faulkner's Big Woods," *Faulkner Journal* 23, no. 1 (2007): 3–25, as well as his article "Iconic Narrative: or, How Faulkner Fought the Second Civil War," in *Faulkner's Discourse* (68–76). Also, for more on the pictorial image in Faulkner, see Barry McCann's article "Faulkner's *As I Lay Dying:* The Coffin Pictogram and the Function of Form," *University of Mississippi Studies in English* 11–12 (1993–1995): 272–81.

56. See chapter 3 in this volume for further discussion of Faulkner's artist figures' interest in the pregnant woman's interior workings.

57. For a critically astute analysis on the connection between the blank space where the dead mother's (Addie Bundren's) virginity used to be and the other pictorial space

filled by the drawing of the coffin, see Carolyn Porter, "Symbolic Fathers and Dead Mothers: A Feminist Approach to Faulkner," in *Faulkner and Psychology: Faulkner and Yoknapatawpha, 1991*, ed. Donald M. Kartiganer and Ann J. Abadie (Jackson: University of Mississippi Press, 1994), 99. As Porter asserts, "The blank space in the text may be filled by phallus or womb, but it is still blank, marking an emptiness, a gap—the gap that has already been textually both filled and emptied by the drawing of her coffin. Further, if this drawing of the coffin is seen as a figure which simultaneously fills in and hollows out a lack, it may serve as a figure for Addie's discourse in the novel as well."

58. Bleikasten, *Ink of Melancholy*, 47.

59. William Faulkner, *The Wild Palms* (1939; New York: Vintage, 1995), 193.

60. For an analysis of the ways in which the female body threatens to imprison men and manhood, see Noel Polk's "The Dungeon Was Mother Herself: William Faulkner, 1927–1931," in *Douze Lectures de* Sanctuaire, ed. André Bleikasten and Nicole Moulinoux (Rennes: PU de Rennes / Fondation William Faulkner, 1995).

61. John Irwin, *Doubling and Incest / Repetition and Revenge* (Baltimore: Johns Hopkins University Press, 1975). Irwin discusses the idea of taking revenge by supplanting the father as the narrative authority and through the telling of the tale.

CHAPTER FIVE. ECHOING BACK TO *ABSALOM*

1. This chapter began as a paper solicited for the "Slow Reading Panel" organized by the Faulkner Society for the American Literature Association Conference in Boston in May 2005. The passage assigned to all of the panelists was the ten pages that I am calling the "reverie" of *The Sound and the Fury*. The talk in Boston was an abbreviated (twenty-minute) version of this chapter. While the chapter has been altered beyond recognition in this version, this extended reading of *Absalom, Absalom!* was gestured toward in a telegraphic form at that event. I benefited from hearing the work of Richard Godden and Phillip Weinstein, who presented papers in Boston on the same passage.

2. William Faulkner, *The Sound and the Fury*, Norton Critical Edition, ed. David Minter (1929; New York: Norton, 1994). All references are to this edition and are included parenthetically in the text. William Faulkner, *Absalom, Absalom!*, The Corrected Text, ed. Noel Polk (1936; New York: Vintage International, 1990). All references are to this edition and are also included parenthetically in the text. To avoid confusion, quotes from *The Sound and the Fury* when necessary for clarity will be indicated by *SF* and those from *Absalom, Absalom!* when necessary for clarity will be designated by *AA!*

3. William Faulkner, "Evangeline," in *The Uncollected Stories of William Faulkner*, ed. Joseph Blotner (New York: Vintage International, 1979). "Evangeline" is the most developed of the stories concerning the Sutpen legends. This story, rejected for publication in 1931, was discovered in the early 1970s.

4. For a reading of the water-splashing scene, see chapter 1 of this volume.

5. Noel Polk, noticing the strangeness of this interlude, describes Quentin as possibly "floating in some twilight zone between consciousness and unconsciousness, having been knocked out by Gerald Bland" (111). See Polk, *Children of the Dark House: Text and Context* (Jackson: University Press of Mississippi, 1996). John Irwin,

referring to the conversation with Shreve and Spoade that follows the reverie, also calls attention to Quentin's altered consciousness, pointing out that Quentin uses "the same words with which he confronted Dalton Ames: 'Did you ever have a sister?'" (Irwin 79). The nuance that I am calling attention to here looks at this repeated line as a bleed-through narrative that reveals not only layers of consciousness but a place of clear contamination in Quentin's reliving of the past.

6. See chapter 4 in this volume, originally published in a much abbreviated form as "The Signifying Eye: Faulkner's Artists and the Engendering of Art," in *Faulkner and the Artist: Faulkner and Yoknapatawpha* (Jackson: University Press of Mississippi, 1996). In this article and in the expanded chapter in this volume, I explicate more fully the symbolism of this wound, detailing the evidence that places it as a feminizing injury which represents the broken ball of Quentin's masculinity as well as the sign of Caddy's broken hymen. This "miniature replica of the whole vast globy earth" (207) as it is described in the 1946 "Appendix Compson" to *The Sound of the Fury* is linked to the bloody eye, the impotence of bloodied men, and the power associated with female blood and bleeding in the novel as a whole. In relation to the rim of Quentin's watch, see the history of the word "watch" and its association with actual seeing and those watchmen who told the time by keeping watch and calling out the hour. As Caddy's hands run over the blood-smeared watch face of her broken-eyed brother, Quentin has already lost Caddy to what cannot be changed. Even were he to have stood his ground in the past in the confrontation with Dalton Ames, the loss of female honor is permanent. Female honor, unlike male honor, is property and, once lost, shares the fate of Humpty Dumpty and the other broken, "frail doomed vessel[s]" (208) of fairy tales and Faulkner. Lost already with regard to what is an impossible ideal of permanence, Caddy is changed and fixed in her unchanging changedness. This fact is seen in the empty and unseeing eyes of the Caddy that the Quentin of the reverie sees as threatening to become a statue.

7. While Quentin Compson is the first-person narrator for the entirety of "June Second, 1910," the characters whose voices are rendered as heard by him in the present emerge with a strong sense of corporeal presence. This is true even in relation to Quentin himself, who is never more than vaguely pictured. Quentin's physicality is underlined by these sensations of physical pain, which call attention to the fact that Quentin, on the final day of his life, still inhabits a living and bleeding body.

8. Here and throughout the novel, the old pun playing on the first-person singular pronoun as an aural and as a visual marker resounds with fury. For more on the importance of this aural, oral, and visual pun of the "I" and the eye in Faulkner's work, see chapter 4 of this volume.

9. Even without the allusions to Father's description of menstruation that follow here, a description that appears earlier in the text, the emphasis on the "bloody rag," the request for "the rag," and the repeated mention of the word "rag" suggest the somewhat vulgar and still-used expression of being "on the rag." Feminine napkins were invented late in the era Anne Goodwyn Jones has named (quoting Faulkner himself) "the Kotex Age." See "'The Kotex Age': Women, Popular Culture, and *The Wild Palms*," *Faulkner and Popular Culture: Faulkner and Yoknapatawpha*, ed. Doreen Fowler and Ann J. Abadie (Jackson: University Press of Mississippi, 1988). This is the era of disposable sanitation products that became revolutionized when it ceased to be

primarily concerned with women's monthlies or periods. This technology was greatly improved by research into absorbent materials created for disposable diapers, a mainstay of modernity. As Jones explains, the invention of modern sanitary napkins was a result of women's experience with the new celluloid bandages used to staunch the blood of wounds during World War I.

10. Just after the single-word sentence "Yellow," this passage continues: "Feet soles with walking like. Then know that some man that all those mysterious and imperious concealed. With all that inside of them shapes an outward suavity waiting for a touch to" (81). This moonlit passage as a whole anticipates the vocabulary and thematic horror of *Light in August* (1932) audible in Joe Christmas's vision of menstruation: "In the notseeing and hardknowing as though in a cave he seemed to see a diminishing row of suavely shaped urns in the moonlight blanched. And not one was perfect. Each one was cracked and from each crack there issued something liquid, deathcoloured, and foul" (189). For a crucial discussion of the threat of female liquidity in Faulkner's fiction, see Anne Goodwyn Jones, "The Kotex Age." For an insightful reading of Joe Christmas's castration as the blood-marked explosion of a menstrual wound, see Joseph Urgo, "Menstrual Blood and 'Nigger' Blood: Joe Christmas and the Ideology of Sex and Race," *Mississippi Quarterly* 41, no. 3 (Summer 1988), and Jay Watson, "Writing Blood: The Art of the Literal in *Light in August*," in *Faulkner and the Natural World: Faulkner and Yoknapatawpha 1996* (Jackson: University Press of Mississippi, 1997). Watson provides an influential discussion of the centrality of blood to this violent narrative of racial identity. There is an understandable focus on conclusiveness and finality in this last and fatal meeting of Joanna and Joe that notes the fixity achieved in their racial and sexually gendered identities here. See Lisa K. Nelson, "Masculinity, Menace, and American Mythologies of Race and Faulkner's Anti-Heroes," *Faulkner Journal* 19, no. 2 (Spring 2004). Nelson (in a comment that speaks profoundly to repetition and racial identity in more than one novel) concludes: "In these nightly ritualized enactments of the myth of the black rapist, a sense of both fatality and necessity dominate Christmas's participation. It is Christmas's blackness and maleness as a despoiling force, his playing of the rapist, that she imagines as she urges 'Negro! Negro! Negro!,' which forms the desire she enacts by acting upon. Yet, as she interpellates him as Negro rapist, she effects the performative correlative: she becomes/is the raped white woman. In this way, in this nightly ritual he effects a black masculinity while she constructs a white femininity. It is for this reason that the narrative must be continually re-enacted: these identities manifest themselves as a result of the continual re-enactment of the rape myth as 'sex-game.' And, in the third phase, the rape myth is violently culminated in murder by 'borrowing' the rage generated from another racial myth altogether—the myth of burden and uplift" (63–64). Racial identity is secured through the construction of race, not though an echo, but rather through repetition itself. In this instance, the ritual of repetition occurs without an appreciable difference. Neither figure is permanently fixed or transformed into a knowable social commodity for the community until they literally are carved into existence. Nelson's point can be applied with significance to the need to repeat that has become located in language, spoken and unspoken, heard and not listened to in *Absalom, Absalom!*

11. Herbert Hoover is associated with the national and international Depression, the economic crash that took place a few weeks after the publication of *The Sound*

and the Fury in October 1929. Hoover was elected president of the United States in November 1928 and was sworn in in January 1929. By "October 1928," the month that Faulkner finished *The Sound and the Fury*, it was a forgone conclusion that Al Smith, a Catholic, would not be elected president of the United States. The economic depression that had long plagued the South reached new lows in the mid-1920s with the collapse of the cotton market. Some readers of Faulkner's *The Sound and the Fury* were surprised at what seemed to be Faulkner's prediction of the market's crash that hit the nation on October 29, 1929.

12. The emphasis on the three shots fired by Dalton Ames before he reloads "the three chambers" is one of those strange details that resound in Quentin's memory of events. (These bullets suggest the three shots that do not take place—just enough ammunition to rid the book of any of its troubling triangles.)

13. In "April Seventh 1928," the Benjy section that precedes the Quentin section, we read: "Caddy smelled like trees. 'We don't like perfume ourselves,' Caddy said." Despite its seeming grammatical eccentricity, my use of the word "themselves" here constitutes a joining that is accurate in terms of the intimacy of relationships and desired relationships in *The Sound and the Fury*.

14. See Nancy Friday, *My Mother / Myself: The Daughter's Search for Identity* (New York: Dell, 1977). In one of the compelling moments of her book, Friday is reluctant to narrate her loss of virginity because it signals the death of the mother. For an archetypal story that insists on the path of replacement in the female life cycle, see versions of the well-known warning tale, "Little Red Riding Hood." See Jack David Zipes's *The Trials and Tribulations of Little Red Riding Hood* (New York: Routledge, 1993).

15. While the completed statement is about a breaking of the phallus, in context it lacks much of the sexual suggestiveness that the phrase "going down" seems to invoke. After biting the gun in half, Gerald proceeds to clean himself with a silk handkerchief that he then throws away. This is all "kitchen"-appropriate behavior.

16. William Faulkner, "There Was a Queen," in *Collected Stories of William Faulkner* (New York: Vintage International, 1995).

17. For a description of the connection between prostitution and the selling of art for money, see Anne Goodwyn Jones, "The Kotex Age." Faulkner used the word "whoring" to describe his efforts to place short stories in popular magazines.

18. See "Appendix Compson 1699–1945," written as what Faulkner called the "fifth section" of *The Sound and the Fury*, first published in Malcolm Cowley's *Portable Faulkner* (1946), page 207 in David Minter's Norton Critical Edition of *The Sound and the Fury* (1994).

19. See Michael Moon, *A Small Boy and Others: Imitation and Initiation in American Culture from Henry James to Andy Warhol* (Durham: Duke University Press, 1998). Moon's powerful insights about the sources of art and the making of artists through acts of initiation that lead to emulation offer a window onto the sadness of Quentin Compson's series of closed doors. In chapter 4, I have discussed Quentin as one of Faulkner's figures of the failed artist, an identity that emerges in part through the history of Faulkner's artist figures and the pattern of their obsessions with chastity.

20. What I am referring to here is the common concept, myriad in Faulkner's fiction, that links the leg to the phallus. See chapter 4 of this volume for a catalog of

displaced body parts that signify castration in a work such as Faulkner's *The Sound and the Fury*.

21. See Nicole Loraux, *Tragic Ways of Killing a Woman* (Cambridge: Harvard University Press, 1987), for an excellent analysis of gendered patterns in the violent deaths that occur in Greek tragedies. There is also a strongly gendered pattern that returns again and again to death by drowning as a motif in the work of nineteenth- and twentieth-century women writers. What awaits Quentin below in the water is not just the "drowned man's shadow" or the womblike embrace with "Little Sister Death." Rather, he has chosen the most female of deaths that has thronging echoes in a well-articulated literary heritage that concerns female sexuality, feminization, and art. (Among others, these include Eliot's Maggie Tulliver [a British example], Chopin's Edna Pontellier, and many of Cather's heroines such as Lucy Gayheart as well as some of Cather's feminized male characters. On other fronts, despite Quentin's disquisitions and questions on being and nonbeing, his decision to escape from sexuality and his choice of death places his suicide closer to that of the drowned Ophelia than to Hamlet. (Quentin, as critics have often noted, has direct ties to both figures.) For an excellent discussion of this coupling of characters to convey complexity, Michael Zeitlin provides a reading of the psychological novel revealed through the analytic writings of Freud. As Zeitlin observes, Freud turned to a contemporary literary critic's reading of Shakespeare's work to explain how paired characters are used to convey psychological dimensions of human being. For this and other insights about the continuing relevance of Freud for understanding Faulkner, see Zeitlin's "Returning to Freud and *The Sound and the Fury*," *Faulkner Journal* 13, nos. 1–2 (Fall 1997): 57.

22. In the signifying, Lutherian act of Faulkner's writing of *The Sound and the Fury*, the message, cum manifesto that the novel itself is, is left by nail, pinned to the self-shut (not slammed, but closed) door of publication. Dilsey is the monumental figure that fills the open door at the opening of the fourth section: "rising like a ruin or a landmark" with "one gaunt hand" (165) outstretched into the weather or, perhaps, toward another historical marker that appears near the section's end: "the Confederate soldier" who gazes "with empty eyes beneath his marble hand in wind and weather" (199). Caddy, particularly when Quentin sees her as a statue, has an affinity with the concluding totems of failed nationalism that appear at the close of the novel; the Confederate monument that recalls the statuelike Caddy's empty eyes concludes by pointing toward the painful innocence of Caddy's aging baby, Benjy, whose "eyes" are said to be "empty and blue and serene again" (199). Bizarrely, it is Dalton Ames, the seeming former soldier, who extends his arm toward Quentin in the longest reverie of *The Sound and the Fury*. In a gesture that opens up a potential ground of equality between them as men—grounds that would justify a duel—Dalton Ames and Quentin Compson shake hands.

23. Estella Schoenberg, *Old Tales and Talking: Quentin Compson in William Faulkner's* Absalom, Absalom! *and Related Works* (Jackson: University Press of Mississippi), 1977), 9.

24. This is an ironic statement on my part that alludes to the rules which govern the practices of the aristocratic "Code of Honor." Meeting on "the field of honor" had long been outlawed. While duels were clearly against the law, the role of the upper-class male, protecting the honor of the family by using a whip or a gun, was to teach those

who were not his equals their "place." The perceived right or responsibility to murder offenders remained as a masculine prerogative, a perceived duty in some families of the American South through the late nineteenth and well into the twentieth centuries.

25. See Eve Kosofsky Sedgwick, *Epistemology of the Closet* (Berkeley: University of California Press, 1990), and Eve Kosofsky Sedgwick, *Between Men: English Literature and Male Homosocial Desire* (New York: Columbia University Press, 1985). The narrative of triangulation in Faulkner's work is analyzed in its multivalenced complexity in John Irwin, *Doubling and Incest / Repetition and Revenge: A Speculative Reading of Faulkner* (Baltimore: Johns Hopkins University Press, 1975). Irwin's work is particularly powerful as it traces the vectors of desire that connect the narrative generated by the characters in *Absalom, Absalom!* to the obsessions of Quentin Compson in *The Sound and the Fury*.

26. See Estella Schoenberg, *Old Tales and Talking*, for the most complete discussion of the timing in relation to the psychic trauma of the Quentin Compson of *The Sound and the Fury*, and the ways in which these past events would be affecting both Father's telling of the story of the Sutpen saga, and the way that that story is being heard by the Quentin of *Absalom, Absalom!*

27. Jean Toomer, *Cane* (New York: Boni & Liveright, 1923). The references here are to the Norton Critical Edition, ed. Rudolph P. Byrd and Henry Louis Gates Jr. (2011), and will be included parenthetically in the body of the paper.

28. Described by one of the Boston boys fishing in the river as a white man who speaks like a black man—like a man in a minstrel show—Quentin is placed in a more subtle way by his friend Shreve. Shreve appears to make a direct reference to the question of racial "passing," a central theme in Toomer's "Bona and Paul," as well as a joking reference to the foibles of Freud's talking cure: "all dressed up and mooning around like the prologue to a suttee. Did you go to Psychology this morning?" (*SF* 64). Toomer's Paul's mysterious melancholy is described as "moony," and this connection may suggest a racializing of gender and a gendering of race in the complex identity formations forged in Toomer's as well as Faulkner's work. "[M]oony" and "mooning" (in the symbolism of *Cane* and *The Sound and the Fury*) may be Quentin's form of feminized fate, PMS, the broken ball of his manhood. Arguably, this may signal the fact that Quentin is no longer pregnant with the monstrously fused and incorporated past that the reverie embodies. As the recurrence of periods brings him back to the present, Quentin has begun to signify nothing—the aversion to and absence of reproduction that takes shape in the anomie and nihilism in his life that is hell-bent on suicide.

29. See Schoenberg, *Old Tales and Talking*, 57–58, for a discussion of the theme of the murdered bridegroom as a repeated motif in Faulkner's fiction.

30. The inscription "To Waldo Frank" stands before what is located as the final third of *Cane*, the long short story in the form of a play, "Kabnis." While Toomer dedicated this piece to Waldo Frank, in the modernist narrative that conceives of the book as a "broken circle," "Kabnis" can also be read as a preface to the "Southern" section, which opens with "Karintha." Waldo Frank accompanied Toomer on this journey south toward art that inspired Toomer's modernist masterpiece.

31. In an essay on patterns entitled "Litotes and Chiasmus: Cloaking Tropes in *Absalom, Absalom!*" James Snead recognizes a "chiasmus" in "the broadly metaphysical point beyond which neither Henry nor Quentin can go." Snead calls this juncture "the

negative hinge of that italicized chiasmus [a juncture found in] the words '*to die.*'" See Snead's analysis in *Faulkner's Discourse: An International Symposium*, ed. Lothar Hönnighausen (Tübingen: Max Niemeyer Verlag, 1989), 23.

32. Peter Brooks, "Incredulous Narration: *Absalom, Absalom!*," in *Reading for the Plot: Design and Intention in Narrative* (Cambridge: Harvard University Press, 1984). See Schoenberg for a description of the way these formations look on the page. This scholar, known for her work elsewhere on visual culture, sees what I am calling the echo formation as looking like "a ragged butterfly." Her description is a visually rendered antecedent to Brooks's more reflective image of the "concave mirror." Alluding to two of the passages that this essay is concerned with, Schoenberg, in passing, sees this form as a *form*, and sees a link between Quentin's dialogues (invented or not), between Henry and Judith at the close of chapter 5, and between Quentin and Henry (in the passage that Brooks has famously dubbed the "almost palindrome") near the close of the novel.

33. François Pitavy, in "Some Remarks on Negation and Denegation," underlines the formal importance of this letter, writing: "The second part of *Absalom, Absalom!* is framed by Mr. Compson's letter, a letter informed precisely by negation, in its two halves ('*I do not know it*,' '*I do not know that either*,' '*It can harm no one to believe*,' '*It will do no harm to hope*' [*AA!* 174, 377]). There is no narrative reason to interrupt this letter in mid-sentence and resume it two hundred pages later, and to fit the whole Harvardian sequence of the novel between its two edges, as if the creased sheet of paper enclosed the whole narrative. The reason can only be poetic; that is, the letter points to, and is consistent with, the state of mind in which Quentin begins his long, painful journey into the night of Southern guilt—a manner of auto-analysis undergone reluctantly, with Shreve as analyst" (*Faulkner's Discourse* 31).

34. Aunt Jenny DuPre of *The Unvanquished* (1938) stops a son (her nephew) from being killed in his honor-driven temptation to avenge his father's murder by recalling the enigmatic courtesy spoken to ladies by a wartime blockade-runner in the drawing rooms of Charleston. This rough figure is known to speak only seven words to these women: "'I'll have rum, thanks' and then, 'No bloody moon'" (282). This narrative has been linked to the profession of rum-running that requires dark nights without a moon as well as being seen as a reference to menstruation and female blood lust. The final words, "No bloody moon," are spoken by this rough figure as he peers across the decorated shelf of a female bosom. Here, Bayard's stepmother, Drusilla, is the blood-driven woman who has handed her stepson the two highly phallicized pistols that would likely have led to his own death (see fig. 10).

35. Part of the resounding echo in this passage comes from the repeating homonym "know" as it syncopates and interleaves with the word "no."

36. For one of the most nuanced discussions of voice in chapter 5 of *Absalom, Absalom!*, see John T. Matthews, *The Play of Faulkner's Language* (Ithaca: Cornell University Press, 1982). As Matthews asserts, chapter 5 "is not Rosa's literal speech, nor is it the narrator's paraphrase or recounting, nor is it Quentin's remembered translation; it is more precisely some collaboration of all three" (121). While this shift into the third person occurs, these are not mistakes on Faulkner's part. The shifts to "she" are most telling. Other instances of a clap or jump-rope rhyme in which "Rosie Coldfield" has become part of a piece of children's taunting is entirely plausible in the first person as

Miss Rosa recounts and includes narrative evidence of her injuries in the aftermath of Sutpen's immodest proposal.

37. See later discussion in this chapter on the connection between "tech" and "teach" in the fatal (and echoing) confrontation between Thomas Sutpen and Wash Jones. Hortense Spillers in "Born Again: Faulkner and the Second Birth," the keynote address for the 2012 Faulkner Conference, addressed the significance of this scene for race and class and class and race. Spillers in a riveting reading of W. E. B. Du Bois's coming to consciousness linked the transformative experience of the young Sutpen to that of the great philosopher. Du Bois, who had felt accepted in school in Great Barrington, Massachusetts, was ruptured into consciousness of race during a playful exercise of making visiting cards. As he presented his to his classmates, his offer of his handmade card to the new girl in class was summarily refused. Du Bois saw himself and race in America in the precise cruelty of her refusal.

38. As Daniel Pecchenino has pointed out in conversation, mathematically speaking, four "no"s appear. This quadruple negative is the double of the double negative, ultimately making this a positive statement. Strangely, what Pecchenino proves is also true of the three "no"s in the narrative economy of the spoken text of the novel that allows the final "no" to affirm the previous double "no" (the double negative). This English usage reverses the Italian "*si*," the nuanced "no" that may mean "yes." Interestingly, the word "*si*" is misheard by Quentin as "see," becoming one of the noted bilingual puns in *The Sound and the Fury*.

39. Jun Liu, "The Judith-Henry-Charles Triangle: The Innermost Kernel of Faulkner's Civil War in the Heart," in *Critical Essays on William Faulkner: The Sutpen Family*, ed. Arthur F. Kinney (New York: G. K. Hall, 1996). Liu centers on the word "civil" to discuss the ways in which the larger historical conflict is intently played out in this family story that becomes the heart of *Absalom, Absalom!* Noting the presence of the echo, he perceptively reads this as a form of personalized history in which form conveys meaning. "The echo-like effect," Liu writes, "reflects the inquisitive mind of a sympathetic outsider; it more than implies that returning to the shot produces echoes that continue to deepen the meanings of a Civil War." Liu's use here of the idea of the echo concludes this paragraph: "Thus echoes signal the continuation of the war in the heart" (184).

40. The absence of a period after the honorific title "Mr" is Faulkner's omission.

41. For a detailed discussion of the connection to Edith Wharton's fiction, see chapters 2 and 6 of this volume.

42. For a discussion of this pictorial connection between Addie Bundren of *As I Lay Dying* and Raby of "Evangeline," see the closing section of chapter 6 in this volume.

43. This (like the word "impression") is an old term denoting a photograph. The camera itself was historically referred to as a "light pencil," emphasizing the process by which the image itself is written, inscribed, through the impression or reflection of light.

44. This is crucial. Whereas Elizabeth Muhlenfeld persuasively argues that "Evangeline" provided the catalyst for the writing of *Absalom, Absalom!*, her concern is that the novel be understood as a "Sutpen" novel, in her essay "'We have waited long enough': Judith Sutpen and Charles Bon," in *Critical Essays on William Faulkner: The Sutpen Family*, ed. Arthur F. Kinney (New York: G. K. Hall, 1996). "Evangeline" read

through Quentin's reverie in *The Sound and the Fury* makes *Absalom, Absalom!* the complex novel that it is. This concept of reverie is present in references to other texts as well. The liquefying, burning house that "rush[es] upward in furious scarlet" after "the whole house seemed to collapse, to fold in upon itself" (69) is clearly the language of the House of Sutpen as Poe's "House of Usher." "Evangeline" is also the work by Faulkner that is closest to Wharton's *Ethan Frome*. As the echoes and reflections "fold in upon [them]selves," these works taken together result in the reflective and projective reverie that reaches its apotheosis in the head game of *Absalom, Absalom!* For a discussion of these and other issues, see chapters 2 and 6 in this volume.

45. See "Appendix Compson 1699–1945."

46. See David Marshall, *The Frame of Art: Fictions of Aesthetic Experience, 1750–1815* (Baltimore: John Hopkins University Press, 2006). Marshall devotes an entire chapter to the theory of "*ut pictura poesis*" that discusses the misuse of Horace's phrase in this theory of aesthetics, which insisted on judging the power of words by whether they were able to evoke pictures in the minds of readers. While Edmund Burke insists on the number of times he has read Milton without seeing a single picture, I know that like the habit of subvocalizing, of hearing the words on the page, that minds haunted by picture-making compulsions do actually exist. The phrase below, "repetition compulsion," comes from Freud; the other phrase, "representation compulsion," comes from Marshall. In relation to Faulkner, Bleikasten sees "Animated descriptions [that] are in fact word-imitations of iconic imitations [which] affect the reader as *tableaux vivants . . . Ut pictorial poesis*: Faulkner probably never quite renounced the old Horatian belief in the commutability of artistic media." See "Faulkner and Paradoxes of Discourse," in *Faulkner's Discourse: An International Symposium*, ed. Lothar Hönnighausen (Tübingen: Max Niemeyer Verlag, 1989), 174.

47. It bears repeating that this chapter originated as a challenge posed by the Faulkner Society—in particular Anne Goodwyn Jones, John Matthews, and others—inviting scholars to present close readings of the same passage at the American Literature Association in Boston (2005). This explains or, to use Wharton's word of defense, "justifies" the method used in most of this chapter.

48. Hoover becomes a synonym for vacuum cleaning quite early. In fact, "to hoover" has become the British verb for this cleaning process. Invented in the United States in 1907 by Murray Spangler, the patent for the vacuum was bought by his brother-in-law, "Boss" Hoover, in 1908. This appliance's new advertising campaign began in the year that Faulkner published his first novel. In 1926 the makers of Hoovers boasted: "It beats as it sweeps and cleans." The strong suction of the vacuum cleaner had been improved by addition of a metal bar that beat the rug first to loosen the caked-in dirt that was then drawn up into the vacuum.

49. Using a place name that sounds salacious, Faulkner chose an actual resort that was a desired and appropriately distant destination for husband hunting in the early twentieth century. The fashionable watering hole that introduced the idea of the tomato juice cocktail, French Lick is now best known as the birthplace of former Boston Celtics basketball star Larry Bird.

50. Blowing out and then backward into the replacement phallus, Dalton Ames is the smoking gun. With his double-barreled nose spewing smoke, his cigarette that he sharpens like a pencil, and (perhaps most of all) the pistol's shaft as he blows the

gun's smoke back into its cylinder, Ames is increasingly a man of metal. Described earlier as "[n]ot quite bronze" in shirts "of heavy Chinese silk or finest flannel" that Quentin has mistaken for "army issue khaki" (59), the Dalton Ames of the reverie is said to look "like he was made out of bronze his khaki shirt" (100). For more on Faulkner's use of a material vocabulary, see the epilogue to this volume as well as Joseph R. Urgo and Ann J. Abadie, eds., *Faulkner and Material Culture: Faulkner and Yoknapatawpha, 2004* (Jackson: University of Mississippi Press, 2007). This extensive note places the early-twentieth-century significance of a simple word such as "khaki"—fabric now seen as an ordinary material—one step up from jeans in boys' dress wear. From the outset, khaki was a military fabric. Invented by the British in India in the mid-1800s to look like dirt and dust, the word khaki comes from "catechu," the name of an existing dye made from the reddish inner wood of trees. Early efforts to achieve this camouflaging color included staining undyed cotton with tea, mud, and other substances. The United States adopted khaki as a military fabric in 1898 for use in uniforms during the Spanish-American War. Khaki, a brownish-beige twill, is in weave and color strongly associated with U.S. imperialism. Dalton Ames stands for, among other things, the male and nationalist interlopers set in motion by U.S. imperialism during the dozen years of southern remilitarization and repatriation that precede Quentin's 1910 leap from a Boston bridge. If Ames's attraction for Caddy lies in the fact that "hes crossed all the oceans all around the world" (95), Quentin's vision of this brown-shirted man in Faulkner's novel (completed in 1928 and published in 1929) has a pointed political resonance as it insists on the sartorial sign most associated with fascism.

51. C. Van Woodward, *Origins of the New South 1877–1913* (Baton Rouge: Louisiana State University Press, 1951).

52. Faulkner often referred publicly and with satisfaction to *The Sound and the Fury* as his "most splendid failure." The word "splendid" is too positive and sparkling a word in its connotations to use in relation to this historical period that saw the rise and violent repression of populism as a movement in the U.S. South.

53. The sartorial sign of the Hitler Youth that was adopted as the uniform of fascism was the brown shirt. Chosen as a political statement for German youth groups in the early 1920s, the brown shirt with a swastika-inscribed armband and black shorts became the uniform of the Hitler Youth, which returned with a vengeance following Hitler's release from prison in December 1924, and a successful, mass-organizing drive led by law student Kurt Gruber in 1925. The particular meaning of the brown shirt would have been well known to Faulkner as he completed *The Sound and the Fury* in 1928. Even before the group was outlawed by German officials, their uniform caused a stir because the storm troopers (the SA) felt that this choice of uniform was too closely modeled on their own, a dispute that was settled by distinctive changes made to the youths' armbands during the reorganization drive of 1925. Laura Yow, who is completing a book on Faulkner and fascism, confirmed my sense that this political symbol, the brown shirt that has been associated with fascism, was not just known but becoming well known by American literati and intellectuals of all stripes by the mid-1920s. For Faulkner, who spent the fall of 1925 in France, familiarity with political developments in Germany would have been even closer to home. For an expanded discussion of canine eugenics in "Evangeline," see chapter 6 in this volume.

1. *Absalom, Absalom!*, 293.

2. See Doreen Fowler's *Faulkner: The Return of the Repressed* (Charlottesville: University of Virginia Press, 1997). Fowler, in her influential work on matricide and Faulkner, builds on the work of Margaret Homans's *Bearing the Word: Language and Female Experience in Nineteenth-Century Women's Writing* (Chicago: University of Chicago Press, 1989), suggesting that Faulkner (like the earlier women writers about whom Homans has written) is concerned with the centrality of the female body in works of literary production by women.

3. See chapter 2 of this volume for an extensive explanation of this parable of art.

4. As this volume and critics such as Louis Rubin, James Snead, Thadious Davis, Eric Sundquist, Noel Polk, and Edouard Glissant acknowledge, race is crucial to Faulkner's development as an artist from the outset. While Rubin rightly insists on the role of *The Sound and the Fury*, Sundquist argues that Faulkner found his great topic, miscegenation and questions of race, in *Light in August*. As Noel Polk provocatively argues in his "Testing Masculinity in the Snopes Trilogy," "Race in Faulkner's fiction often serves as a mask for gender. In fact, race occupied him in only four of his nineteen novels and in only one or two of over 120 short stories, so that race, statistically at any rate, is a very minor part of his concerns, whereas sexual and sexualized relationships are everywhere, on nearly every page, in one way or another, even in three of the racial Big Four—*Absalom, Absalom!*, *Go Down, Moses*, and *Light in August*, less so in *Intruder in the Dust*" (*Faulkner Journal* 16, no. 3 [Fall 2000–2001]: 3). Traditionally, *As I Lay Dying* has been overlooked as a work that is substantially concerned with race, what I earlier call the "coloring of class." Color is at the center of the Bundrens' experience of their literalized fall in class standing.

5. Edgar Allan Poe, "The Fall of the House of Usher," in *Edgar Allan Poe: Poetry, Tales, and Selected Essays* (New York: Library of America, 1996), 317–36. Further references are to this edition and are included parenthetically in the text.

6. See chapter 2 in this volume for a linking of Darl's being sent to a mental institution to this phrase from Shakespeare that was so important to Faulkner. Chapter 6 in a different form and context appeared formerly as an extension in a version of chapter 2, which appeared in *The Faulkner Journal*.

7. For a description of the importance of this head game, see chapter 2 of this volume.

8. "June Second, 1910." Shades of Roderick and Madeline Usher, Quentin imagines his own incestuous joining with his sister Caddy, an act of wholeness and horror that would erase the noise of being.

9. This may be—as the title of Suzan-Lori Parks's send-up of *As I Lay Dying* as an African American comedic novel, *Getting Mother's Body* (New York: Random House, 2004), suggests—what it means to "get," to "understand," racially gendered embodiment.

10. This statement by Charlotte Rittenmeyer to her lover Harry Wilbourne addresses his unusually happy mood; she does not know he has just made and then burned his painting of a calendar based on her menstrual cycles. Excised, the quotation is pointedly equivocal: either the "human race" has been relieved from the perceived

necessity, the unaccountable drive to make art, or whether art is something that will be generated whether human beings "try" or not.

11. Edith Wharton, *The Age of Innocence*, ed. Candace Waid (New York: Norton, 2003), 208. Further references are to this edition and are included parenthetically in the text.

12. In "Darl Bundren's Cubist Vision," in *William Faulkner's* As I Lay Dying: *A Critical Casebook*, ed. Dianne L. Cox (New York: Garland, 1985), 117, Branch follows the lead of Panthea Reid Broughton who has recognized the whole of *As I Lay Dying* as "an exercise in pure design," a "quintessential cubist novel [that is itself] like a cubist painting." See "Faulkner's Cubist Novels," in *"A Cosmos of My Own": Faulkner and Yoknapatawpha, 1980*, ed. Doreen Fowler and Ann Abadie (Jackson: University Press of Mississippi, 1981), 93.

13. Like Stowe's *Uncle Tom's Cabin* (1851), this commemorative stamp of Whistler's *Mother* was dedicated to those called the "Mothers of America."

14. *Nocturne in Black and Gold, The Falling Rocket* and *Nocturne in Blue and Gold—Old Battersea Bridge* appear in black-and-white photographic prints back-to-back on an unnumbered plate between pages 232 and 233. Whistler, who himself was a pioneer in the processes that allowed color printing in books, saw his own paintings replicated in beautifully colored plates at the beginning of the twentieth century. See T. Martin Wood, *Whistler: Illustrated with Eight Reproductions in Color*, presumed to have been published in 1909.

15. The rising tensions and disagreement in what was acceptable in terms of subject as well as composition in artists' paintings resulted in the radical break with established views of acceptable art that gave birth to the influential Salon des Refusés in Paris in 1863. This year marked a revolt against the conservative view that insisted only paintings in the classical tradition were worthy of being shown in the powerful Salon. This nationally authorized exhibit had long been the French venue that determined whether artists would be recognized or even able to sell their works. The infamous Salon of 1863 established a place for new art in France. Through his libel suit against Ruskin in 1878, Whistler publicized what had been seen as a largely French dispute over the unseating of the reigning tradition of representational art.

16. *Selected Letters of William Faulkner*, 12.

17. For a full discussion of the development of the political vectors of *The House of Mirth* and that novel's efforts at mounting a political critique by adding a strain of anti-Semitism and a plotline that exposed women's sexual vulnerability in relation to their social class, see Waid, "Building *The House of Mirth*," in *The House of the Mirth*, ed. Tom Quirk (Columbia: University of Missouri Press, 1996).

18. See Ann Douglas's *Terrible Honesty: Mongrel Manhattan in the 1920s* (New York: Farrar, Straus & Giroux, 1996), in which she exposes the cultural grounds that bred Wharton's own version of a grotesquely animal and miscegenated culture, which she links to art in *Twilight Sleep*.

19. The "races" that are referred to in the sentences that immediately follow this remark include French, Anglo-Saxon, Mongol, Semitic, Italian, English, and American (*Mosquitoes* 239–40). Eva Wiseman asks about the weakly masculine but amorous sycophant Talliaferro, "I mean, what—ah—race does he belong to?"

20. It should be noted that Faulkner's next novel, *Flags in the Dust* (edited and

published as *Sartoris* in 1929) is an apprentice novel on many levels. This work shows Faulkner beginning to deal with race much more directly, although more stereotypically than he would in later novels. He begins to map out Yoknapatawpha County, but calls it "Yocona." And as Daniel Pecchenino contends in conversation, he even writes a proto-Jewel figure in the character of young Bayard Sartoris.

21. "Exhibit A," Jim's father, the aristocratic and chivalric Arthur, who refers to Klawhammer as "the dirty Jew," adds that he is "the kind we used to horsewhip." This reference to horsewhipping, extremely unusual in relation to Wharton's oeuvre, signals Twain's presence again as it recalls Injun Joe's outrage in *The Adventures of Tom Sawyer* at the judge who has had him "horsewhipped in front of the jail, like a nigger!" See also Faulkner's "Evangeline," in which a newspaper writer is told of the "whup[ping]" of an earlier, similarly prying newspaper reporter.

22. I discuss this scene and others in a 1995 paper on incest in Wharton's later novels, linking the chiastic resolution (a Cavellian comedy of "marriage" and "remarriage") accomplished through daughter sacrifice in *Twilight Sleep* to the conclusion of Walpole's *Castle of Otranto*. This reading inspired a paper on eugenics in *Twilight Sleep*, given July 2004 at the International Gothic Society in Paris.

23. Wharton's first book (coauthored with the architect Ogden Codman) was *The Decoration of Houses* (1897), through which she hoped to rescue the much-abused art of interior decoration from the realm of dressmakers and stuffed furniture by applying structural principles associated with architecture.

24. The presence of anti-Semitism in Wharton's fiction and personal letters has benefited from insightful papers given by Annette Zilversmitt. See Waid, "Building *The House of Mirth*," for a discussion of Wharton's manuscript revisions to include a gesture toward anti-Semitism in what is arguably, in the end, a positive portrait of a socially climbing, blond Jewish man, the roseate Rosedale. Crossing out the descriptive phrase the "new man" (a valorized term in the history and mythos of the U.S.), Wharton replaced it with a phrase alluding to Rosedale as the "little Jew."

25. For further discussion of the similarities between Faulkner's drawings in *The Marionettes* and Beardsley's drawings for Wilde's *Salome*, see Noel Polk's introduction to *The Marionettes* (1977). In his reading, Polk also recounts the history of Herodias as a recent nineteenth-century subject. For other analyses of Faulkner's connection to and interest in the work of Aubrey Beardsley, see Lothar Hönnighausen's "Faulkner's Graphic Work in Historical Context," in *Faulkner, International Perspectives: Faulkner and Yoknapatawpha, 1982*, ed. Doreen Fowler and Ann J. Abadie (Jackson: University Press of Mississippi, 1984), 139–73. For other discussions of this noted connection, see Timothy Conley's "Beardsley and Faulkner," *Journal of Modern Literature* 5, no. 3 (September 1976): 339–56, and Addison C. Bross's "*Soldiers' Pay* and the Art of Aubrey Beardsley," *American Quarterly* 19 (1967): 3–23.

26. Wharton, who denied ever having seen a film (she is known to have seen at least one), definitely did not see *Salomé*. However, *Salomé*, an event in the history of avant-garde aesthetics and a cult film even prior to its debut, would have been known by Wharton and, very likely, seen by Faulkner. While this argument does not depend on Faulkner having seen the film, the likelihood that he did is increased exponentially by the film's connection to Beardsley. See Lind for a detailed discussion of Faulkner's obsession with Beardsley, to whom he alludes in three of his novels. It is significant

that Faulkner owned a Beardsley-illustrated edition of Wilde's *Salome*, a fact that is clearly visible in Faulkner's early drawings, in particular his hand-drawn and lettered play *The Marionettes* (1920).

27. For a discussion of the vacillating pronouns that make this a passage not only about Joanna but also Joe, see Laura Doyle's "The Body against Itself in Faulkner's Phenomenology of Race," *American Literature* 73, no. 2 (June 2001): 339–64.

28. See Anne Goodwyn Jones's "The Kotex Age" for an account of Faulkner's obsession with the terrifying and engulfing power of female liquidity in his fiction, particularly *The Wild Palms*. See Noel Polk's *Children of the Dark House* for the most complete account of Faulkner's use of the Medusa figure, which he argues is used most often in relation to older women. Finally, Philip Weinstein's "'If I Could Say Mother': Construing the Unsayable about Faulknerian Maternity" offers a compelling analysis of female liquidity that concludes: "The mother's threat seems most to inhere in her leaky and fluctuating wetness, a female wetness that menaces all projects of male enclosure and mastery" (11).

29. The small man, representing Lacedaemon whose dominating city was the bellicose Sparta, negotiates a settlement with the taller Athenians who seek peace in Aristophanes' play because of a successful sex strike mounted by the women of Athens.

30. Faulkner's image of struggling sisters rising to the surface of a suggestively black pool may allude to Beardsley's illustration of what Wilde's play explicitly calls a "*cistern*" on several levels. Playing on the old and misogynistic pun that connects female bodies to vessels of filth, the homonyms "cistern" and "sistern" are based on a folk neologism that invents a feminine word which parallels "brethren."

31. As "*[a] huge black arm, the arm of the Executioner, comes forth from the cistern,*" the head of John the Baptist ("Iokanaan") is served to Salome on a "*silver shield*" (Wilde 72).

32. Salome holds the head of John the Baptist ("Iocanaan") as she rises above the black cistern.

33. In an old and racist connection linking race with sexuality and filth, Amory Dwight Mayo, arguing for the "uplift," calls the "daughters of . . . emancipated slaves" "the great American sewer under the back windows of every respectable home" ("The Women's Movement in the South," *New England Magazine*, no. 5 (1891): 259. This idea, as disturbing and illogical as it is, was part of standard racism and the fecalization and blackening of sexuality itself. For a detailed analysis on the association of femaleness with liquidity in Faulkner, see Philip Weinstein's "If I Could Say Mother," in *A Cosmos That No One Owns* (New York: Cambridge University Press, 1992). Also see Anne Goodwyn-Jones, "'The Kotex Age': Woman, Popular Culture, and *The Wild Palms*," in *Faulkner and Popular Culture* (Jackson: University Press of Mississippi, 1990), 142–62.

34. See Du Bois for his proposal on the necessity of the "race man." This idea of racial uplift depends on the dedication of an educated elite, the "talented tenth," that could bring the economically and socially depressed African American community up from their lowly positions determined by prejudice and poverty.

35. Lisa Nelson sees Joe and Joanna's sexual relationship in its three stages, noting that the middle one where they meet in bed constitutes a type of marriage. While many have discussed the way that the deaths of Joe and Joanna determine their once inde-

terminate racial and sexual identities, Nelson makes the point that death itself makes these conversions final. Lisa K. Nelson, "Masculinity, Menace, and American Mythologies of Race in Faulkner's Anti-Heroes," *The Faulkner Journal* 19, no. 2 (2004): 49–68.

36. Referring to this military-styled vigilante, Percy Grimm of *Light in August*, Faulkner stirred controversy by publicly announcing that he had invented a Nazi before Adolph Hitler had. Grimm provides a case study in masculine loss as he enforces whiteness as the color of masculinity and domination.

37. See Roberts for an explication of this concept. I offer an extensive reading of the practical and deadly functioning of this race-based cultural narrative in the "The Strange Career of the Black Lady" ("Blood Union," unpublished book manuscript).

38. Marc D. Baldwin, "Faulkner's Cartographic Method: Producing the Land through Cognitive Mapping," *The Faulkner Journal* 7, nos.1–2 (1991/1992): 193–214.

39. For more on Faulkner's use of this trope to describe his magazine fiction, see James Carothers's article "Faulkner's Short Story Writing and the Oldest Profession," in *Faulkner and the Short Story: Faulkner and Yoknapatawpha, 1990* (Jackson: University Press of Mississippi, 1992).

40. This allusion to a "dead dog in a ditch" replicates the exact language used to refer to the animal-like mountain mother of Edith Wharton's *Summer* (1917), who is said to be "like a dead dog in a ditch." Faulkner's "Evangeline" is his closest work to Wharton's *Ethan Frome*. In fact, many of the Whartonian elements of *Absalom, Absalom!* appear in their most condensed form in "Evangeline." In 1931 the strangeness of having the final purebred German dog die only to be immediately and mysteriously replaced by a living dog points to an awareness of a grotesque Aryan-obsession (Sutpen's and Hitler's) mapped onto canine eugenics. This animal genealogy focuses on the whelps of the original German dogs that eventually lead to the last "son" ("Evangeline" 593).

41. In an act of replication and replacement, the unnamed but racially determinate German shepherd dog takes the place of the unnamed writer of "Evangeline" (the character based on the door-obsessed narrator of Wharton's *Ethan Frome* and an ironic avatar of the young Thomas Sutpen of *Absalom, Absalom!* who has been refused entry at the plantation house). The writer/narrator who has successfully breached the front door may inspire Raby to set the fire. Yet in this scene of sacrifice, after the loyal animal hurls himself repeatedly against the front door, he circles around, springing (in resonant words that recall "The Fall of the House of Usher") as the loyal dog jumps "into the roaring dissolution of the house" (607).

42. This sense of the canine gatekeeper has been mapped onto Clytie's role as the watchdog of *Absalom, Absalom!* Called a "Cerberus," Clytie is linked to the famed hellhound of Hades.

43. For a discussion of the threshold scenes, see chapter 2, "The Woman Behind the Door," in Waid, *Edith Wharton's Letters from the Underworld: Fictions of Women and Writing*. The closest allusion in Faulkner's work to this repeated motif in *Ethan Frome* of a door whose distant frame is marked by light is in *The Unvanquished* (1938). The boy narrator tripped by a high threshold falls into the dark room to discover the dead body of the elderly Granny. Here, the narrator discovers the beloved maternal figure rather than the feared crone of Wharton's novel.

44. Wharton's *Ethan Frome* repeats the word "then" as doors open to disclose women, whether reviled or desired, hidden from sight. This "then" is shocking, particularly as the "then" is used to introduce the appearance of the dreaded wife's face followed by the smashing of the characters' sled against a tree, framed by the words "and then the elm." See Waid's "The Woman Behind the Door."

45. The passage continues: "The inscription was in French: *A mon mari. Toujours. 12 Août, 1860*. And I looked again quietly at the doomed passionate face with its thick, surfeitive quality of magnolia petals—the face which had unawares destroyed three lives—and I knew now why Charles Bon's guardian had sent him all the way to North Mississippi to attend school, and what to a Henry Sutpen born, created by long time, with what he was and what he believed and thought, would be worse than the marriage and which compounded the bigamy to where the pistol was not only justified, but inescapable" (608–09). This story's melodramatic search for an ending anticipates some of the problems of law and custom, as they are pointedly contorted and distorted through the prism of race and the cruel vagaries of love that continue to plague those seeking historically explicable resolutions of the plot in *Absalom, Absalom!*

46. See chapter 2 in this volume for an extensive and detailed discussion of the formal and thematic connections between and among these works by Wharton and Cather as they directly influenced Faulkner's fictions' obsessions with the mother in his developing paradigms of art.

47. Seen once from the window with her hands on the sill as a "composite picture of all time" and once again as she is boxed and hidden in the revised picture of the geometrically framed painting that alludes to "a cubistic bug," the encoffined and multiply framed Addie is the centerpiece of Darl's cubist vision that is being consumed by the "red glare" which lights the dark. The writer in "Evangeline" sees the "redglared pasture" through a nocturnal, Whistler-like vision as the fire "swirling upward like scraps of burning paper, burning out zenithward like inverted shooting stars" ("Evangeline" 607). This view of disaster explicitly recalls Vardaman's astral vision of the barn-burning in *As I Lay Dying* as "the red went swirling up . . . swirling up in little red pieces, against the sky and the stars so that the stars moved backward" (*AILD* 223).

CHAPTER SEVEN. DE KOONING'S FAULKNER TRILOGY

1. Elaine de Kooning, "de Kooning Memories" [1983], in *Elaine de Kooning: The Spirit of Abstract Expressionism* (New York: George Braziller, 1994), 208.

2. This collage portrait, characteristic of those that were a prominent feature during de Kooning's Faulkner period, has not been seen or discussed in the criticism. This chapter contains the only discussion of *Asheville* and its relationship to the thinking and dreaming man of Gorky's late paintings—his *Betrothal* series. In *Betrothal I*, this male head in the lower-left quadrant is seen from the top while the head's imaginative space in the recognizable objects above consists of, among other things, a pair of satin pumps and a columnar bride on the right side of the canvas. The bride is an elusive, miragelike figure that has been swiped in two or, more precisely, divided by the continuity of the background. Martin Ries, in his article "Arshile Gorky Centaurmachia: Betrothal and Betrayal," *Art Criticism Journal* 22, no. 1 (2007), quotes Hayden Herrera's insight that Gorky "did not see an object and proceed to obfuscate or disguise it.

Rather, he saw objects as full of visual and metamorphic possibility, so that one image might have several referents." Herrera's understanding is particularly interesting in relation to what this chapter sees as the centrality of metamorphoses to several of de Kooning's paintings, works that are concerned with the problem of inscribing motion in the stillness that threatened to frame, dry, and kill his art. For a well-researched and insightful account of Gorky's life and art, see Hayden Herrera, *Arshile Gorky: His Life and Work* (New York: Farrar, Straus & Giroux, 2003). His comment on Gorky's metamorphoses is located in a note to this compelling work (708, note 567).

3. Originally written as "Ashville," de Kooning added the "e" to "Asheville" in a letter to the Phillips Gallery sent at the time of their acquisition of this painting.

4. Mark Stevens and Annalyn Swann, *De Kooning: An American Master* (New York: Alfred A. Knopf, 2007), 39.

5. Storm de Hirsch, "A Talk with de Kooning," *Intro Bulletin*, Oct. 1955, 3. Quoted in Charles F. Stuckey, "Bill de Kooning and Joe Christmas," *Art in America* (1980): 71.

6. In the late 1940s, de Kooning (along with his friend Franz Kline) purchased five-gallon cans of black and white house enamel and substantial stacks of treated paper. This was an aesthetic that both he and Kline had decided to explore not due to poverty, as some critics have suggested, but rather as a way to be able to paint in excess. De Kooning's paintings referred to as the great "black-and-white paintings" included some paintings in which dark predominated and others that were primarily light. The words "black" and "white," as the color plate of de Kooning's *Light in August* included in this volume demonstrates, are a misnomer. The paintings shown in 1948 at the Egan Gallery were not all rigidly black and white attenuated with shades of gray. Some like *Black Friday* had pops of color, while others featured blood-tinctured whites, roseate-siennas, browns, and valentine-pinks. *Black Untitled*, a largely black-and-white composition, has some touches, brushed swipes of pink paint.

7. For more on the Bird lynching, see J. Douglas Smith's *Managing White Supremacy: Race, Politics, and Citizenship in Jim Crow Virginia* (Chapel Hill: University of North Carolina Press, 2002), 167–72. The timing in relation to de Kooning's arrival suggests that he may have been in Virginia for more than a week before he began to go north up the Eastern Seaboard, working for his passage on a boat that made numerous stops, taking approximately a week before it docked in northern New Jersey. Although Maryland was a slave state, it was north of Washington, D.C., and did not secede from the Union. The next state between Maryland and New Jersey is of course Delaware, the last slaveholding state in the United States. The slaves in the North were not freed by Lincoln's Emancipation Proclamation. This note is meant to add perspective and geographic range to speculations about how far north this barbershop conversation might reasonably have taken place. The story of the "Grubb girls" (neither of the parents was aware that either of the daughters were pregnant before the first child was born) and the brutal torture of Raymond Bird before he was dragged back to their homeplace to be hung and desecrated at the scene of his "crime" was a sensationalist horror and would have remained memorable for de Kooning, who was well aware that he had landed in Virginia. *Time* magazine printed an account of the stories surrounding this ritualized lynching, which became national news by the end of August. While no one from the mob was convicted for this heinous murder, the lynching of Raymond

Bird was important to the passing of an antilynching statute that was codified into the law of Virginia two years later in 1928.

8. Harold Rosenberg, *De Kooning* (New York: Harry N. Abrams, 1973), 51. Quoted in Stuckey, "Bill de Kooning," 71.

9. Clement Greenberg, "'American-Type' Painting," in *Art and Culture: Critical Essays* (Boston: Beacon Press, 1961), 214. This essay originally appeared in a Spring 1955 issue of the *Partisan Review*. To understand what was at stake for Greenberg, it is important to recall (as many observers have) that the key word "abstract" was included in quotation marks as the critic declared, "De Kooning is an outright 'abstract' painter" in his review for *The Nation* of de Kooning's first solo-artist show in 1948 ("Review of an Exhibition of Willem de Kooning," *The Nation* 166, no. 17, April 24, 1948). Greenberg, who was trained in literature and who was an early translator of Kafka, insisted on the "purity" of abstract art as a medium in itself. Figural elements, even inanimate objects, were deemed to tell a story and to taint this pure medium with the narrative stain of literature.

10. See Richard Schiff's article "Water and Lipstick: De Kooning in Transition," originally printed in *Willem de Kooning: Paintings,* ed. Marla Prather (Washington, D.C.: National Gallery of Art, 1994).

11. Allan Stone, *Willem de Kooning: Liquefying Cubism*, Allan Stone Gallery catalog (New York, 1994), iii.

12. See Rosemary Franklin, "Animal Magnetism in *As I Lay Dying*," *American Quarterly* 18 (Spring 1966): 24–34.

13. Panthea Reid, "The Cubist Novel: Toward Defining the Genre," in *"A Cosmos of My Own": Faulkner and Yoknapatawpha, 1980*, eds. Doreen Fowler and Ann J. Abadie (Jackson: University Press of Mississippi, 1981), 36–58.

14. While the "ekphrastic" in its root meaning refers to the idea of giving voice to a silent work of art (which favors descriptions of visual arts given voice through the words of poetry and prose), here I am using the term in its older and more encompassing meaning: the giving voice to one art form through another. In this sense, de Kooning's paintings cause Faulkner's novels to speak through a different medium.

15. For a detailed discussion of these drawings, see the introduction to this volume.

16. Randall S. Wilhelm, the only scholar to have recognized (or even to have seen) a field/space drawing in Faulkner's illustrations, saw this phallus. For more on this, see his articles "Faulkner's Big Picture Book: Word and Image in *The Marionettes*," *The Faulkner Journal* 19, no. 2 (Spring 2004), and "Visual to Verbal Art: William Faulkner's Domain of Images," *Proteus: A Journal of Ideas* 21, no. 2 (Fall 2004).

17. Faulkner uses this word that still has the force of an obscenity in his 1939 novel, *The Wild Palms*. For a discussion of this reference to the sexlessness of puppets and its literary antecedent in *Bartholomew's Fair*, see chapter 4 of this volume.

18. Richard Schiff extracted this quotation from a 1968 interview. See *Reading Abstract Expressionism: Context and Critique*, ed. Ellen G. Landau (New Haven: Yale University Press, 2005), 597.

19. See "Willem de Kooning's Parables of Art," appendix 1 to this volume, which discusses *Untitled* ("Still Life with Matches"), *Weil Plaza*, and *Woman, Sag Harbor* as paintings that accomplish major metamorphoses through bodies that construct faces in the form of field/space drawings. This parable of art is driven by a narrative of hid-

den metamorphoses that is part of the power of these paintings, yet the significance of this parable (or even the fact of these metamorphoses) has not been articulated in criticism of de Kooning's work.

20. Renée Arb, "Spotlight on de Kooning," *ArtNews* 47 (April 1948).

21. *William Faulkner: Three Decades of Criticism*, ed. and with an introduction by Frederick J. Hoffman and Olga W. Vickery (New York: Harcourt, Brace & World, 1963), 251–52. Essay first published in *Twelve Original Essays on Great American Novels*, ed. Charles Shapiro (Detroit: Wayne State University Press, 1958), 257–83.

22. Panthea Reid Broughton, "Faulkner's Cubist Novels," in *"A Cosmos of My Own": Faulkner and Yoknapatawpha, 1980*, ed. Doreen Fowler and Ann J. Abadie (Jackson: University Press of Mississippi, 1981), 93.

23. Thomas Hess, *Willem de Kooning Drawings* (Greenwich, Conn.: New York Graphic Society, 1972). Quoted in Stuckey, "Bill de Kooning, " 71.

24. For a discussion of the cultural milieu and biographical background of de Kooning during this period, see Mark Stevens and Annalyn Swan's *De Kooning: An American Master* (New York: Knopf, 2007), 243–69.

25. Phyllis Tuchman, oral history interview with Elaine de Kooning, Aug. 27, 1981, Archives of American Art, Smithsonian Institution.

26. Stuckey, "Bill de Kooning," 72.

27. Stuckey, "Bill de Kooning," 70.

28. Stuckey, "Bill de Kooning," 72.

29. Stuckey, "Bill de Kooning," 74.

30. William Faulkner, *Light in August* (1932; New York: Random House, 1991). All further citations refer to this edition. In terms of this photograph, it is more than useful to consult Judith Sensibar's article, "Popular Culture Invades Jefferson: Faulkner's Real and Imagined Photos of Desire," in *Faulkner and the Craft of Fiction: Faulkner and Yoknapatawpha, 1987* (Jackson: University Press of Mississippi, 1989), 124–47, to speculate on the desire and terror that is contained in the shocking whiteness of Joe Christmas's torso as it emerges from the darkness for the couple in the car and for the reader as well.

31. Charles F. Stuckey, "Bill de Kooning and Joe Christmas," *Art in America*, 1980. Protecting the uninformed, if not the innocent, Stuckey does not include the name of the original owner. In their Pulitzer Prize–winning biography, Swan and Stevens report that Charles Egan (the gallery owner who mounted the black-and-white show) had asked his mother-in-law to buy the painting as a wedding present for him and his wife. This appears to have been a highly profitable deal in that Egan not only got the painting, he also never gave de Kooning any part of the $700 he received for it. Commenting on what he calls "a quality of enigma," Stuckey adds: "But this is not to say that de Kooning would necessarily consider one explanation to be as good as any other . . . I imagine the artist would be disappointed to learn . . . the contents of a letter I solicited from the original owner of his *Light in August*" (70). I, too, see the team of horses or mules entering a space hung with a clearly articulated frying pan while the ribbon-held balloon shape as well as the other circles evoke circuits of visceral as well as mental interiority. De Kooning sometimes painted with caricatured lines reminiscent of his taste for comic strips.

32. Harry F. Gaugh, *Willem de Kooning* (New York: Abbeville Press, 1983), 31.

33. As Holland Carter writes in his review "Tall, Dark and Fragile" about Ad Reinhardt's paintings done in the 1960s: "Reinhardt's series of 'Black Paintings,' which he sometimes referred to as 'Ultimate Paintings,' . . . took abstraction as far as it could go in terms of color and form. Done in shades of black, with subliminal traces of underlying grids, these were endgame objects, versions of an absolutist art. They embodied no narratives, projected no emotions, broadcast no beliefs; they absorbed light, gave off no heat. The primary reward they offered was the experience of being with them, which, to be an experience (as opposed to a mere walkby sighting), required patience and concentration. You let your eyes rest on them, and what you see changes, constantly. Blacks change shades; reds and blues appear and fade. One minute you think you are looking at a grid or a cruciform; the next a cloudy sky or a Monet landscape, dark like the negative of a photograph. Your vision is changing things; you are changing. The paintings are not. But they are leaving their trace on your psyche and memory. The mark may be permanent, whatever permanent means" (*New York Times*, August 1, 2008, B23, 25).

34. Stuckey, "Bill de Kooning," 71.

35. When I looked at de Kooning's *Light in August*, the first thing that I saw was the alternately male and female, external and internal, reproductive system rendered in a large form occupying the lower-right quadrant of the painting. This structure has a strong, black vector streaming downward toward the edge of the canvas. Beside this (what seems to be a relatively abstract construct that literally maps male on top of female), there is a roman numeral "V" closed off at the top, like an upside-down delta. While Faulkner's "Delta Autumn" immediately follows Cowley's excerpt from *Light in August*, "Percy Grimm," the following passage appears to be a template for this configuration in de Kooning's painting: "He had watched it, not being conquered, destroyed, so much as retreating since its purpose was served now and its time an outmoded time, retreating southward through this inverted apex, this V-shaped section of earth between hills and River until what was left of it seemed now to be gathered and for the time arrested in one tremendous density of brooding and inscrutable impenetrability at the ultimate funneling tip" (*GDM* 326–27). Interestingly, while this passage, with its reference to the flow from the funneling tip, suggests the possibility of a direct correspondence between Faulkner's writing and de Kooning's painting, it is important to note that Cowley's abbreviated edition of "Delta Autumn" did not include this striking passage. This may have been due to the expense or difficulty of picturing the pictorial element of the upside-down delta. For a discussion of Faulkner's pictorial insertions, see chapter 4 of this volume.

36. William Faulkner, "Dilsey," in *The Portable Faulkner*, ed. Malcolm Cowley (New York: Viking Press, 1946). "Dilsey" was originally published as the fourth section of *The Sound and the Fury* (1929), and is an edited and shortened version of that chapter. This chapter will quote from "Dilsey," as opposed to "April Eighth, 1928."

37. De Kooning worked only briefly as a sign painter in New Jersey; he was not familiar with the American style of lettering. His skills were more valued in the highest levels of the house painting trades. De Kooning was a painter who was assigned to make faux wood and faux marble surfaces as well as other *trompe l'oeil* finishes for elite homes and office buildings. See Stevens and Swan for a detailed account of de Kooning's skills and his early work history. After he was put in charge of windows for

A. S. Beck, a chain of large department stores, he oversaw the making of many signs and likely lettered some as a matter of course in his daily dressing of displays.

38. The eating potential of this shape, long recognizable, is now a semiotic certainty confirmed as a Pac-Man fact. See any archive of early video game characters.

39. It is interesting that the Phoenician letters which are not related to the human body are not as precise a pictorial rendering of the body part. For instance, the Phoenician letter for "C" stands for "camel," a shape possibly drawn from that of the distinctive hump or the high arc between the front and back legs.

40. As Hoke Perkins has pointed out: "There is no shortage of black razor murderers in Faulkner's fiction; they show up in *Sanctuary*, *Light in August*, 'That Evening Sun,' and *Go Down, Moses*." If we expand Perkins's list to include white men with knives such as Percy Grimm of *Light in August* and the more abstract concept of *The Sound and the Fury* that time itself might be dismembered to become a clock with no or only one hand, then what emerges is a list of the works that de Kooning had read or read in part by 1946. This only slightly expanded list of works, an expansion that includes the readily available *Sanctuary,* details Faulkner's narratives concerning dismemberment and threatened dismemberment within the pages of Cowley's *Portable Faulkner*. For more on Faulkner's black razor murderers, see Perkins, "'Ah Just Cant Quit Thinking': Faulkner's Black Razor Murderers," in *Faulkner and Race* (Jackson: University Press of Mississippi, 1987), as well as Martha Banta's "The Razor, the Pistol, and the Ideology of Race Etiquette," in *Faulkner and Ideology* (Jackson: University Press of Mississippi, 1995).

41. See Jay Watson, "The Art of the Literal in *Light in August,*" in *Faulkner and the Natural World* (Jackson: University Press of Mississippi, 1999), for an argument that discusses Joe Christmas's castration and the violent spurting of blood as having created a menstrual wound. Watson's insight into this chiastic connection between these dismembered bodies, key to the structuring of this novel, is also broached in Deborah Clarke's *Robbing the Mother* (1994). For one of the most profound readings of Joe Christmas's body as he perceives it as a blood-filled "cage," see Joseph Urgo's "Menstrual Blood and 'Nigger' Blood: Joe Christmas and the Ideology of Sex and Race," *Mississippi Quarterly* 41 (1988): 391–401. In Urgo's remarkable reading of the related bodies, he links the sacrifice of the sheep, which is Joe's ritualized response to learning about menstruation, to the need to let blood from the menopausal body of Joanna Burden and his openness to Grimm's castrating knife. Urgo makes a subtle and entirely convincing claim that these cuttings enact rituals of purification and cleansing that Joe sees as necessary to purging the blood of femaleness and blackness.

42. David L. Shirey, "Don Quixote and Springs," *Newsweek*, November 20, 1967, 80.

43. This is an allusion to a line in Faulkner's *The Wild Palms* (1939): "grave-womb or womb-grave, it's all one" (138).

44. Sally Yard, "The Angel and Demoiselle: Willem de Kooning's 'Black Friday,'" *Record of the Art Museum, Princeton University* 50, no. 2 (1991): 9.

45. William Faulkner, "That Evening Sun," in *Collected Stories of William Faulkner* (1948; New York: Random House, 1995). All further citations to this story refer to this edition.

46. "Black Friday" was long the term used by Christians to refer to the Friday of

the Crucifixion. This is now a lesser-known term because of the Catholic Church's decision to celebrate the sacrifice by changing the designation to "Good Friday." This title has long been linked by critics to that of de Kooning's later work *Easter Monday*. These writers argued that such titles were Christological references without a referent. *Easter Monday* has been exposed by Kirsten Hoving Powell, in an essay entitled "Resurrecting Content: de Kooning's *Easter Monday*," *Smithsonian Studies in American Art* 4, nos. 3/4 (Summer/Fall 1990), as a heretically raucous painting that uses these newsprint transfers (previously assumed to be random results from using newspaper to slow the drying process) to narrate a devastating and witty critique of materialism. Among the inked-in pictures and words, de Kooning's *Easter Monday* includes a holiday bunny holding a paint brush and a palette, an advertisement for a film that featured gladiators, as well as an ad for the film *Invasion of the Body Snatchers*. Among Powell's notable discoveries is that de Kooning blacked out food items that had emphasized door storage in an ad that featured an open and otherwise empty refrigerator to emphasize the emptiness of the tomb on Easter morning. This narrative embedded as the ink transferred onto the wet paint collates a critique of consumer society in which the hope of salvation to be achieved through sacrifice has been replaced by material desires. The savings promised by a sale, the reversed letters "SAV," provides the largest caption, which proves that *Easter Monday* was not a randomly selected title, chosen to commemorate the day on which the painting was finished. This argument about the randomness of titles had been made despite evidence that the painting had not even been finished on Easter Monday. Powell's essay in many ways exposes the proscriptive vision that has made randomness itself a fetish in de Kooning criticism. A number of de Kooning's paintings remained untitled or were given titles like "Painting" (the only work from the 1948 show that sold, but sold to a high-profile client, New York's Museum of Modern Art). His *Woman* series is distinguished as a sequence because he chose to use roman numerals. Some titles were random or, like *Orestes*, renamed to serve an ulterior motive. In a statement that suggests there is content to be resurrected in some of his work, de Kooning quipped that "a painter who always has titles for his paintings must not have a very good idea of what he is painting." John Elderfield, arguing against this convincing interpretation, makes a telling appeal to precedence: "There is neither precedent nor anything subsequent in de Kooning's art" to justify this narrative reading of the painting as about Christianity. Elderfield quotes de Kooning as testifying against the idea of his use of "newspaper imprints" to convey meaning: "when I used the newspapers in the paintings, it was just an accident. When I took it off . . . I thought it was nice. That's about all. It had no social significance that way like Rauschenberg used it or something" (*De Kooning: A Retrospective*, ed. John Elderfield [New York: Museum of Modern Art, 2011], 294). See appendix 1 for yet another context that underlines de Kooning's close attention to certain of his titles. The analysis in this appendix also speaks strongly to de Kooning's investment in distinguishing himself from Robert Rauschenberg.

47. Interview with Phyllis Tuchman, Smithsonian Institution Archive. *Black Untitled* is not a huge painting, but it may have seemed to be in comparison with *Asheville*, the small painting on which de Kooning had expended so much time. De Kooning was not working on large compositions in 1948. The major misstatement in this interview is a slip in terms of sequence: Elaine de Kooning refers to "the following year" in

relation to *Light in August*. De Kooning's *Light in August* has been considered by some to be the major work of his first solo show in the spring of 1948. This was the spring immediately before the summer that the de Koonings spent at Black Mountain College in rural North Carolina. The "Faulkner connection," as Elaine de Kooning refers to it, was actively pursued—in temporal terms—on both sides of *Asheville* from 1946 through the fall of 1948.

48. These quotations are taken directly from the epigraph above, which is from *The Heilbrunn Timeline of Art*, the most public and most disseminated of the Metropolitan Museum of Art's synoptic descriptions of this painting housed in their permanent collection.

49. De Kooning presented several high-profile talks on the history of art, including "The Renaissance in Order" (*trans/formation* 1 [1951]). In discussion, he contrasted the stone fragments of the art of classical antiquity to the more vulnerable work of the Renaissance that, like potatoes, was distinguished by the potential for rot.

50. For readings of works by de Kooning that demonstrate his interest in making paintings which transform stasis through invoking visual metamorphoses, see appendix 1.

51. This head emerges into shape in reproductions, because reproductions reproduce the distance of a museum-mandated viewing that from impressionism forward has been a perquisite of envisioning forms that are composite compositions.

52. See Michael Fried, "Jackson Pollock," *Artforum*, Sept. 1965, for a riveting essay on the significance of lines as containers in art. Strong lines signal the presence of something contained or excluded. Fried sees Pollock's experiment as going beyond this function of the line to create a new aesthetic of fluidity that did not seek to limit, to delimit, or to form conforming shapes.

53. For those unable to locate the Africanist head discussed in the previous paragraph, the calypso dancer provides a helpful clue. The unsourced light that demarcates the left side of this beautifully rendered head accomplishes a dual function when the painting is turned upside down by forming the buttons on this dancing sailor's shirt.

54. Sally Yard, "The Angel and the Demoiselle—Willem de Kooning's *Black Friday*," *Record of the Art Museum, Princeton University* 50, no. 2 (1991): 13.

55. As John Elderfield writes, Thomas Hess in 1959 recalled de Kooning saying that *Black Untitled* "reminded him of 'seventeenth-century naval prints'" (*De Kooning: A Retrospective* 183). This comment by de Kooning confirms the palpable sense that this painting pictures wind blowing across a stormy sea.

56. This in itself was not unusual. De Kooning, particularly around this time, did not sign a number of his large paintings on the front of the canvas.

57. While de Kooning once slipped and referred to Keats as Shelley, this reasonable error in relation to the leading Romantic poets becomes even more understandable when it is remembered that the young Dutchman made his illegal crossing to the United States on the S.S. *Shelley*.

58. The formal construction of the novel, which stations Lena Grove in the role of what a student from my distant past called "pregnant bookends," is a perennial realization by those who understand the book. For this and other early and influential insights about the structure of Faulkner's *Light in August*, see Eric J. Sundquist's *Faulkner: A House Divided* (Baltimore: Johns Hopkins University Press), 1983.

59. The tip of this "vee" is cut off by the magnificently curved and classically shaped body of a black woman, the vertical torso whose form, in turn, is cut off or elegantly draped by the shadow of the reclining, headless nude who has already been distinguished by her proximity to the carefully modeled Africanist head.

60. The first sign of Joanna Burden's death is the column of yellow smoke rising from her burning house seen by Lena Grove and the driver of the wagon, as they approach Jefferson at the close of the first chapter of *Light in August*.

61. Frank O'Hara, "Personism: A Manifesto," 1951.

62. Faulkner, *Selected Letters*, 202.

63. This crescent moon is a direct quotation from Arshile Gorky's *Betrothal* series, which features a crescent moon at the neck of the man whose thoughts fill the paintings.

64. This scene, which introduces a godlike and personified force called the "Player" that seems to control both Percy Grimm and Joe Christmas, indicates why de Kooning would picture the chess piece as a pawn while these characters are played in this violent cultural script. See chapter 6 of this volume for a discussion of the significance of the blood that rises like a "rocket" from Joe's castrated body.

65. See Martin Ries, "De Kooning's *Asheville* and Zelda's Immolation," *Art Criticism* 20, no. 1 (2005).

66. This is Lauren Mahoney's description in "At Black Mountain," in *De Kooning: A Retrospective*, 196. Mahoney, in addition to acknowledging the large recognizable eye on the right side of the painting, sees a possible eye above the abbreviated profile that she describes here.

67. This painting is part of a series in which other versions reconfigure the primary elements of Gorky's composition, including the puzzle piece and the puppy. De Kooning's *Secretary* (1948) echoes the shape of *Night*'s bone as a form.

68. De Kooning used this evocative word to refer to Joe Christmas in his 1962 interview for *Newsweek*. Joe Christmas's racial heritage remains unknown to him as well as to others in Faulkner's *Light in August*.

69. Willem de Kooning, "What Abstract Art Means to Me," Symposium, Museum of Modern Art, Feb. 5, 1951, *Pittsburgh International Series*, 22–23.

70. This quotation from Harry F. Gaugh refers to de Kooning's supposed process for getting ideas for painting his black and whites (Gaugh, *Willem de Kooning*, 31).

EPILOGUE. COLLATERAL DAMAGE, COLLATING STRANGE

1. William Faulkner, *As I Lay Dying* (1931; New York: Random House, 1991), 207.

2. William Faulkner, *Intruder in the Dust* (1948; New York: Random House, 1991), 206–7.

3. Samuel Beckett, "Dante . . . Vico. Bruno . . . Joyce," in *Our Exagamination Round His Factification for Incamination of Work in Progress* (New York: Faber & Faber, 1929), 3. In 1929 Beckett wrote the opening essay for an unusual work of criticism after having heard Joyce read aloud from the book that Joyce called "Work in Progress." This volume, of which Beckett's essay was an important part, was comprised of twenty essays and two "dissenting" letters (possibly authored by Joyce himself) that responded to fragments of Joyce's novel ten years before the publication of *Finnegans Wake*.

4. Bruce Kawin, "The Montage Element in Faulkner's Fiction," in *Faulkner, Modernism, and Film: Faulkner and Yoknapatawpha, 1978*, ed. Evans Harrington and Ann Abadie (Jackson: University Press of Mississippi, 1979). Kawin offers a sophisticated analysis of montage, categorizing five different types of this powerful form of making meaning in relation to Faulkner's fiction.

5. *Go Down, Moses* 132. Also see note 6 to this epilogue for a discussion of Rider's hope that his marriage can attain the lasting love of Molly and Lucas Beauchamp, a relationship presented with its private tensions and triumphs in "The Fire and the Hearth," the story that precedes "Pantaloon in Black" in this, Faulkner's finest, story-cycle novel.

6. "The Fire and the Hearth," the second story in *Go Down, Moses*, is the title of Faulkner's most detailed story of the lifelong love of a man and a woman in which Lucas is faced with dousing the fire that represents his and Molly's marriage or killing his white cousin who has commandeered Molly's milk-filled breast for his motherless son. This hearth, by far the most valorized site of domestic love between a man and a woman in Faulkner's oeuvre, becomes the model for Rider in his death-ended marriage to Mannie in "Pantaloon in Black," the story that follows "The Fire and the Hearth" in *Go Down, Moses*.

7. The ailanthus, with its scented flowers, is commonly known for its sweet pleasures as "heaven's tree." For a sophisticated and insightful reading of trash art that is unflinchingly embodied, see Patricia Yeager's "Dematerializing Culture: Faulkner's Trash Aesthetic," in *Faulkner and Material Culture: Faulkner and Yoknapatawpha, 2004*, ed. Joseph R. Urgo and Ann J. Abadie (Jackson: University Press of Mississippi, 2007).

8. Ratliff's economic assessment of what can be embezzled from a saw mill in retrospect critiques the stealing of lumber that precipitates the murder of the Gowrie son, which is so crucial to the plot of *Intruder in the Dust*.

9. The horror of modernity is demonstrated by Mink Snopes, who himself has a perfectly respectable Hollywood rodent's name, when he is offered "lunch meat" and must ask the question that sooner or later could be addressed to all forms of sausage: "What is lunch meat?" To pursue the point, "galmeat" is "gal," but what in the mid-twentieth century—colloquially translated "what in the hell"—is a "lunch"?

10. See the concluding coda to chapter 2 in this volume.

11. For a telling discussion of Faulkner's position on nymphets and the related alignment of "capitalism and sexual exploitation" through "their mutual history as social institutions," see John T. Matthews, *William Faulkner: Seeing through the South* (New York: John Wiley & Sons, 2011). While Gavin Stevens imagines the young Eula as a nymphet, Matthews acutely argues that "the most iconic representation of these matters [is found] in the portrait of the young Linda Snopes, who stands in a long line in American literature of fetishized nymphets representing a national psychosis: the transgressive consumption of unspoiled goods" (262).

12. Marcel Duchamp's description here (recorded in 1966) was published in *Dialogues with Marcel Duchamp: Interview with Pierre Cabanne* (New York: Da Capo Press 1971), 48–49. After 1925, T. S. Eliot's "hollow men," "stuffed men," had articulated the state of the male container for modernism. See fig. 33, Duchamp's *La Boîte-en-valise*, to understand the significance of the "moulded" males folding out from the right of this collated display, which is a museum of miniaturized reproductions,

Duchamp's life's work enclosed in a box in a suitcase. This print picturing the "Nine Malic Moulds" (described in the epigraph) was conceived of earlier in the eight shapes Duchamp called his "Cemetery of Uniforms and Liveries." Duchamp's "Nine Malic Moulds"—the source for his famous "bachelors"—was originally a sartorial "cemetery" of official abstractions identified by occupations: "a priest, delivery man, cuirasser, policeman, pall bearer, footman, stationmaster, and page boy." This translation favors the archaic terms. Speaking and writing about these abstractions of men whose work is traditionally signaled by insignia, armor, or just different "hats," Duchamp himself occasionally named these figures of the punningly "malic moulds" (*mal* or "bad" in French, "male" in English) in more current occupations that could be translated as "busboy" or "waiter's assistant." Said to be lead moulds filled with "malic," illuminating, gas, the cuirraser (sometimes called a "cavalry soldier") is already designated by his metal mould, the armored breast plate known as a "cuirass." Notably, the pall bearer and page boys are those who serve as formal attendants at established rituals, funerals and weddings, respectively.

Duchamp's *Boîte-en-valise* is an active collation in which his famous "readymades" are stacked on the left side of the suitcase's lifted lid: the diminutive urinal designated as the *Fountain* (1917) (signed by the pseudonym "R. Mutt") is at the bottom, the tiny black typewriter cover inscribed "Underwood" next, and at the top a fragile glass bubble with writing that attests to the claim that it holds a precise and measured amount of Parisian air. Folding out at the left is a color print of his painting *La mariée (The Bride)*. What does not change in the *Boîte* is the centrally displayed image of this opened suitcase that reveals his *La mariée mise à nu par ses célibataires, même* or *Le grand verre (The Bride Stripped Bare by Her Bachelors, Even*, or *The Large Glass* [1915–23]). This dynamic work painted and affixed onto upper and lower panes of glass, according to Duchamp, was both humorous and erotic. In these two realms, beneath the "stripped" "bride" the lower image recycles the "Nine Malic Moulds" (formerly the eight figures of his "cemetery") into the bachelors identified collectively as the "bachelor machine." These bachelors inhabit a factory-driven underworld that contains, among other things, a "chocolate grinder," a "water mill," and an optically mesmeric "eye-chart" in which saucer-like disks begin as an iris and diminish upward to culminate in a small circle. These repeating disks (said to be illuminated by the gas in the male moulds, "the bachelors") have been described as the "eye-witness." While critics emphasize that this gas is used for street lights and other types of illumination, Duchamp was sometimes more visceral in his description that claims that these hollow lead torsos—his nine bachelors—are "the projections of the main points of a three-dimensional body" (quoted in *Great Modern Masters—Duchamp*, ed., Jose Maria Faerna [New York: Harry N. Abrams Inc., Publishers, 1996], 5). The bachelors replication of the "malic moulds" is the source of the illuminating gas that moves to a common point through the curved vectors Duchamp called "capillary tubes."

The forms for these "capillary tubes" originated in a Duchampian experiment that questioned standard measures by reifying their randomness. Cutting a three-meter length of tailor's thread into three equal parts, Duchamp preserved what he claimed was their random forms as they fell, varnishing their three different shapes onto a stable surface. These three shapes were then modeled by being carved into the upper edge of slats, wooden guides that allowed the initially random curves to be reproduced with precision. Duchamp's curving threads, called the "Three Standard Stoppages," became preserved as strict forms denominated by a titular equation that Duchamp actually called "tinned" or "canned chance." Both simple and complex, Duchamp made a painting in which these three rigidly established, curving lines radiate outward. Meanwhile, in this construction, these three lines themselves contain two other points of origin in which these identical lines begin again—overlapping each other or branching to make nine lines in all. Here, the three standard lengths with their fixed random curves form a spectral fingering of formal beauty. Duchamp then used this representation of the repeating threads as a model, cutting the painted strings from a canvas and configuring them in this prearranged conceptual form to become the "capillary tubes" of his *Large Glass*. *The Large Glass*, Duchamp's culminating collage, was made with paint, lead, foil, dust, two colors of glass, and other things applied to glass. The other things included these pieces of carefully cut canvas "threads" in threes, an element that underlines the presence of the mythical "Three Fates" (who made, measured, and cut the thread of life) in this large glass work that Duchamp repeatedly associated with fate and desire. Chance has been "canned" in these cut out representations as they become the "capillary tubes" that siphon the gas, light and life, from the "hats" of these seemingly headless "moulds" based on the abstract sartorial torsos that Duchamp claims to have designed to conceal their interiors. Echoing Duchamp's own description of his "malic moulds" as male vessels "built on a common horizontal plane, where lines intersect at the point of their sex," Duchamp's reprised "bachelors" are linked by these "tubes," the capillaries of fate that have incorporated them into a "bachelor machine." These tubes designed by the random curves of thread join the "bachelors" in a draining system, even as they originate as nine forms in the "uniforms" signaling their varied shapes and social roles.

What this opened box reveals is a randomness arranged by an active viewer: the *Boîte* is a collation, represented here in photographic fixity. Meanwhile, part of the arrangement of this collection is fixed—*The Large Glass* that unfolds with the opening lid is immediately revealed, as are the "readymades," while other parts can be opened out and made visible as the "museum" is displayed. *The Large Glass* flanked by the "readymades"—the urinal, the typewriter cover, and the glass bubble of breath claiming to be Parisian, all bizarrely Faulknerian and related containers for human output—forms a dynamic composition. While *The Bride* herself (the painting of that name), unfolding to the left of the box, is part of a series, she is also the dominant portrait shown in this particular opening of the suitcase that conceals prints of other paintings behind her in an accordion fold. *The Bride*'s cubist beauty with its golds, yellows, and rich darknesses is painted in the tonal and visual aesthetics that characterize and join Duchamp's most celbrated paintings including *Sad Young Man on a Train* (reprinted in this volume in black and white, figure 9) and his most famous work in this vein, *Nude Descending a Staircase, No. 2*. Profoundly related, these art paintings convey Duchamp's early experiments in translating emotion as well as motion. In his boxed collations where diminutive versions of his manufactured "readymades" are seen alongside prints of his works of high art, Duchamp replicates replication in a modernity that pictures men as containers filled with gas, abstractions already boxed in a valise: canned men who may "strip[. . .] bare" the bride but who are also on their way to a museum certified death or factory regulated fixity in their mechanical reproductions. The violently exposed pieces of *The Bride* in the upper half of *The Big Glass* reveal recognizable fragments of her portrait of the same name on the lower left, but her animacy, among these scattered pieces and parts, has become that of mechanically rendered dog (there is an engraved dog comb conveniently among the "readymades" to the right in the lower part of the valise), albeit with a bird's beak for a head. After the attack or "stripp[ing]" "by her bachelors," she is a disassembled bride, a stripped chassis, a woman of leftover metallic parts who is unveiled as more "bitch" (English, female dog) than "*biche*" (French, female deer and term of endearment). This junkyard bride with her canine tail lacks the cubist grace of a misplaced breast, buttock, or eye. Duchamp's bride "stripped bare by her bachelors, even" lacks the humanity or genuine animality achieved by the most pained and fierce of Piccasso's figures. Duchamp's *La Boîte-en-valise*, an archive of representations of some sixty-nine pieces of his work in miniature form, is meant to be seen here as a visual epigraph for the epilogue and for my book as a whole. It is impossible not to think of Addie Bundren boxed and ripe like "a cheese," wearing her wedding dress in Faulkner's 1930 novel: this book was certainly on the French intellectual and modernist table by the mid-1930s. The Duchamp works analyzed here precede Faulkner's fiction, but their boxing and recycling is crucial to a narratively driven visual circuit that amounts to a cogently collated critique of art in modernity. This is finally less about influence and more about the political aesthetics that define an era. *Boîte-en-valise* (fig. 33), Duchamp's multiply produced museum in a box, a box that is itself inside a valise or suitcase, is the signifying work of art, the aesthetic corollary for the collage portraits and images of "canned death" present in Faulkner's works, early and late.

13. James G. Watson, *William Faulkner: Self-Presentation and Performance* (Austin: University of Texas Press, 2002), 51. For an essay notable for its efforts to see, to visualize, the literal scene of Faulkner's fiction, see Webb Salmon, "On Quentin's Absence from Caddy's Tree-Climbing Scene," *Faulkner Journal* 3, no. 2 (Spring 1988): 48–52. The sense of Quentin's narrating presence as an absence has been gestured toward more than once in the criticism. For a classic essay that addresses this aspect, see Phillip Novak, "Meaning, Mourning, and the Form of Modern Narrative: The Inscription of Loss in Faulkner's *The Sound and the Fury*," *Faulkner Journal* 12, no. 1 (Fall 1996).

14. It is not enough for Benjy to beller and stop bellering at the close of *The Sound and the Fury*. Faulkner's idiot must be given a proper ending. It is no accident but destiny that insists on Benjy having burned himself alive in the Compson house: this leftover history is both listed and closed off in *The Mansion*, the concluding work of the Snopes Trilogy.

15. Michael Millgate quoting "Faulkner at Nagano," in *The Achievement of William Faulkner* (New York: Random House, 1966), 109.

16. Clifford Geertz, "Thick Description: Toward an Interpretive Theory of Culture," in *The Interpretation of Cultures: Selected Essays* (1973; New York: Basic Books, 2000).

17. This Burliuk painting appears on the cover and also as the frontispiece to this volume.

APPENDIX 1. WILLEM DE KOONING'S PARABLES OF ART

1. Quoted in *Modern Artists in America*, First series, ed. Robert Motherwell et al. (New York: Wittenborn, Schultz, 1951), 12.

2. See Thomas B. Hess, *Willem de Kooning: Recent Paintings* (New York: M. Knoedler, 1967). This conversation (reported to have taken place in 1949) overheard and recounted by Hess came to be viewed as a critical touchstone, marking a major divergence in Abstract Expressionism.

3. Mieke Bal theorizes that de Kooning's "emphatic inscription of the hand comes close to 'first-person' narrative" as de Kooning speaks in the stroke of his brush to assert his presence as the maker. If one defines narrative as "sequence" (as Bal and others do), the de Kooning of *Light in August*, as well as in his other Faulkner works, is a narrative painter. See Bal, *Looking In: The Art of Viewing* (Amsterdam: Gordon and Breach Publishing Group, 2001), 215.

Index of Subjects

Index of Faulkner's Characters

The New Southern Studies

The Nation's Region: Southern Modernism, Segregation, and U.S. Nationalism
by Leigh Anne Duck

Black Masculinity and the U.S. South: From Uncle Tom to Gangsta
by Riché Richardson

Grounded Globalism: How the U.S. South Embraces the World
by James L. Peacock

Disturbing Calculations: The Economics of Identity in Postcolonial Southern Literature, 1912–2002
by Melanie R. Benson

American Cinema and the Southern Imaginary
edited by Deborah E. Barker and Kathryn McKee

Southern Civil Religions: Imagining the Good Society in the Post-Reconstruction Era
by Arthur Remillard

Reconstructing the Native South: American Indian Literature and the Lost Cause
by Melanie Benson Taylor

Apples and Ashes: Literature, Nationalism, and the Confederate States of America
by Coleman Hutchison

Reading for the Body: The Recalcitrant Materiality of Southern Fiction, 1893–1985
by Jay Watson

Latining America: Black-Brown Passages and the Coloring of Latino/a Studies
by Claudia Milian

Finding Purple America: The South and the Future of American Cultural Studies
by Jon Smith

The Signifying Eye: Seeing Faulkner's Art
by Candace Waid

Sacral Grooves, Limbo Gateways: Travels in Deep Southern Time, Circum-Caribbean Space, Afro-creole Authority
by Keith Cartwright

Jim Crow, Literature, and the Legacy of Sutton E. Griggs
edited by Tess Chakkalakal and Kenneth W. Warren

Sounding the Color Line: Music and Race in the Southern Imagination
by Erich Nunn

Borges's Poe: The Influence and Reinvention of Edgar Allan Poe in Spanish America
by Emron Esplin

Eudora Welty's Fiction and Photography: The Body of the Other Woman
by Harriet Pollack

Keywords for Southern Studies
edited by Scott Romine and Jennifer Rae Greeson

www.ingramcontent.com/pod-product-compliance
Lightning Source LLC
LaVergne TN
LVHW030907080826
845145LV00010B/2801

* 9 7 8 0 8 2 0 3 5 0 5 5 4 *